Pages **72–73**

75

74

SOUTH AMERICA

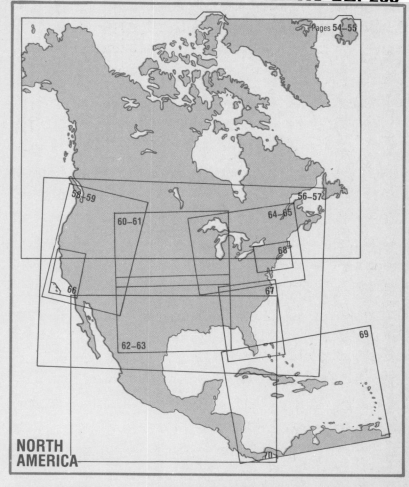

Pages **54–55**

58–59

56–57

60–61

64–65

68

66

67

62–63

69

70

NORTH AMERICA

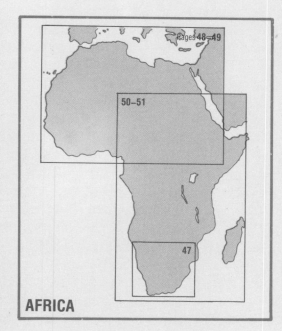

Pages **48–49**

50–51

47

AFRICA

GENERAL MAPS

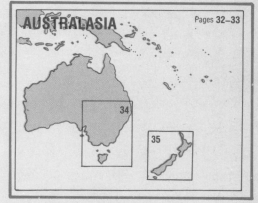

AUSTRALASIA

Pages **32–33**

34

35

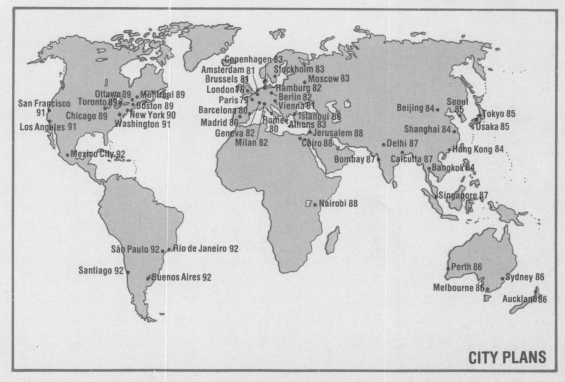

Copenhagen 83
Amsterdam 81   Stockholm 83
Brussels 81   Moscow 83
London 78   Hamburg 82
Paris 79   Berlin 82
Barcelona 80   Vienna 81
Madrid 80   Rome Istanbul 88   Beijing 84   Seoul 85   Tokyo 85
Geneva 82   80 Athens 83
Milan 82   Jerusalem 88   Shanghai 84   Osaka 85
Cairo 88   Hong Kong 84
Delhi 87
Ottawa 89   Montreal 89
Toronto 89   Boston 89
San Francisco 91
Chicago 89   New York 90
Los Angeles 91   Washington 91
Bombay 87   Calcutta 87   Bangkok 84
Mexico City 92
Singapore 87
Nairobi 88

São Paulo 92   Rio de Janeiro 92
Perth 86
Santiago 92   Buenos Aires 92
Sydney 86
Melbourne 86
Auckland 86

CITY PLANS

THE TIMES
FAMILY ATLAS
OF THE WORLD
FIRST EDITION

Salem House

First published in the United States by
SALEM HOUSE PUBLISHERS, 1988,
462 Boston Street, Topsfield,
Massachusetts, 01983.

Reprinted with revisions 1989

2nd reprint 1989

Copyright © Times Books Ltd and
John Bartholomew & Son Ltd 1988 , 1989

Maps prepared by
John Bartholomew & Son Ltd, Edinburgh
Times Books Ltd, London
with the assistance of
Thames Cartographic Services, Maidenhead
Cosmographics, Watford

Index and statistical data prepared by
Geographical Research Associates,
Maidenhead

Geographical Dictionary prepared by
Professor B.W. Atkinson

Index processed and typeset by
Computaprint Data Services,
Haywards Heath

Physical Earth Maps
Duncan Mackay

Design
Ivan Dodd
Vivienne Hookings

Editorial Direction
Alison Ewington
H.A.G. Lewis, O.B.E.
Paul Middleton
Barry Winkleman

Printed and bound in Italy by
Mondadori, Verona.

Library of Congress Cataloging-in-
Publication Data
Times Books (Firm)
 The Times family atlas of the world.
 Includes index.
 I. Atlases.   I. Title.
G1021. T565 1988 912 88-675200

ISBN: 0 88162 346 6

The Times Family Atlas of the World is a reference work for use in the home, office or school, for those who travel the world and also those, like Francis Bacon, who journey only "in map and chart".

An index of no fewer than 30,000 entries, keyed to the main map plates, will aid those who, whilst familiar with the name of a place, are uncertain of just where it lies on the map.

It is by no means always easy to ascertain the correct title and status of a country as distinct from its everyday name used on maps. The list of states and territories gives in addition to name, title and status, the population and area, the national currency, the major religions and the national flag.

Maps, being an efficient way of storing and displaying information, are used to amplify the list of states and territories and the geographical comparisons of continents, oceans, lakes and islands. They form the basis of the section on earthquakes, volcanoes, economic minerals, vegetation, temperature, rainfall and population.

Maps are also, by nature, illustrative and a 14-page section shows the world's major physical features in the way they appear from space but with the names of the features added.

Amongst the statistical data contained in the Atlas is a listing of the major metropolitan areas with their populations. For the past several decades there has been, throughout the world, an accelerating flow of people from the land to towns and cities and especially the major cities, some of which now contain the bulk of the national population. Growth in air travel has turned those same cities into centres of tourism. Influx of population and the demands of tourism have enhanced the status of cities. Generous space has, therefore, been allocated to maps of major cities and their environs.

Geographical names in this Atlas are given in their anglicized (convention-al) form where such a form is in current use. Other names are given in their national Roman alphabet or else converted into English by transliteration (letter-to-letter) or transcription (sound-to-sound). Because Roman alphabet letters, sometimes modified, are pronounced in a variety of ways, a brief guide to pronunciation has been included. The whole is supplemented by a dictionary of geographical terms.

In the names, in the portrayal of international boundaries and in the list of states and territories, the aim has been to show the situation as it pertains in the area at the time of going to press. This must not be taken as endorsement by the publishers of the status of the territories concerned. The aim throughout has been to show things as they are. In that way the Atlas will best serve the reader to whom, it is hoped, it will bring interest, benefit and continuing pleasure.

H.A.G. Lewis, OBE
Geographical Consultant to *The Times*

CONTENTS

ABU DHABI
(see **UNITED ARAB EMIRATES**)

AFGHANISTAN

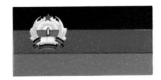

STATUS: Republic
AREA: 652,225 sq km (251,773 sq miles)
POPULATION: 18,614,000
ANNUAL NATURAL INCREASE: 2.4%
DENSITY: 28.6 per sq km
CAPITAL: Kabul
LANGUAGE: Pushtu, Dari (Persian dialect)
RELIGION: 90% Sunni and 9% Shiah Moslem. Hindu, Sikh and Jewish minorities
CURRENCY: afghani (Af)
ORGANISATIONS: UN, Col. Plan

Afghanistan is a mountainous landlocked country in south-west Asia with a climate of extremes. In summer the lowland south-west reaches a temperature of over 40°C (104°F); in winter this may drop to −26°C (−15°F) in the northern mountains. Rainfall varies between 10 and 40cm (4–16in). The country is one of the poorest in the world with hardly 10% of the land suitable for agriculture. Main crops are wheat, fruit and vegetables. Sheep and goats are the main livestock. Mineral resources are rich but underdeveloped with natural gas, coal and iron ore deposits predominating. The main industrial area is centred on Kabul.

AJMAN
(see **UNITED ARAB EMIRATES**)

ÅLAND

STATUS: Self-governing Island Province of Finland
AREA: 1,505 sq km (581 sq miles)
POPULATION: 23,595

ABBREVIATIONS	
ANZUS	Australia, New Zealand, United States Security Treaty
ASEAN	Association of South East Asian Nations
CACM	Central American Common Market
CARICOM	Caribbean Community and Common Market
CEAO	West African Economic Community
Col. Plan	Colombo Plan
COMECON	Council for Mutual Economic Assistance
Comm	Commonwealth
Council of Eur	Council of Europe
ECOWAS	Economic Community of West African States
EEC	European Economic Community
EFTA	European Free Trade Association
NATO	North Atlantic Treaty Organisation
OAS	Organization of American States
OAU	Organization of African Unity
OECD	Organisation of Economic Co-operation and Development
OPEC	Organization of Petroleum Exporting Countries
UN	United Nations
WEU	Western European Union

ALBANIA

STATUS: People's Socialist Republic
AREA: 28,750 sq km (11,100 sq miles)
POPULATION: 3,022,000
ANNUAL NATURAL INCREASE: 2.0%
DENSITY: 105.2 per sq km
CAPITAL: Tirana (Tiranë)
LANGUAGE: Albanian (Gheg, Tosk)
RELIGION: mainly atheist. Moslem, Roman Catholic and Greek Orthodox minorities
CURRENCY: new lek
ORGANISATIONS: UN

Situated between Yugoslavia and Greece on the eastern seaboard of the Adriatic, Albania is politically and economically isolated from the rest of Europe. The climate is Mediterranean type with a high rainfall of more than 180cm (7in) in the mountains which cover most of the country. There are considerable mineral resources of chrome, copper, and iron ores; also oil and natural gas. Major exports are now metal products, textiles and grain. Albania became a people's republic in 1946, drifted away from Soviet influence towards China in the 1960's, but since the death of Mao Zedong in 1976 has slowly improved relations with western Europe.

ALEUTIAN ISLANDS

STATUS: Territory of USA
AREA: 17,665 sq km (6,820 sq miles)
POPULATION: 6,730

ALGERIA

STATUS: Democratic and Popular Republic
AREA: 2,381,745 sq km (919,355 sq miles)
POPULATION: 22,971,000
ANNUAL NATURAL INCREASE: 3.2%
DENSITY: 9.7 per sq km
CAPITAL: Algiers (El-Djezaïr)
LANGUAGE: Arabic, French, Berber
RELIGION: Moslem
CURRENCY: Algerian dinar (AD)
ORGANISATIONS: UN, Arab League, OAU, OPEC

Physically the country is divided between the coastal Atlas mountain ranges of the north and the Sahara desert to the south. Arable land occupies small areas of the northern valleys and coastal strip with wheat, barley and vines leading crops. Sheep, goats and cattle are the most important livestock. Although oil from the southern deserts dominates the economy it is now declining. Economic policy has concentrated on encouraging smaller manufacturing industries. Tourism is a growth industry and now earns important foreign exchange.

AMERICAN SAMOA
STATUS: Unincorporated Territory of USA
AREA: 197 sq km (76 sq miles)
POPULATION: 34,000
CAPITAL: Pago Pago

ANDORRA

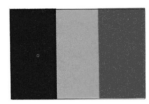

STATUS: Principality
AREA: 465 sq km (180 sq miles)
POPULATION: 47,000
ANNUAL NATURAL INCREASE: n.a.
DENSITY: 101.1 per sq km
CAPITAL: Andorra la Vella

LANGUAGE: Catalan, French, Spanish
RELIGION: mainly Roman Catholic
CURRENCY: French franc, Spanish peseta

Andorra is a tiny alpine state high in the Pyrenees between France and Spain. Agriculture and tourism are the main occupations. Tobacco and potatoes are the principal crops, sheep and cattle the main livestock. Important sources of revenue are the sale of hydro-electricity, stamps and duty-free goods.

ANGOLA

STATUS: People's Republic
AREA: 1,246,700 sq km (481,225 sq miles)

POPULATION: 8,981,000
ANNUAL NATURAL INCREASE: 2.5%
DENSITY: 7.2 per sq km
CAPITAL: Luanda
LANGUAGE: Portuguese, tribal dialects
RELIGION: mainly traditional beliefs. Large Roman Catholic and Protestant minorities
CURRENCY: kwanza (K)
ORGANISATIONS: UN, OAU

Independent from the Portuguese since 1975, Angola is a large country south of the equator in south-western Africa. Much of the interior is savannah plateaux with rainfall varying from 25cm (10in) in the north to 60cm (24in) in the south. Most of the population is engaged in agriculture producing cassava, maize and coffee, but Angola is very rich in minerals. Petroleum, diamonds, iron ore, copper and manganese are exported with petroleum accounting for at least 50% of earnings. The small amount of industry is concentrated around Luanda. Most consumer products and textiles are imported.

ANGUILLA

STATUS: UK Dependent Territory
AREA: 91 sq km (35 sq miles)
POPULATION: 7,014
CAPITAL: The Valley

ANTIGUA & BARBUDA

STATUS: Commonwealth Nation
AREA: 442 sq km (171 sq miles)
POPULATION: 81,000
ANNUAL NATURAL INCREASE: 1.0%

DENSITY: 183.3 per sq km
CAPITAL: St John's (on Antigua)
LANGUAGE: English
RELIGION: Anglican Christian majority
CURRENCY: East Caribbean dollar (EC$)
ORGANISATIONS: Comm., UN, CARICOM, OAS

The country consists of two main islands in the Leeward group in the West Indies. Tourism is the main activity but local agriculture is being encouraged to reduce food imports. The production of rum is the main manufacturing industry.

ARGENTINA

STATUS: Republic
AREA: 2,766,889 sq km (1,068,302 sq miles)
POPULATION: 31,029,694
ANNUAL NATURAL INCREASE: 1.6%
DENSITY: 11.2 per sq km
CAPITAL: Buenos Aires
LANGUAGE: Spanish
RELIGION: 90% Roman Catholic, 2% Protestant
CURRENCY: austral (A)
ORGANISATIONS: UN, OAS

The country stretches over 30 degrees of latitude from the thick sub-tropical forests of the north through the immense flat grass plains of the pampas to the cool desert plateaux of Patagonia in the south. The economy of Argentina was long dominated by the produce of the rich soils of the pampas, beef and grain. Agricultural products account for over 60% of export revenue with grain crops pre-dominating, although the late 1980's have seen a decline due to competition and falling world grain prices. Beef exports, the mainstay of the economy from 1850, decreased by over 50% between 1970 and 1983, again due to strong competition from Western Europe. Industry has also declined during the last decade. Shortage of raw materials and foreign aid debts have meant lower production, unemployment and a strong decline in home demand. The expansion of the oil and gas industry and the steady growth of coal, hydro-electricity and nuclear power, is providing a base for industrial expansion but internal inflation and foreign financial sanctions have not yet allowed this expansion.

ARUBA

STATUS: Self-governing Island of Netherlands Antilles
AREA: 193 sq km (75 sq miles)
POPULATION: 67,000
CAPITAL: Oranjestad

ASCENSION

STATUS: Island Dependency of St Helena
AREA: 88 sq km (34 sq miles)
POPULATION: 1,075
CAPITAL: Georgetown

ASHMORE AND CARTIER ISLANDS

STATUS: External Territory of Australia
AREA: 3 sq km (1.2 sq miles)
POPULATION: No permanent population

AUSTRALIA

STATUS: Commonwealth Nation
AREA: 7,682,300 sq km (2,965,370 sq miles)
POPULATION: 16,531,900
ANNUAL NATURAL INCREASE: 0.8%
DENSITY: 2.1 per sq km
CAPITAL: Canberra
LANGUAGE: English
RELIGION: 88% Christian. Aboriginal beliefs. Jewish minority
CURRENCY: Australian dollar ($A)
ORGANISATIONS: Comm, UN, ANZUS, Col. Plan, OECD

AUSTRALIAN CAPITAL TERRITORY (CANBERRA)

STATUS: Federal Territory
AREA: 2,432 sq km (939 sq miles)
POPULATION: 244,500
CAPITAL: Canberra

NEW SOUTH WALES

STATUS: State
AREA: 801,430 sq km (309,350 sq miles)
POPULATION: 5,406,900
CAPITAL: Sydney

NORTHERN TERRITORY

STATUS: Territory
AREA: 1,346,200 sq km (519,635 sq miles)
POPULATION: 138,800
CAPITAL: Darwin

QUEENSLAND

STATUS: State
AREA: 1,727,000 sq km (666,620 sq miles)
POPULATION: 2,505,300
CAPITAL: Brisbane

SOUTH AUSTRALIA

STATUS: State
AREA: 984,380 sq km (79,970 sq miles)
POPULATION: 1,352,900
CAPITAL: Adelaide

TASMANIA

STATUS: State
AREA: 68,330 sq km (26,375 sq miles)
POPULATION: 437,300
CAPITAL: Hobart

VICTORIA

STATUS: State
AREA: 227,600 sq km (87,855 sq miles)
POPULATION: 4,075,500
CAPITAL: Melbourne

WESTERN AUSTRALIA

STATUS: State
AREA: 2,525,500 sq km (974,845 sq miles)
POPULATION: 1,382,500
CAPITAL: Perth

Australia is both a continent and a country and is the sixth largest country in terms of area. The centre and the west, over 50% of the land area, are desert and scrub with less than 25cm (10in) of rain. Only in the sub-tropical north and the eastern highlands does rainfall exceed 100cm (39in) annually. Australia is rich in both agricultural and natural resources. Wool, wheat, meat, sugar and dairy products account for over 40% of export revenue despite the immense growth in mineral exploitation. The country has vast reserves of coal, oil, natural gas, nickel, iron ore, bauxite and uranium ores. Gold, silver, lead, zinc and copper ores are also exploited. In 1984 minerals accounted for about 38% of export revenue. Recent high deficits in balance of trade have been caused by fluctuations in world demand, competition from the E.E.C. and recent unfavourable climatic conditions affecting agricultural surpluses. Increasing trade with eastern Asia, and Japan in particular has opened up new areas of commerce to counteract the sharp decline in Europe as a market.

AUSTRALIAN ANTARCTIC TERRITORY

STATUS: Territory
AREA: 6,120,000 sq km (2,320,000 sq miles)
POPULATION: No permanent population

AUSTRIA

STATUS: Republic
AREA: 83,855 sq km (32,370 sq miles)
POPULATION: 7,571,000
ANNUAL NATURAL INCREASE: 0.0%
DENSITY: 90.3 per sq km
CAPITAL: Vienna (Wien)
LANGUAGE: German
RELIGION: 89% Roman Catholic, 6% Protestant
CURRENCY: Schilling (Sch)
ORGANISATIONS: UN, Council of Europe, EFTA, OECD

Austria is an alpine, land-locked country in central Europe. The mountainous Alps which cover 75% of the land consist of a series of east-west ranges enclosing lowland basins. The climate is continental with cold winters and warm summers. About 25% of the country, in the north and north-east, is lower foreland or flat land containing most of Austria's fertile farmland. Half is arable and the remainder is mainly for root or fodder crops. Manufacturing and heavy industry however, account for the majority of export revenue particularly pig-iron, steel, chemicals and vehicles. Over 70% of the country's power is hydroelectric. Tourism and forestry are also important to the economy.

AZORES

STATUS: Self-governing Island Region of Portugal

AREA: 2,335 sq km (901 sq miles)
POPULATION: 251,352
CAPITAL: Ponta Delgada

BAHAMAS

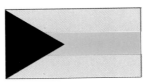

STATUS: State
AREA: 13,865 sq km (5,350 sq miles)
POPULATION: 236,000
ANNUAL NATURAL INCREASE: 1.9%
DENSITY: 17.1 per sq km
CAPITAL: Nassau (on New Providence)
LANGUAGE: English
RELIGION: mainly Anglican Christian, Baptist and Roman Catholic
CURRENCY: Bahamian dollar (B$)
ORGANISATIONS: Comm, UN, CARICOM, OAS

About 700 islands and over 2000 coral sand cays (reefs) constitute the sub-tropical Commonwealth of The Bahamas. The island group extends from the coast of Florida to Cuba and Haiti in the south. Only 29 islands are inhabited. Most of the 100cm (39in) of rainfall falls in the summer. The tourist industry is the main source of income and although fluctuating through recession, still employs over 70% of the working population. Recent economic plans have concentrated on reducing imports by developing fishing and domestic agriculture. Other important sources of income are ship registration (the world's third largest open-registry fleet), income generated by offshore finance and banking and export of rum, salt and cement.

BAHRAIN

STATUS: State
AREA: 661 sq km (225 sq miles)
POPULATION: 412,000
ANNUAL NATURAL INCREASE: 2.8%
DENSITY: 623.3 per sq km
CAPITAL: Al Manāmah (Manama)
LANGUAGE: Arabic, English
RELIGION: 60% Shiah and 40% Sunni Moslem. Christian minority
CURRENCY: Bahrain dinar (BD)
ORGANISATIONS: UN, Arab League

The sheikdom is a barren island in the Persian Gulf with less than 8cm (3in) rainfall. Summer temperatures average 32°C (89°F). Bahrain was the first country in the Arabian peninsula to strike oil, in 1932. In 1985, oil accounted for 65% of revenue, but a decline in value of the product and lower production is now causing the government to diversify the economy with expansion of light and heavy industry and chemical plants, and the subsequent encouragement of trade and foreign investment.

BALEARIC ISLANDS (BALEARES)

STATUS: Island Province of Spain
AREA: 5,015 sq km (1,935 sq miles)
POPULATION: 685,088
CAPITAL: Palma de Mallorca

BANGLADESH

STATUS: People's Republic
AREA: 144,000 sq km (55,585 sq miles)
POPULATION: 100,616,000
ANNUAL NATURAL INCREASE: 2.7%

DENSITY: 698.8 per sq km
CAPITAL: Dhaka (Dacca)
LANGUAGE: Bengali (Bangla), Bihari, Hindi, English
RELIGION: 85% Moslem. Hindu, Buddhist and Christian minorities
CURRENCY: taka (tk)
ORGANISATIONS: Comm, UN, Col. Plan

Bangladesh is one of the world's poorest countries. Life expectancy averages only 48 years. Most of the territory of Bangladesh comprises the vast river systems of the Ganges and Brahmaputra which drain from the Himalayas into the Bay of Bengal, frequently changing course and flooding the flat delta plain. The climate is tropical, and agriculture is dependent on monsoon rainfall. When the monsoon fails there is drought. 82% of the population of Bangladesh are farmers, the main crops being rice and jute. There are no extensive mineral deposits, although large reserves of natural gas under the Bay of Bengal have not yet been exploited. The main export goods are jute, animal skins and tea.

BARBADOS

STATUS: State
AREA: 430 sq km (166 sq miles)
POPULATION: 253,000
ANNUAL NATURAL INCREASE: 0.9%
DENSITY: 588 per sq km
CAPITAL: Bridgetown
LANGUAGE: English
RELIGION: Anglican Christian majority.
Methodist and Roman Catholic minorities
CURRENCY: Barbados dollar (BDs$)
ORGANISATIONS: Comm, UN, CARICOM, OAS

The former British colony of Barbados in the Caribbean is the easternmost island of the

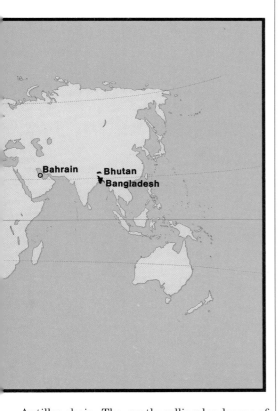

Antilles chain. The gently rolling landscape of the island is lush and fertile, the temperature ranging from 25°–28°C(77°–82°F) with 127–190cm(50–75in) rainfall per year. Sugar and its by-products, molasses and rum, form the mainstay of the economy. Tourism has become a growing industry in recent years.

BASUTOLAND
(see **LESOTHO**)

BEAR ISLAND (BJØRNØYA)

STATUS: Island of Svalbard, Norway
AREA: 176 sq km (68 sq miles)
POPULATION: 14

BECHUANALAND
(see **BOTSWANA**)

BELGIUM

STATUS: Kingdom
AREA: 30,520 sq km (11,780 sq miles)
POPULATION: 9,913,000
ANNUAL NATURAL INCREASE: 0.1%
DENSITY: 324.8 per sq km
CAPITAL: Brussels (Bruxelles/Brussel)
LANGUAGE: French, Dutch, German
RELIGION: Roman Catholic majority. Protestant, Jewish minorities
CURRENCY: Belgian franc
ORGANISATIONS: UN, Council of Europe, EEC, NATO, OECD, WEU

Belgium is situated between the hills of Northern France and the North European plain. Over two thirds of the country comprises the Flanders plain, a flat plateau covered by fertile wind-blown loess which extends from the North Sea coast down to the forested mountains of the Ardennes in the south, which rise to a height of 692m(2270ft). The climate is mild and temperate, although the country's proximity to the Atlantic means that low pressure fronts bring changeable weather and frequent rainfall (72–120cm or 28–47in per annum). Over half the country is intensively farmed – cereals (mainly wheat), root crops, vegetables and flax are the main crops. Extensive pastureland ensures that Belgium is self-sufficient in meat and dairy products. Belgium lacks mineral resources, except for coal, but its metal and engineering industries account for nearly one third of its exports. The Flanders region is famous for its textiles. Most of Belgium's trade passes through the North sea port of Antwerp, and an efficient communications network links the port with the rest of Europe.

BELIZE

STATUS: State
AREA: 22,965 sq km (8,865 sq miles)
POPULATION: 171,000
ANNUAL NATURAL INCREASE: 2.5%
DENSITY: 7.5 per sq km
CAPITAL: Belmopan
LANGUAGE: English, Spanish, Maya
RELIGION: 60% Roman Catholic, 40% Protestant
CURRENCY: Belizean dollar (BZ$)
ORGANISATIONS: Comm, UN, CARICOM

Bordering the Caribbean Sea, sub-tropical Belize is dominated by its dense forest cover. Principal crops for export are sugar-cane, fruit, rice, maize and timber products. Since independence from Britain in 1973 the country has developed agriculture to lessen reliance on imported food products. Fish is a staple diet and also provides valuable foreign exchange.

BENIN

STATUS: People's Republic
AREA: 112,620 sq km (43,470 sq miles)
POPULATION: 4,042,000
ANNUAL NATURAL INCREASE: 3.0%
DENSITY: 35.9 per sq km
CAPITAL: Porto Novo
LANGUAGE: French, Fon, Adja
RELIGION: traditional beliefs majority, 15% Roman Catholic and 13% Moslem
CURRENCY: CFA franc
ORGANISATIONS: UN, CEAO, ECOWAS, OAU

Benin, formerly Dahomey, is a small strip of country descending from the wooded savannah hills of the north to the forested and cultivated lowlands fringing the Bight of Benin. The economy is dominated by agriculture with palm oil, cotton, coffee, groundnuts and copra as main exports. The developing off-shore oil industry has proven reserves of over 20 million barrels.

BERMUDA
STATUS: Self-governing UK Crown Colony
AREA: 54 sq km (21 sq miles)
POPULATION: 56,000
CAPITAL: Hamilton

BHUTAN

STATUS: Kingdom
AREA: 46,620 sq km (17,995 sq miles)
POPULATION: 1,447,000
ANNUAL NATURAL INCREASE: 2.0%
DENSITY: 31.1 per sq km
CAPITAL: Thimphu
LANGUAGE: Dzongkha, Nepali, English
RELIGION: Mahayana Buddhist. Hindu minority
CURRENCY: ngultrum, Indian rupee
ORGANISATIONS: UN, Col. Plan

The country spreads across the Himalayan foothills between China and India east of Nepal. Rainfall is high at over 300cm (118in) per year but temperatures vary between extreme cold of the northern ranges to a July average of 27°C (81°F) in the southern forests. Long isolated, the economy of Bhutan is dominated by agriculture and small local industries. All manufactured goods are imported.

BIOKO (FERNANDO PÓO)
STATUS: Island of Equatorial Guinea
AREA: 2,034 sq km (785 sq miles)
POPULATION: 304,000
CAPITAL: Malabo (Sta. Isabel)

BJØRNØYA

(see **BEAR ISLAND**)

BOLIVIA

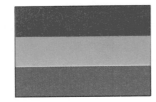

STATUS: Republic
AREA: 1,098,575 sq km (424,050 sq miles)
POPULATION: 6,547,000
ANNUAL NATURAL INCREASE: 2.8%
DENSITY: 6 per sq km
CAPITAL: La Paz
LANGUAGE: Spanish, Quechua, Aymara
RELIGION: large Roman Catholic majority
CURRENCY: Boliviano
ORGANISATIONS: UN, OAS

With an average life expectancy of 51 years, Bolivia is one of the world's poorest nations. Landlocked and isolated, the country stretches from the eastern Andes across high cool plateaux before dropping to the dense forest of the Amazon basin and the grasslands of the south-east. Development of the economy relies on the growth of exploitation of mineral resources as subsistence agriculture occupies the majority of the population. Crude oil, natural gas, tin, zinc and iron ore are the main mineral deposits.

BONAIRE

STATUS: Self-governing Island of Netherlands Antilles
AREA: 288 sq km (111 sq miles)
POPULATION: 8,845
CAPITAL: Kralendijk

BONIN ISLANDS (OGASAWARA-SHOTO)

STATUS: Islands of Japan
AREA: 104 sq km (40 sq miles)
POPULATION: 200

BOTSWANA

STATUS: Republic
AREA: 582,000 sq km (224,652 sq miles)
POPULATION: 1,131,000
ANNUAL NATURAL INCREASE: 3.3%
DENSITY: 1.9 per sq km
CAPITAL: Gaborone
LANGUAGE: Setswana, English
RELIGION: traditional beliefs majority. Christian minority

CURRENCY: pula (P)
ORGANISATIONS: Comm, UN, OAU

The arid high plateau of Botswana with its poor soils and low rainfall, supports little arable agriculture, but over 2.5 million cattle graze the dry grasslands. Diamonds, copper, nickel and gold are mined in the east and are the main mineral exports. The growth of light industries around the capital has stimulated trade with neighbouring countries.

BOUGAINVILLE ISLAND

STATUS: Part of Papua New Guinea
AREA: 10,620 sq km (4,100 sq miles)
POPULATION: 77,880

BRAZIL

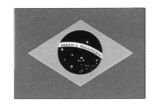

STATUS: Federative Republic
AREA: 8,511,965 sq km (3,285,620 sq miles)
POPULATION: 138,493,000
ANNUAL NATURAL INCREASE: 2.3%
DENSITY: 16.3 per sq km
CAPITAL: Brasília
LANGUAGE: Portuguese
RELIGION: 90% Roman Catholic. Protestant minority
CURRENCY: Cruzado (CZ$)
ORGANISATIONS: UN, OAS

Brazil is not only the largest country in South America but also has the fastest growing economy. Brazil is now an industrial power but with development limited to the heavily populated urban areas of the eastern coastal lowlands. The Amazon basin tropical rain forest covers roughly one third of the country; savannah grasslands of the centre west give way to light forest – now much cleared – of the eastern Brazilian Highlands, and the cool southern plateau of the south. This varied landscape is dominated by three river systems of the Amazon, São Francisco and Paraguay/Paraná. Economic variety reflects the changing landscape. In agricultural production Brazil is one of the world's leading exporters with coffee, soya beans, sugar, bananas, cocoa, tobacco, rice and cattle major commodities. Mineral resources, except for iron ore, at the moment do not play a significant role in the economy, but recent economic policies have concentrated on developing the industrial base – road and rail communications, of light and heavy industry and expansion of energy resources, particularly hydro-electric power harnessed from the great river systems.

BRITISH INDIAN OCEAN TERRITORY

STATUS: British Dependency comprising the Chagos Archipelago
AREA: 52 sq km (20 sq miles)
POPULATION: 2,000

BRUNEI

STATUS: Sultanate
AREA: 5,765 sq km (2,225 sq miles)
POPULATION: 244,000
ANNUAL NATURAL INCREASE: 2.6%
CAPITAL: Bandar Seri Begawan
DENSITY: 42.4 per sq km
LANGUAGE: Malay, English, Chinese
RELIGION: 65% Sunni Moslem. Buddhist and Christian minorities
CURRENCY: Brunei dollar (B$)
ORGANISATIONS: Comm, UN, ASEAN

The Sultanate of Brunei is situated on the north-west coast of Borneo. Its tropical climate is hot and humid with annual rainfall ranging from 250cm(98in) on the thin coastal strip to

500cm(197in) in the mountainous interior. Oil, both on-shore and off-shore is the mainstay of the Brunei economy. Other exports include natural gas, which is transported to Japan, rubber and timber. Apart from oil, most other industries are local.

BULGARIA

STATUS: People's Republic
AREA: 110,910 sq km (42,810 sq miles)
POPULATION: 8,959,000
ANNUAL NATURAL INCREASE: 0.2%
DENSITY: 80.8 per sq km

CAPITAL: Sofia (Sofiya)
LANGUAGE: Bulgarian
RELIGION: atheist, Eastern Orthodox and Moslem
CURRENCY: lev
ORGANISATIONS: UN, Warsaw Pact, COMECON

Most of the landscape consists of low alpine mountain ranges with broad fertile valleys. The climate is continental with hot summers and cold winters. Rainfall ranges between 45 and 120cm (18–47in) per year. Tobacco is the main export crop but rice, wine, fruit and vegetables are also important. Bulgaria has experienced significant industrial growth since the end of the Second World War and been transformed from an agricultural economy to one based on light and heavy engineering and manufacturing. Most of this industry is concentrated around Sofia. Nuclear power is expected to provide up to 60% of electricity by the end of the century. Copper, lead, zinc and coal mining have helped stimulate this transformation. Tourism is a developing industry.

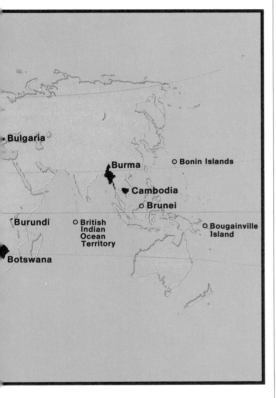

BURKINA

STATUS: People's Democratic Republic
AREA: 274,122 sq km (105,811 sq miles)
POPULATION: 6,754,000
ANNUAL NATURAL INCREASE: 2.6%
DENSITY: 24.7 sq km
CAPITAL: Ouagadougou
LANGUAGE: French, Moré (Mossi), Dyula
RELIGION: 60% animist, 30% Moslem, 10% Roman Catholic
CURRENCY: franc CFA
ORGANISATIONS: UN, CEAO, ECOWAS, OAU

Situated on the southern edge of the Sahara in West Africa, Burkina is a poor, landlocked republic with thin soils supporting savannah grasslands. Frequent droughts, particularly in the north, seriously affect exports of cattle and cotton and the economy which is mainly subsistence agriculture. There is virtually no industry.

BURMA

STATUS: Socialist Republic
AREA: 678,030 sq km (261,720 sq miles)
POPULATION: 39,411,000
ANNUAL NATURAL INCREASE: 2.0%
DENSITY: 58.2 per sq km
CAPITAL: Rangoon
LANGUAGE: Burmese
RELIGION: 85% Buddhist. Animist, Moslem, Hindu and Christian minorities
CURRENCY: kyat
ORGANISATIONS: UN, Col. Plan

Much of Burma is covered by tropical rain forest divided by the central valley of the Irrawaddy, the Sittang and the Salween rivers. The western highlands are an extension of the Himalayas; hills to the east and south are a continuation of the Yunnan Plateau of China. The Burmese economy is based on export of rice and forestry products. The irrigated central basin and the coastal region to the east of the Irrawaddy delta are the major rice-growing areas. Hardwoods, particularly teak, cover the highlands. There is potential for growth in areas of tin, copper, oil and natural gas exploitation, as there are significant deposits. The small amount of industry concentrates on food processing.

BURUNDI

STATUS: Republic
AREA: 27,835 sq km (10,745 sq miles)
POPULATION: 4,852,000
ANNUAL NATURAL INCREASE: 3.0%
DENSITY: 174.4 sq km
CAPITAL: Bujumbura
LANGUAGE: French, Kirundi, Swahili
RELIGION: 60% Roman Catholic. Large minority Animist
CURRENCY: Burundi franc
ORGANISATIONS: UN, OAU

This central African republic is one of the world's poorest nations. Manufacturing industry is almost non-existent as the population barely produces enough food for itself. Burundi is close to the equator but because of its altitude temperatures range between 17° and 23°C (63° and 74°F). The poverty has two basic causes – repetitive droughts and slow recovery from tribal conflicts.

CAMBODIA

STATUS: People's Republic
AREA: 181,000 sq km (69,865 sq miles)
POPULATION: 7,492,000
ANNUAL NATURAL INCREASE: 2.3%
DENSITY: 41.4 per sq km
CAPITAL: Phnom Penh
LANGUAGE: Khmer
RELIGION: Buddhist majority. Roman Catholic and Moslem minorities
CURRENCY: riel
ORGANISATIONS: UN, Col. Plan

Cambodia is a potentially rich country in S.E. Asia whose economy has been damaged since the 1970's by the aftermath of the Vietnam War. The central plain of the river Mekong covers over 70% of the country and provides ideal conditions for rice production and harvesting of fish. Over 50% of Cambodia is covered by monsoon rain forest.

CAMEROON

STATUS: Republic
AREA: 475,500 sq km (183,545 sq miles)
POPULATION: 10,446,000
ANNUAL NATURAL INCREASE: 2.7%
DENSITY: 22 per sq km
CAPITAL: Yaoundé
LANGUAGE: English, French
RELIGION: 40% Christian, 39% traditional beliefs, 21% Moslem
CURRENCY: CFA franc
ORGANISATIONS: UN, OAU

Cameroon is situated on the coast of West Africa just north of the equator. Coastal lowlands rise to densely forested plateaux. Rainfall varies from over 1000 to only 50cm per year. The majority of the population are farmers with agricultural products accounting for over 80% of export revenue. Coffee and cocoa are the main cash crops. Mineral resources are underdeveloped but Cameroon already is Africa's greatest producer of bauxite, aluminium ore. Oil exploitation is playing an increasing role in the economy.

CANADA

STATUS: Dominion
AREA: 9,922,385 sq km (3,830,840 sq miles)
POPULATION: 25,612,000

ANNUAL NATURAL INCREASE: 0.8%
DENSITY: 2.6 per sq km
CAPITAL: Ottawa
LANGUAGE: English, French
RELIGION: 46% Roman Catholic. Protestant and Jewish minority
CURRENCY: Canadian dollar (C$)
ORGANISATIONS: Comm, UN, Col. Plan, NATO, OECD

ALBERTA

STATUS: Province
AREA: 661,190 sq km (255,220 sq miles)
POPULATION: 2,358,000
CAPITAL: Edmonton

BRITISH COLUMBIA

STATUS: Province
AREA: 948,595 sq km (366,160 sq miles)
POPULATION: 2,884,700
CAPITAL: Victoria

MANITOBA

STATUS: Province
AREA: 650,090 sq km (250,935 sq miles)
POPULATION: 1,070,600
CAPITAL: Winnipeg

NEW BRUNSWICK

STATUS: Province
AREA: 73,435 sq km (28,345 sq miles)
POPULATION: 719,600
CAPITAL: Fredericton

NEWFOUNDLAND AND LABRADOR

STATUS: Province
AREA: 404,520 sq km (156,145 sq miles)
POPULATION: 405,720
CAPITAL: St. John's

NORTHWEST TERRITORIES

STATUS: Territory
AREA: 3,379,685 sq km (1,304,560 sq miles)
POPULATION: 51,000
CAPITAL: Yellowknife

NOVA SCOTIA

STATUS: Province
AREA: 55,490 sq km (21,420 sq miles)
POPULATION: 879,800
CAPITAL: Halifax

ONTARIO

STATUS: Province
AREA: 1,068,630 sq km (412,490 sq miles)
POPULATION: 9,064,200
CAPITAL: Toronto

PRINCE EDWARD ISLAND

STATUS: Province
AREA: 5,655 sq km (2,185 sq miles)
POPULATION: 124,000
CAPITAL: Charlottetown

QUEBEC

STATUS: Province
AREA: 1,540,680 sq km (594,705 sq miles)
POPULATION: 6,582,700
CAPITAL: Quebec

SASKATCHEWAN

STATUS: Province
AREA: 651,900 sq km (251,635 sq miles)
POPULATION: 1,017,800
CAPITAL: Regina

YUKON TERRITORY

STATUS: Territory
AREA: 482,515 sq km (186,250 sq miles)
POPULATION: 23,200
CAPITAL: Whitehorse

Canada is the world's second largest country stretching from the great barren islands of the Arctic north to the vast grasslands of the central south, and from the Rocky Mountain chain of the west to the farmlands of the Great Lakes in the east. This huge area experiences great climatic differences but basically a continental climate prevails with extremes of heat and cold particularly in the central plains. The Arctic tundra of the far north provides summer grazing for caribou. Further south coniferous forests grow on the thin soils of the ancient shield landscape and on the extensive foothills of the Rocky Mountains. In contrast, the rich soils of the central prairies support grasslands and grain crops. The Great Lakes area provides fish, fruit, maize, root crops and dairy products; the prairies produce over 20% of the world's wheat; and the grasslands of Alberta support a thriving beef industry. Most minerals are mined and exploited in Canada with oil and natural gas, iron ore, bauxite, nickel, zinc, copper, gold and silver the major exports. The country's vast rivers provide huge amounts of hydro-electric power but most industry is confined to the Great Lakes and St Lawrence margins. The principal manufactured goods for export are steel products, motor vehicles, and paper for newsprint. Despite economic success, Canada still remains one of the world's most under-exploited countries so vast are the potential mineral resources and areas of land for agricultural development.

CANARY ISLANDS

STATUS: Island Province of Spain
AREA: 7,275 sq km (2,810 sq miles)
POPULATION: 1,444,626
CAPITAL: Las Palmas (Gran Canaria) and Santa Cruz (Tenerife)

CAPE VERDE

STATUS: Republic
AREA: 4,035 sq km (1,560 sq miles)
POPULATION: 333,000
ANNUAL NATURAL INCREASE: 2.4%
DENSITY: 82.6 per sq km
CAPITAL: Praia
LANGUAGE: Portuguese, Creole
RELIGION: 98% Roman Catholic
CURRENCY: Cape Verde escudo
ORGANISATIONS: UN, ECOWAS, OAU

Independent since 1975, the ten inhabited volcanic islands of the republic are situated in the Atlantic 500km (310 miles) west of Senegal. Rainfall is low but irrigation encourages growth of sugar-cane, coconuts, fruit and maize. Fishing accounts for about 70% of export revenue. All consumer goods are imported and trading links continue to be maintained with Portugal.

CAROLINE ISLANDS

(see **MICRONESIA, FEDERATED STATES OF, AND PALAU**)

CAYMAN ISLANDS

STATUS: UK Dependent Territory
AREA: 259 sq km (100 sq miles)
POPULATION: 22,000
CAPITAL: George Town

CELEBES (SULAWESI)

STATUS: Island Province of Indonesia
AREA: 229,110 sq km (88,435 sq miles)
POPULATION: 10,409,533

CENTRAL AFRICAN REPUBLIC

STATUS: Republic
AREA: 624,975 sq km (241,240 sq miles)
POPULATION: 2,740,000
ANNUAL NATURAL INCREASE: 2.8%
DENSITY: 4.4 per sq km
CAPITAL: Bangui
LANGUAGE: French, Sango
RELIGION: animist majority. 33% Christian. Moslem minority
CURRENCY: CFA franc
ORGANISATIONS: UN, OAU

The republic is landlocked and remote from both east and west Africa. The natural vegetation is tropical savannah on the rolling plateaux but despite 100cm (39in) or more rainfall per year, the economy is based on subsistence agriculture. A small amount of crops are exported – cotton, coffee, oil palm and cocoa. Diamonds and uranium ore are the major mineral exports. Hardwood forests in the south-west provide timber for export.

CEUTA
STATUS: Spanish External Territory
AREA: 19.5 sq km (7.5 sq miles)
POPULATION: 70,172

CEYLON
(see **SRI LANKA**)

CHAD

STATUS: Republic
AREA: 1,284,000 sq km (495,625 sq miles)
POPULATION: 5,139,000
ANNUAL NATURAL INCREASE: 2.0%
DENSITY: 4 per sq km
CAPITAL: Ndjamena
LANGUAGE: French, Arabic, local languages
RELIGION: 50% Moslem, 45% animist, 5% Christian
CURRENCY: CFA franc
ORGANISATIONS: UN, OAU

Chad is a vast state of central Africa stretching deep into the Sahara. The economy is based on agriculture but only the south with 100cm (39in) of rainfall can support crops for export – cotton, rice and groundnuts. Severe droughts, increasing desertification and border disputes have severely restricted development. Life expectancy at birth is still only 43 years. Salt is mined around Lake Chad.

CHANNEL ISLANDS
STATUS: British Crown Dependency
AREA: 194 sq km (75 sq miles)
POPULATION: 136,000
CAPITAL: St Helier (Jersey), St Peter Port (Guernsey)

CHILE

STATUS: Republic
AREA: 751,625 sq km (290,125 sq miles)
POPULATION: 12,466,000
ANNUAL NATURAL INCREASE: 1.6%
DENSITY: 16.6 per sq km
CAPITAL: Santiago
LANGUAGE: Spanish
RELIGION: 85% Roman Catholic. Protestant minority
CURRENCY: Chilean peso
ORGANISATIONS: UN, OAS

Chile is a long thin country on the west coast of South America stretching throughout 38 degrees of latitude from the Atacama desert of the north to the ice deserts of Tierra del Fuego. Apart from a thin coastal strip of lowland, the country is dominated by the Andes mountains. The economy is based upon the abundance of mineral resources with copper (the world's largest reserve), iron ore, nitrates, coal, oil and gas all major exports. Most energy is provided by hydro-electric power. Light and heavy industries are based around Concepción and Santiago.

CHINA

STATUS: People's Republic
AREA: 9,597,000 sq km (3,704,440 sq miles)
POPULATION: 1,066,293,000
ANNUAL NATURAL INCREASE: 1.0%
DENSITY: 111.1 per sq km
CAPITAL: Beijing (Peking)
LANGUAGE: Mandarin Chinese, regional languages
RELIGION: Confucianist, Buddhist, Taoist. Small Christian and Moslem minority
CURRENCY: Renminbi or yuan
ORGANISATIONS: UN

ANHUI (ANHWEI)
STATUS: Province
AREA: 139,900 sq km (54,000 sq miles)
POPULATION: 51,030,000
CAPITAL: Hefei

BEIJING (PEKING)
STATUS: Municipality
AREA: 17,800 sq km (6,870 miles)
POPULATION: 9,470,000

FUJIAN (FUKIEN)
STATUS: Province
AREA: 123,000 sq km (47,515 sq miles)
POPULATION: 26,770,000
CAPITAL: Fuzhou

GANSU (KANSU)
STATUS: Province
AREA: 530,000 sq km (204,580 sq miles)
POPULATION: 20,160,000
CAPITAL: Lanzhou

GUANGDONG (KWANGTUNG)
STATUS: Province
AREA: 231,400 sq km (89,320 sq miles)
POPULATION: 61,660,000
CAPITAL: Guangzhou

GUANGXI-ZHUANG (KWANGSI-CHUANG)
STATUS: Autonomous Region
AREA: 220,400 sq km (85,075 sq miles)
POPULATION: 38,060,000
CAPITAL: Nanning

GUIZHOU (KWEICHOW)
STATUS: Province
AREA: 174,000 sq km (67,165 sq miles)
POPULATION: 29,320,000
CAPITAL: Guiyang

HEBEI (HOPEI)
STATUS: Province
AREA: 202,700 sq km (78,240 sq miles)
POPULATION: 54,870,000
CAPITAL: Shijiazhuang

HEILONGJIANG (HEILUNGKIANG)
STATUS: Province
AREA: 710,000 sq km (274,060 sq miles)
POPULATION: 32,950,000
CAPITAL: Harbin

HENAN (HONAN)
STATUS: Province
AREA: 167,000 sq km (64,460 sq miles)
POPULATION: 76,460,000
CAPITAL: Zhengzhou

HUBEI (HUPEH)
STATUS: Province
AREA: 187,500 sq km (72,375 sq miles)
POPULATION: 48,760,000
CAPITAL: Wuhan

HUNAN (HUNAN)
STATUS: Province
AREA: 210,500 sq km (81,255 sq miles)
POPULATION: 55,610,000
CAPITAL: Changsha

JIANGSU (KIANGSU)
STATUS: Province
AREA: 102,200 sq km (39,450 sq miles)
POPULATION: 61,710,000
CAPITAL: Nanjing

JIANGXI (KIANGSI)
STATUS: Province
AREA: 164,800 sq km (63,615 sq miles)
POPULATION: 34,210,000
CAPITAL: Nanchang

JILIN (KIRIN)
STATUS: Province
AREA: 290,000 sq km (111,940 sq miles)
POPULATION: 22,840,000
CAPITAL: Changchun

LIAONING (LIAONING)
STATUS: Province
AREA: 230,000 sq km (88,780 sq miles)
POPULATION: 36,550,000
CAPITAL: Shenyang

NEI MONGOL (INNER MONGOLIA)
STATUS: Autonomous Region
AREA: 450,000 sq km (173,700 sq miles)
POPULATION: 19,850,000
CAPITAL: Hohhot

NINGXIA HUI (NINGHSIA)
STATUS: Autonomous Region
AREA: 170,000 sq km (65,620 sq miles)
POPULATION: 4,060,000
CAPITAL: Yinchuan

QINGHAI (CHINGHAI)
STATUS: Province
AREA: 721,000 sq km (278,305 sq miles)
POPULATION: 4,020,000
CAPITAL: Xining

SHAANXI (SHENSI)
STATUS: Province
AREA: 195,800 sq km (75,580 sq miles)
POPULATION: 29,660,000
CAPITAL: Xian

SHANDONG (SHANTUNG)
STATUS: Province
AREA: 153,300 sq km (59,175 sq miles)
POPULATION: 76,370,000
CAPITAL: Jinan

SHANGHAI
STATUS: Municipality
AREA: 5,800 sq km (2,240 sq miles)
POPULATION: 12,050,000

SHANXI (SHANSI)
STATUS: Province
AREA: 157,100 sq km (60,640 sq miles)
POPULATION: 26,000,000
CAPITAL: Taiyuan

SICHUAN (SZECHWAN)
STATUS: Province
AREA: 569,000 sq km (219,635 sq miles)
POPULATION: 101,120,000
CAPITAL: Chengdu

TIANJIN (TIENTSIN)
STATUS: Municipality
AREA: 4,000 sq km (1,545 sq miles)
POPULATION: 7,990,000

YUNNAN (YUNNAN)
STATUS: Province
AREA: 436,200 sq km (168,375 sq miles)
POPULATION: 33,620,000
CAPITAL: Kunming

XINJIANG UYGUR (SINKIANG UIGHUR)
STATUS: Autonomous Region
AREA: 1,646,800 sq km (635,665 sq miles)
POPULATION: 13,440,000
CAPITAL: Urumqi

XIZANG (TIBET)
STATUS: Autonomous Region
AREA: 1,221,600 sq km (471,540 sq miles)
POPULATION: 1,970,000
CAPITAL: Lhasa

ZHEJIANG (CHEKIANG)
STATUS: Province
AREA: 101,800 sq km (39,295 sq miles)
POPULATION: 39,930,000
CAPITAL: Hangzhou

With population over one billion and vast mineral and agricultural resources China has made a tremendous effort during the late 1970's and 80's to erase the negative economic effects of the collectivisation policy implemented from 1955, and the cultural revolution of the late 1960's.

The land of China is one of the most diverse on Earth. The majority of the people live in the east where the economy is dictated by the great drainage basins of the Huang He and the Chang Jiang (Yangtze). Here, intensive irrigated agriculture produces one third of the world's rice as well as wheat, maize, sugar, soya beans and oil seeds. Pigs are reared and fish caught throughout China. The country is basically self-sufficient in cereals, livestock and fish.

Western and northern China are far less densely populated areas as cultivation is restricted to oases and sheltered valleys. In the south-west, the Tibetan plateau averages 4,900 m (16,000 ft) and supports scattered sheep herding. To the north are Sinkiang and the desert basins of Tarim and Dzungaria, and bordering Mongolia the vast dry Gobi desert. In the far north only in Manchuria does the rainfall allow extensive arable cultivation, mainly wheat, barley and maize.

The natural mineral resources of China are immense, varied and under-exploited. The Yunnan Plateau of the south-east is rich in tin, copper, and zinc; Manchuria possesses coal and iron ore; and oil is extracted from beneath the Yellow Sea. The main industrial centres are situated close to the natural resources and concentrate on the production of iron, steel, cement, light engineering and textile manufacturing. The economy is being built on this industrial base, with stable and adequate food production and increasing trade with the United States, Western Europe and Japan.

CHRISTMAS ISLAND
STATUS: External Territory of Australia
AREA: 135 sq km (52 sq miles)
POPULATION: 3,214

COCOS (KEELING) ISLANDS
STATUS: External Territory of Australia
AREA: 14 sq km (5 sq miles)
POPULATION: 585

COLOMBIA

STATUS: Republic
AREA: 1,138,915 sq km (439,620 sq miles)
POPULATION: 29,188,000
ANNUAL NATURAL INCREASE: 2.1%
DENSITY: 25.7 per sq km
CAPITAL: Bogotá
LANGUAGE: Spanish, Indian languages
RELIGION: 95% Roman Catholic. Small Protestant and Jewish minorities
CURRENCY: Colombian peso
ORGANISATIONS: UN, OAS

The landscape of Colombia falls into two distinct parts: the northern Andes and the

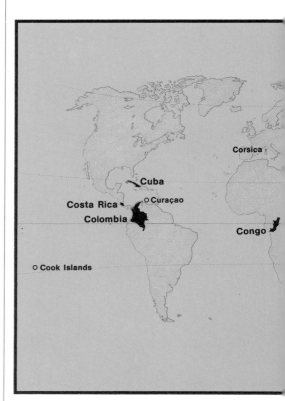

rain forests of the east.

Fertile river valleys in the Andean range produce tobacco, coffee, cotton, and rice.

Coffee has always been the major export crop, but manufacturing industry and mining of coal, iron ore, copper and precious stones are becoming more dominant in the economy. Immense illegal quantities of cocaine are exported.

COMOROS

STATUS: Federal Islamic Republic
AREA: 1,860 sq km (718 sq miles)
POPULATION: 484,000

ANNUAL NATURAL INCREASE: 3.1%
DENSITY: 260.2 per sq km
CAPITAL: Moroni
LANGUAGE: French, Arabic, Comoran
RELIGION: large Moslem majority. Christian minority
CURRENCY: Comoros franc (CF)
ORGANISATIONS: UN, OAU

The Comoro Islands, comprising Moheli, Grand Comore, and Anjouan, are situated between Madagascar and the east African coast. In 1974, the island of Mayotte voted in referenda to remain a French dependency. A cool, dry season alternates with hot, humid monsoon weather between November and April, and annual rainfall ranges from 100–114cm(40–45in). Mangoes, coconuts and bananas are grown around the coastal lowlands. The island's economy is based on the export of coffee, vanilla, copra, sisal, cacao and cloves. Timber and timber products are important to local development. There is no manufacturing.

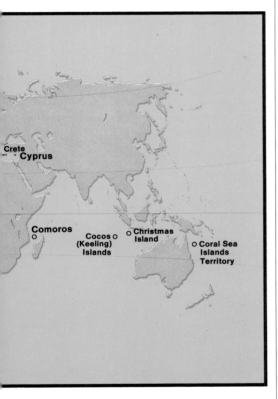

CONGO

STATUS: People's Republic
AREA: 342,000 sq km (132,010 sq miles)
POPULATION: 1,787,000
ANNUAL NATURAL INCREASE: 2.6%
DENSITY: 5.3 per sq km
CAPITAL: Brazzaville
LANGUAGE: French, Kongo, Teke, Sanga
RELIGION: 50% traditional beliefs, 30% Roman Catholic. Small Protestant and Moslem minority
CURRENCY: CFA franc
ORGANISATIONS: UN, OAU

The Congo, Africa's first Communist State still has strong economic ties with the west, especially France its former colonial ruler. Situated on the coast of West Africa it contains over two-thirds swamp and forest, with wooded savannah on the highlands of the Batéké plateau near the Gabon border. Its climate is hot and humid with average rainfall of 122–128cm(48–50in). Over 60% of the population are employed in subsistence farming, the main crops being plantains, maize and cassava, while coffee, groundnuts and cocoa are all exported. Timber and timber products accounts for 60% of all the Congo's exports. Its mineral resources are considerable including industrial diamonds, gold, lead, zinc and extensive coastal oilfields. Manufacturing industry is concentrated in the major towns and is primarily food processing and textiles.

COOK ISLANDS

STATUS: Self-governing Overseas Territory in free association with New Zealand
AREA: 233 sq km (90 sq miles)
POPULATION: 20,000
CAPITAL: Rarotonga

CORAL SEA ISLANDS TERRITORY

STATUS: External Territory of Australia
AREA: 22 sq km (8.5 sq miles)
POPULATION: 3

CORSICA (CORSE)

STATUS: Island Region of France
AREA: 8,680 sq km (3,350 sq miles)
POPULATION: 240,178
CAPITAL: Ajaccio

COSTA RICA

STATUS: Republic
AREA: 50,900 sq km (19,650 sq miles)
POPULATION: 2,666,000
ANNUAL NATURAL INCREASE: 2.6%
DENSITY: 52.4 per sq km
CAPITAL: San José
LANGUAGE: Spanish
RELIGION: 95% Roman Catholic
CURRENCY: Costa Rican colón
ORGANISATIONS: UN, CACM, OAS

Costa Rica is a narrow country, situated between Nicaragua and Panama, with both a Pacific and a Caribbean coastline. The mountain chains that run the length of the country form the fertile uplands where coffee (one of the main crops and exports) and cattle flourish. Bananas are grown on the Pacific coast. Although gold, silver, iron ore and bauxite are mined, the principal industries are food processing and manufacture of textiles and chemicals, fertilizers and furniture.

CRETE (KRÍTI)

STATUS: Island Province of Greece
AREA: 8,330 sq km (3,215 sq miles)
POPULATION: 502,165
CAPITAL: Iráklion

CUBA

STATUS: Republic
AREA: 114,525 sq km (44,205 sq miles)
POPULATION: 10,268,000
ANNUAL NATURAL INCREASE: 1.1%
DENSITY: 89.7 per sq km
CAPITAL: Havana (Habana)
LANGUAGE: Spanish
RELIGION: Roman Catholic majority
CURRENCY: Cuban peso
ORGANISATIONS: UN, COMECON

Cuba, consisting of one large island and over fifteen hundred small ones, dominates the entrance to the Gulf of Mexico. It is a mixture of fertile plains, mountain ranges and gentle countryside with temperatures ranging from 22°–28°C(72°–82°F) and an average annual rainfall of 120cm(47in). Being the only Communist state in the Americas, most of Cuba's trade relations are with the USSR and Comecon countries. Sugar, tobacco and nickel are the main exports and the mining of manganese, chrome, copper and oil is expanding. Cuba has enough cattle and coffee for domestic use but many other food products are imported.

CURAÇAO

STATUS: Self-governing Island of Netherlands Antilles
AREA: 444 sq km (171 sq miles)
POPULATION: 170,000
CAPITAL: Willemstad

CYPRUS

STATUS: Republic
AREA: 9,250 sq km (3,570 sq miles)
POPULATION: 673,000
ANNUAL NATURAL INCREASE: 1.3%
DENSITY: 72.8 per sq km
CAPITAL: Nicosia
LANGUAGE: Greek, Turkish, English
RELIGION: Greek Orthodox majority. Moslem minority
CURRENCY: Cyprus pound (C£),Turkish Lira (TL)
ORGANISATIONS: Comm, UN, Council of Europe

Cyprus is a prosperous Mediterranean island. The summers are very hot (38°C, 100°F) and dry and the winters warm and wet. About two-thirds of the island is under cultivation and produces citrus fruit, potatoes, barley, wheat and olives. Sheep, goats and pigs are the principal livestock. The main exports are minerals (including copper and asbestos), fruit, wine and vegetables. Tourism is also an important source of foreign exchange, despite Turkish occupation of the north. Most industry consists of local manufacturing.

CZECHOSLOVAKIA

STATUS: Socialist Republic
AREA: 127,870 sq km (49,360 sq miles)
POPULATION: 15,534,000
ANNUAL NATURAL INCREASE: 0.3%
DENSITY: 121.5 per sq km
CAPITAL: Prague (Praha)
LANGUAGE: Czech, Slovak
RELIGION: 70% Roman Catholic,
15% Protestant
CURRENCY: koruna (Kcs)
ORGANISATIONS: UN, Warsaw Pact, COMECON

At the heart of central Europe, Czechoslovakia is fringed by forested uplands in the west and the Carpathians to the east. Winters are cold and wet, while summers are hot and humid with frequent thundery showers. Agriculture accounts for 65% of the land use and ranges from cereal crops, cattle and pig farming in the fertile lowlands, to the cultivation of oats, potatoes and rye and sheep farming in the less hospitable uplands. Czechoslovakia is rich in natural resources including coal, zinc, lead, mercury, iron ore, copper and tin. Timber and timber products are also important. These have been extensively exploited and Czechoslovakia's only industrial competitor in the Communist block is East Germany. Exports include machinery, industrial chemicals, coal, lignite, iron, steel and textiles.

DAHOMEY
(see **BENIN**)

DENMARK

STATUS: Kingdom
AREA: 43,075 sq km (16,625 sq miles)
POPULATION: 5,116,273
ANNUAL NATURAL INCREASE: −0.1%
DENSITY: 119 per sq km
CAPITAL: Copenhagen (København)
LANGUAGE: Danish
RELIGION: 94% Lutheran. Small Protestant and Roman Catholic minority

CURRENCY: Danish krone
ORGANISATIONS: UN, Council of Europe, EEC,
NATO, OECD

Denmark acts as a bridge between West Germany and Scandinavia. It consists of the Jutland Peninsula and over 400 islands. The low-lying landscape was scarred by retreating glaciers leaving distinctive 'moraines' (accumulations of earth and stones carried by glaciers). The climate is mild, especially in the North Sea area, with rainfall at all seasons. Exports are predominantly meat and dairy products – beef, butter, cheese, eggs, bacon and pork. Cereals, sugar beet and pototoes are also grown. An extensive fishing industry is centred on the shallow lagoons which have formed along the indented western coastline. Over 30% of the total workforce are involved in industry, and machinery and electrical products are amongst the most important.

DJIBOUTI

STATUS: Republic
AREA: 23,000 sq km (8,800 sq miles)
POPULATION: 456,000
ANNUAL NATURAL INCREASE: 2.5%
DENSITY: 19.9 per sq km
CAPITAL: Djibouti
LANGUAGE: French, Somali, Dankali, Arabic
RELIGION: mainly Moslem. Roman Catholic
minority
CURRENCY: Djibouti franc
ORGANISATIONS: UN, Arab League, OAU

The former French colony of Djibouti, strategically situated at the mouth of the Red Sea, acts as a trade outlet for Ethiopia, as well as serving Red Sea shipping. Its climate is extremely hot and arid – average annual temperatures are 30°C(86°F) and the annual rainfall on the coast is as low as 38cm(15in), and there is consequently very little cultivation. Cattle, hides and skins are the main exports. The port of Djibouti is an important transit point for Red Sea trade.

DOMINICA

STATUS: Commonwealth Nation
AREA: 751 sq km (290 sq miles)
POPULATION: 77,000
ANNUAL NATURAL INCREASE: 1.7%
DENSITY: 102.3 per sq km
CAPITAL: Roseau
LANGUAGE: English, French patois
RELIGION: 80% Roman Catholic
CURRENCY: East Caribbean dollar (EC$)
ORGANISATIONS: Comm, UN, CARICOM, OAS

Dominica is located in the Windward Islands of the east Caribbean between Martinique and Guadeloupe. Tropical rain forest covers the island which obtains foreign revenue from sugar-cane, bananas, coconuts, soap, vegetables and citrus fruits. Main livestock are cattle, pigs and poultry. Tourism is the most rapidly expanding industry.

DOMINICAN REPUBLIC

STATUS: Republic
AREA: 48,440 sq km (18,700 sq miles)
POPULATION: 6,416,000

ANNUAL NATURAL INCREASE: 2.5%
DENSITY: 132.5 per sq km
CAPITAL: Santo Domingo
LANGUAGE: Spanish
RELIGION: 90% Roman Catholic. Small
Protestant and Jewish minority
CURRENCY: Dominican Republic peso
ORGANISATIONS: UN, OAS

The Caribbean island of Hispaniola is divided between Haiti and the Dominican Republic. The landscape is dominated by a series of mountain ranges, thickly covered with rain forest, reaching up to 3000m(9840ft). To the south there is a coastal plain where the capital, Santo Domingo, lies. The annual rainfall exceeds 100cm(40in). Agriculture forms the backbone of the economy – sugar, coffee, cocoa and tobacco are the staple crops. Minerals include bauxite, nickel, gold and silver.

DUBAI
(see **UNITED ARAB EMIRATES**)

ECUADOR

STATUS: Republic
AREA: 461,475 sq km (178,130 sq miles)
POPULATION: 9,647,107
ANNUAL NATURAL INCREASE: 2.8%
DENSITY: 20.9 per sq km
CAPITAL: Quito
LANGUAGE: Spanish, Quechua, other Indian languages
RELIGION: 90% Roman Catholic
CURRENCY: sucre
ORGANISATIONS: UN, OAS, OPEC

Ecuador falls into two distinctive geographical zones, the coastal lowlands which border the Pacific Ocean and, inland the Andean highlands. The highlands stretch about 400km(250

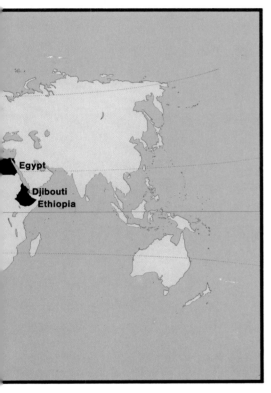

miles) north-south, and here limited quantities of maize, wheat and barley are cultivated. Ecuador's main agricultural exports—bananas, coffee and cocoa, are all grown on the fertile coastal lowlands. Large resources of crude oil have been found in the thickly forested lowlands on the eastern border. Ecuador is now South America's second largest oil producer after Venezuela.

EGYPT

STATUS: Arab Republic
AREA: 1,000,250 sq km (386,095 sq miles)
POPULATION: 48,205,000
ANNUAL NATURAL INCREASE: 2.6%
DENSITY: 48.2 per sq km
CAPITAL: Cairo (El Qâhira)
LANGUAGE: Arabic, Berber, Nubian, English, French
RELIGION: 80% Moslem (mainly Sunni), Coptic Christian minority
CURRENCY: Egyptian pound (£E)
ORGANISATIONS: UN, Arab League (suspended), OAU

The focal point of Egypt situated on the Mediterranean coast of north-east Africa is the fertile, irrigated Nile Valley, sandwiched between two deserts. Egypt is virtually dependent on the River Nile for water as average annual rainfall varies between only 20cm(8in) in the north and zero in the deserts. Cotton and Egyptian clover are the two most important crops with an increasing cultivation of cereals, fruits, rice, sugar-cane and vegetables. Buffaloes, cattle, sheep, goats and camels are the principal livestock. Tourism is an important source of revenue together with tolls from the Suez Canal. Major manufactures include cement, cotton goods, iron and steel, and processed foods. The main mineral deposits are phosphates, iron ore, salt, manganese and chrome.

EL SALVADOR

STATUS: Republic
AREA: 21,395 sq km (8,260 sq miles)
POPULATION: 4,913,000
ANNUAL NATURAL INCREASE: 2.4%
DENSITY: 229.7 per sq km
CAPITAL: San Salvador
LANGUAGE: Spanish
RELIGION: 80% Roman Catholic
CURRENCY: Salvadorean colón (C)
ORGANISATIONS: UN, CACM, OAS

Independent from Spain since 1821, El Salvador is a small, densely populated country on the Pacific coast of Central America. Temperatures range from 24 to 26°C(75–79°F) with an average, annual rainfall of 178cm(70in). Coffee and cotton are important exports and the country is the main producer of balsam. Industry has expanded considerably with the production of textiles, shoes, cosmetics, cement, processed foods, chemicals and furniture.

EQUATORIAL GUINEA

STATUS: Republic
AREA: 28,050 sq km (10,825 sq miles)
POPULATION: 401,000
ANNUAL NATURAL INCREASE: 2.3%
DENSITY: 14.3 per sq km
CAPITAL: Malabo
LANGUAGE: Spanish, Fang, Bubi, other tribal languages
RELIGION: 96% Roman Catholic. 4% animist
CURRENCY: CFA franc
ORGANISATIONS: UN, OAU

Independent from Spain since 1968, Equatorial Guinea is made up of two separate provinces – mainland Mbini with hot, wet climate and dense rain forest but little economic development, and the volcanic island of Bioko. Agriculture is the principal source of revenue. Cocoa and coffee from the island plantations are the main exports with wood products, fish and processed foods manufactured near the coast in Mbini.

ETHIOPIA

STATUS: People's Democratic Republic
AREA: 1,023,050 sq km (394,895 sq miles)
POPULATION: 44,927,000
ANNUAL NATURAL INCREASE: 2.1%
DENSITY: 44 per sq km
CAPITAL: Adis Abeba (Addis Ababa)
LANGUAGE: Amharic, English, Arabic
RELIGION: Ethiopian Orthodox, Moslem and animist
CURRENCY: Birr
ORGANISATIONS: UN, OAU

Situated off the Red Sea coast, the landscape of Ethiopia consists of heavily dissected plateaux and plains of arid desert. Rainfall in these latter areas is minimal and unreliable. Drought and starvation are an ever-present problem. Farming, in the high rural areas, accounts for 90% of export revenue with coffee as the principal crop and main export together with fruit and vegetables, oil-seeds, hides and skins. Gold and salt are mined on a small scale. The most important industries are cotton textiles, cement, canned foods, construction materials and leather goods. These are concentrated around the capital, and Asmara in the north. Difficulty of communication has hindered development. In recent years the economy has been devastated by droughts and civil wars.

FAEROES (FØROYAR)
STATUS: Self-governing Island Territory of Denmark
AREA: 1,399 sq km (540 sq miles)
POPULATION: 46,000
CAPITAL: Tórshavn

FALKLAND ISLANDS (MALVINAS)
STATUS: UK Crown Colony
AREA: 12,175 sq km (4,700 sq miles)
POPULATION: 1,900
CAPITAL: Port Stanley

FIJI

STATUS: Republic
AREA: 18,330 sq km (7,075 sq miles)
POPULATION: 714,548
ANNUAL NATURAL INCREASE: 2.4%
DENSITY: 39 per sq km
CAPITAL: Suva
LANGUAGE: Fijian, English, Hindi
RELIGION: 51% Methodist Christian,
40% Hindu, 8% Moslem
CURRENCY: Fiji dollar ($F)
ORGANISATIONS: UN, Col. Plan

A country of some 320 tropical islands, of which over 100 are inhabited, in the south central Pacific Ocean. Fiji's economy is geared to production of sugar-cane, coconut oil, bananas and rice. Main industries are sugar processing, gold-mining, copra processing and fish canning. Important livestock are cattle, goats, pigs and poultry. Tourism is a major developing industry.

FINLAND

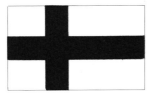

STATUS: Republic
AREA: 337,030 sq km (130,095 sq miles)
POPULATION: 4,929,000
ANNUAL NATURAL INCREASE: 0.4%
DENSITY: 14.7 per sq km
CAPITAL: Helsinki
LANGUAGE: Finnish, Swedish
RELIGION: 90% Evangelical Lutheran. Eastern
Orthodox minority
CURRENCY: markka (Finnmark)
ORGANISATIONS: UN, EFTA, OECD

Finland is a flat land of lakes and forests stretching from 60° to 70°N. The soils are thin and poor on the ice-scarred granite plateau, but ⅘ths of the country supports coniferous forest. Timber and timber products such as paper and dairy goods make up most of Finnish exports. Because of the harsh northern climate most of the population live in towns in the far south. Manufacturing industry has been developing rapidly in recent years.

FRANCE

STATUS: Republic
AREA: 543,965 sq km (209,970 sq miles)
POPULATION: 55,392,000
ANNUAL NATURAL INCREASE: 0.4%
DENSITY: 101.8 per sq km
CAPITAL: Paris
LANGUAGE: French
RELIGION: 90% Roman Catholic. Protestant,
Moslem and Jewish minorities
CURRENCY: French franc
ORGANISATIONS: UN, Council of Eur, EEC,
OECD, WEU

France encompasses a great variety of landscapes, a series of high plateaux, mountain ranges and lowland basins. The Pyrenees form the border with Spain in the south-west, and the Jura mountains form a border with Switzerland. The highest mountain range is the Alps, south of the Jura.

The highest plateau is the Massif Central which rises to 1886m(6188ft). The Vosges plateau borders the plain of Alsace, and the third major plateau, Armorica, occupies the Brittany peninsula.

The French climate is moderated by proximity to the Atlantic, and is generally mild. The south has a mediterranean climate with hot dry summers, the rest of the country has rain all year round. Much of the French countryside is agricultural. France is self-sufficient in cereals, dairy products, meat, fruit and vegetables, and a leading exporter of wheat, barley and sugarbeet. Wine is also a major export. France has reserves of coal, oil and natural gas, and is one of the world's leading producers of iron ore. It has large steel-making and chemical refining industries. Its vehicle, aeronautical and armaments industries are among the worlds most important. Leading light industries are fashion, perfumes and luxury goods. Most of its heavy industry is concentrated in the major industrial zone of the north-east. Tourism is a major source of revenue.

FRANZ JOSEF LAND

STATUS: Islands of USSR
AREA: 16,575 sq km (6,400 sq miles)
POPULATION: No reliable figure available

FRENCH GUIANA

STATUS: Overseas Department of France
AREA: 91,000 sq km (35,125 sq miles)
POPULATION: 84,000
CAPITAL: Cayenne

FRENCH POLYNESIA

STATUS: Overseas Territory of France
AREA: 3,940 sq km (1,520 sq miles)
POPULATION: 172,000
CAPITAL: Papeete

FRENCH SOUTHERN AND ANTARCTIC TERRITORIES

STATUS: Overseas Territory of France
AREA: 439,580 sq km (169,680 sq miles)
POPULATION: 210

FUJAIRAH
(see UNITED ARAB EMIRATES)

GABON

STATUS: Republic
AREA: 267,665 sq km (103,320 sq miles)
POPULATION: 1,172,000
ANNUAL NATURAL INCREASE: 1.6%
DENSITY: 4.4 per sq km
CAPITAL: Libreville
LANGUAGE: French, Bantu dialects, Fang
RELIGION: 60% Roman Catholic
CURRENCY: CFA franc
ORGANISATIONS: UN, OAU, OPEC

Gabon, which lies on the equator, consists of the Ogooúe river basin covered with tropical rain forest. It is hot and wet all year with average

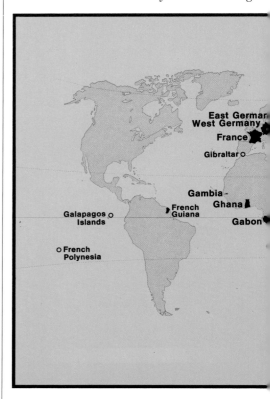

annual temperatures of 25°C(77°F). It is one of the most prosperous states in Africa with valuable timber and mineral resources.

GALAPAGOS ISLANDS

STATUS: Territory of Ecuador
AREA: 7,845 sq km (3,030 sq miles)
POPULATION: 6,201

GAMBIA, THE

STATUS: Republic
AREA: 10,690 sq km (4,125 sq miles)
POPULATION: 656,000

ANNUAL NATURAL INCREASE: 2.0%
DENSITY: 61.4 per sq km
CAPITAL: Banjul
LANGUAGE: English, Madinka, Fula, Wolof
RELIGION: 85% Moslem. Christian and animist minorities
CURRENCY: dalasi
ORGANISATIONS: Comm, UN, ECOWAS, OAU

The Gambia is the smallest country in Africa and, apart from its Atlantic coastline, is entirely surrounded by Senegal. It is 470km(292 miles) long, averages 24km(15 miles) wide and is divided by the Gambia river. The climate has two distinctive seasons. November to May is dry but July to October sees monsoon rainfall up to 130cm(51in). The temperatures average about 23°–27°C(73°–81°F) throughout the year. Groundnuts and subsidiary products are the mainstay of the economy but tourism is developing rapidly. The production of cotton, livestock, fish and rice is increasing to change the present economic reliance on a single crop – groundnuts.

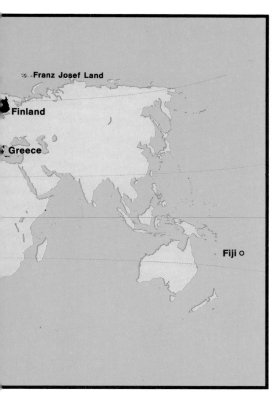

GERMANY, EAST

STATUS: Democratic Republic
AREA: 108,175 sq km (41,755 sq miles)
POPULATION: 16,624,000
ANNUAL NATURAL INCREASE: 0%
DENSITY: 153.7% per sq km
CAPITAL: Berlin (East)
LANGUAGE: German
RELIGION: atheist. 50% Evangelical Protestant, 8% Roman Catholic
CURRENCY: Mark of the GDR (DDR-M)
ORGANISATIONS: UN, COMECON, Warsaw Pact

East Germany is a leading European industrial nation and one of the most developed of the east European socialist bloc. Most of the northern part is flat or rolling hills covered with dark soils. Further south the Central Highlands rise towards the Erzgebirge (500–1000m or 1640–3280ft). The climate is central European with cold, wet winters and warm summers. The country trades predominantly with other Comecon members but is not rich in minerals although potash, copper and uranium are mined successfully and East Germany is the world's largest producer of lignite. Within the eastern bloc East Germany is also the leading supplier and producer of chemicals, synthetic fibres and plastics. There is also a thriving engineering industry and the manufacture of consumer goods is expanding. Although it is a largely urban-industrial economy, agriculture employs 10% of the workforce producing mainly cereal crops, potatoes and sugar-beet. Cattle, pigs, sheep and poultry are the main livestock.

GERMANY, WEST

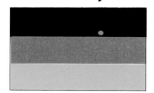

STATUS: Federal Republic
AREA: 248,665 sq km (95,985 sq miles)
POPULATION: 59,576,000
ANNUAL NATURAL INCREASE: −0.2%
DENSITY: 239.6 per sq km
CAPITAL: Bonn
LANGUAGE: German
RELIGION: 50% Protestant, 50% Roman Catholic
CURRENCY: Deutsche Mark (DM)
ORGANISATIONS: UN, EEC, NATO

West Germany consists of three main areas – the Northern plain, the Central Uplands (the largest area) and the Bavarian Alps. It has extremely fertile farmland and although less than 10% of the population work in agriculture over 50% of the land is farmed. West Germany produces huge amounts of dairy products, pork, bacon, beef and ham. The main crops are barley, oats, wheat, rye, sugar-beet and potatoes. The iron, steel and chemical industries of the Ruhr are at the heart of the economy. West Germany is one of the world's leading producers of vehicles, machine tools, electrical and electronic goods and consumer products. Exploitation of the vast resources of coal, iron ore and lignite continues to be a priority. They also help Germany produce its vast electricity supply. The chemical industry relies on the country's great reserves of potash. The textile manufacturing industry is also important.

GHANA

STATUS: Republic
AREA: 238,305 sq km (91,985 sq miles)
POPULATION: 14,045,000

ANNUAL NATURAL INCREASE: 3.4%
DENSITY: 58.9 per sq km
CAPITAL: Accra
LANGUAGE: English, tribal languages
RELIGION: 42% Christian
CURRENCY: new cedi (C)
ORGANISATIONS: Comm, UN, ECOWAS, OAU

Ghana, the West African state once known as the Gold Coast, gained independence from Britain in 1957. The landscape varies from tropical rain forest to dry scrubland, with the annual rainfall ranging from over 200cm(79in) to less than 100cm(40in). The temperature averages 27°C(81°F) all year. Cocoa is the principal crop and chief export but although most Ghanaians farm, there is also a thriving industrial base around Tema, where local bauxite is smelted into aluminium, the largest artificial harbour in Africa. Other exports include gold and diamonds and principal imports are fuel and manufactured goods.

GIBRALTAR

STATUS: UK Crown Colony
AREA: 6.5 sq km (2.5 sq miles)
POPULATION: 29,000

GILBERT ISLANDS
(see **KIRIBATI**)

GREAT BRITAIN
(see **UNITED KINGDOM**)

GREECE

STATUS: Hellenic Republic
AREA: 131,985 sq km (50,945 sq miles)
POPULATION: 9,966,000
ANNUAL NATURAL INCREASE: 0.44%
DENSITY: 75.5 per sq km
CAPITAL: Athens (Athina)
LANGUAGE: Greek
RELIGION: 97% Greek Orthodox
CURRENCY: drachma
ORGANISATIONS: UN, Council of Eur, EEC, NATO, OECD

Mainland Greece and the many islands are dominated by mountains and sea. The climate is predominantly Mediterranean with hot, dry summers and mild winters. Poor irrigation and drainage mean that much of the agriculture is localised but the main crop, olives, is exported and agricultural output generally is increasing. The surrounding seas are important, providing two-thirds of Greece's fish and supporting an active merchant fleet. Athens is the manufacturing base and at least one-quarter of the population live there. Greece is a very popular tourist destination which helps the craft industries in textiles, metals and ceramics and other local products.

GREENLAND

STATUS: Self-governing Island Territory of Denmark
AREA: 2,175,600 sq km (839,780 sq miles)
POPULATION: 53,406
CAPITAL: Godthåb (Nuuk)

GRENADA

STATUS: Commonwealth Nation
AREA: 345 sq km (133 sq miles)
POPULATION: 113,000
ANNUAL NATURAL INCREASE: 1.8%
DENSITY: 327.5 per sq km
CAPITAL: St George's
LANGUAGE: English, French patois
RELIGION: Roman Catholic majority
CURRENCY: E. Caribbean dollar (EC$)
ORGANISATIONS: Comm, UN, CARICOM, OAS

The Caribbean island of Grenada is the southernmost of the Windward islands. It is mountainous and thickly forested with a settled warm climate, (average temperature of 27°C or 81°F), which ensures that its tourist industry continues to expand. Bananas are the main export, although the island is also famous for its spices, especially nutmeg and cloves. Cocoa is also exported.

GUADELOUPE

STATUS: Overseas Department of France
AREA: 1,780 sq km (687 sq miles)
POPULATION: 333,000
CAPITAL: Basse-Terre

GUAM

STATUS: Unincorporated Territory of USA
AREA: 450 sq km (174 sq miles)
POPULATION: 115,756
CAPITAL: Agaña

GUATEMALA

STATUS: Republic
AREA: 108,890 sq km (42,030 sq miles)
POPULATION: 8,195,000
ANNUAL NATURAL INCREASE: 3.1%
DENSITY: 75.3 per sq km
CAPITAL: Guatemala
LANGUAGE: Spanish, Indian languages
RELIGION: 75% Roman Catholic, 25% Protestant
CURRENCY: quetzal (Q)
ORGANISATIONS: UN, CACM, OAS

The central American country of Guatemala has both a Pacific and a Caribbean coastline. The mountainous interior, with peaks reaching up to 4000m (13,120ft), covers two-thirds of the country; in addition there are coastal lowlands and a thickly forested mainland to the north known as the Petén. Agricultural products form the bulk of Guatemala's exports, notably coffee, sugar-cane and bananas. Mineral resources including nickel, antimony, lead, silver and, in the north, crude oil, are only just beginning to be exploited.

GUINEA

STATUS: Republic
AREA: 245,855 sq km (94,900 sq miles)
POPULATION: 6,225,000
ANNUAL NATURAL INCREASE: 2.3%
DENSITY: 25.3 per sq km
CAPITAL: Conakry
LANGUAGE: French, Susu, Manika (Official languages: French and 8 others)
RELIGION: mainly Moslem, some animist, 1% Roman Catholic
CURRENCY: Guinea franc
ORGANISATIONS: UN, ECOWAS, OAU

Guinea, a former French colony is situated on the West African coast. Its drowned coastline, lined with mangrove swamps contrasts strongly with its interior highlands containing the headwaters of the Gambia, Niger and Senegal rivers. Agriculture occupies 80% of the workforce, the main exports being coffee, bananas, pineapple and palm products. Guinea has some of the largest resources of bauxite (aluminium ore) in the world as well as gold and diamonds. Both bauxite and aluminium are exported.

GUINEA-BISSAU

STATUS: Republic
AREA: 36,125 sq km (13,945 sq miles)
POPULATION: 906,000
ANNUAL NATURAL INCREASE: 1.9%
DENSITY: 25.1 per sq km
CAPITAL: Bissau
LANGUAGE: Portuguese, Crioulo, Guinean dialects
RELIGION: Animist and Moslem majorities. Roman Catholic minority
CURRENCY: Guinea-Bissau peso
ORGANISATIONS: UN, ECOWAS, OAU

Guinea-Bissau, on the West African coast was once a centre for the Portuguese slave trade. The coast is swampy and lined with mangroves, and the interior consists of a low-lying plain densely covered with rain forest. The coast is hot and humid with annual rainfall of 200–300cm (79–118in) a year, although the interior is cooler and drier. 80% of the country's exports comprise groundnuts, groundnut oil, palm kernels and palm oil. Fish, fish products and coconuts also make an important contribution to trade.

GUYANA

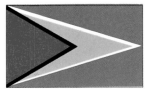

STATUS: Co-operative Republic
AREA: 214,970 sq km (82,980 sq miles)
POPULATION: 971,000
ANNUAL NATURAL INCREASE: 2.2%
DENSITY: 4.6 per sq km
CAPITAL: Georgetown
LANGUAGE: English, Hindu, Urdu, Amerindian dialects

RELIGION: mainly Christian, Moslem and Hindu
CURRENCY: Guyana dollar ($G)
ORGANISATIONS: Comm, UN, CARICOM

The ex-British colony of Guyana borders both Venezuela and Brazil. Its Atlantic coast, the most densely-populated area, is flat and marshy, while towards the interior the landscape gradually rises to the Guiana Highlands – a region densely covered in rain forest. Sugar, molasses and rum, once Guyana's main exports, are now being outstripped by bauxite.

HAITI

STATUS: Republic
AREA: 27,750 sq km (10,710 sq miles)
POPULATION: 5,358,000

ANNUAL NATURAL INCREASE: 2.3%
DENSITY: 193.1 per sq km
CAPITAL: Port-au-Prince
LANGUAGE: French, Creole
RELIGION: 80% Roman Catholic. Some Voodoo folk religion
CURRENCY: gourde
ORGANISATIONS: UN, OAS

Haiti occupies the western part of the island of Hispaniola in the Caribbean. It is the poorest country in Central America. The country is mountainous with three main ranges, the highest reaching 2680m(8793ft). Agriculture is restricted to the plains which divide the ranges. The climate is tropical. 85% of the workforce are farmers, and coffee is the main export. Light manufacturing industries are concentrated around the capital.

HAWAIIAN ISLANDS
(see UNITED STATES OF AMERICA)

HEARD AND McDONALD ISLANDS

STATUS: External Territory of Australia
AREA: 412 sq km (159 sq miles)
POPULATION: No permanent population

HISPANIOLA

STATUS: Island of the West Indies comprising Haiti & Dominican Republic
AREA: 76,170 sq km (29,400 sq miles)
POPULATION: 10,868,780

HOKKAIDO

STATUS: Island of Japan
AREA: 78,460 sq km (30,285 sq miles)
POPULATION: 5,338,206

HONDURAS

STATUS: Republic
AREA: 112,085 sq km (43,265 sq miles)
POPULATION: 4,514,000
ANNUAL NATURAL INCREASE: 3.2%
DENSITY: 40.3 per sq km
CAPITAL: Tegucigalpa
LANGUAGE: Spanish, Indian dialects
RELIGION: large Roman Catholic majority
CURRENCY: lempira or peso
ORGANISATIONS: UN, CACM, OAS

The Central American republic of Honduras consists substantially of rugged mountains and high plateaux with, on the Caribbean coast, an area of hot and humid plains, densely covered with tropical vegetation. These low-lying plains are subject to high annual rainfall, an average of 250cm(98in), and it is in this region that bananas, accounting for half the nation's exports, are grown. Other crops include coffee, sugar, rice, maize, beans and tobacco. Exploitation of lead, iron, tin and oil may lead, however, to a change in the traditional agriculture-based economy. Most industries are concerned with processing local products.

HONG KONG
(INCLUDING KOWLOON & THE NEW TERRITORIES)

STATUS: UK Dependent Territory
AREA: 1,067 sq km (412 sq miles)
POPULATION: 5,533,000
CAPITAL: Victoria

HONSHU

STATUS: Main Island of Japan
AREA: 230,455 sq km (88,955 sq miles)
POPULATION: 89,101,702

HUNGARY

STATUS: People's Republic
AREA: 93,030 sq km (35,910 sq miles)
POPULATION: 10,611,000
ANNUAL NATURAL INCREASE: −0.2%
DENSITY: 114.1 per sq km
CAPITAL: Budapest
LANGUAGE: Hungarian
RELIGION: 60% Roman Catholic, 20% Hungarian Reformed Church, Lutheran and Orthodox minorities
CURRENCY: forint
ORGANISATIONS: UN, Warsaw Pact, COMECON

The undulating fertile plains of Hungary are bisected by the River Danube, and the country is surrounded by mountains – the northern highlands reach a height of 1000m(3280ft). In the centre of the country, Lake Balaton (600sq km or 232sq miles) is the largest lake in Europe. Winters in Hungary are severe, though in summer the enclosed plains can become very hot. Just over 50% of land is arable. Main crops are wheat and maize, and rice, sugar-beet and sunflowers are also grown. Bauxite is Hungary's only substantial mineral deposit. Engineering forms the basis of the economy and most of this industry is concentrated around the capital, Budapest, which is linked by road, rail and river to the rest of eastern Europe. Heavy industry specialises in the production of pig-iron, crude steel, cement and chemicals.

ICELAND

STATUS: Republic
AREA: 102,820 sq km (39,690 sq miles)
POPULATION: 243,000
ANNUAL NATURAL INCREASE: 1.0%
DENSITY: 2.4 per sq km
CAPITAL: Reykjavik
LANGUAGE: Icelandic
RELIGION: 93% Evangelical Lutheran
CURRENCY: Icelandic krona
ORGANISATIONS: UN, Council of Eur, EFTA, NATO, OECD

The northernmost island in Europe, Iceland is 850km(530 miles) away from Scotland, its nearest neighbour. The landscape is entirely volcanic – compacted volcanic ash has been eroded by the wind and there are substantial ice sheets and lava fields as well as many still active volcanoes, geysers and hot springs. The climate is cold, with average summer temperatures of 9°–10°C(48°–50°F), and vegetation is sparse. An average of 950,000 tonnes of fish are landed each year and 95% of Iceland's exports consist of fish and fish products.

INDIA

STATUS: Republic
AREA: 3,166,830 sq km (1,222,395 sq miles)
POPULATION: 766,135,000
ANNUAL NATURAL INCREASE: 2.3%
DENSITY: 242 per sq km
CAPITAL: New Delhi
LANGUAGE: Hindi, English, regional languages
RELIGION: 83% Hindu, 11% Moslem
CURRENCY: Indian rupee (R)
ORGANISATIONS: Comm, UN, Col. Plan

India has the world's second largest population. This vast country contains an extraordinary variety of landscapes, climates and resources.

The Himalaya in the north is the world's highest mountain range with many peaks reaching over 6000m(19,685ft). The Himalayan foothills are covered with lush vegetation, water is in abundant supply (rainfall in Assam reaches 1,070cm or 421in a year) and the climate is hot, making this region the centre for tea cultivation. To the south lies the vast expanse of the Indo-Gangetic plain, 2500km(1550 miles) east-west, divided by the Indus, Ganges and Brahmaputra rivers. This is one of the world's most fertile regions, although it is liable to flooding and failure of monsoon rainfall (June to September) can result in severe drought. In the pre-monsoon season the heat becomes intense – average temperatures in New Delhi reach 38°C(100°F). Rice, wheat, cotton, jute, tobacco and sugar are the main crops. To the south lies the Deccan plateau. India's natural resources are immense – timber, coal, iron ore and nickel, and oil has been discovered in the Indian Ocean. Nevertheless, 80% of the population live by subsistence farming. Main exports by value are precious stones, clothing, tea, iron ore, machinery and cotton.

INDONESIA

STATUS: Republic
AREA: 1,919,445 sq km (740,905 sq miles)
POPULATION: 166,940,000
ANNUAL NATURAL INCREASE: 2.1%
DENSITY: 87 per sq km
CAPITAL: Jakarta
LANGUAGE: Bahasa Indonesia
RELIGION: 78% Moslem, 11% Christian, 11% Hindu and Buddhist
CURRENCY: rupiah
ORGANISATIONS: UN, ASEAN, Col. Plan, OPEC

Indonesia is an arc of islands along the equator which includes Kalimantan (the central and southern part of Borneo), Sumatra, Irian Jaya (the western part of New Guinea), Sulawesi and Java. It is a Moslem nation and has the fifth largest population in the world. Most people live on Java, leaving parts of the other islands virtually uninhabited. The climate is tropical: hot, wet and subject to monsoons. Over three-quarters of the people live in villages and farm but the crops produced are hardly enough for the increasing population and the fishing industry needs developing. Timber and oil production are becoming very important as sources of foreign exchange and there are also rich mineral deposits, as yet not fully exploited.

IRAN

STATUS: Republic
AREA: 1,648,000 sq km (636,130 sq miles)
POPULATION: 49,765,000

ANNUAL NATURAL INCREASE: 2.9%
DENSITY: 30.2 per sq km
CAPITAL: Tehrān
LANGUAGE: Farsi, Kurdish, Arabic, Baluchi, Turkic
RELIGION: Shiite Moslem majority. Sunni Moslem and Armenian Christian minorities
CURRENCY: Iranian rial
ORGANISATIONS: UN, Col. Plan, OPEC

Iran is a large mountainous country situated between the Caspian Sea and the Persian Gulf. The climate is one of extremes with temperatures ranging from −20° to 55°C(−4° to 131°F) and rainfall varies from 200cm(79in) to almost zero. Agricultural conditions are poor except around the Caspian Sea and wheat is the main crop though fruit (especially dates) and nuts are grown and exported. The main livestock is sheep and goats. Iran is oil rich and the revenues have been used to improve communications and social conditions generally. War with neighbouring Iraq has restricted economic growth and particularly affected the Iranian oil industry in the Persian Gulf.

IRAQ

STATUS: Republic
AREA: 438,317 sq km (169,235 sq miles)
POPULATION: 16,450,000
ANNUAL NATURAL INCREASE: 3.3%
DENSITY: 37.6 per sq km
CAPITAL: Baghdad
LANGUAGE: Arabic Kurdish, Turkoman
RELIGION: 50% Shiite, 45% Sunni Moslem
CURRENCY: Iraqi dinar (ID)
ORGANISATIONS: UN, Arab League, OPEC

Iraq is mostly desert but because of the two great rivers, the Tigris and the Euphrates, there are pockets of fertile land. The two rivers join and become the Shatt al Arab which flows into the Persian Gulf. Iraq has a very short coastline making Basra, the principal port, very important. Oil is the major export and oil revenues enable agriculture to be improved and increased. Dates are the other main export. Light industry is situated around Baghdad, the capital, Basra and Kirkuk, the large oilfield. War with Iran has placed great strains on the economy with exports of oil, oil products and natural gas severely restricted.

IRELAND (EIRE)

STATUS: Republic
AREA: 68,895 sq km (26,595 sq miles)
POPULATION: 3,537,195
ANNUAL NATURAL INCREASE: 0.9%
DENSITY: 51.4 per sq km

CAPITAL: Dublin (Baile Átha Cliath)
LANGUAGE: Irish, English
RELIGION: 95% Roman Catholic, 5% Protestant
CURRENCY: punt or Irish pound (I£)
ORGANISATIONS: UN, Council of Eur, EEC, OECD

The Irish Republic forms 80% of the island of Ireland. It is a country where the cool, damp climate makes for rich pastureland, and livestock farming predominates. Meat and dairy produce is processed in the small market towns where there are also breweries and mills. Large-scale manufacturing is centred round Dublin, the capital and main port. Ireland also possesses reserves of oil and natural gas, peat and deposits of lead and zinc. Tourism is also important to the Irish economy.

IRIAN JAYA

STATUS: Province of Indonesia
AREA: 421,980 sq km (162,885 sq miles)
POPULATION: 1,173,875

ISRAEL

STATUS: State
AREA: 20,770 sq km (8,015 sq miles)
POPULATION: 4,296,000
ANNUAL NATURAL INCREASE: 1.6%
DENSITY: 206.9 per sq km
CAPITAL: Jerusalem
LANGUAGE: Hebrew, Arabic
RELIGION: 85% Jewish, 13% Moslem
CURRENCY: new shekel
ORGANISATIONS: UN

This narrow country on the eastern Mediterranean littoral contains a varied landscape – a coastal plain bounded by foothills in the south and the Galilee Highlands in the north; a deep trough extending from the River Jordan to the Dead Sea, and the Negev, a desert region in the south extending to the Gulf of Aqaba. Economic development in Israel is the most advanced in the Middle East. Manufacturing, particularly diamond finishing and electronics, and mining are the most important industries although Israel also has a flourishing agricultural industry exporting fruit, flowers and vegetables to Western Europe.

ITALY

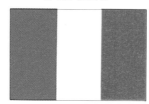

STATUS: Republic
AREA: 301,245 sq km (116,280 sq miles)

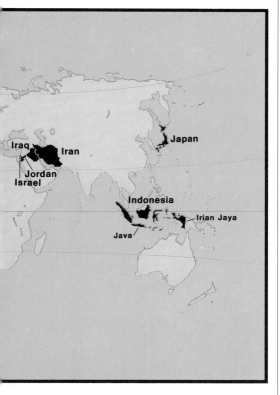

POPULATION: 57,221,000
ANNUAL NATURAL INCREASE: 0.1%
DENSITY: 190 per sq km
CAPITAL: Rome (Roma)
LANGUAGE: Italian, German
RELIGION: 90% Roman Catholic
CURRENCY: Italian lira
ORGANISATIONS: UN, Council of Eur, EEC, NATO, OECD, WEU

Over 75% of the landscape of Italy is hill or mountain, with the north dominated by the flat plain of the River Po rising to the high Alps. Climate varies from hot summers and mild winters in the south and lowland areas, to mild summers and cold winters in the Alps. Agriculture flourishes with cereals, vegetables, olives and vines the principal crops. Italy is the world's largest wine producer. Cheese is also an important commodity. In spite of the lack of mineral and power resources textiles, manufacturing industry: cars, machine tools, textile machinery and engineering, mainly in the north, are expanding rapidly and account for nearly 50%

of the work force. This is increasing the imbalance between the north and south where the average income is far less per head, and where investment is lacking.

IVORY COAST (CÔTE D'IVOIRE)

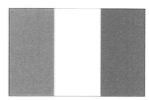

STATUS: Republic
AREA: 322,465 sq km (124,470 sq miles)
POPULATION: 10,165,000
ANNUAL NATURAL INCREASE: 3.0%
DENSITY: 31.6 per sq km
CAPITAL: Yamoussoukro
LANGUAGE: French, tribal languages
RELIGION: 65% traditional beliefs, 23% Moslem, 12% Roman Catholic
CURRENCY: CFA franc
ORGANISATIONS: UN, CEAO, ECOWAS, OAU

Independent from the French since 1960, the Ivory Coast is divided between the low plains of the south and the plateaux of the north. The climate is tropical with rainfall all year round in the south. Much of the population is engaged in agriculture producing rice, cassava, maize, sorghum, plantains and yams. Exports include coffee, timber and cocoa. The main industrial area and leading port is centred on Abidjan. Important industries are food-processing, textiles and timber products.

JAMAICA

STATUS: State
AREA: 11,425 sq km (4,410 sq miles)
POPULATION: 2,372,000
ANNUAL NATURAL INCREASE: 1.8%
DENSITY: 207.7 per sq km
CAPITAL: Kingston
LANGUAGE: English, local patois
RELIGION: Anglican Christian majority. Rastafarian minority
CURRENCY: Jamaican dollar (J$)
ORGANISATIONS: Comm, UN, CARICOM, OAS

Jamaica, part of the Greater Antilles chain of islands in the Caribbean is formed from the peaks of a submerged mountain range. The climate is tropical with an annual rainfall of over 500cm(197in) on the high ground. There is a plentiful supply of tropical fruits such as melons, bananas and guavas. Principal crops include sugar-cane, bananas and coffee. Jamaica is rich in bauxite which provides over half foreign-exchange earnings. Main manufacturing industries are food processing, textiles, cement and agricultural machinery.

JAN MAYEN

STATUS: Island Territory of Norway
AREA: 380 sq km (147 sq miles)
POPULATION: No permanent population

JAPAN

STATUS: Imperial monarchy
AREA: 369,700 sq km (142,705 sq miles)
POPULATION: 121,492,000
ANNUAL NATURAL INCREASE: 0.7%
DENSITY: 328.7 per sq km
CAPITAL: Tokyo
LANGUAGE: Japanese
RELIGION: Shintoist, Buddhist, Christian minority
CURRENCY: yen
ORGANISATIONS: UN, Col. Plan, OECD

Japan consists of the main islands of Hokkaido, Honshu, Shikoku and Kyushu which stretch over 1,600km(995 miles). The land is mountainous and heavily forested with small, fertile patches and a climate ranging from harsh to tropical. The archipelago is also subject to monsoons, earthquakes, typhoons and tidal waves. Very little of the available land is cultivable and although many of the farmers only work part-time Japan manages to produce enough rice for the growing population. Most food has to be imported but the Japanese also catch and eat a lot of fish. Japan is a leading economic power and most of the population are involved in industry. Because of the importance of trade, industry has grown up round the major ports especially Yokohama and Osaka and Tokyo, the capital. The principal exports are electronic, electrical and optical equipment. To produce these goods Japan relies heavily on imported fuel and raw materials and is developing the country's nuclear power resources to reduce this dependence. Production of coal, oil and natural gas is also being increased.

JAVA

STATUS: Island of Indonesia
AREA: 134,045 sq km (51,740 sq miles)
POPULATION: 91,269,528

JORDAN

STATUS: Kingdom
AREA: 90,650 sq km (35,000 sq miles)
POPULATION: 3,656,000
ANNUAL NATURAL INCREASE: 3.7%
DENSITY: 40.4 per sq km
CAPITAL: Amman

LANGUAGE: Arabic
RELIGION: 90% Sunni Moslem. Christian and Shiite Moslem minorities
CURRENCY: Jordanian dinar (JD)
ORGANISATIONS: UN, Arab League

Jordan is one of the few remaining kingdoms in the middle east. It is mostly desert, but has fertile pockets. Temperatures rise to 49°C(120°F) in the valleys but it is cooler and wetter in the east. Fruit and vegetables account for 20% of Jordan's exports and phosphate, the most valuable mineral, accounts for over 40% of export revenue. Amman is the manufacturing centre, processing bromide and potash from the Dead Sea. Other important industries are food processing and textiles.

KALIMANTAN

STATUS: Indonesian Province in Borneo
AREA: 550,205 sq km (212,380 sq miles)
POPULATION: 6,723,086

KAMPUCHEA

(see **CAMBODIA**)

KENYA

STATUS: Republic
AREA: 582,645 sq km (224,900 sq miles)
POPULATION: 21,163,000
ANNUAL NATURAL INCREASE: 4.2%
DENSITY: 36.4 per sq km
CAPITAL: Nairobi
LANGUAGE: Kiswahili, English, Kikuyu, Luo
RELIGION: traditional beliefs majority, 25% Christian, 6% Moslem
CURRENCY: Kenya shilling (KSh)
ORGANISATIONS: Comm, UN, OAU

Kenya lies on the equator but as most of the country is on a high plateau the temperatures range from 10° to 27°C (50° to 81°F). Rainfall varies from 76 to 250cm(30 to 98in) depending on altitude. Poor soil and a dry climate mean that little of the land is under cultivation but exports are nonetheless dominated by farm products – coffee, tea, sisal and meat. Nairobi and Mombasa are the manufacturing centres. The tourist industry is growing. Electricity is generated from both geothermal sources and hydro-electric power stations on the Tana river.

KERGUELEN ISLANDS

STATUS: Part of French Southern and Antarctic Territories
AREA: 7,215 sq km (2,785 sq miles)
POPULATION: 92

KHMER REPUBLIC

(see **CAMBODIA**)

KIRIBATI

STATUS: Republic
AREA: 717 sq km (277 sq miles)
POPULATION: 65,000
ANNUAL NATURAL INCREASE: 2.0%
DENSITY: 90.7 per sq km
CAPITAL: Bairiki (in Tarawa Atoll)
LANGUAGE: I-Kiribati, English
RELIGION: Christian majority
CURRENCY: Australian dollar ($A)
ORGANISATIONS: Comm

Kiribati consists of sixteen Gilbert Islands, eight Phoenix Islands, three Line Islands and Ocean Island. These four groups are spread over 5 million sq km(1,930,000 sq miles) in the central and west Pacific. The temperature is a constant 27° to 32°C (80° to 90°F). The islanders grow coconut, breadfruit, bananas and babai (a coarse vegetable). Copra is the only major export. Main imports are machinery and manufactured goods.

KOREA, NORTH

STATUS: Democratic People's Republic
AREA: 122,310 sq km (47,210 sq miles)
POPULATION: 20,883,000
ANNUAL NATURAL INCREASE: 2.3%
DENSITY: 170.8 per sq km
CAPITAL: Pyongyang
LANGUAGE: Korean
RELIGION: mainly Buddhist, Confucianist, Daoist and Chundo Kyo
CURRENCY: won

High, rugged mountains and deep valleys typify North Korea. Climate is extreme with severe winters and warm, sunny summers. Cultivation is limited to the river valley plains where rice, millet, maize and wheat are the principal crops. North Korea is rich in minerals including iron ore, coal and copper and industrial development has been expanding. Further potential exists in the exploitation of the plentiful resources of hydro-electricity. Main exports are metal ores and metal products.

KOREA, SOUTH

STATUS: Republic
AREA: 98,445 sq km (38,000 sq miles)
POPULATION: 41,569,000
ANNUAL NATURAL INCREASE: 1.6%

DENSITY: 422.3 per sq km
CAPITAL: Seoul (Sŏul)
LANGUAGE: Korean
RELIGION: 26% Mahayana Buddhism, 22% Christian. Confucianist minority
CURRENCY: won
ORGANISATIONS: Col. Plan

The terrain of South Korea is less rugged than the North and the climate is less extreme. Agriculture is still very primitive, with rice the principal crop. Tungsten, coal and iron ore are the main mineral deposits. The country is a major industrial nation with iron and steel, chemicals, machinery, shipbuilding, vehicles and electronics dominating. South Korea builds more ships than any other nation except Japan.

KURIL ISLANDS

STATUS: Islands of USSR
AREA: 15,540 sq km (6,000 sq miles)
POPULATION: No reliable figure available

KUWAIT

STATUS: State
AREA: 24,280 sq km (9,370 sq miles)
POPULATION: 1,791,000
ANNUAL NATURAL INCREASE: 3.2%
DENSITY: 73.8 per sq km
CAPITAL: Kuwait (Al Kuwayt)
LANGUAGE: Arabic, English
RELIGION: 95% Moslem, 5% Christian and Hindu
CURRENCY: Kuwaiti dinar (KD)
ORGANISATIONS: UN, Arab League, OPEC

Situated at the mouth of the Persian Gulf, Kuwait comprises low, undulating desert, with summer temperatures as high as 52°C(126°F). Annual rainfall fluctuates between 1 and

37cm(½–15in). Severe dust storms are a frequent occurrence in winter. Since the discovery of oil in 1946, Kuwait has been transformed into one of the world's wealthiest nations, exporting oil to Japan, France, the Netherlands and the UK. Apart from the sale of crude oil, Kuwait also refines and sells oil products. The natural gas fields have also been developed. Other industries include fishing (particularly shrimp), food processing, chemicals and building materials. However, it is the prolific public services which account for over 65% of the country's work force. In agriculture, the aim is to produce half the requirements of domestic vegetable consumption by expanding the irrigated area. Major crops are melons, dates and vegetables.

KYUSHU

STATUS: Island of Japan
AREA: 42,010 sq km (16,215 sq miles)
POPULATION: 13,459,665

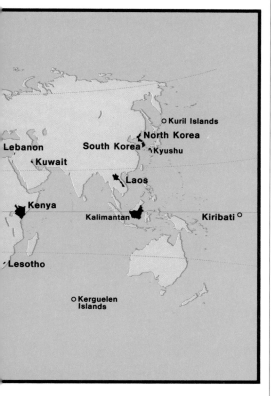

LAOS

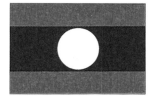

STATUS: People's Democratic Republic
AREA: 236,725 sq km (91,375 sq miles)
POPULATION: 4,218,000
ANNUAL NATURAL INCREASE: 2.3%
DENSITY: 17.9 per sq km
CAPITAL: Vientiane (Viangchan)
LANGUAGE: Lao, French, tribal languages
RELIGION: Buddhist majority, Christian and animist minorities
CURRENCY: kip (K)
ORGANISATIONS: UN, Col. Plan

Laos is a poor, landlocked country in Indo-China. Temperatures range from 15°C (59°F) in winter, to 32°C (90°F) before the rains, and 26°C (79°F) during the rainy season from May to October. Most of the sparse population are farmers growing small amounts of rice, maize, sweet potatoes and tobacco. The major exports are tin and teak, the latter floated down the Mekong river. Almost constant warfare since 1941 has hindered any possible industrial development. Main exports are timber products and coffee.

LEBANON

STATUS: Republic
AREA: 10,400 sq km (4,015 sq miles)
POPULATION: 2,707,000
ANNUAL NATURAL INCREASE: 2.1%
DENSITY: 260.3 per sq km
CAPITAL: Beirut (Beyrouth)
LANGUAGE: Arabic, French, English
RELIGION: 58% Shiite and Sunni Moslem, 42% Roman Catholic and Maronite Christian
CURRENCY: Lebanese pound (£L)
ORGANISATIONS: UN, Arab League

Physically, Lebanon can be divided into four main regions: a narrow coastal plain; a narrow, fertile, interior plateau; the west Lebanon and Anti-Lebanon mountains. The climate is of Mediterranean type with an annual rainfall ranging between 92cm (36in) on the coast and 230cm (91in) in the mountains. Trade and tourism have been severely affected by civil war since 1975. Agriculture accounts for nearly half the employed people. Cement, fertilisers, jewellery, sugar and tobacco products are all manufactured on a small scale.

LEEWARD ISLANDS
(see ANGUILLA, ANTIGUA, GUADELOUPE, MONTSERRAT & ST KITTS-NEVIS)

LESOTHO

STATUS: Kingdom
AREA: 30,345 sq km (11,715 sq miles)
POPULATION: 1,559,000
ANNUAL NATURAL INCREASE: 2.5%
DENSITY: 51.4 per sq km
CAPITAL: Maseru
LANGUAGE: Sesotho, English
RELIGION: 80% Christian
CURRENCY: loti
ORGANISATIONS: Comm, UN, OAU

Lesotho, formerly Basutoland, is completely encircled by South Africa. This small country is rugged and mountainous, and southern Africa's highest mountain, Thabana Ntlenyana (3482m or 11,424ft) is to be found in the east Drakensberg. Because of the terrain, agriculture is limited to the lowlands and foothills and sorghum, wheat, barley, maize, oats and legumes are the main crops. Cattle, sheep and goats graze on the highlands.

LIBERIA

STATUS: Republic
AREA: 111,370 sq km (42,990 sq miles)
POPULATION: 2,221,000
ANNUAL NATURAL INCREASE: 3.1%
DENSITY: 20 per sq km
CAPITAL: Monrovia
LANGUAGE: English, tribal languages
RELIGION: Christian majority, 5% Moslem
CURRENCY: Liberian dollar (L$)
ORGANISATIONS: UN, ECOWAS, OAU

The West African republic of Liberia is the only nation in Africa never to have been ruled by a foreign power. The hot and humid coastal plain with its savannah vegetation and mangrove swamps rises gently towards the Guinea Highlands, and the interior is densely covered by tropical rain forest. Rubber, formerly Liberia's main export has now been supplemented by iron, discovered in the Bomi Hills. Liberia has the world's largest merchant fleet of over 2,500 ships due to its flag of convenience tax regime.

LIBYA

STATUS: Socialist People's Jamahiriyah
AREA: 1,759,180 sq km (679,180 sq miles)
POPULATION: 3,742,000
ANNUAL NATURAL INCREASE: 3.3%
DENSITY: 2.2 per sq km
CAPITAL: Tripoli (Tarabulus)
LANGUAGE: Arabic, Italian, English
RELIGION: Sunni Moslem
CURRENCY: Libyan dinar (LD)
ORGANISATIONS: UN, Arab League, OAU, OPEC

Libya is situated on the lowlands of North Africa which rise southwards from the Mediterranean Sea. 95% of its territory is hot and dry desert or semi-desert with average rainfall of less than 13cm(5in). The coastal plains, however, have a moister Mediterranean climate with rainfall of 20–61cm(8–24in), and this is the most densely populated region. In these areas, a wide range of crops are cultivated including grapes, groundnuts, oranges, wheat and barley. Dates are grown in the desert oases. Only 30 years ago Libya was classed as one of the world's poorest nations but the exploitation of oil has transformed Libya's economy and now accounts for over 95% of its exports. Most imported goods come from Italy.

LIECHTENSTEIN

STATUS: Principality
AREA: 160 sq km (62 sq miles)
POPULATION: 27,000
ANNUAL NATURAL INCREASE: 1.1%
DENSITY: 168.8 per sq km
CAPITAL: Vaduz
LANGUAGE: Alemannish, German
RELIGION: 87% Roman Catholic
CURRENCY: Franken (Swiss franc)
ORGANISATIONS: Council of Eur

Situated in the central Alps between Switzerland and Austria, Liechtenstein is one of the smallest states in Europe. Its territory is divided into two zones – the flood plains of the Rhine to the north and Alpine mountain ranges to the south where cattle are reared. Liechtenstein's other main sources of revenue comprise light industry chiefly the manufacture of precision instruments, also textile production, food products and tourism.

LUXEMBOURG

STATUS: Grand Duchy
AREA: 2,585 sq km (998 sq miles)
POPULATION: 367,200
ANNUAL NATURAL INCREASE: 0%
DENSITY: 142 per sq km
CAPITAL: Luxembourg
LANGUAGE: Letzeburgish, French, German
RELIGION: 95% Roman Catholic
CURRENCY: Luxembourg franc, Belgian franc
ORGANISATIONS: UN, Council of Eur, EEC, NATO, OECD, WEU

The Grand Duchy of Luxembourg is strategically situated between France, Belgium and Germany. In the north the Oesling region is an extension of the Ardennes which are cut through by thickly forested river valleys. The Gutland to the south is an area of rolling lush pastureland. The climate is mild and temperate with rainfall ranging from 70–100cm(28–40in) a year. Just over half the land is arable, mainly cereals, dairy produce and potatoes, and wine is produced in the Moselle Valley. Iron ore is found in the south and is the basis of the thriving steel industry. Other major industries are textiles, chemicals, metal goods and pharmaceutical products.

MACAU (MACAO)

STATUS: Overseas Territory of Portugal
AREA: 16 sq km (6 sq miles)
POPULATION: 392,000
CAPITAL: Macau

MADAGASCAR

STATUS: Democratic Republic
AREA: 594,180 sq km (229,345 sq miles)
POPULATION: 10,303,000
ANNUAL NATURAL INCREASE: 2.8%
DENSITY: 17.4 per sq km
CAPITAL: Antananarivo
LANGUAGE: Malagasy, French, English
RELIGION: 57% animist, 40% Christian, 3% Moslem
CURRENCY: Malagasy franc (FMG)
ORGANISATIONS: UN, OAU

Madagascar is the world's fourth largest island, situated 400km(250 miles) east of the Mozambique coast. The terrain consists largely of a high plateau reaching 1500m(4920ft), with steppe and savannah vegetation. The mountains of the Tsaratanana Massif to the north reach up to 2876m(9435ft). Much of the hot humid east coast is covered by tropical rain forest – here rainfall reaches 150–200cm(59–79in) per annum. Although farming is the occupation of about 85% of the population, only 3% of the land is cultivated. Coffee and rice are the main products. Forestry is rapidly gaining in importance.

MADEIRA

STATUS: Self-governing Island Region of Portugal
AREA: 796 sq km (307 sq miles)
POPULATION: 267,400
CAPITAL: Funchal

MALAWI

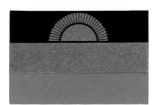

STATUS: Republic
AREA: 94,080 sq km (36,315 sq miles)
POPULATION: 7,278,925
ANNUAL NATURAL INCREASE: 3.2%
DENSITY: 77.4 per sq km
CAPITAL: Lilongwe
LANGUAGE: Chichewa, English
RELIGION: traditional beliefs majority, 10% Roman Catholic, 10% Protestant
CURRENCY: kwacha (K)
ORGANISATIONS: Comm, UN, OAU

Malawi, formerly Nyasaland, is located at the southern end of the East African Rift Valley. The area around Lake Malawi is hot and humid with swampy vegetation, gradually supplemented by highlands to the west and southeast, where conditions are cooler. Temperatures vary between 15° and 32°C(58° to 89°F). Average annual rainfall is 73–100cm(29–39in). Malawi has an intensely rural economy –

96% of the population work on the land. Maize is the main subsistence crop, and tea, tobacco, sugar and groundnuts are the main exports. Malawi has deposits of both coal and bauxite, but they are, as yet, largely unexploited. Manufacturing industry concentrates on consumer goods (mainly clothing) and building and construction material. All energy is produced by hydro-electric power stations.

MALAYSIA

STATUS: Federation
AREA: 332,965 sq km (128,525 sq miles)
POPULATION: 16,109,000
ANNUAL NATURAL INCREASE: 2.4%
DENSITY: 48.4 per sq km

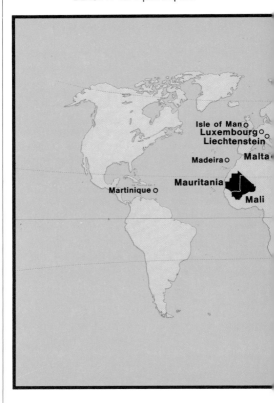

CAPITAL: Kuala Lumpur
LANGUAGE: Bahasa Malaysia, English
RELIGION: 53% Moslem, 25% Buddhist, Hindu, Christian and animist, minorities
CURRENCY: ringgit/Malaysian dollar
ORGANISATIONS: Comm, UN, ASEAN, Col. Plan

PENINSULAR MALAYSIA

STATUS: States
AREA: 131,585 sq km (50,790 sq miles)
POPULATION: 11,138,227

SABAH

STATUS: State
AREA: 76,115 sq km (29,380 sq miles)
POPULATION: 1,002,608
CAPITAL: Kota Kinabalu

SARAWAK

STATUS: State
AREA: 124,965 sq km (48,235 sq miles)
POPULATION: 1,294,753
CAPITAL: Kuching

The federation of Malaysia consists of two separate parts; West Malaysia is located on the Malay Peninsula, while East Malaysia consists of Sabah and Sarawak on the island of Borneo 700km(435 miles) across the South China Sea. Despite this distance, both areas share a similar landscape, which is mountainous and covered with lush tropical rain forest. The climate is tropical, hot and humid all the year round, with annual average rainfall of 250cm(98in). Malaysia is the world's main tin producer, and also produces over 40% of the world's rubber, and is also a leading source of palm oil, bauxite and gold.

Chief exports by value are manufactured goods, rubber, crude oil, palm oil, timber and timber products and tin. Most industries are concerned with production and processing of local products – palm oil, furniture, food processing and petroleum products. Most of the population are engaged in agriculture for local needs but crops grown for export include pineapples, tobacco, cocoa and spices. Livestock is imported to the home economy with pigs, cattle, goats, buffaloes and sheep predominant.

MALDIVES

STATUS: Republic
AREA: 298 sq km (115 sq miles)
POPULATION: 189,000
ANNUAL NATURAL INCREASE: 3.1%
DENSITY: 634.3 per sq km
CAPITAL: Malé
LANGUAGE: Divehi
RELIGION: Sunni Moslem majority
CURRENCY: rufiyaa
ORGANISATIONS: Comm, UN, Col. Plan

The Maldive Islands are listed as one of the world's poorest nations. They consist of a series of coral atolls stretching 885km(550 miles)

across the Indian Ocean. Although there are 2000 islands, only about 215 are inhabited. The main island, Malé, is only 1½ miles long. Fishing is the main activity and fish and coconut fibre are both exported. Most staple foods have to be imported but coconuts, millet, cassava, yams and fruit are grown locally. Tourism is developing.

MALI

STATUS: Republic
AREA: 1,240,140 sq km (478,695 sq miles)
POPULATION: 8,438,000
ANNUAL NATURAL INCREASE: 2.8%
DENSITY: 6.8 per sq km
CAPITAL: Bamako
LANGUAGE: French, native languages
RELIGION: 65% Moslem, 30% traditional beliefs, 5% Christian
CURRENCY: CFA franc
ORGANISATIONS: UN, CEAO, ECOWAS, OAU

Mali is one of the world's most undeveloped countries. Over half the area is barren desert. South of Tombouctou the savannah covered plains support a wide variety of wildlife. Most of the population live in the Niger valley and grow cotton, oil seeds and groundnuts. Fishing is important. Mali has few mineral resources. Recent droughts have taken their toll of livestock and agriculture. Main exports are cotton and livestock. There is no industry.

MALTA

STATUS: Republic
AREA: 316 sq km (122 sq miles)
POPULATION: 341,179
ANNUAL NATURAL INCREASE: 0.8%
DENSITY: 1079.7 per sq km
CAPITAL: Valletta
LANGUAGE: Maltese, English, Italian
RELIGION: Great majority Roman Catholic
CURRENCY: Maltese lira (LM)
ORGANISATIONS: Comm, UN, Council of Eur

Malta lies about 96km(60 miles) south of Sicily, and consists of three islands; Malta, Gozo and Comino. Malta has a Mediterranean climate with mild winters, hot dry summers and an average rainfall of 51cm(20in). About 40% of the land is under cultivation with wheat, potatoes, tomatoes and vines the main crops. The large natural harbour at Valletta has made it a major transit port. Tourism is also an important source of revenue. Principal exports are machinery, beverages, tobacco, flowers, wine, leather goods and potatoes.

MAN, ISLE OF
STATUS: British Crown Dependency
AREA: 572 sq km (221 sq miles)
POPULATION: 64,282
CAPITAL: Douglas

MARIANA ISLANDS, NORTHERN
STATUS: Freely Associated State with USA
AREA: 471 sq km (182 sq miles)
POPULATION: 19,635

MARQUESAS ISLANDS
(see **FRENCH POLYNESIA**)

MARSHALL ISLANDS
STATUS: Freely Associated State with USA
AREA: 181 sq km (70 sq miles)
POPULATION: 34,923
CAPITAL: Majuro

MARTINIQUE
STATUS: Overseas Department of France
AREA: 1,079 sq km (417 sq miles)
POPULATION: 329,500
CAPITAL: Fort-de-France

MAURITANIA

STATUS: Islamic Republic
AREA: 1,030,700 sq km (397,850 sq miles)
POPULATION: 1,946,000
ANNUAL NATURAL INCREASE: 2.9%
DENSITY: 1.9 per sq km
CAPITAL: Nouakchott
LANGUAGE: Arabic, French
RELIGION: Moslem
CURRENCY: ouguiya
ORGANISATIONS: UN, CEAO, ECOWAS, Arab League, OAU

Situated on the west coast of Africa, Mauritania consists of savannah, steppes and desert with high temperatures, low rainfall and frequent droughts. There is very little arable farming except in the Senegal river valley where millet and dates are grown. Most Mauritanians raise cattle, sheep, goats or camels. The country has only one railway which is used to transport the chief export, iron ore, from the mines to the coast at Nouadhibou. Severe drought during the last decade decimated the livestock population and forced many nomadic tribesmen into the towns. Coastal fishing contributes nearly 50% of foreign earnings. Exports are almost exclusively confined to iron ore, copper and fish products.

MAURITIUS

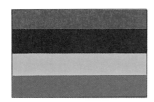

STATUS: State
AREA: 1,865 sq km (720 sq miles)
POPULATION: 1,029,000
ANNUAL NATURAL INCREASE: 1.5%
DENSITY: 551.8 per sq km
CAPITAL: Port Louis
LANGUAGE: English, French, Creole, Hindi, Bhojpuri
RELIGION: 51% Hindu, 31% Christian, 17% Moslem
CURRENCY: Mauritian rupee (R)
ORGANISATIONS: Comm, UN, OAU

Mauritius is a mountainous island in the Indian Ocean. It has a varied climate with temperatures ranging from 7° to 36°C(45° to 97°F) and annual rainfall of between 153 and 508cm(60 to 200in). Sugar-cane and its by-products are the mainstay of the economy and tourism is developing rapidly.

MAYOTTE

STATUS: French 'Territorial Collectivity', claimed by Comoros
AREA: 376 sq km (145 sq miles)
POPULATION: 67,138
CAPITAL: Dzaoudzi

MELILLA

STATUS: Spanish External Territory
AREA: 12.5 sq km (4.8 sq miles)
POPULATION: 57,622

MEXICO

STATUS: Federal Republic
AREA: 1,972,545 sq km (761,400 sq miles)
POPULATION: 81,163,000
ANNUAL NATURAL INCREASE: 2.6%
DENSITY: 41.2 per sq km
CAPITAL: Mexico City
LANGUAGE: Spanish
RELIGION: 96% Roman Catholic
CURRENCY: Mexican peso
ORGANISATIONS: UN, OAS

The landscape of Mexico consists of mountain ranges and dissected plateaux. As much of the land is above 500m(1640ft) temperature and rainfall are modified. The north is arid but the south is humid and tropical. Maize and beans are grown for local consumption. The population has outstripped food production and many Mexicans have moved to the cities. Minerals, especially silver, uranium and gold, are the main source of Mexico's wealth but the mines are mostly foreign-owned and Mexico aims to lessen this dependence on foreign investment as the country develops. Oil, natural gas and coal all have considerable reserves and are gradually becoming more important. Main exports are crude oil, and machinery.

MICRONESIA, FEDERATED STATES OF

STATUS: Freely Associated State with USA
AREA: 330 sq km (127 sq miles)
POPULATION: 88,375
CAPITAL: Kolonia

MOLUCCAS

STATUS: Island Group of Indonesia
AREA: 83,675 sq km (32,300 sq miles)
POPULATION: 1,411,006

MONACO

STATUS: Principality
AREA: 1.6 sq km (0.6 sq miles)
POPULATION: 27,000
ANNUAL NATURAL INCREASE: 1.4%
DENSITY: 16875 per sq km
CAPITAL: Monaco-ville
LANGUAGE: French, Monegasque, Italian, English
RELIGION: 90% Roman Catholic
CURRENCY: French franc

The tiny Principality is the world's smallest independent state after the Vatican City. It occupies a thin strip of the French Mediterranean coast near the Italian border and is backed by the Maritime Alps. It comprises the towns of Monaco, la Condamine, Fontvieille and Monte Carlo. Most revenue comes from tourism, casinos and light industry. Land has been reclaimed from the sea to extend the area available for commercial development.

MONGOLIA

STATUS: People's Republic
AREA: 1,565,000 sq km (604,090 sq miles)
POPULATION: 1,965,300
ANNUAL NATURAL INCREASE: 2.5%
DENSITY: 1.3 per sq km
CAPITAL: Ulaanbaatar (Ulan Bator)
LANGUAGE: Khalkha Mongolian
RELIGION: some Buddhist Lamaism
CURRENCY: togrog (tughrik)
ORGANISATIONS: UN, COMECON

Situated between China and the USSR, Mongolia has one of the lowest population densities in the world. Much of the country consists of a high undulating plateau (1500m or 4920ft) covered with grassland. To the north, mountain ranges reaching 4231m(13,881ft) bridge the border with the USSR, and to the south is the large expanse of the Gobi desert where rainfall averages only 10–13cm(4–5in) a year. The climate is very extreme with January temperatures falling to −34°C(−29°F). Mongolia is predominantly a farming economy, its main exports being cattle and horses, and wheat, barley, millet and oats are also grown. Its natural resources include some oil, coal, iron ore, gold, tin and copper.

MONTSERRAT

STATUS: UK Crown Colony
AREA: 106 sq km (41 sq miles)
POPULATION: 12,000
CAPITAL: Plymouth

MOROCCO

STATUS: Kingdom
AREA: 710,895 sq km (274,414 sq miles)
POPULATION: 22,476,000
ANNUAL NATURAL INCREASE: 2.6%
DENSITY: 31.7 per sq km
CAPITAL: Rabat
LANGUAGE: Arabic, French, Spanish, Berber
RELIGION: Moslem majority, Christian and Jewish minorities
CURRENCY: Moroccan dirham (DH)
ORGANISATIONS: UN, Arab League

One third of Morocco, on the north-west coast of Africa, consists of the Atlas mountains reaching 4165m(13,665ft). Between the Atlas and the Atlantic coastal strip is an area of high plateau bordered on the south by the Sahara desert. The north has a Mediterranean climate and vegetation, and west-facing slopes of the Atlas have high annual rainfall and are thickly forested. Morocco has the world's largest phosphate deposits. The main crops are wheat and barley, and tourism is a major source of revenue.

MOZAMBIQUE

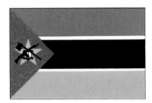

STATUS: People's Republic
AREA: 784,755 sq km (302,915 sq miles)

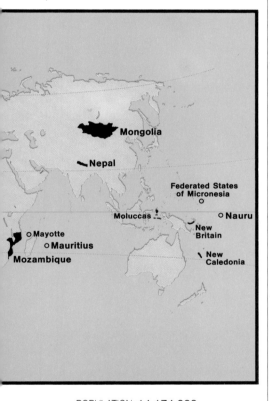

POPULATION: 14,174,000
ANNUAL NATURAL INCREASE: 2.5%
DENSITY: 18.1 per sq km
CAPITAL: Maputo
LANGUAGE: Portuguese, tribal languages
RELIGION: mainly traditional beliefs,
15% Christian, 15% Moslem
CURRENCY: metical
ORGANISATIONS: UN, OAU

The ex-Portuguese colony of Mozambique consists of a large coastal plain, rising towards the interior to the plateaux and mountain ranges which border Malawi, Zambia and Zimbabwe. The highlands in the north reach 2436m (7992ft). The climate is tropical on the coastal plain, although high altitudes make it cooler inland. Over 90% of the population are subsistence farmers cultivating coconuts, cashews, cotton, maize and rice. Mozambique also acts as an entrepôt, handling exports from South Africa, and landlocked Zambia and Malawi. Coal is the main mineral deposit and there are large reserves. Other underexploited minerals are iron ore, bauxite and gold.

NAMIBIA (S.W. AFRICA)

STATUS: UN Trust Territory
AREA: 824,295 sq km (318,180 sq miles)
POPULATION: 1,595,000
ANNUAL NATURAL INCREASE: 2.9%
DENSITY: 2 per sq km
CAPITAL: Windhoek
LANGUAGE: Afrikaans, German, English,
regional languages
RELIGION: 90% Christian
CURRENCY: South African rand (R)

The south-west African country of Namibia is one of the driest in the world. The Namib desert on the coast has less than 5cm(2in) average rainfall a year, the Kalahari to the north-east 10–25cm(4–10in). The vegetation is sparse. Maize and sorghum are grown in the northern highlands and sheep are reared in the south. Namibia is, however, rich in mineral resources, with large deposits of diamonds, lead, tin and zinc, and the world's largest uranium mine.

NAURU

STATUS: Republic
AREA: 21 sq km (8 sq miles)
POPULATION: 8,000
ANNUAL NATURAL INCREASE: −0.3%
DENSITY: 381 per sq km
CAPITAL: Yaren
LANGUAGE: Nauruan, English
RELIGION: Nauruan Protestant majority
CURRENCY: Australian dollar ($A)
ORGANISATIONS: Comm (special member)

Nauru is one of the smallest republics in the world. Its great wealth is entirely derived from the phosphate deposits. The flat coastal lowlands encircled by coral reefs rise gently to the central plateau where the phosphate is mined. Most phosphate is exported to Australasia and Japan. Deposits may be exhausted by 1993.

NEPAL

STATUS: Kingdom
AREA: 141,415 sq km (54,585 sq miles)
POPULATION: 17,131,000
ANNUAL NATURAL INCREASE: 2.3%
DENSITY: 121.2 per sq km
CAPITAL: Kathmandu
LANGUAGE: Nepali, Maithir, Bhojpuri
RELIGION: 90% Hindu, 5% Buddhist,
3% Moslem
CURRENCY: Nepalese rupee (NR)
ORGANISATIONS: UN, Col. Plan

Nepal is a Himalayan kingdom sandwiched between China and India. The climate changes sharply with altitude from the southern Tarai plain to the northern Himalayas. Central Kathmandu varies between 2°C(35°F) and 30°C(86°F). Most rain falls between June and October and can reach 250cm(100in). Agriculture concentrates on rice, maize and cattle, buffaloes, sheep and goats. The small amount of industry processes local products.

NETHERLANDS

STATUS: Kingdom
AREA: 33,940 sq km (13,105 sq miles)
POPULATION: 14,562,924
ANNUAL NATURAL INCREASE: 0.4%
DENSITY: 429.1 per sq km
CAPITAL: Amsterdam (seat of Government:
The Hague)
LANGUAGE: Dutch
RELIGION: 40% Roman Catholic,
30% Protestant. Jewish minority
CURRENCY: gulden (guilder) or florin
ORGANISATIONS: UN, Council of Eur, EEC,
NATO, OECD, WEU

The Netherlands is situated at the western edge of the North European plain. The country is exceptionally low-lying, and about 25% of its territory has been reclaimed from the sea. The wide coastal belt consists of flat marshland, mud-flats, sand-dunes and dykes. Further inland, the flat alluvial plain is drained by the Rhine, Maas and Ijssel. A complex network of dykes and canals prevents the area from flooding. To the south and east the land rises. Flat and exposed to strong winds, the Netherlands has mild winters and cool summers.

The Dutch are leading world producers of dairy goods and also cultivate crops such as wheat, barley, oats and potatoes. Lacking mineral resources, much of the industry of the Netherlands is dependent on natural gas. Most manufacturing industry has developed around Rotterdam. Here are oil refineries, steel-works and chemical and food processing plants.

NETHERLANDS ANTILLES

STATUS: Self-governing part of Netherlands
Realm
AREA: 993 sq km (383 sq miles)
POPULATION: 261,850
CAPITAL: Willemstad

NEW BRITAIN

STATUS: Island of Papua New Guinea
AREA: 36,500 sq km (14,090 sq miles)
POPULATION: 222,759

NEW CALEDONIA

STATUS: Overseas Territory of France
AREA: 19,105 sq km (7,375 sq miles)
POPULATION: 154,000
CAPITAL: Noumea

NEW GUINEA

STATUS: Island comprising Irian Jaya and part of Papua New Guinea
AREA: 808,510 sq km (312,085 sq miles)
POPULATION: 3,763,300

NEW HEBRIDES

(see **VANUATU**)

NEW ZEALAND

STATUS: Dominion
AREA: 265,150 sq km (102,350 sq miles)
POPULATION: 3,307,084
ANNUAL NATURAL INCREASE: 0.8%
DENSITY: 12.5 per sq km
CAPITAL: Wellington
LANGUAGE: English, Maori
RELIGION: 35% Anglican Christian, 22% Presbyterian, 16% Roman Catholic
CURRENCY: New Zealand dollar ($NZ)
ORGANISATIONS: Comm, UN, ANZUS, Col. Plan, OECD

The two main islands that make up New Zealand lie in the South Pacific Ocean. The Southern Alps run the length of South Island with a narrow coastal strip in the west and a broader plain to the east. Stewart Island lies beyond the Foreaux Strait to the south. North Island is less mountainous. Most of the country enjoys a temperate climate. Nearly 20% of the land is forested and 50% pasture. New Zealand is one of the world's leading exporters of beef, mutton and wool. Most exploited minerals are for industrial use – clay, iron sand, limestone, sand and coal. Manufacturing industries and tourism are of increasing importance. New trading links are developing with countries bordering the Pacific.

NICARAGUA

STATUS: Republic
AREA: 148,000 sq km (57,130 sq miles)
POPULATION: 3,384,000
ANNUAL NATURAL INCREASE: 3.4%
DENSITY: 22.9 per sq km
CAPITAL: Managua
LANGUAGE: Spanish
RELIGION: Roman Catholic
CURRENCY: cordoba (C$)
ORGANISATIONS: UN, CACM, OAS

Nicaragua is the largest of the Central American republics south of Mexico situated between the Caribbean and the Pacific. Active volcanic mountains parallel the western coast. The south is dominated by Lakes Managua and Nicaragua. Climate is tropical with rains May to October. Agriculture is the main occupation with cotton, coffee, sugar-cane and fruit the main exports. Gold, silver and copper are mined.

NIGER

STATUS: Republic
AREA: 1,186,410 sq km (457,955 sq miles)
POPULATION: 6,698,000
ANNUAL NATURAL INCREASE: 2.8%
DENSITY: 5.7 per sq km
CAPITAL: Niamey
LANGUAGE: French. Hausa and other native languages
RELIGION: 85% Moslem, 15% traditional beliefs
CURRENCY: CFA franc
ORGANISATIONS: UN, CEAO, ECOWAS, OAU

Niger is a vast landlocked south Saharan republic with rainfall gradually decreasing from 56cm(22in) in the south to near zero in the north. Temperatures are above 35°C(95°F) for much of the year. Most of the population are farmers particularly cattle, sheep and goat herders. Recent droughts have affected both cereals and livestock. Large deposits of uranium ore and phosphates are being exploited. The economy depends largely on foreign aid.

NIGERIA

STATUS: Federal Republic
AREA: 923,850 sq km (356,605 sq miles)
POPULATION: 98,517,000
ANNUAL NATURAL INCREASE: 3.0%
DENSITY: 106.7 per sq km
CAPITAL: Lagos
LANGUAGE: English, Hausa, Yoruba, Ibo
RELIGION: Moslem majority, 30% Christian, animist minority
CURRENCY: naira (N)
ORGANISATIONS: Comm, UN, ECOWAS, OAU, OPEC

The most populous nation in Africa, Nigeria is bounded to the north by the Sahara and to the west, east and south-east by tropical rain forest. The southern half of the country is dominated by the Niger and its tributaries, the north by the interior plateaux. Temperature averages 32°C(90°F) with high humidity. From a basic agricultural economy, Nigeria is slowly being transformed by oil discoveries in the Niger delta which account for 95% of exports.

NIUE

STATUS: Self-governing Overseas Territory in free association with New Zealand
AREA: 259 sq km (100 sq miles)
POPULATION: 3,032
CAPITAL: Alofi

NORFOLK ISLAND

STATUS: External Territory of Australia
AREA: 36 sq km (14 sq miles)
POPULATION: 2,367
CAPITAL: Kingston

NORWAY

STATUS: Kingdom
AREA: 323,895 sq km (125,025 sq miles)
POPULATION: 4,169,000
ANNUAL NATURAL INCREASE: 0.2%
DENSITY: 12.9 per sq km
CAPITAL: Oslo

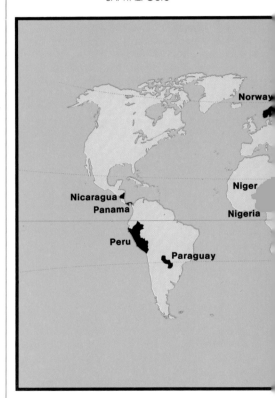

LANGUAGE: Norwegian (Bokmal and Nynorsk), Lappish
RELIGION: 92% Evangelical Lutheran Christian
CURRENCY: Norwegian krone
ORGANISATIONS: UN, Council of Eur, EFTA, NATO, OECD

Norway is a mountainous country stretching from 58° to 72°N. The climate on the indented western coast is modified by the Gulf Stream with high rainfall and relatively mild winters with temperatures averaging −3.9°C(25°F) in January and 17°C(63°F) in July. Rainfall may be as high as 196cm(79in). Most settlements are scattered along the fjords, the coast and around Oslo in the south. Norway is rich in natural resources. Coal, petroleum, natural gas predominate in exports but are supplemented by forestry products and fishing. By value, the most important exports are crude oil and natural gas, food manufacturing and machinery. The advanced production of hydro-electric power has helped develop industry, particularly chemicals, metal products and paper processing.

OMAN

STATUS: Sultanate
AREA: 271,950 sq km (104,970 sq miles)
POPULATION: 2,000,000
ANNUAL NATURAL INCREASE: 3.3%
DENSITY: 7.4 per sq km
CAPITAL: Muscat (Masqat)
LANGUAGE: Arabic, English
RELIGION: 75% Ibadi Moslem, 25% Sunni Moslem
CURRENCY: rial Omani (RO)
ORGANISATIONS: UN, Arab League

The Sultanate occupies the north-east coast of Arabia with a detached portion overlooking the

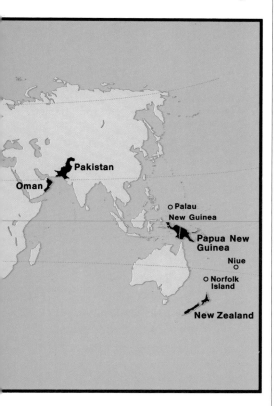

Straits of Hormuz. The desert landscape consists of a coastal plain and low hills rising to plateau in the interior. The two fertile areas are the Batimah in the north and Dhofar in the south. The main crop is dates. Oil provides over 95% of export revenue.

PAKISTAN

STATUS: Islamic Republic
AREA: 803,940 sq km (310,320 sq miles)
POPULATION: 99,163,000
ANNUAL NATURAL INCREASE: 2.8%
DENSITY: 123.4 per sq km

CAPITAL: Islamabad
LANGUAGE: Urdu, Punjabi, Sindhi, Pushtu
RELIGION: 90% Moslem
CURRENCY: Pakistani rupee (R)
ORGANISATIONS: UN, Col. Plan

The landscape and the economy of Pakistan are dominated by the river Indus and its tributaries which flow south flanked by the plateau of Baluchistan and the Sulaiman mountains to the west and the Thar desert to the east. The climate is dry and hot averaging 27°C(80°F). Rainfall reaches 90cm(36in) in the northern mountains. Over 50% of the population are engaged in agriculture which is confined to the irrigated areas near the great rivers. Main crops are wheat, cotton, maize, rice and sugarcane. There are many types of low-grade mineral deposits, such as coal and copper, but these are little developed. Main industries are food-processing and metals but these only contribute about 20% to the economy.

PALAU

STATUS: UN Trustee Territory
AREA: 497 sq km (192 sq miles)
POPULATION: 13,000
CAPITAL: Koror

PANAMA

STATUS: Republic
AREA: 78,515 sq km (30,305 sq miles)
POPULATION: 2,227,000
ANNUAL NATURAL INCREASE: 2.1%
DENSITY: 28.4 per sq km
CAPITAL: Panama
LANGUAGE: Spanish, English
RELIGION: large Roman Catholic majority
CURRENCY: balboa (B)
ORGANISATIONS: UN, OAS

Panama is situated at the narrowest part of Central America and has both Pacific and Caribbean coastlines. The climate is tropical with little variation throughout the year – average temperature 27°C(80°F). The rainy season is from April to December. Panama probably has the world's largest copper reserves but these are hardly developed. Most foreign revenue is earned from the Panama Canal, and export of petroleum products.

PAPUA NEW GUINEA

STATUS: Independent State
AREA: 462,840 sq km (178,655 sq miles)

POPULATION: 3,400,000
ANNUAL NATURAL INCREASE: 2.6%
DENSITY: 7.4 per sq km
CAPITAL: Port Moresby
LANGUAGE: Pidgin English, English, native languages
RELIGION: Pantheist, Christian minority
CURRENCY: kina (K)
ORGANISATIONS: Comm, UN, Col. Plan

Papua New Guinea (the eastern half of New Guinea and neighbouring islands) is a mountainous country. It has an equatorial climate with temperatures of 21° to 32°C(70° to 90°F) and annual rainfall of over 200cm(79in). Copper is the major mineral deposit with large reserves on Bougainville, one of the neighbouring islands. Sugar and beef-cattle are developing areas of production. Major exports are copra, timber, coffee, rubber and tea.

PARAGUAY

STATUS: Republic
AREA: 406,750 sq km (157,005 sq miles)
POPULATION: 3,807,000
ANNUAL NATURAL INCREASE: 2.8%
DENSITY: 9.4 per sq km
CAPITAL: Asunción
LANGUAGE: Spanish, Guarani
RELIGION: 90% Roman Catholic
CURRENCY: guarani (G)
ORGANISATIONS: UN, OAS

Paraguay is a landlocked country in South America with temperatures which average 15°C(59°F) all year. The country divides into lush, fertile plains and heavily forested plateau east of the River Paraguay and marshy scrubland (the Chaco) west of the river. Cassava, cotton, soyabeans and maize are the main crops but the rearing of livestock – cattle, horses, pigs and sheep – and food processing, dominate the export trade. The largest hydro-electric dam in the world is at Itaipú. This was constructed as a joint project with Brazil and will eventually have a capacity of 12.6 million kw.

PERU

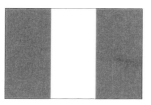

STATUS: Republic
AREA: 1,285,215 sq km (496,095 sq miles)
POPULATION: 20,207,100
ANNUAL NATURAL INCREASE: 2.5%
DENSITY: 15.8 per sq km
CAPITAL: Lima
LANGUAGE: Spanish, Quechua
RELIGION: large Roman Catholic majority
CURRENCY: inti
ORGANISATIONS: UN, OAS

Peru divides into three geographical regions. The coastal region is very dry but fertile oases produce cotton, sugar, fruit and fodder crops. This is the most prosperous and heavily populated area which includes the industrial centres around Lima. In the ranges and plateaux of the Andes and the Amazon lowlands the soil is thin but the inhabitants depend on cultivation and grazing. Poor communications have hindered the development of Peru and there are great differences between rich and poor. Peru has rich mineral deposits of copper, lead, zinc and silver. There are oil reserves in the interior.

PHILIPPINES

STATUS: Republic
AREA: 300,000 sq km (115,800 sq miles)
POPULATION: 56,004,000
ANNUAL NATURAL INCREASE: 2.5%
DENSITY: 186.7 per sq km
CAPITAL: Manila
LANGUAGE: Pilipino (Tagalog), English, Spanish, Cebuano
RELIGION: 90% Christian, 70% Moslem
CURRENCY: Philippine peso (P)
ORGANISATIONS: UN, ASEAN, Col. Plan

The Philippines consists of three main island groups, the Luzon and its neighbours, the Visayas and Mindanao, including the Sulus. The archipelago is subject to earthquakes and typhoons. It has a monsoon climate and over 40% of the country is covered by rain forest. Fishing is important but small farms dominate the economy, producing rice and copra for domestic consumption and other coconut and sugar products for export. Forestry is becoming an important industry but main exports are textiles, fruit and electronic products. Fishing is an important local industry.

PITCAIRN ISLAND

STATUS: UK Dependent Territory
AREA: 45 sq km (17.25 sq miles)
POPULATION: 62
CAPITAL: Adamstown

POLAND

STATUS: Republic
AREA: 312,685 sq km (120,695 sq miles)
POPULATION: 37,626,000
ANNUAL NATURAL INCREASE: 0.9%
DENSITY: 120.4 per sq km
CAPITAL: Warsaw
LANGUAGE: Polish
RELIGION: 90% Roman Catholic
CURRENCY: zloty
ORGANISATIONS: UN, Warsaw Pact, COMECON

Poland occupies most of the southern coast of the Baltic Sea. Part of the North European Plain, the flat well-drained landscape rises gently towards the foothills of the Carpathians in the far south. The climate is continental with long severe winters. Average winter temperatures are below freezing point; rainfall averages between 52 and 73cm(21 and 29in). Both agriculture and natural resources play an important part in the economy and Poland is nearly self-sufficient in cereals sugar-beet and potatoes. There are large reserves of coal, copper, sulphur and natural gas. Major industries are ship-building in the north and production of metals and chemicals in the major mining centres in the south.

PORTUGAL

STATUS: Republic
AREA: 91,630 sq km (35,370 sq miles)
POPULATION: 10,291,000
ANNUAL NATURAL INCREASE: 0.5%
DENSITY: 112.4 per sq km
CAPITAL: Lisbon (Lisboa)
LANGUAGE: Portuguese
RELIGION: large Roman Catholic majority
CURRENCY: escudo
ORGANISATIONS: UN, Council of Eur, EEC, NATO, OECD

Portugal occupies the western, Atlantic coast of the Iberian Peninsula. The Mediterranean climate is modified by westerly winds and the Gulf Stream. This is reflected in the lusher mixed deciduous/coniferous forest in the northern mountains and the Mediterranean scrub in the far south. The rolling hills along the western coasts rise gently to the interior plateaux. A quarter of the population are farmers growing vines, olives, wheat, maize and beans, and rearing cattle and sheep. Minerals are coal, copper, kaolin and uranium. Over 9 million tourists visit the country each year.

PORTUGUESE GUINEA
(see **GUINEA-BISSAU**)

PUERTO RICO

STATUS: Self-governing commonwealth associated with USA
AREA: 8,960 sq km (3,460 sq miles)
POPULATION: 3,270,000
CAPITAL: San Juan

QATAR

STATUS: State
AREA: 11,435 sq km (4,415 sq miles)
POPULATION: 335,000

ANNUAL NATURAL INCREASE: 2.9%
DENSITY: 29.3 per sq km
CAPITAL: Doha (Ad Dawhah)
LANGUAGE: Arabic, English
RELIGION: Moslem
CURRENCY: Qatar riyal (QR)
ORGANISATIONS: UN, Arab League, OPEC

The country occupies all of the Qatar peninsula which reaches north from the north-east Arabian coast into the Persian Gulf. The land is flat and dry desert; the climate is hot and humid. July temperatures average 37°C(98°F) and annual rainfall averages 62mm(2.5in). Irrigation schemes are expanding production of fruit and vegetables for home consumption. The main source of revenue is from the exploitation of oil and gas reserves. The N.W. Dome oilfield contains 15% of known world gas reserves.

RAS AL KHAIMAH
(see **UNITED ARAB EMIRATES**)

RÉUNION

STATUS: Overseas Department of France
AREA: 2,510 sq km (969 sq miles)
POPULATION: 538,000
CAPITAL: Saint-Denis

ROMANIA

STATUS: Republic
AREA: 237,500 sq km (91,675 sq miles)
POPULATION: 23,174,000
ANNUAL NATURAL INCREASE: 0.4%
DENSITY: 97.6 per sq km
CAPITAL: Bucharest (Bucureşti)

LANGUAGE: Romanian, Magyar
RELIGION: 85% Romanian Orthodox
CURRENCY: leu
ORGANISATIONS: UN, Warsaw Pact, COMECON

The landscape of Romania is dominated by the great curve of the Carpathian mountains. Lowlands to the west, east and south contain rich agricultural land, especially north of Bucharest either side of the Danube. The climate is continental with variable rainfall, hot summers and cold winters. The economy, once mainly agricultural, is now based on mineral resources and the policy of industrialisation. Coal, oil and natural gas provide power; iron ore, manganese, lead, copper and uranium are mined.

ROSS DEPENDENCY

STATUS: Antarctic Territory Overseas of New Zealand
AREA: 425,000 sq km (164,050 sq miles)
POPULATION: No permanent population

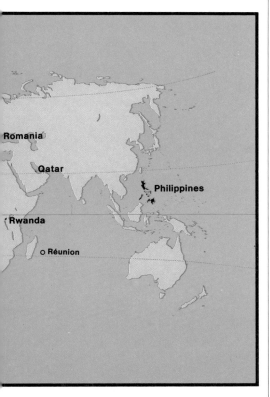

RWANDA

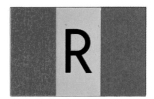

STATUS: Republic
AREA: 26,330 sq km (10,165 sq miles)
POPULATION: 6,275,000
ANNUAL NATURAL INCREASE: 3.8%
DENSITY: 238.4 per sq km
CAPITAL: Kigali
LANGUAGE: French, tribal languages, Kinyarwanda (Bantu)
RELIGION: 50% animist, 50% Roman Catholic
CURRENCY: Rwanda franc
ORGANISATIONS: UN, OAU

Small and isolated Rwanda supports a high density of population on the moist plateaux east of the Rift Valley. Agriculture is basically subsistence with coffee the major export. Few minerals have been discovered, and manufacturing is confined to food processing and construction materials.

SABAH

(see **MALAYSIA**)

ST HELENA

STATUS: UK Dependent Territory
AREA: 122 sq km (47 sq miles)
POPULATION: 6,000
CAPITAL: Jamestown

ST KITTS (ST CHRISTOPHER)-NEVIS

STATUS: Commonwealth Nation
AREA: 262 sq km (101 sq miles)
POPULATION: 47,000
ANNUAL NATURAL INCREASE: 1.8%
DENSITY: 180 per sq km
CAPITAL: Basseterre
LANGUAGE: English
RELIGION: Christian
CURRENCY: E. Caribbean dollar (EC$)
ORGANISATIONS: Comm, UN, CARICOM, OAS

St Kitts-Nevis, in the Leeward Islands, comprises two volcanic islands: St Christopher (St Kitts) and Nevis. The climate is tropical and humid with temperatures between 16°C and 33°C(61°F and 91°F) and an average annual rainfall of 140cm(55in). Main exports are sugar and molasses and cotton. Tourism is an important source of revenue.

ST LUCIA

STATUS: Commonwealth Nation
AREA: 616 sq km (238 sq miles)
POPULATION: 132,000
ANNUAL NATURAL INCREASE: 2.5%
DENSITY: 217.5 per sq km
CAPITAL: Castries
LANGUAGE: English, French patois
RELIGION: 80% Roman Catholic
CURRENCY: E. Caribbean dollar (EC$)
ORGANISATIONS: Comm, UN, CARICOM, OAS

Independent since 1979 this small tropical Caribbean island in the Lesser Antilles grows coconuts, cocoa, citrus fruit and bananas. Most of the population are small farmers. Main industries are food and drink processing and all consumer goods are imported. There are no commercial mineral deposits. Tourism is a rapidly developing industry.

ST PIERRE & MIQUELON

STATUS: Overseas Department of France
AREA: 241 sq km (93 sq miles)
POPULATION: 6,000
CAPITAL: St Pierre

ST VINCENT

STATUS: Commonwealth Nation
AREA: 389 sq km (150 sq miles)
POPULATION: 105,000
ANNUAL NATURAL INCREASE: 2.5%
DENSITY: 316.2 per sq km
CAPITAL: Kingstown
LANGUAGE: English
RELIGION: Christian
CURRENCY: E. Caribbean dollar (EC$)
ORGANISATIONS: Comm, UN, CARICOM, OAS

St Vincent in the Lesser Antilles comprises the main island and a chain of small islands called the Northern Grenadines. The climate is tropical. Most exports are foodstuffs: arrowroot, sweet potatoes, bananas, coconut products and yams. Some sugar-cane is grown for the production of rum and other drinks. Tourism is an expanding industry.

SAMOA

(see **AMERICAN SAMOA & WESTERN SAMOA**)

SAN MARINO

STATUS: Republic
AREA: 61 sq km (24 sq miles)
POPULATION: 22,000
ANNUAL NATURAL INCREASE: 1.2%
DENSITY: 360.7 per sq km
CAPITAL: San Marino
LANGUAGE: Italian
RELIGION: Roman Catholic
CURRENCY: Italian lira, San Marino lire

An independent state within Italy, San Marino straddles a limestone peak in the Apennines south of Rimini. The economy is centred around tourism and sale of postage stamps. Most of the population are farmers growing cereals, olives and vines and tending herds of sheep and goats. Wine and textiles are exported.

SÃO TOMÉ AND PRINCIPE

STATUS: Democratic Republic
AREA: 964 sq km (372 sq miles)
POPULATION: 110,000
ANNUAL NATURAL INCREASE: 2.9%
DENSITY: 114.1 per sq km
CAPITAL: São Tomé
LANGUAGE: Portuguese
RELIGION: Roman Catholic majority
CURRENCY: dobra (Db)
ORGANISATIONS: UN, OAU

Independent from Portugal since 1975, two large and several small islands make up this tiny state situated near the equator 200km(125 miles) off the west coast of Africa. The climate is tropical with temperatures averaging 25°C(77°F) and rainfall between 100 and 500cm (40 and 197in). Cocoa, coconuts and palm oil are the main crops grown on the rich volcanic soil. Other foods and consumer goods are imported.

SARAWAK
(see MALAYSIA)

SARDINIA (SARDEGNA)

STATUS: Island Region of Italy
AREA: 24,090 sq km (9,300 sq miles)
POPULATION: 1,617,265
CAPITAL: Cagliari

SAUDI ARABIA

STATUS: Kingdom
AREA: 2,400,900 sq km (926,745 sq miles)
POPULATION: 13,612,000
ANNUAL NATURAL INCREASE: 3.0%
DENSITY: 5.7 per sq km
CAPITAL: Riyadh (Ar Riyad)
LANGUAGE: Arabic
RELIGION: Moslem (85% Sunni)
CURRENCY: riyal
ORGANISATIONS: UN, Arab League, OPEC

Saudi Arabia occupies the heart of the vast arid Arabian Peninsula. To the east, high mountains fringe the Red Sea but even here rainfall rarely exceeds 38cm(15in). Temperatures rise beyond 44°C(111°F) in the summer. The interior plateau slopes down gently eastwards to the Persian Gulf and supports little vegetation. Only in coastal strips and oases are cereals and date-palms grown. Oil is the most important resource and export commodity and economic development is dependent on its revenue. Irrigation schemes and land reclamation projects are attempting to raise food production.

SENEGAL

STATUS: Republic
AREA: 196,720 sq km (75,935 sq miles)
POPULATION: 6,614,000
ANNUAL NATURAL INCREASE: 2.9%
DENSITY: 33.7 per sq km
CAPITAL: Dakar
LANGUAGE: French, native languages
RELIGION: 90% Moslem, 5% Roman Catholic
CURRENCY: CFA franc
ORGANISATIONS: UN, CEAO, ECOWAS, OAU

Senegal on the coast of West Africa, is a flat, dry country cut through by the Gambia, Casamance and Senegal rivers. Rainfall rarely exceeds 58cm(23in) on the wetter coast. The interior savannah supports varied wildlife but little agriculture. Groundnuts, cotton and millet are the main crops, but frequent droughts have reduced their value as cash crops. Phosphate mining, ship-repairing and food processing are the major industries.

SEYCHELLES

STATUS: Republic
AREA: 404 sq km (156 sq miles)
POPULATION: 66,000
ANNUAL NATURAL INCREASE: 1.9%
DENSITY: 163.4 per sq km
CAPITAL: Victoria
LANGUAGE: Creole
RELIGION: 90% Roman Catholic
CURRENCY: Seychelles rupee (SR)
ORGANISATIONS: Comm, UN, OAU

This archipelago in the Indian Ocean comprises some 86 granite or coral islands. Mahe, the largest covers 155sq km(60sq miles) rising steeply to over 900m(2953ft). The coral islands rise only a few metres above sea level. Temperatures are a constant 24°–29°C(75°–84°F), and rainfall is in the range 180–345cm(71–135in). Main exports are copra, coconuts and cinnamon. Fishing is also important to the economy. Tourism has expanded greatly since the opening of the international airport in 1978.

SHARJAH
(see UNITED ARAB EMIRATES)

SHIKOKU

STATUS: Island Prefecture of Japan
AREA: 18,755 sq km (7,240 sq miles)
POPULATION: 4,040,070

SIERRA LEONE

STATUS: Republic
AREA: 72,325 sq km (27,920 sq miles)
POPULATION: 3,670,000
ANNUAL NATURAL INCREASE: 1.8%
DENSITY: 50.8% per sq km
CAPITAL: Freetown
LANGUAGE: English, (also Krio Temne, Mende)
RELIGION: animist majority. Moslem and Christian minorities
CURRENCY: leone (Le)
ORGANISATIONS: Comm, UN, ECOWAS, OAU

A former British colony, the coastline of Sierra Leone is dominated by swamps broken only by

the mountainous peninsula south of Freetown. A wide coastal plain extends inland to the foothills of the interior plateaux and mountains. The land is not fertile due to the poor soils with most of the population farming at subsistence level. Mineral deposits include diamonds, iron ore and bauxite with manufacturing only developed around the capital. Oil-, rice- and timber-mills process these products for export.

SINGAPORE

STATUS: Republic
AREA: 616 sq km (238 sq miles)
POPULATION: 2,600,000

ANNUAL NATURAL INCREASE: 1.1%
DENSITY: 4220.8 per sq km
CAPITAL: Singapore City
LANGUAGE: Malay, Chinese (Mandarin), Tamil, English
RELIGION: Daoist, Buddhist, Moslem, Christian, Hindu
CURRENCY: Singapore dollar (S$)
ORGANISATIONS: Comm, UN, ASEAN, Col. Plan

Founded by Sir Stamford Raffles, the state of Singapore has been transformed from an island of mangrove swamps into one the world's major entrepreneurial centres. The island, connected to Peninsular Malaysia by a man-made causeway, has a hot, humid climate with 224cm(96in) of rain per year. With few natural resources, Singapore depends on manufacturing precision goods and electronic products along with financial services.

SOCIETY ISLANDS
(see **FRENCH POLYNESIA**)

SOCOTRA
STATUS: Island of South Yemen
AREA: 3,625 sq km (1,400 sq miles)
POPULATION: No reliable figure available

SOLOMON ISLANDS

STATUS: Commonwealth Nation
AREA: 29,790 sq km (11,500 sq miles)
POPULATION: 285,796
ANNUAL NATURAL INCREASE: 3.7%
DENSITY: 9.6 per sq km
CAPITAL: Honiara
LANGUAGE: English, native languages
RELIGION: 95% Christian

CURRENCY: Solomon Islands dollar (SI$)
ORGANISATIONS: Comm, UN

Situated in the South Pacific Ocean the Solomon Islands consist of six main and many smaller islands. The mountainous large islands are covered by tropical rain forest reflecting the high temperatures and heavy rainfall. The main crops are coconuts, cocoa and rice with copra, timber and palm oil being the main exports. This former British protectorate became independent in 1978. There are reserves of bauxite, phosphate and gold.

SOMALIA

STATUS: Democratic Republic
AREA: 630,000 sq km (243,180 sq miles)
POPULATION: 4,760,000
ANNUAL NATURAL INCREASE: 2.5%
DENSITY: 7.6 per sq km
CAPITAL: Mogadishu (Muqdisho)
LANGUAGE: Somali, Arabic, English, Italian
RELIGION: Moslem. Roman Catholic minority
CURRENCY: Somali shilling (Som. Sh.)
ORGANISATIONS: UN, Arab League, OAU

Independent since 1960, Somalia, is a hot and arid country in north-east Africa. The semi-desert of the northern mountains contrasts with the plains of the south where the bush country is particularly rich in wildlife. Most of the population are nomadic, following herds of camels, sheep, goats and cattle. Little land is cultivated but cotton, maize, millet and sugar-cane are grown. Bananas are a major export. Iron ore, gypsum and uranium deposits are found but none are yet exploited.

SOUTH AFRICA

STATUS: Republic
AREA: 1,184,825 sq km (457,345 sq miles)
POPULATION: 33,221,000
ANNUAL NATURAL INCREASE: 2.3%
DENSITY: 28.1 per sq km
CAPITAL: Pretoria (administrative)
Cape Town (legislative)
LANGUAGE: Afrikaans, English, various African languages
RELIGION: mainly Christian. Hindu, Jewish and Moslem minorities
CURRENCY: rand (R)
ORGANISATIONS: UN

BANTU HOMELANDS
STATUS: Self-governing Territories of South Africa
AREA: 93,690 sq km (36,165 sq miles)
POPULATION: 6,890,000

BOPHUTHATSWANA
STATUS: Self-governing Republic within South Africa
AREA: 40,000 sq km (15,440 sq miles)
POPULATION: 1,433,424

CAPE PROVINCE
STATUS: Province
AREA: 656,640 sq km (253,465 sq miles)
POPULATION: 5,041,137

CISKEI
STATUS: Self-governing Republic within South Africa
AREA: 4,000 sq km (1,545 sq miles)
POPULATION: 728,441

NATAL
STATUS: Province
AREA: 86,965 sq km (33,570 sq miles)
POPULATION: 2,145,018

ORANGE FREE STATE
STATUS: Province
AREA: 127,990 sq km (49,405 sq miles)
POPULATION: 1,776,903

TRANSKEI
STATUS: Self-governing Republic within South Africa
AREA: 43,190 sq km (16,670 sq miles)
POPULATION: 2,524,353

TRANSVAAL
STATUS: Province
AREA: 268,915 sq km (103,800 sq miles)
POPULATION: 7,532,179

VENDA
STATUS: Self-governing Republic within South Africa
AREA: 6,500 sq km (2,510 sq miles)
POPULATION: 376,470

The Republic of South Africa is the most highly developed country in Africa. Geographically, the interior consists of a plateau of over 900m(2955ft) drained by the Orange and Limpopo rivers. Surrounding the plateau is a pronounced escarpment below which the land descends by steps to the sea. Rainfall in most areas is less than 50cm(20in) becoming increasingly drier in the west. Agriculture is limited by poor soils but sheep and cattle are extensively grazed. Main crops are maize, wheat, sugar-cane, vegetables, cotton and vines. Wine is an important export commodity. South Africa abounds in minerals. Diamonds, gold, platinum, silver, uranium, copper, manganese and asbestos are mined and nearly 80% of the continent's coal reserves are in South Africa. Manufacturing and engineering is concentrated in southern Transvaal and around the ports. Most foreign revenue is earned through exports of minerals, metals, precious stones, textiles and chemicals and tobacco.

SOUTHERN & ANTARCTIC TERRITORIES
STATUS: Overseas Territory of France
AREA: 439,580 sq km (169,680 sq miles)
POPULATION: 210

SOUTH GEORGIA
STATUS: Dependency of Falkland Islands
AREA: 3,755 sq km (1,450 sq miles)
POPULATION: No permanent population

SOUTH SANDWICH ISLANDS

STATUS: Dependency of Falkland Islands
AREA: 337 sq km (130 sq miles)
POPULATION: No permanent population

SPAIN

STATUS: Kingdom
AREA: 504,880 sq km (194,885 sq miles)
POPULATION: 38,853,000
ANNUAL NATURAL INCREASE: 0.5%
DENSITY: 77 per sq km
CAPITAL: Madrid
LANGUAGE: Spanish, Catalan, Basque
RELIGION: Roman Catholic
CURRENCY: peseta
ORGANISATIONS: UN, Council of Eur, EEC, NATO, OECD

Once a great colonial power, Spain occupies most of the Iberian Peninsula. Mountain ranges fringe the meseta, a vast plateau averaging 600m(1970ft). Climate is affected regionally by latitude and proximity to the Atlantic Ocean and Mediterranean Sea. Much of the land is covered by Mediterranean scrub but wheat, barley, maize, grapes and olives are cultivated. Main cash crops are cotton, olives, tobacco and citrus fruit. Textile manufacturing in the north-east and steel, chemicals, consumer goods and vehicle manufacturing in the towns and cities has proved a magnet for great numbers of the rural population. Other major industries are cement, fishing and forestry. Main minerals are coal, iron ore, uranium and zinc. Tourism is of vital importance to the economy.

SPITSBERGEN

STATUS: Main Island of Svalbard
AREA: 39,045 sq km (15,070 sq miles)
POPULATION: 3,477

SRI LANKA

STATUS: Democratic Socialist Republic
AREA: 65,610 sq km (25,325 sq miles)
POPULATION: 16,117,000
ANNUAL NATURAL INCREASE: 2.0%
DENSITY: 245.7 per sq km
CAPITAL: Colombo
LANGUAGE: Sinhala, Tamil, English
RELIGION: 70% Buddhist, 15% Hindu. Roman Catholic and Moslem minorities
CURRENCY: Sri Lanka rupee (R)
ORGANISATIONS: Comm, UN, Col. Plan

Situated only 19km(12 miles) from mainland India, Sri Lanka (also called Ceylon) is an island of undulating coastal plain encircling the central highlands. The climate is divided accordingly between tropical on the coast and temperate in the hills. Annual rainfall averages only 100cm(39in) in the north and east while the south and west receive over 200cm(79in). Natural resources are limited but the rich agricultural land produces tea, rubber and coconuts. Gem-stones (sapphire, ruby, beryl, topaz), graphite and salt are mined. The main industries are food processing, textiles, chemicals and rubber. Tourism is a steadily growing area of foreign exchange earnings.

SUDAN

STATUS: Republic
AREA: 2,505,815 sq km (967,245 sq miles)
POPULATION: 22,178,000
ANNUAL NATURAL INCREASE: 2.9%
DENSITY: 8.9 per sq km
CAPITAL: Khartoum
LANGUAGE: Arabic, tribal languages
RELIGION: Moslem, animist and Christian
CURRENCY: Sudanese pound (£S)
ORGANISATIONS: UN, Arab League, OAU

Sudan, in the upper Nile basin, is Africa's largest country. The land is mostly flat and infertile with a hot, arid climate. The White and Blue Niles are invaluable, serving not only to irrigate cultivated land but also as a potential source of hydro-electric power. Subsistence farming accounts for 80% of the Sudan's total production. Major exports include cotton, groundnuts, sugar-cane and sesame seed. The principal activity is nomadic herding with over 20 million cattle and sheep and 14 million goats. Gum arabic is the only forest product exported.

SUMATRA (SUMATERA)

STATUS: Island of Indonesia
AREA: 524,100 sq km (202,305 sq miles)
POPULATION: 28,016,160

SURINAM

STATUS: Republic
AREA: 163,820 sq km (63,235 sq miles)
POPULATION: 380,000
ANNUAL NATURAL INCREASE: 2.0%
DENSITY: 2.4 per sq km
CAPITAL: Paramaribo
LANGUAGE: Dutch, English, Surinamese (Sranang Tongo), and others

RELIGION: 45% Christian, 28% Hindu, 20% Moslem
CURRENCY: Suriname guilder
ORGANISATIONS: UN, OAS

Independent from the Dutch since 1976, Surinam is a small state lying on the north-east coast in the tropics of South America. Physically, there are three main regions: a low-lying, marshy coastal strip; undulating savannah; densely forested highlands. Rice growing takes up 75% of all cultivated land. The introduction of cattle-raising for meat and dairy products is not yet complete. Bauxite accounts for 90% of Surinam's foreign earnings. Rice and timber products are also important. Timber resources are largely untapped.

SVALBARD

STATUS: Archipelago Territory of Norway
AREA: 62,000 sq km (23,930 sq miles)
POPULATION: 3,914

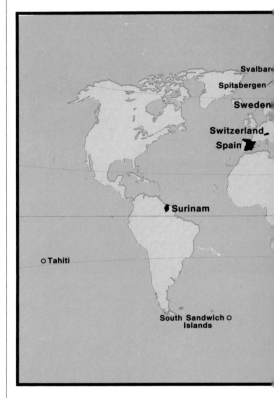

SWAZILAND

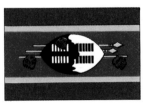

STATUS: Kingdom
AREA: 17,365 sq km (6,705 sq miles)
POPULATION: 676,000
ANNUAL NATURAL INCREASE: 3.0%
DENSITY: 39 per sq km
CAPITAL: Mbabane
LANGUAGE: English, SiSwati
RELIGION: 60% Christian, 40% traditional beliefs
CURRENCY: emalangeni (E) S. African rand
ORGANISATIONS: Comm, UN, OAU

Landlocked Swaziland in southern Africa, is a sub-tropical, savannah country. It is divided into four main regions: the High, Middle and Low Velds and the Lebombo Mountains. Rainfall is abundant promoting good pastureland for the many cattle and sheep. Major exports include sugar, meat, citrus fruits, textiles, wood products and asbestos.

SWEDEN

STATUS: Kingdom
AREA: 449,790 sq km (173,620 sq miles)
POPULATION: 8,370,000
ANNUAL NATURAL INCREASE: 0%
DENSITY: 18.6 per sq km
CAPITAL: Stockholm

LANGUAGE: Swedish, Finnish, Lappish
RELIGION: 95% Evangelical Lutheran
CURRENCY: Swedish krona (kr)
ORGANISATIONS: UN, Council of Eur, EFTA, OECD

Glacial debris, glacier-eroded valleys and thick glacial clay are all dominant features of Sweden. Physically, Sweden comprises four main regions: Norrland the northern forested mountains; the Lake District of the centre south; the southern Uplands of Jönköping; and the extremely fertile Scania plain of the far south. Summers are short and hot with long, cold winters. Annual rainfall varies between 200cm(79in) in the west and south-west, to 50cm(20in) in the east and south-east.

Over half the land area is forested resulting in a thriving timber industry, but manufacturing industry, particularly cars and trucks, metal products and machine tools, is becoming increasingly dominant. Mineral resources are also rich and plentiful – iron-ore production alone exceeds 17 million tons a year. There are also deposits of copper, lead and zinc.

SWITZERLAND

STATUS: Confederation
AREA: 41,285 sq km (15,935 sq miles)
POPULATION: 6,504,000
ANNUAL NATURAL INCREASE: 0.2%
DENSITY: 157.6 per sq km
CAPITAL: Bern (Berne)
LANGUAGE: German, French, Italian, Romansch
RELIGION: 44% Protestant, 48% Roman Catholic. Jewish minority
CURRENCY: Swiss franc
ORGANISATIONS: Council of Eur, EFTA, OECD

Switzerland is a mountainous, landlocked country in the Alps. Winters are very cold with heavy snowfall. Summers are mild with an average July temperature of 18–19°C(64°–66°F). Rainfall is normally restricted to the summer months. Agriculture is based mainly on dairy farming. Major crops include hay, wheat, barley and potatoes. Industry plays a major role in Switzerland's economy, centred on metal engineering, watchmaking, food processing, textiles and chemicals. Tourism is also an important source of income and employment. The financial services sector, especially banking, is also of great importance.

SYRIA

STATUS: Arab Republic
AREA: 185,680 sq km (71,675 sq miles)
POPULATION: 10,612,000
ANNUAL NATURAL INCREASE: 3.8%
DENSITY: 57.2 per sq km
CAPITAL: Damascus (Dimashq)
LANGUAGE: Arabic
RELIGION: 80% Sunni Moslem. Christian minority
CURRENCY: Syrian pound (£Syr)
ORGANISATIONS: UN, Arab League

Syria is situated at the heart of the Middle East bordered by Turkey, Iraq, Jordan, Israel and Lebanon. Its most fertile areas lie along the coastal strip, and in the depressions and plateaux of the north-east which are cut through by the rivers Orontes and Euphrates. In the south the Anti-Lebanon range is bordered to the east by the Syrian desert. While the coast has a Mediterranean climate, the interior becomes increasingly hot and arid – average summer temperatures in the desert reach 43°C(109°F). Rainfall varies between 22 and 40cm(9 and 16in). Cotton is Syria's main export crop, and wheat and barley are also grown. Cattle, sheep and goats are the main livestock. The country is rapidly becoming industrialised as oil, natural gas and phosphates are exploited. Salt and gypsum are mined.

TAHITI

STATUS: Main Island of French Polynesia
AREA: 1,042 sq km (402 sq miles)
POPULATION: 95,604

TAIWAN

STATUS: Republic
AREA: 35,990 sq km (13,890 sq miles)
POPULATION: 19,258,053
ANNUAL NATURAL INCREASE: 1.5%
DENSITY: 535.1 per sq km
CAPITAL: Taipei
LANGUAGE: Mandarin Chinese
RELIGION: Buddhist majority. Moslem, Daoist and Christian minorities
CURRENCY: New Taiwan dollar (NT$)

Taiwan is situated off the coast of China and the East China Sea. It is a mountainous island with the interior reaching a height of 4000m (13,125ft). The mountains on the eastern side have been terraced for agriculture. Monsoon rain falls for eleven months of the year (annual average 260cm or 102in) and summers are long and hot. Main crops include rice, tea, fruit, sugar-cane and sweet potatoes. Highly industrialised, its principal exports are textiles, electrical goods and consumer goods. Coal, copper, sulphur, oil and natural gas are exploited.

TANZANIA

STATUS: United Republic
AREA: 939,760 sq km (362,750 sq miles)
POPULATION: 22,462,000
ANNUAL NATURAL INCREASE: 3.5%
DENSITY: 24 per sq km
CAPITAL: Dodoma
LANGUAGE: Kiswahili, English
RELIGION: Christian, Hindu, Moslem
CURRENCY: Tanzanian shilling
ORGANISATIONS: Comm, UN, OAU

Much of this East African country consists of high interior plateaux covered by scrub and grassland, bordered to the north by the volcanic Kilimanjaro region, to the east by Lake Tanganyika, and by highlands to the south. Despite its proximity to the equator, the altitude of much of Tanzania means that temperatures are reduced, and only on the narrow coastal plain is the climate truly tropical. Average temperatures vary between 19° and 28°C(67° and 82°F), and rainfall 57 to 106cm(23 to 43in). Subsistence farming is the main way of life, although coffee, cotton and sisal are exported. Industry is limited to textiles, food processing and tobacco.

THAILAND

STATUS: Kingdom
AREA: 514,000 sq km (198,405 sq miles)
POPULATION: 53,605,000
ANNUAL NATURAL INCREASE: 2.0%
DENSITY: 104.3 per sq km
CAPITAL: Bangkok (Krung Thep)
LANGUAGE: Thai
RELIGION: Buddhist, 4% Moslem
CURRENCY: baht
ORGANISATIONS: UN, ASEAN, Col. Plan

Thailand consists of a flat undulating central plain fringed by mountain ranges, and by a flat plain drained by the River Mekong. From May to October monsoon rains are heavy with an annual average rainfall of 150cm(59in). The climate is tropical with temperatures reaching 36°C(97°F). Over 50% of the country is covered by dense rain forest. Rice is the main export crop, although maize, beans, coconut and groundnuts are also grown. Thailand is one the world's largest producers of rubber and tin.

TIMOR

STATUS: Island of Indonesia
AREA: 33,915 sq km (13,090 sq miles)
POPULATION: 555,350

TOGO

STATUS: Republic
AREA: 56,785 sq km (21,920 sq miles)
POPULATION: 3,052,000
ANNUAL NATURAL INCREASE: 3.1%
DENSITY: 53.8 per sq km
CAPITAL: Lomé
LANGUAGE: French, Kabre, Ewe
RELIGION: 60% animist, 25% Christian, 7.5% Moslem
CURRENCY: CFA franc
ORGANISATIONS: UN, ECOWAS, OAU

This small African republic between Ghana and Benin has only 65km(40 miles) of coast. The interior consists of mountains and high infertile tableland. The climate is tropical with an average temperature of 27°C(81°F). Most of Togo's farmers grow maize, cassava, yams, groundnuts and plantains. Main exports are phosphates, cotton and coffee.

TOKELAU ISLANDS

STATUS: Overseas Territory of New Zealand
AREA: 10 sq km (4 sq miles)
POPULATION: 1,627

TONGA

STATUS: Kingdom
AREA: 699 sq km (270 sq miles)
POPULATION: 111,000
ANNUAL NATURAL INCREASE: 0.9%
DENSITY: 158.8 per sq km
CAPITAL: Nuku'alofa
LANGUAGE: Tongan, English
RELIGION: Christian
CURRENCY: pa'anga ($T)
ORGANISATIONS: Comm

Tonga consists of an archipelago of 169 islands in the Pacific 180km(112 miles) north of New Zealand. There are seven groups of islands, but the most important are Tongatapu, Ha'apai and Vava'u. All the islands are covered with dense tropical vegetation, and temperatures range from 11° to 29°C(52° to 84°F). Main exports are coconut products and bananas.

TRINIDAD & TOBAGO

STATUS: Republic
AREA: 5,130 sq km (1,980 sq miles)
POPULATION: 1,204,000
ANNUAL NATURAL INCREASE: 1.8%
DENSITY: 234.7 per sq km
CAPITAL: Port of Spain
LANGUAGE: English
RELIGION: 60% Christian, 25% Hindu, 6% Moslem
CURRENCY: Trinidad & Tobago $ (TT$)
ORGANISATIONS: Comm, UN, CARICOM, OAS

These Caribbean islands lie only 11 and 30km(7 and 19 miles) respectively from the Venezuelan coast. Both islands have mountainous interiors – the central range of Trinidad reaches 940m(3084ft) – and are densely covered with tropical rain forest. Sugar was once the mainstay of the economy but oil is now the leading source of revenue.

TRISTAN DA CUNHA

STATUS: Dependency of St Helena
AREA: 98 sq km (38 sq miles)
POPULATION: 310

TUAMOTU-GAMBIER ARCHIPELAGO

(see **FRENCH POLYNESIA**)

TUBAI ISLANDS

(see **FRENCH POLYNESIA**)

TUNISIA

STATUS: Republic
AREA: 164,150 sq km (63,378 sq miles)
POPULATION: 7,234,000
ANNUAL NATURAL INCREASE: 2.7%
DENSITY: 44 per sq km
CAPITAL: Tunis
LANGUAGE: Arabic, French
RELIGION: Moslem
CURRENCY: Tunisian dinar (TD)
ORGANISATIONS: UN, Arab League, OAU

The flat central plains of Tunisia are fringed to the north-east and south-west by mountains and to the west by the sahel, a broad plain

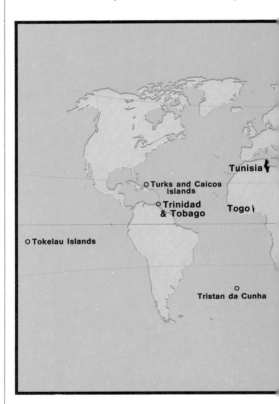

which leads to the Sahara. Average annual temperature ranges from 10° to 27°C(50° to 81°F) and while the coastal area has Mediterranean scrub, the interior is desert. Wheat, barley, olives and citrus fruit are the main crops and oil, natural gas and sugar refining are the main industries. Tourism is growing rapidly.

TURKEY

STATUS: Republic
AREA: 779,450 sq km (300,870 sq miles)
POPULATION: 50,301,000
ANNUAL NATURAL INCREASE: 2.5%
DENSITY: 64.6 per sq km

CAPITAL: Ankara
LANGUAGE: Turkish, Kurdish
RELIGION: Sunni Moslem. Christian minority
CURRENCY: Turkish Lira (TL)
ORGANISATIONS: UN, Council of Eur, NATO, OECD

Turkey has always occupied a strategically important position linking Europe and Asia. The central Anatolian plateau, is bordered to the north and south by mountain ranges which converge in the eastern Anatolian mountains crowned by Mt Ararat 5165m(16,945ft). The north, south and west coastlines are fringed by Mediterranean vegetation and have short, mild and wet winters and long, hot summers. The interior is arid with average rainfall less than 25cm(10in). The main crops are wheat and barley, but tobacco, olives, sugar-beet, tea and fruit are also grown, and sheep, goats and cattle are raised. Turkey is becoming increasingly industrialised and now leads the Middle East in the production of iron, steel, chrome, coal and lignite. Tourism is a rapidly growing industry.

TURKS & CAICOS ISLANDS

STATUS: UK Dependent Territory
AREA: 430 sq km (166 sq miles)
POPULATION: 8,000
CAPITAL: Cockburn Town

TUVALU

STATUS: State
AREA: 24.6 sq km (9.5 sq miles)
POPULATION: 8,000
ANNUAL NATURAL INCREASE: 1.5%
DENSITY: 325.2 per sq km
CAPITAL: Funafuti
LANGUAGE: Tuvaluan, English

RELIGION: 98% Protestant
CURRENCY: Australian and Tuvaluan $A
ORGANISATIONS: Comm (Special member)

Tuvalu consists of nine dispersed coral atolls 600–1200km(372–745 miles) north of Fiji in the Pacific Ocean. The climate is tropical; hot, with heavy annual rainfall (c300cm or 118in). Fish is the staple food but coconuts and bread-fruits are cultivated.

UGANDA

STATUS: Republic
AREA: 236,580 sq km (91,320 sq miles)
POPULATION: 16,018,000
ANNUAL NATURAL INCREASE: 3.4%
DENSITY: 67.7 per sq km
CAPITAL: Kampala
LANGUAGE: English, tribal languages
RELIGION: 60% Christian. Moslem minority
CURRENCY: Uganda shilling
ORGANISATIONS: Comm, UN, OAU

Uganda is bordered to the west by the African Rift valley and to the east by Kenya. The central high plateau is savannah, while the area around Lake Victoria has been cleared for cultivation. To the west are mountain ranges reaching 5110m(16,765ft). The climate is warm (21°–24°C or 70°–75°F), and rainfall ranges from 75–150cm(30–59in). The main export crop is coffee. Lake Victoria has great supplies of freshwater fish.

UMM AL QAIWAIN
(see UNITED ARAB EMIRATES)

UNION OF SOVIET SOCIALIST REPUBLICS (USSR)

STATUS: Union of Soviet Socialist Republics
AREA: 22,400,000 sq km (8,646,400 sq miles)
POPULATION: 278,719,000
ANNUAL NATURAL INCREASE: 0.9%
DENSITY: 12.4 per sq km
CAPITAL: Moscow (Moskva)
LANGUAGE: Russian, regional languages
RELIGION: Russian Orthodox with Christian, Jewish and Moslem minorities
CURRENCY: rouble
ORGANISATIONS: UN, Warsaw Pact, COMECON

ARMENIA
STATUS: Union Republic
AREA: 30,000 sq km (11,580 sq miles)
POPULATION: 3,369,000
CAPITAL: Yerevan

AZERBAYDZHAN
STATUS: Union Republic
AREA: 87,000 sq km (33,580 sq miles)
POPULATION: 6,718,000
CAPITAL: Baku

BYELORUSSIA
STATUS: Union Republic
AREA: 208,000 sq km (80,290 sq miles)
POPULATION: 10,002,000
CAPITAL: Minsk

ESTONIA
STATUS: Union Republic
AREA: 45,100 sq km (17,410 sq miles)
POPULATION: 1,541,500
CAPITAL: Tallinn

GEORGIA
STATUS: Union Republic
AREA: 69,700 sq km (26,905 sq miles)
POPULATION: 5,239,000
CAPITAL: Tbilisi

KAZAKHSTAN
STATUS: Union Republic
AREA: 2,717,300 sq km (1,048,880 sq miles)
POPULATION: 16,036,000
CAPITAL: Alma-Ata

KIRGHIZIA
STATUS: Union Republic
AREA: 198,500 sq km (76,620 sq miles)
POPULATION: 4,055,000
CAPITAL: Frunze

LATVIA
STATUS: Union Republic
AREA: 63,700 sq km (24,590 sq miles)
POPULATION: 2,621,000
CAPITAL: Riga

LITHUANIA
STATUS: Union Republic
AREA: 65,200 sq km (25,165 sq miles)
POPULATION: 3,603,000
CAPITAL: Vilnius

MOLDAVIA
STATUS: Union Republic
AREA: 33,700 sq km (13,010 sq miles)
POPULATION: 4,142,000
CAPITAL: Kishinev

RUSSIAN SOVIET FEDERAL SOCIALIST REPUBLIC (RSFSR)
STATUS: Union Republic
AREA: 17,078,005 sq km (6,592,110 sq miles)
POPULATION: 144,027,000
CAPITAL: Moscow

TADZHIKISTAN
STATUS: Union Republic
AREA: 143,100 sq km (55,235 sq miles)
POPULATION: 4,643,000
CAPITAL: Dushanbe

TURKMENISTAN
STATUS: Union Republic
AREA: 488,100 sq km (188,405 sq miles)
POPULATION: 3,271,000
CAPITAL: Ashkhabad

UKRAINE
STATUS: Union Republic
AREA: 603,700 sq km (233,030 sq miles)
POPULATION: 50,973,000
CAPITAL: Kiev

UZBEKISTAN

STATUS: Union Republic
AREA: 447,400 sq km (172,695 sq miles)
POPULATION: 18,479,000
CAPITAL: Tashkent

The Union of Soviet Socialist Republics is the largest country in the world, covering one fifth of the earth's surface. After China and India, it has the world's third largest population. From Moscow, in European Russia, to Vladivostok on the Sea of Japan is a journey of 9200km(5720 miles) which crosses eleven time zones.

The country encompasses a great diversity of different climates and environments ranging from the frozen wastes of eastern Siberia to the deserts of Central Asia. Nearly half of the USSR falls north of 60°, and large areas of its territory lie within the Arctic Circle.

European Russia, west of the Ural mountains, is an area of undulating lowlands cut through by broad rivers. To the south and west of this region lie the mountain ranges of the Caucasus, Carpathians and Crimea. East of the Urals lies the West Siberian plain, a vast tract of low-lying marshy land, drained by the great rivers Ob and Irtysh. This gradually rises towards the Central Siberian plateau which reaches a height of 1500m(4920ft), and lies between the Yenisey and Lena rivers. East of the River Lena the mountains reach a height of 3000m(9840ft). In the south of this region is Lake Baikal, at 1611m(5285ft), the world's deepest lake. South of the West Siberian plain is Soviet Central Asia.

The vegetation and climate of the USSR reflect this great diversity. Within the Arctic Circle there is a belt of tundra – sparse, scrubby vegetation. Here, reindeer herding is the only means of subsistence. South of the tundra lies the taiga belt, an area of thick coniferous forest which stretches from the Baltic to the Pacific. European Russia is an area of mixed and deciduous woodland while the steppe lands immediately to the east of the Urals are Russia's 'black soil' lands, the most fertile areas of the USSR. The climate of the USSR is one of extremes.

These conditions become more extreme towards the east; in Moscow, for example, annual snow cover is five months, on the east coast nine months. In the north-east January temperatures can fall to −60°C(−76°F). The central Siberian plateau is covered with permafrost – the ground is permanently frozen, and only the top soil thaws in the spring. Rainfall is erratic, particularly to the east of the Urals, where drought is common, and this can undermine the agricultural potential of the blacksoil belts. The steppes do, however, account for much of the 10% of Russian territory which is under cultivation. About 60% of this area is given over to cereals – wheat, barley, oats and rye – which are transported vast distances to supply the most far-flung regions of the USSR. In general fruit and vegetables are grown and consumed locally. In addition to cereals industrial crops are also grown in the steppe regions – sunflowers, sugar-beet, cotton, flax, hemp and potatoes.

The 12th Five Year Plan adopted in 1986, is dedicated to raising the living standards, implementing scientific and technical progress, greater economy in use of energy and natural resources and placing greater emphasis on energy, food programmes and development of consumer goods and services.

The Soviet economy is self-sufficient in energy requirements. Coal is in plentiful supply – the USSR has about 58% of the world's reserves – but is now being supplemented by oil and natural gas as the country's main source of energy. Over 80% of electricity is produced by fuel-burning power stations. The remainder is generated by hydro-electric schemes using the latent power of the great rivers of Siberia, in particular the rivers Yenisey, Angara and Kureyka. There are also at least four potential and one working tidal electric generation schemes in the White Sea. These could eventually provide electricity to the Moscow region and to the heavy industry of the southern Urals. Nuclear and nuclear thermal power stations also make an important contribution.

Recent discoveries of vast reserves of oil in the area of Saratov in West Siberia, supplement the supplies from the longer established Volga-Urals oilfields. A network of pipelines over 71,000km(44,120 miles) in length distributes oil to the industrial centres and to eastern European countries. The natural gas pipelines total over 124,000km(77,055 miles) and distribute to eastern Europe and Italy, West Germany and Austria. The USSR also has large reserves of iron ore and non-ferrous metals such as manganese, though it is not self-sufficient in copper, lead, zinc and tin. Uranium is mined in the Altai mountains.

Heavy industry is concentrated in the Urals around Sverdlovsk, Chelyabinsk and Magnitogorsk producing steel, turbines, piping, heavy machinery, chemicals and vehicles. Lighter, consumer industries are concentrated around Moscow with cotton and woollen textiles, leather goods, precision instruments, electric and electronic goods, and processed foods.

UNITED ARAB EMIRATES (UAE)

STATUS: United Arab Emirates
AREA: 75,150 sq km (29,010 sq miles)
POPULATION: 1,384,000
ANNUAL NATURAL INCREASE: 2.3%
DENSITY: 18.5 per sq km
CAPITAL: Abu Dhabi
LANGUAGE: Arabic, English
RELIGION: Sunni Moslem
CURRENCY: UAE dirham (Dh)
ORGANISATIONS: UN, Arab League, OPEC

ABU DHABI

STATUS: State
AREA: 64,750 sq km (24,995 sq miles)
POPULATION: 670,125

ÁJMĀN

STATUS: State
AREA: 260 sq km (100 sq miles)
POPULATION: 64,318

DUBAI

STATUS: State
AREA: 3,900 sq km (1,505 sq miles)
POPULATION: 419,104

FUJAIRAH

STATUS: State
AREA: 1,170 sq km (452 sq miles)
POPULATION: 54,425

RAS AL-KHAIMAH

STATUS: State
AREA: 1,690 sq km (652 sq miles)
POPULATION: 116,470

SHARJAH

STATUS: State
AREA: 2,600 sq km (1,005 sq miles)
POPULATION: 268,722

UMM AL QAIWAIN

STATUS: State
AREA: 780 sq km (300 sq miles)
POPULATION: 29,229

Seven emirates stretched along the south eastern shores of the Persian Gulf constitute this oil rich Arab state. Flat deserts cover most of the landscape rising to the Hajar mountains of the Musandam Peninsula. Summer temperatures reach 40°C(104°F) and winter rainfall 13cm(5in). Only the desert oases are fertile, producing fruit and vegetables. Trade is dominated by exports of oil and natural gas.

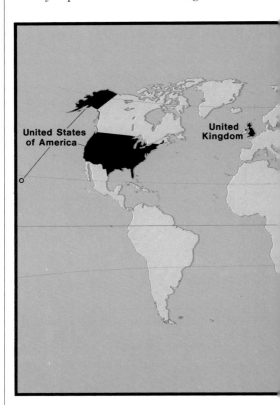

UNITED KINGDOM OF GREAT BRITAIN & NORTHERN IRELAND (UK)

STATUS: Kingdom
AREA: 244,755 sq km (94,475 sq miles)
POPULATION: 56,617,900
ANNUAL NATURAL INCREASE: 0.2%
DENSITY: 231.4 per sq km
CAPITAL: London
LANGUAGE: English, Welsh, Gaelic
RELIGION: Protestant majority, Roman Catholic, Jewish, Moslem and Hindu minorities

CURRENCY: Pound Sterling (£)
ORGANISATIONS: Comm, UN, Col. Plan, Council of Eur, NATO, OECD, WEU

ENGLAND

STATUS: Constituent Country
AREA: 130,360 sq km (50,320 sq miles)
POPULATION: 47,254,500
CAPITAL: London

NORTHERN IRELAND

STATUS: Constituent Region
AREA: 14,150 sq km (5,460 sq miles)
POPULATION: 1,557,800
CAPITAL: Belfast

SCOTLAND

STATUS: Constituent Country
AREA: 78,750 sq km (30,400 sq miles)
POPULATION: 5,136,500
CAPITAL: Edinburgh

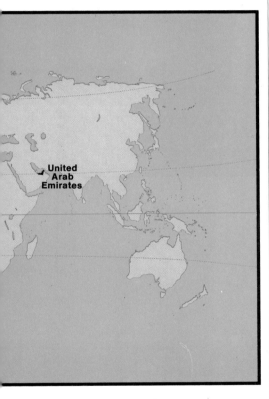

WALES

STATUS: Principality
AREA: 20,760 sq km (8,015 sq miles)
POPULATION: 2,821,000
CAPITAL: Cardiff

The United Kingdom is part of the British Isles which are situated off the coast of north-west Europe separated from France by the English Channel and from Belgium, the Netherlands and Scandinavia by the North Sea. There are two main islands: the larger, Great Britain, comprises England, Scotland and Wales; the smaller, the island of Ireland separated from Britain by the Irish Sea, comprises Northern Ireland and the Irish Republic.

The Highland zone of Britain consists of ancient uplifted rocks which now form the mountainous dissected and glaciated areas of Wales, the Lake District in the north-west, and the Southern Uplands and Grampians of Scotland which rise to the highest point in the UK to 1344m(4409ft) at Ben Nevis. The latter are divided by the wide Central Lowland rift valley.

Central England is dominated by the Pen-nine mountain chain which stretches southwards from the Southern Uplands down the centre of England to the river Trent. The landscape of the south-west consists of the ancient uplifted granite domes of Dartmoor and Bodmin Moor.

Lowland Britain is a very contrasting landscape. Limestone and sandstone hills are separated by flat clay vales, east of a line joining the rivers Humber and Exe. Here is found both the richest agricultural land and the densest population.

The climate of the British Isles is mild, wet and variable. Summer temperatures average 13°–17°C(55°–63°F), and winter temperatures 5°–7°C(41°–45°F). Annual rainfall varies between 65 and 500cm(26 and 200in) with the highest in the central Lake District and the lowest on the coasts of East Anglia.

Although a tiny percentage of the nation's workforce are employed in agriculture, farm produce is important to both home and export markets. 78% of the total UK land area is farmland. The main cereal crops are wheat, barley and oats. Potatoes, sugar-beet and green vegetable crops are widespread.

About 20% of the land is permanent pasture for raising of dairy and beef stock; and 28% of the land, mainly hill and mountain areas, is used for rough grazing of sheep. Pigs and poultry are widespread in both England and lowland Britain. The best fruit-growing areas are the south-east, especially Kent, and East Anglia and the central Vale of Evesham for apples, pears and soft-fruit. Both forestry and fishing industries contribute to the economy.

The major mineral resources of the UK are coal, oil and natural gas. Most of coal output goes towards the generation of electricity but oil and natural gas from the North Sea, and to a lesser extent nuclear power, are divided between the needs of industry and the consumer. Iron ore, once mined in sufficient quantity to satisfy industry, is now imported to support the iron and steel manufacturing sector.

The UK produces a great range of industrial goods for home consumption and export. Heavy industry particularly the production of iron and steel is traditionally located close to fuel sources (coal) in South Wales, the North-East at Tees-side and South Yorkshire. The majority of iron ore is imported. The main shipbuilding areas are Clydeside in western Scotland, Belfast in Northern Ireland and Tyneside in the North-East. Other heavy industrial goods, vehicles, engines and machinery are produced on Merseyside in Lancashire, Derby/Nottingham in the North Midlands, Birmingham in the West-Midlands, Cardiff in South Wales, Clydeside and Belfast.

General and consumer good manufacturing is located in all heavy industrial areas but the London area, West Midlands and Lancashire/Merseyside predominate. Main products are food and drinks, chemicals, light engineering products, cotton and woollen textiles, electrical and electronic goods.

The UK is a trading nation. The balance of trade has changed during the last 30 years because of stronger economic, military and political ties within Europe – the EEC and NATO – and consequently reduced trading links with former colonies particularly in Australasia. Major exports are cereals, meat, dairy products, beverages, tobacco products, textiles, metalliferous ores, petroleum and petroleum products, chemicals, pharmaceutical goods, plastics, leather goods, rubber, paper, iron and steel, other metal goods, engines and vehicles, machinery, electrical goods and transport equipment.

The UK has a highly developed transport network to move goods and services. Motorways, trunk roads and principal roads total over 50,000km(31,070 miles), the railway network covers 16,730km(10,395 miles). The inland waterway system, once a major freight carrier, totals only 563km(350 miles) but still carries over 4 million tonnes of goods annually.

UNITED STATES OF AMERICA (USA)

STATUS: Federal Republic
AREA: 9,363,130 sq km (3,614,170 sq miles)
POPULATION: 238,740,000
ANNUAL NATURAL INCREASE: 0.7%
DENSITY: 25.5 per sq km
CAPITAL: Washington, DC
LANGUAGE: English, Spanish
RELIGION: Christian majority. Jewish minority
CURRENCY: US dollar ($)
ORGANISATIONS: UN, ANZUS, Col. Plan, NATO, OECD, OAS

ALABAMA

STATUS: State
AREA: 131,485 sq km (50,755 sq miles)
POPULATION: 4,021,000
CAPITAL: Montgomery

ALASKA

STATUS: State
AREA: 1,478,450 sq km (570,680 sq miles)
POPULATION: 521,000
CAPITAL: Juneau

ARIZONA

STATUS: State
AREA: 293,985 sq km (113,480 sq miles)
POPULATION: 3,187,000
CAPITAL: Phoenix

ARKANSAS

STATUS: State
AREA: 134,880 sq km (52,065 sq miles)
POPULATION: 2,359,000
CAPITAL: Little Rock

CALIFORNIA

STATUS: State
AREA: 404,815 sq km (156,260 sq miles)
POPULATION: 26,365,000
CAPITAL: Sacramento

COLORADO

STATUS: State
AREA: 268,310 sq km (103,570 sq miles)
POPULATION: 3,231,000
CAPITAL: Denver

CONNECTICUT

STATUS: State
AREA: 12,620 sq km (4,870 sq miles)
POPULATION: 3,174,000
CAPITAL: Hartford

DELAWARE
STATUS: State
AREA: 5,005 sq km (1,930 sq miles)
POPULATION: 622,000
CAPITAL: Dover

DISTRICT OF COLUMBIA
STATUS: Federal District
AREA: 163 sq km (63 sq miles)
POPULATION: 626,000
CAPITAL: Washington

FLORIDA
STATUS: State
AREA: 140,255 sq km (54,140 sq miles)
POPULATION: 11,366,000
CAPITAL: Tallahassee

GEORGIA
STATUS: State
AREA: 150,365 sq km (58,040 sq miles)
POPULATION: 5,976,000
CAPITAL: Atlanta

HAWAII
STATUS: State
AREA: 16,640 sq km (6,425 sq miles)
POPULATION: 1,054,000
CAPITAL: Honolulu

IDAHO
STATUS: State
AREA: 213,455 sq km (82,390 sq miles)
POPULATION: 1,005,000
CAPITAL: Boise

ILLINOIS
STATUS: State
AREA: 144,120 sq km (55,630 sq miles)
POPULATION: 11,535,000
CAPITAL: Springfield

INDIANA
STATUS: State
AREA: 93,065 sq km (35,925 sq miles)
POPULATION: 5,499,000
CAPITAL: Indianapolis

IOWA
STATUS: State
AREA: 144,950 sq km (55,950 sq miles)
POPULATION: 2,884,000
CAPITAL: Des Moines

KANSAS
STATUS: State
AREA: 211,805 sq km (81,755 sq miles)
POPULATION: 2,450,000
CAPITAL: Topeka

KENTUCKY
STATUS: State
AREA: 102,740 sq km (39,660 sq miles)
POPULATION: 3,726,000
CAPITAL: Frankfort

LOUISIANA
STATUS: State
AREA: 115,310 sq km (44,510 sq miles)
POPULATION: 4,481,000
CAPITAL: Baton Rouge

MAINE
STATUS: State
AREA: 80,275 sq km (30,985 sq miles)
POPULATION: 1,164,000
CAPITAL: Augusta

MARYLAND
STATUS: State
AREA: 25,480 sq km (9,835 sq miles)
POPULATION: 4,392,000
CAPITAL: Annapolis

MASSACHUSETTS
STATUS: State
AREA: 20,265 sq km (7,820 sq miles)
POPULATION: 5,822,000
CAPITAL: Boston

MICHIGAN
STATUS: State
AREA: 147,510 sq km (56,940 sq miles)
POPULATION: 9,088,000
CAPITAL: Lansing

MINNESOTA
STATUS: State
AREA: 206,030 sq km (79,530 sq miles)
POPULATION: 4,193,000
CAPITAL: St Paul

MISSISSIPPI
STATUS: State
AREA: 122,335 sq km (47,220 sq miles)
POPULATION: 2,613,000
CAPITAL: Jackson

MISSOURI
STATUS: State
AREA: 178,565 sq km (68,925 sq miles)
POPULATION: 5,029,000
CAPITAL: Jefferson City

MONTANA
STATUS: State
AREA: 376,555 sq km (145,350 sq miles)
POPULATION: 826,000
CAPITAL: Helana

NEBRASKA
STATUS: State
AREA: 198,505 sq km (76,625 sq miles)
POPULATION: 1,606,000
CAPITAL: Lincoln

NEVADA
STATUS: State
AREA: 284,625 sq km (109,865 sq miles)
POPULATION: 936,000
CAPITAL: Carson City

NEW HAMPSHIRE
STATUS: State
AREA: 23,290 sq km (8,990 sq miles)
POPULATION: 998,000
CAPITAL: Concord

NEW JERSEY
STATUS: State
AREA: 19,340 sq km (7,465 sq miles)
POPULATION: 7,562,000
CAPITAL: Trenton

NEW MEXICO
STATUS: State
AREA: 314,255 sq km (121,300 sq miles)
POPULATION: 1,450,000
CAPITAL: Santa Fé

NEW YORK
STATUS: State
AREA: 122,705 sq km (47,365 sq miles)
POPULATION: 17,783,000
CAPITAL: Albany

NORTH CAROLINA
STATUS: State
AREA: 126,505 sq km (48,830 sq miles)
POPULATION: 6,255,000
CAPITAL: Raleigh

NORTH DAKOTA
STATUS: State
AREA: 179,485 sq km (69,280 sq miles)
POPULATION: 685,000
CAPITAL: Bismarck

OHIO
STATUS: State
AREA: 106,200 sq km (40,995 sq miles)
POPULATION: 10,744,000
CAPITAL: Columbus

OKLAHOMA
STATUS: State
AREA: 177,815 sq km (68,635 sq miles)
POPULATION: 3,301,000
CAPITAL: Oklahoma City

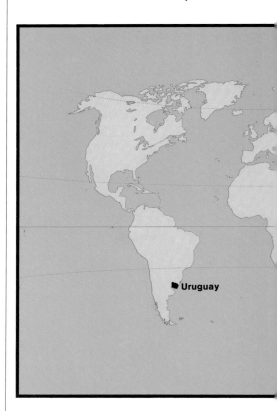

Uruguay

OREGON
STATUS: State
AREA: 249,115 sq km (96,160 sq miles)
POPULATION: 2,687,000
CAPITAL: Salem

PENNSYLVANIA
STATUS: State
AREA: 116,260 sq km (44,875 sq miles)
POPULATION: 11,853,000
CAPITAL: Harrisburg

RHODE ISLAND
STATUS: State
AREA: 2,730 sq km (1,055 sq miles)
POPULATION: 968,000
CAPITAL: Providence

SOUTH CAROLINA
STATUS: State
AREA: 78,225 sq km (30,195 sq miles)
POPULATION: 3,347,000
CAPITAL: Columbia

SOUTH DAKOTA

STATUS: State
AREA: 196,715 sq km (75,930 sq miles)
POPULATION: 708,000
CAPITAL: Pierre

TENNESSEE

STATUS: State
AREA: 106,590 sq km (41,145 sq miles)
POPULATION: 4,762,000
CAPITAL: Nashville

TEXAS

STATUS: State
AREA: 678,620 sq km (261,950 sq miles)
POPULATION: 16,370,000
CAPITAL: Austin

UTAH

STATUS: State
AREA: 212,570 sq km (82,050 sq miles)
POPULATION: 1,645,000
CAPITAL: Salt Lake City

VERMONT

STATUS: State
AREA: 24,900 sq km (9,612 sq miles)
POPULATION: 535,000
CAPITAL: Montpelier

VIRGINIA

STATUS: State
AREA: 102,835 sq km (39,695 sq miles)
POPULATION: 5,706,000
CAPITAL: Richmond

WASHINGTON

STATUS: State
AREA: 172,265 sq km (66,495 sq miles)
POPULATION: 4,409,000
CAPITAL: Olympia

WEST VIRGINIA

STATUS: State
AREA: 62,470 sq km (24,115 sq miles)
POPULATION: 1,936,000
CAPITAL: Charleston

WISCONSIN

STATUS: State
AREA: 140,965 sq km (54,415 sq miles)
POPULATION: 4,775,000
CAPITAL: Madison

WYOMING

STATUS: State
AREA: 251,200 sq km (96,965 sq miles)
POPULATION: 508,000
CAPITAL: Cheyenne

The United States of America is the world's fourth largest country after USSR, Canada and China, with the world's fourth largest population. The 19th and 20th centuries have brought 42 million immigrants to its shores, and the population of the USA now has the highest living standard of any country in the world. The large land area covers a huge spectrum of different landscapes, environments and climates. The eastern coast of New England where the European settlers first landed, is rocky, mountainous and richly wooded. South of New England is the Atlantic coastal plain, rising to the west towards the Appalachian mountain system. Beyond the Appalachians lie the central lowlands, a large undulating plain cut through by the Mississippi and Ohio rivers. Further west lie the Great Plains crossed by the Missouri, Red and Arkansas rivers and rising gently towards the mighty Rockies a spine of mountains running south from Alaska. The highest point is Mt. Whitney in California, at 4418m(14,495ft). Beyond the Rockies lies the Great Valley of California and the Pacific coast.

Climatic variety within this vast region is enormous, ranging from the Arctic conditions of Alaska to the desert of the south-west — winter temperatures in Alaska plummet to −28°C(−19°F), whereas in Florida they maintain a steady 19°C(66°F). In California the weather varies little, being constantly mild with a range of only 9°C(48°F), whereas in the central lowlands winters are severe and the summers very hot. The centre of the continent is dry, but both the north-west Pacific and the New England Atlantic coast are humid with heavy rainfall. Many areas of the USA fall prey to exceptional, often disastrous, weather conditions: the north-eastern seaboard is susceptible to heavy blizzards, the southern lowlands are vulnerable to spring thaw flooding and the Mississippi valley is prone to tornadoes.

The natural vegetation of the USA reflects it's climatic diversity. The north-west coast is rich in coniferous forest, especially Douglas fir, while its Appalachian mountain region is well endowed with hardwoods, notably maple and oak. In the arid south-west, vegetation is limited to desert scrub whereas the Gulf and South Atlantic coast are fringed with swampy wetlands. The central lowlands are endowed with rich black-earth soils (the agricultural heartland), gradually supplanted – towards the Rockies, by tall-grass prairie. The north-eastern states of Illinois, Iowa, Indiana and Nebraska form the so-called corn belt, whereas further west wheat supplements corn as the main crop. Spring wheat is grown in the northern states of North and South Dakota and Minnesota. The north-eastern corner of the USA is predominantly dairy country, and the states of the deep south are famous for their cotton, though cotton cultivation is declining. Rice is grown in Texas, California and Louisiana, and fruit and vegetables in Florida, Texas and California.

The USA consumes 30% of all the world's energy resources but is well endowed with energy reserves. There are substantial coal resources in Pennsylvania, the Appalachian region, the Dakotas and Wyoming, and oil and natural gas regions in Texas, Louisiana, Alaska, and off-shore, in the Gulf of Mexico. The vast resources of America's great rivers have been harnessed extensively for hydro-electric power. In the west, mineral deposits include copper, lead, zinc and silver, and there is iron ore around Lake Superior. Most specialist industrial minerals are imported. Diamonds, tin, chromite, nickel, asbestos, platinum, manganese, mercury, tungsten, cobalt, antimony and cadmium are not found in sufficient quantities for home demand. Main non-metallic minerals extracted within the USA are cement, clays, gypsum, lime, phosphate, salt, sand, gravel and sulphur.

About one fifth of the land area of the USA is covered by commercially usable coniferous and deciduous forest. Exploitation and re-planting are closely controlled. Atlantic and Pacific fishing, particularly around Alaska, is mainly carried out within the 200 mile fishery zone.

America's first industrialised area lies to the south of the Great Lakes, and has gradually extended south and west to form one of the largest industrial zones in the world. Chicago is the main steel-producing town, while Pennsylvania and Pittsburgh are famous for their steel and chemical industries. Manufacturing industries are more predominant towards the east of this zone.

Most of the fastest growing industrial areas are along the west coast. These stretch from Seattle and Portland in the north to San Francisco, Oakland and San Jose in central California and to Los Angeles, Anaheim, Santa Ana and San Diego in the south. The main industries are vehicle manufacture, armaments, machinery, electrical goods, electronics, textiles and clothing and entertainment.

UPPER VOLTA
(see BURKINA)

URUGUAY

STATUS: Republic
AREA: 186,925 sq km (72,155 sq miles)
POPULATION: 2,983,000
ANNUAL NATURAL INCREASE: 0.9%
DENSITY: 16 per sq km
CAPITAL: Montevideo
LANGUAGE: Spanish
RELIGION: Roman Catholic
CURRENCY: Uruguayan new peso (N$)
ORGANISATIONS: UN, OAS

Situated on the coast of South America, Uruguay consists of a narrow coastal plain with rolling hills inland. Maximum elevation is around 200m(656ft). The temperate climate and adequate rainfall provide good agricultural potential but most of the land is given over to the grazing of sheep and cattle. The entire economy relies on the production of meat and wool. Most industry is devoted to food processing. 89% of the land area is farmed.

VANUATU

STATUS: Republic
AREA: 14,765 sq km (5,700 sq miles)
POPULATION: 140,000
ANNUAL NATURAL INCREASE: 3.6%
DENSITY: 9.5 per sq km
CAPITAL: Port Vila
LANGUAGE: Bislama, English, French, many
Melanesian languages
RELIGION: Christian
CURRENCY: Vatu
ORGANISATIONS: Comm, UN

Vanuatu is a chain of densely forested, mountainous, volcanic islands in the South Pacific. Climate is tropical and cyclonic. Copra, cocoa and coffee are grown mainly for export. Fish, pigs and sheep are important for home consumption as well as yam, taro, manioc and bananas. Manganese is the only mineral.

VATICAN CITY

STATUS: Ecclesiastical State
AREA: 0.44 sq km (0.17 sq miles)
POPULATION: 1,000
DENSITY: 2272.8 per sq km
LANGUAGE: Italian, Latin
RELIGION: Roman Catholic
CURRENCY: Italian lira, Papal coins

The headquarters of the Roman Catholic church, the Vatican in Rome is the world's smallest independent state. The papal residence since the 5th century AD, it is the destination for pilgrims and tourists from all over the world. Most income is derived from voluntary contributions and interest on investments. The only industries are those connected with the Church.

VENEZUELA

STATUS: Republic
AREA: 912,045 sq km (352,050 sq miles)
POPULATION: 17,791,412
ANNUAL NATURAL INCREASE: 2.7%
DENSITY: 19.5 per sq km
CAPITAL: Caracas
LANGUAGE: Spanish
RELIGION: Roman Catholic

CURRENCY: bolívar (B)
ORGANISATIONS: UN, OAS, OPEC

Venezuela, one of the richest countries of Latin America is divided into four topographic regions: the continuation of the Andes in the west; the humid lowlands around Lake Maracaibo in the north; the savannah-covered central plains (llanos) and the extension of the Guiana Highlands covering almost half the country. The climate varies between tropical in the south to warm temperate along the northern coasts. The economy is built around oil production in the Maracaibo region. Bauxite and iron ore are also important. The majority of employment is provided by industrial and manufacturing developments.

VIETNAM

STATUS: Socialist Republic
AREA: 329,566 sq km (127,246 sq miles)
POPULATION: 60,919,000
ANNUAL NATURAL INCREASE: 2.5%
DENSITY: 184.9 per sq km
CAPITAL: Hanoi
LANGUAGE: Vietnamese, French, Chinese
RELIGION: Buddhist
CURRENCY: dong
ORGANISATIONS: UN, COMECON

A long narrow country in South-East Asia, Vietnam has a mountainous backbone and two extensive river deltas: the Song Hong (Red River) in the north and the Mekong in the south. Monsoons bring 150cm(59in) of rain every year and rice is grown extensively throughout the north. Vietnam possesses a wide range of minerals including coal, lignite, anthracite, iron ore and tin. Industry is expanding rapidly, but decades of warfare and internal strife have impeded development.

VIRGIN ISLANDS (UK)

STATUS: UK Dependent Territory
AREA: 153 sq km (59 sq miles)
POPULATION: 11,858
CAPITAL: Road Town

VIRGIN ISLANDS (USA)

STATUS: External Territory of USA
AREA: 345 sq km (133 sq miles)
POPULATION: 100,000
CAPITAL: Charlotte Amalie

WALLIS & FUTUNA ISLANDS

STATUS: Self-governing Overseas Territory of France
AREA: 274 sq km (106 sq miles)
POPULATION: 13,000
CAPITAL: Mata-Utu

WESTERN SAMOA

STATUS: Independent state
AREA: 2,840 sq km (1,095 sq miles)
POPULATION: 163,000
ANNUAL NATURAL INCREASE: 3.0%
DENSITY: 57.4 per sq km
CAPITAL: Apia
LANGUAGE: English, Samoan
RELIGION: local beliefs
CURRENCY: talà dollar ($WS)
ORGANISATIONS: Comm, UN

Nine volcanic tropical islands constitute this south Pacific state, of which only four are populated – Savaii, Upolu, Manono and Apolima. Annual rainfall is often 250cm(100in) per year. Temperatures average 26°C(79°F) for

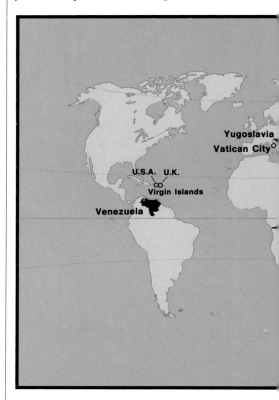

most months. Main exports are copra, timber, taro, cocoa and fruit. The only industries are food processing and timber products. Main imports are food products, consumer goods, machinery and animals.

WEST IRIAN
(see **IRIAN JAYA**)

WINDWARD ISLANDS
(see **DOMINICA, GRENADA, MARTINIQUE, ST LUCIA & ST VINCENT**)

WRANGEL ISLAND (VRANGELYA OSTROV)

STATUS: Island Territory of USSR
AREA: 7,250 sq km (2,800 sq miles)
POPULATION: No permanent population

YEMEN

STATUS: Arab Republic
AREA: 189,850 sq km (73,280 sq miles)
POPULATION: 9,274,173
ANNUAL NATURAL INCREASE: 3.0%
DENSITY: 48.9 per sq km
CAPITAL: San'a
LANGUAGE: Arabic
RELIGION: Sunni and Shiite Moslem
CURRENCY: Yemeni riyal
ORGANISATIONS: UN, Arab League

Situated in the extreme south-west corner of the Arabian Peninsula, the Yemen Arab Republic is mountainous and relatively wet.

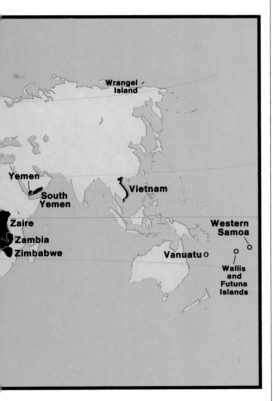

Temperatures vary between 14° and 22°C(57° and 70°F). Rainfall reaches 89cm(35in) inland and this helps to irrigate the cereals, cotton, coffee, fruits and vegetables which are mainly grown above 1500m(4920ft). Most of the population are farmers and herders of sheep and cattle. The main industries are textiles, cement and salt mining.

YEMEN, SOUTH

STATUS: People's Democratic Republic
AREA: 287,680 sq km (111,045 sq miles)
POPULATION: 2,294,000
ANNUAL NATURAL INCREASE: 3.0%

DENSITY: 8 per sq km
CAPITAL: Aden
LANGUAGE: Arabic
RELIGION: Sunni Moslem
CURRENCY: Yemeni dinar (YD)
ORGANISATIONS: UN, Arab League

This desert country stretches for 1100km(685 miles) along the south-east coast of Arabia from the mouth of the Red Sea to Oman. The narrow coastal plain fringes the wide irrigated Hadhramaut valley in which are grown sorghum, millet, wheat and barley. Main livestock are sheep, goats, cattle and poultry. Rainfall rarely exceeds 46mm(2in). Altitude of the inland desert restricts summer average temperature to 32°C(90°F). The country's major exports are cotton and fish.

YUGOSLAVIA

STATUS: Socialist Federal Republic
AREA: 255,805 sq km (98,740 sq miles)
POPULATION: 23,259,000
ANNUAL NATURAL INCREASE: 0.7%
DENSITY: 91 per sq km
CAPITAL: Belgrade (Beograd)
LANGUAGE: Serbo-Croat, Albanian, Macedonian, Slovene
RELIGION: 40% Orthodox Christian, 30% Roman Catholic
CURRENCY: dinar
ORGANISATIONS: UN

Yugoslavia is a federal union of very diverse republics. The long mountainous coastline, popular with tourists, enjoys a typical Mediterranean climate. The interior limestone 'karst' region has more extreme temperatures. The most productive areas, both agriculturally and industrially, are in the north and east. Cereals, root crops, cotton and fruit are grown. Mineral resources include iron ore, chrome, manganese, copper and lead.

ZAIRE

STATUS: Republic
AREA: 2,345,410 sq km (905,330 sq miles)
POPULATION: 30,850,000
ANNUAL NATURAL INCREASE: 2.8%
DENSITY: 13.2 per sq km
CAPITAL: Kinshasa
LANGUAGE: French, Kiswahili, Tshiluba, Kikongo, Lingala
RELIGION: traditional beliefs, 48% Roman Catholic, 13% Protestant
CURRENCY: zaïre
ORGANISATIONS: UN, OAU

Zaire, formerly the Belgian Congo, is Africa's second largest country and is dominated by the drainage basin of the Zaire river. The climate is very variable but basically equatorial with high temperatures and high rainfall. Soils are poor with the majority of the population engaged in shifting agriculture. Cassava, cocoa, coffee, cotton, millet, rubber and sugar-cane are grown. 60% of exports are minerals – copper, cobalt, diamonds, gold, manganese, uranium and zinc, with copper being the most important with 40% of total foreign exchange earnings. Zaire has abundant wildlife with tourism becoming increasingly important.

ZAMBIA

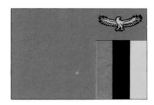

STATUS: Republic
AREA: 752,615 sq km (290,510 sq miles)
POPULATION: 6,898,000
ANNUAL NATURAL INCREASE: 3.3%
DENSITY: 9.2 per sq km
CAPITAL: Lusaka
LANGUAGE: English, African languages
RELIGION: 70% Christian, animist minority
CURRENCY: Kwacha (K)
ORGANISATIONS: Comm, UN, OAU

Mineral-rich Zambia consists mainly of high rolling plateaux. Altitude moderates the potentially tropical climate so that the summer temperature averages only 13°–27°C(55°–81°F). The north receives over 125cm(49in) of rain per annum, the south, less. Most of the country is grassland with some forest in the north. Farming is mainly at subsistence level. Copper, lead, zinc, cobalt and tobacco are the main exports. Wildlife is diverse and abundant and contributes to expanding tourism.

ZIMBABWE

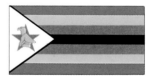

STATUS: Republic
AREA: 390,310 sq km (150,660 sq miles)
POPULATION: 8,406,000
ANNUAL NATURAL INCREASE: 3.5%
DENSITY: 21.6 per sq km
CAPITAL: Harare
LANGUAGE: English, Chishona, Sindebele
RELIGION: traditional beliefs, 20% Christian
CURRENCY: Zimbabwe dollar (Z$)
ORGANISATIONS: Comm, UN, OAU

Landlocked Zimbabwe consists of rolling plateaux (the high veld) 1,200–1,500m(3940–4920ft) and the low veld (the valleys of the Zambezi and Limpopo rivers). Altitude moderates the tropical climate of the high veld to temperate with low humidity. Mineral deposits include chrome, nickel, platinum and coal with gold and asbestos especially important. Tobacco, maize, tea and sugar-cane are grown. Manufacturing industry is slowly developing and now provides a wide range of consumer products.

North and Central America
25 349 000
9 785 000

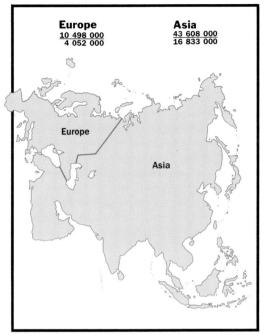

CONTINENTS

land area ☐ = **1 000 000** sq kms
386 000 sq miles

Europe
10 498 000
4 052 000

Asia
43 608 000
16 833 000

Europe

Asia

Africa
30 335 000
11 709 000

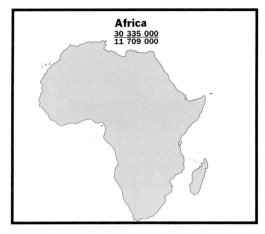

South America
17 611 000
6 798 000

Antarctica
13 340 000
5 149 240

Australasia
8 923 000
3 444 278

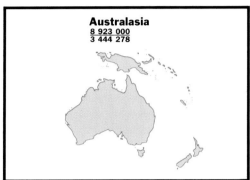

Population	City	Country
19,396,000	**Mexico City**	*Mexico*
17,968,000	**New York**	*USA*
15,910,913	**Tokyo–Yokohama**	*Japan*
15,280,375	**Sao Paulo**	*Brazil*
13,300,000	**Cairo**	*Egypt*
12,050,000	**Shanghai**	*China*
10,232,000	**Los Angeles**	*USA*
10,217,269	**Rio de Janeiro**	*Brazil*
9,969,826	**Buenos Aires**	*Argentina*
9,645,824	**Seoul**	*South Korea*
9,470,000	**Beijing (Peking)**	*China*
9,194,018	**Calcutta**	*India*
9,050,654	**London**	*United Kingdom*
8,815,000	**Moscow**	*USSR*
8,594,000	**Osaka–Kōbe**	*Japan*
8,510,000	**Paris**	*France*
8,243,405	**Bombay**	*India*
7,990,000	**Tianjin**	*China*
7,347,800	**Jakarta**	*Indonesia*
6,720,050	**Manila–Quezon City**	*Philippines*
6,511,130	**Chongqing**	*China*
6,188,000	**Chicago**	*USA*
6,022,029	**Tehran**	*Iran*
5,729,283	**Delhi**	*India*
5,705,230	**Changchun**	*China*
5,669,640	**Guangzhou (Canton)**	*China*
5,613,400	**Hong Kong**	*UK Colony*
5,494,916	**Istanbul**	*Turkey*
5,446,708	**Bangkok**	*Thailand*
5,180,562	**Karachi**	*Pakistan*
5,054,640	**Shenyang**	*China*
5,008,400	**Lima**	*Peru*
4,948,000	**Leningrad**	*USSR*
4,826,000	**Philadelphia**	*USA*
4,486,000	**Bogotá**	*Colombia*
4,335,000	**Detroit**	*USA*
4,318,305	**Santiago**	*Chile*
4,289,347	**Madras**	*India*
4,273,080	**Wuhan**	*China*
4,200,000	**Lagos**	*Nigeria*
4,025,180	**Chengdu**	*China*
4,000,000	**Ho Chi Minh (Saigon)**	*Vietnam*
4,000,000	**Alexandria**	*Egypt*
3,962,000	**Budapest**	*Hungary*
3,844,608	**Baghdad**	*Iraq*
3,655,000	**Dallas–Fort Worth**	*USA*
3,563,000	**Washington DC**	*USA*
3,522,000	**San Francisco**	*USA*
3,516,768	**Pusan**	*South Korea*
3,430,600	**Sydney**	*Australia*
3,430,312	**Dhaka**	*Bangladesh*
3,427,168	**Toronto**	*Canada*
3,247,698	**Caracas**	*Venezuela*
3,231,000	**Houston**	*USA*
3,188,297	**Madrid**	*Spain*
3,091,009	**Berlin**	*E & W Germany*
3,059,727	**Belo Horizonte**	*Brazil*
3,027,331	**Athens**	*Greece*
2,993,000	**Yokohama**	*Japan*

METROPOLITAN AREAS

2,952,689	**Lahore**	*Pakistan*
2,942,000	**Melbourne**	*Australia*
2,921,751	**Bangalore**	*India*
2,921,357	**Montreal**	*Canada*
2,912,000	**Miami**	*USA*
2,911,580	**Xian**	*China*
2,878,000	**Hanoi**	*Vietnam*
2,824,000	**Boston**	*USA*
2,815,457	**Rome**	*Italy*
2,708,100	**Essen–Dortmund**	*West Germany*
2,653,558	**Kinshasa**	*Zaire*
2,636,249	**Osaka**	*Japan*
2,630,000	**Harbin**	*China*
2,600,000	**Algiers**	*Algeria*
2,580,111	**Manchester**	*United Kingdom*
2,575,180	**Taipei**	*Taiwan*
2,561,000	**Atlanta**	*USA*
2,558,000	**Singapore**	*Singapore*
2,554,000	**Kiev**	*USSR*
2,548,057	**Ahmadabad**	*India*
2,500,000	**Damascus**	*Syria*
2,458,712	**Rangoon**	*Burma*
2,435,000	**Casablanca**	*Morocco*
2,401,000	**Dallas**	*USA*
2,315,400	**Birmingham**	*United Kingdom*
2,295,000	**Minneapolis–St. Paul**	*USA*
2,251,533	**Ankara**	*Turkey*
2,201,000	**San Diego**	*USA*
2,197,702	**Bucharest**	*Romania*
2,123,000	**Pittsburg**	*USA*
2,025,700	**Havana**	*Cuba*
2,000,000	**Ibadan**	*Nigeria*
2,000,000	**Kābul**	*Afghanistan*
2,000,000	**Abidjan**	*Ivory Coast*
1,911,521	**Cape Town**	*South Africa*
1,816,300	**San Juan**	*Puerto Rico*
1,754,900	**Barcelona**	*Spain*
1,751,000	**Seattle**	*USA*
1,664,700	**Warsaw**	*Poland*
1,639,064	**Kanpur**	*India*
1,633,000	**Denver**	*USA*
1,611,887	**Lisbon**	*Portugal*
1,609,408	**Johannesburg**	*South Africa*
1,587,000	**Kharkov**	*USSR*
1,576,657	**Brasilia**	*Brazil*
1,575,700	**Hamburg**	*West Germany*
1,555,427	**Tel Aviv**	*Israel*
1,536,095	**Stockholm**	*Sweden*
1,518,000	**Kansas City**	*USA*
1,500,000	**Mashad**	*Iran*
1,495,260	**Milan**	*Italy*
1,481,399	**Vienna**	*Austria*

1,470,073	**Belgrade**	*Yugoslavia*
1,464,901	**Addis Ababa**	*Ethiopia*
1,425,000	**Gorky**	*USSR*
1,400,000	**Dakar**	*Senegal*
1,397,000	**Haiphong**	*Vietnam*
1,380,729	**Vancouver**	*Canada*
1,380,000	**Milwaukee**	*USA*
1,355,312	**Montevideo**	*Uruguay*
1,346,666	**Copenhagen**	*Denmark*
1,343,651	**Khartoum**	*Sudan*
1,334,000	**New Orleans**	*USA*
1,331,000	**Sverdlovsk**	*USSR*
1,314,794	**Oporto**	*Portugal*
1,291,000	**Sacramento**	*USA*
1,280,000	**Pyongyang**	*North Korea*
1,276,000	**San Antonio**	*USA*
1,269,400	**Munich**	*West Germany*
1,204,211	**Naples**	*Italy*
1,200,000	**Luanda**	*Angola*
1,200,000	**Nairobi**	*Kenya*
1,194,000	**Tbilisi**	*USSR*
1,193,513	**Prague**	*Czechoslovakia*
1,182,000	**Dnepropetrovsk**	*USSR*
1,174,512	**Zagreb**	*Yugoslavia*
1,171,300	**Brisbane**	*Australia*
1,168,000	**Yerevan**	*USSR*
1,160,000	**Shijiazhuang**	*China*
1,145,117	**Aleppo**	*Syria*
1,141,000	**Odessa**	*USSR*
1,134,000	**Omsk**	*USSR*
1,120,777	**Belem**	*Brazil*
1,108,000	**Alma-Ata**	*USSR*
1,104,209	**Faisalabad**	*Pakistan*
1,101,828	**Sofia**	*Bulgaria*
1,096,000	**Dar-es-Salaam**	*Tanzania*
1,093,278	**Quito**	*Ecuador*
1,092,000	**Ufa**	*USSR*
1,090,000	**Donetsk**	*USSR*
1,080,000	**Marseilles**	*France*
1,075,000	**Perm**	*USSR*
1,056,000	**Kitakyushu**	*Japan*
1,050,000	**Luoyang**	*China*
1,044,118	**Hiroshima**	*Japan*
1,041,000	**Salt Lake City**	*USA*
1,035,565	**Turin**	*Italy*
1,030,696	**Rotterdam**	*Netherlands*
1,025,300	**Perth**	*Australia*
1,020,796	**Dublin**	*Ireland*
1,015,916	**Amsterdam**	*Netherlands*
1,015,160	**Jaipur**	*India*
1,000,000	**Kano**	*Nigeria*
988,000	**Volgograd**	*USSR*
973,499	**Brussels**	*Belgium*
937,875	**Kuala Lumpur**	*Malaysia*
915,000	**Al Basrah**	*Iraq*
914,000	**Cologne**	*West Germany*
678,173	**The Hague**	*Netherlands*
643,000	**Colombo**	*Sri Lanka*
457,700	**Jerusalem**	*Israel*
285,800	**Canberra**	*Australia*

metres feet

8,848	29,028	**Everest (Qomolangma Feng)** *China–Nepal*
8,611	28,250	**K2 (Qogir Feng) (Godwin Austen)** *India–China*
8,598	28,170	**Kangchenjunga** *India–Nepal*
8,481	27,824	**Makalu** *China–Nepal*
8,167	26,795	**Dhaulagiri** *Nepal*
8,156	26,758	**Manaslu** *Nepal*
8,153	26,749	**Cho Oyu** *China–Nepal*
8,125	26,657	**Nanga Parbat** *India*
8,091	26,545	**Annapurna** *Nepal*
8,088	26,470	**Gasherbrum** *India–China*
8,027	26,335	**Xixabangma Feng (Gosainthan)** *China*
7,885	25,869	**Distaghil Sar** *India, Kashmir*
7,820	25,656	**Masherbrum** *India*
7,816	25,643	**Nanda Devi** *India*
7,788	25,550	**Rakaposhi** *India*
7,756	25,446	**Kamet** *China–India*
7,756	25,447	**Namjagbarwa Feng** *China*
7,728	25,355	**Gurla Mandhata** *China*
7,723	25,338	**Muztag** *China*
7,719	25,325	**Kongur** *China*
7,690	25,230	**Tirich Mir** *Pakistan*
7,546	24,757	**Muztagata** *China*
7,514	24,652	**Gongga Shan (Minya Konka)** *China*
7,495	24,590	**Pik Kommunizma** *USSR*
7,439	24,406	**Pik Pobedy (Tomur Feng)** *USSR–China*
7,313	23,993	**Chomo Lhari** *Bhutan–Tibet*
7,134	23,406	**Pik Lenina** *USSR*
6,960	22,834	**Aconcagua** *Argentina*
6,908	22,664	**Ojos del Salado** *Argentina–Chile*
6,872	22,546	**Bonete** *Argentina*
6,800	22,310	**Tupungato** *Argentina–Chile*

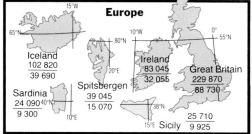

MOUNTAIN HEIGHTS

6,770	22,211	**Mercedario** *Argentina*
6,768	22,205	**Huascarán** *Peru*
6,723	22,057	**Llullaillaco** *Argentina–Chile*
6,714	22,027	**Kangrinboqê Feng (Kailas)** *China, Tibet*
6,634	21,765	**Yerupaja** *Peru*
6,542	21,463	**Sajama** *Bolivia*
6,485	21,276	**Illampu** *Bolivia*
6,425	21,079	**Coropuna** *Peru*
6,402	21,004	**Illimani** *Bolivia*
6,310	20,702	**Chimborazo** *Ecuador*
6,194	20,320	**McKinley** *USA*
5,951	19,524	**Logan** *Canada*
5,896	19,344	**Cotopaxi** *Ecuador*
5,895	19,340	**Kilimanjaro** *Tanzania*
5,775	18,947	**Santa Marta (Cristobal Colon)** *Colombia*
5,775	18,947	**Bolivar** *Colombia*
5,671	18,605	**Damāvand** *Iran*
5,642	18,510	**El'brus** *USSR*
5,610	18,405	**Citlatépetl (Orizaba)** *Mexico*
5,489	18,008	**Mt St. Elias** *Canada*
5,227	17,149	**Mt Lucania** *Canada*
5,200	17,058	**Kirinyaga (Kenya)** *Kenya*
5,140	16,860	**Vinson Massif** *Antarctica*
5,123	16,808	**Büyük Ağri (Ararat)** *Turkey*
5,110	16,763	**Stanley (Margherita)** *Uganda–Zaire*
5,030	16,503	**Jaya (Carstensz)** *Indonesia*

5,005	16,421	**Mt Bona** *USA*
4,996	16,391	**Mt Blackburn** *Canada*
4,949	16,237	**Sanford** *USA*
4,807	15,770	**Mont Blanc** *France–Italy*
4,750	15,584	**Klyuchevskaya Sopka** *USSR*
4,634	15,203	**Monte Rosa (Dufour)** *Italy–Switzerland*
4,620	15,157	**Ras Dashen** *Ethiopia*
4,565	14,979	**Meru** *Tanzania*
4,545	14,910	**Dom (Mischabel)** *Switzerland*
4,528	14,855	**Kirkpatrick** *Antarctica*
4,508	14,790	**Wilhelm** *Papua, New Guinea*
4,507	14,786	**Karisimbi** *Rwanda–Zaire*
4,478	14,691	**Matterhorn** *Italy–Switzerland*
4,418	14,495	**Whitney** *USA*
4,398	14,431	**Elbert** *USA*
4,392	14,410	**Rainier** *USA*
4,351	14,275	**Markham** *Antarctica*
4,321	14,178	**Elgon** *Kenya–Uganda*
4,307	14,131	**Batu** *Ethiopia*
4,205	13,796	**Mauna Kea** *USA, Hawaii*
4,169	13,677	**Mauna Loa** *USA, Hawaii*
4,165	13,664	**Toubkal** *Morocco*
4,095	13,435	**Caméroun** *Cameroon*
4,094	13,431	**Kinabalu** *Malaysia*
3,794	12,447	**Erebus** *Antarctica*
3,776	12,388	**Fuji** *Japan*
3,764	12,349	**Cook** *New Zealand*
3,718	12,198	**Teide** *Canary Is*
3,482	11,424	**Thabana Ntlenyana** *Lesotho*
3,482	11,424	**Mulhacén** *Spain*
3,415	11,204	**Emi Koussi** *Chad*
3,323	10,902	**Etna** *Italy, Sicily*
2,743	9,000	**Mt Balbi** *Bougainville, Papua, New Guinea*
2,655	8,708	**Gerlachovsky stit (Tatra)** *Czechoslovakia*
2,230	7,316	**Kosciusko** *Australia*

ISLANDS

land area □ = $\dfrac{10\,000 \text{ sq kms}}{3\,860 \text{ sq miles}}$

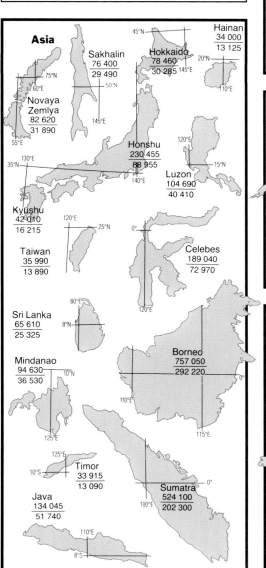

Asia

Sakhalin 76 400 / 29 490
Hokkaido 78 460 / 30 285
Hainan 34 000 / 13 125
Novaya Zemlya 82 620 / 31 890
Honshu 230 455 / 88 955
Luzon 104 690 / 40 410
Kyushu 42 010 / 16 215
Taiwan 35 990 / 13 890
Celebes 189 040 / 72 970
Sri Lanka 65 610 / 25 325
Borneo 757 050 / 292 220
Mindanao 94 630 / 36 530
Timor 33 915 / 13 090
Java 134 045 / 51 740
Sumatra 524 100 / 202 300

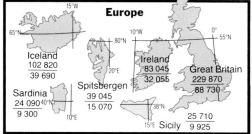

Europe

Iceland 102 820 / 39 690
Ireland 83 045 / 32 055
Great Britain 229 870 / 88 730
Sardinia 24 090 / 9 300
Spitsbergen 39 045 / 15 070
Sicily 25 710 / 9 925

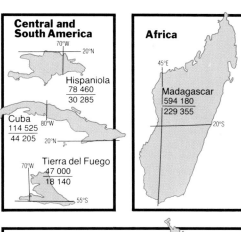

Central and South America

Hispaniola 78 460 / 30 285
Cuba 114 525 / 44 205
Tierra del Fuego 47 000 / 18 140

Africa

Madagascar 594 180 / 229 355

Australasia

Tasmania 68 330 / 26 375
N. Island 114 690 / 44 270
New Zealand
New Britain 36 500 / 14 090
S. Island 150 460 / 58 080
New Guinea 808 510 / 312 085

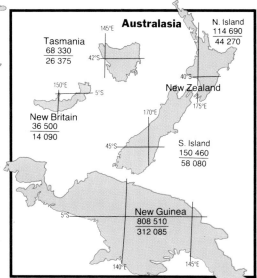

North America

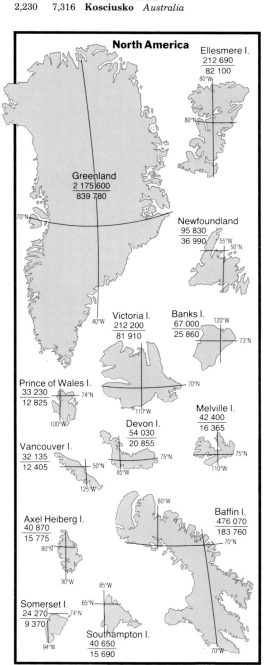

Ellesmere I. 212 690 / 82 100
Greenland 2 175 600 / 839 780
Newfoundland 95 830 / 36 990
Victoria I. 212 200 / 81 910
Banks I. 67 000 / 25 860
Prince of Wales I. 33 230 / 12 825
Melville I. 42 400 / 16 365
Devon I. 54 030 / 20 855
Vancouver I. 32 135 / 12 405
Axel Heiberg I. 40 870 / 15 775
Baffin I. 476 070 / 183 760
Somerset I. 24 270 / 9 370
Southampton I. 40 650 / 15 690

OCEANS AND SEAS

water area ☐ = $\frac{1\,000\,000 \text{ sq km}}{386\,000 \text{ sq miles}}$

OCEAN FACTS AND FIGURES

The area of the Earth covered by sea is estimated to be 361,740,000 sq km (139,670,000 sq miles), or 70.92% of the total surface. The mean depth is estimated to be 3554 m (11,660 ft), and the volume of the oceans to be 1,285,600,000 cu. km (308,400,000 cu. miles).

INDIAN OCEAN

Mainly confined to the southern hemisphere, and at its greatest breadth (Tasmania to Cape Agulhas) 9600 km. Average depth is 4000 m; greatest depth is the Amirante Trench (9000 m).

ATLANTIC OCEAN

Commonly divided into North Atlantic (36,000,000 sq km) and South Atlantic (26,000,000 sq km). The greatest breadth in the North is 7200 km (Morocco to Florida) and in the South 9600 km (Guinea to Brazil). Average depth is 3600 m; the greatest depths are the Puerto Rico Trench 9220 m, S. Sandwich Trench 8264 m, and Romansh Trench 7728 m.

PACIFIC OCEAN

Covers nearly 40% of the world's total sea area, and is the largest of the oceans. The greatest breadth (E/W) is 16,000 km and the greatest length (N/S) 11,000 km. Average depth is 4200 m; also the deepest ocean. Generally the west is deeper than the east and the north deeper than the south. Greatest depths occur near island groups and include Mindanao Trench 11,524 m, Mariana Trench 11,022 m, Tonga Trench 10,882 m, Kuril-Kamchatka Trench 10,542 m, Philippine Trench 10,497 m, and Kermadec Trench 10,047 m.

Comparisons (where applicable)	greatest distance N/S (km)	greatest distance E/W (km)	maximum depth (m)
Indian Ocean	—	9600	9000
Atlantic Ocean	—	9600	9220
Pacific Ocean	11,000	16,000	11,524
Arctic Ocean	—	—	5450
Mediterranean Sea	960	3700	4846
S. China Sea	2100	1750	5514
Bering Sea	1800	2100	5121
Caribbean Sea	1600	2000	7100
Gulf of Mexico	1200	1700	4377
Sea of Okhotsk	2200	1400	3475
E. China Sea	1100	750	2999
Yellow Sea	800	1000	91
Hudson Bay	1250	1050	259
Sea of Japan	1500	1100	3743
North Sea	1200	550	661
Red Sea	1932	360	2246
Black Sea	600	1100	2245
Baltic Sea	1500	650	460

EARTH'S SURFACE WATERS

Total volume	c.1400 million cu. km
Oceans and seas	1370 million cu. km
Ice	24 million cu. km
Interstitial water (in rocks and sediments)	4 million cu. km
Lakes and rivers	230 thousand cu. km
Atmosphere (vapour)	c.140 thousand cu. km

to convert metric to imperial measurements:
1 m = 3.281 feet
1 km = 0.621 miles
1 sq km = 0.386 sq miles

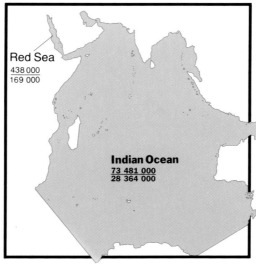

Red Sea
438 000
169 000

Indian Ocean
73 481 000
28 364 000

Arctic Ocean
14 056 000
5 426 000

Baltic Sea
422 000
163 000

Hudson Bay
1 233 000
476 000

North Sea
575 000
222 000

Black Sea
461 000
178 000

Gulf of Mexico
1 544 000
596 000

Mediterranean Sea
2 505 000
967 000

Caribbean Sea
1 943 000
750 000

Atlantic Ocean
82 217 000
31 736 000

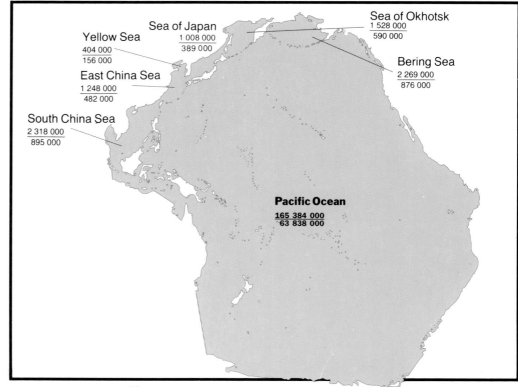

Sea of Japan
1 008 000
389 000

Sea of Okhotsk
1 528 000
590 000

Yellow Sea
404 000
156 000

East China Sea
1 248 000
482 000

Bering Sea
2 269 000
876 000

South China Sea
2 318 000
895 000

Pacific Ocean
165 384 000
63 838 000

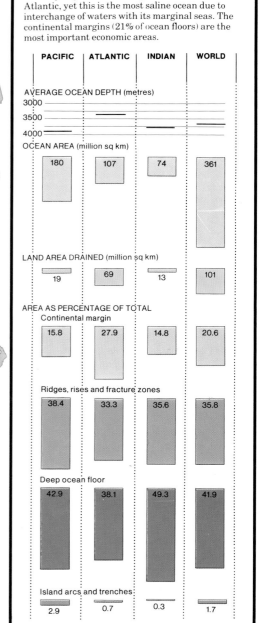

FEATURES OF THE OCEAN BASIN

The majority of land drainage occurs in the Atlantic, yet this is the most saline ocean due to interchange of waters with its marginal seas. The continental margins (21% of ocean floors) are the most important economic areas.

	PACIFIC	ATLANTIC	INDIAN	WORLD
AVERAGE OCEAN DEPTH (metres) 3000 / 3500 / 4000				
OCEAN AREA (million sq km)	180	107	74	361
LAND AREA DRAINED (million sq km)	19	69	13	101
AREA AS PERCENTAGE OF TOTAL Continental margin	15.8	27.9	14.8	20.6
Ridges, rises and fracture zones	38.4	33.3	35.6	35.8
Deep ocean floor	42.9	38.1	49.3	41.9
Island arcs and trenches	2.9	0.7	0.3	1.7

RIVER LENGTHS

km	miles	
6,695	4,160	**Nile** *Africa*
6,515	4,050	**Amazon** *South America*
6,380	3,965	**Chang Jiang (Yangtze)** *Asia*
6,019	3,740	**Mississippi-Missouri** *North America*
5,570	3,460	**Ob'-Irtysh** *Asia*
5,550	3,450	**Yenisey-Angara** *Asia*
5,464	3,395	**Huang He (Yellow River)** *Asia*
4,667	2,900	**Zaire (Congo)** *Africa*
4,500	2,800	**Paraná** *South America*
4,440	2,775	**Irtysh** *Asia*
4,425	2,750	**Mekong** *Asia*
4,416	2,744	**Amur** *Asia*
4,400	1,730	**Lena** *Asia*
4,250	2,640	**Mackenzie** *North America*
4,090	2,556	**Yenisey** *Asia*
4,030	2,505	**Niger** *Africa*
3,969	2,466	**Missouri** *North America*
3,779	2,348	**Mississippi** *North America*
3,750	2,330	**Murray-Darling** *Australasia*
3,688	2,290	**Volga** *Europe*
3,218	2,011	**Purus** *South America*
3,200	1,990	**Madeira** *South America*
3,185	1,980	**Yukon** *North America*
3,180	1,975	**Indus** *Asia*
3,078	1,913	**Syrdar'ya** *Asia*
3,060	1,901	**Salween** *Asia*
3,058	1,900	**St Lawrence** *North America*
2,900	1,800	**São Francisco** *South America*
2,870	1,785	**Rio Grande** *North America*
2,850	1,770	**Danube** *Europe*
2,840	1,765	**Brahmaputra** *Asia*
2,815	1,750	**Euphrates** *Asia*
2,750	1,710	**Pará-Tocantins** *South America*
2,750	1,718	**Tarim** *Asia*
2,650	1,650	**Zambezi** *Africa*
2,620	1,630	**Amudar'ya** *Asia*
2,620	1,630	**Araguaia** *South America*
2,600	1,615	**Paraguay** *South America*
2,570	1,600	**Nelson-Saskatchewan** *North America*

RIVER LENGTHS & DRAINAGE BASINS

2,534	1,575	**Ural** *Asia*
2,513	1,562	**Kolyma** *Asia*
2,510	1,560	**Ganges (Ganga)** *Asia*
2,500	1,555	**Orinoco** *South America*
2,490	1,550	**Shabeelle** *Africa*
2,490	1,550	**Pilcomayo** *South America*
2,348	1,459	**Arkansas** *North America*
2,333	1,450	**Colorado** *North America*
2,285	1,420	**Dnepr** *Europe*
2,250	1,400	**Columbia** *North America*
2,150	1,335	**Irrawaddy** *Asia*
2,129	1,323	**Xi Jiang (Pearl)** *Asia*
2,032	1,270	**Kama** *Europe*
2,000	1,240	**Negro** *South America*
1,923	1,195	**Peace** *North America*
1,899	1,186	**Tigris** *Asia*
1,870	1,162	**Don** *Europe*
1,860	1,155	**Orange** *Africa*
1,809	1,124	**Pechora** *Europe*
1,800	1,125	**Okavango** *Africa*
1,609	1,000	**Marañón** *South America*
1,609	1,005	**Uruguay** *South America*
1,600	1,000	**Volta** *Africa*
1,600	1,000	**Limpopo** *Africa*
1,550	963	**Magdalena** *South America*
1,515	946	**Kura** *Asia*
1,480	925	**Oka** *Europe*
1,445	903	**Godavari** *Asia*
1,430	893	**Senegal** *Africa*
1,480	925	**Belaya** *Europe*
1,410	876	**Dnestr** *Europe*
1,400	875	**Chari** *Africa*
1,368	850	**Fraser** *North America*
1,320	820	**Rhine** *Europe*
1,314	821	**Vyatka** *Europe*
1,183	735	**Donets** *Europe*
1,159	720	**Elbe** *Europe*
1,151	719	**Kizilirmak** *Asia*

1,130	706	**Desna** *Europe*
1,094	680	**Gambia** *Africa*
1,080	675	**Yellowstone** *North America*
1,049	652	**Tennessee** *North America*
1,024	640	**Zelenga** *Asia*
1,020	637	**Duena** *Europe*
1,014	630	**Wisła (Vistula)** *Europe*
1,012	629	**Loire** *Europe*
1,006	625	**Tejo (Tagus)** *Europe*
977	607	**Tisza** *Europe*
925	575	**Meuse (Maas)** *Europe*
909	565	**Oder** *Europe*
761	473	**Seine** *Europe*
354	220	**Severn** *Europe*
346	215	**Thames** *Europe*
300	186	**Trent** *Europe*

DRAINAGE BASINS

sq km	sq miles	
7,050,000	2,721,000	**Amazon** *South America*
3,700,000	1,428,000	**Congo** *Africa*
3,250,000	1,255,000	**Mississippi-Missouri** *North America*
3,100,000	1,197,000	**Paraná** *South America*
2,700,000	1,042,000	**Yenisey** *Asia*
2,430,000	938,000	**Ob'** *Asia*
2,420,000	934,000	**Lena** *Asia*
1,900,000	733,400	**Nile** *Africa*
1,840,000	710,000	**Amur** *Asia*
1,765,000	681,000	**Mackenzie** *North America*
1,730,000	668,000	**Ganges-Brahmaputra** *Asia*
1,380,000	533,000	**Volga** *Europe*
1,330,000	513,000	**Zambezi** *Africa*
1,200,000	463,000	**Niger** *Africa*
1,175,000	454,000	**Chang Jiang** *Asia*
1,020,000	394,000	**Orange** *Africa*
980,000	378,000	**Huang He** *Asia*
960,000	371,000	**Indus** *Asia*
945,000	365,000	**Orinoco** *South America*
910,000	351,000	**Murray-Darling** *Australasia*
855,000	330,000	**Yukon** *North America*
815,000	315,000	**Danube** *Europe*
810,000	313,000	**Mekong** *Asia*
225,000	86,900	**Rhine** *Europe*

North and Central America

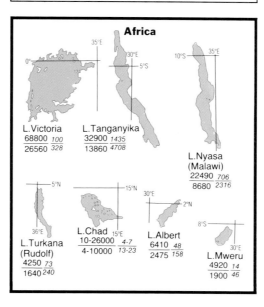

L.Superior
83270 *393*
32140 *1289*

L.Huron
60700 *229*
23430 *751*

L.Ontario
19230 *237*
7425 *778*

L.Michigan
58020 *281*
22395 *922*

L.Erie
25680 *64*
9915 *210*

L.de Nicaragua
8270 *70*
3190 *230*

Great Bear Lake
31790 *319*
12270 *1047*

L.Athabasca
8080 *91*
3120 *299*

Great Slave Lake
28440 *140*
10980 *459*

Nettilling Lake
5250
2030

L.Winnipeg
24510 *21*
9460 *69*

Reindeer Lake
6390
2470

INLAND WATERS

water surface area ▢ = $\frac{1\,000 \text{ sq km}}{386 \text{ sq miles}}$

deepest point $\frac{229 \text{ metres}}{751 \text{ feet}}$

Africa

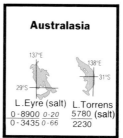

L.Victoria
68800 *100*
26560 *328*

L.Tanganyika
32900 *1435*
13860 *4708*

L.Nyasa (Malawi)
22490 *706*
8680 *2316*

L.Turkana (Rudolf)
4250 *73*
1640 *240*

L.Chad
10-26000 *4-7*
4-10000 *13-23*

L.Albert
6410 *48*
2475 *158*

L.Mweru
4920 *14*
1900 *46*

South America

L.Titicaca
8340 *304*
3220 *997*

Australasia

L.Eyre (salt)
0-8900 *0-20*
0-3435 *0-66*

L.Torrens (salt)
5780
2230

Europe

L.Onega
9600 *124*
3705 *407*

L.Vänern
5580 *98*
2155 *322*

L.Ladoga
18390 *230*
7100 *755*

Asia

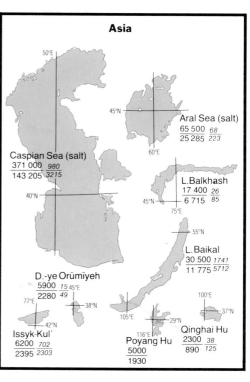

Aral Sea (salt)
65 500 *68*
25 285 *223*

Caspian Sea (salt)
371 000 *980*
143 205 *3215*

L.Balkhash
17 400 *26*
6 715 *85*

L.Baikal
30 500 *1741*
11 775 *5712*

D.-ye Orūmīyeh
5900 *15*
2280 *49*

Issyk-Kul'
6200 *702*
2395 *2303*

Poyang Hu
5000
1930

Qinghai Hu
2300 *38*
890 *125*

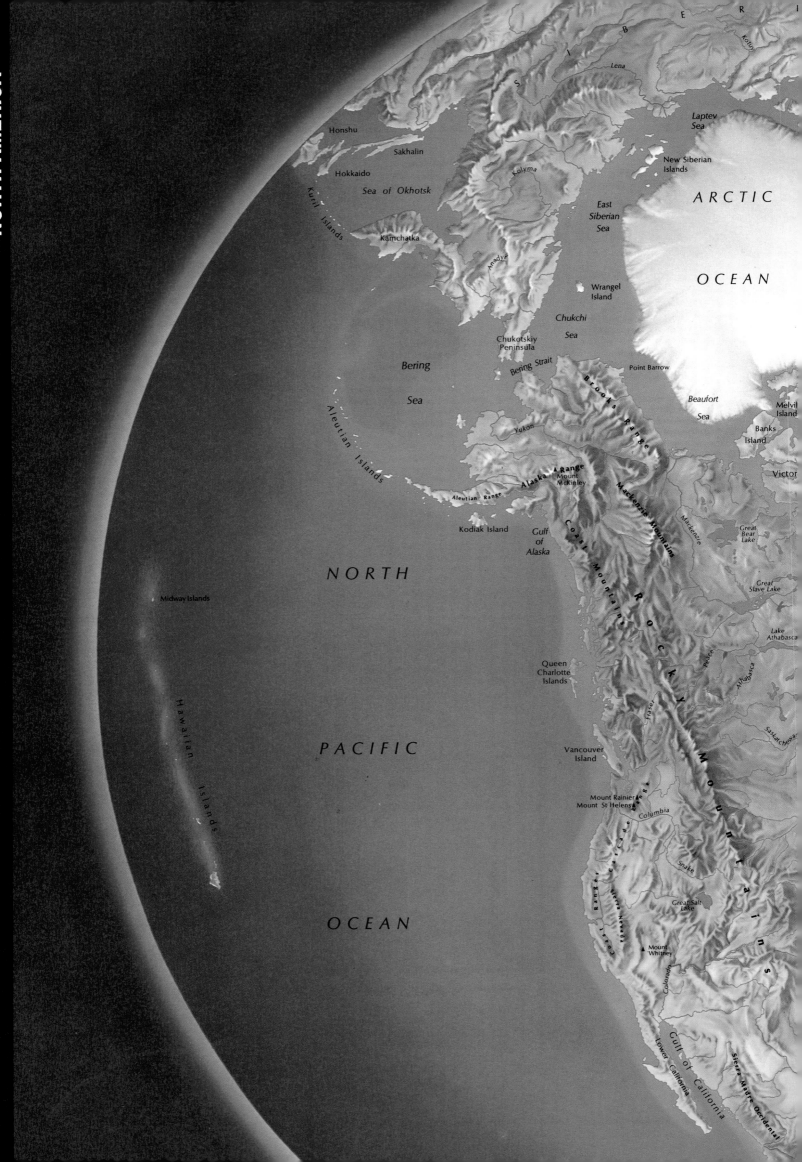

S I B E R I A

Kotuy

Lena

Laptev
Sea

Honshu

Sakhalin

Kolyma

New Siberian
Islands

ARCTIC

Hokkaido

Sea of Okhotsk

East
Siberian
Sea

Kamchatka

Kuril Islands

Anadyr

Wrangel
Island

OCEAN

Chukchi
Sea

Chukotskiy
Peninsula

Bering Strait

Point Barrow

Beaufort
Sea

Melvil
Island

Bering

Sea

Brooks Range

Banks
Island

Aleutian Islands

Yukon

Victor

Aleutian Range

Alaska Range
Mount
McKinley

Mackenzie Mountains

Mackenzie

Great
Bear
Lake

Kodiak Island

Gulf
of
Alaska

Coast Mountains

Great
Slave
Lake

NORTH

R O C K Y

Lake
Athabasca

Midway Islands

Peace

Athabasca

Queen
Charlotte
Islands

Saskatchewan

PACIFIC

Vancouver
Island

Fraser

Hawaiian Islands

M o u n t a i n s

Mount Rainier
Mount St Helens

Columbia

Snake

OCEAN

Cascade Range

Sierra Nevada

Great Salt
Lake

Coast Ranges

Mount
Whitney

Colorado

Gulf of California

Sierra Madre Occidental

Lower California

Gulf of California

Sierra Madre Occidental

Rio Grande

Sierra Madre Oriental

Popocatépetl

Islas Revillagigedo

Sierra Madre del Sur

Clipperton
Island

GULF
OF
MEXICO

Gulf of Campeche

Yucatan

Gulf
of
Honduras

Florida

W

GREA

Lake
Nicaragua

Isthmus of

Gulf
of
Panama

PACIFIC

Isla del Coco

Isla de Malpelo

Galapagos Islands

Cotopax

Chimborazo

OCEAN

Bermuda

N O R T H

B A H A M A S

Sargasso
Sea

A T L A N T I C

*W
E
S
T
Cuba*

*I
N
D
I
E
S*

O C E A N

Hispaniola

Jamaica

*R
A
N
T
I
L
L
E
S*

Puerto
Rico

C A R I B B E A N

L E S S E R

A N T I L L E S

S E A

Gulf
of
Darien

Panama

Lake
Maracaibo

Trinidad

Cordillera Occidental

Cauca

Magdalena

Cordillera Oriental

Orinoco

L L A N O S

G u i a n a

Roraima ▲

H i g h l a n d s

Branco

Mouths
of the
Amazon

Negro

Japurá

Putumayo

Amazon

Amazon

Marañón

Juruá

Ucayali

Purus

Madeira

Tapajós

Xingu

Tocantins

Parnaíba

▲ Huascarán

Araguaia

Tocantins

São Francisco

Madre de Dios

Lake
Titicaca

M A T O

▲ Ancohuma

G R O S S O

A
N
D
E
S

Lake
Poopó

B r a z i l i a n   H i g h l a n d s

Salar
de
Uyuni

Atacama Desert

G R A N   C H A C O

Paraguay

Paraná

Pilcomayo

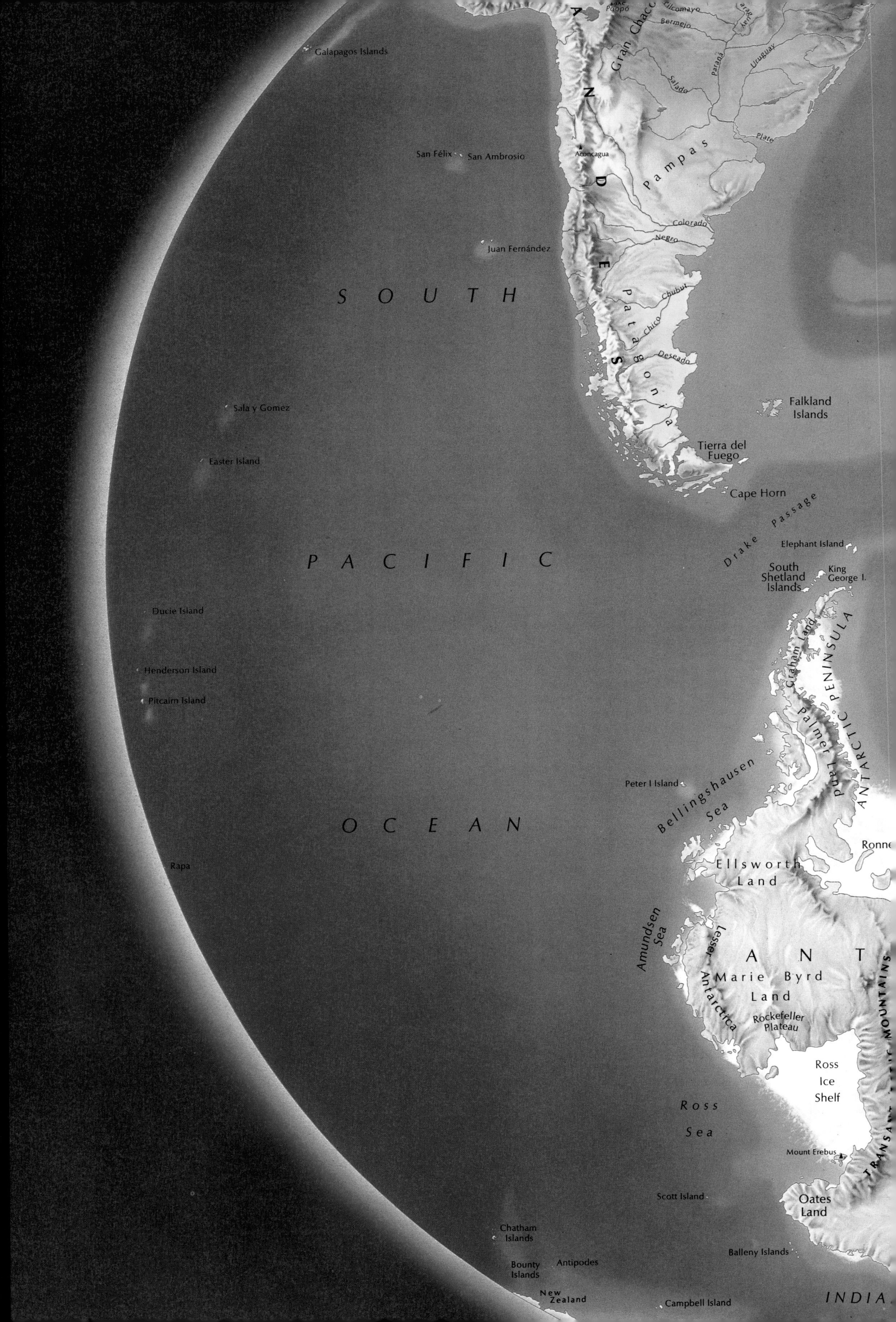

Galapagos Islands

ANDES

Gran Chaco
Bermejo
Poopó
Pilcomayo
Paraná
Salado
Uruguay
Plate

San Félix   San Ambrosio

Aconcagua
Pampas
Colorado
Negro

Juan Fernández

S O U T H

Chico
Chubut
Patagonia
Deseado

Sala y Gomez

Falkland
Islands

Easter Island

Tierra del
Fuego

Cape Horn

Drake Passage

Elephant Island

P A C I F I C

South
Shetland
Islands

King
George I.

Ducie Island

Graham Land

ANTARCTIC PENINSULA

Palmer Land

Henderson Island

Pitcairn Island

Peter I Island

Bellingshausen
Sea

O C E A N

Ronne

Ellsworth
Land

Rapa

Amundsen
Sea

Lesser Antarctica

A N T

Marie Byrd
Land

Rockefeller
Plateau

Ross
Ice
Shelf

Ross

Sea

TRANSANTARCTIC MOUNTAINS

Mount Erebus

Scott Island

Oates
Land

Chatham
Islands

Bounty
Islands

Antipodes

Balleny Islands

New
Zealand

Campbell Island

INDIA

St Helena

S O U T H

Tristan da Cunha

Gough Island

Cumane

South Georgia

South
Sandwich
Islands

South Orkney
Islands

A T L A N T I C

Kalahari
Desert

Orange River

Cape
of
Good Hope

Limpopo

Bouvet Island

Weddell

Sea

Madagascar

Lazarev
Sea

Limit of permanent pack ice

Prince Edward
Islands

O C E A N

Ice Shelf

Queen Maud Land

A R C T I C A

Antarctica

Enderby Land

Îles Crozet

· SOUTH POLE

Greater

Îles Kerguelen

· Macdonald Islands
Heard Island

George V
Land

Wilkes Land

St Paul
Amsterdam Island

OCEAN

Azores

Strait of Gibraltar

Mediterra

Madeira

Chott
Melrhir

El Jerid

Gulf of
Sirte

ATLAS MOUNTAINS

Libyan

Canary Islands

NORTH

ATLANTIC

OCEAN

Hoggar

S A H A R A

Tibesti

Lac Faguibine

Sénégal

Niger

S A H E L

Cape Verde
Islands

Jebel
Marra

Cape
Verde

Gambia

Lake
Chad

Grain Coast

Lake
Volta

Benue

**Adamawa
Highlands**

Ubangi

Uele

Ivory Coast

Gold Coast

Slave Coast
Bight of
Benin

Sanaga

Zaire

Mouths
of the Niger

St Paul Rocks

Gulf of Guinea

Bioko

Príncipe

São Tomé

Pagalu

Lac
Mai-Ndombe

Kasai

Congo

SOUTH AMERICA

Ascension

Cuango

Cuanza

S O U T H

Bie
Plateau

St Helena

Cubango

Okavango

Cunene

A T L A N T I C

Etosha Pan

Okavango

Lake
Ngami

Walvis
Bay

K a l a h a r i

O C E A N

Namib Desert

D e s e r t

Orange River

**Great
Karoo**

Cape of Good Hope

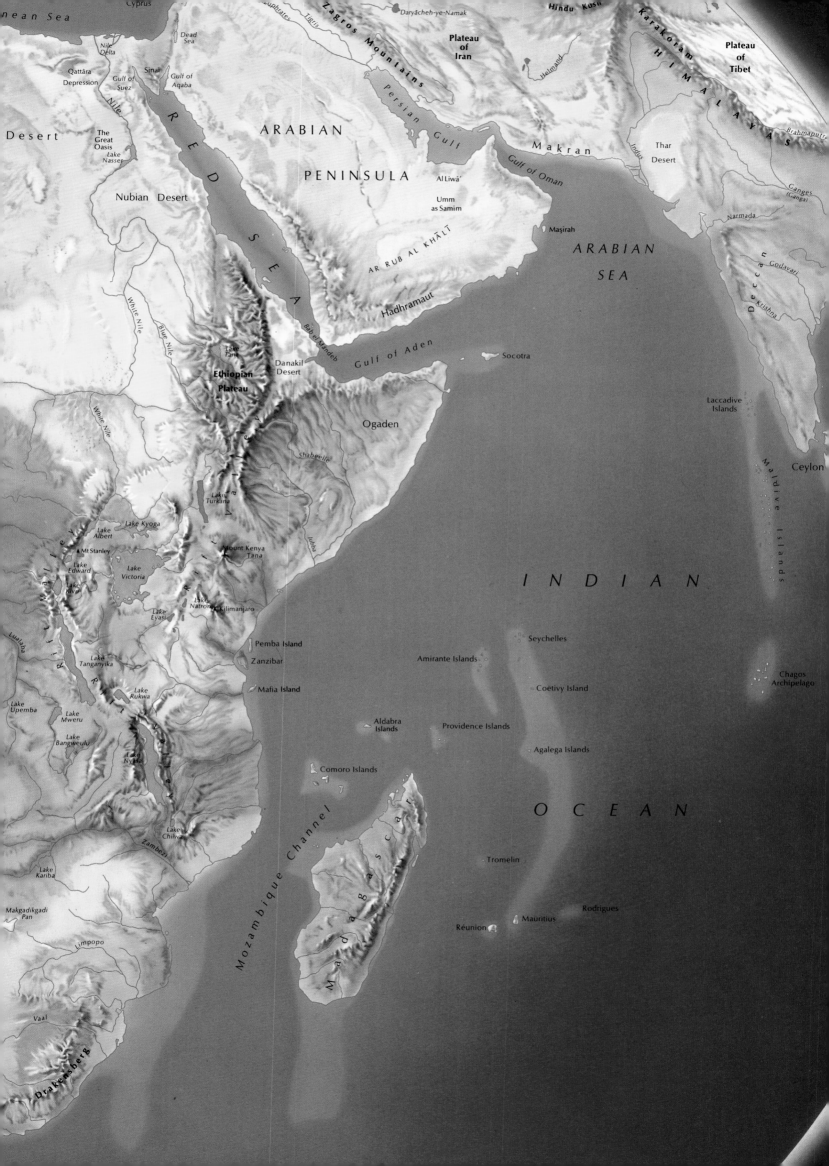

nean Sea
Cyprus
Zagros Mountains
Daryácheh-ye-Namak
Hindu Kush
Karakoram
Plateau
of
Tibet

Nile
Delta
Qattâra
Depression
Dead
Sea
Gulf of
Suez
Sinai
Gulf of
Aqaba
Euphrates
Tigris
Plateau
of
Iran
HIMALAYAS
Brahmaputra

Desert
The
Great
Oasis
Lake
Nasser
RED
SEA
ARABIAN
PENINSULA
Persian Gulf
Makran
Gulf of Oman
Thar
Desert
Indus
Ganges
(Ganga)

Nubian Desert
Al Liwá'
Umm
as Samim
Maşirah
ARABIAN
SEA
Narmada
Deccan
Godavari

AR RUB AL KHĀLĪ
Hadhramaut
Krishna

Lake
Tana
Danakil
Desert
Bâb el Mandeb
Gulf of Aden
Socotra
Laccadive
Islands
Ceylon

Ethiopian
Plateau
Ogaden

White Nile
Blue Nile
Shabeelle
Maldive Islands

White Nile
Lake
Turkana
Jubba
Chagos
Archipelago

Lake Kyoga
Lake
Albert
Mt Stanley
Mount Kenya
Tana
INDIAN

Rift Valley
Lake
Edward
Lake
Kivu
Lake
Victoria
Lake
Natron
Kilimanjaro
Lake
Eyasi

Lualaba
Pemba Island
Zanzibar
Seychelles
Amirante Islands
Coëtivy Island

Lake
Tanganyika
Mafia Island

Lake
Upemba
Lake
Mweru
Lake
Rukwa
Aldabra
Islands
Providence Islands
Agalega Islands

Lake
Bangweulu
Rift Valley
Lake
Nyasa
OCEAN

Makgadikgadi
Pan
Lake
Kariba
Lake
Chilwa
Zambezi
Mozambique Channel
Madagascar
Tromelin

Limpopo
Comoro Islands
Rodrigues
Réunion
Mauritius

Vaal
Drakensberg

NORTH POLE .

ARCTIC

Ellesmere Island

Greenland
Sea

Svalbard

Bear
Island

Hudson Bay

Baffin Island

G r e e n l a n d

Davis Strait

Jan Mayen

N o r w e g i a n

Denmark Strait

S e a

Iceland

LABRADOR

Cape Farewell

N O R T H

Faeroe Islands

Shetland

Lake
Vänern

Orkney

Lake
Vättern

Rockall

British
Isles

Grampians

N o r t h

S e a

Ba

Irish Sea

Elbe

Oder

Ness

A T L A N T I C

Severn

Thames

Rhine

N O R

English Channel

Seine

Danub

Loire

O C E A N

Bay
of
Biscay

Massif
Central

Mt. Blanc

A L P S

Po

Azores

Cantabrian Mts

Pyrenees

Rhône

Garonne

Adriatic

Apennines

Dinari

Ebro

Corsica

Se

Tagus

Balearic Islands

Sardinia

Guadalquivir

M E D I T E R

Strait of Gibraltar

Madeira

Sicily

Malta

R

A T L A S   M O U N T A I N S

Chott Melrhir

Canary Islands

El Jerid

OCEAN

Severnaya
Zemlya

Limit of permanent pack ice

Franz
Josef
Land

Spitsbergen

*Kara
Sea*

Novaya

*Barents
Sea*

Zemlya

North Cape

Lena

CENTRAL SIBERIAN PLATEAU

Nizhnyaya Tunguska

Lena

Yenisey

WEST SIBERIAN PLAIN

Ob'

Angara

Lake
Baikal

Pechora

URAL MOUNTAINS

Ob'

Irtysh

White
Sea

Severnaya Dvina

Lake
Onega

PLAZ

Lake
Ladoga

Gulf of Finland

Gulf of Bothnia

AVIA

Volga

EUROPEAN PLAIN

Central

Russian

Uplands

KIRGHIZ STEPPE

Lake
Balkhash

tic Sea

Dvina

Ural

Syrdar'ya

Vistula

H

Dnieper

Volga

Aral
Sea

Kyzylkum

CARPATHIANS

Dniester

Don

K

Amudar'ya

Hungarian Plain

Tisza

Sea of Azov

Caspian Sea

Karakumy

Danube

Caucasus

Balkan Mountains

Rhodope

Black Sea

Bosporus

Thrace

Arases

Elbruz Mts

Alps

Pindus

Dardanelles

Sea of
Marmara

ASIA MINOR

Kızıl Irmak

Lake
Van

Lake
Urmia

Zagros Mountains

Daryācheh-ye-Namak

Aegean
Sea

Tuz
Gölü

Taurus

Plateau
of
Iran

Crete

Cyprus

Mesopotamia

Tigris

ANEAN SEA

Jordan

Syrian Desert

Euphrates

Dead Sea

Persian Gulf

Gu
of
Om

Baltic Sea

Lake Ladoga

Lake Onega

Pechora

Kheta

CENTRAL

NORTH EUROPEAN PLAIN

Ob

WEST

SIBERIAN

PLATEAU

SIBERIAN

Nizhnyaya Tunguska

Dnieper

Ural Mountains

Volga

Tobol

PLAIN

S   I   B

PLATEAU

Don

Ural

Ishim

Ob

Lena

Volga

KIRGHIZ

Irtysh

Ozero Tengiz

Angara

Yenisey

Black Sea

Caucasus

Caspian Sea

Steppe

Lake Baikal

Hövsgöl Nuur

Selenga

Yablonoyy

Ustyurt Plateau

Aral Sea

Ozero Zaysan

ALTAI

Kyzylkum

Syrdar'ya

Lake Balkhash

Ozero Alakol'

MONGOLI

Kerulen

Karakumy

Amudar'ya

Ili

Ebi Nor

Dzungaria

GOBI

Issyk Kul

Tian   Shan

Bosten Hu

Yellow River (Huang He)

Plateau of Iran

▲Pik Kommunizma

Tarim

Lop Nur

Ordos

Pamirs

Hindu Kush

Takla Makan

Altun Shan

Qaidam Pendi

Qinghai Hu

Karakoram

▲K2

Kunlun   Shan

Qin Ling

Helmand

HIMALAYA

Plateau

Moron Us He (Chang Jiang)

Yellow River (Huang He)

Chenab

of

Yalong He

Red Basin

Indus

Sutlej

Tibet

Tongban He

Indo-Gangetic

Salween

Lancang Jiang

Thar Desert

Brahmaputra

Yangtze Kiang (Chang Jiang)

Dongting Hu

Plain

Everest

Kangchenjunga▲

Narmada

Ganges (Ganga)

Khasi Hills

Naga Hills

Nan Ling

Arabian

Mahanadi

Pearl River (Xi Jiang)

Sea

Mouths of the Ganges

Arakan

Red River (Song Hong)

Western Ghats

Godavari

Irrawaddy

Gulf of Tongking

Deccan

Krishna

Eastern Ghats

Bay

Salween

INDOCHINA

Hainan

Laccadive Islands

Cauvery

of

Paracel Islands

Bengal

Chao Phraya

Palk Strait

Gulf of Martaban

Mekong

Maldive Islands

Ceylon

Andaman Islands

Andaman

Gulf of Thailand

Mouths of the Mekong

Sea

Kra Isthmus

Nicobar Islands

Malay Peninsula

INDIAN   OCEAN

Yana

Indigirka

Kolyma

Anadyr

Nunivak
Island

Verkhoyanskiy Khrebet

Lena

Vilyuy

B e r i n g
S e a

Aleutian Islands

A

R

Aldan

Kamchatka

Komandorskiye
Ostrova

Kht. Dzhungdzhur

Sea
of
Okhotsk

Sakhalin

Khrebet

Shilka

Greater Khingan Range

Hulun
Nur

Manchuria

Amur

Tatarskiy Proliv

Kuril Islands

A

Songhua

Ussuri

Sikhote Alin

North Pacific Ocean

Midway
Islands

Changbai Shan

Oz
Khanka

Hokkaido

NORTH

Korea

Sea
of
Japan

Honshu

Bo Hai

Yellow River
(Huang He)

Yellow
Sea

PACIFIC

Korea Strait

Great Plain of China

Shikoku

Yangtze Kiang
(Chang Jiang)

Kyushu

OCEAN

Poyang Hu

East

Bonin Islands

China

Volcano
Islands

Taiwan Strait

Sea

Ryukyu Islands

Marshall Islands

Taiwan

Marianas

South

PHILIPPINES

China

Guam

Kiribati

Sea

Luzon

Mindoro

Samar

Caroline Islands

Panay

Palawan

Negros

Spratly
Islands

Sulu

Mindanao

Sea

Borneo

New Ireland

Nicobar
Islands

South
China
Sea

Celebes

N O R I

Celebes
Sea

Malay Peninsula

Strait of Malacca

Borneo

Makassar Strait

Halmahera

Moluccas

Seram

S u m a t r a

B a n d a
S e a

J a v a
Sea

E

Bali   Sumbawa   Flores

A r a f u r a
Sea

J a v a

Sumba

Timor

S

T

Christmas Island

I

N

D

I

E

Timor

S

Timor
Sea

Cocos–Keeling Island

Arnhem Land

Victoria

Barkly Tableland

I N D I A N

Kimberley
Plateau

Fitzroy

Tanami
Desert

Great
Sandy
Desert

Lake
Mackay

Macdonnell Ranges

Ashburton

Gibson
Desert

Lake
Amadeus

Simpson
Desert

Gascoyne

Finke

Murchison

Great Victoria Desert

Lake
Eyre

Lake
Barlee

Lake
Torrens

Lake
Moore

Nullarbor Plain

Lake
Gairdner

O C E A N

Great Australian Bight

Spencer
Gulf

Amsterdam Island

St Paul

Kerguelen

Heard Island
Macdonald Islands

A N T A R C T I C A

H PACIFIC OCEAN MICRONESIA SOUTH

Marshall
Islands

M E L A N

Admiralty Islands

New Ireland

Bismarck
Sea

New Guinea

New Britain

Bougainville

Solomon Islands

E S I A

Nauru

Banaba

Kiribati

P O L Y N

Tokelau
Islands

Tuvalu

Torres Strait

Great Barrier Reef

Coral

Sea

Santa
Cruz
Islands

Vanuatu

PACIFIC

E S I A

Samoan
Islands

Fiji

Tahiti

Gulf of
Carpentaria

Cape
York
Peninsula

Flinders

Georgina

Great Dividing Range

Diamantina

Cooper Creek

Warrego

Culgoa

Barwon

Darling

Lake
Frome

Lachlan

Murrumbidgee

Murray

Murray

Murray

Mount Kosciusko

Australian Alps

Fraser
Island

New
Caledonia

Tonga

OCEAN

Norfolk Island

Lord Howe Island

Kermadec Islands

King
Island

Bass Strait

Flinders
Island

Tasmania

Tasman

Sea

New Zealand

Cook
Strait

Chatham Islands

Foveaux Strait

Stewart
Island

Bounty Islands

Antipodes Islands

Auckland Islands

Campbell Island

Macquarie Island

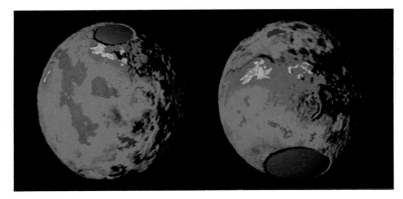

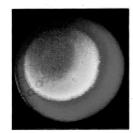

Top left The two hemispheres of Venus constructed from radar altimetry data from Pioneer. High areas are yellow and green and low areas blue in these false colour images. There is no data for the polar regions.

Top right Io and Europa are clearly visible as they cross the face of Jupiter. The Great Red Spot of Jupiter has been observed for 300 years but the white ovals nearby did not appear until the 1930s. They are all centres of high pressure.

Far left The Caloris basin of Mercury is the largest impact feature on the planet.
Right The rings of Saturn lie in the equatorial plane and consist of countless small ice-covered particles.
Left This Viking Lander 2 photograph shows a thin coating of ice that has accumulated at the base of rocks on the Martian soil.

Left This photograph of Uranus in false colour was taken from 9.1 million km (5.7 million miles) by Voyager 2. The planet's atmosphere is deep, cold and remarkably clear, but the false colours enhance the polar region. Here, the suggestion is that a brownish haze of smog is concentrated over the pole.

Current theory suggests that the solar system condensed from a primitive solar nebula of gas and dust during an interval of a few tens of millions of years about 4600 million years ago. Gravity caused this nebula to contract, drawing most of its mass into the centre. Turbulence gave the original cloud a tendency to rotate faster and faster, forcing the remainder of the cloud into a disc shape.

The centre of the cloud heated up as it compressed, and so eventually became hot enough for the Sun to begin to shine, through nuclear energy released at its core. Meanwhile the surrounding disc of cloud cooled, allowing material to condense into solid form. Particles stuck together as they collided and progressively larger bodies were built up. These swept up most of the debris to form the planets, which now orbit the Sun.

EARTHLIKE PLANETS

Mercury is the nearest planet to the Sun, spinning three times for every two orbits around the Sun. It has an exceptionally large metallic core which may be responsible for Mercury's weak magnetic field. Mercury is an airless world subject to vast extremes of temperature, from −180°C (−292°F) at night to 430°C (806°F) near the middle of its long day. The Mariner 10 space probe, during the mid-1970s, revealed the surface to be dominated by heavily cratered areas.

Venus has a dense atmosphere of 96% carbon dioxide mixed with nitrogen, oxygen, sulphur dioxide and water vapour which hides the surface under permanent cloud and maintains a mean surface temperature of about 480°C (896°F). The planet's slow rotation means that weather systems are driven mostly by solar heat, rather than by spin. Westerly winds may blow up to 100 m/sec (328 ft/sec).

Mars has a thin atmosphere of about 96% carbon dioxide mixed with other minor gases. The polar caps consist of semi-permanent water-ice and solid carbon dioxide. Day and night surface temperatures vary between about −120°C (−184°F) and −20°C (−4°F). Mars has two small satellites, Phobos and Deimos, each less than about 25km (15.5 miles) across, probably captured asteroids.

Mars also shows evidence of erosional processes. The effect of winds is seen in the form of the deposition of sand dunes. Dust storms frequently obscure the surface. The large channels, such as the 5000km (3107 miles) long Valles Marineris, may have been cut by flowing water. Water is abundant in the polar caps and may be widespread, held in as permafrost.

GAS GIANTS

Jupiter has at least 16 satellites and a debris ring system about 50,000km (31,070 miles) above the cloud tops. The outer atmosphere is all that can be directly observed of the planet itself. It is mostly hydrogen with lesser amounts of helium, ammonia, methane and water vapour. Jupiter's rapid rotation causes it to be flattened towards the poles. This rotation and heat flow from the interior cause complex weather patterns. Where cloud systems interact vast storms can occur in the form of vortices. Some last only a few days, but the most persistent of these, the Great Red Spot, has been present since it was first detected in the 17th century.

Saturn is the least dense of the planets. It has a stormy atmosphere situated above a 30,000km (18,640 miles) layer of liquid hydrogen and helium distorted by rotation.

The rings of Saturn are thought to be mostly made of icy debris, from 10m (33 ft) down to a few microns in size, derived from the break-up of a satellite. The rings are less than 1km thick.

Uranus was little known until Voyager 2 flew by it in January 1986. It has a cloud cover even more featureless than Jupiter and Saturn, and consists mostly of hydrogen. Voyager 2 discovered ten new satellites and provided detailed images of the planet's eleven rings of icy debris.

Neptune has only been studied from Earth. Its composition is thought to be similar to that of Uranus. Its two satellites are very different. Triton is large, with considerable mass; Neroid is small and on an eccentric orbit.

Pluto is usually the most distant planet from the Sun, but since 1983 the eccentricity of its orbit has brought it temporarily within the orbit of Neptune. The atmosphere is thought to be composed mostly of methane and smaller amounts of other gases.

	SUN	MERCURY	VENUS	EARTH	(MOON)	MARS	JUPITER	SATURN	URANUS	NEPTUNE	PLUTO
Mass (Earth=1)	333 400	0.055	0.815	1 (5.97 10²⁴kg)	0.012	0.107	317.8	95.2	14.5	17.2	0.003
Volume (Earth=1)	1 306 000	0.06	0.88	1	0.020	0.150	1 319	751	62	54	0.015?
Density (water=1)	1.41	5.43	5.24	5.52	3.34	3.94	1.33	0.70	1.30	1.76	1.1?
Equatorial diameter (km)	1 392 000	4 878	12 104	12 756	3 476	6 787	142 796	120 000	50 800	48 600	3 000?
Polar flattening	0	0	0	0.003	0	0.005	0.065	0.108	0.030	0.026	?
'Surface' gravity (Earth=1)	27.9	0.37	0.88	1	0.16	0.38	2.64	1.15	1.17	1.18	0.45?
Number of satellites greater than 100 km diameter	—	0	0	1	—	0	4	10	6	2	1
Total number of satellites	—	0	0	1	—	2	16	17	c.15	2	1
Period of rotation (in Earth days)	25.38	58.65	−243 (retrograde)	23hr 56m 4 secs	27.32	1.03	0.414	0.438	−0.72 (retrograde)	0.77	−6.39 (retrograde)
Length of year (in Earth days and years)	—	88 days	224.7 days	365.26 days	—	687 days	11.86 years	29.46 years	84.01 years	164.8 years	247.7 years
Distance from Sun (mean) Mkm	—	57.9	108.2	149.6	—	227.9	778 3	1 427	2 870	4 497	5 900

EARTH STRUCTURE

Internally, the Earth may be divided broadly into crust, mantle and core (*see right*).

The crust is a thin shell constituting only 0.2% of the mass of the Earth. The continental crust varies in thickness from 20 to 90km (12 to 56 miles) and is less dense than ocean crust. Two-thirds of the continents are overlain by sedimentary rocks of average thickness less than 2km (1.2 miles). Ocean crust is on average 7km (4.4 miles) thick. It is composed of igneous rocks, basalts and gabbros.

Crust and mantle are separated by the Mohorovičić Discontinuity (Moho). The mantle differs from the crust. It is largely igneous. The upper mantle extends to 350km (218 miles). The lower mantle has a more uniform composition. A sharp discontinuity defines the meeting of mantle and core. The inability of the outer core to transmit seismic waves suggests it is liquid. It is probably of metallic iron with other elements – sulphur, silicon, oxygen, potassium and hydrogen have all been suggested. The inner core is solid and probably of nickel-iron. Temperature at the core-mantle boundary is about 3700°C (5430°F) and 4000°–4500°C (7230°–8130°F) in the inner core.

THE ATMOSPHERE

The ancient atmosphere lacked free oxygen. Plant life added oxygen to the atmosphere and transferred carbon dioxide to the crustal rocks and the hydrosphere. The composition of air today at 79% nitrogen and 20% oxygen remains stable by the same mechanism.

Solar energy is distributed around the Earth by the atmosphere. Most of the weather and climate processes occur in the troposphere at the lowest level. The atmosphere also shields the Earth. Ozone exists to the extent of 2 parts per million and is at its maximum at 30km (19 miles). It is the only gas which absorbs ultra-violet radiation. Water-vapour and CO_2 keep out infra-red radiation.

Above 80km (50 miles) nitrogen and oxygen tend to separate into atoms which become ionized (an ion is an atom lacking one or more of its electrons). The ionosphere is a zone of ionized belts which reflect radio waves back to Earth. These electrification belts change their position dependent on light and darkness and external factors.

Beyond the ionosphere, the magnetosphere extends to outer space. Ionized particles form a plasma (a fourth state of matter, ie. other than solid, liquid, gas) held in by the Earth's magnetic field.

ORIGIN AND DEVELOPMENT OF LIFE

Primitive life-forms (blue-green algae) are found in rocks as old as 3500Ma (million years) and, although it cannot yet be proved, the origin of life on Earth probably dates back to about 4000Ma. It seems likely that the oxygen levels in the atmosphere increased only slowly at first, probably to about 1% of the present amount by 2000Ma. As the atmospheric oxygen built up so the protective ozone layer developed to allow organisms to live in shallower waters. More highly developed photosynthesising organisms led to the development of oxygen breathing animals. The first traces of multicellular life occur about 1000Ma; by 700Ma complex animals, such as jellyfish, worms and primitive molluscs, had developed.

Organisms developed hard parts that allowed their preservation as abundant fossils at about 570Ma. This coincided with a

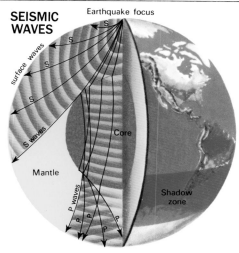

THE EARTH'S SHELLS

oceanic crust — Lithosphere — continental crust
depth (km) 350 — transition zone — Moho
900 — — upper mantle
lower mantle — seismic discontinuities
2900 — core-mantle discontinuity
outer core
4700 — transition zone
5150
inner core
6370

SEISMIC WAVES

Earthquake focus

surface waves

S waves

P waves

Mantle

Core

Shadow zone

Above In an earthquake the shock generates vibrations, or seismic waves, which radiate in all directions from the focus. Surface waves travel close to the surface of the Earth. They cause most damage in the ground and most damage to structures.

Other waves known as body waves pass through the body of the Earth. Primary (P) waves are compressional. They are able to travel through solids and fluids and cause the particles of the Earth to vibrate in the direction of travel. Secondary (S) waves are transverse, or shear, waves. They can only pass through solids.

period of explosive evolution of marine life. Fishes appeared about 475Ma and by 400Ma land plants had developed. Between 340 and 305Ma dense vegetation covered the land, amphibians emerged from the sea, and by about 250Ma had given rise to reptiles and the first mammals. These expanded hugely about 65Ma.

EARTHQUAKES

Earthquakes are the manifestation of a slippage at a geological fault. The majority occur at tectonic plate boundaries. The interior of a plate tends to be stable and less subject to earthquakes. When plates slide past each other strain energy is suddenly released. Even though the amount of movement is very small the energy released is colossal. It

is transferred in shock waves.

Most earthquakes originate at not very great depths – 5km (3 miles) or so. Some, however, may be as deep as 700km (435 miles). The precise cause of these very deep earthquakes is not known. The point from which the earthquake is generated is the focus and the point on the surface immediately above the focus is the epicentre.

The Richter Scale is used to define the magnitude of earthquakes. In the Scale each unit is ten times the intensity of the next lower on the scale. The intensity is recorded by seismographs. There is no upper limit but the greatest magnitude yet recorded is 8.9.

VOLCANOES

Almost all the world's active volcanoes, numbering 500–600 are located at convergent plate boundaries. Those are the volcanoes which give spectacular demonstrations of volcanic activity. Yet far greater volcanic activity continues unnoticed and without cessation at mid-ocean ridges where magma from the upper mantle is quietly being extruded on to the ocean floor to create new crustal material.

Chemical composition of magmas and the amount of gas they contain determine the nature of a volcanic eruption. Gas-charged basalts produce cinder cones. Violent eruptions usually occur when large clouds of lava come into contact with water to produce fine-grained ash. When andesites are charged with gas they erupt with explosive violence.

Nuées ardentes (burning clouds) are extremely destructive. They are produced by magmas which erupt explosively sending molten lava fragments and gas at great speeds down the mountain sides.

In spite of the destructiveness of many volcanoes people still live in their vicinity because of the fertile volcanic soils. Geothermal energy in regions of volcanic activity is another source of attraction.

GRAVITY AND MAGNETISM

The Earth is spheroidal in form because it is a rotating body. Were it not so it would take the form of a sphere. The shape is determined by the mass of the Earth and its rate of rotation. Centrifugal force acting outwards reduces the pull of gravity acting inwards so that gravity at the equator is less than at the poles. Uneven distribution of matter within the Earth distorts the shape taken up by the mean sea-level surface (the geoid). Today the belief is that electric currents generated in the semi-molten outer core are responsible for the magnetic field. The Earth's magnetic poles have experienced a number of reversals, the north pole becoming the south and vice-versa.

ROCK AND HYDROLOGICAL CYCLES

Right In the most familiar cycle rain falls onto the land, drains to the sea, evaporates, condenses into cloud and is precipitated onto the land again. Water is also released and recirculated. In the rock cycle rocks are weathered and eroded, forming sediments which are compacted into rocks that are eventually exposed and then weathered again.

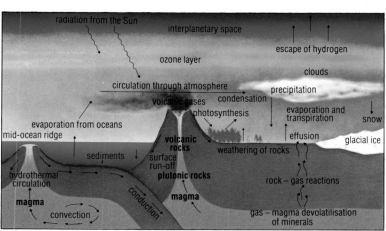

radiation from the Sun
interplanetary space
escape of hydrogen
ozone layer
clouds
circulation through atmosphere
precipitation
volcanic gases
condensation
photosynthesis
evaporation and transpiration
snow
evaporation from oceans
mid-ocean ridge
volcanic rocks
effusion
glacial ice
sediments
weathering of rocks
surface run-off
hydrothermal circulation
plutonic rocks
rock – gas reactions
conduction
magma
magma
gas – magma devolatilisation of minerals
convection

EARTHQUAKES AND VOLCANOES

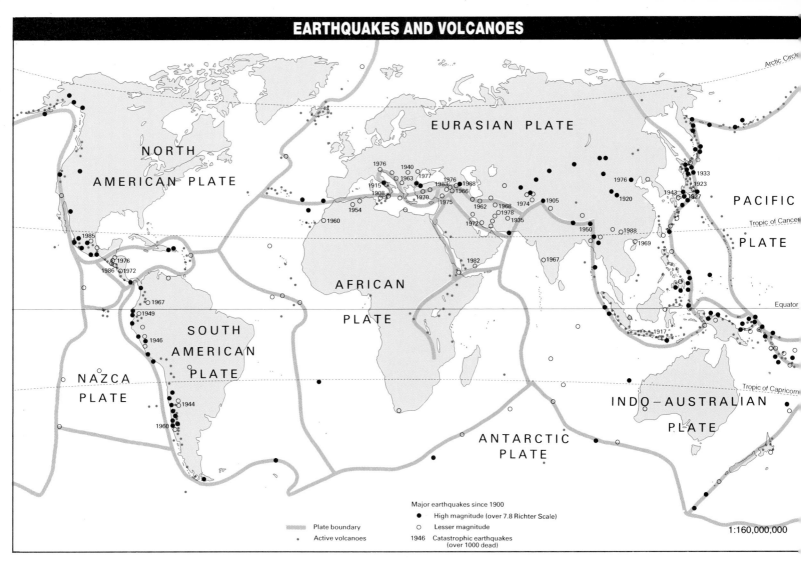

Major earthquakes since 1900

● High magnitude (over 7.8 Richter Scale)

○ Lesser magnitude

1946 Catastrophic earthquakes (over 1000 dead)

Plate boundary

Active volcanoes

1:160,000,000

ECONOMIC MINERALS

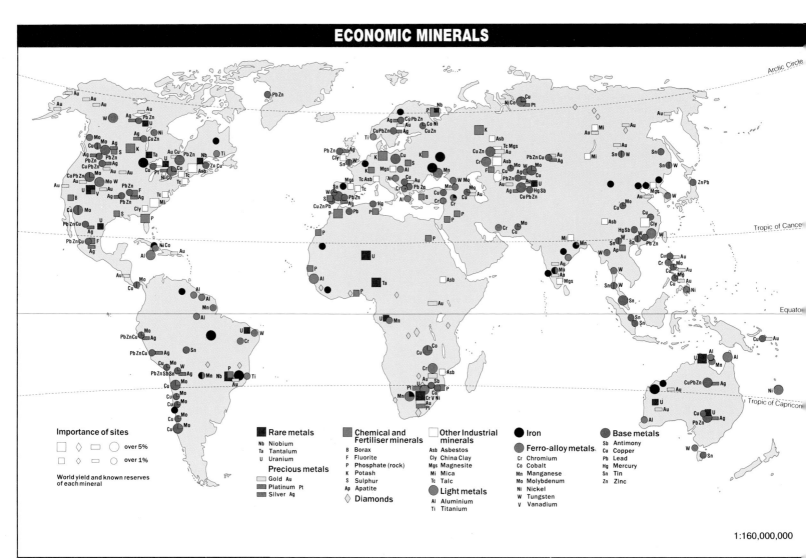

Importance of sites

□ ◇ ▭ ○ over 5%
□ ◇ ▭ ○ over 1%

World yield and known reserves of each mineral

Rare metals
Nb Niobium
Ta Tantalum
U Uranium

Precious metals
Gold Au
Platinum Pt
Silver Ag

Chemical and Fertiliser minerals
B Borax
F Fluorite
P Phosphate (rock)
K Potash
S Sulphur
Ap Apatite

◇ Diamonds

Other Industrial minerals
Asb Asbestos
Cly China Clay
Mgs Magnesite
Mi Mica
Tc Talc

● Light metals
Al Aluminium
Ti Titanium

● Iron

● Ferro-alloy metals
Cr Chromium
Co Cobalt
Mn Manganese
Mo Molybdenum
Ni Nickel
W Tungsten
V Vanadium

● Base metals
Sb Antimony
Cu Copper
Pb Lead
Hg Mercury
Sn Tin
Zn Zinc

1:160,000,000

64

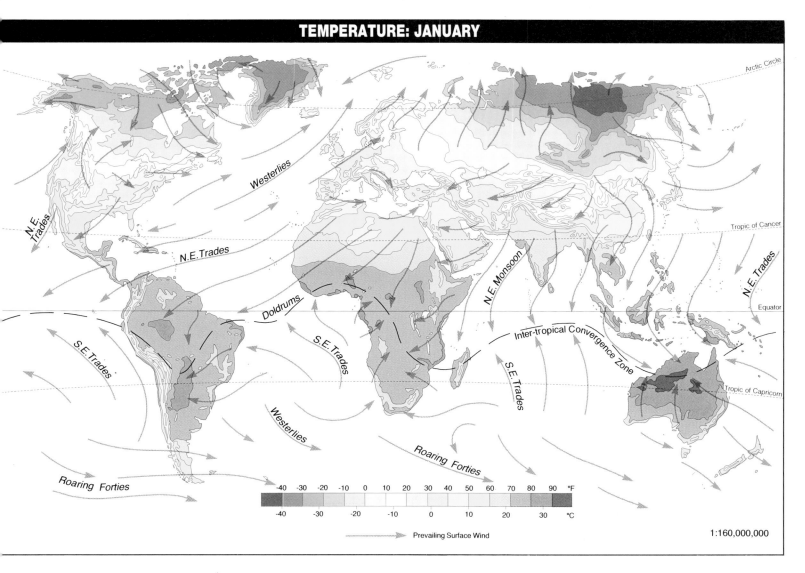

Arctic Circle

Westerlies

N.E. Trades

N.E. Trades

N.E. Monsoon

N.E. Trades

Tropic of Cancer

N.E. Trades

Doldrums

Equator

S.E. Trades

S.E. Trades

Inter-tropical Convergence Zone

S.E. Trades

Tropic of Capricorn

Westerlies

Roaring Forties

Roaring Forties

| -40 | -30 | -20 | -10 | 0 | 10 | 20 | 30 | 40 | 50 | 60 | 70 | 80 | 90 | °F |
| -40 | | -30 | | -20 | | -10 | | 0 | | 10 | | 20 | | 30 | | °C |

Prevailing Surface Wind

1:160,000,000

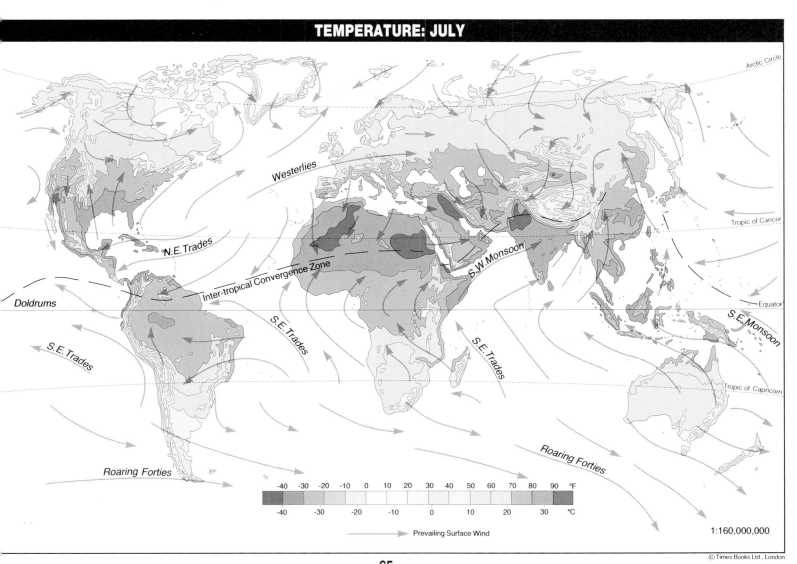

Arctic Circle

Westerlies

N.E. Trades

Tropic of Cancer

Inter-tropical Convergence Zone

S.W. Monsoon

Doldrums

S.E. Trades

Equator

S.E. Monsoon

S.E. Trades

S.E. Trades

Tropic of Capricorn

Roaring Forties

| -40 | -30 | -20 | -10 | 0 | 10 | 20 | 30 | 40 | 50 | 60 | 70 | 80 | 90 | °F |
| -40 | | -30 | | -20 | | -10 | | 0 | | 10 | | 20 | | 30 | | °C |

Prevailing Surface Wind

1:160,000,000

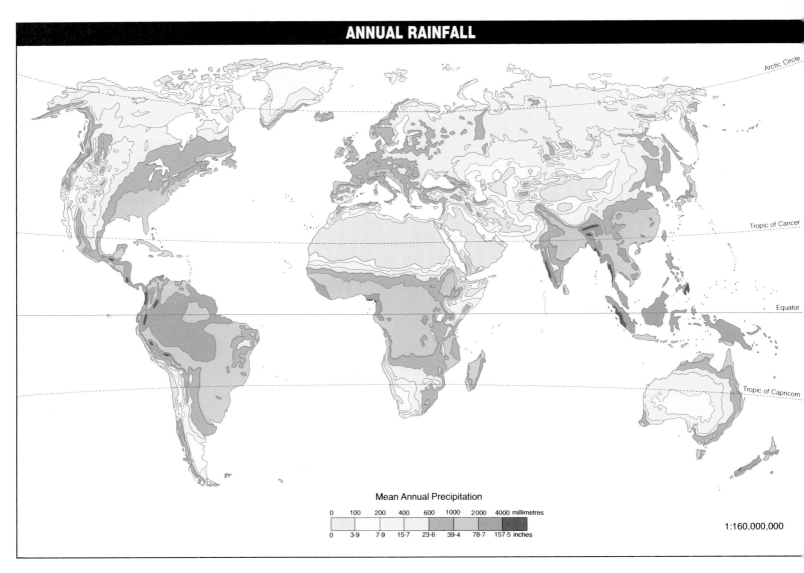

Mean Annual Precipitation

0	100	200	400	600	1000	2000	4000 millimetres
0	3·9	7·9	15·7	23·6	39·4	78·7	157·5 inches

1:160,000,000

NATURAL VEGETATION

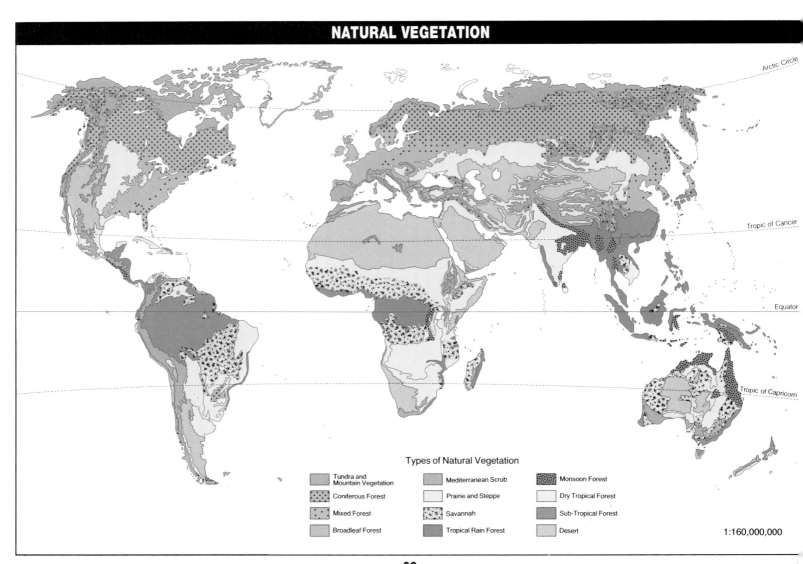

Types of Natural Vegetation

Tundra and Mountain Vegetation	Mediterranean Scrub	Monsoon Forest
Coniferous Forest	Prairie and Steppe	Dry Tropical Forest
Mixed Forest	Savannah	Sub-Tropical Forest
Broadleaf Forest	Tropical Rain Forest	Desert

1:160,000,000

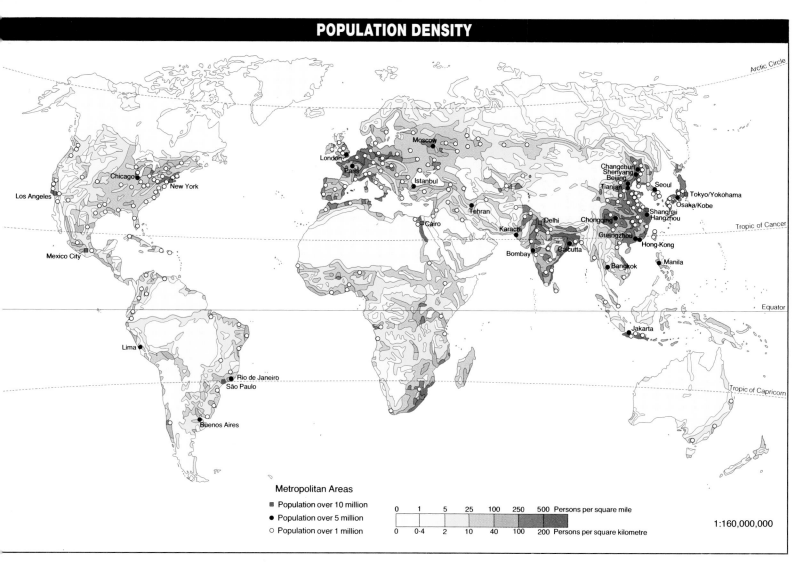

Metropolitan Areas

■ Population over 10 million
● Population over 5 million
○ Population over 1 million

| 0 | 1 | 5 | 25 | 100 | 250 | 500 | Persons per square mile |
| 0 | 0·4 | 2 | 10 | 40 | 100 | 200 | Persons per square kilometre |

1:160,000,000

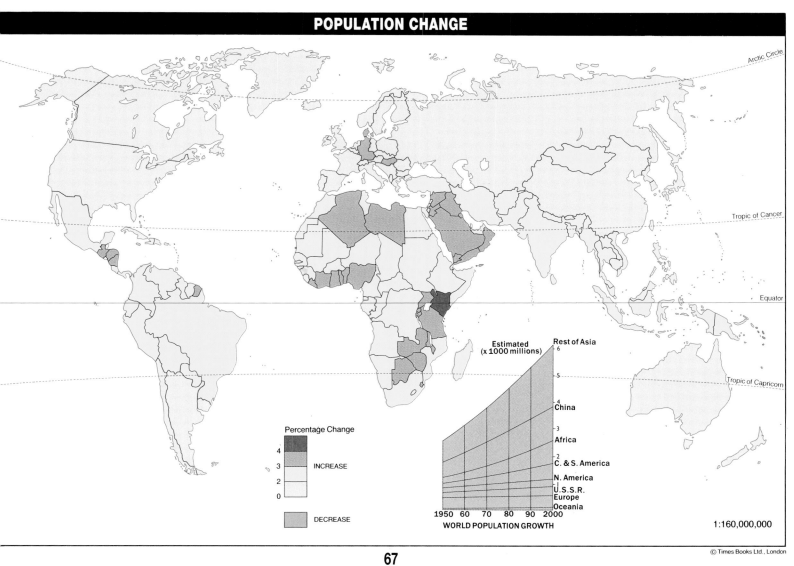

Percentage Change

4
3   INCREASE
2
0

DECREASE

Estimated
(x 1000 millions)

Rest of Asia
China
Africa
C. & S. America
N. America
U.S.S.R.
Europe
Oceania

1950 60 70 80 90 2000
WORLD POPULATION GROWTH

1:160,000,000

67

© Times Books Ltd., London

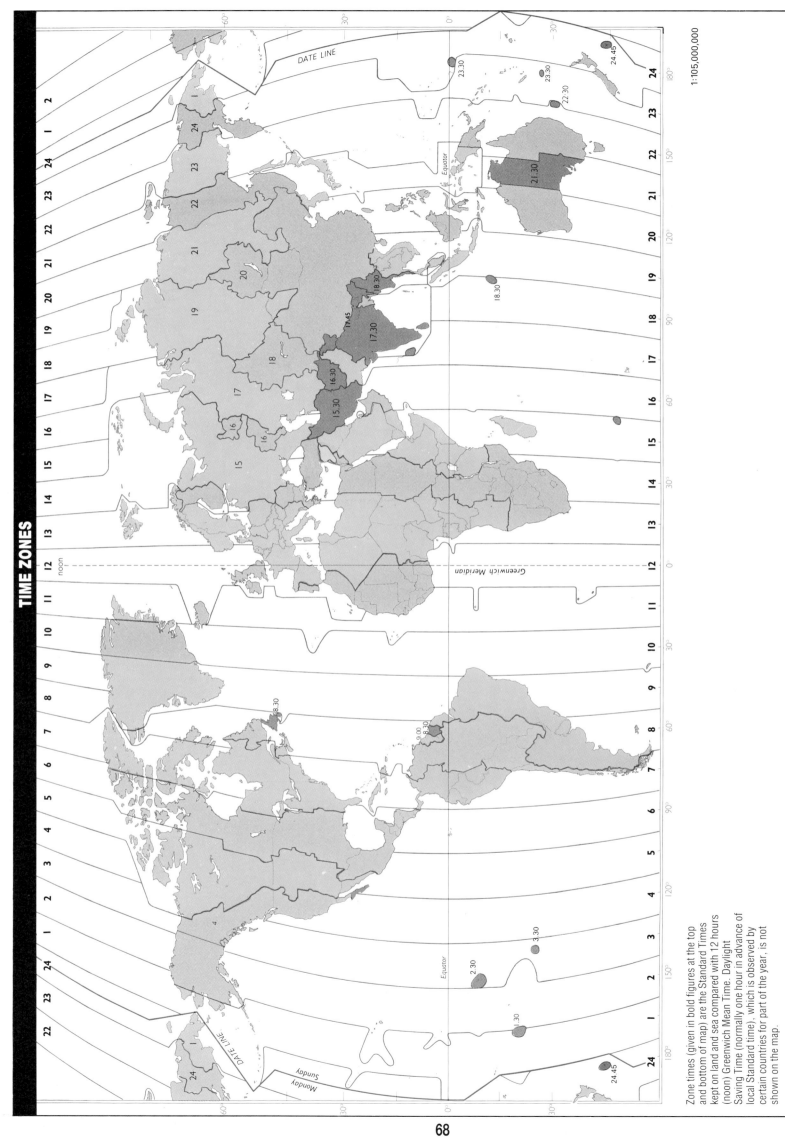

TIME ZONES

DATE LINE

Equator

Greenwich Meridian

noon

Monday
Sunday

DATE LINE

Equator

1:105,000,000

Zone times (given in bold figures at the top
and bottom of map) are the Standard Times
kept on land and sea compared with 12 hours
(noon) Greenwich Mean Time. Daylight
Saving Time (normally one hour in advance of
local Standard time), which is observed by
certain countries for part of the year, is not
shown on the map.

68

This page explains the main symbols, lettering style and height/depth colours used on the reference maps on pages 2 to 76. The scale of each map is indicated at the foot of each page. Abbreviations used on the maps appear at the beginning of the index.

BOUNDARIES

	International
	International under Dispute
	Cease Fire Line
	Autonomous or State
	Administrative
	Maritime (National)
	International Date Line

COMMUNICATIONS

	Motorway/Express Highway
	Under Construction
	Major Highway
	Other Roads
	Under Construction
	Track
	Road Tunnel
	Car Ferry
	Main Railway
	Other Railway
	Under Construction
	Rail Tunnel
	Rail Ferry
	Canal
⊕	International Airport
+	Other Airport

LAKE FEATURES

	Freshwater
	Saltwater
	Seasonal
	Salt Pan

LANDSCAPE FEATURES

	Glacier, Ice Cap
	Marsh, Swamp
	Sand Desert, Dunes

OTHER FEATURES

	River
	Seasonal River
⁼	Pass, Gorge
	Dam, Barrage
	Waterfall, Rapid
	Aqueduct
	Reef
▲ 4231	Summit, Peak
. 217	Spot Height, Depth
ᵕ	Well
Δ	Oil Field
▲	Gas Field
Gas / Oil	Oil/Natural Gas Pipeline
Gemsbok Nat. Pk	National Park
∴ᵁᴿ	Historic Site

LETTERING STYLES

CANADA	Independent Nation
FLORIDA	State, Province or Autonomous Region
Gibraltar (U.K.)	Sovereignty of Dependent Territory
Lothian	Administrative Area
LANGUEDOC	Historic Region
Loire **Vosges**	Physical Feature or Physical Region

TOWNS AND CITIES

Square symbols denote capital cities

Population

■ ●	**New York**	over 5 000 000
■ ●	**Montréal**	over 1 000 000
□ ○	Ottawa	over 500 000
■ ●	Québec	over 100 000
□ ○	St John's	over 50 000
□ ○	Yorkton	over 10 000
□ ○	Jasper	under 10 000
		Built-up-area

Height

- 6000m
- 5000m
- 4000m
- 3000m
- 2000m
- 1000m
- 500m
- 200m

0 — Sea Level

Depth

- 200m
- 2000m
- 4000m
- 6000m
- 8000m

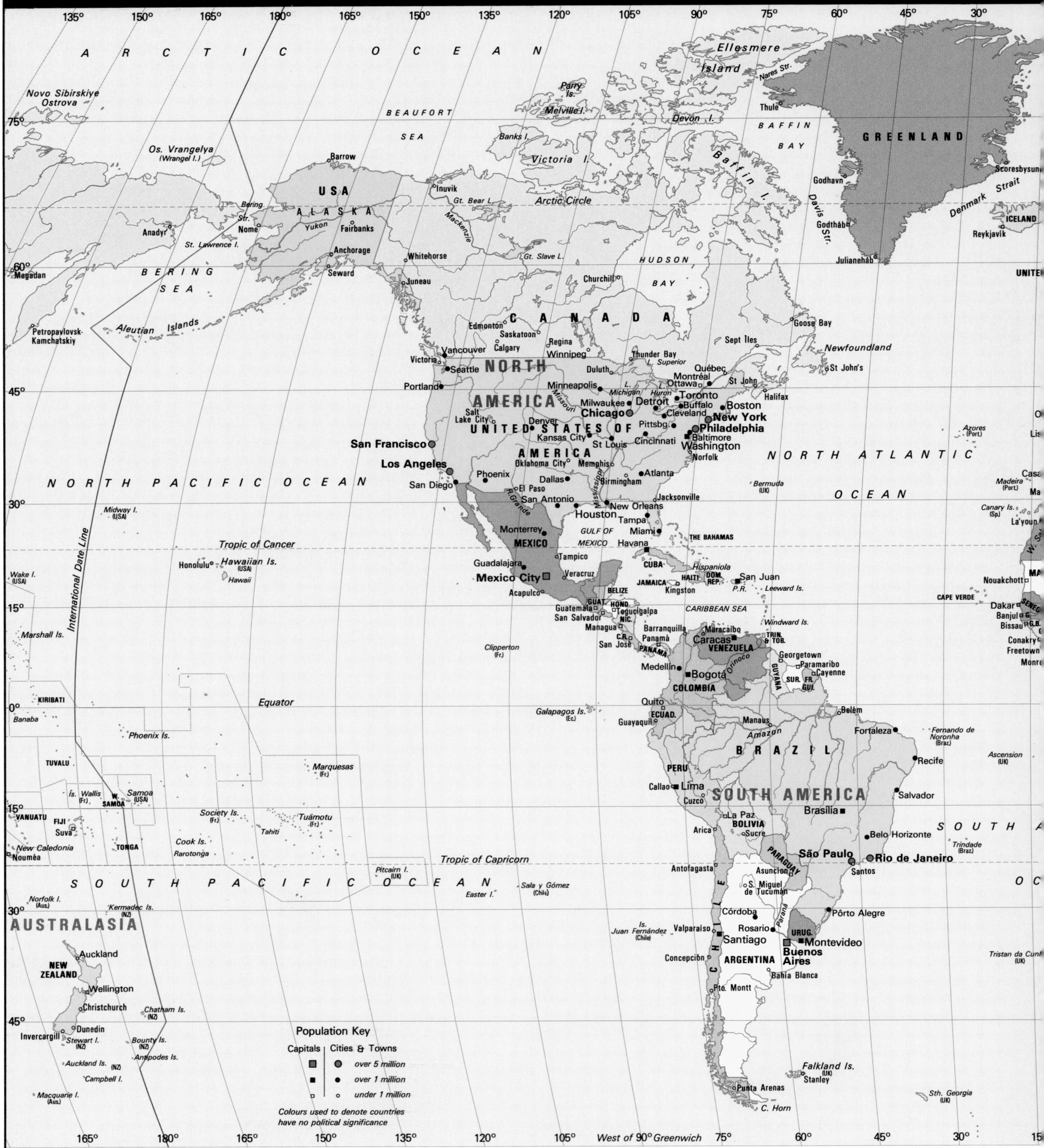

ARCTIC OCEAN

Novo Sibirskiye Ostrova

Os. Vrangelya (Wrangel I.)

75°

BEAUFORT SEA

Parry Is.
Melville I.
Banks I.

Victoria I.

Devon I.

BAFFIN BAY

Nares Str.

Thule

ELLesmere Island

GREENLAND

Scoresbysund

Godhavn

Denmark Strait

60°

Magadan

Petropavlovsk-Kamchatskiy

BERING SEA

Barrow

Inuvik
Gt. Bear L.
Mackenzie

Arctic Circle

Godthåb

Julianehåb

ICELAND

Reykjavík

UNITE

Aleutian Islands

Bering Str.

Nome
Yukon
Fairbanks

Anchorage
Seward

Whitehorse

Juneau

Gt. Slave L.

HUDSON BAY

Churchill

Goose Bay

Sept Iles

Newfoundland

St John's

45°

NORTH PACIFIC OCEAN

USA
ALASKA

Anadyr'
St. Lawrence I.

Victoria
Vancouver
Seattle
Portland

Edmonton
Calgary
Saskatoon
Regina
Winnipeg

CANADA

NORTH

Thunder Bay
L. Superior

Duluth
Minneapolis
L. Michigan
Milwaukee
Chicago

Québec
Montréal
Ottawa
Toronto
Buffalo
Detroit
Cleveland
Pittsbg.

St John
Halifax

Boston
New York
Philadelphia
Baltimore
Washington

NORTH ATLANTIC OCEAN

Azores (Port.)

Lis

30°

San Francisco

Los Angeles

AMERICA

UNITED STATES OF
AMERICA

Salt Lake City
Denver
Kansas City
St Louis
Cincinnati

Oklahoma City
Memphis

Norfolk

Bermuda (UK)

OCEAN

Casa
Madeira (Port.)
Ma

Phoenix
San Diego
El Paso
San Antonio

Dallas
Birmingham
Atlanta
Jacksonville

Canary Is. (Sp.)
La'youn

Tropic of Cancer

Houston
Monterrey

New Orleans
Tampa
Miami

GULF OF MEXICO
Havana

THE BAHAMAS

Midway I. (USA)

Honolulu
Hawaiian Is. (USA)
Hawaii

Guadalajara
MEXICO
Tampico

Mexico City
Veracruz
Acapulco

CUBA
HAITI
JAMAICA
Kingston

Hispaniola
DOM. REP.
San Juan
P.R.
Leeward Is.

Nouakchott

CAPE VERDE

MA

Wake I. (USA)

15°

Marshall Is.

GUAT.
HOND.
Guatemala
Tegucigalpa
San Salvador
NIC.
Managua
C.R.
San José

BELIZE

CARIBBEAN SEA

Windward Is.

Dakar
Banjul
Bissau
G.B.

Conakry
Freetown
Monr

KIRIBATI
Banaba

Equator

Clipperton (Fr)

Barranquilla
Panamá
PANAMA

Maracaibo
Caracas
VENEZUELA

Medellín
Bogotá
COLOMBIA

TRIN. TOB.
Georgetown
Paramaribo
Cayenne
GUYANA SUR. FR. GUI.

0°

TUVALU

Phoenix Is.

Galapagos Is. (Ec.)

Quito
ECUAD.
Guayaquil

Manaus
Amazon

Belém

Fernando de Noronha (Braz.)

BRAZIL

Fortaleza

Ascension (UK)

15°

VANUATU

Marquesas (Fr.)

Is. Wallis (Fr.)
Samoa (USA)
W. SAMOA

Society Is. (Fr.)
Tahiti

Tuámotu (Fr.)

PERU
Callao
Lima
Cuzco

SOUTH AMERICA

Recife

Salvador

FIJI
Suva

Cook Is.

La Paz
BOLIVIA
Sucre

Brasília

Belo Horizonte

Trindade (Braz.)

SOUTH

New Caledonia
Nouméa

TONGA

Rarotonga

Tropic of Capricorn

Pitcairn I. (UK)

Easter I.

Sala y Gómez (Chile)

Arica

Antofagasta

Asunción
PARAGUAY

São Paulo
Santos

Rio de Janeiro

OC

30°

AUSTRALASIA

Norfolk I. (Aus.)
Kermadec Is. (NZ)

S O U T H   P A C I F I C   O C E A N

S. Miguel de Tucumán

Córdoba
Rosario
URUG.
Montevideo

Tristan da Cunh (UK)

NEW ZEALAND

Auckland

Valparaiso
Santiago
Concepción

CHILE
ARGENTINA

Porto Alegre

Buenos Aires

Bahía Blanca

Wellington

Juan Fernández (Chile)

Pto. Montt

45°

Invercargill
Dunedin
Stewart I. (NZ)
Bounty Is. (NZ)
Antipodes Is.
Auckland Is. (NZ)
Campbell I.

Chatham Is. (NZ)

Macquarie I. (Aus.)

Population Key

	Capitals	Cities & Towns
■	●	over 5 million
■	●	over 1 million
□	○	under 1 million

Colours used to denote countries have no political significance

Falkland Is. (UK)
Stanley

Punta Arenas

C. Horn

Sth. Georgia (UK)

Map (1:70 000 000, 45° N & S)

Longitude labels (top): 0° 15° 30° 45° 60° 75° 90° 105° 120° 135° 150° 165° 180° 165°

Latitude labels (right): 75° 60° 45° 30° 15° 0° 15° 30° 45°

ARCTIC OCEAN
Zemlya Frantsa Josifa
Severnaya Zemlya
Novo Sibirskiye Ostrova
Os. Vrangelya (Wrangel I.)
International Date Line
SVALBARD
Novaya Zemlya
BARENTS SEA
KARA SEA
Bjørnøya (Nor.)
Jan Mayen (Nor.)
Hammerfest
Tromsø
Narvik
Arctic Circle
Nordvik
Khatanga
Tiksi
Anadyr'
BERING SEA
Murmansk
Salekhard
Urengoy
Noril'sk
Magadan
Petropavlovsk-Kamchatskiy
Aleutian Is.
NORWAY SWEDEN FINLAND
Trondheim
Bergen Oslo
Stockholm
Umeå
Helsinki
Leningrad
Archangel
Sev. Dvina
Petrozavodsk
Kirov
Perm
Sverdlovsk
Tomsk
Krasnoyarsk
Yakutsk
Magadan
SEA OF OKHOTSK
Sakhalin
Kuril Is.
UNION OF SOVIET SOCIALIST REPUBLICS
BALTIC SEA
Tallinn
Riga
Vilnius
Minsk
Moscow
Yaroslavl
Gor'kiy
Kazan
Chelyabinsk
Omsk
Novosibirsk
Novokuznetsk
Irkutsk
L. Baikal
Chita
Ulan Ude
Blagoveshchensk
Khabarovsk
Vladivostok
Sapporo
Hokkaidō
UNITED KINGDOM
Glasgow Edinburgh
Belfast Aberdeen Newc.SEA
NORTH SEA
Göteborg Copenhagen
Liverpool Manch.
Dublin B'ham
London Amst.
Le Havre Brux. GERM. Berlin POLAND Warsaw
Paris Bonn CZECH. Cracow Kiev Khar'kov Donetsk Volgograd Gur'yev
Munich Vienna Budapest
EUROPE FRANCE Berne Milan AUS. HUN. Belgrade Bucharest ROMANIA Odessa Rostov Krasnodar
Bordeaux Lyon Genoa YU. Sofia BULG. Sevastopol Novorossiysk Groznyy
Bilbao Marseilles Venice Adriatic Sea Tirana GREECE Istanbul BLACK SEA Batumi Tbilisi Baku
SPAIN Rome ITALY Naples Athens Izmir Ankara TURKEY Yerevan Krasnovodsk
Madrid Barcelona Palermo Crete Halab Mosul Tabriz Mashhad
PORT. Gibraltar (UK) MEDITERRANEAN SEA CYPRUS Beirut SYRIA LEB. Baghdad Tehrān Herat
Tunis MALTA Tripoli Benghāzi Damascus Amman ISR. IRAQ IRAN AFGHANISTAN Kabul Islāmābād Rawalpindi
Rabat Algiers TUNISIA Alexandria Cairo Jerusalem Suez Kuwait Basra Abadan Shīrāz Quetta Lahore
Tangier Casablanca MOROCCO ALGERIA LIBYA EGYPT Aswān Medina SAUDI Ar Riyāḑ Bandar 'Abbās PAKISTAN Delhi Agra
In Salah RED SEA Wadi Halfa Port Sudan Jiddah Mecca ARABIA Muscat OMAN Karachi Ahmadābād Kānpur Lucknow Patna NEPAL
MAURITANIA MALI NIGER CHAD Omdurman Khartoum Asmara Sanʿā YEM. SOUTH YEMEN Aden ARABIAN SEA Bombay INDIA Nāgpur Calcutta BANGLADESH Dhākā Chittagong
Tombouctou Niamey Agades SUDAN DJIBOUTI Djibouti Socotra (S.Y.) Muscat Pune Hyderābād Bay of Bengal BURMA
Bamako Kano NIGERIA Addis Ababa ETHIOPIA SOMALIA Mogadishu MALDIVES Bangalore Madras Rangoon THAILAND
IVORY COAST GHANA BENIN TOGO Ibadan Lagos CAMEROON CENT. AFR. REP. Bangui UGANDA KENYA Nairobi SEYCHELLES Colombo SRI LANKA (CEYLON) Bangkok CAMBODIA
LIB. Abidjan Accra Lomé SAO TOME EQ. GU. GABON Libreville CONGO Yaoundé ZAIRE Kisangani Kampala Victoria Mombasa Kigoma Dodoma TANZANIA Equator MALAYSIA Kuala Lumpur
Brazzaville Pointe-Noire Kinshasa Ilebo Kindu Kigoma Dar es Salaam Chagos Arch. (UK) SINGAPORE Sumatra Borneo
Luanda ANGOLA Lubumbashi MALAWI COMOROS JAVA SEA Jakarta Bandung INDONESIA Java Surabaya
Huambo ZAMBIA Lilongwe Lusaka Livingstone Harare ZIMBABWE MOZAMBIQUE Moçambique MADAGASCAR MAURITIUS Réunion (Fr.)
NAMIBIA BOTSWANA Bulawayo Sofala Antananarivo Toamasina Tropic of Capricorn
Windhoek (S.W. AFRICA) Gaborone Pretoria Johannesburg SOUTH AFRICA Maputo Cocos (Aus.)
Walvis Bay Kimberley Bloemfontein Durban TIMOR SEA ARAFURA SEA Darwin
Cape Town Cape of Good Hope Port Elizabeth East London INDIAN OCEAN AUSTRALASIA
St. Helena (UK) ATLANTIC OCEAN
Gough I. (UK)
CHINA
Ürümqi Kashi Alma Ata Frunze Tashkent Samarkand Dushanbe Ashkhabad
MONGOLIA Ulaanbaatar Hovd Harbin Changchun Shenyang Beijing (Peking) N. KOR. P'yŏngyang S. KOR. Seoul Pusan JAPAN Tōkyō Yokohama
Lanzhou Xi'an Taiyuan Tianjin Lüda SEA OF JAPAN Kita-Kyūshū Kōbe Ōsaka
ASIA Chengdu Wuhan Nanjing Shanghai EAST CHINA SEA Honshū
Lhasa TIBET Chongqing Changsha Fuzhou Okinawa
Kunming Guangzhou HONG KONG (UK) Taipei TAIWAN Tropic of Cancer
Hanoi Haiphong Victoria Hainan PACIFIC OCEAN
Chiang Mai LAOS VIETNAM Wake I. (USA) Northern Marianas
THAILAND Bangkok CAMBODIA Phnom Penh Ho Chi Minh City SOUTH CHINA SEA Luzon Manila PHILIPPINES Guam (USA)
BRUNEI Mindanao Palau Caroline Is. Truk Marshall Is.
MALAYSIA CELEBES SEA Sulawesi Moluccas Halmahera New Guinea
Kuala Lumpur SINGAPORE Borneo PAPUA NEW GUINEA New Ireland NAURU
New Britain Port Moresby New Britain SOLOMON IS. Guadalcanal
AUSTRALASIA Cairns VANUATU CORAL SEA New Caledonia (Fr.) Nouméa
Alice Springs AUSTRALIA Townsville
Fremantle Perth Brisbane Norfolk I. (Aus.)
Adelaide Newcastle Sydney
Melbourne Canberra TASMAN SEA NEW ZEALAND Auckland Wellington
TASMANIA Hobart Christchurch
Invercargill Dunedin Stewart I. (NZ) Auckland Is. (NZ) Campbell I.
St. Paul I. (Fr.) Amsterdam I. (Fr.) Crozet Is. (Fr.) Kerguelen (Fr.) Heard I. (Aus.)
Pr. Edward I. (S.A.) Marion I. (S.A.) FRENCH SOUTHERN AND ANTARCTIC LANDS
Bouvet I. Macquarie I. (Aus.)

Bottom longitude labels: Meridian of 0° Greenwich 15° 30° 45° 60° 75° East of 90° Greenwich 105° 120° 135° 150° 165° 180°

Index

Peru **29** *72*	Japan **21** *28–29*	Taiwan **35** *31*	Vanuatu **42** *33*	Ireland **20** *9*
Surinam **34** *73*	Jordan **21** *40*	Thailand **36** *30*	Western Samoa **42** *33*	Italy **21** *16*
Uruguay **41** *74*	North Korea **22** *28*	Turkey **36** *40*		Liechtenstein **24** *16*
Venezuela **42** *72*	South Korea **22** *28*	USSR **37** *24–25*	**EUROPE**	Luxembourg **24** *13*
	Kuwait **22** *41*	UAE **38** *41*	Albania **4** *17*	Malta **25** *16*
ASIA	Laos **23** *30*	Vietnam **42** *30*	Andorra **4** *15*	Monaco **26** *14*
Afghanistan **4** *42*	Lebanon **23** *45*	Yemen **43** *50*	Austria **6** *18*	Netherlands **27** *13*
Bahrain **6** *41*	Malaysia **24** *30*	Yemen, South **43** *38*	Belgium **7** *13*	Norway **28** *12*
Bangladesh **6** *43*	Maldives **25** *44*		Bulgaria **8** *17*	Poland **30** *18–19*
Bhutan **7** *43*	Mongolia **26** *26*	**AUSTRALASIA**	Cyprus **13** *45*	Portugal **30** *15*
Brunei **8** *27*	Nepal **27** *43*	Australia **5** *32–34*	Czechoslovakia **14** *18–19*	Romania **30** *17*
Burma **9** *30*	Oman **29** *38*	Fiji **21** *33*	Denmark **14** *11*	San Marino **31** *16*
Cambodia **9** *30*	Pakistan **29** *42*	Kiribati **22** *33*	Finland **16** *12*	Spain **34** *15*
China **11** *31*	Philippines **30** *27*	Nauru **27** *33*	France **16** *14*	Sweden **35** *12*
India **19** *42–44*	Qatar **30** *41*	New Zealand **28** *35*	East Germany **17** *18*	Switzerland **35** *16*
Indonesia **20** *27*	Saudi Arabia **32** *40–41*	Papua New Guinea **29** *32*	West Germany **17** *18*	UK **38** *6–9*
Iran **20** *41*	Singapore **32** *30*	Solomon Islands **33** *33*	Greece **17** *17*	Vatican City **42**
Iraq **20** *40–41*	Sri Lanka **34** *44*	Tonga **36** *33*	Hungary **19** *18–19*	Yugoslavia **43** *16–17*
Israel **20** *45*	Syria **35** *40*	Tuvalu **37** *33*	Iceland **19** *12*	

Ⓐ 40 Ⓑ ② 30 Ⓒ 20 Ⓓ 10 Ⓔ 0 Ⓕ 10 Ⓖ

Greenland
(Dan.)
Capo Farewell

Jan Mayen
(Nor.)

A R C T I C

Vesterålen

Lofoten
Narvik

ICELAND

Reykjavik

Arctic Circle

N O R W E G I A N

S E A

Trondheim

③

N O R W A Y

Sundsva

Faeroes

Bergen

Stavanger

Uppsala
Oslo
Västerås

Örebro Norrköping
S Stockholm
Vänern

Borås Linköping
Jönköping

Rockall

Shetland

N O R T H

S E A

Göteborg

Gotland

Öland

Orkney

UNITED KINGDOM
OF GREAT BRITAIN AND
NORTHERN IRELAND

Dundee Aberdeen

Glasgow
Edinburgh

Ålborg

Århus

Kiel Rostock Schwerin

DENMARK
Copenhagen
(København) Malmö

Bornholm

B a l t i c

Gdańsk

Szczecin

Belfast

IRELAND

Newcastle
Middlesborough

Blackpool Leeds
Liverpool Manchester Hull

Bremerhaven
Wilhelmshaven
Lübeck
Hamburg

E A S T

Gorzow Wlkp.

Poznań

Dublin

Sheffield Derby

Cork

Wolverhampton

Birmingham
Northampton Leicester Norwich

Swansea Cardiff Oxford
Reading Luton

Bristol

Plymouth Southampton Brighton

Isles of Scilly

Groningen

Enschede

Amsterdam

The Hague
's-Gravenhage
Rotterdam

Bremen

Hannover Wolfsburg

Paderborn Hildesheim

GERMANY

Berlin

Leipzig Dresden

Cottbus

Zielona Gora

Wroclaw

P O L

Antwerp
London Ipswich

English Channel

Channel Islands

Le Havre

Brest

Bruxelles Düsseldorf
BELGIUM Cologne
(Köln)

Lille Bonn
Valenciennes Namur Koblenz

Essen Dortmund
Kassel

Göttingen

Jena
Karl Marx
Stadt

Frankfurt

Zwickau

Prague
(Praha)

Brno

C Z E C H O S L O

Brussels

Amiens

Boulogne

Mainz

Offenbach

Darmstadt

Rouen

Reims Luxembourg LUXEMBOURG Mannheim Heidelberg

Caen

Paris Metz

Nürnberg Erlangen

Plzen

Heilbronn Regensburg

Lorient

Rennes

W E S T

Karlsruhe

Nancy Strasbourg

Vienna
(Wien)

St. Nazaire

Le Mans

Troyes

Stuttgart

Bratislava

Nantes

Angers Orléans

Ulm Augsburg

Tours

Freiburg Mulhouse

Munich
(München)

Gyö

Loire

Dijon
Montbéliard

Salzburg

H U N

Bay of
Biscay

Besançon Berne
(Bern) Basle

Innsbruck

A U S T R I A

La Coruña

F R A N C E

Limoges

Clermont-
Ferrand

Lyon

Geneva
(Genève) Zurich

SWITZERLAND

Graz

Lausanne LIECHTENSTEIN

Bolzano

Gijón
Oviedo Santander Baracaldo

St-Étienne Villeurbanne

Novara Bergamo Udine
Brescia

Ljubljana Pécs

Trieste Zagreb

Vigo

León Bilbao
Vitoria

Bayonne Pau

Burgos

Valence

Milan
(Milano)
Verona

Turin
(Torino)

Padova
Venice
(Venezia)

Y U G O S

Oporto
(Porto)

Valladolid

Logroño

San Sebastián

Toulouse

Ebro

Montpellier

Nîmes

Rhône

Piacenza

Parma

Alessandria

Reggio

La
Spezia

Ferrara

Bologna

Florence
(Firenze)

Rimini

Split Sarajevo

P O R T U G A L

Salamanca

ANDORRA

Sabadell

Zaragoza

Marseilles
(Marseille)
Perpignan

Nice

Genoa
(Genova)

MONACO

Pisa Livorno

I T A L Y

SAN
MARINO

Ancona

A D R I A T I C S E A

Toulon

Lisbon
(Lisboa)

S P A I N
Madrid

Alcalá de H.

Tarrasa
Tarragona

Corsica
(Corse)

Perugia

Terni

Pescara

Foggia

Bari

Badajoz

Toledo

Barcelona
Badalona

Bastia

Rome
(Roma)

Faro

Córdoba

Albacete

Castellon
de la P.

Valencia

Balearic Islands

Sardinia
(Sardegna)

Ajaccio

Sassari

Olbia

Naples
(Napoli)

Taranto

T Y R R H E N I A N
S E A

Sevilla Huelva
Jerez de la F.

Granada

Murcia

Elche

Alicante

Ibiza

Minorca
(Menorca)

Majorca
(Mallorca)

Cagliari

Cosenza

Cádiz

Málaga

Cartagena

Almería

M E D I T E R

Palermo

Messina

Tangiers
(Tanger)

Gibraltar (U.K.)

Casablanca Rabat

Ceuta (Sp.)
Tetouan

Melilla
(Sp.)

Oran

Algiers
(Alger)

Sicily
(Sicilia)

Reggio di Calabria

Syracuse

R A N E A N S E A

Madeira
(Port.)

M O R O C C O

Marrakech

A L G E R I A

Tunis

MALTA

TUNISIA

Canary Is.

Ⓓ 10 Ⓔ 0 Ⓕ 10 Ⓖ

1:15M

200 400 600 km
100 200 300 mis

50

40

④

⑤

50

40

30

Grid references (top)

H 30 J 40 K 50 L 60 M 70 ② N 80 90

Water bodies and geographic features

OCEAN

Barents Sea

O.Kolguyev

White Sea

Gulf of Bothnia

Lake Onega

Lake Ladoga

Gulf of Finland

Rybinskoye Vdkhr.

Kamskoye Vdkhr.

Kuybyshevskoye Vdkhr.

Volgogradskoye Vdkhr.

Kremenchugskoye Vdkhr.

Kakhovskoye Vdkhr.

Tsimlyanskoye Vdkhr.

BLACK SEA

CASPIAN SEA

Aral Sea (Aral'skoye More)

AEGEAN SEA

Dodecanese

Cyclades

Crete

The Gulf

Rivers

Pechora, Ob', Irtysh, Ishim, Tavda, Sev. Dvina, Kama, Volga, Ural, Don, Dnepr, Daugava, Neman, Danube (Danubel), Dunav, Firat, Tigris, Euphrates

Countries

FINLAND

UNION OF SOVIET SOCIALIST REPUBLICS

POLAND (...ND)

...KIA

HUNGARY (...RY)

ROMANIA

...AVIA (YUGOSLAVIA)

BULGARIA

ALBANIA

GREECE

TURKEY

SYRIA

IRAQ

IRAN

LEBANON

CYPRUS

Cities

Murmansk, Apatity, Luleå, Oulu, Umeå, Vaasa, Koupio, Jyväskylä, Petrozavodsk, Pori, Tampere, Åland, Turku, Helsinki, Tallinn, Vyborg, Leningrad, Pskov, Riga, Daugavpils, Kaliningrad, Kaunas, Vilnius, Grodno, Minsk, Orsha, Warsaw (Warszawa), Łódź, Brest, Cracow, L'vov, Budapest, Oradea, Cluj, Tirgu Mureş, Szeged, Arad, Timişoara, Belgrade (Beograd), Niš, Pleven, Sofiya, Skopje, Plovdiv, Edirne, Tirane, Thessaloniki, Lárisa, Pátrai, Kalámai, Khaniá, Athens (Athina)

Severodvinsk, Arkhangel'sk, Syktyvkar, Kotlas, Ukhta, Pechora, Vorkuta, Sverdlovsk, Perm', Chelyabinsk, Magnitogorsk, Ufa, Kirov, Kazan', Kuybyshev, Tol'yatti, Cherepovets, Vologda, Yaroslavl', Gor'kiy, Kalinin, Zagorsk, Moscow, Tula, Voronezh, Saratov, Kursk, Kiev, Khar'kov, Donetsk, Dnepropetrovsk, Rog, Zaporozh'ye, Zhdanov, Rostov, Volgograd, Astrakhan', Gur'yev, Shevchenko, Makhachkala, Ordzhonikidze, Krasnodar, Kerch', Sevastopol', Odessa, Constanta, Galaţi, Bucharest (Bucureşti), Varna, Burgas, Istanbul, Uskudar, Bursa, Eskişehir, Ankara, Izmir, Denzil, Antlaya, Adana, Samsun, Trabzon, Erzurum, Batumi, Tbilisi, Yerevan, Baku, Tabriz, Tehrān, Urumtyeh, Mosul, Halab, Himṣ, Beirūt, Damascus, Nicosia, Baghdād, Basra, Abadan, Estahān, Omsk

N (Narvik area?)

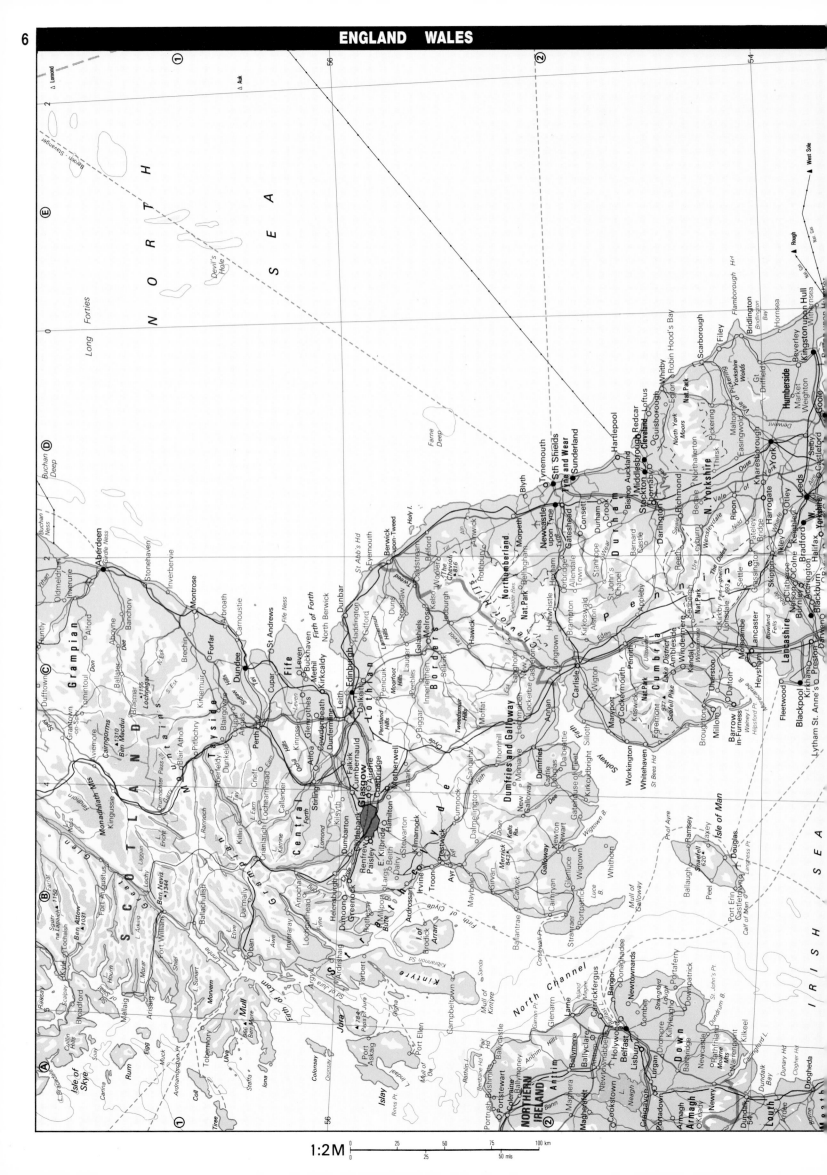

1:2M

ENGLAND

WALES

Dyfed · Powys · Clwyd · Gwynedd · Glamorgan · Gwent

Norfolk · Suffolk · Essex · Kent · East Sussex · West Sussex · Hampshire · Isle of Wight · Dorset · Somerset · Devon · Cornwall · Wilts. · Berks. · Oxon · Hereford and Worcester · Shropshire · Staffordshire · Cheshire · Lincoln · Clwyd · Avon

London · Gtr London · Westminster · Croydon

Birmingham · Dudley · Walsall · W. Bromwich · Wolverhampton

ENGLISH CHANNEL

Bristol Channel

Celtic Sea

Cardigan Bay

St George's Channel

Liverpool Bay

The Wash

Major towns: Dublin · Dún Laoghaire · Bray · Wicklow · Arklow · Wexford · Rosslare · Holyhead · Bangor · Caernarfon · Pwllheli · Aberystwyth · Cardigan · Fishguard · Haverfordwest · Milford Haven · Pembroke · Tenby · Carmarthen · Llanelli · Swansea · Neath · Port Talbot · Bridgend · Porthcawl · Cardiff · Penarth · Barry · Newport · Cwmbran · Pontypool · Merthyr Tydfil · Aberdare · Rhondda · Pontypridd · Caerphilly · Chepstow · Monmouth · Abergavenny · Brecon · Builth Wells · Llandrindod Wells · Rhayader · Newtown · Welshpool · Montgomery · Knighton · Leominster · Hereford · Ross-on-Wye · Ledbury · Great Malvern · Worcester · Droitwich · Kidderminster · Stourport · Bromsgrove · Redditch · Stratford-on-Avon · Warwick · Leamington Spa · Rugby · Coventry · Nuneaton · Hinckley · Tamworth · Cannock · Stafford · Stone · Stoke-on-Trent · Newcastle-under-Lyme · Crewe · Nantwich · Northwich · Middlewich · Winsford · Knutsford · Altrincham · Stockport · Manchester · Salford · Bolton · Bury · Rochdale · Oldham · Wigan · St Helens · Warrington · Widnes · Runcorn · Ellesmere Port · Chester · Flint · Mold · Wrexham · Ruabon · Oswestry · Shrewsbury · Telford · Wellington · Market Drayton · Whitchurch · Ludlow · Bishops Castle · Church Stretton

Plymouth · Saltash · Looe · Fowey · St Austell · Newquay · Padstow · Wadebridge · Bodmin · Liskeard · Launceston · Bude · Okehampton · Tavistock · Truro · Redruth · Camborne · St Ives · Hayle · Helston · Penzance · Land's End · Lizard Pt · St Mary's · Isles of Scilly

Exeter · Exmouth · Sidmouth · Seaton · Axminster · Lyme Regis · Bridport · Dorchester · Weymouth · Portland · Swanage · Wareham · Poole · Bournemouth · Christchurch · Lymington · Lyndhurst · Southampton · Eastleigh · Fareham · Gosport · Portsmouth · Havant · Chichester · Bognor Regis · Littlehampton · Worthing · Brighton · Newhaven · Seaford · Eastbourne · Bexhill · Hastings · St Leonards · Rye · New Romney · Folkestone · Dover · Deal · Sandwich · Ramsgate · Broadstairs · Margate · Herne Bay · Whitstable · Faversham · Canterbury · Ashford · Maidstone · Tonbridge · Royal Tunbridge Wells · Sevenoaks · Rochester · Chatham · Gillingham · Sheerness · Gravesend · Dartford

Boulogne · Calais · Dunkerque · Dieppe · Le Havre · Cherbourg

Rotterdam · Zeebrugge · Hook van Holland

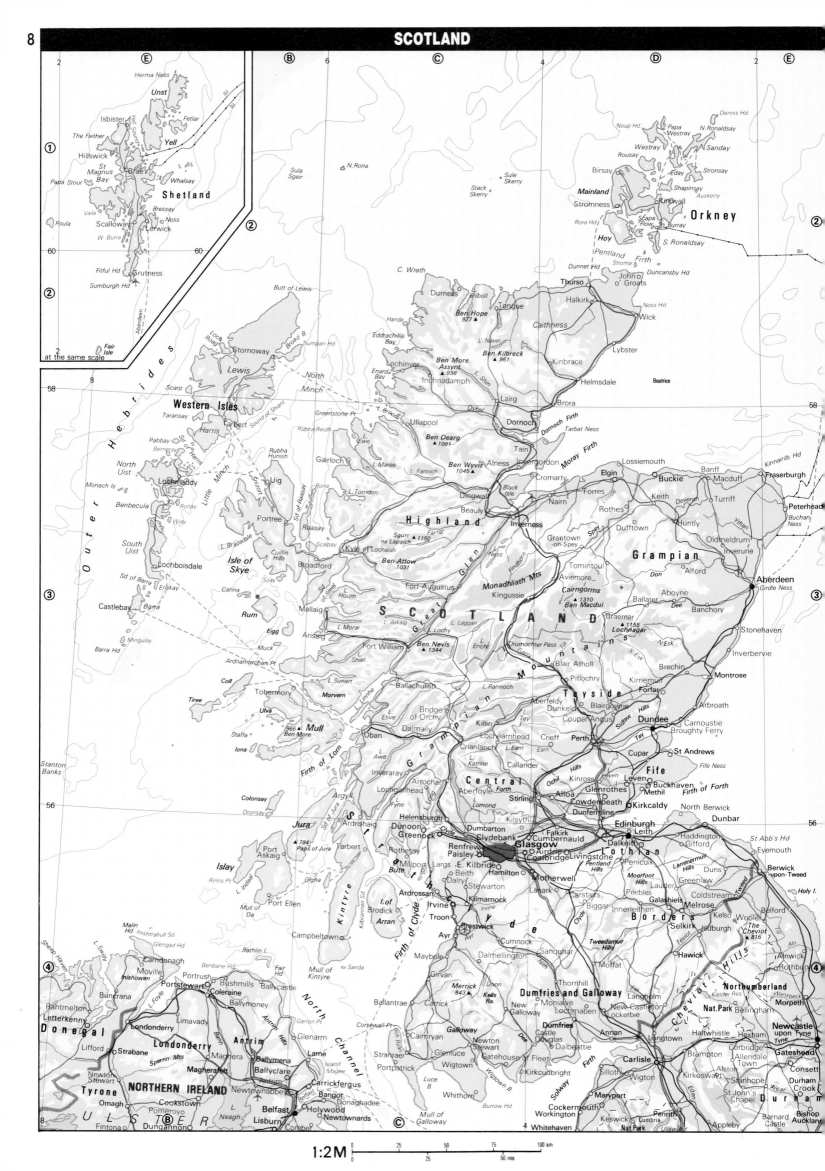

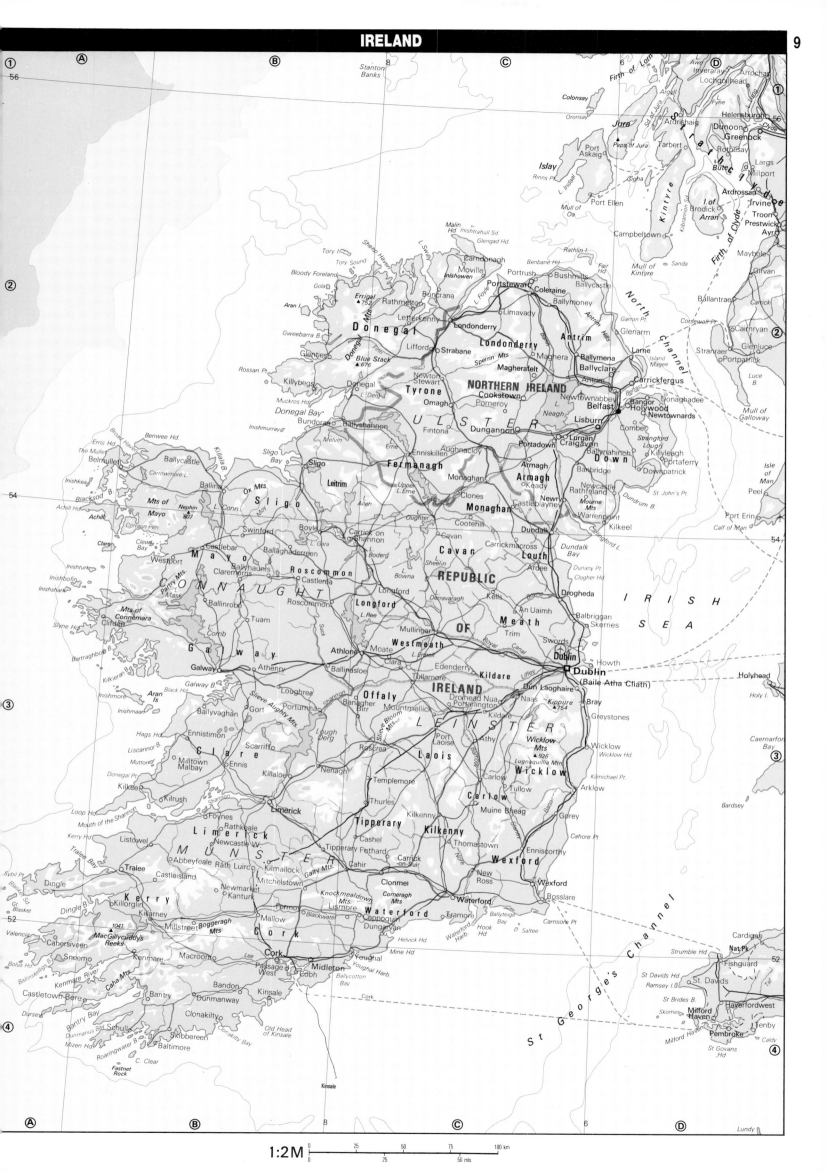

Herma Ness
Isbister
Fetlar
Yell   Unst
Nordhordland
Bergen
Whalsay
St Magnus B.
Shetland
Sotra
Viking Bank
Lerwick
Foula
Sunnhordland
Sumburgh Hd
Leirvik
Bømlo
Skj
Haugesund
Karmøy

Westray
Rousay   Sanday
Sula Sgeir
N.Rona
Sule Skerry
Stronsay
Fair Isle
Stromness
Stack Skerry
Kirkwall
Hoy   Scapa Flow   Orkney

Flannan Is
Butt of Lewis
C. Wrath
Duncansby Hd
Thurso
Ben Hope
927
Wick
Helmsdale
St Kilda
Lewis
Stornoway
Ben More
Assynt
998
Outer Hebrides
Harris
Ullapool
Dornoch
Dornoch Firth
N.Uist
Dingwall
Moray Firth
Elgin
Banff
Fraserburgh
S.Uist
Portree
Skye
Inverness
Peterhead
Barra
Kyle
of Lochalsh
L.Ness
Spey
Buchan Ness
Rum
Mallaig
Fort
Augustus
Ben Macdui
1309
Don
Aberdeen
Coll
Fort William
SCOTLAND
Ben Nevis
1344
Dee
Braemar
Stonehaven
Tiree
Ben
Lawers
1214
Pitlochry
Grampian   Mts
Montrose
Mull
Oban
L.Awe
Perth
Dundee
Arbroath
L. Lomond
Colonsay
Jura
Stirling
St Andrews
Islay
Greenock
Paisley
Kirkcaldy
F.of Lorn
L.Tay
Glasgow
Edinburgh
Long Forties
Motherwell
Berwick-upon-Tweed
Campbeltown
Arran
Irvine
Kilmarnock
White
Coomb
822
Galashiels
Holy I.
St Abbs Hd
Tory I.
Malin Hd
Ayr
Moffat
Hawick
Great Fisher Bank
Rathlin I.
F.of Clyde
Merrick
843
Alnwick
Aran I.
Errigal
752
Coleraine
Girvan
Dumfries
Cheviots
Morpeth
N   O   R   T   H
Londonderry
Ballymena
Stranraer
Nith
Blyth
Rossan Pt
Donegal
N. IRELAND
Larne
Kirkcudbright
Carlisle
Newcastle upon Tyne
S E A
Donegal B.
L.Erne
Omagh
Belfast
Solway Firth
Gateshead
S.Shields
Enniskillen
Bangor
Penrith
Durham
Sunderland
Erris Hd
L.Neagh
Portadown
Luce B.
Scafell Pike
977
Darlington
Hartlepool
Sligo B.
Sligo
Armagh
Newry
Douglas
Isle of Man
Kendal
Middlesbrough
Achill
Ballina
Monaghan
Dundalk
Barrow-
in-Furness
Yorkshire Moors
Dogger Bank
Clew B.
Castlebar
Cavan
Morecambe
Lancaster
Scarborough
L.Conn
Boyle
Drogheda
Blackpool
Harrogate
Ouse
Flamborough Hd
L.Mask
Roscommon
Longford
IRISH   SEA
Preston
Bradford
York
Slyne
Hd
L.Ree
Athlone
Mullingar
Bolton
Leeds
Hull
Galway
Shannon
Liverpool
Huddersfield
Spurn Hd
Aran Is
Galway B.
Monasterevan
Dublin
(Baile Atha Cliath)
Birkenhead
Manchester
Doncaster
Grimsby
Ennis
Nenagh
Port
Laoise
Dun Laoghaire
Holyhead
Anglesey
Warrington
Sheffield
Humber
Mouth of
the Shannon
Kilrush
REP. OF
IRELAND
Carlow
Bray
Bangor
Snowdon
1085
Chester
Crewe
Stoke
on-Trent
Lincoln
The Wash
Tralee
Limerick
Tipperary
Kilkenny
Wicklow Mts
Wicklow
Pwllheli
Dee
Shrewsbury
Derby
Nottingham
Dingle
Clonmel
Arklow
Trent
Dingle B.
Blackwater
Waterford
Barrow
Cardigan
Aberystwyth
Wolverhampton
Leicester
Nene
Ouse
King's Lynn
Norwich
Carrauntoohill
1041
Killarney
Dungarvan
Youghal
Bay
WALES
Birmingham
Coventry
Peterborough
Great Yarmouth
Cork
St George's Channel
St David's
Hd
Builth
Wells
ENGLAND
Worcester
Northampton
Bedford
Newmarket
Lowestoft
Bantry B.
Bantry
Old Hd
of Kinsale
Fishguard
Carmarthen
Brecon
Wye
Severn
Gloucester
Milton
Keynes
Cambridge
Ipswich
C. Clear
Pembroke
Swansea
Newport
Oxford
Luton
Colchester
Felixstowe
Harwich
Lundy I.
Cardiff
Bristol
Swindon
Windsor
London
Chelmsford
Southend-
on-Sea
Bristol Chan.
Bath
Reading
Thames
Maidstone
Barnstaple
Weston-
super-Mare
Canterbury
Dover
Bude
Taunton
Salisbury
Guildford
Winchester
Crawley
Folkestone
Dover
Exeter
Bournemouth
Southampton
Brighton
Hastings
Eastbourne Str.
Boulogne
Newquay
Dartmoor
Weymouth
Portsmouth
Penzance
Truro
Plymouth
Torbay
Isle of Wight
English   Channel
Isles of Scilly
Falmouth
Prawle Pt
Land's End
Lizard Pt

NORDHORDLAND area (right side):
Terschelling
Harlingen
Vlieland
Texel
Den Helder
Hoorn
Alkmaar
Zaanstad
Amsterdam
Haarlem
Leiden   Hilversum
Amersfoort
The Hague
('s-Gravenhage)
Utrecht
Rotterdam
Dordrecht
's-Hertogenbosch
Breda
Tilburg
Eindhoven
Vlissingen
Antwerp
Antwerpen
Zeebrugge
Bruges
Mechelen
Hasselt
Oostende
Gent
Brussels
(Bruxelles)
Leuven
Calais
Dunkirk
St-Omer
Tourcoing
Roubaix
Lille
Tournai
Soignies
Namur
Charleroi
Béthune
Lens
Mons
Montreuil
Douai
Valenciennes
Maubeuge
Abbeville
Cambrai
Denain
Fourmies
Le Tréport
C. de la Hague
Dieppe
Amiens
St-Quentin
Charleville-
Mézières
Sedan
Alderney
Pte de Barfleur
Neufchâtel
Montdidier
Laon
Aisne
Guernsey
Sark
Channel Is
(U.K.)
Jersey
St Helier
Cherbourg
Valognes
Fécamp
Bolbec
Rouen
Beauvais
Compiègne
Senlis
Reims
Verdun
St-Lô
Bayeux
Deauville
Le Havre
Seine
Soissons
Château-
Thierry
Epernay
Caen
Lisieux
Elbeuf
Louviers
Mantes
Cergy-
Pontoise
Meaux
Chalons
-s.-M.
Golfe de St-Malo
Granville
Coutances
Evreux
Eure
Dreux
Versailles
Paris
Sézanne
Vitry-l.-F.
Roscoff
Morlaix
St-Malo
Dinan
Mont-
St-Michel
Domfront
Argentan
Alençon
Chartres
Etampes
Melun
Provins
Romilly-s.-S.
St-Diz
Brest
St-Brieuc
Carhaix-
Plouguer
Fougères
Mayenne
Fontainebleau
Troyes
Châteaulin
Loudéac
Pontivy
Vitré
Laval
Le Mans
Sens
Bar-s-A
Quimper
Quimperlé
Rennes
FRANCE
Chaumont
Concarneau
Ploërmel
Lorient

NORTH
SEA

ICELAND

Bolungarvik Isafjörður Drangajökull Grimsey
Siglufjörður Olafsfjörður Bakkaflói
Dalvik Húsavik
Sauðárkrókur Akureyri Njarðvik
Blönduós Seyðisfjörður
Biargtangar Glama 845 Húnaflói Neskaupstaður
Breiðafjörður Stykkishólmur Langjökull Hofsjökull Eskifjörður
Faxaflói Akranes Tungnafellsjökull Snæfell 1833
Reykjavik Kópavogur Vatnajökull
Hafnarfjörður Öræfajökull 2119
Keflavík Selfoss Mýrdalsjökull Ingólfshöfði
Grindavik Surtsey Vestmannaeyjar

Faeroes (Faerøerne) (Den.)
Streymoy
Vágar Tórshavn
Sandoy
Suðuroy
at the same scale 7W

N O R W E G I A N   S E A

A R C T I C   O C E A N

B A R E N T S   S E A

Nordkapp Honningsvåg Vardø
Hammerfest Vadsø
Tromsø Lakselv Kirkenes Murmansk
Harstad Karasjok Nikel
Narvik Kiruna Rovaniemi
Bodø Gällivare Kemijärvi
Luleå Oulu
Sundsvall

F I N L A N D

Vaasa Kuopio Joensuu
Pori Tampere
Turku Helsinki (Helsingfors) Leningrad

Trondheim
Östersund
Bergen Oslo Uppsala
Stockholm
Göteborg

B A L T I C   S E A

ESTONIAN S.S.R.
Tallinn Narva
Pärnu Tartu Pskov

Gulf of Riga
Ventspils Riga LATVIAN S.S.R.
Liepāja Daugavpils

Klaipēda LITHUANIAN S.S.R.
Kaunas Vilnius

DENMARK
Copenhagen Malmö
Kolding Odense

Kiel Kaliningrad Minsk
Lübeck Gdynia BELORUSSIAN S.S.R.
Rostock Gdańsk (Danzig)
Hamburg Szczecin
Bremen P O L A N D
WEST EAST Berlin Poznań Warsaw
GERMANY GERMANY

1 : 7.5 M
100 200 300 km
100 150 mls

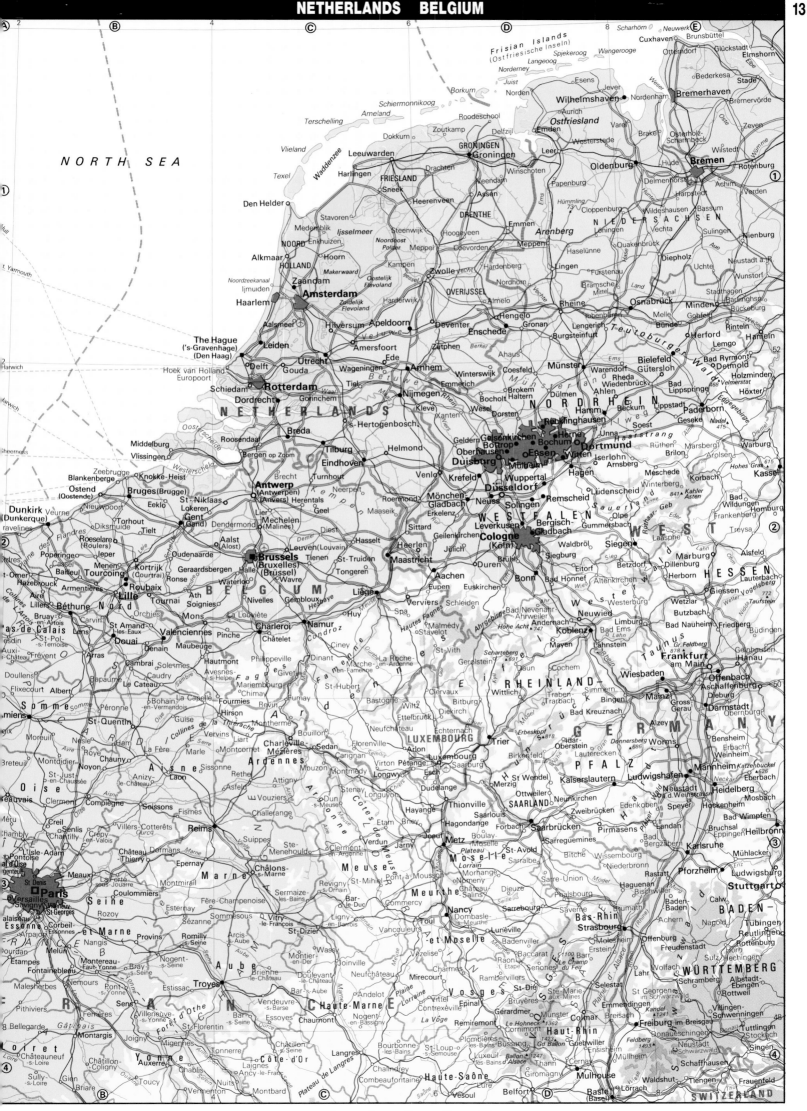

NORTH SEA

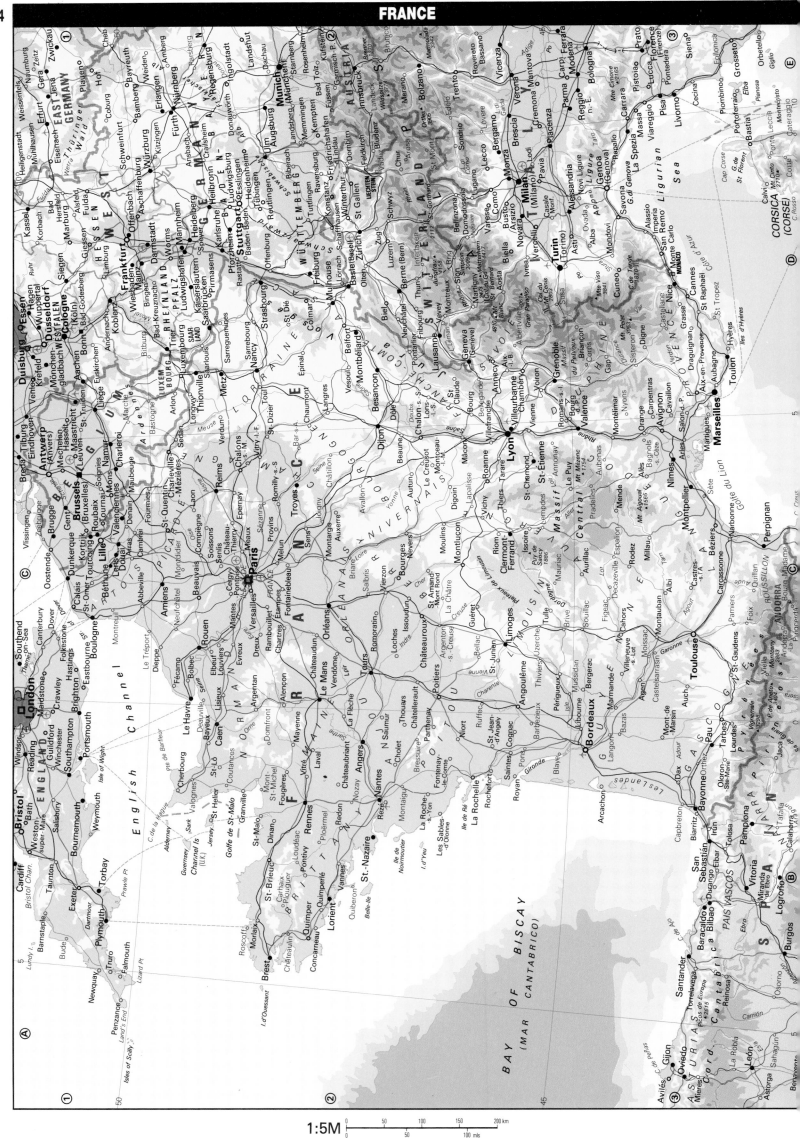

1:5M

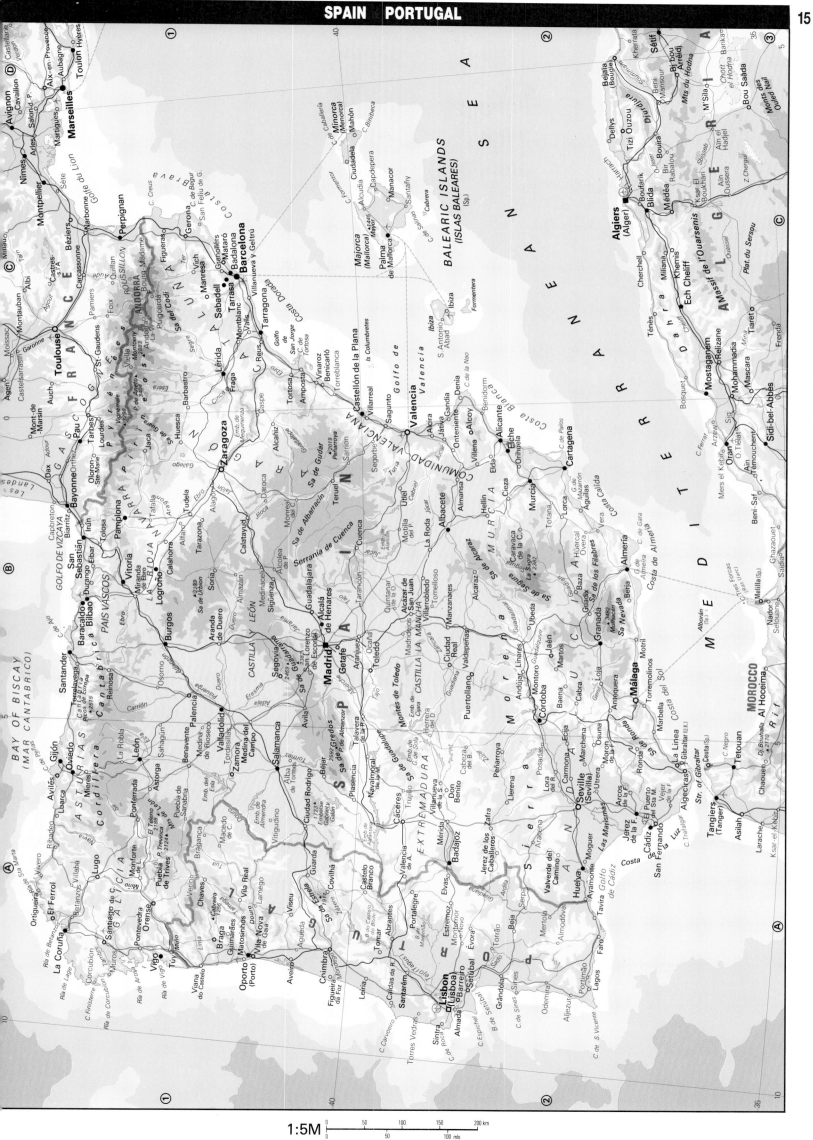

1:5M
50 100 150 200 km
0 50 100 mls

1:5M

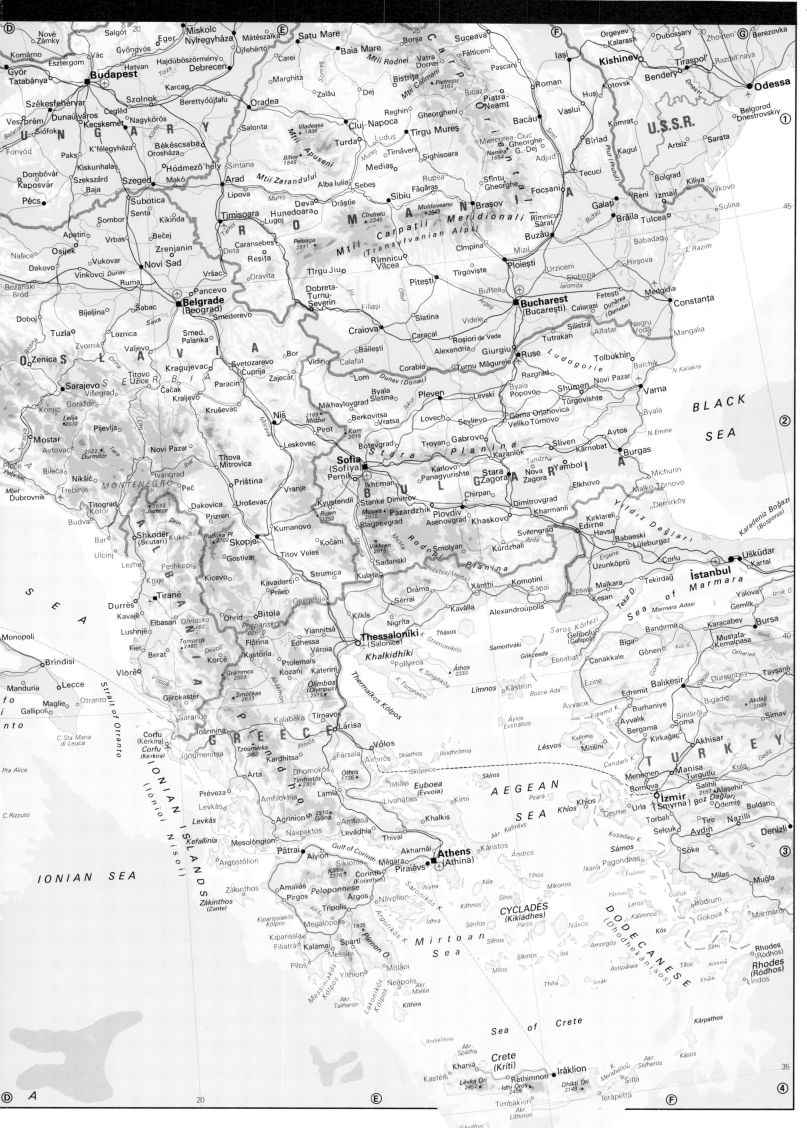

1:5M

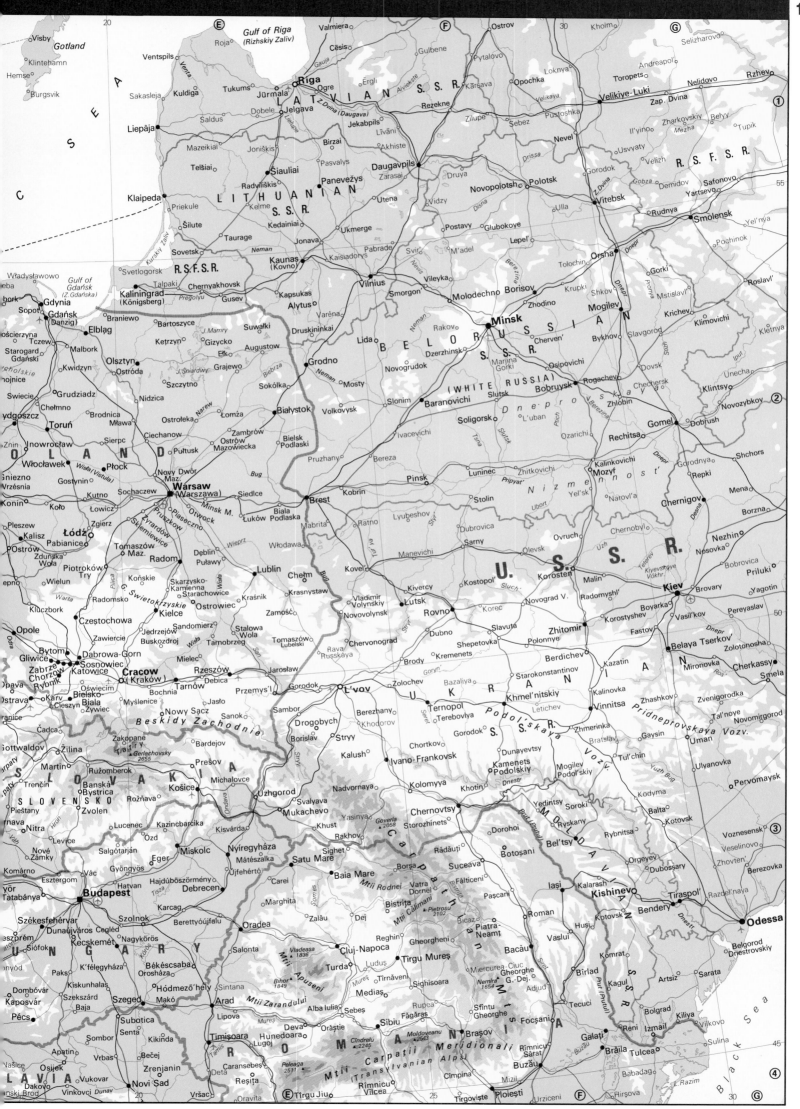

BARENTS SEA
(Barentsovo More)

Pechorskoye More

NORWEGIAN SEA

WHITE SEA (Beloye More)

Novaya Zemlya

Kol'skiy Poluostrov

Timanskiy Kryazh

Severnyy Ural

Zapadno Sibirskaya Nizmennost'

Komi A.S.S.R.

Karelian A.S.S.R.

Udmurt A.S.S.R.

Tatar A.S.S.R.

Mari A.S.S.R.

Chuvash A.S.S.R.

Mordovian A.S.S.R.

R.S.F.S.R.

Bashkir A.S.S.R.

Bashkir

R U S S I A N   S . F . S . R .

FINLAND

SWEDEN

NORWAY

Lappland

ESTONIAN S.S.R.

LATVIAN S.S.R.

LITHUANIAN S.S.R.

BELORUSSIAN S.S.R.

RUSSIAN S.F.S.R.

POLAND

BALTIC SEA

Gulf of Bothnia

Gulf of Finland

Gulf of Riga

Lake Ladoga

Lake Onega

Arctic Circle

MOSCOW (Moskva)

Leningrad

Murmansk

Archangel

Sverdlovsk

Chelyabinsk

Perm

Ustinov

Kazan'

Gor'kiy

Kuybyshev

Yoshkar Ola

Cheboksary

Saransk

Stockholm

Helsinki

Tallinn

Riga

Vilnius

Minsk

Warsaw (Warszawa)

Trondheim

Vorkuta

Salekhard

Syktyvkar

Ukhta

Pechora

Vologda

Kirov

Novgorod

Pskov

Smolensk

Tula

Ryazan'

1:10M

0   100   200   300   400 km

0   100   200 mls

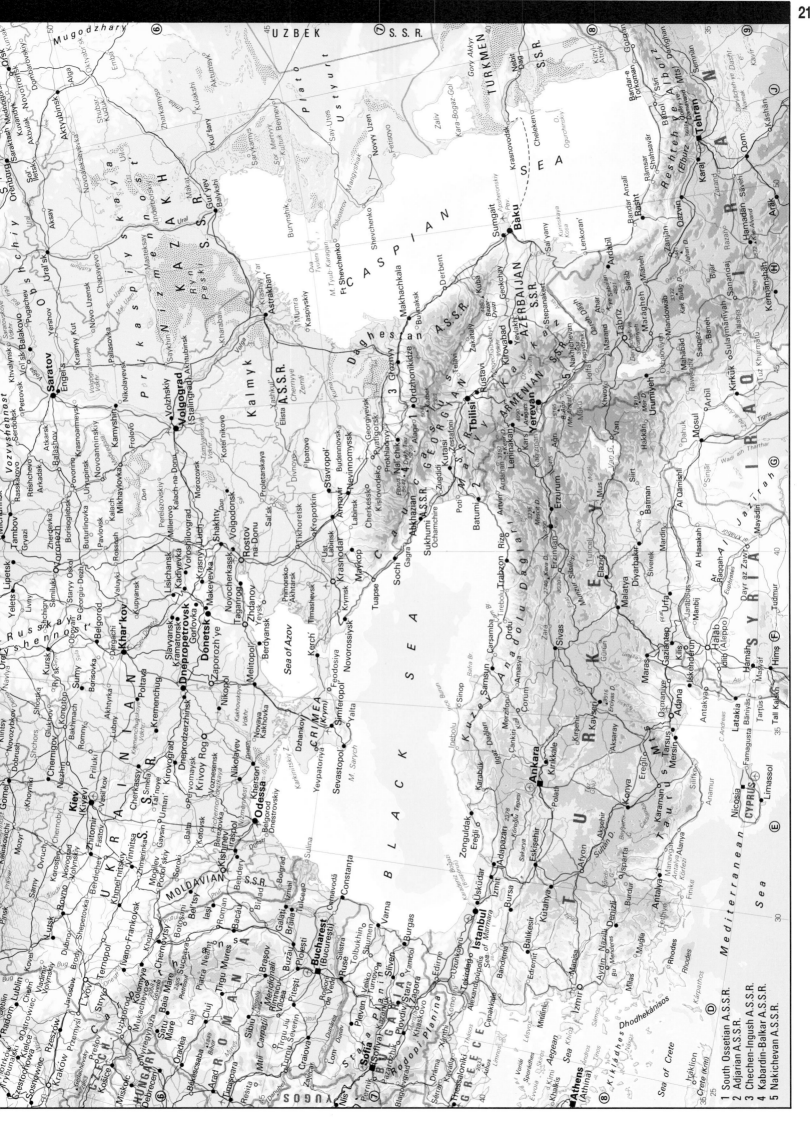

ICELAND

ARCTIC OCEAN

Greenland (Den.)

③ ② ①

Ⓐ

Ⓑ

Ⓒ Svalbard (Nor.)

Ⓛ

Ⓚ

Ⓙ

Ⓗ

Ⓖ

Ⓔ Ⓕ

Barents Sea

Novaya Zemlya

Severnaya Zemlya

Faeroes (Den.)

Novosibirskiye Ostrova

Ⓐ PORT.

SPAIN

IRELAND

Dublin □

Edinburgh □

London ■ UNITED KINGDOM

NORWAY Oslo □

DENMARK

NETH.

W. LUX.

GERMANY

FRANCE

Paris ■

SWITZ.

Marseilles ○

Corsica ITALY

Sardinia

Rome ■

Ⓑ Tunis ○

Sicily

AUSTRIA HUNGARY

CZECHOSLOVAKIA

POLAND

Warsaw ■

Copenhagen ■

Stockholm ■

Baltic Sea

Riga ○

Helsinki □

SWEDEN

FINLAND

Murmansk ○

Arkhangel'sk ○

White Sea

L. Onega

L. Ladoga

Leningrad ●

Yaroslavl' ○

Moscow ● Gorkiy ○

Perm ○

Vorkuta ○

Noril'sk ○

Lena

Yakutsk ○

Arctic Circle

ALB.

YUGOSLAVIA

ROMANIA

Bucureşti ●

BULGARIA

GREECE

Athens ■

Crete

Minsk ●

Kiev ●

Dnepropetrovsk ●

Odessa ●

Black Sea

Istanbul ●

Ankara ●

TURKEY

Khar'kov ●

Rostov ●

Voronezh ○

Saratov ●

Volgograd ●

Volga

Ufa ○

Kuybyshev ●

Ural'sk ○

Astrakhan' ○

UNION OF SOVIET SOCIALIST REPUBLICS

Sverdlovsk ●

Chelyabinsk ●

Omsk ○

Ob'

Karaganda ○

Semipalatinsk ○

L. Balkhash

Krasnoyarsk ○

Novosibirsk ●

Barnaul ○

Bratsk ○

Irkutsk ○

L. Baikal

Ulan 'Ude ○

Yenisey

CYPRUS

Beirut ○ LEB.

Jerusalem □ ISRAEL

Adana ○

Halab ○

Damascus ● SYRIA

Amman ○ JOR.

Baghdad ■

IRAQ

Mosul ○

Tbilisi ●

Yerevan ●

Tabrīz ○

Baku ●

Caspian Sea

Ashkhabad ○

Tehrān ●

Mashhad ○

Esfahān ○

Herat ○

Aral Sea

Aral'sk ○

Oz. Issyk Kul'

Alma Ata ●

Tashkent ●

Ürümqi ○

SINKIANG

Qinghai Hu

Ⓑ LIBYA

Alexandria ○

Cairo ■

EGYPT

Aswān ○

Nile

RED SEA

Ⓒ

SUDAN

Khartoum □

Asmara ○

SAUDI ARABIA

Makkah ○

Riyadh ●

BAHRAIN

QATAR

Abū Dhabi □

U.A.E.

KUWAIT

The Gulf

Basra ○

Ābādān ○

Kermān ○

IRAN

Kabul □

AFGHANISTAN

Islamabad □

Kashmir

Lahore ●

PAKISTAN

Indus

TIBET

Lhasa ○

CHINA

Lanzhou ○

Chengdu ●

Chongqing ●

Xi'an ●

Zhengzhou ○

Wuhan ●

Changsha ○

Chang Jiang

Guiyang ○

Kunming ○

INNER MONGOLIA

MONGOLIA

Ulaanbaatar (Ulan Bator) ○

Beijing ■

Tianjin ●

Taiyuan ●

Qiqihar

Oihi

Guangzhou ●

Ⓒ

LIBYA

ETHIOPIA

Ādis Ābeba ■

DJIBOUTI

Aden ○

G. of Aden

YEMEN

San'ā ○

S. YEMEN

OMAN

Muscat ○

ARABIAN SEA

Socotra (S.Yemen)

Karachi ●

Hyderābād ○

Ahmadābād ●

Bombay ●

Delhi ●

Agra ○

Jaipur ○

Kānpur ●

Lucknow ○

Allahabad ○

Jabalpur ○

Nāgpur ○

INDIA

Godavari

Krishna

Hyderabad ●

Bangalore ●

Madras ●

NEPAL

Kathmandu ○

BHUTAN

Thimphu ○

Patna ○

Ganga

BANGLA DESH

Dhaka ■

Calcutta ●

Chittagong ○

Imphal ○

Brahmaputra

Mandalay ○

BURMA

Rangoon ■

Moulmein ○

Chiang Mai ○

THAILAND

Bangkok ■

Hanoi □

Haiphong ○

Haina Dao

LAOS

Vientiane ○

Da Nang ○

VIETNAM

Mekong

CAMBODIA

Phnom Penh ●

Ho-Chi-Minh ●

Surat Thani ○

SOUT

Ⓓ

KENYA

SOMALIA

Mogadishu (Muqdisho) ○

Mombasa ○

Equator

Dar es Salaam ■

TANZANIA

SEYCHELLES

Laccadive Is. (Ind.)

Madurai ○

Jaffna ○

SRI LANKA

Colombo □ Kandy ○

MALDIVES

Bay of Bengal

Andaman Is. (Ind.)

Nicobar Is. (Ind.)

INDIAN OCEAN

Kota Bharu ○

George Town ○

Medan ○

MALAY

Kuala Lumpur ○

SINGAPORE

SUMATERA

Padang ○

Palembang ○

Ⓔ

MOZAMBIQUE

COMOROS

Aldabra Is (Sey.)

MADAGASCAR

Antananarivo ○

Chagos Arch. (U.K.)

Cocos Is (Aust.)

Christmas I (Aust.)

Jakarta ■

Ⓓ Ⓔ Ⓕ

1:40M

| 0 | 400 | 800 | 1200 | 1600 km |

| 0 | 400 | 800 mls |

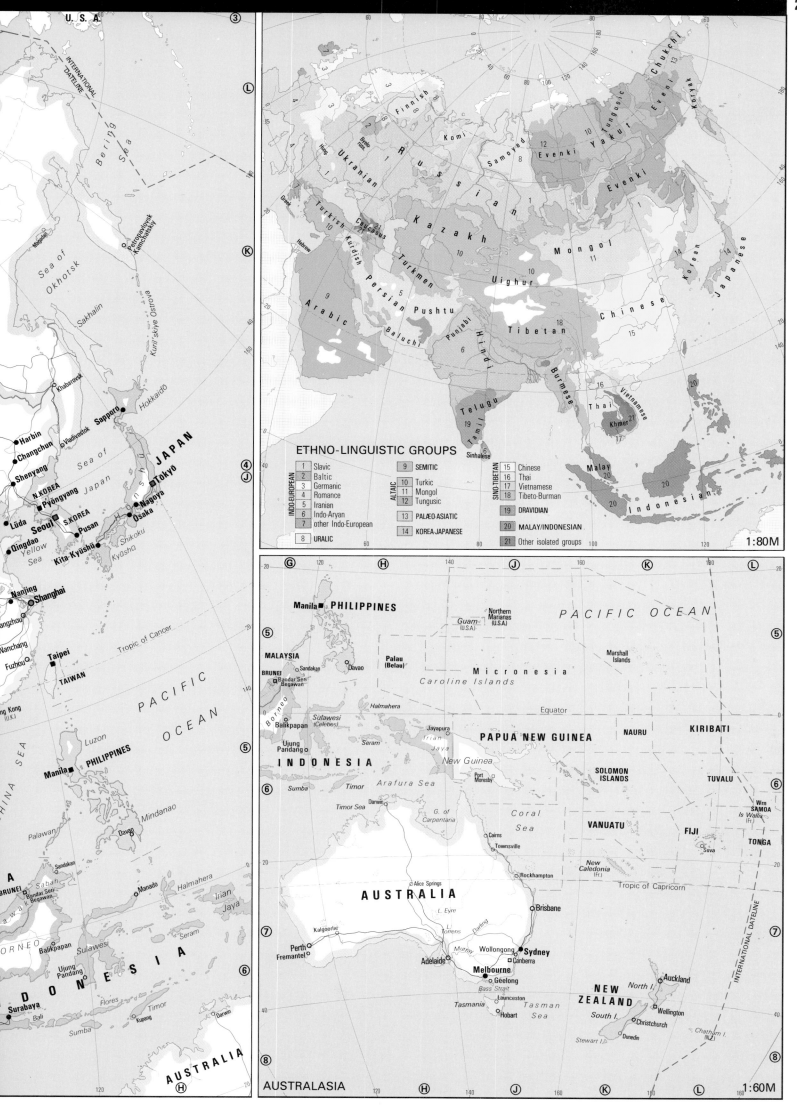

U.S.A.

INTERNATIONAL DATELINE

Bering Sea

Magadan

Petropavlovsk-Kamchatskiy

Sea of Okhotsk

Sakhalin

Kuril'skiye Ostrova

Khabarovsk

Vladivostok

Harbin

Changchun

Shenyang

Sea of Japan

Sapporo

Hokkaidō

JAPAN

N.KOREA

Pyŏngyang

Lüda

Seoul

S.KOREA

Pusan

Tōkyō

Nagoya

Ōsaka

Shikoku

Kita-Kyūshū

Kyūshū

Qingdao

Yellow Sea

Nanjing

Shanghai

Hangzhou

Nanchang

Fuzhou

Taipei

TAIWAN

ong Kong (U.K.)

PACIFIC OCEAN

SOUTH CHINA SEA

Luzon

PHILIPPINES

Manila

Mindanao

Palawan

Davao

Sandakan

BRUNEI

Sabah

Bandar Seri Begawan

awak

ORNEO

Balikpapan

Sulawesi

Ujung Pandang

Manado

Halmahera

Irian Jaya

Seram

INDONESIA

Surabaya

Bali

Flores

Timor

Kupang

Sumba

Darwin

AUSTRALIA

ETHNO-LINGUISTIC GROUPS

Finnish

Komi

Samoyed

R u s s i a n

Evenki

Yakut

Chukchi

Evenki

Kazakh

Korean

Japanese

Ukranian

Greek

Hebrew

Turkish

Caucasus

Kurdish

Persian

Turkmen

Pushtu

Baluchi

A r a b i c

Punjabi

Hindi

Uighur

Mongol

Chinese

Tibetan

Telugu

Tamil

Sinhalese

Burmese

Thai

Vietnamese

Khmer

Malay

I n d o n e s i a n

INDO-EUROPEAN	1	Slavic		
	2	Baltic		
	3	Germanic		
	4	Romance		
	5	Iranian		
	6	Indo-Aryan		
	7	other Indo-European		
	8	**URALIC**		

9	**SEMITIC**	
ALTAIC	10	Turkic
	11	Mongol
	12	Tungusic
13	**PALÆO-ASIATIC**	
14	**KOREA-JAPANESE**	

SINO-TIBETAN	15	Chinese
	16	Thai
	17	Vietnamese
	18	Tibeto-Burman
19	**DRAVIDIAN**	
20	**MALAY/INDONESIAN**	
21	Other isolated groups	

1:80M

Manila **PHILIPPINES**

Northern Marianas

Guam (U.S.A.)

PACIFIC OCEAN

MALAYSIA

Palau (Belau)

Marshall Islands

BRUNEI

Sandakan

Davao

Bandar Seri Begawan

M i c r o n e s i a

Caroline Islands

Borneo

Balikpapan

Sulawesi (Celebes)

Halmahera

Equator

PAPUA NEW GUINEA

NAURU

KIRIBATI

Ujung Pandang

Seram

I N D O N E S I A

Jayapura

Irian Jaya

New Guinea

Port Moresby

SOLOMON ISLANDS

Sumba

Timor

Arafura Sea

TUVALU

Wm SAMOA

Is Wallis (Fr.)

Timor Sea

Darwin

G. of Carpentaria

Coral Sea

VANUATU

FIJI

TONGA

Cairns

Townsville

New Caledonia (Fr.)

Suva

Alice Springs

Rockhampton

Tropic of Capricorn

A U S T R A L I A

L. Eyre

Brisbane

Kalgoorlie

L. Torrens

Darling

Perth

Fremantel

Murray

Wollongong

Sydney

Adelaide

Canberra

Melbourne

Geelong

Bass Strait

Auckland

North I.

N E W ZEALAND

Launceston

Tasman Sea

Tasmania

Wellington

Hobart

South I.

Christchurch

Chatham I. (NZ)

Dunedin

Stewart I.

INTERNATIONAL DATELINE

AUSTRALASIA

1:60M

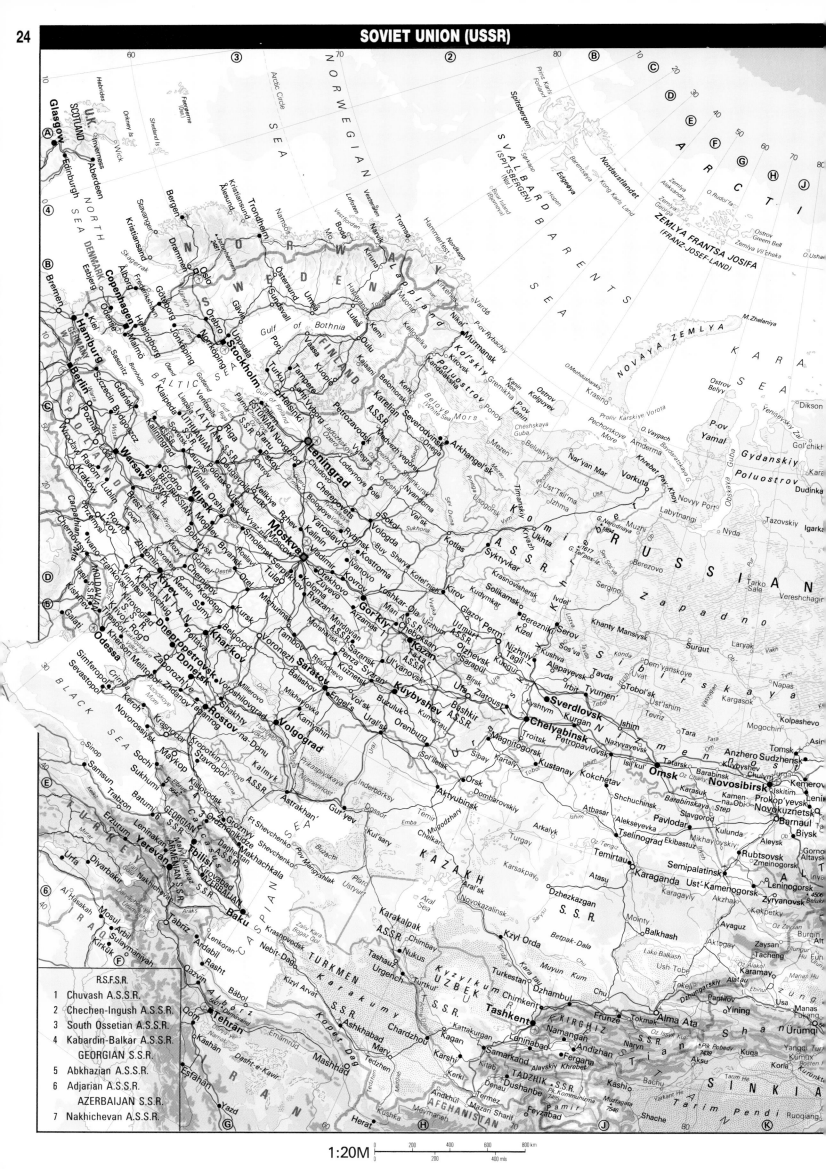

Map (Northeast Asia / Far East)

O C E A N

SEVERNAYA ZEMLYA (NORTH LAND)

NOVOSIBIRSKYE OSTROVA (NEW SIBERIAN ISLANDS)

LAPTEV SEA

EAST SIBERIAN SEA

CHUKCHI SEA

Bering Str.

BERING SEA

Gory Byrranga

Poluostrov Taymyr

Gory Putorana

Kolymskoye Nagor'ye

KAMCHATKA

Sredinnyy Khrebet

Petropavlovsk-Kamchatskiy

SEA OF OKHOTSK

Khrebet Cherskogo

Verkhoyanskiy Khrebet

Yakut A.S.S.R.

Yakutsk

Magadan

SAKHALIN

Kuril Islands (Kuril'skiye Ostrova)

R.S.F.S.R.

Sredne Sibirskoye Ploskogor'ye

Stanovoy Khrebet

Komsomol'sk-na-Amure

Khabarovsk

Yuzhno-Sakhalinsk

HOKKAIDO

Sapporo

Hakodate

Bratsk

Krasnoyarsk

Irkutsk

Ulan Ude

Chita

Buryat A.S.S.R.

Vladivostok

Nakhodka

SEA OF JAPAN

Tuva A.S.S.R.

Kyzyl

M O N G O L I A

Ulaanbaatar

MANCHURIA

Harbin

Changchun

Qiqihar

Mudanjiang

NORTH KOREA

P'yŏngyang

SOUTH KOREA

Seoul (Sŏul)

Taegu

Pusan

HONSHU

TOKYO

Yokohama

Nagoya

Kyoto

Osaka

Kobe

KYUSHU

Fukuoka

Nagasaki

Kagoshima

SHIKOKU

INNER MONGOLIA

Beijing (Peking)

Tianjin (Tientsin)

Shenyang

Luda

Baotou

Hohhot

Datong

Taiyuan

Jinan

Qingdao

YELLOW SEA

Bo Hai

GREAT WALL

GOBI DESERT

QILIAN SHAN

KAMCHATKA

SEA OF OKHOTSK

Kuril Islands (Kuril'skiye Ostrova)

SAKHALIN

HOKKAIDŌ

J A P A N

SEA OF JAPAN

N O R T H   K O R E A

S O U T H   K O R E A

Seoul (Sŏul)
P'yŏngyang

M A N C H U R I A

Harbin
Changchun
Shenyang
Beijing (Peking)
Tianjin (Tientsin)

I N N E R   M O N G O L I A

M O N G O L I A

C I S   S . S . R .

SINKIANG AUT. REG.

TSINGHAI

TIBET AUT. REG.

C H I N A

Shanghai
Wuhan
Chengdu
Chongqing
Guangzhou (Canton)
HONG KONG (U.K.)
Macau (Port.)

TAIWAN (FORMOSA)
Taipei
Kaohsiung

RYUKYU ISLANDS

P A C I F I C   O C E A N

EAST CHINA SEA

YELLOW SEA

BURMA

INDIA

Tropic of Cancer

1:20M

0   200   400   600   800 km
0   200   400 mls

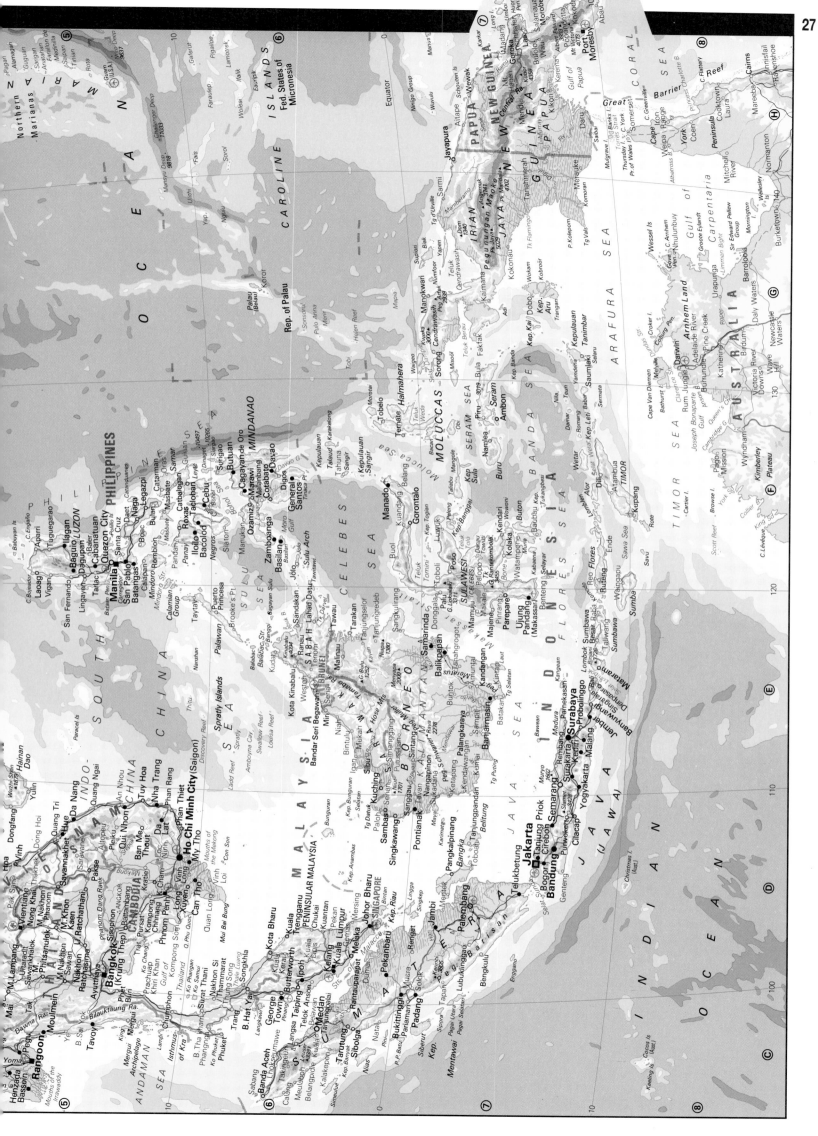

27

China

Jilin

Liaoning

Qian Shan

Liaodong Bandao

Liaodong Wan

North Korea

Korea Bay

Yellow Sea

(Huang Hai)

South Korea

Kyūshū

Kita-Kyūshū

Fukuoka

Nagasaki

Kumamoto

Kagoshima

Miyazaki

Hiroshima

Yamaguchi

Shimonoseki

Seoul (Sŏul)

P'yŏngyang

Pusan

Taegu

Taejŏn

Kwangju

Mokp'o

Cheju do

Cheju haehyŏp

Korea Strait (Tsushima Kaikyō)

Tsushima

Changchun

Shenyang

Vladivostok

Nakhodka

Ussuriysk

1:5M

50   100   150   200 km

50   100 mls

U.S.S.R.

135

140

continued on inset

145

Asahikawa

Kutcharo-ko

Teshikaga

Nemuro

Arkhipovka

Ol'ga

Takikawa

Fukagawa

Asahi dake 2290

1503

Me-akan dake

Vangou

Lazo

Margaritovo

Sunagawa

Akabira

Ashibetsu

Furano

Shakotan-misaki

Ishikari- wan

Furubira

Bibai

Iwamizawa

Yubari

Ikeda

Kushiro

Otaru

Sapporo

Ebetsu

Chitose

Obihiro

HOKKAIDŌ

Iwanai

Kutchan

Eniwa

Tomakomai

Mukawa

Hidaka-sammyaku

Suttsu

Shikotsu-ko

Date

Monbetsu

Tokachi

Oshamambe

Tōya-ko

Noboribetsu

Urakawa

Samani

Setana

Uchiura- wan

Muroran

Taiki

Hiroo

Yakumo

Komaga take 1133

Erimo-misaki

Okushiri-tō

Mori

Esashi

Kikonai

Esan-misaki

Hakodate

Ōma-saki

Ōhata

Shiriya-saki

Matsumae

Mutsu

Tsugaru-kaikyō

Ōminato

Kodomari-misaki

Mimmaya

Mutsu- wan

Nobeji

O F

Goshogawara

Ajigasawa

Aomori

Towada

Iwaki-san 1625

Kuroishi

Henashi-zaki

Hirosaki

Towada- ko

Hachinohe

Odate

Kuji

Mi-zaki

Noshiro

J

Oga

Koma

Morioka

Miyako

Akita

Tazawa- ko

P

Tazawako

Honjō

Hanamaki

Yokote

Tōno

Kamaishi

A

Tobi-shima

Kitakami

Yuzawa

Mizusawa

Ofunato

N

Chōkai-san 2230

Yokobori

Ichinoseki

Rikuzen- Tanaka

Sakata

Narugo

Kesennuma

O F

Shinjō

Tsuruoka

Obanazawa

Murayama

Higashine

Furukawa

Ishinomaki

H

Tendo

Sendai

Shiogama

Awa-shima

Hajiki-saki

Murakami

Yamagata

Natori

Sado-shima

Nagai

Kaminoyama

Aikawa

Ryōtsu

Yonezawa

Kakuda

Sōma

Mano-wan

O

Niigata

Shibata

Iide-san 2105

Fukushima

Haramachi

Niitsu

Kitakata

Nihommatsu

Teradomari

Sanjō

Aizu

Kōriyama

Hegura-jima

Nagaoka

Wakamatsu

Sukagawa

Taira

N

Ojiya

Koide

Shirakawa

Iwaki

Nanatsu-jima

Naoetsu

Tokamachi

Sammyaku

Kuroiso

Otawara

S

Suzu-misaki

Takada

Arai

Nakano

Shirane-san 2369

Nikkō

Imaichi

Suzu

Noto- hantō

Nanao

Itoigawa

Mikuni-

Yaita

Hitachi

Himi

Takaoka

Kurobe

Nagano

Suzaka

Utsonomiya

Hitachi-Ota

Hakui

Toyama- wan

Shibukawa

Maebashi

Mito

Katsuta

Kanazawa

Toyama

Omachi

Ueda

Kiryū

Nakaminato

Komatsu

Tsurugi

Yariga-take 3180

Matsumoto

Komoro

Ōta

Oyama

Ishioka

Kaga

Haku-san 2702

Katsuyama

Takasaki

Hok

Tsuchiura

Fukui

Ono

Okaya

Takayama

Suwa

Chichibu

Kumagaya

Konosu

Sawara

Sabae

Osaka

Ina

Chino

Kawagoe

Omiya

Narita

Chōshi

Takefu

Shirotori

Hachiman

3063 Ontake-san

3192 Shirani-san

Enzan

Kawaguchi

Urawa

Tokyo

Inubo-saki

Kasumi

Obama

Ogaki

Kofu

Hachioji

Funabashi

Kurayoshi

Maizuru

Biwa- ko

Hikone

Ichinomiya

Kasugai

Fuji- Yoshida

Yokohama

Chiba

Yonago

Tottori

Miyazu

Ayabe

Seto

Toyota

Akaishi- sanchi

Fujinomiya

Kawasaki

Bōsō- hantō

Fukuchiyama

Ōtsu

Kuwana

Fuji-san 3776

Fujisawa

Mobara

Niimi

Tsushima

Yokkaichi

Nakatsu-

Fuji

Yokosuka

Katsuura

Takahashi

Aioi

Nishiwaki

Handa

Shimada

Shimizu

Odawara

Miura

Kamogawa

Nagashima

Sanchi

Kyōto

Uji

Toyonaka

Nagoya

Okazaki

Shizuoka

Numazu

Tateyama

Tsuchima

Chizu

Himeji

Nara

Suzuka

Toyohashi

Ito

Sagami- nada

Nojima-zaki

Okayama

Kakogawa

Kōbe

Akashi

Nabari

Matsusaka

Hamamatsu

Suruga- wan

Ō-shima

Naikai

Sakai

Osaka

Ise

Shimoda

Urashiki

Harima- nada

Awaji- shima

Kishiwada

Izumi-Sano

Toba

Ise- wan

Omae-zaki

Iro-zaki

To-shima

Onomichi

Tamano

Sakaide

Sumoto

Hashimoto

Wakayama

Nii-jima

Marugame

Takamatsu

Naruto

Kainan

Nagashima

Owase

Kōzu-shima

Miyake-jima

Niihama

Tokushima

Komatsushima

Gobo

Kumano

Shikoku- sanchi

Hiwasa

Anan

Tanabe

Shingū

Ōnohara-jima

Mikura- jima

Inamba-jima

Kōchi

Nankoku

Aki

Kushimoto

Shiono-saki

Kii-suidō

J A P A N

Tosa- wan

Susaki

Muroto

Muroto-zaki

S H I K O K U

P A C I F I C

Ōhara-jima

Wakkanai

Sōya-misaki

145 at the same scale

Rishiri-tō

Rebun-tō

Hama-Tombetsu

Kitami-Esashi

Otoineppu

Yagishiri-tō

Teuri-tō

Ōmu

Okoppe

Mombetsu

M. Dokuchayevo

Nayoro

Rudnaya

Rumoi

Uryū-ko

Takinoue

Shiretoko-misaki

O. Kunashir (U.S.S.R.)

Shibetsu

Engaru

Teshio dake 1558

Abashiri

Abashiri- wan

Golovnino

Asahi dake 2290

Asahikawa

Soranuma-ko

Kitami

Shari

Rausu

Takikawa

Fukagawa

Akabira

Ashibetsu

Furano

1503 Me-akan dake

Kutcharo-ko

Teshikaga

Shibetsu

Sunagawa

Bibai

HOKKAIDŌ

Otaru

Ishikari- wan

Iwamizawa

Yūbari

Nemuro

Shakotan-misaki

Sapporo

Ebetsu

Ikeda

Kushiro

Furubira

Iwanai

Kutchan

Eniwa

Obihiro

Nemuro-kaikyō

P A C I F I C   O C E A N

1:10M

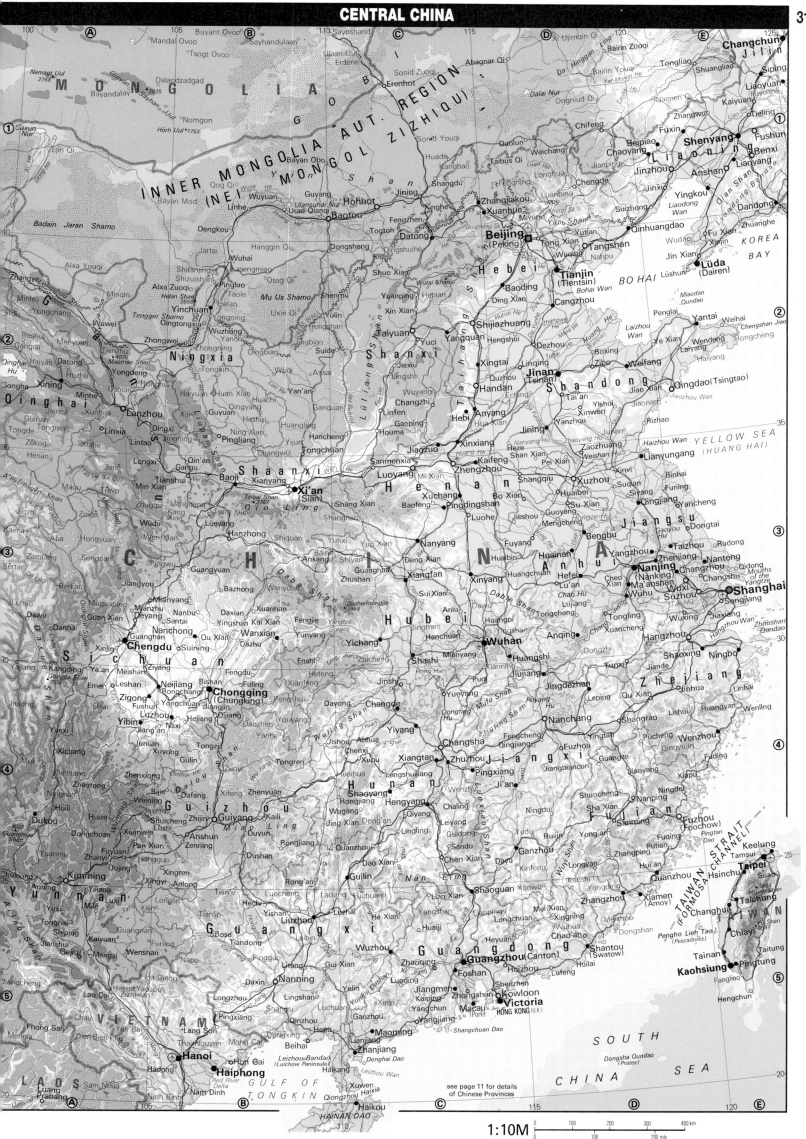

1:10M

see page 11 for details of Chinese Provinces

BORNEO

Tajungselor
Tanjungredeb
Kelolokan
Samarinda
Balikpapan
Tanjung
Banjarmasin
Kintap
Tg Selatan

Makassar Strait

SULAWESI
(CELEBES)
Palopo
Majene
Parepare
Teluk Bone
Watampone
Ujung Pandang
(Makassar)
Bonthain
Selayar
Kep. Takabonerate

Manado
Belang
Tolitoli
Gorontalo
Togian Is
Luwuk
Peleng
Banggai
Kep. Sula
Donggala
Poso
Palu
Teluk Tolo
Teluk Tomini

Morotai
Tubelo
Ternate
Halmahera
Molucca Sea
Weda
Teluk Weda

MOLUCCAS

Kep. Asia
Kep. Ayu
Mapia

Waigeo
Sorong
Salawati
Misool
Kep. Gorong
Adi
Kep. Watubela
Kep. Kai
Kep. Aru
Dobo
Kep. Tanimbar

Manokwari
Biak
Numfoor
Yapen
Cendrawasih
Teluk Cendrawasih
Teluk Berau
Fakfak
Babo
Kaimana
Kokonau

IRIAN JAYA

Pegunungan Maoke
Pk Jaya 5029

Sarmi
Jayapura
Aitape
Wewak

NEW GUINEA

Mt Wilhelm
Mt Hagen
Goroka
Mendi

PAPUA NEW GUINEA

Madang
Sepik
Central Ra
Tanahmerah
Merauke
Dolak
Digul
Fly
Daru
Saibai I.
Torres Strait
Pr. of Wales I.
C. York
Somerset

Ninigo Is
Hermit Is
Admiralty Is
Manus
Schouten Is
Mussau
Saint Matthias Group
New Hanover
Kavieng
New Ireland

Bismarck Archipelago
Bismarck Sea
Rabaul
New Britain

Bulolo
Lae
Morobe
Kerema
Gulf of Papua
Mt St Mary
Popondetta
Kokoda
Owen Stanley Ra
Port Moresby
Kupiano
Samarai
Alotau
Tobriand Is
D Entrecasteaux Is

Arafura Sea

INDONESIA

Bali
Denpasar
Mataram
Lombok
Sumbawa
Raba
Ruteng
Ende
Flores
Waingapu
Sumba

Flores Sea

Wetar
Roma
Kep. Leti
Sermata
Kep. Damar
Kep. Babar

Timor Sea

Timor
Kupang
Oekusi
Alor
Savu
Rote

Banda Sea

Timor
Melville I.
Bathurst I.
Clarence Str.
Darwin
Rum Jungle
Van Diemen G.
Cobourg Pen
Croker I.
C. Arnhem
Nhulunbuy
Wessel Is

Cartier I.
C. Londonderry
Joseph Bonaparte Gulf
Adelaide River
Burrundie
Pine Creek
Katherine
Roper

Scott Reef
Pago Mission
Wyndham
Daly
Victoria
Birdum
Daly Waters
Limmen Bight

Arnhem Land

Gulf of Carpentaria

Groote Eylandt
Sir Edward Pellew Group
Borroloola
Mornington
Wellesley Is
Weipa
Mitchell River
Gilbert
Normanton
Croydon
Burketown
Leichhardt

Cape York Peninsula
Iron Range
Coen
Laura
Cooktown
Willis Group
Coringa I.

Princess Charlotte B.

INDIAN OCEAN

Java Trench

Rowley Shoals
Monte Bello Is
Barrow I.
North West C.
Dampier
Roebourne

King Sound
C. Lévêque
Derby
Broome
Lagrange
Eighty Mile Beach

Collier B.
King Leopold Ra
Mt Ord 936
Kimberley Plateau
Fitzroy Crossing
Hall's Creek
Sturt Ck

L. Argyle
Victoria River Downs
Ord

Wave Hill
Powell Creek
Newcastle Waters

NORTHERN TERRITORY

Tennant Creek
Barrow Creek

Camooweal
Mount Isa
Cloncurry
Dajarra
Georgina
Selwyn
Winton

QUEENSLAND

Croydon
Richmond
Hughenden
Charters Towers
Townsville
Ayr
Bowen
Proserpine
Collinsville
Mackay
Sarina
Marlborough
Rockhampton
Gladstone
Mount Morgan
Barcaldine
Blackall
Clermont
Emerald

Great Dividing Range

Great Barrier Reef

Coral Sea

Port Hedland
Shay Gap
Marble Bar
De Grey
Nullagine

Great Sandy Desert

L. Mackay
L. Disappointment

WESTERN AUSTRALIA

Onslow
Hamersley Ra
Mt Bruce 1226
Wittenoom
Paraburdoo
Newman
Ashburton
Fortescue

Carnarvon
Gascoyne
Mt Augustus 1106
Barlee Ra
Lyons
McLeod

Shark B.
Dirk Hartog I.

Murchison
Meekatharra
Wiluna
Cue
Sandstone
Mt Magnet
Leonora
Mullewa
Barlee

Gibson Desert
L. Carnegie
L. Wells

Mt Aloysius 981
Tomkinson Ra
Petermann Ra

Macdonnell Ranges
Mt Ziel 1510
Alice Springs
Finke
Musgrave Ra
Mt Woodroffe 1440

Simpson Desert

Lake Eyre Basin
L. Eyre
Oodnadatta
Birdsville
Windorah
Diamantina
Thomson
Barcoo
Cooper Ck
Charleville
Quilpie
Roma
Miles
Toowoomba
Goondiwindi
St George
Cunnamulla
Warrego
Paroo
Bourke
Walgett
Moree
Narrabri
Armidale
Tamworth

AUSTRALIA

Coober Pedy

SOUTH AUSTRALIA

Great Victoria Desert

Marree
L. Frome
Leigh Ck
Milparinka
Wilcannia
Cobar
Darling
Nyngan
Dubbo
Gondobolin
Orange
Bathurst
Lithgow
Newcastle

NEW SOUTH WALES

Menindee
Broken Hill
Ivanhoe
Griffith
Hay
Lachlan
Cootamundra
Junee
Wagga Wagga
Goulburn
Sydney
Wollongong
Canberra
A.C.T.
Mt Kosciusko 2230

Wiluna
Sandstone
Northampton
Mt Magnet
Leonora
Barlee
Kalgoorlie
Coolgardie
Southern Cross
Bulfinch
Merredin
Northam
Nullarbor Plain
Rawlinna
Forrest
Eyre
Norseman
Esperance
C. Pasley
Arch. of the Recherche

Geraldton
Dongara
Houtman Abrolhos
Moora
Goomalling
Moore
Bencubbin
Wongan
Corrigin
York
Perth
Fremantle
Pinjarra
Mandurah
Bunbury
Busselton
Augusta
C. Leeuwin
C. Naturaliste
Collie
Narrogin
Wagin
Katanning
Manjimup
Bluff Knoll
C. Knob
Albany

Ceduna
Ooldea
Tarcoola
Penong
Gawler Ranges
Iron Knob
Whyalla
Port Pirie
Port Augusta
Quorn
Peterborough
Port Lincoln
Eyre Pen.
Spencer Gulf
Flinders I.
Investigator Str.
Kangaroo I.
Victor Harbour
Murray Bridge
Elizabeth
Adelaide
Renmark
Mildura
Swan Hill
Balranald
Deniliquin
Shepparton
Benalla
Albury

L. Torrens
L. Gairdner
L. Everard
St Mary Pk 1189
Woomera
Walaroo
Kingoonya

Great Australian Bight

VICTORIA

Horsham
Ararat
Ballarat
Bendigo
Hamilton
Mount Gambier
Portland
Port Fairy
Warrnambool
Colac
Geelong
Melbourne
Morwell
Sale
Bairnsdale
Orbost
Australian Alps
C. Howe
Bombala
Wonthaggi
Wilson's Prom.
Naracoorte
Kingston

Bass Strait

King I.
Furneaux Group
Flinders I.
C. Barren

TASMANIA

Smithton
C. Grim
Burnie
Devonport
Launceston
St Mary's
Queenstown
Mt Ossa
Hobart
Geeveston
South West C.
South East C.

INDIAN OCEAN

200   400   600   800 km
200   400 mils

1:7.5M

Three Kings Is
B
C. Maria
van Diemen
North Cape
A
170
Rangaunu B.
175
Doubtless B.
Ahipara B.
Tauroa Pt
Kaitaia
Bay of Islands
C.Brett
Russell
35
35
Kaikohe
Kawakawa
Hokianga Har.
Hikurangi
Whangarei
Hen & Chickens Is
Dargaville
Bream B.
Little
Barrier I.
Great Barrier I.
Wellsford
Kaipara Har.
Hauraki
Gulf
C.Colville
Mercury Is
Manly
Mercury Bay
Takapuna
NORTH
Auckland
Coromandel
Peninsula
①
Papatoetoe
Manukau
Papakura
Pukekohe
Thames
ISLAND
Waiuku
Paeroa
Waihi
Mayor I.
TASMAN
Huntly
Te Aroha
Matakana I.
White I.
C. Runaway
Hicks
Bay
①
Glen Afton
Morrinsville
Tauranga Har.
Ngaruawahia
Tauranga
East C.
Hamilton
Cambridge
Te Puke
Bay of
Plenty
Te Awamutu
Putaruru
Rotorua
Whakatane
Kawhia
Opotiki
SEA
Otorohanga
Rotorua
Kawerau
Taneatua
Waitomo
Waikato
Tokomaru
Te Kuiti
Mangakino
Murupara
Tolaga
Bay
N. Taranaki Bight
Ohura
Mangaweka
Taupo
Gisborne
Waitara
Taumarunui
Taupo
Poverty Bay
New Plymouth
Inglewood
Mt
Ngauruhoe
2291
Mt
Makorako
1727
Wairoa
Hawke
Bay
Mahia Peninsula
C. Egmont
Mt Egmont
2518
Stratford
Mt Ruapehu
2797
Tarawera
Eltham
Raetihi
Ohakune
Eskdale
Portland I.
Opunake
Hawera
Waiouru
Taradale
Napier
S. Taranaki Bight
Patea
Wanganui
Taihape
Hastings
C. Kidnappers
Havelock North
Marton
②
40
Feilding
Dannevirke
40
Palmerston N
Woodville
C. Farewell
Farewell Spit
COOK
Foxton
Pahiatua
C. Stephens
Levin
Eketahuna
C.Turnagain
Herbertville
C. Farewell
Golden
Bay
Collingwood
Separation Pt
D'Urville I.
Otaki
Rocks Pt
Takaka
Tasman
Mts
G.Jackson
Paraparaumu
Masterton
Mt
1529
Hector
Carterton
The Twins
1826
Tasman
Bay
Picton
Porirua
Upper Hutt
Karamea
Motueka
Tawa
L. Wairarapa
Martinborough
Bight
Nelson
Wellington
Lower
Hutt
Mt Ross
983
Karamea
Richmond
Blenheim
Richmond Ra.
Wairau
Palliser Bay
Seddonville
C. Palliser
Westport
Murchison
L. Rotoiti
Awatere
C. Foulwind
Buller
L. Rotoroa
Victoria
Ra.
Spenser
Mts
Mt Travers
2338
Kaikoura
Ra.
Tapuaenuku
2885
C. Campbell
Reefton
Clarence
Grey
Lewis
Pass
Hanmer
Springs
Kaikoura
Runanga
Brunner
Waiau
Kaikoura Pen.
Greymouth
Waiau
Hokitika
L. Sumner
Culverden
②
Ross
Hurunui
Cheviot
②
SOUTH
Arthurs
Pass
Puketeraki
Ra.
Waipara
Pegasus
Bay
Abut Hd
Waimakariri
Rangiora
Franz Josef Gl.
Coleridge
Rakaia
Kaiapoi
ISLAND
2764
Mt Cook
Waimakariri
Christchurch
Jackson Hd
Mt Sefton
3157
Methven
Hornby
Lyttelton
Cascade Pt
Hermitage
Rangitata
Lincoln
Banks
Peninsula
Ellesmere
Akaroa
L. Tekapo
Geraldine
Awarua Pt
Pollux
2542
Young Ra.
Pukaki
Lake
Fairlie
Ashburton
Canterbury
Plains
Canterbury
Bight
Ohau
Temuka
Mt Aspiring
3027
Wanaka
L. Benmore
Milford Sd
Hawea
Timaru
Milford
Mt Pyramid
2326
Homer
Tunnel
Wanaka
L. Aviemore
George Sd
Arrowtown
Omarama
Waimate
Caswell Sd
Kurow
45
Cromwell
Hawkdun Ra.
Waitaki
45
Secretary
Fiordland
Queenstown
Clyde
Ranfurly
Oamaru
Doubtful
Sd
Wakatipu
Alexandra
Hampden
Breaksea
Nat. Park
Te Anau
Kingston
Roxburgh
Palmerston
Sd
Manapouri
Te Anau
Waikouaiti
Resolution
I.
Mt Ward
718
Waiau
Port Chalmers
Dusky
Sd
Lumsden
Heriot
Clutha
Otago Peninsula
Puysegur
Pt
Mt Ward
Oreti
Riversdale
Lawrence
Mosgiel
Dunedin
Te
Waewae
Bay
Winton
Tapanui
Milton
Cameron
Mts
Ohai
Mataura
Balclutha
Truatapere
Edendale
Kaitangata
③
Riverton
Owaka
③
Invercargill
Solander I.
Bluff
Foveaux
Strait
Codfish I.
Mt Allen
730
Oban
Paterson Inlet
Stewart Island
Shelter Pt
A
170
B
Port Pegasus
175
C

TASMAN
SEA

NORTH
ISLAND

SOUTH
ISLAND

PACIFIC
OCEAN

1:5M
0   50   100   150   200 km
0   50   100 mils

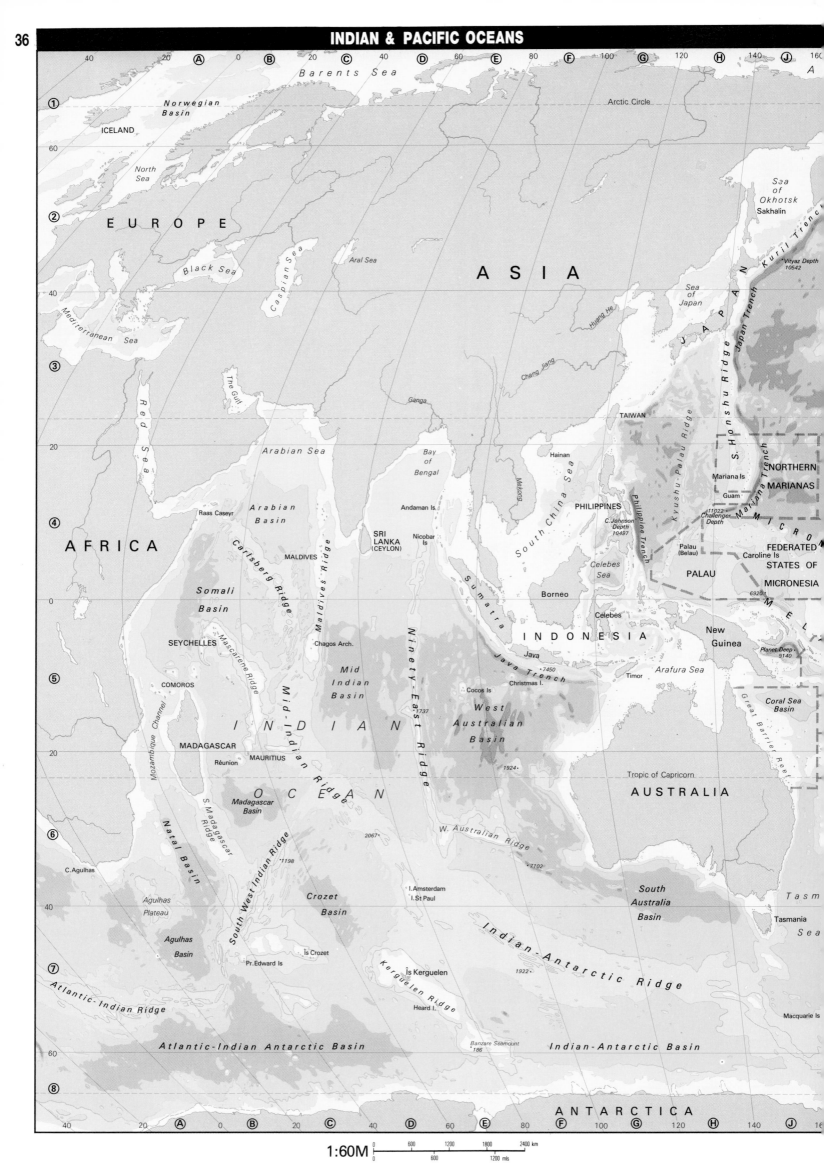

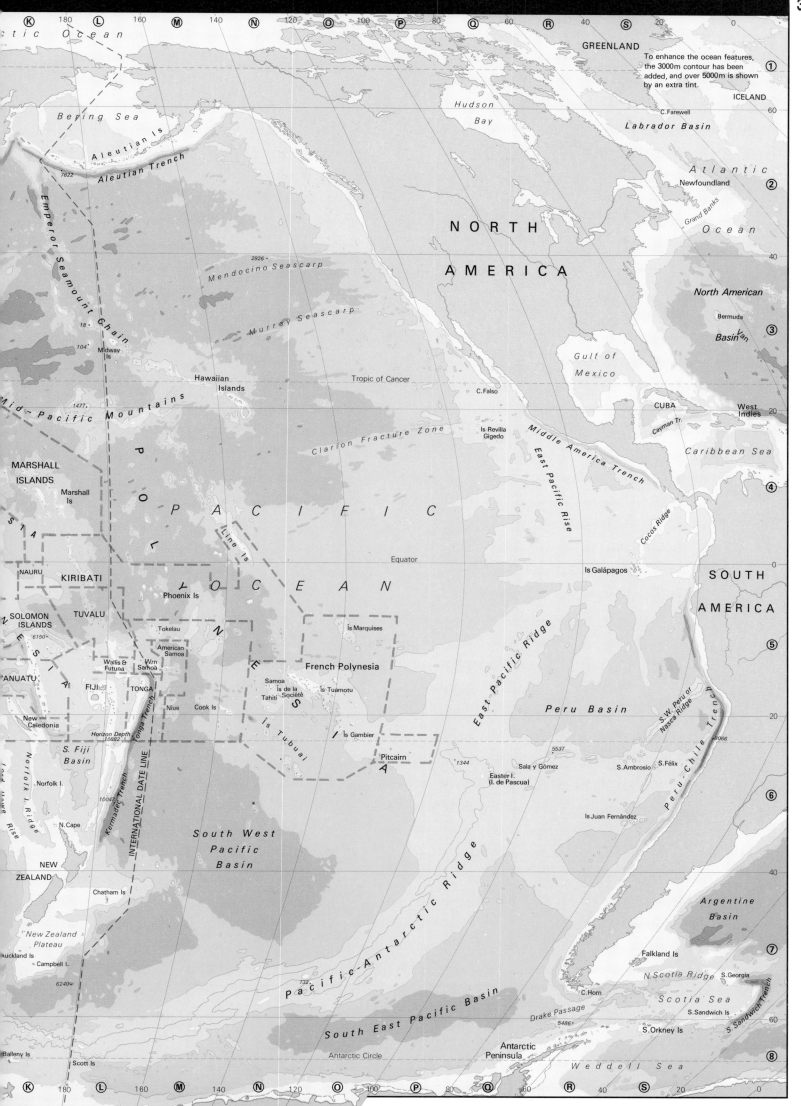

K 180 L 160 M 140 N 120 O 100 P 80 Q 60 R 40 S 20 0

tic Ocean

GREENLAND

To enhance the ocean features,
the 3000m contour has been
added, and over 5000m is shown
by an extra tint.

ICELAND ①

Hudson
Bay

C.Farewell 60

Labrador Basin

Bering Sea

A t l a n t i c

Newfoundland ②

Aleutian Is

7822

Aleutian Trench

Grand Banks

Ocean

NORTH

AMERICA 40

North American

Bermuda

2926

Mendocino Seascarp

Basin Van ③

Murray Seascarp

18°

104°

Midway Is

Gulf of
Mexico

Tropic of Cancer

C.Falso

Hawaiian
Islands

West 20
Indies

CUBA

Caribbean Sea

1477

Mid-Pacific Mountains

Clarion Fracture Zone

Is Revilla
Gigedo

Middle America Trench

Cayman Tr.

MARSHALL
ISLANDS

P
O

PACIFIC

④

Marshall
Is

East Pacific Rise

L

Cocos Ridge

NAURU

Line Is

Y

Equator

Is Galápagos

SOUTH

KIRIBATI

N

O C E A N

AMERICA

TUVALU

Tokelau

Îs Marquises

⑤

6150

American
Samoa

E

French Polynesia

East Pacific Ridge

Wallis &
Futuna

Wrn
Samoa

Samoa
Îs de la Société
Tahiti

Îs Tuamotu

Peru Basin

S.W. Peru or
Nasca Ridge

FIJI

TONGA

Niue

Cook Is

S

⑥

ANUATU

New
Caledonia

Îs Tubuai

Îs Gambier

20

Peru-Chile Trench

8066

Horizon Depth
10882

Tonga Trench

Pitcairn

1344

5537

S.Ambrosio

S.Félix

Norfolk I.

S. Fiji
Basin

A

Easter I.
(I. de Pascua)

Sala y Gómez

Norfolk
I.

10047

Kermadec Trench

Is Juan Fernández

N.Cape

INTERNATIONAL DATE LINE

South West
Pacific
Basin

Pacific-Antarctic Ridge

NEW

Argentine ⑥

ZEALAND 40

Basin

Chatham Is

Falkland Is ⑦

"New Zealand
Plateau

N.Scotia Ridge S.Georgia

Auckland Is

Scotia Sea

Campbell I.

S.Sandwich Is

6240

South East Pacific Basin

South East Pacific Basin

C.Horn

S.Orkney Is 60

Drake Passage

5486

S.Sandwich Trench

Balleny Is

Antarctic
Peninsula ⑧

Scott Is

Antarctic Circle

W e d d e l l   S e a

K 180 L 160 M 140 N 120 O 100 P 80 Q 60 R 40 S 20 0

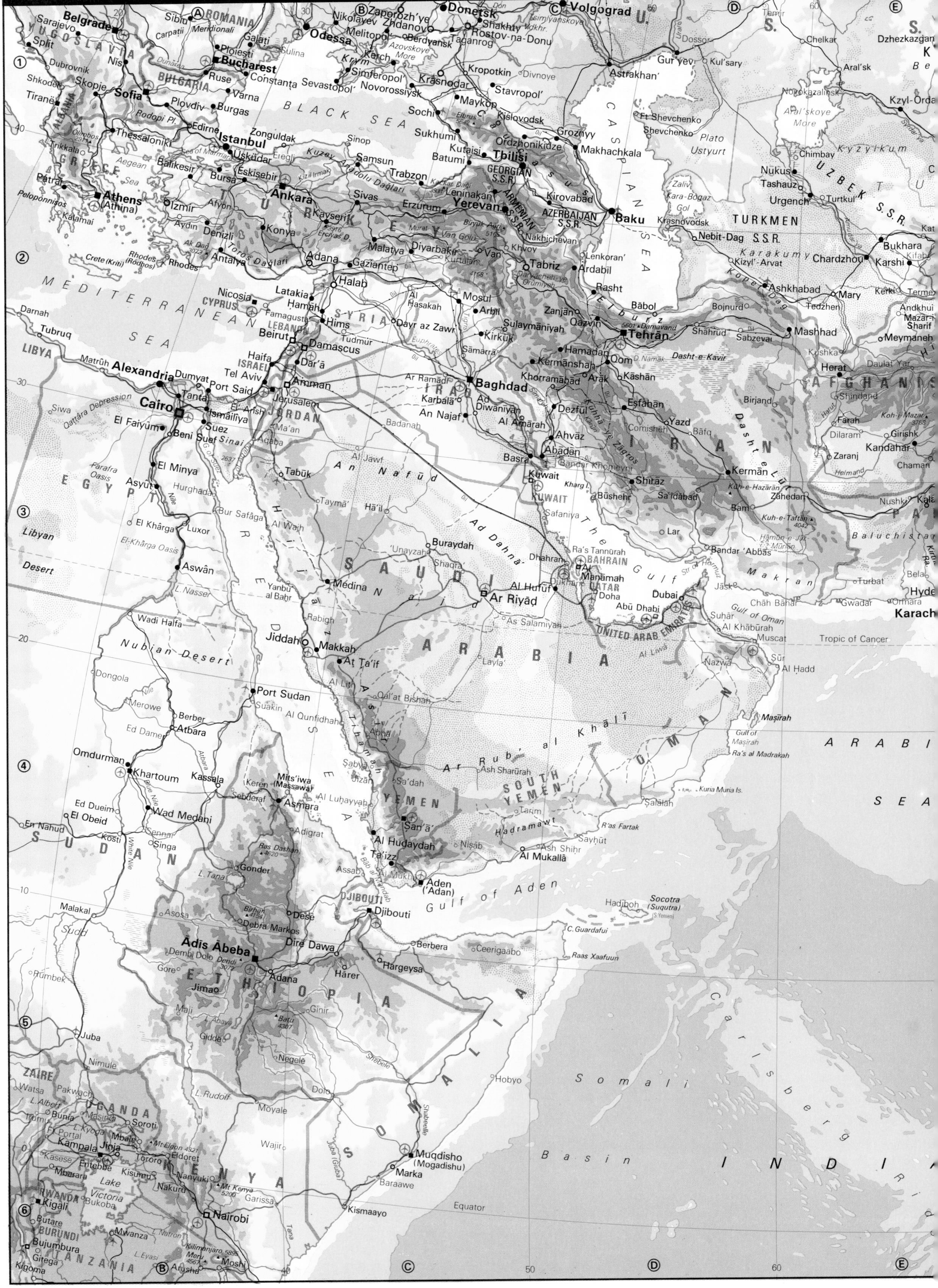

YUGOSLAVIA
Belgrade
Split
Sarajevo
Dubrovnik
Nis
Skopje
Tiranë
Shkodër
ALBANIA
Sofia
BULGARIA
Plovdiv
Burgas
Varna
Ruse
Rodopi Pl.
Thessaloniki
GREECE
Trikkala
Olympos
Pátrai
Peloponnisos
Kalamai
Athens (Athína)
Aegean Sea
Crete (Kríti)
Rhodes (Ródhos)

ROMANIA
Sibiu
Carpatii Meridionali
Galati
Ploiesti
Bucharest
Dunărea
Constanta
Sulina
Meridionali

Nikolayev
Zhdanov
Melitopol'
Berdyansk
Odessa
Kerch
Krym
Azovskoye More
Taganrog
Zaporozh'ye
Donetsk
Shakhty
Rostov-na-Donu
Don
Simferopol'
Sevastopol'
Novorossiysk
Krasnodar
Kropotkin
Stavropol'
Divnoye

Volgograd
U.S.S.R.
Astrakhan'
Gur'yev
Kul'sary
Chelkar
Aral'sk
Aral'skoye More
Novokazalinsk
Kzyl-Orda

BLACK SEA
Zonguldak
Istanbul
Üsküdar
Sea of Marmara
Bursa
Eskisehir
Ankara
Kuzey Anadolu Dağları
Sinop
Samsun
Ordu
Trabzon
Sukhumi
Batumi
Tbilisi
GEORGIAN S.S.R.
Kutaisi
Ordzhonikidze
Groznyy
Makhachkala
Kislovodsk
Elbrus
Sochi
Maykop
CASPIAN SEA

Balikesir
Izmir
Aydin
Denizli
Antalya
Toros Dağlari
Konya
Adana
Gaziantep
Kayseri
Sivas
Erzurum
Yerevan
ARMENIAN S.S.R.
Leninakan
Kirovabad
AZERBAIJAN S.S.R.
Baku
Nakhichevan
Tabriz
Ardabil
Rasht
Qazvin
Bābol
Krasnovodsk
Nebit-Dag
Bojnurd
Mashhad
Herat
AFGHANISTAN

Nicosia
CYPRUS
Famagusta
Latakia
Hamah
Hims
Beirut
LEBANON
Damascus
Dar'ā
Amman
ISRAEL
Haifa
Tel Aviv
Jerusalem
JORDAN
SYRIA
Halab
Al Hasakah
Mosul
Arbil
Sulaymaniyah
Kirkūk
Dayr az Zawr
Tudmur
Sāmarrā
Baghdad
Ad Diwaniyah
An Najaf
Karbala'
Al Amārah
Hamadan
Kermānshāh
Arāk
Qom
Tehrān
Shāhrūd
Sabzevar
Dasht-e-Kavir
Esfahān
Yazd
IRAN
Birjand
Farah
Girishk
Kandahar
Chaman

MEDITERRANEAN SEA
Darnah
Tubruq
LIBYA
Matrūh
Alexandria
Dumyat
Port Said
Cairo
Tanta
Ismailiya
Suez
El Faiyûm
Beni Suef
El Minya
Asyût
El Khârga
El-Khârga Oasis
Farafra Oasis
Siwa
Qattâra Depression
EGYPT
Libyan Desert
Aswân
Luxor
Hurghada
Bur Safâga
L. Nasser
Wadi Halfa
Yanbu al Bahr
Medina
Rabigh
Jiddah
Makkah
At Ta'if
SAUDI ARABIA
An Nafūd
Tabūk
Taymâ'
Hā'il
Buraydah
'Unayzah
Shaqra'
Ar Riyād
Al Hufuf
As Salamiyah
Ad Dahnā'
ARABIA
Rub' al Khālī
Layla'

Nubian Desert
Dongola
Merowe
Berber
Atbara
Port Sudan
Suakin
Al Qunfidhah
SUDAN
Khartoum
Omdurman
Kassala
Ed Damer
Wad Medani
El Obeid
Ed Dueim
Kosti
Sennar
Singa
En Nahud
Malakal
Sudd
Rumbek
Juba
Nimule
ZAIRE
UGANDA
L. Albert
Kampala
Jinja
L. Kyoga
Mt. Elgon
Soroti
Eldoret
KENYA
Mt. Kenya 5200
Nakuru
Nanyuki
Nairobi
Garissa

ETHIOPIA
Ādis Ābeba
Dembi Dolo
Gore
Jimao
Mali
Dendi
Ras Dashan 4620
Gonder
L. Tana
Debra Markos
Dese
Mits'iwa (Massawa)
Asmara
Keren
Sebderat
Adigrat
Adana
Hārer
Dire Dawa
Ginir
Batu 4307
Negele
Abaya
Dolo
Moyale
Wajir
Shebele
SOMALIA
Hobyo
Muqdisho (Mogadishu)
Marka
Baraawe
Kismaayo
Equator

ERITREA
YEMEN
San'a
Al Hudaydah
Ta'izz
Al Mukhā
Aden ('Adan)
Zabid
Sa'dah
Nisāb
SOUTH YEMEN
Hadramawt
Tarim
Ash Shihr
Al Mukallā
Sayhūt
Ra's Fartak
OMAN
Salalah
Kuria Muria Is.

Al Luhayyah
Jizan
Abha
Najrān
Qal'at Bishah
Al Lith
Tihamah

DJIBOUTI
Djibouti
Berbera
Ceerigaabo
C. Guardafui
Hadiboh
Socotra (Suqutra) (S. Yemen)
Raas Xaafuun
Gulf of Aden
Ras Xaafuun
Somali Basin
Carlsberg
INDIAN

RED SEA

PERSIAN GULF
The Gulf
Basra
Abādān
Kuwait
KUWAIT
Kharg I.
Bushehr
Dhahran
BAHRAIN
Manāmah
QATAR
Doha
Abū Dhabi
UNITED ARAB EMIRATES
Dubai
Al Khābūrah
Muscat
Nazwa
Sūr
Al Hadd
Masirah
Gulf of Masirah
Ra's al Madrakah
ARABIAN SEA
Gulf of Oman
Bandar 'Abbas
Str. of Hormuz
Jāsk
Chāh Bahār
Gwadar
Turbat
Karachi
PAKISTAN
Baluchistan
Makran
Kermān
Shīrāz
Bam
Zāhedān
Zaranj
Dezfūl
Ahvāz
Bandar Khomeyni
Safaniya
Al Lwā

Ismailiya
El 'Arish
Sinai
Aqaba
Ma'an
Badanah
Al Jawf
HIJAZ
NEJD
ASIR

TURKMEN S.S.R.
UZBEK S.S.R.
Nukus
Chimbay
Tashauz
Urgench
Turtkul
Bukhara
Karshi
Chardzhou
Ashkhabad
Kizyl-Arvat
Tedzhen
Mary
Kerki
Termez
Andkhui
Mazar-i Sharif
Meymaneh
Kushka

BURUNDI
Bujumbura
RWANDA
Kigali
Butare
TANZANIA
Bukoba
Mwanza
Lake Victoria
Kigoma
Kilimanjaro 5895
Moshi
Arusha
Meru

1:20M
0 200 400 600 800 km
0 200 400 mls

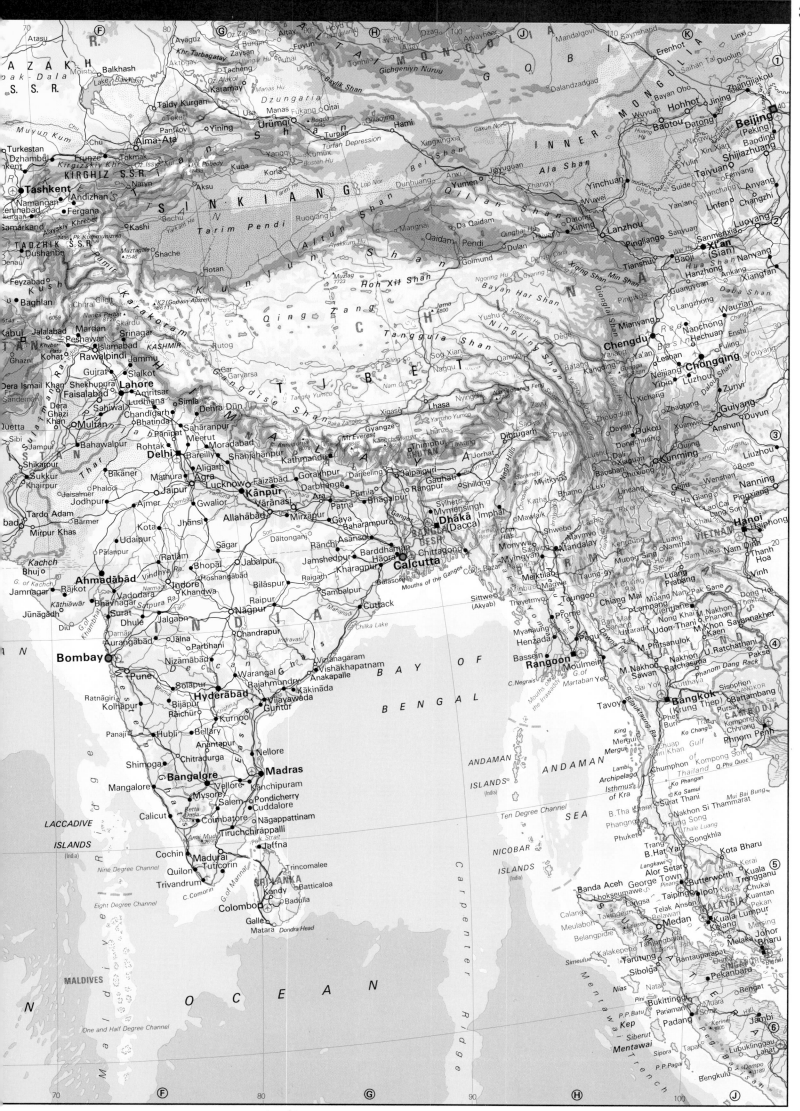

BLACK SEA

Khaskovo
Edirne
Kırklareli
Babaeski
Uzunköprü
Çorlu
İstanbul
Üsküdar
Adapazarı
Zonguldak
Bartın
Kastamonu
İnebolu
Sinop
Samsun
Terme
Ünye
Ordu
Giresun
Tirebolu
Trabzon
Çayeli
Rize
Artvin
Batumi
Akhalkalaki
Makharadze
Zestafoni

Tekirdağ
İzmit
Düzce
Bolu
Karabük
Ereğli
Kalecik
Delice
Tosya
İskilip
Merzifon
Amasya
Taşova
Niksar
Gümüşhane
Bayburt
Ardahan
Kağızman
Horasan
Sarıkamış

Gelibolu
Biga
Bandırma
Gemlik
İznik
İnegöl
Bilecik
Çankırı
Çorum
Turhal
Tokat
Refahiye
Erzincan
Erzurum
Aşkale
Eleşkirt

Eceabat
Çanakkale
Gönen
Bursa
Kütahya
Eskişehir
Sivrihisar
Polatlı
Balâ
Yozgat
Boğazlıyan
Gemerek
Sivas
Zara
Tunceli
Bingöl
Muş
Süphan D.
Malazgirt

Ankara
Kırıkkale
Kırşehir
Nevşehir
Kayseri
Gürün
Elazığ
Palu
Ergani

TURKEY

İzmir (Smyrna)
Manisa
Akhisar
Bergama
Ayvalık
Balıkesir
Tavşanlı
Emirdağ
Afyon
Bolvadin
Kulu
Tuz Gölü
Aksaray
Niğde
Bor
Erciyes D. 3916
Gölbaşı
Elbistan
Göksun
Kahramanmaraş
Adıyaman
Besni
Hilvan
Diyarbakır
Siverek
Batman
Silvan
Bitlis
Siirt

Çeşme
Khios
Sámos
EPHESUS
Aydın
Nazilli
Saraköy
Denizli
Burdur
Isparta
Akşehir
Konya
Karapınar
Ereğli
Karaman
Tarsus
Adana
Ceyhan
Osmaniye
Gaziantep
Nizip
Urfa
Ceylanpınar
Mardin
Nusaybin
Al Qāmishlī

Söke
Muğla
Köyceğiz
Korkuteli
Antalya
Akseki
Beyşehir
Çumra
Mersin
Kilis
Jarābulus
A'zāz
Manbij
Al Bāb
Ar Raqqah
Al Ḥasakah
Tall 'Afar
Sinjār

GREECE
Rhodes
Kárpathos
Crete

Mediterranean Sea

CYPRUS
Nicosia
Famagusta
Limassol
Larnaca

Latakia (Al Lādhiqīyah)
Idlib
Aleppo (Halab)
Ma'arret an Nu'mān
Ar Raqqah
As Sabkhah
Al Badi
Al Haḍr

Tripoli (Trâblous esh Shem)
Ṭarṭūs
Bāniyās
Maşyāf
Ḥamāh
As Salamīyah
SYRIA
Dayr az Zawr
Mayādīn

Beirut (Beyrouth)
Ba'albek
An Nabk
Al Qaryatayn
Tudmur
Al Bū Kamāl
Al Qā'im
Ānah

LEBANON
Zahle
Saïda
Damascus (Dimashq)
Al Quṭayfah
Sab'Bi'ār
Muḥaywir

Tyr
'Akko (Acre)
Haifa
Zefat
Al Qunayṭirah
Az Zilaf
As Suwaydā'
 Şalkhad
Ar Rutbah

ISRAEL
Nazareth
Irbid
Mafraq
JORDAN
Badiyat ash Shām

Netanya
Nāblus
Zarqa
Al Azraq

Tel Aviv-Yafo
Ashdod
Jerusalem
Amman
Turayf

Gaza
Hebron
Dead Sea
Al Jālāmīd
Badanah

Beersheba
Kārak
Qaṭrāna
An Nabk

Negev
Ma'ān
Al Jafr

SINAI
Elat
Aqaba
At Tubayq
AN NAFŪD

Matrûh
Ras el Kenâyis
Alexandria (El Iskandariya)
Rashîd
Baltîm
Dumyât
Port Said (Bûr Sa'îd)

El 'Alamein
Damanhûr
El Mahalla el Kubra
El Mansûra
Tanta
Ismâ'îlîya
El 'Arîsh

Libyan Plateau
Benha
Zagazig
Suez Canal
Bitter Lakes
El Qantara

Qattâra Depression
El Giza
Cairo (El Qâhira)
Helwân
Suez (El Suweis)
Nakhl

Qara
Birkat Qârûn
El Faiyûm
'Ain Sukhna
El Kuntilla

El Beni Suef
El Fashn
Biba

Bawiti
Baharîya Oasis
El Harra
Beni Mazar
Maghâgha

EGYPT
El Minya
Mallawi
Dairût
Manfalût
Asyût
Abu Tig

RED SEA

Farâfra
Tahta
Akhmîm
Sohâg
Girga
Dishna
Qena
Quseir

Mût
Balât
El Balyana
Qus
Luxor
Isna

El Khârga
Bâris
Idfu
Marsa Alam

Aswân
Saad el Aali (Aswân High Dam)
Berenice
Ras Banâs

Libyan Desert
Khazzan an-Nasr (Lake Nasser)

HIJAZ
Tabūk
Al Qalībah
Taymā'
Jabal Shammar
Ḥā'il
Khaybar
Medīna (Al Madīnah)

SAUDI ARABIA

1:7.5M

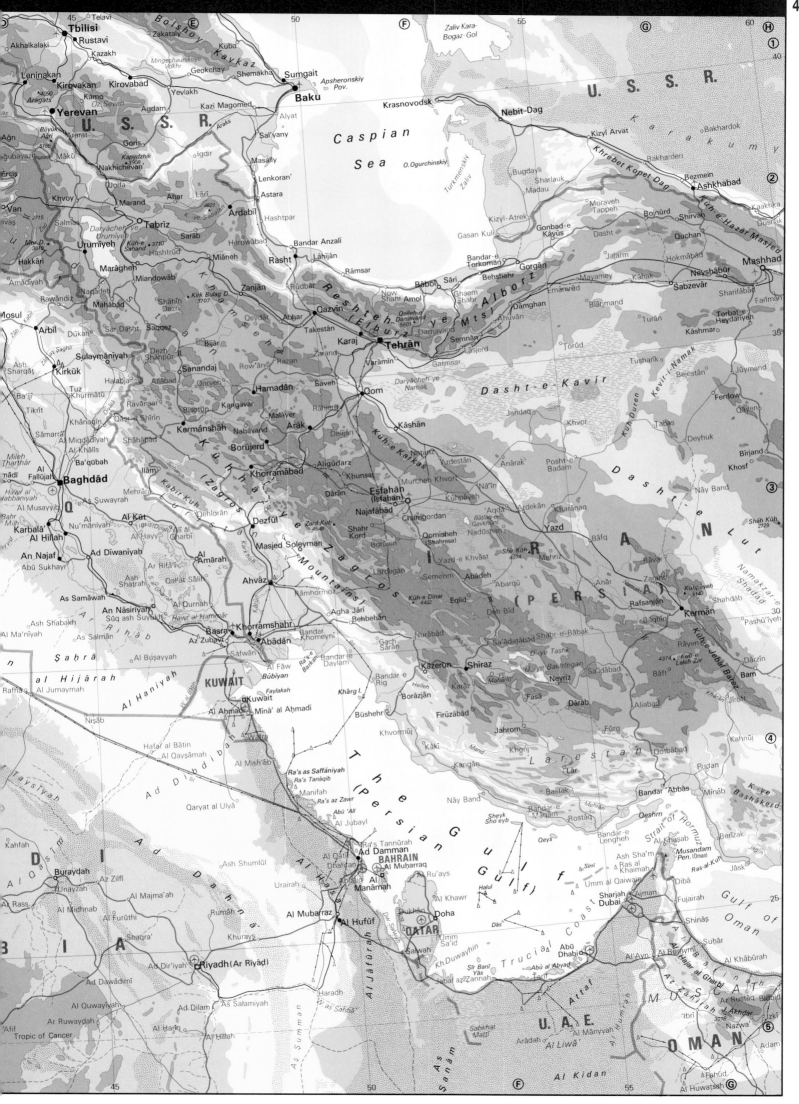

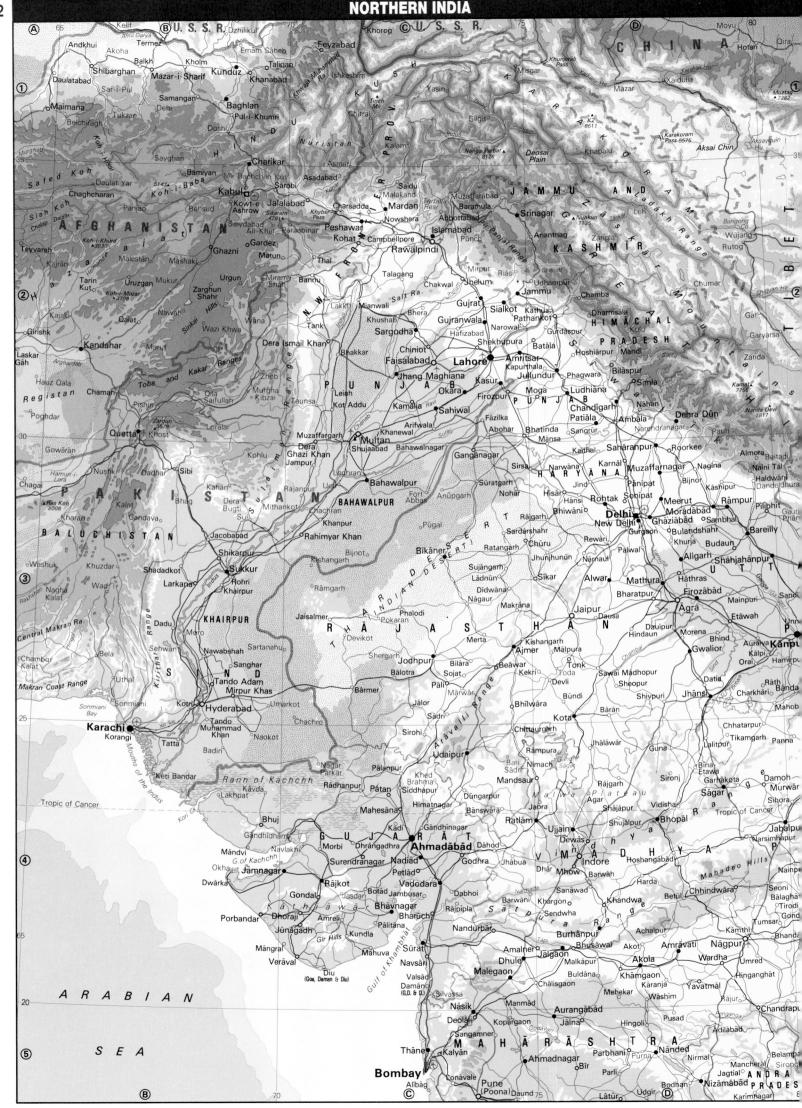

1:7.5M

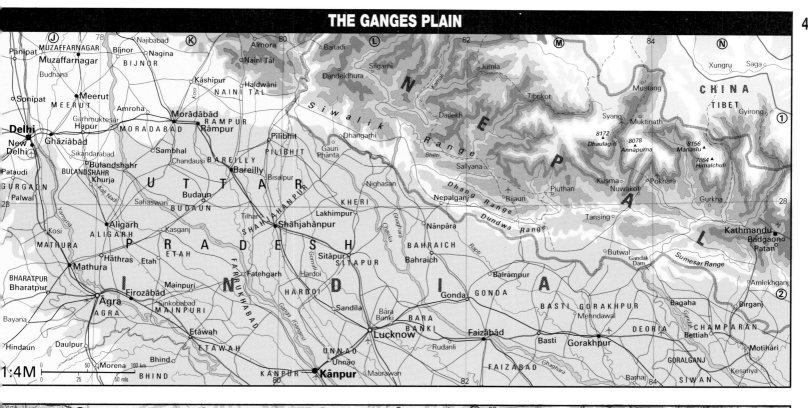

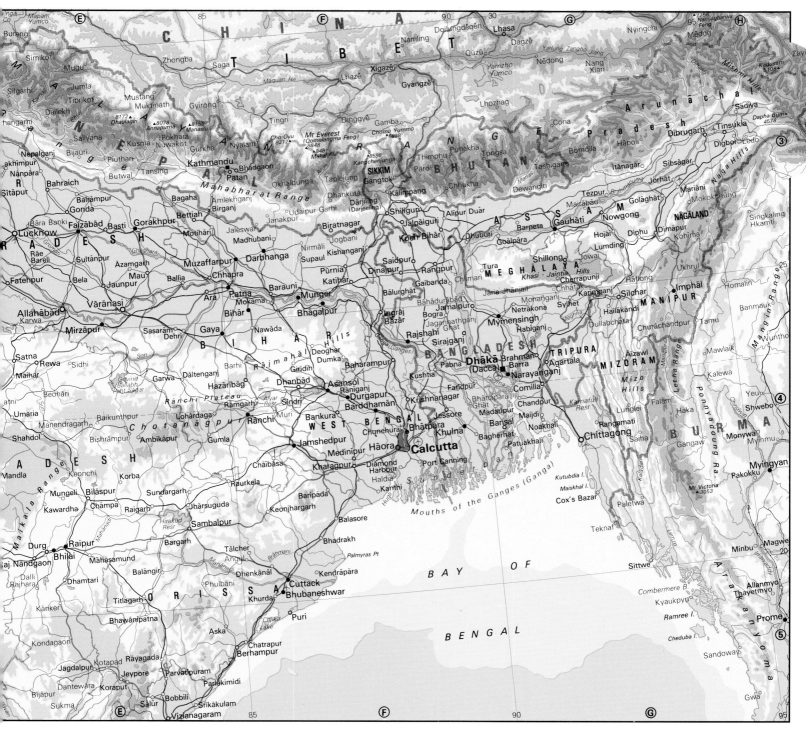

1:7.5M

0 50 100 200 300 km
0 50 100 150 mils

CYPRUS

C.A. Andreas
Yialousa
Rizokaipaso
Leonarisso
C. Kormakiti
Lapithos
Kyrenia
Akanthou
C.Elea
Morphou
Kythrea
Trikomo
Famagusta Bay
Khrysokhou Bay
Karavostasi
Lefka
Morphou
SALAMIS
Famagusta
C. Arnauti
Polis
Nicosia
Dhali
Athna
Pedhoulas
IDALION
C.Greco
Paphos (Pefos)
Mt Olympus 1951
Troodos Range
Platres
Paleokhorio
Larnaca
Larnaca Bay
C. Kiti
Lefkara
Zyvi
Episkopi
Akrotiri
Limassol
C.Zevgari
Episkopi B
Akrotiri Bay
C. Gata

ATTILA LINE

MEDITERRANEAN

SEA

SYRIA

Al Bayḍiyah
Serai
Jisr ash Shughur
Ra's Ibn Hani
Al Haffah
Shinfah
Ma'arrat an Nu'man
Latakia (Al Lādhiqīyah)
SAHYŪN
Shathah
Khan Shaykhun
Al Qardāḥah
At Tahta
Jablah
Suqaylibīyah
'Arab al Mulk
(Orontes) Suran
1385
Banias
Al Qadmūs
Dayr Shumayyil
QAL'AT AL MARQAB
Ḥamāh
Tartūs
Duraykīsh
Kafrūn Bashūr
Al Behum
Arwad
Ṣāfītā
An Nāṣirah Tall Bīsah
Birin
Al Qusayr
Qal'at al Hisn (KRAK-DES CHEVALIERS)
Hims (Homs)
Tall Kalakh
Shinshār
Kleia
Kebir
Qoubayat
El Mīna
Halba
Al Qusayr
Ūsīyah
Tripoli (Trâblous)
Zghorta
El Hermel
Hisyan

LEBANON

Batroûn
Amioune
Bcharre
Laboue
Jabal Halimah 2464
Jubail BYBLOS
Kartaba
Deir el Ahmar
2659
Dayr 'Atīyah
Rhazir
Ba'albek
An Nabk
Yabrūd
Jounié
Qornet es Saouda 3086
Bikfaya 2628
Beirut (Beyrouth)
Ba'abda
Zahle
Al J. Ma'lūla
Jayrūd
Baie de St Georges
Rayak
Aley
Az. Zabdāni
Qutayfah 1910
Damour
Beit ed Dīne
Ayn al Fījah
Dūma 'Adhra
Sidon (Saida)
Mâchghârab
At Tall
Barada
Damascus (Dimashq)
Jezzine
Rachaya
Qatana
Hasbaiya
Mt. Hermon (Jebel esh Sheikh)
A'waj Al Ḥījānah
Tyre (Tyr,Sour)
Q. Shemona
Marjayoun
Al Kiswah
Litāni
Jouai'ya
Mas'adah
Dayr 'Ali
Enn Nâqoûra
Baniyas
CEASE FIRE LINES 1974
Ghabāghib
Burāq
Nahariya
Al Qunaytirah
As Sanamayn
Mismīyah
Bennt Jbail
1208
Hama'ala
Khabab
Ma'alot Tarshīhā
Har Meron
Golan
Al Lajāh 863
Shaqqā
'Akko (Acre)
Zefat (Safad)
Nawa
Haifa (Hefa)
Q. Yam
Shefar'am
Rama
Tiberias (Yam Kinneret) (Sea of Galilee)
Izra
Shahbā
'Atlit
Tasil
Mt Carmel
Nazareth
Fiq
Shaykh Miskīn
Jabal al 'Arab 1735
528
Q. Qishon
Ma'agan
Zikhron Ya'aqov
MEGIDDO ARMAGEDDON
Afula
Deir Abu Sa'id
Dar'a
CAESAREA
Beyt Shean
Husn
Pardes Hanna
Jenin
Irbid
Hadera
Qabatiya
Ajlun
Ramtha
Netanya
Tubas
Jarash
Es Samrā
Tulkarm
J. Umm ed Daraj 1247
ISRAEL
Sabastiya
Zarqa
Er Rummān
Qa Khanna
Herzliyya
Nablus
Salt
Suweileh
Zarqa
Kefar Sava
Ramat Gan
Petah Tiqwa
Tel Aviv-Yafo (Jaffa)
Ba'al Hazor 1016
Karama
Marka
Amman
Holon
Lod
Ramallah
Wadi es Sir
Sahāb
Bat Yam
Jericho ('Arīha)
Rishon le Zion
Ramla
Na'ur
Rehovot
Latrun
Jiza
Ashdod
Jerusalem (El Quds) (Yerushalayim)
Madaba
Ashqelon
Beit Jala
Qasr el Kharana
Bethlehem (Bayt Laḥm)
Qiryat Gat
Bet Guvrin
Hebron (El Khalil)
Dab'a
Jebel Mudeisisat 962
Gaza
LACHISH
Dura
En Gedi
Wad edh Dhab'i
Sederot
Yatta
Dhībān
Khan ez Zabib
Gaza Strip
Edh Dhahiriya
Gerar
Khan Yunis
Rafah
Beersheba (Be'er Sheva)
MEZADA
Mazra
Qatrâna
Ofaqim
Be'er Sheva
Nevatim
Arad
Zeelim
El Līsan
Haluza
Sedom
Karak
Qâ'el Ḥafīra
Revivim
Dimona
MAMSHIT
Saff
Qaṣed Deir
Qezi'ot
Yeroham
SHIVTA
Sede Boqer
El Ghor
1305
T. el Meise Mazār
Manzil
NIZANA
AVEDAT
Oron
1356
Tafila
El Quseima
Mizpe Ramon
Neqarot
Ein Yahav
Rashādīya
Danā
Ḥāṣa
1641 J. el Atā'ita
Negev
1082

JORDAN

EDOM

Dead Sea

SINAI

Gulf of Suez

EGYPT

Cairo (El Qâhira)

1:2.5M
0   25   50   75   100 km
0   25   50 mls

NORWAY
SWEDEN
FINLAND
Oslo
Helsinki
Stockholm
Leningrad
Gor'kiy
Kuybyshev
Magnitogorsk
Lake Balkhash
U. S. S. R.
UNITED KINGDOM
Edinburgh
North Sea
DENMARK
Riga
Minsk
Moscow
Ural
Kharkov
Volgograd
Tashkent
Aral Sea
IRELAND
Dublin
Copenhagen
Hamburg
Gdansk
Warsaw
Kiev
Kharkov
Rostov
Don
London
NETH.
The Hague
Berlin
POLAND
Cracow
Dnepr
Volga
Brussels
BELG.
GERMANY
EAST
Prague
Odessa
Black Sea
Tbilisi
Baku
Caspian Sea
Lux.
WEST
Bonn
CZECHOSLOVAKIA
Vienna
Budapest
Bucharest
ROMANIA
Sofia
Istanbul
Ankara
Tabrīz
Mashhad
Paris
FRANCE
Berne
SWITZ.
AUSTRIA
HUNGARY
Belgrade
YUGOSLAVIA
BULGARIA
TURKEY
Tehrān
AFGHANISTAN
Bordeaux
Bay of Biscay
Milan
Rhône
ITALY
Adriatic Sea
GREECE
Athens
CYPRUS
Nicosia
SYRIA
Baghdād
IRAN
Oporto
Marseilles
Corsica
Rome
Crete
Beirut
LEB.
Damascus
IRAQ
Basra
PAK.
Madrid
Barcelona
Naples
Sardinia
Mediterranean Sea
Sicily
Jerusalem
Port Said
ISR.
JORDAN
Amman
KUWAIT
Kuwait
Shirāz
Lisbon
PORTUGAL
Tajo
SPAIN
Balearic Is.
Ebro
Azores (Port.)
Madeira (Port.)
Tangiers
Rabat
Oran
Algiers
Skikda
Annaba
Tunis
Sfax
Tripoli
Benghāzī
Tobruk
Alexandria
Cairo
Suez
Sinai
SAUDI
BAHRAIN
QATAR
Abū Dhabi
UNITED ARAB EMIRATES
Muscat
Marrakesh
Casablanca
Fès
Oujda
Béchar
Constantine
Misrātah
El Faiyûm
El Minya
Tabuk
Medina
Riyadh
ARABIA
OMAN
Kuria Muria Is.
Agadir
MOROCCO
TUNISIA
Touggourt
Ouargla
Ghadāmis
Asyût
Aswân
Mecca (Makkah)
Canary Is. (Sp.)
Tarfaya
Tindouf
Timmoun
In Salah
Ghāt
Sabhā
L. Nasser
Nile
Wadi Halfa
Jiddah
Red Sea
La'youn
Western Sahara
ALGERIA
Reggane
Tamanrasset
LIBYA
EGYPT
Atbara
Medina
San'ā
YEMEN
SOUTH YEMEN
Bir Moghrein
Nouadhibou
Atar
F'Dérik
Zouérat
SAHARA
Port Sudan
Omdurman
Khartoum
Asmara
Aden
Gulf of Aden
Socotra (S.Y.)
Nouakchott
MAURITANIA
Tombouctou
Agadez
NIGER
CHAD
Ndjamena
L. Chad
Kassala
Wad Medani
Ta'izz
Djibouti
DJIBOUTI
Dakar
St-Louis
Sénégal
MALI
Niger
Bamako
Kayes
Niamey
Zinder
Kano
Maiduguri
El Obeid
SUDAN
White Nile
Blue Nile
Hargeysa
THE GAMBIA
Banjul
SENEGAL
Tambacounda
BURKINA (UPPER VOLTA)
Ouagadougou
Kaduna
Jos
Wau
Ādīs Ābeba
ETHIOPIA
Jimma
Dire Dawa
SOMALIA
GUINEA-BISSAU
GUINEA
Mamou
Kankan
Bobo Dioulasso
BENIN
Ilorin
NIGERIA
Juba
L. Turkana
Mogadishu (Muqdisho)
Conakry
SIERRA LEONE
Freetown
Bo
IVORY COAST (CÔTE D'IVOIRE)
Tamale
TOGO
Niger
Ogbomosho
Ibadan
Enugu
Onitsha
CENTRAL AFRICAN REPUBLIC
Ngaoundéré
Bangassou
Bambari
Gulu
L Albert
UGANDA
Kampala
KENYA
Marka
Monrovia
LIBERIA
Buchanan
GHANA
Kumasi
Bouaké
Yamoussoukro
Volta
Porto Novo
Lomé
Accra
Lagos
Port Harcourt
Aba
CAMEROON
Douala
Yaoundé
Garoua
Bouar
Bangui
Zaire (Congo)
Kisangani
L Edward
Goma
RWANDA
Kigali
Entebbe
Lake Victoria
Nairobi
Kisumu
Mombasa
INDIAN
Abidjan
Bioko
Malabo
Bata
EQUAT. GUINEA
Gulf of Guinea
Príncipe
SÃO TOMÉ & PRINCIPE
Libreville
GABON
CONGO
Congo
Mbandaka
ZAIRE
Kindu
BURUNDI
Bujumbura
Kigoma
L Tanganyika
Mwanza
Arusha
Dodoma
Zanzibar
Dar es Salaam
OCEAN
Seychelles Arch.
Amirante Is
SEYCHELLES
Aldabra Is
São Tomé
Annobon (Eq.G)
Lambaréné
Equator
Brazzaville
Kinshasa
Bandundu
Kikwit
Ilebo
Kananga
Mbuji Mayi
Kalémié
L Mweru
Mbala
Kasai
L Bangweulu
Mbeya
TANZANIA
Lake Nyasa
Lichinga
Pemba
COMOROS
Mayotte (Fr.)
Antseranana
Farquhar Is
Tromelin (Fr.)
Pointe Noire
Cabinda (Ang.)
Matadi
Luanda
Malanje
Kwango
Kwilu
Kamina
Kolwezi
Likasi
Lubumbashi
Ndola
ZAMBIA
Lusaka
Lilongwe
MALAWI
Blantyre
Zomba
Nampula
MOZAMBIQUE
Mozambique
Ascension (U.K.)
SOUTH
ATLANTIC
OCEAN
St Helena (U.K.)
Namibe
Lobito
Bié
Huambo
Lubango
Cunene
ANGOLA
Cubango
Zambezi
Livingstone
L Kariba
Harare
ZIMBABWE
Hwange
Gweru
Mutare
Sofala (Beira)
Quelimane
Mozambique Channel
Mahajanga
MADAGASCAR
Antananarivo
Toamasina
Namibia
Tsumeb
Otjiwarongo
Francistown
Bulawayo
Limpopo
Fianarantsoa
Réunion (Fr.)
MAURITIUS
Walvis Bay (S.A.)
Windhoek
BOTSWANA
Serowe
Inhambane
Tropic of Capricorn
NAMIBIA (S.W. AFRICA)
Lüderitz
Keetmanshoop
Gaborone
Pretoria
Pietersburg
Xai Xai
Maputo
SWAZILAND
Mbabane
Grunau
Johannesburg
Mbombela
Welkom
Bloemfontein
Kimberley
Pietermaritzburg
Durban
LESOTHO
Maseru
SOUTH AFRICA
Orange
Bitterfontein
Paarl
Worcester
Mossel Bay
Port Elizabeth
East London
Cape Town

NORTH ATLANTIC OCEAN

Tropic of Cancer

SOUTH ATLANTIC OCEAN

Tristan da Cunha (U.K.)

1:40M
0 400 800 1200 1600 km
0 400 800 mils

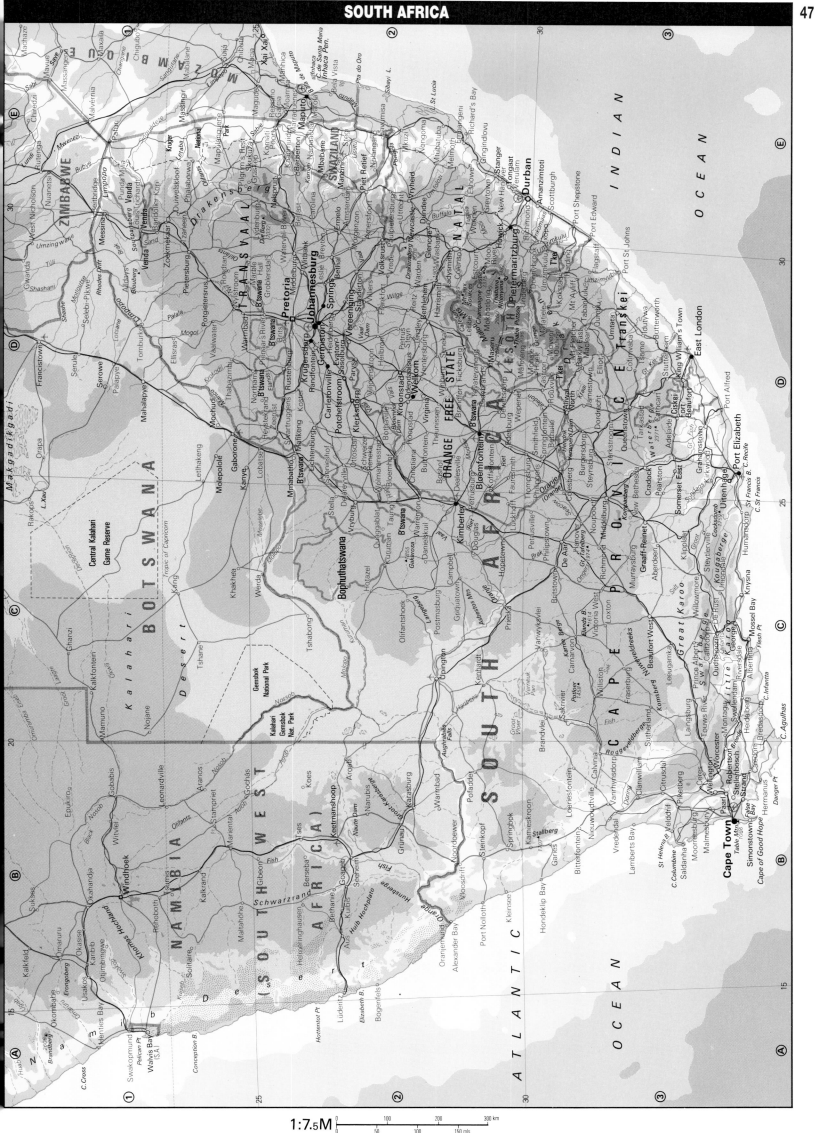

1:7.5M

| 0 | 100 | 200 | 300 km |
| 0 | 50 | 100 | 150 mls |

MEDITERRANEAN

Azores (Açores) (Portugal)
at the same scale

Flores
São Jorge
Faial Pico Terceira
Graciosa
Angra Do Heroismo
São Miguel
Ponta Delgada
Santa Maria
Formigas

PORTUGAL
Lisbon (Lisboa)
Beja Badajoz
Faro Sierra Morena Córdoba Ciudad Real Albacete
Huelva Seville (Sevilla) Granada Linares Murcia Alicante
Cádiz Málaga Almería Cartagena
Str. of Gibraltar
SPAIN
Ibiza
BALEARIC ISLANDS (Islas Baleares)
Sardinia (Sardegna)
Cagliari
La Galite
Bizerte Tunis
Tangier (Tanger) Gibraltar (U.K.) Melilla (SP.) Oran Mostaganem Algiers (Alger) Tizi Ouzou Bejaïa (Bougie) Skikda (Philippeville) Annaba (Bône) Béja Souk Ahras
Tetouan Ceuta (Sp.) Al Hoceima Mascara Cherchell Ech Cheliff Blida Constantine Sétif Souk Ahras Tunisia
Ksar-El-Kebir Taza Oujda Tlemcen Sidi-bel-Abbès Ignil-Izane Tiaret Bou Saâda M'Sila Batna Kairouan Mahdia El Jem
Kenitra Fès Aïn Beni Mathar Saïda Ksar El Boukhari Djelfa Aurès Biskra Kasserine Sfax
Rabat Meknès Azrou Missour Mecheria des Ksout Laghouat Ghardaïa Berriane Chott Melrhir Tozeur Mahrès Gabès
Casablanca (El-Dar-El-Beida) Settat Oued Zem Beni Mellal Midelt Bouârfa Figuig Berriane El Oued Touggourt Medenine Zarzis
El Jadida Safi Marrakech Toubkal 4165 Ouarzazate El Rachida Béchar Abadla Ghadaïa Ouargla Dehibat Tataouine
Essaouira **MOROCCO** Jbel Sarhro Zagora Beni Abbès El Golea El Gassi Ghadames Daraj
Agadir Anti Atlas Tata Hamada du Dra Tabelbala Timimoun Grand Erg Oriental Hassi Inifel Ohanet
Tiznit Bou Izakarn Tinfouchy Kerzaz Grand Erg Occidental In Salah Bordj Omar Driss In Amenas Idehan
Tan-Tan Jbel Ouarkziz Hamada Tounassine Hassi Mdakane Adrar In Belbel Reggane Aoulef Plateau du Tademaït Arak Hamada de Tinhert Hammâda
La'youn Saguia el Hamra El Farsia Mcherran El Eglab Chenachèn Tropic of Cancer Plaine du Tidikelt Tassili N'Ajjer Tarat

Canary Islands (Islas Canarias) (Spain)
Santa Cruz De La Palma La Palma Gomera Hierro Tenerife Santa Cruz De Tenerife Las Palmas De Gran Canaria Gran Canaria Lanzarote Arrecife Fuerteventura Pto Del Rosario C. Yubi

Madeira (Portugal) Funchal Porto Santo Deserta Grande Ilhas Selvagens (Port.)
C. Bojador B. de Rio de Oro Smara
Dakhla
Zouerate Fdérik Tourine Bir Zreigat Troudenni Bidon 5 (Ruins) Tamanrasset In Ebeggi Djanet In Ezzane
WESTERN SAHARA Tiris Ausert Aguenit Tichla Adrar Soutouf El Mreiti El Mzereb El Haricha In Dagouber Abalessa Tamanrasset (Ahaggar) Hoggar Tahat 3016 In Afaleleh
Nouadhibou Ras Nouadhibou Atar Chinguetti Ouadâne Ouarane El Djouf Oguilet Khenachich El Guettâra Taguenout Haggueret Tessalit Tin Zaouaten Mt Gréboun 1944 Iférouane Aïr
I. Tidra C. Mirik Akjoujt Araouane Guir Azaouad Ardar des Iforas In Guezzam Timia
Nouakchott Trarza Tidjikja Tichitt Néma Tombouctou Gourma Rharous Gao Kidal Anéfis Talak Timia Fach
Boutilimit Brakna Aleg Kiffa Aklé Aouana Hodh L. Faguibine Goundam Bourem Zaguere Ingal Agadez Erg du Ténéré
Rosso Kaédi El Atrouss Aïoun Dhar Oualata Niafounké Ménaka Tillia Tchin Tabaradene Tasker
St-Louis Dagana Matam Mbout Nampala Nara Douentza Ansongo Say Dosso Abala Tahoua Tanout
Louga Linguère Du Sahel Diéma Sokolo Mopti Bandiagara Djibo Téra Ouallam Birnin N'Konni Madaoua Mayahi Zinder Gouré Goudoumaria Diffa
Thies Kébémer Touba Nioro Nampala Massina Ke Macina Aribinda Dori Tillabéri Niamey Dogondoutchi Illéla Keita Dakoro Tessaoua Matameye Nguru Gashua Geidam
Dakar Diourbel Bakel Kidira Nampala Ségou Bani Djenné Dédougou Yako Kaya Bogandé Koupéla Sokoto Maradi Daura Kano Hadeija Nguigmi
Rufisque **SENEGAL** Tambacounda Kayes Koulikoro San Bani Ségou Nouna Ouagadougou Fada N'Gourma Gaya Birnin-Kebbi Gusau Kaura Namoda Katsina Kano Damaturu
Kaolack Kaffrine Bafoulabé Kolokani Bamako Kangaba Sikasso Bobo Dioulasso Boromo **BURKINA** Tenkodogo Pama Malanville Yelwa Zaria Funtua Zaria Gombe
THE GAMBIA Banjul Georgetown Velingara Kita Siguiri Kouroussa Bougouni Diébougou Tumu Bolgatanga Mango Kandi Kontagora Zungeru Kaduna Jos Bauchi Biu
Ziguinchor Bignona Kolda Sédhiou Kédougou Kangaba Kankan Gaoua Batié Bawku Gambaga Bembéréké Nikki Kainji Resr Minna **NIGERIA** Numan Yola
GUINEA-BISSAU Bissau Bafatá Gaoual Labé Touba Faranah Tingrela Wa Bolgatanga Bémberéké Parakou Jebba Shaki Keffi Wamba Shendam Jalingo Shebshi Mts 2042
Bolama Catió Fouta Djallon Kindia Kissidougou Odienné Korhogo Bouna Bole Yendi Djougou Bassila Savalou Baro Ilorin Lafiagi Nasarawa Lafia Wukari Gashaka Gotel Mts
Arquipélago dos Bijagós Boké Dalaba Dabola Kankan Niakaramandougou Ferkéssédougou Kanté Kouandé Yashikera Bida Ogbomosho Oshogbo Oyo Okene Makurdi Katsina Ala
C. Verga Boffa Fria Mamou **GUINEA** Faranah Séguéla Sokodé Djougou Parakou Save Abomey Iwo Ife Okene Otukpo Ogoja Abakaliki Wum Mamfé
Conakry Forécariah Kabala Beyla Kissidougou Bouaké Katiola Bondoukou Wenchi Atakpamé Kpalimé Pobé Sakété Abéokuta Ibadan Ondo Owo Benin City Enugu Nkambe Bamenda Foumban Bafoussam
Kambia **SIERRA LEONE** Makeni Kenema Voinjama Zorzor Man Daloa Bouaké Mampong Volta Ho Tsévié Cotonou Lagos Ijebu Ode Sapele Onitsha Aba Mamfé **CAMEROON**
C. Sierra Leone Freetown Moyamba Bo Mano Nzérékoré Touba Danané Duékoué Gagnoa Yamoussoukro Kumasi Bibiani Koforidua Nsawam Accra Porto Novo Warri Owerri Calabar Kumba Nkongsamba Douala Yaoundé
Sherbro Bonthe Robertsport **LIBERIA** Buchanan Greenville Chiehn Sassandra San Pédro Harper C. Palmas **IVORY COAST (CÔTE D'IVOIRE)** Abidjan Grand Bassam Sekondi Takoradi Cape Coast Bight of Benin Mouths of the R. Niger Port Harcourt Bonny Mt Cameroun 4095 Buea Limbe Malabo Edea
Monrovia Mt Niete River Cess Dabou Three Points Forcados **EQUATORIAL GUINEA** Bata Ebebiyin Mbalmayo Ebolowa Sangmélima
GULF OF GUINEA Bight of Biafra Kribi Campo Principe S. TOME & PRINCIPE São Tomé Río Benito Libreville **GABON**

Cape Verde at the same scale
Sto Antão S Vicente Sta Luzia S Nicolau Sal Boa Vista S Tiago Fogo Maio Brava Praia
Pagalu (Equat. Guinea)

Scale 1:15M
0 200 400 600 km
0 100 200 300 mls

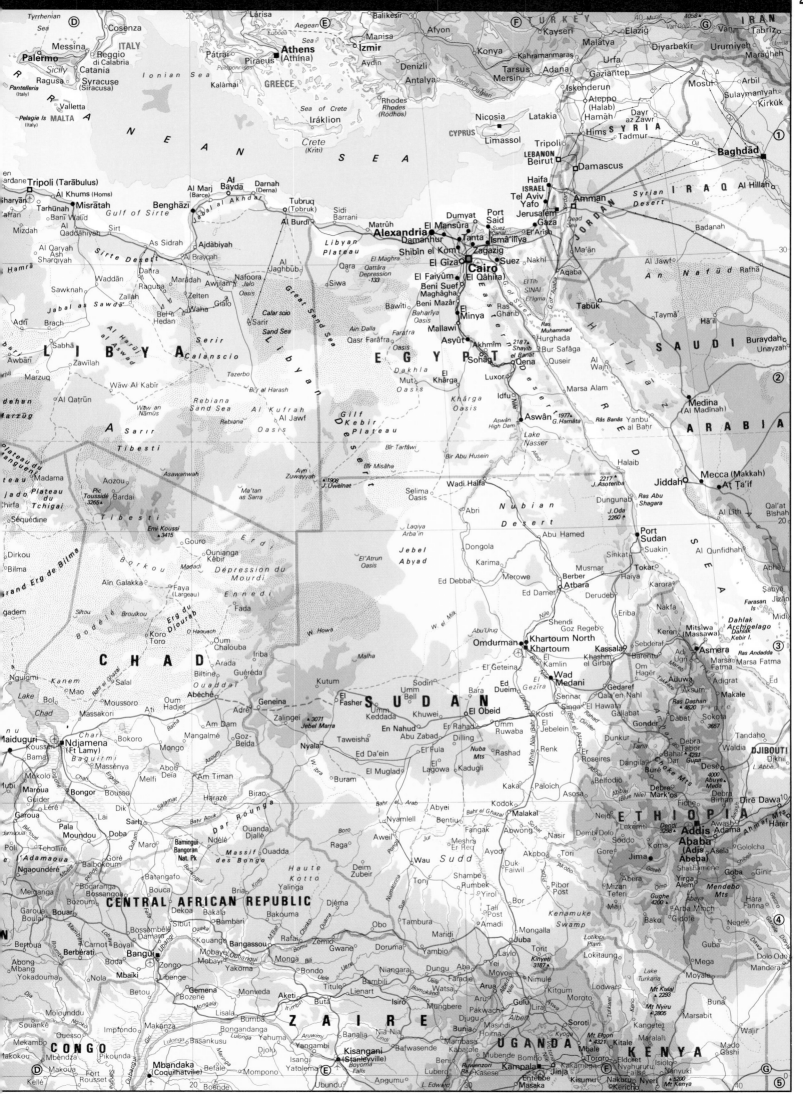

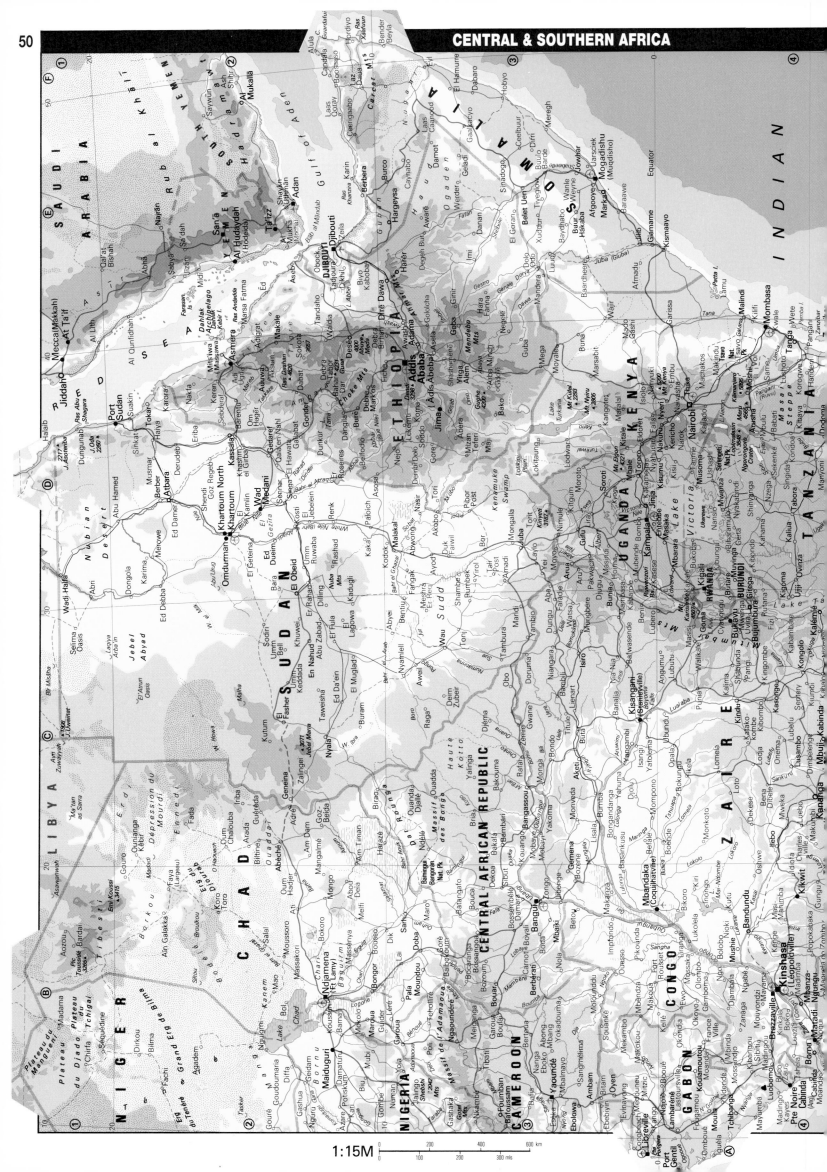

1:15M

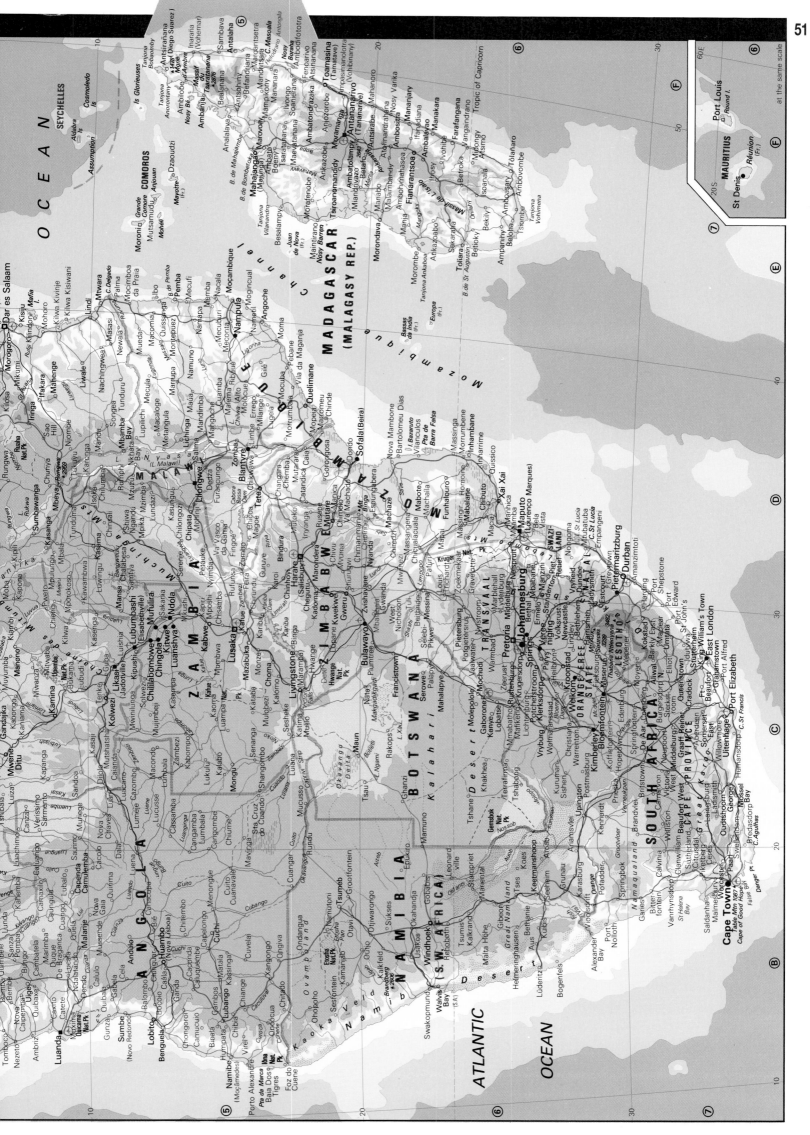

ATLANTIC OCEAN

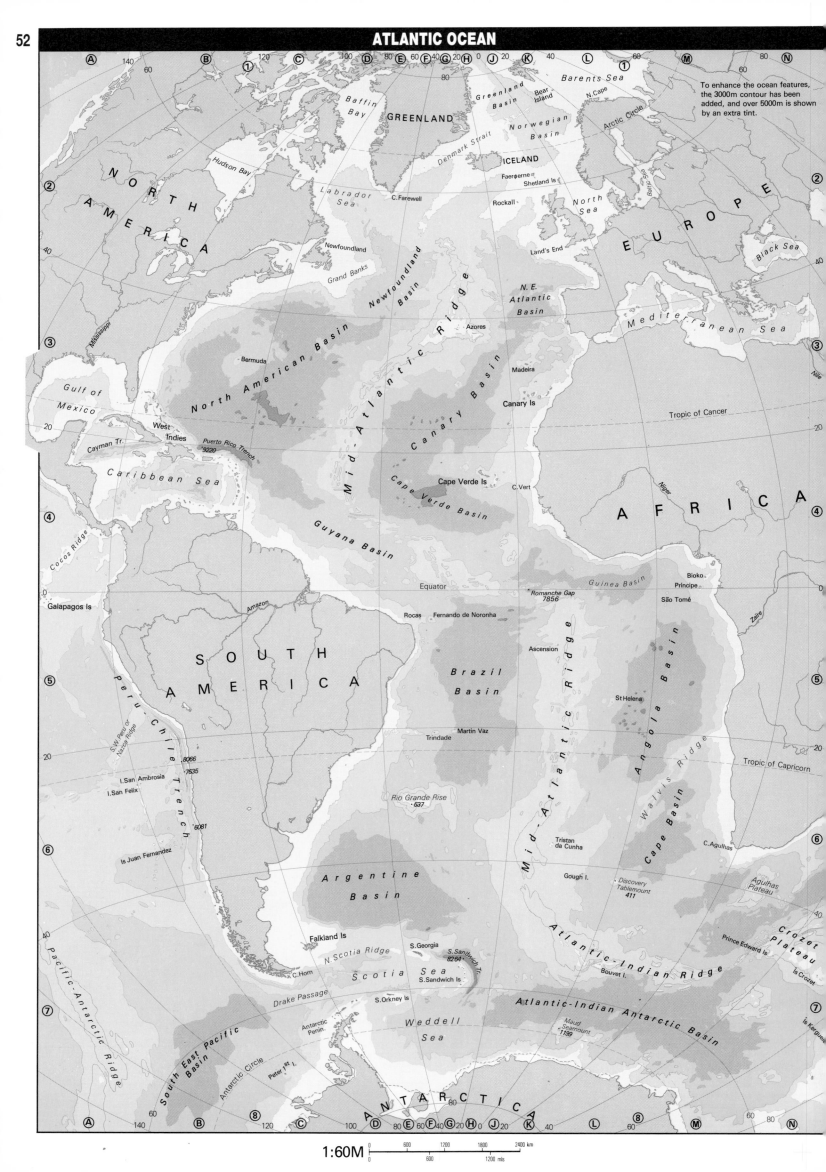

To enhance the ocean features,
the 3000m contour has been
added, and over 5000m is shown
by an extra tint.

NORTH AMERICA

EUROPE

SOUTH AMERICA

AFRICA

ANTARCTICA

GREENLAND

ICELAND

Baffin Bay

Hudson Bay

Labrador Sea

Newfoundland

Grand Banks

Gulf of Mexico

Mississippi

West Indies

Cayman Tr.

Caribbean Sea

Puerto Rico Trench
·9220

Bermuda

Galapagos Is

Cocos Ridge

Amazon

Rocas
Fernando de Noronha

Peru-Chile Trench

S.W.Peru or Nazca Ridge

·8066
·7635

I.San Ambrosia
I.San Felix

·6081

Is Juan Fernandez

Pacific-Antarctic Ridge

South East Pacific Basin

Antarctic Circle

Peter 1st I.

C.Horn

Drake Passage

Falkland Is

Argentine Basin

N.Scotia Ridge

S.Georgia

S.Sandwich Tr.
8264

Scotia Sea

S.Sandwich Is

S.Orkney Is

Antarctic Penin.

Weddell Sea

Maud Seamount
1199

North American Basin

Newfoundland Basin

Mid-Atlantic Ridge

Azores

N.E. Atlantic Basin

Canary Basin

Canary Is

Madeira

Cape Verde Is

Cape Verde Basin

C.Vert

Guyana Basin

Equator

Brazil Basin

Ascension

Trindade

Martin Vaz

Rio Grande Rise
·637

Mid-Atlantic Ridge

Tristan da Cunha

Gough I.

Discovery Tablemount
411

Atlantic-Indian Ridge

Bouvet I.

Atlantic-Indian Antarctic Basin

Romanche Gap
7856

Guinea Basin

São Tomé

Bioko
Príncipe

Zaïre

Niger

St Helena

Angola Basin

Walvis Ridge

Cape Basin

C.Agulhas

Agulhas Plateau

Prince Edward Is

Crozet Plateau

Is Crozet

Is Kerguelen

Greenland Basin

Bear Island

Barents Sea

N.Cape

Arctic Circle

Norwegian Basin

Denmark Strait

C.Farewell

Faerøerne
Shetland Is

North Sea

Rockall

Land's End

Baltic Sea

Mediterranean Sea

Black Sea

Nile

Tropic of Cancer

Tropic of Capricorn

1:60M

0   600   1200   1800   2400 km
0   600   1200 mls

U.S.S.R.

Arctic Ocean

ICELAND
Reykjavík

Bering Strait

Chukchi Sea

Bering Sea

Beaufort Sea

Aleutian Islands

A L A S K A
Prudhoe Bay
Barrow
Fairbanks
Anchorage
Archangel
Juneau
C. Juneau
Yukon

Banks I.

Victoria I.

Queen Elizabeth Islands

Ellesmere I.

Thule

GREENLAND
(Denmark)

Godthåb

Denmark Strait

Davis Strait

Baffin Bay

Baffin I.

Resolute
Devon I.
Inuvik

Whitehorse
Dawson
Prince Rupert
Q. Charlotte Is
Prince George
Vancouver I.
Victoria
Vancouver
Seattle
Portland
Columbia

Dawson Creek
Peace
Athabasca
Uranium City
Great Slave L.
Yellowknife
Hay River
Great Bear L.
Mackenzie

C A N A D A

Hudson Bay

Churchill

Inukjuac

Hudson Strait

Southampton I.

Labrador Sea

Schefferville
Goose Bay
Churchill Falls

Newfoundland
Anticosti I.
St John's
Charlottetown

Edmonton
Calgary
Saskatoon
Regina
Medicine Hat
Saskatchewan
Athabasca

Spokane
Great Falls
Butte
Snake

San Francisco
Sacramento
Reno
Salt Lake City
Los Angeles
San Bernadino
San Diego
Tijuana
Phoenix
Tucson

U N I T E D   S T A T E S
O F   A M E R I C A

Denver
Pueblo
Arkansas
Albuquerque
Amarillo
Oklahoma City
Wichita

Omaha
Kansas City
St Louis
Missouri
Colorado

Winnipeg
Kenora
L. Winnipeg
Fargo
Duluth
Thunder Bay
Minneapolis
St Paul
Milwaukee
Chicago
L. Superior
L. Michigan
Sault Ste Marie
Sudbury
Huron
Detroit
Cleveland
Indianapolis
Cincinatti
Nashville
Memphis
Birmingham
Jackson
Ohio
Mississippi
Red

Moosonee
Chibougamau
Québec
Montréal
Ottawa
Toronto
Ontario
L. Erie
Buffalo
Boston
New York
Philadelphia
Baltimore
Washington
Newport News
Norfolk

Sept Îles
Moncton
Fredericton
St. John
Halifax

ATLANTIC OCEAN

Bermuda (U.K.)

Phoenix
Ciudad Juárez
El Paso
Fort Worth
Dallas
Austin
San Antonio
Houston
Corpus Christi
Hermosillo
Chihuahua
Monterrey
Torreón
Durango
Mazatlán

Atlanta
Charleston
Savannah
Tallahassee
Mobile
Baton Rouge
New Orleans
Jacksonville
Tampa
Miami

Tropic of Cancer

M E X I C O

G. de California

Revilla Gigedo Is. (Mex.)

Guadalajara
México
Veracruz
Tampico
Acapulco
Mérida

Gulf of Mexico

Nassau
THE BAHAMAS

Habana
CUBA
Guantánamo

HAITI
Port-au-Prince
DOMINICAN REP.
Santo Domingo
Pto Rico (U.S.A.)
San Juan

ANTIGUA & BARBUDA
St Kitts - Nevis
DOMINICA
ST LUCIA
ST VINCENT
BARBADOS
GRENADA
TRINIDAD & TOBAGO

JAMAICA
Kingston

CARIBBEAN SEA

Sargasso Sea

PACIFIC

OCEAN

Clipperton (Fr.)

GUATEMALA
Guatemala
BELIZE
Belmopan
HONDURAS
Tegucigalpa
EL SALVADOR
S.Salvador
NICARAGUA
Managua

COSTA RICA
S.José
PANAMA
Panamá

Sta Marta
Barranquilla
Maracaibo
Caracas
Cd Guayana
Orinoco

Netherlands Antilles

VENEZUELA

I. del Coco (C.R.)

Medellín
Bogotá
Bueraventura
Cali
Malpelo (Col.)
COLOMBIA

Quito
ECUADOR
Galapagos Is (Ecu.)

PERU

BRAZIL
Negro

Equator

1:35M

0 250 500 750 1000 1250 km

0 250 500 750 mls

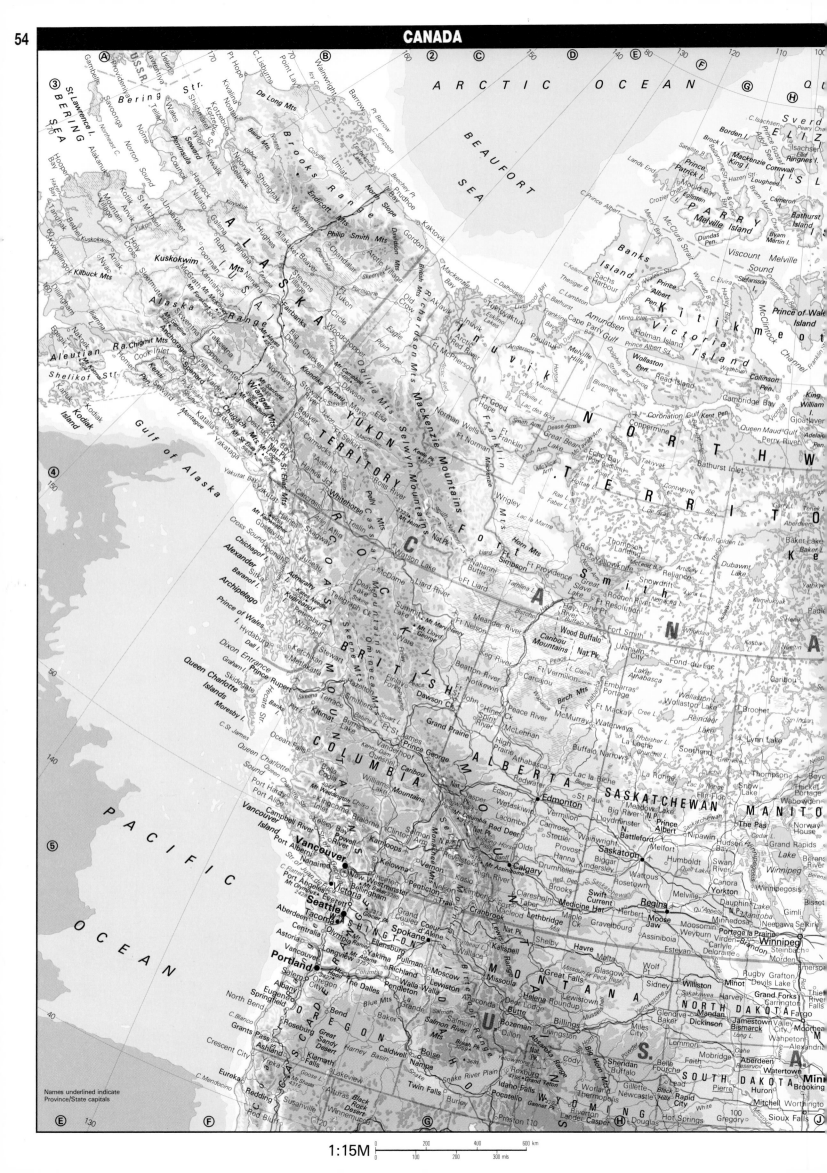

ARCTIC OCEAN

BEAUFORT SEA

U.S.S.R.

BERING SEA

Bering Str.

St. Lawrence I.

ALASKA (U.S.A.)

Brooks Range

Alaska Range

Mt. McKinley

Kuskokwim

Aleutian Ra.

Kodiak Island

Gulf of Alaska

PACIFIC OCEAN

YUKON TERRITORY

Whitehorse

BRITISH COLUMBIA

Queen Charlotte Islands

Vancouver Island

Vancouver

Victoria

Seattle

Tacoma

Portland

WASHINGTON

OREGON

NORTHWEST TERRITORIES

Banks Island

Victoria Island

Kitikmeot

PARRY ISLS.

Melville Island

Prince of Wales Island

Great Bear Lake

Great Slave Lake

Yellowknife

Lake Athabasca

ALBERTA

Edmonton

Calgary

SASKATCHEWAN

Saskatoon

Regina

Prince Albert

MANITOBA

Winnipeg

MONTANA

NORTH DAKOTA

Bismarck

SOUTH DAKOTA

Pierre

WYOMING

Casper

U.S.A.

Names underlined indicate Province/State capitals

1:15M

0   200   400   600 km

0   100   200   300 mls

BRITISH COLUMBIA

ALBERTA

SASKATCHEWAN

MANITOBA

ROCKY MOUNTAINS

WASHINGTON

OREGON

IDAHO

MONTANA

NORTH DAKOTA

WYOMING

SOUTH DAKOTA

NEVADA

UTAH

UNITED

COLORADO

NEBRASKA

KANSAS

CALIFORNIA

ARIZONA

NEW MEXICO

OKLAHOMA

TEXAS

BAJA CALIFORNIA

SONORAN DESERT

MEXICO

SIERRA MADRE OCCIDENTAL

SIERRA MADRE ORIENTAL

PACIFIC OCEAN

GULF OF CALIFORNIA

Vancouver Island

Vancouver
Seattle
Tacoma
Portland
Salem
Eugene
San Francisco
Oakland
San Jose
Sacramento
Los Angeles
San Diego
Tijuana
Mexicali
Las Vegas
Phoenix
Tucson
Salt Lake City
Provo
Denver
Colorado Springs
Pueblo
Albuquerque
Santa Fe
El Paso
Cd Juárez
Dallas
Fort Worth
Austin
San Antonio
Corpus Christi
Monterrey
Chihuahua
Durango
Mazatlán
Culiacán

Tropic of Cancer

Names underlined indicate
Province/State capitals

1:12.5M

0   100   200   300   400   500 km
0   100   200   300 mils

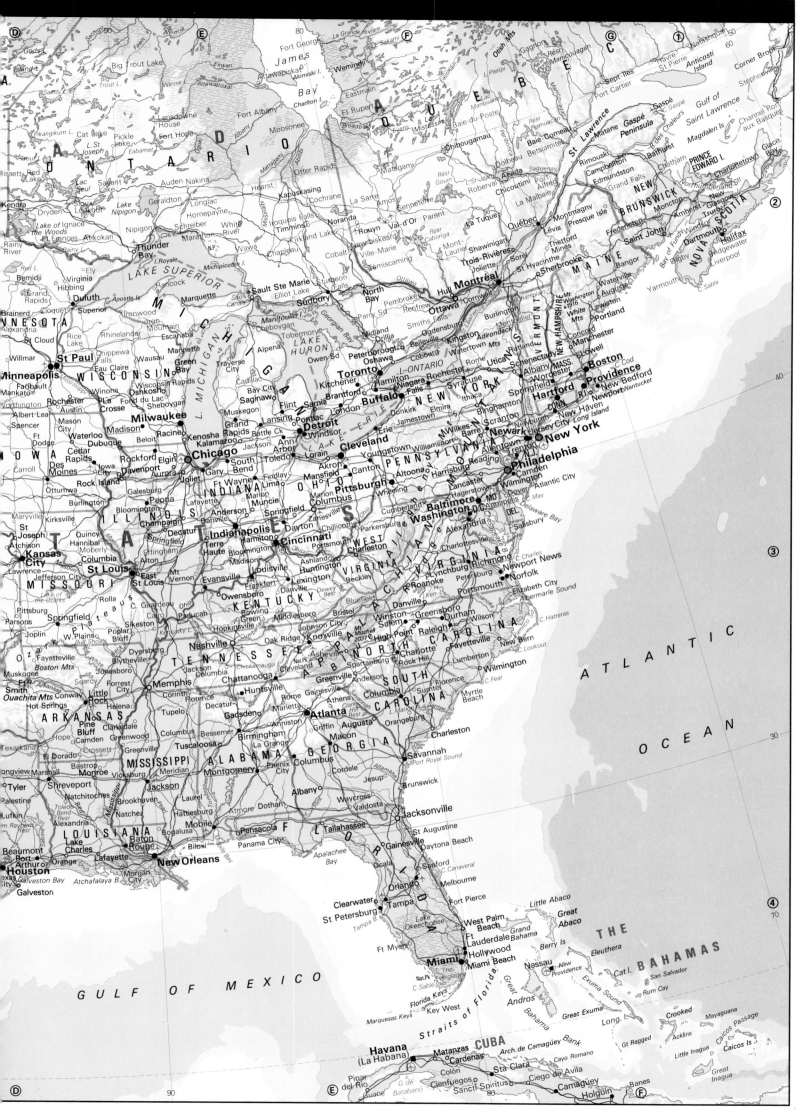

SASKATCHEWAN
ALBERTA
BRITISH COLUMBIA
CANADA
WASHINGTON
OREGON
MONTANA
IDAHO
WYOMING
ROCKY MOUNTAINS
BITTERROOT RANGE
Salmon River Mountains
Clearwater Mountains
Beaverhead Mts
Columbia Plateau
Snake River Plain
Blue Mountains
Wind River Range
Absaroka
Gros Ventre Range
Teton Range
Lewis Range
Cabinet Mts
Little Belt Mts
Big Belt Mts
Crazy Mts
Cypress Hills
Uinta Mts
Klamath Mts
Steens Mtn
Santa Rosa Mts
Independence Mts
High Desert
Harney Basin
Black Rock Desert
Great Salt Lake Desert

Vancouver
Victoria
Seattle
Tacoma
Olympia
Portland
Salem
Spokane
Salt Lake City
Ogden
Billings
Great Falls
Helena
Butte
Missoula
Boise
Pocatello
Idaho Falls
Yellowstone Nat. Park
Glacier Nat. Park
Mount Rainier Nat. Park
Olympic Nat. Park
North Cascades Nat. Park

1:5M

0   50   100   150   200 km
0   50   100 mls

ALBERTA
SASKATCHEWAN
CANADA
MANI...

Milk   Wild Horse   Consul   Govenlock   Climax   Val Marie   Willow Bunch   Rockglen   Radville   Carlyle   Souris   Melita   Boissevain   Mani...
Cut Bank   Shelby   Chester   Gildford   Fresno Resr   Havre   Harlem   Opheim   Scobey   Plentywood   Fortuna   Portal   Bowbells   Mohall   Bottineau   Dunseith   Langdon   Edmo...
Two Medicine   Conrad   Teton   Big Sandy   Tiber Resr   Malta   Saco   Glasgow   Wolf Point   Poplar   Culbertson   Williston   Tioga   Stanley   Kenmare   Towner   Rugby   Cando
Chouteau   Black Eagle   Fort Benton   Baldy Mtn 2116   Missouri   Fort Peck   Sidney   Watford City   New Town   Lake Sakakawea   Max   Garrison   Velva   Drake   Harvey   Shey...   Devils L.
Fairfield   Sun   Cascade   Great Falls   Stanford   Royo   Jordan   Circle   Lindsay   Glendive   Wibaux   Beach   Belfield   Halliday   Underwood   Carrington   Devils Lake
Helena   Townsend   White Sulphur Springs   Harlowtown   Lewistown   Grassrange   Roundup   Rock Springs   Terry   Yellowstone   Dickinson   Hebron   Mandan   Bismarck   Medina   Jamestown
MONTANA   NORTH DAKOTA
Three Forks   Belgrade   Bozeman   Livingston   Big Timber   Columbus   Laurel   Billings   Hardin   Custer   Forsyth   Miles City   Rosebud   Baker   Marmarth   White Butte 1076   Mott   Elgin   Sterling   Dawson   Napoleon
Madison   Gallatin   Gardiner   Red Lodge   Bridger   Bighorn   Ashland   Broadus   Hammond   Ekalaka   Bowman   Cannonball   Hettinger   Lemmon   McIntosh   Linton   Edgeley   Ellendale
ROCK   Electric Peak   Mt Washburn   Granite Peak 3901   Lovell   Ranchester   Tongue   Powder   Buffalo   McLaughlin   Mobridge   Selby   Ashley   Eureka   Aberdeen
West Yellowstone   Yellowstone Nat. Park   Absaroka Range   Cody   Greybull   Story   Sheridan   Clearmont   Belle Fourche   Faith   Dupree   Moreau   La Plant   Eagle Butte   Gettysburg   Redfield   Miller
Island Park   Shoshone   Trout Peak 3732   Basin   Cloud Peak 4016   Buffalo   Gillette   Sundance   Spearfish   Enning   Lake Oahe   Blunt
Targhee Pass   Jackson Lake   Grand Teton Nat. Park   Moran   Meeteetse   Worland   Francs Pk 4005   Owl Creek Mts   Moorcroft   Lead   Deadwood   Black Hills   Rapid City   SOUTH DAKOTA   Fort Pierre   Pierre   Wessington Springs
Gros Ventre   Jackson   Dubois   Thermopolis   Osage   Newcastle   Custer   Nat. Pk   Hot Springs   Philip   Wall   Kadoka   Presho   Chamberlain
Alpine   Gannett Peak 4202   Boysen Resr   Riverton   Shoshoni   Kaycee   Midwest   Mule Creek   Edgemont   Oelrichs   White River   Murdo   Oacoma   Plankinto...
Afton   Daniel   3480 Wyoming Peak   Lander   Powder River   Wind River Range   Wounded Knee   Winner   Gregory   Lake Andes   Platte
La Barge   Pinedale   WYOMING   Casper   Douglas   Shawnee   Pine Ridge   Martin   Mission   Bonesteel
Cokeville   Eden   Sweetwater   Evansville   Lusk   Glendo Resr   Chadron   Merriman   Valentine   Niobrara   Stuart
Kemmerer   Diamondville   Reliance   Wamsutter   Muddy Gap Pass   Pathfinder Resr   Lamont   Guernsey   Crawford   Rushville   Ainsworth   Bassett
Green   Rock Springs   Seminoe Resr   Wheatland   Lingle   NEBRASKA   Hyannis   Thedford   Dunning   Bartlett   Burwell   Ord
Lyman   Evanston   Flaming Gorge Resr   Green River   Saratoga   Elk Mtn 3400   Medicine Bow   Rock River   Fort Laramie   Torrington   Morrill   Scottsbluff   Bayard   Alliance   N. Platte   Bridgeport   Broadwater   Stapleton   Broken Bow
Manila   Kings Peak 4114   Uinta Mts   Vernal   Baggs   Bridger Peak 3662   Medicine Bow Pk 3661   Laramie   Foxpark   Gering   Chugwater   Kimball   Potter   Sidney   Ushkosh   L. McConaughy   Ogallala   Big Springs   Paxton   North Platte   Ansley   St Paul
Roosevelt   Medicine Bow Mts   Pine Bluffs   Chappell   Ovid   Julesburg   Sutherland   Gothenburg   Cozad   Lexington   Grand Island
Duchesne   Dinosaur   Craig   Hayden   Steamboat Springs   Fall River Pass   Fort Collins   Wellington   Cheyenne   Sterling   Holyoke   Imperial   Maywood   Gibb...   Kearney   Hasti...
Price   Roan Plateau   Meeker   Kremmling   Rocky Mtn Nat. Park   Estes Park   Loveland   Greeley   S. Platte   Brush   Otis   Arapahoe   Holdrege   Blu... Hill
UTAH   Green River   Rangely   White   Granby   Longs Peak 4345   Boulder   Longmont   Fort Morgan   Wray   Benkelman   McCook   Alma   Red Cloud   Republican
Mack   Fruita   Glenwood Springs   Eagle   Idaho Springs   Lafayette   Las Vegas   Denver   Byers   Akron   Cope   St Francis   Norton   Lebanon   Oberlin   Phillipsburg   Stockton
Grand Junction   Minturn   Loveland Pass   Berthoud Pass   Mt Evans 4348   Lakewood   Aurora   Englewood   Littleton   Limon   Burlington   Colby   Goodland   Hill City   Stockton
Grand Valley   Rifle   Palisade   Leadville   Sawatch Mts   Tennessee Pass   Castle Rock   Kanorado   Oakley   Saline
Brendel   Moab   Delta   Mt Elbert 4399   Buena Vista   COLORADO   Simla   Cheyenne Wells   Weskan   WaKeeney   Russell   Smoky Hill
Arches N.P.   Green River   Mt Harvard 4378   Manitou Springs   Pikes Peak 4301   Colorado Springs   Kit Carson   Tribune   Scott City   Ness City   Hosington   Wilso...
Canyonlands Nat. Pk   Mt Peale 3957   Gunnison   Monarch Pass   Salida   Canon City   Garden City   Kinsley   KANSAS
Monticello   Abajo Mts   Dove Creek   Uravan   Montrose   Uncompahgre Plateau   Ouray   Saguache   Florence   Arkansas   Pueblo   Boone   Ordway   Wiley   Lamar   Syracuse   Lakin   Great Bend
Blanding   Mt Wilson 4342   Silverton   San Juan Mts   Monte Vista   Blanca Peak 4364   Sangre de Cristo Mts   Rocky Ford   John Martin Resr   Las Animas   La Junta   Montezuma   Dodge City   Pratt   Greensburg
Bluff   Cortez   Mesa Verde N.P.   Durango   Wolf Creek Pass   South Fork   Alamosa   Walsenburg   Delhi   Purgatoire   Ulysses   Red Hills   Meade   Medicine Lodge
Mexican Hat   Monument Valley   COLORADO   Pagosa Springs   Antonito   Trinidad   Springfield   Hugoton   Plains   Liberal   Ashland
Kayenta   Shiprock   Aztec   Bloomfield   Farmington   Navajo Resr   Chama   Tierra Amarilla   Raton

1:5M   0   50   100   150   200 km   0   50   100 mls

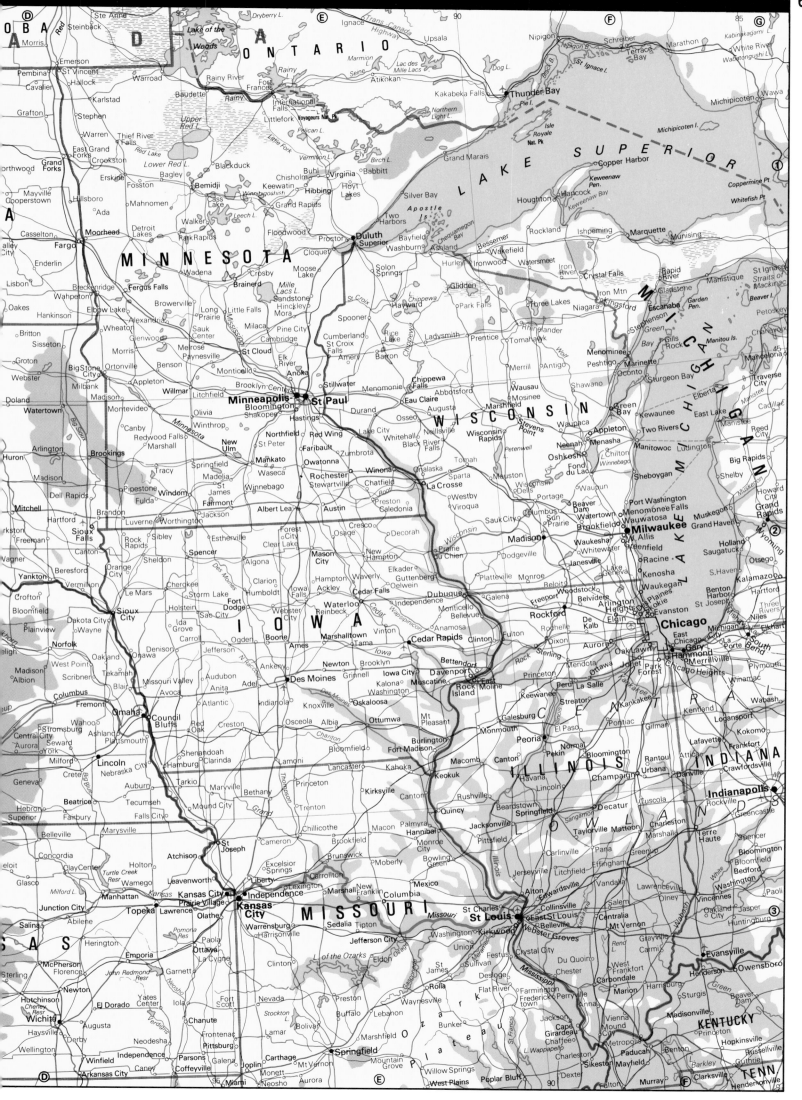

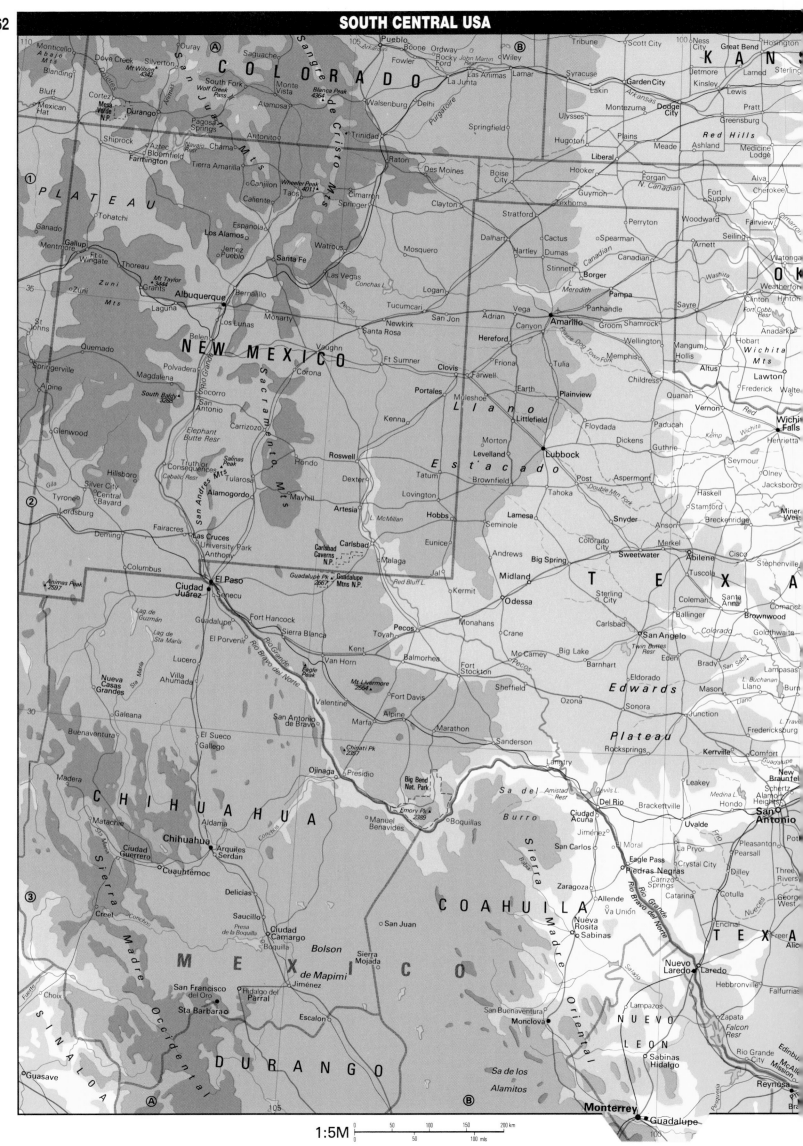

1:5M

0   50   100   150   200 km
0   50   100 mls

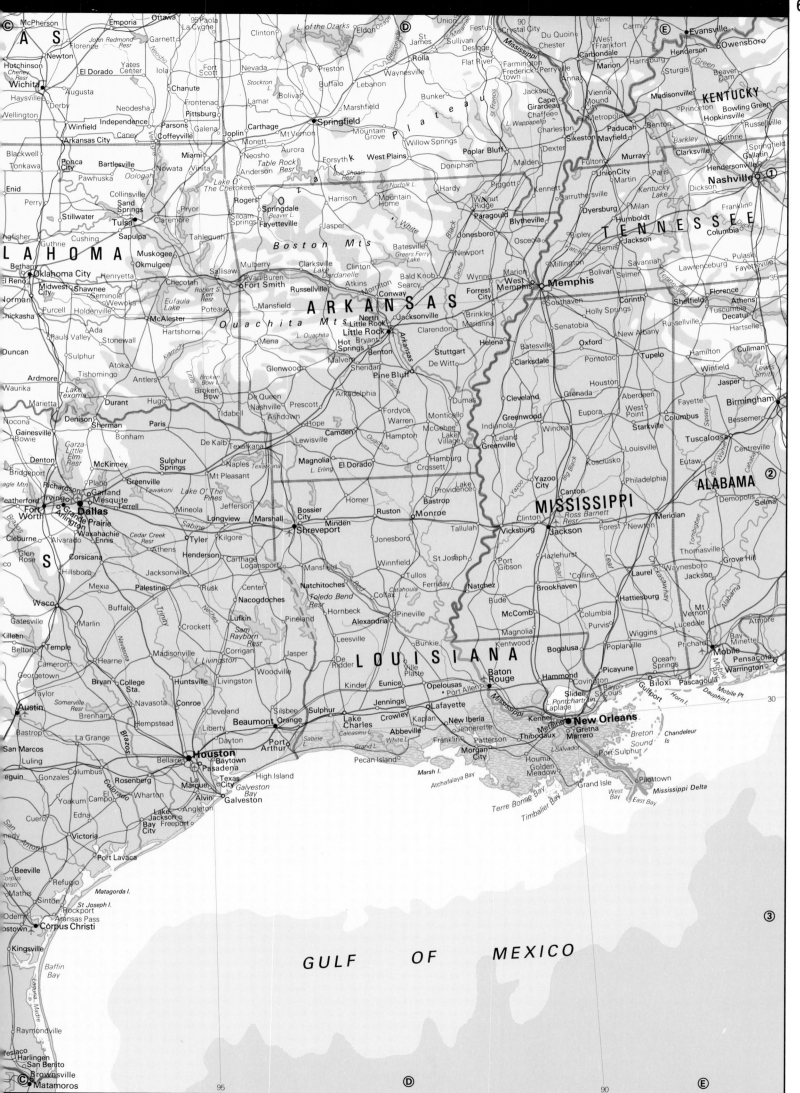

1:5M

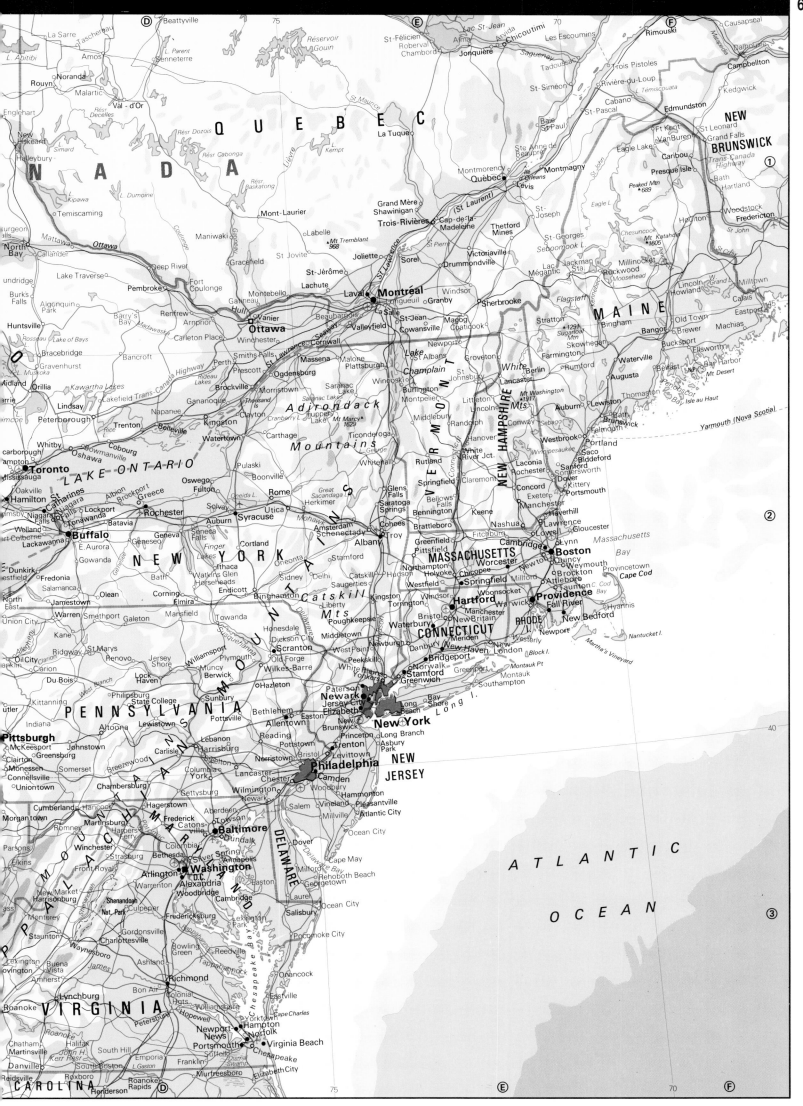

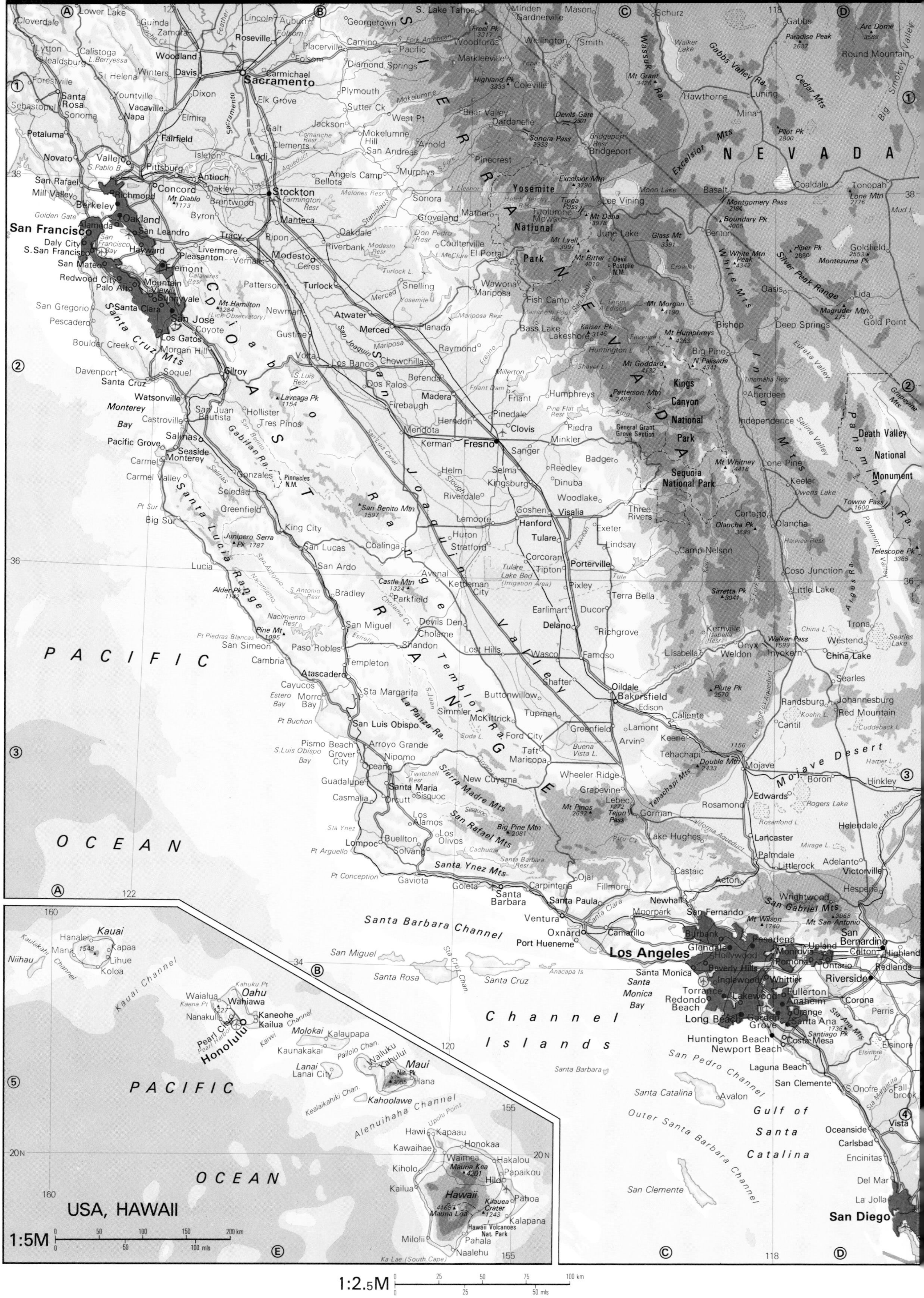

NEVADA

CALIFORNIA

PACIFIC OCEAN

San Francisco · Oakland · Berkeley · San Jose · Sacramento · Stockton · Modesto · Fresno · Bakersfield · Los Angeles · San Diego

Yosemite National Park · Kings Canyon National Park · Sequoia National Park · Death Valley National Monument · Mojave Desert

SIERRA NEVADA · Santa Lucia Range · Gabilan Ra. · Santa Cruz Mts · Temblor Ra. · San Rafael Mts · Santa Ynez Mts · San Gabriel Mts

Mt Whitney 4418 · Mauna Kea 4201 · Mauna Loa 4169

Santa Barbara Channel · Channel Islands · Gulf of Santa Catalina · Outer Santa Barbara Channel · San Pedro Channel

USA, HAWAII

Kauai · Niihau · Oahu · Honolulu · Molokai · Lanai · Maui · Kahoolawe · Hawaii

Hawaii Volcanoes Nat. Park · Kilauea Crater 1243

PACIFIC OCEAN

1:5M

0 50 100 150 200 km
0   50   100 mls

1:2.5M

0 25 50 75 100 km
0   25   50 mls

1:5M

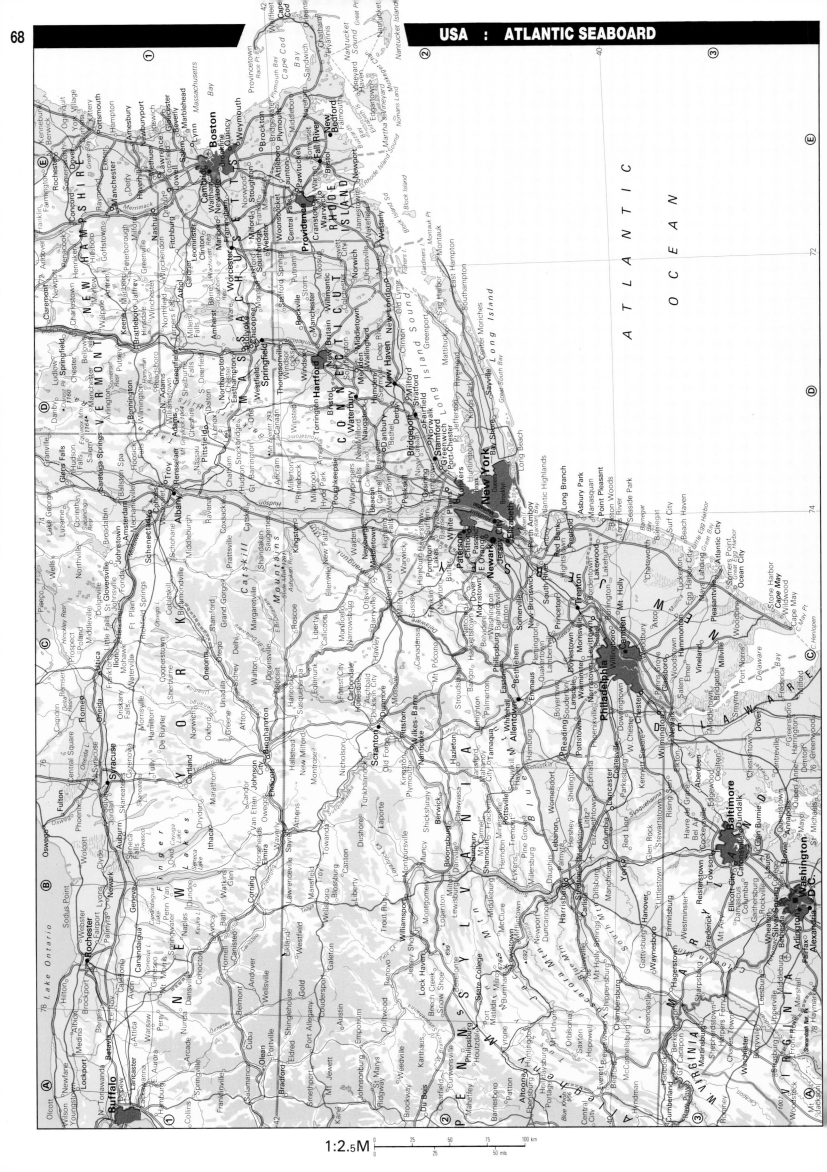

1:2.5M

TRINIDAD

Galera Pt · Matura Bay · Matelot · Northern Mt Aripo Range · Cocos Bay · St Joseph · Upper Manzanilla · Arima · Chupara Pt · Toco · Tunapuna · Princes Town · Guayaguayare · Cocos Bay · Galeota Pt · Port of Spain · San Juan · Chaguanas · Rio Claro · Débé · Siparia · San Fernando · Gulf of Paria · Point Fortin · Fullarton · Moruga · 61 · 62

TOBAGO 1:2.5 M
Charlotteville · Speyside · Moriah · Scarborough · Canaan · Crown Pt · 60°30' · 11°15' · K · 18

DOMINICA 1:2.5 M
C. Melville · Mangot · Morne Diablotin · 1447 · Portsmouth · Roseau · Rosalie · Grand Bay · 61°30' · Q

BARBADOS 1:2.5 M
North Pt · Speightstown · Holetown · Bridgetown · Ragged Pt · Blackman's · Mt Hillaby 340 · South Pt · 59°30' · 13°15' · R

ST LUCIA 1:2.5 M
Gros Islet · Cap Pt · Castries · Dennery · Soufrière · Mt Gimie 958 · Vieux Fort · C. Moule à Chique · 61 · P

ST VINCENT 1:2.5 M
Porter Pt · Georgetown · Soufrière 1234 · Barrouallie · Kingstown · Johnston Pt · 13°15' · 61°15' · N

GRENADA 1:2.5 M
Bedford Pt · Sauteurs · Grenville · Mt St Catherine 840 · St George's · Prickly Pt · Pt Salines · 61°45' · 12 · M

JAMAICA 1:2.5 M
St Ann's Bay · Falmouth · Galina Pt · Annotto Bay · Pt Antonio · Ocho Rios · Moneague · Portland Pt · The Blue Mts · Blue Mtn Pk 2256 · Kingston · Port Royal · Spanish Town · Chapelton · Wakefield · Cambridge · The Cockpit Country · Dry Harbour Mts · Mandeville · May Pen · Salt River · Mt Denham 986 · Montego Bay · Black River · Southfield · Long Bay · S. Negril Point · Savanna la Mar · 77 · 78 · 18 · H · J

ATLANTIC OCEAN

THE BAHAMAS
Marsh Harbour · Grand Bahama · Freeport · Palm Beach · L. Worth · Delray Beach · Pompano Beach · Ft Lauderdale · Miami · Hollywood · FLORIDA · Naples · Belle Glade · The Everglades · Florida Bay · Key West · Marquesas Keys · Florida Keys · Straits of Florida · Tropic of Cancer · Dunmore Town · Nassau · New Providence · Nicholl's Town · Kemps Bay · Andros · Great Bahama Bank · Eleuthera · Great Abaco · Cat I. · Long I. · New Bight · San Salvador · Rum Cay · Deadman's Cay · Acklins · Mayaguana · Crooked I. · Great Exuma · Great Inagua · Little Inagua · Matthew Town · Anguilla Cays · 85 · 75 · 25 · A · B · C · 1

CUBA
Pinar del Río · C. San Antonio · Havana · Guanabacoa · S. Antonio de los Baños · Güines · Matanzas · Cienfuegos · Santa Clara · Nueva Gerona · I. de la Juventud (I. de Pinos) · G. de Batabanó · Sancti Spíritus · Ciego de Ávila · Morón · Camagüey · Arch. de Camagüey · Nuevitas · Sagua la Grande · Sta Cruz del Sur · Jardines de la Reina · Victoria de las Tunas · Holguín · Banes · Sagua de Tánamo · Baracoa · Guantánamo · Santiago de Cuba · Manzanillo · Palma Soriano · Bayamo · C. Cruz · Guacanayabo · Cayman Islands (U.K.) · Little Cayman · Cayman Brac · Grand Cayman · G. de Guacanayabo · 70 · 2

CAYMAN TRENCH

PUERTO RICO TRENCH

HISPANIOLA
Turks Is. (U.K.) · Caicos Is. (U.K.) · Puerto Plata · Santiago · Montecristi · S. Francisco · Santo Domingo · DOMINICAN REPUBLIC · La Romana · Samaná · Miches · Cordillera Central · Pico Duarte 3175 · La Vega · La Selle 2680 · Barahona · Cap-Haïtien · Port-de-Paix · Gonaïves · HAITI · I. de la Gonâve · Port-au-Prince · Massif de la Hotte · Les Cayes · Jacmel · I. Beata · C. Beata · Anse d'Hainault · Mona Passage · Aguadilla · Arecibo · Mayagüez · PUERTO RICO (U.S.A.) · San Juan · Caguas · Ponce · Cerro de Punta 1338 · Mona I. · 20 · 65 · D · 3

JAMAICA
Montego Bay · Savanna la Mar · Mandeville · Blue Mts · Spanish Town · Kingston · Port Antonio · Pedro Cays (Jam.) · 4

Windward Passage · Jamaica Channel · Windward Channel

Leeward Islands
Anguilla (U.K.) · St Martin (Fr. & Neth.) · St Kitts · Nevis · Barbuda · ANTIGUA & BARBUDA · St John's · Montserrat (U.K.) · Guadeloupe (Fr.) · Basse Terre · Pointe-à-Pitre · Marie Galante · DOMINICA · Roseau · Martinique (Fr.) · Fort-de-France · ST LUCIA · Castries · ST VINCENT · Kingstown · The Grenadines · GRENADA · St George's · BARBADOS · Bridgetown · Virgin Is (U.S.A. & U.K.) · St Croix (U.S.A.) · Los Testigos · I. Blanquilla (Ven.) · 15 · 60 · E · F · 3 · 4

Windward Islands

LESSER ANTILLES

CARIBBEAN SEA

Bonaire (Neth.) · Islas los Roques (Ven.) · Curaçao (Neth.) · Willemstad · Aruba (Neth.) · Isla Margarita · Isla la Tortuga · La Asunción · Porlamar · Isla la Orchila · 15 · 65 · 70

TRINIDAD AND TOBAGO
Tobago · Scarborough · Trinidad · Port of Spain · San Fernando · Pta de Paria · G. of Paria · 60 · F · 5

VENEZUELA
Güiria · G. of Paria · Carúpano · Cumaná · Barcelona · Anaco · El Tigre · Ciudad Guayana · Cd Bolívar · Maturín · Temblador · Tucupita · Barrancas · Caripito · Carúpano · Pto la Cruz · Maiquetía · Caracas · Maracay · V. de la Pascua · Altagracia de Orituco · Calabozo · Valencia · Puerto Cabello · Pto Fijo · Coro · Dabajuro · S. Juan de los Cayos · Acarigua · S. Felipe · Barquisimeto · Cabimas · Cd. Ojeda · Maracaibo · Lago de Maracaibo · Pen. de la Guajira · G. de Venezuela · Pto López · Valera · Trujillo · Cerro 1980 · Mérida · Pico Bolívar 5007 · Barinas · El Baúl · Guanare · El Banco · 65 · 70 · 75 · C · D · E

COLOMBIA
Riohacha · Sta Marta · S. Nevada de Sta Marta 5775 · Ciénaga · Barranquilla · Soledad · Cartagena · Sabanalarga · Plato · El Banco · Valledupar · Sincelejo · Montería · S. Onofre · Gulf of Darién · 75 · B · C

PANAMA
Panamá · La Chorrera · Colón · Panama Canal · Arch. de las Perlas · Acandí · Penonomé · 80 · A · B

NICARAGUA
Cabo Gracias à Dios · Puerto Cabezas · Cayos Miskito · Bonanza · Río Grande · Bluefields · Lago de Managua · Lago de Nicaragua · San Juan del Norte · 85 · 2 · 3

HONDURAS
Trujillo · Catacamas · Caratasca · Brus Laguna · Iriona · Lag. de Caratasca · Swan I. (Hond.) · Is de Maíz (Nic. & U.S.A.) · 20 · 2

COSTA RICA
Limón · Cartago · San José · Heredia · Alajuela · Pto Armuelles · David · B. de Coronado · Pta Mala · 3800 · A · 5

I. de Providencia (Col.) · I. de San Andrés (Col.) · 80 · 15

1:10M
0 · 100 · 200 · 300 · 400 km
0 · 100 · 200 mls

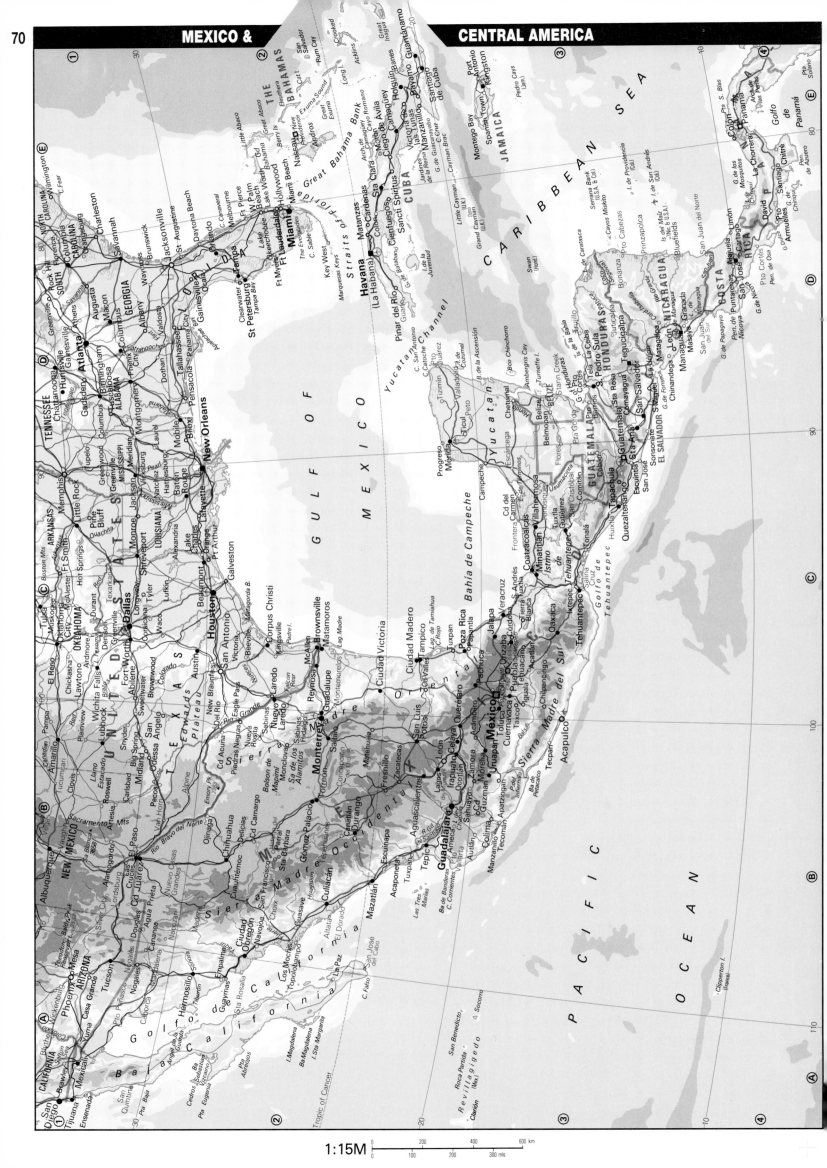

1:15M

Ⓐ 90 Ⓑ U.S.A. 80 Ⓒ 70 Ⓓ 60 Ⓔ 50 Ⓕ 40 Ⓖ 30

① Gulf of Mexico ● Miami THE BAHAMAS Tropic of Cancer ①

20

Mérida Habana ■

CUBA Guantanamo DOMINICAN REP. Pto Rico (U.S.A.)

② MEXICO BELIZE Santiago de Cuba HAITI Santiago San Juan ANTIGUA & BARBUDA ②
Belmopan JAMAICA Port-au-Prince Santo Domingo St Kitts – Nevis Guadeloupe (Fr.)
GUATEMALA HONDURAS Kingston DOMINICA
Guatemala Tegucigalpa Martinique (Fr.)
S.Salvador ST LUCIA
EL SALVADOR NICARAGUA ST VINCENT BARBADOS
Managua CARIBBEAN SEA GRENADA Port of Spain TRINIDAD & TOBAGO

COSTA RICA Neth. Antilles Barcelona
S.José Barranquilla Sta Marta Curaçao Caracas ■
I. del Coco (C.R.) Colón Cartagena Maracaibo Barquisimeto
③ PANAMA Panamá S.Cristóbal Cd. Bolívar Cd. Guayana ③
Medellín VENEZUELA Georgetown
Malpelo (Col.) Manizales Orinoco GUYANA Paramaribo Cayenne
Buenaventura Bogotá ● Boa Vista SURINAM FR. GUIANA
Galápagos Is (Ecu.) Cali COLOMBIA Branco
S.Lorenzo Popayán Pasto Negro S.Pedro e S.Paulo (Braz.)
Quito Putumayo Macapá I. de Marajó Equator
ECUADOR Amazon Belém I. Fernando de Noronha (Braz.)
Guayaquil Iquitos Manaus Santarém São Luís Rocas
④ Piura Juruá Tapajós Codó Sobral Fortaleza ④
Chiclayo Purus Xingu Teresina Natal
Trujillo Marañón Madeira Tocantins Juazeiro João Pessoa
Chimbote PERU Rio Branco Pto Velho Araguaia Recife ■
Ucayali B R A Z I L Maceió
Callao ■ Pto Maldonado Alagoinhas Aracajú
Lima ■ Huancayo Salvador ●
Cuzco Ilhéus
⑤ Arequipa La Paz Cáceres Cuiabá Brasília São Francisco Montes Claros ⑤
Oruro BOLIVIA Goiânia Cotinto
Arica Cochabamba Sta Cruz Belo Horizonte ●
Sucre Corumbá Vitória
Iquique Campo Grande Dourados Ribeirão Prêto Campos
Juiz de Fora
SOUTH PARAGUAY Paraná Campinas Rio de Janeiro ●
Antofagasta Concepción São Paulo ●
Salta Asunción Foz do Iguaçu Santos
⑥ PACIFIC S.Félix (Chile) CHILE Salado Resistencia Posadas Ponta Grossa ⑥
S.Miguel de Tucumán Curitiba
OCEAN A R G E N T I N A Paraná Florianópolis
Tropic of Capricorn Córdoba Uruguay SOUTH
Juan Fernández Is. (Chile) Mendoza Sante Fe Rivera Pto Alegre
Viña del Mar Rosario Paysandú Pelotas ATLANTIC
Valparaíso Paraná URUGUAY Rio Grande
⑦ Santiago ■ Buenos Aires ■ Montevideo ● OCEAN ⑦
Talca R.de la Plata
Concepción Colorado Mar del Plata
Temuco Bahía Blanca
Valdivia Negro
Pto Montt Chico
⑧ Deseado Falkland Is (U.K.) S.Georgia (U.K.) ⑧
Cmd. Rivadavia Stanley
G.San Jorge
Pto Natales Trindade (Braz.)
Rio Gallegos
Punta Arenas Cape Horn S.Sandwich Is (U.K.)
Tierra del Fuego
⑨ ⑨
50 110 100 Ⓐ 60 90 80 Ⓒ 70 Ⓓ S.Shetland Is (U.K.) Ⓔ S.Orkney Is (U.K.) Ⓖ
Ⓑ ANTARCTICA Ⓗ

1:35M

0 250 500 750 1000 1250 km

0 250 500 750 mls

A B C 75 D 70 E 65 (F) Roseau
Fort-de-France
Martinique (Fr.)

ST LUCIA
Castries

ST VINCENT
Kingstown

The Grenadines

GRENADA
St George

① Siguatepeque
Comayagua
Tegucigalpa
San Miguel
La Unión Somoto Estelí
Choluteca Chinandega Matagalpa
León NICARAGUA
Managua Granada
Masaya L. de Nicaragua
Rivas S. Carlos
G. del Papagaya
Alajuela Heredia Limón
Puntarenas San José
Pen. de Nicoya Cartago
COSTA RICA David
G. Dulce Chirripó Grande 3475
Pto Armuelles Chitré
G. de Chiriquí Pen. de Azuero
Barú

Pto Cabezas
Coco (Segovia)
I. de Providencia (Col.)
I. de San Andrés (Col.)
Laguna de Perlas
Bluefields
San Juan
Colón
PANAMA Panamá
La Chorrera
La Palma
Arch. de las Perlas
I. Coiba G. de Panamá
I. del Rey
Pta Mariato

Pta Gallinas
Pen. de Guajira
Aruba Curaçao (Neth.)
Bonaire Is Los Roques (Ven.)
I. de Margarita
Neth. Antilles
Willemstad

Ríohacha
Maicao G. de Venezuela
Sta Marta Pto Fijo Coro Riecito
Ciénaga Sa Nevada de Sta Marta 5800
Barranquilla Valledupar Maracaibo Cabimas Puerto Cabello Maiquetía Caracas
Cartagena Machiques L. de Maracaibo Valencia Maracay
S. Jacinto Trujillo Barquisimeto S. Juan
Sincelejo El Banco Ocaña Valera Acarigua
Magangué Cúcuta Mérida Cord. de Mérida Barinas V. de la Pascua
Montería Pamplona San Cristóbal Bolívar 5775 Guanare
Caucasia Bucaramanga Arauca Apure
Turbo Barrancabermeja LLANOS
Quibdó Yarumal Málaga
Bello Pto Berrío Sogamoso Orocué
Itagüí Medellín Barbosa Tunja Meta Pto Carreño
Manizales Chocontá Vichada
Pereira Cartago Armenia Bogotá Villavicencio Guaviare Inírida
Tuluá Ibagué Girardot Granada
Buenaventura Buga Palmira Guania
Cali COLOMBIA Meta Pto Ayacucho
Santander Huila 5750 Neiva Vaupés
Popayán Vol. Puracé 4700 Pto Rico
Tumaco Pitalito Florencia
S. Lorenzo El Diviso Pasto Belén Caquetá
Esmeraldas Ibarra Ipiales Mocoa Pto Asís
Cojimíes Otavalo Tulcán Leguizamo
Jama Quito Coca Putumayo
Manta Chone Cotopaxi Napo
C. San Lorenzo Ambato Tena
Jipijapa ECUADOR Chimborazo 6310
Guayaquil Guaranda Riobamba
La Libertad Milagro Babahoyo Macas
Playas Cuenca Azogues
I. Puná Gualaceo
G. de Guayaquil Machala
Tumbes Zaruma Loja
Talara Zamora
Negritos Sullana Marañón
Paita Chulucanas
Piura Huancabamba
Catacaos Jaén
Pta Aguja Ferreñafe Chachapoyas Moyobamba
Lambayeque Cajamarca Tarapoto
Chiclayo Cajabamba
Chepén Huamachuco
Pacasmayo Otusco
Trujillo CORDILLERA Pomabamba Tingo María
Chimbote Huaráz Huascarán 6768 La Unión
Casma Huánuco
Huarmey Pativilca
Barranca Oxapampa Cerro de Pasco La Merced
Huacho Tarma
Ancón La Oroya Jauja Acobamba
Callao Lima Huancayo Parque Nac. de Manú
Huancavelica
Chincha Alta Ayacucho MACHU PICCHU Cuzco
Pisco Andahuaylas Abancay
Ica Apurímac Sicuani
Pen. de Paracas Ayaviri
Nazca Juliaca
Chala Arequipa Puno L. Titicaca
Coropuna 6425 Misti 5822 Juli
Camaná Majes
Matarani Moquegua Guaqui La Paz
Mollendo Desaguadero
Ilo Sajama 6542 Oruro
Tacna Poopó
Arica BOLIVIA

AMAZONAS
SELVAS
Iquitos
Leticia Tabatinga
Caxias
Elvira
Yavarí (Javari)
Marañón
Yurimaguas
Ucayali
Pucallpa
Cruzeiro do Sul
Feijó
ACRE
Sena Madureira
Rio Branco
Brasiléia
Cobija Porvenir
Riberalta
Guajará-Mirim RONDÔNIA
Pôrto Velho
Abunã
Madre de Dios
Pto Maldonado
Pto Heath
Quillabamba
Rurrenabaque Trinidad
Huanay Sta Ana
Ancohuma 6388 Coripco
Chulumani
Cochabamba
Quillacollo Santa Cruz
Oruro
Potosí Sucre

P A C I F I C   O C E A N

Malpelo (Col.)
I. del Coco (C.R.)

Tropic of Capricorn
Antofagasta
Iquique
CHILE
ARGENTINA

1:15M
200 400 600 km
100 200 300 mls

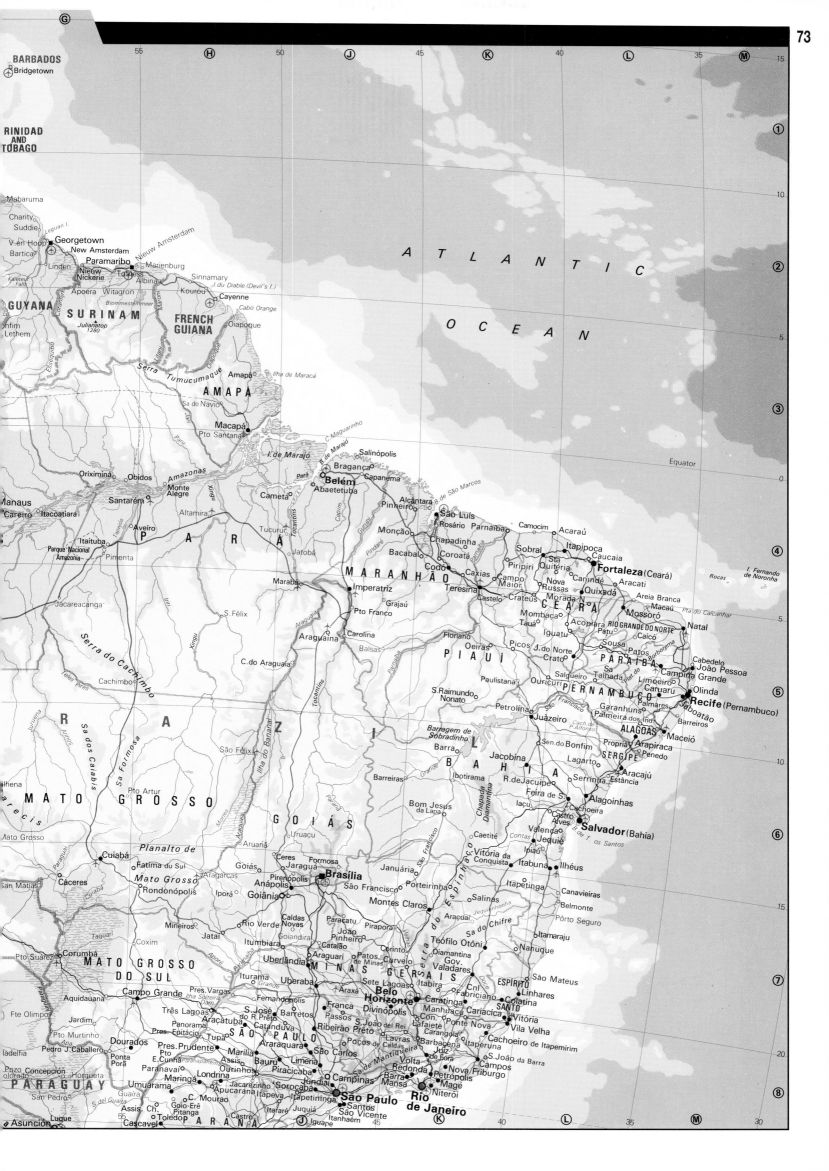

BOLIVIA

BRAZIL

MATO GROSSO DO SUL

MINAS GERAIS

PARAGUAY

GRAN CHACO

SÃO PAULO

PARANÁ

SANTA CATARINA

RIO GRANDE DO SUL

ARGENTINA

URUGUAY

Asunción

Buenos Aires

Montevideo

Santiago

São Paulo

Rio de Janeiro

Belo Horizonte

Curitiba

Porto Alegre

Córdoba

Rosario

Mendoza

La Pampa

Río Negro

Chubut

Santa Cruz

PATAGONIA

CORDILLERA

LOS ANDES

ATLANTIC OCEAN

FALKLAND ISLANDS
(ISLAS MALVINAS)
(U.K.)

West Falkland

East Falkland

Stanley

Jason Is

C. Dolphin

Weddell

Beauchene Is

South Georgia
(U.K.)

Tierra del Fuego

Isla Grande de Tierra del Fuego

Ushuaia

Punta Arenas

C. de Hornos
(C. Horn)

1:15M

200   400   600 km
100   200   300 mls

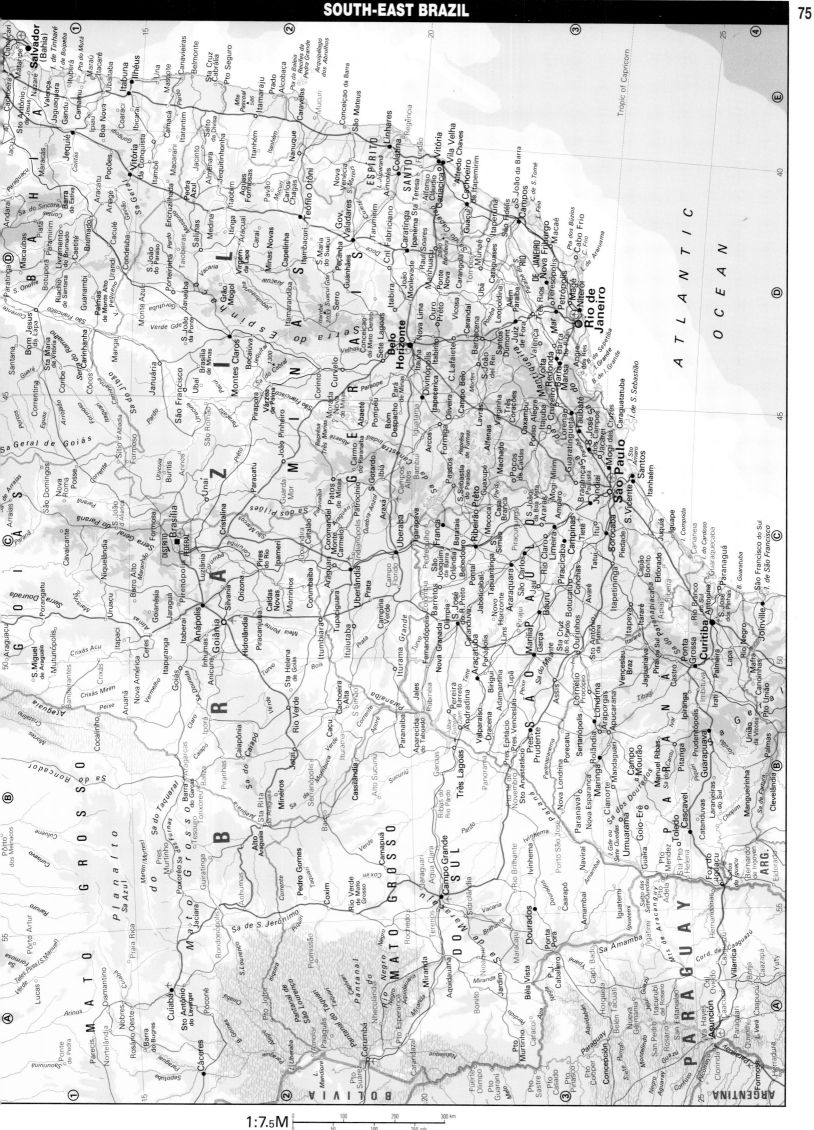

1:7.5M

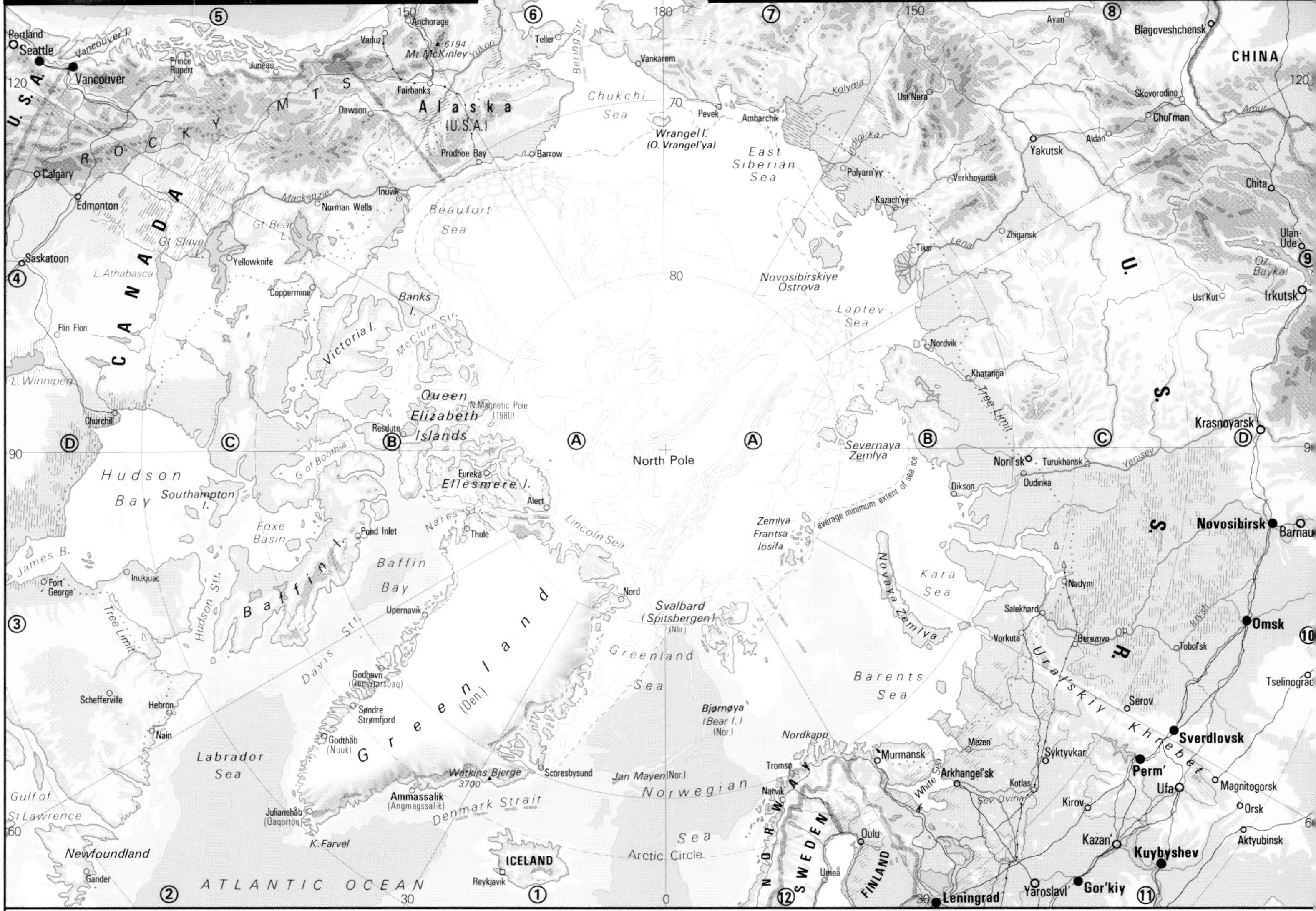

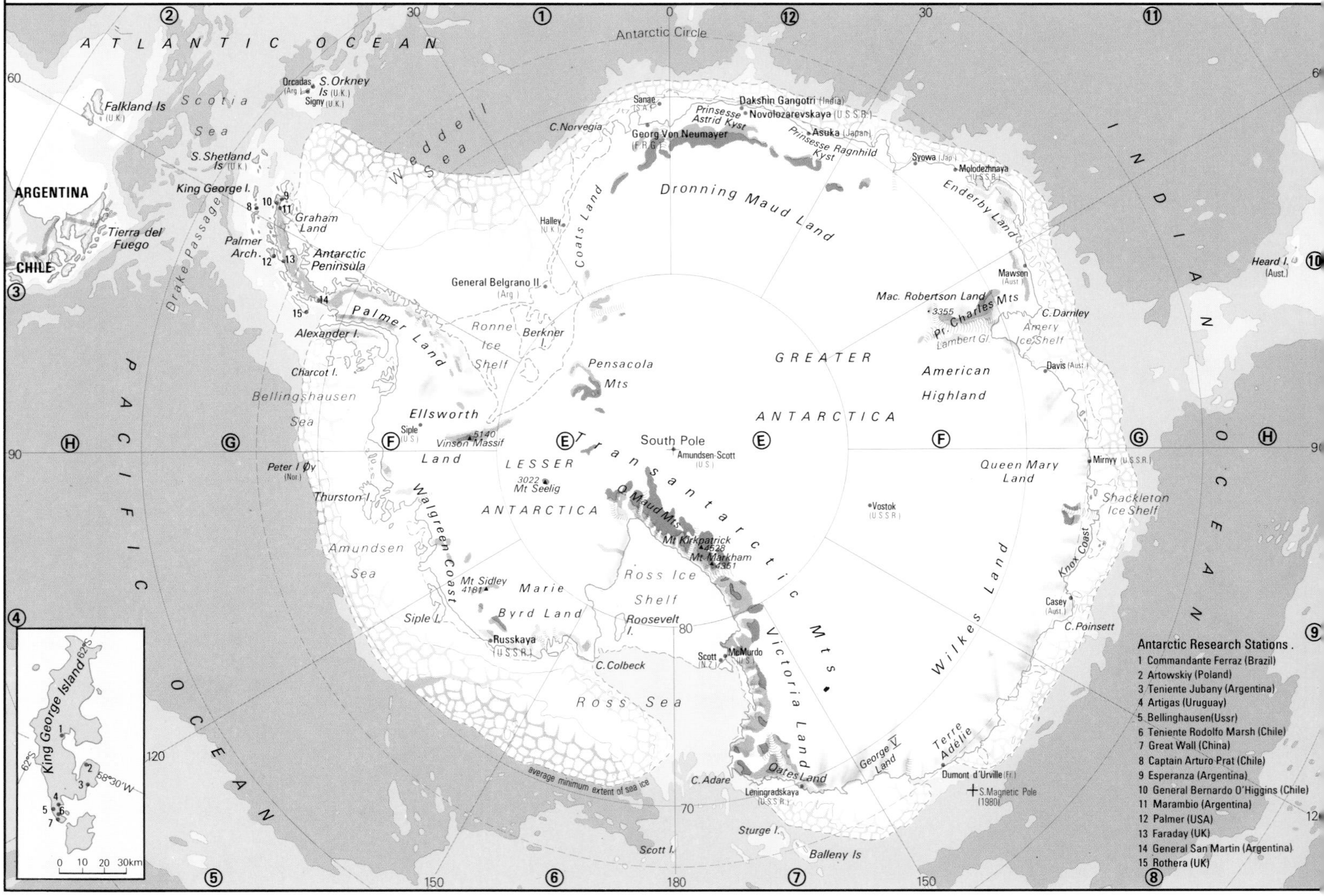

Portland
Seattle
Vancouver I.
Prince Rupert
Vancouver
Vaduz
Anchorage
Mt McKinley 6194
Teller
Juneau
Fairbanks
Dawson
Ayan
Blagoveshchensk
CHINA
Skovorodino
Chul'man
Amur
Calgary
Edmonton
Coppermine
Norman Wells
Inuvik
Prudhoe Bay
Barrow
Chukchi Sea
Pevek
Ambarchik
Kolyma
Ust'Nera
Aldan
Chita
Ulan Ude
Oz. Baykal
CANADA
Saskatoon
L. Athabasca
Yellowknife
Gt Bear L.
Mackenzie
Gt Slave L.
Wrangel I. (O. Vrangel'ya)
East Siberian Sea
Vankarem
Indigirka
Polyarn'yy
Verkhoyansk
Yakutsk
Chul'man
Irkutsk
U. S. S. R.
Flin Flon
L. Winnipeg
Churchill
Banks I.
Victoria I.
McClure Str.
Beaufort Sea
Kazach'ye
Tiksi
Lena
Zhigansk
Ust Kut
Krasnoyarsk
Hudson Bay
Southampton I.
Queen Elizabeth Islands
N. Magnetic Pole (1980)
Resolute
Eureka
80
North Pole
Severnaya Zemlya
Novosibirskiye Ostrova
Laptev Sea
Nordvik
Khatanga
Nordik
Noril'sk
Turukhansk
Yenisey
Dikson
Dudinka
James B.
Fort George
Inukjuac
Foxe Basin
G. of Boothia
Ellesmere I.
Nares Str.
Thule
Alert
Lincoln Sea
Nord
Zemlya Frantsa Iosifa
average minimum extent of sea ice
Novaya Zemlya
Kara Sea
Berezovo
Salekhard
Vorkuta
Nadym
Tobol'sk
Omsk
Tselinograd
Baffin I.
Baffin Bay
Pond Inlet
Upernavik
Godhavn (Qeqertarsuaq)
Davis Str.
Svalbard (Spitsbergen)
Greenland Sea
Bjørnøya (Bear I.) (Nor.)
Barents Sea
Novosibirsk
Barnaul
Scheffeville
Hebron
Nain
Sandre Stromfjord
Godthåb (Nuuk)
Greenland (Den.)
Watkins Bjerge 3700
Scoresbysund
Jan Mayen (Nor.)
Nordkapp
Nordkapp
Murmansk
White Sea
Mezen'
Arkhangel'sk
Sev Dvina
Syktyvkar
Kotlas
Perm'
Sverdlovsk
Magnitogorsk
Labrador Sea
Julianehåb (Qaqortoq)
Ammassalik (Angmagssalik)
Denmark Strait
K. Farvel
Norwegian Sea
Tromsø
Narvik
NORWAY
SWEDEN
Kirov
Kazan'
Orsk
Aktyubinsk
Gulf of St Lawrence
Newfoundland
Gander
ICELAND
Reykjavik
Arctic Circle
Oulu
Umeå
FINLAND
Kuybyshev
Ufa
Ural'skiy Khrebet
ATLANTIC OCEAN
Leningrad
Yaroslavl
Gor'kiy

ATLANTIC OCEAN
Antarctic Circle
INDIAN OCEAN
Falkland Is (U.K.)
Scotia Sea
Orcadas (Arg.) S. Orkney Is (U.K.)
Signy (U.K.)
Sanae (S.A.)
Dakshin Gangotri (India)
Novolazarevskaya (U.S.S.R.)
Prinsesse Astrid Kyst
Asuka (Japan)
Syowa (Jap.)
ARGENTINA
S. Shetland Is
King George I.
Drake Passage
Graham Land
Palmer Arch.
Antarctic Peninsula
Weddell Sea
C. Norvegia
Georg Von Neumayer (F.R.G.)
Dronning Maud Land
Prinsesse Ragnhild Kyst
Enderby Land
Molodezhnaya (U.S.S.R.)
Heard I. (Aust.)
CHILE
Tierra del Fuego
Alexander I.
Palmer Land
Halley (U.K.)
Coats Land
Mawson (Aust.)
Mac. Robertson Land
3355
Pr. Charles Mts
C. Darnley
Lambert Gl.
Amery Ice Shelf
General Belgrano II (Arg.)
Ronne Ice Shelf
Berkner
Pensacola Mts
GREATER
American Highland
Davis (Aust.)
Charcot I.
Bellingshausen Sea
Ellsworth Land
Vinson Massif 5140
Siple (U.S.)
South Pole
Amundsen-Scott (U.S.)
ANTARCTICA
Queen Mary Land
Mirnyy (U.S.S.R.)
PACIFIC OCEAN
Peter I Øy (Nor.)
Thurston I.
LESSER
ANTARCTICA
Mt Seelig 3022
Maud Mts
Vostok (U.S.S.R.)
Shackleton Ice Shelf
Knox Coast
Amundsen Sea
Walgreen Coast
Mt Sidley 4181
Marie Byrd Land
Siple I.
Russkaya (U.S.S.R.)
Mt Kirkpatrick
Mt Markham 4351
Ross Ice Shelf
Roosevelt I.
Transantarctic Mts
Victoria Land
Wilkes Land
Casey (Aust.)
C. Poinsett
Ross Sea
C. Colbeck
Scott McMurdo
George V Land
Terre Adélie
Dumont d'Urville (Fr.)
C. Adare
Oates Land
Leningradskaya (U.S.S.R.)
S. Magnetic Pole (1980)
Sturge I.
Balleny Is
Scott I.

King George Island
0 10 20 30 km

Antarctic Research Stations
1 Commandante Ferraz (Brazil)
2 Artowskiy (Poland)
3 Teniente Jubany (Argentina)
4 Artigas (Uruguay)
5 Bellinghausen (Ussr)
6 Teniente Rodolfo Marsh (Chile)
7 Great Wall (China)
8 Captain Arturo Prat (Chile)
9 Esperanza (Argentina)
10 General Bernardo O'Higgins (Chile)
11 Marambio (Argentina)
12 Palmer (USA)
13 Faraday (UK)
14 General San Martin (Argentina)
15 Rothera (UK)

1:40M
0 400 800 1200 1600 km
0 400 800 mls

	International Boundary
	State Boundary
	Department Boundary
	City Limits
	Borough, District Boundary
	Military Zones
	Armistice, Ceasefire Line
	Demilitarised Zone
Station	Main Railways
Bridge	Other Railways
	Projected Railways
Station	Underground Railway
	Aerial Cableway, Funicular
M	Metro Stations
Projected	Special Highway
	Main Road
	Secondary Road
	Other Road, Street
	Track
	Road Tunnel
	Bridge, Flyover

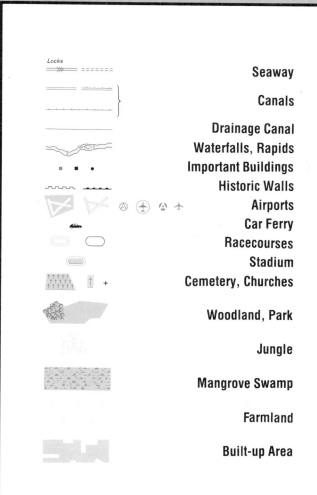

Locks	Seaway
	Canals
	Drainage Canal
	Waterfalls, Rapids
	Important Buildings
	Historic Walls
	Airports
	Car Ferry
	Racecourses
	Stadium
	Cemetery, Churches
	Woodland, Park
	Jungle
	Mangrove Swamp
	Farmland
	Built-up Area

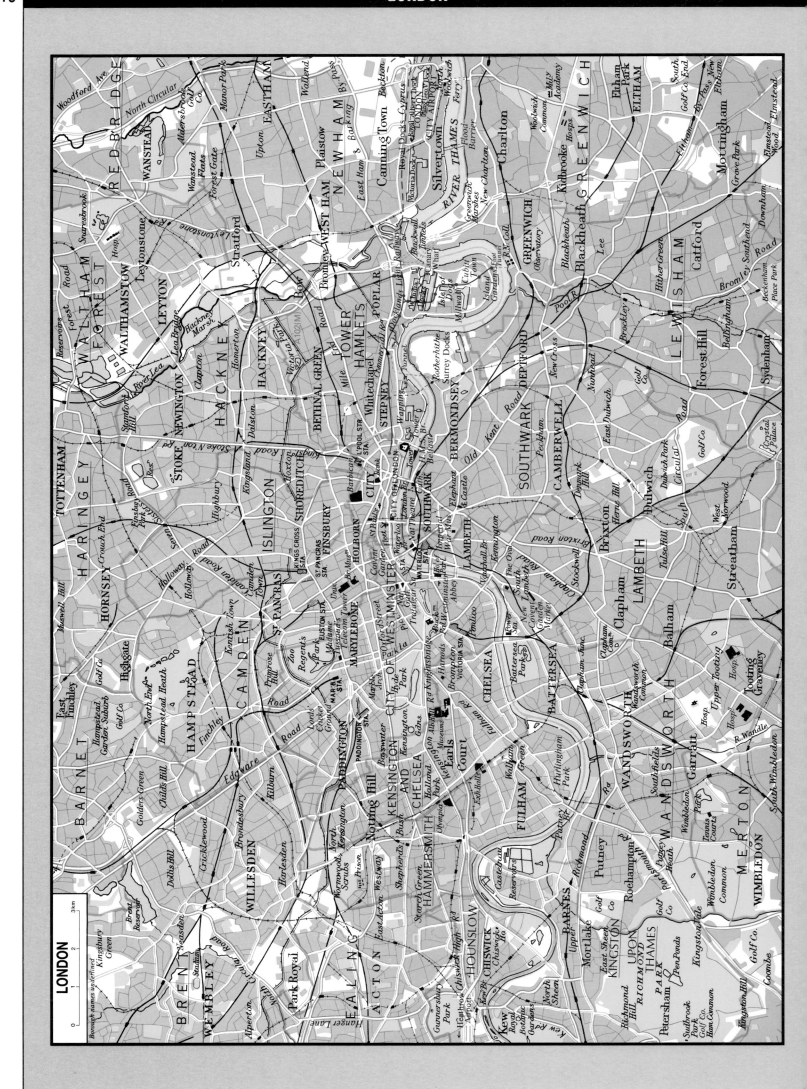

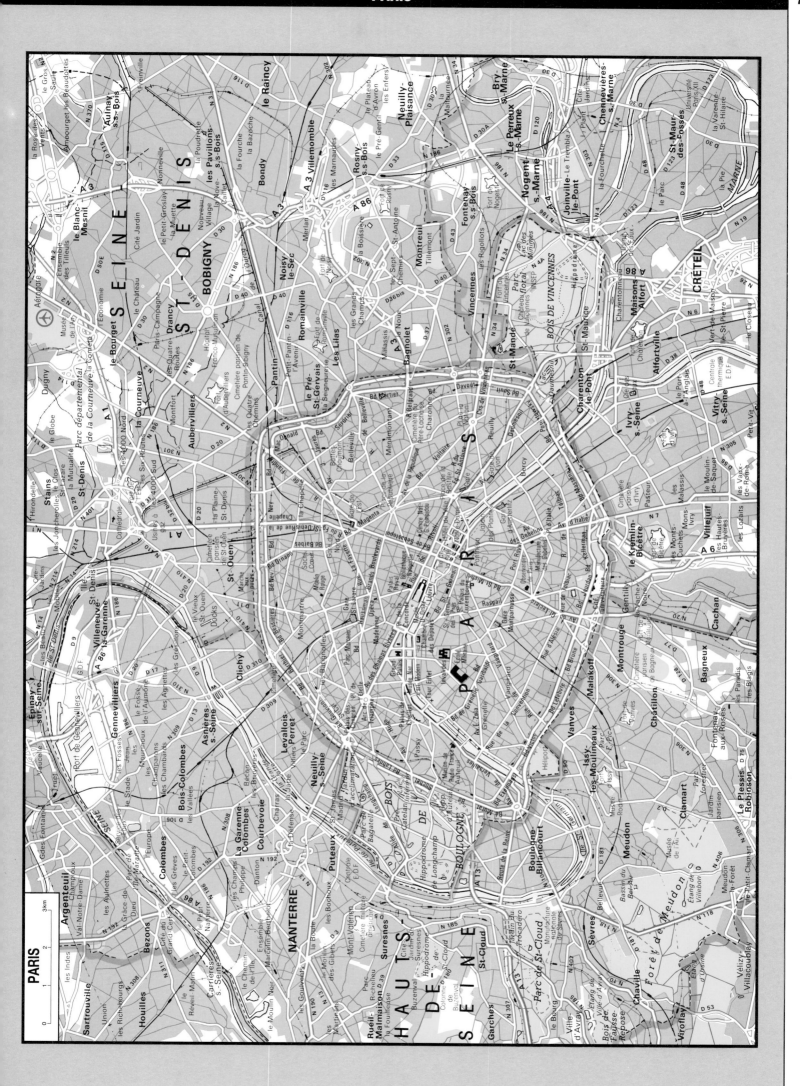

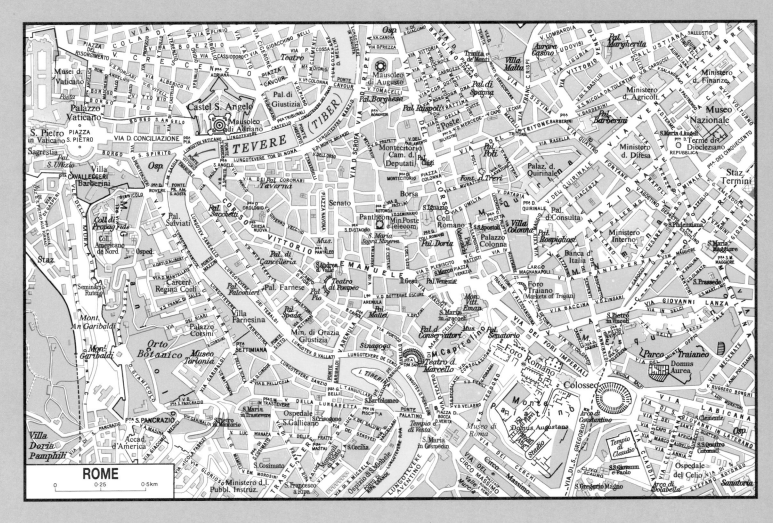

ROME

0   0·25   0·5km

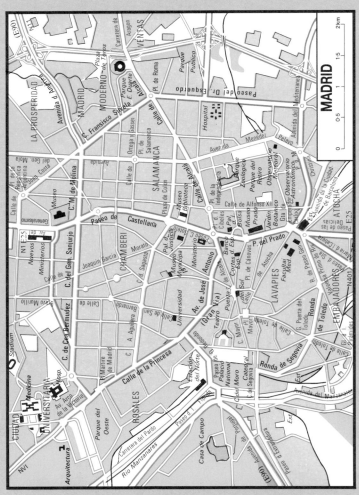

MADRID

2km
1·5
1
0·5
0

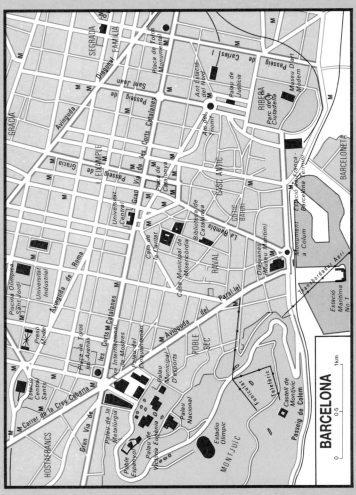

BARCELONA

1km
0·5
0

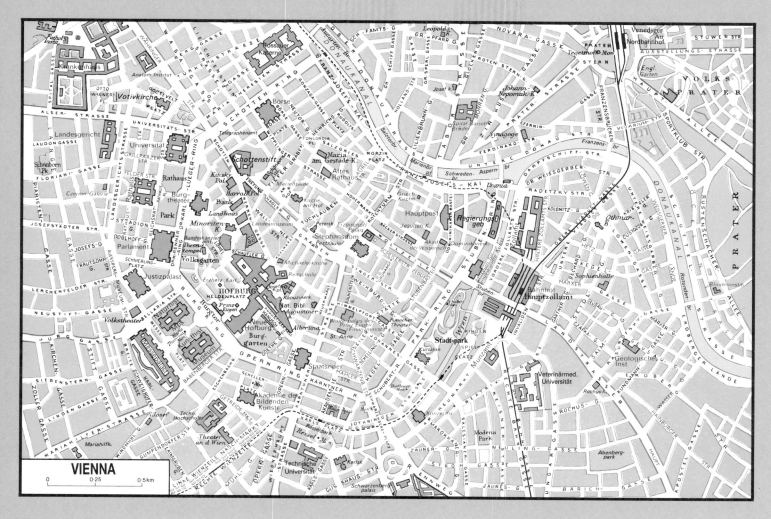

VIENNA

0   0·25   0·5km

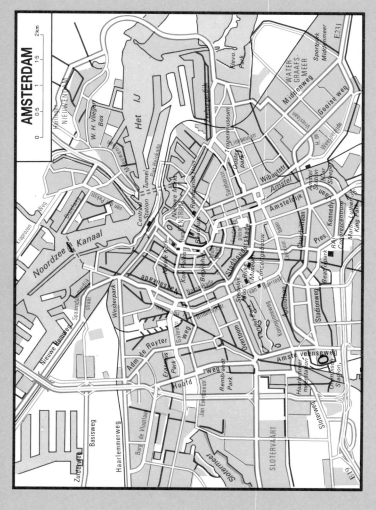

AMSTERDAM

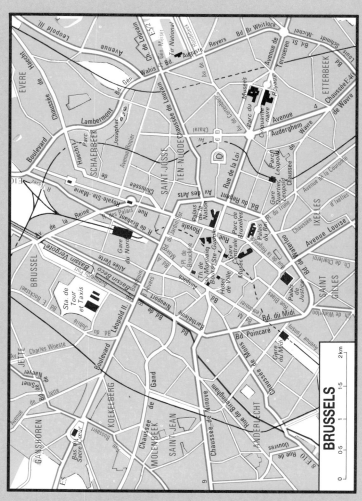

BRUSSELS

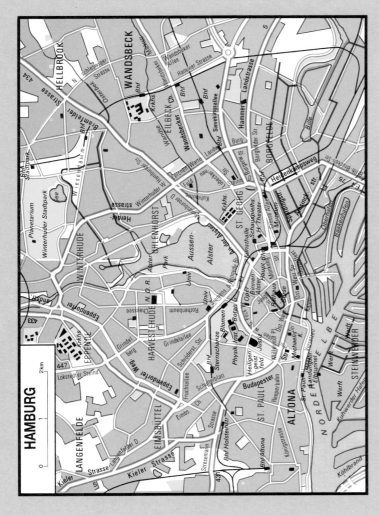

HAMBURG

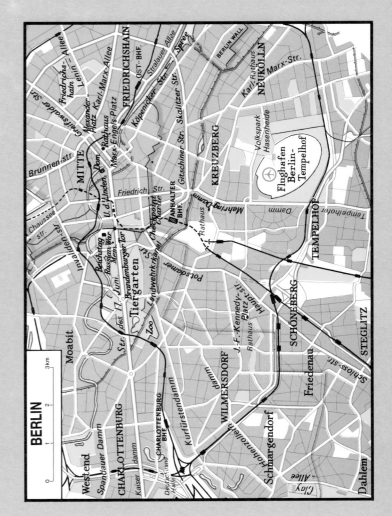

BERLIN

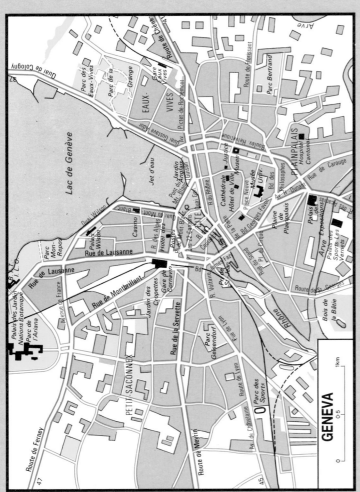

GENEVA

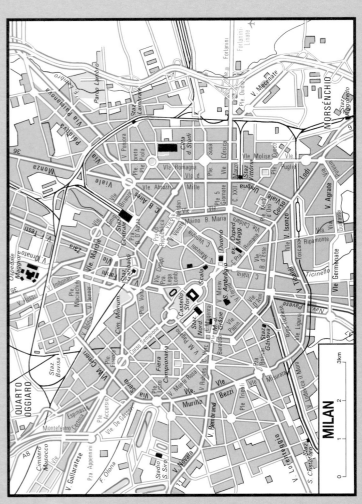

MILAN

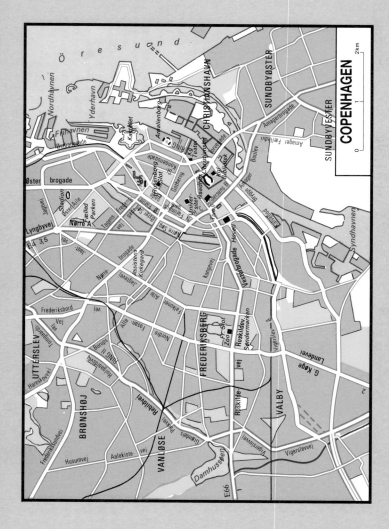

COPENHAGEN

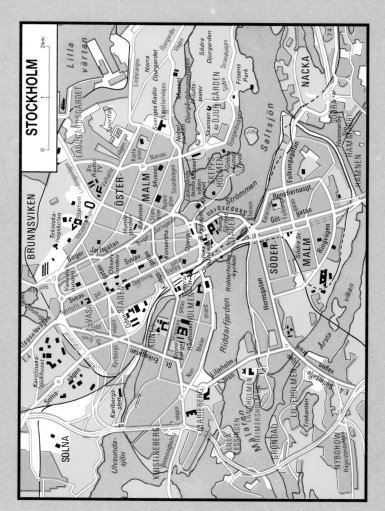

STOCKHOLM

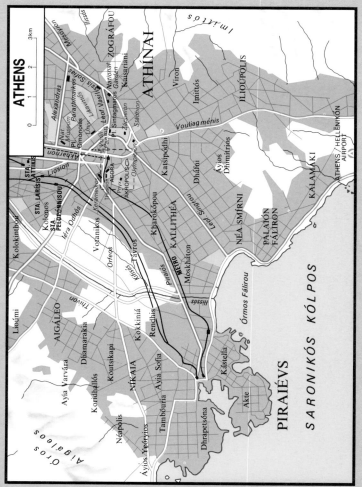

ATHENS

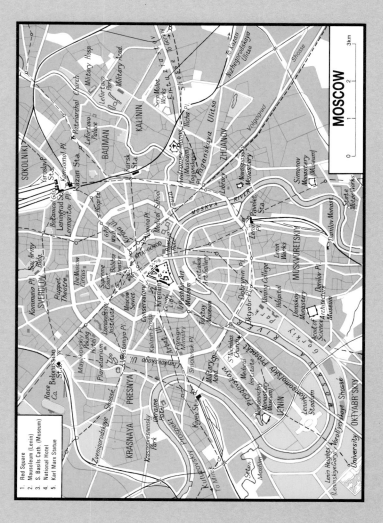

MOSCOW

1. Red Square
2. Mausoleum (Lenin)
3. S. Basil's Cath. (Museum)
4. National Hotel
5. Karl Marx Statue

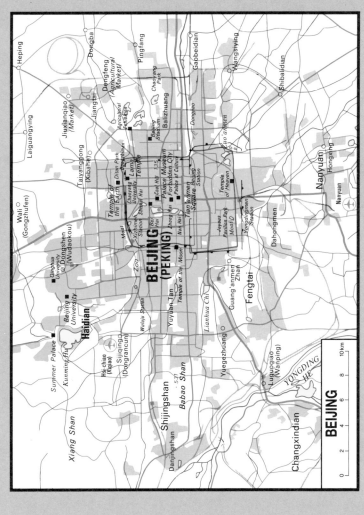

BEIJING

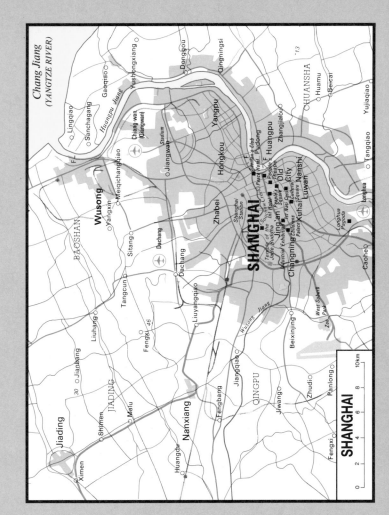

SHANGHAI

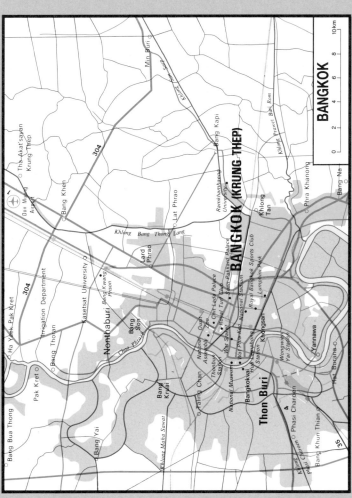

BANGKOK

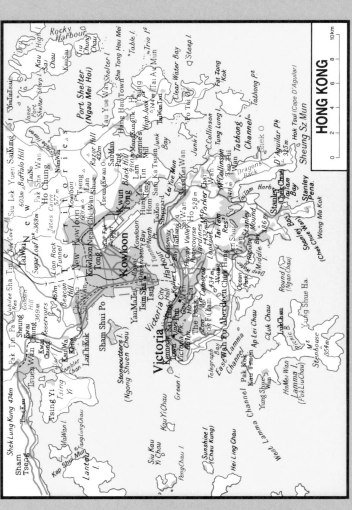

HONG KONG

TOKYO

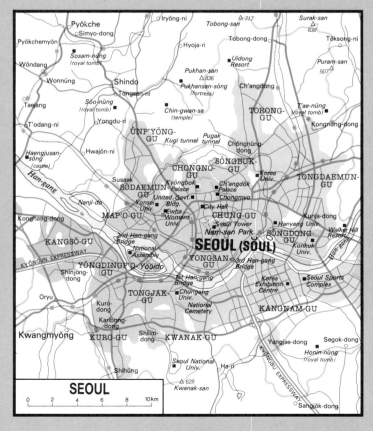

SEOUL

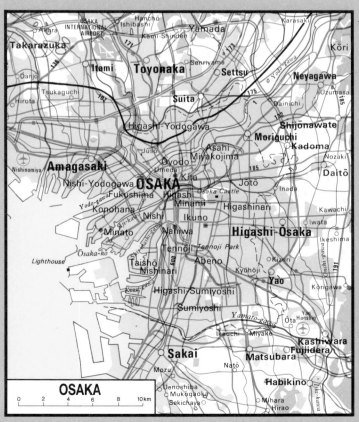

OSAKA

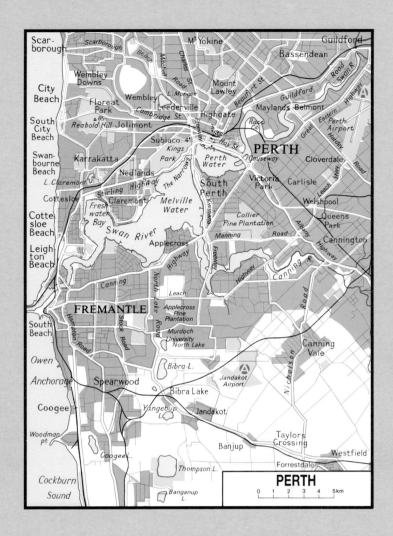

PERTH

Scarborough, Scarborough Beach, Mt Yokine, Guildford, Bassendean, Wembley Downs, City Beach, Floreat Park, Mount Lawley, Wembley, L. Monger, Leederville, Highgate, Maylands, Belmont, Beaufort St, Guildford Road, Perth Airport, Great Eastern Highway, South City Beach, Reabold Hill, Jolimont, Subiaco, Kings Park, Perth Water, Race Co., Causeway, PERTH, Cloverdale, Hardey Road, Swanbourne Beach, Karrakatta, Nedlands, South Perth, Victoria Park, Carlisle, Welshpool, Cottesloe, L. Claremont, Stirling Highway, Claremont, Freshwater Bay, Melville Water, Swan River, Applecross, Manning, Road, Collier Pine Plantation, Queens Park, Cannington, Canning R., Leighton Beach, Canning, North Lake Road, Applecross Pine Plantation, Leach, Albany Highway, Canning Highway, Canning Vale, FREMANTLE, Murdoch University North Lake, Nicholson Road, South Beach, Hampton Road, Stock Road, Bibra L., Jandakot Airport, Owen Anchorage, Spearwood, Bibra Lake, Yangebup L., Jandakot, Coogee, Taylors Crossing, Woodman Pt, Coogee L., Banjup, Westfield, Cockburn Sound, Thompson L., Forrestdale, Banganup L.

0 1 2 3 4 5km

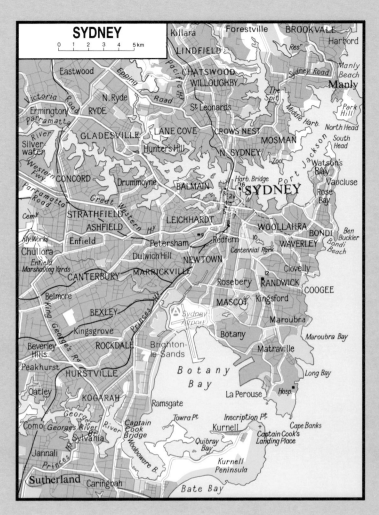

SYDNEY

0 1 2 3 4 5km

Killara, Forestville, BROOKVALE, Harbord, LINDFIELD, Eastwood, Epping, CHATSWOOD, WILLOUGHBY, Manly Beach, Manly, Victoria Road, N. Ryde, St Leonards, The Spit, Middle Harb., North Head, Ermington, RYDE, Silverwater, Parramatta River, GLADESVILLE, LANE COVE, CROWS NEST, MOSMAN, South Head, Western Fwy, CONCORD, Hunter's Hill, N. SYDNEY, Zoo, Port Jackson, Watson's Bay, Vaucluse, Parramatta Road, Drummoyne, BALMAIN, Harb. Bridge, SYDNEY, Rose Bay, Great Western Hy, STRATHFIELD, LEICHHARDT, WOOLLAHRA, BONDI, Ben Buckler, ASHFIELD, Petersham, Redfern, WAVERLEY, Bondi Beach, Enfield, Dulwich Hill, NEWTOWN, Centennial Park, Chullora, Enfield Marshalling Yards, CANTERBURY, MARRICKVILLE, Roseberry, RANDWICK, Clovelly, Belmore, Rosebery, MASCOT, Kingsford, COOGEE, BEXLEY, Kingsgrove, Sydney Airport, Botany, Maroubra, Beverley Hills, Princes Hy, ROCKDALE, Brighton-le-Sands, Maroubra Bay, Peakhurst, King Georges Rd, HURSTVILLE, Matraville, Oatley, Botany Bay, Long Bay, KOGARAH, Ramsgate, La Perouse, Hosp., Como, Georges River, Inscription Pt, Cape Banks, Sylvania, Captain Cook Bridge, Kurnell, Captain Cook's Landing Place, Jannali, Towra Pt, Quibray Bay, Sutherland, Princes Hy, Caringbah, Kurnell Peninsula, Bate Bay

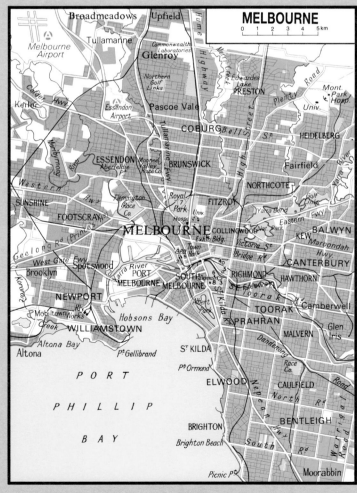

MELBOURNE

0 1 2 3 4 5km

Broadmeadows, Upfield, Melbourne Airport, Tullamarine, Commonwealth Laboratories, Glenroy, Hume Highway, Merri Creek, Edwardes Lake, Keilor, Calder Hwy, Northern Golf Links, PRESTON, Plenty Road, Mont. Park Hosp., Pascoe Vale, Univ., Essendon Airport, COBURG, Bell St, HEIDELBERG, Western Hwy, ESSENDON, Moonee Valley Race Co., Aberfeldie Pt, BRUNSWICK, Tullamarine Fwy, Fairfield, Maribyrnong, NORTHCOTE, Yarra Bend, Golf Links, Sunshine, Royal Park, FITZROY, Eastern Fwy, Hwy, Flemington Race Co., Univ., BALWYN, FOOTSCRAY, Park, Town Hall, COLLINGWOOD, KEW, Maroondah Hwy, Geelong Rd (Prince's), MELBOURNE, Exhb. Bldg, CANTERBURY, West Gate Fwy, Spotswood, Yarra River, Town Hall, Victoria St, Bridge Rd, HAWTHORN, Brooklyn, PORT, SOUTH MELBOURNE, RICHMOND, Kororoit Creek, NEWPORT, Rly Wks, Mobiltown Works, Hobsons Bay, Albert Park, St Kilda Rd, TOORAK, Camberwell, WILLIAMSTOWN, Glen Iris, Altona Bay, Pt Gellibrand, PRAHRAN, MALVERN, Altona, St KILDA, Pt Ormond, Dandenong Road, Race Co., PORT PHILLIP BAY, ELWOOD, Nepean Hwy, CAULFIELD, North Rd, South Rd, Waverley Road, BRIGHTON, BENTLEIGH, Picnic Pt, Brighton Beach, Moorabbin

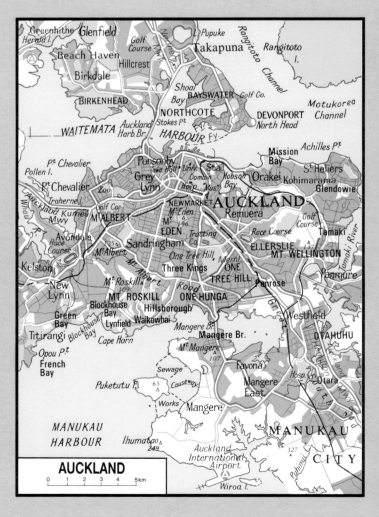

AUCKLAND

0 1 2 3 4 5km

Greenhithe, Glenfield, Herald I., L. Pupuke, Rangitoto Channel, Rangitoto I., Golf Course, Takapuna, Beach Haven, Hillcrest, Birkdale, BAYSWATER, Golf Co., Motukorea, Shoal Bay, BIRKENHEAD, NORTHCOTE, Stokes Pt, DEVONPORT, Devonport Channel, WAITEMATA, Auckland Harb. Br., North Head, HARBOUR FY., Achilles Pt, Pt Chevalier, Ponsonby, Town Hall, Univ., Sta., Hobson Bay, Mission Bay, Pollen I., Pt Chevalier, Zoo, Grey Lynn, Domain, Hosp. Mus., Orakei, St Heliers, Traherne I., Golf Co., NEWMARKET, AUCKLAND, Kohimarama, Glendowie, Auckland Race Co., Kumeu Mwy, Mt ALBERT, Remuera, Avondale, Race Course, Mt EDEN, Golf Course, Kelston, Mt ALBERT, Sandringham, Tranting Co., ELLERSLIE, MT WELLINGTON, Tamaki, New Lynn, Mt ROSKILL, One Tree Hill, ONE TREE HILL, Panmure, Tamaki River, Green Bay, MT. ROSKILL, Three Kings, Meml Road, Penrose, Blockhouse Bay, Hillsborough, ONE HUNGA, Westfield, Titirangi, Lynfield, Waikowhai, Mangere Br., OTAHUHU, Opou Pt, Blockhouse Bay, Cape Horn, Mt Mangere, French Bay, Favona, Mangere East, Hosp., Otara, Puketutu I., Causeway, Mangere, MANUKAU CITY, MANUKAU HARBOUR, Ihumatao, Sewage, Works, Auckland International Airport, Wiroa I., Puhinui Rd

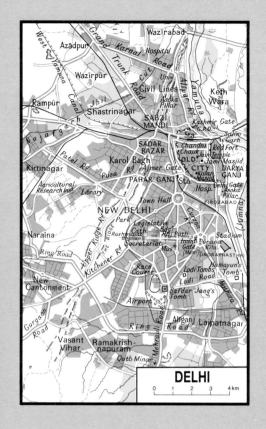

DELHI

West Yamuna
Azadpur
Wazirabad
Grand Karnal Road
Hospital
Wazirpur
Keth Wara
Civil Lines
Asoka Pillar
Univ.
Rampur
Jhil
Shastrinagar
SABZI MANDI
Kashmir Gate
Sta.
Salim Garh
SADAR BAZAR
Chandni Chauk
Red Fort
OLD
Jain Temple
DELHI
Karol Bagh
Jami Masjid
Kalan Masjid
DARYA GANJ
Kirtinagar
Ajmer Gate
CITY
Patel Rd
Pusa Rd
PAHAR GANJ
Sta.
Delhi Gate
Delhi Gate
Hosp.
Agricultural Research Inst.
Library
Town Hall
Asoka Pillar
Firozabad
NEW DELHI
Naraina
Park
Legislative
Bldg
Rashtrapati bhavan
Secretariat
Ridge Road
Kitchener Rd
Purana Qila
(Fort)
Mus.
INDRAPRASTHA
Stadium
New Cantonment
Ring Road
Race Course
Lodi Tombs
Lodi
Humayun's Tomb
Mehrauli Road
Jamuna
Airport
Safdar Jang's Tomb
Gurgaon Road
Ring Road
Aliganj Laipatnagar
Vasant Vihar
Ramakrishnanapuram
Mehrauli Road
Qutb Minar

0 1 2 3 4km

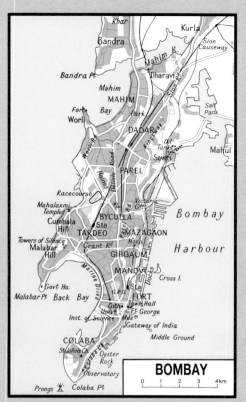

BOMBAY

Khar
Bandra
Kurla
Mahim R.
Bandra Pt
Sion Causeway
MAHIM
Mahim Bay
Dharavi
Fort Worli
Park
DADAR
Salt Pans
Worli Rd
Old Tanks
PAREL
Sewri
Mahul
Racecourse
Victoria Gdns
Mahalaxmi Temples
BYCULLA
Sta.
Cumbala Hill
TARDEO
MAZAGAON
Bombay Harbour
Towers of Silence
Grant Rd
Hosp.
Malabar Hill
GIRGAUM
MANDVI
Sta.
Cross I.
Marine Drive
Govt Ho.
G.P.O.
FORT
Malabar Pt
Back Bay
Univ.
Town Hall
Ft George
Caths.
Inst. of Science
Mus.
Gateway of India
COLABA
Middle Ground
St John's Ch.
Oyster Rock
Observatory
Prongs
Colaba Pt

0 1 2 3 4km

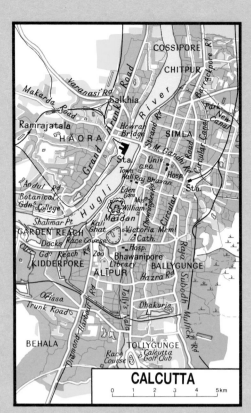

CALCUTTA

COSSIPORE
CHITPUR
Varanasi Rd
Makarda Road
Salkhia
Barrackpore Rd
Grand Trunk Road
River
Ramrajatala
HAORA
Howrah Bridge
SIMLA
New Canal
Strand Rd
M. Gandhi Rd
Andul Rd
Sta.
Town Hall
G.P.O.
Univ.
Hosp.
Botanical Gdn
College
Raj Bhavan
Sta.
Hugli
Eden Gdns
Shalimar Pt
Ft William
Circular Rd
GARDEN REACH
Maidan
Kali Ghat
Victoria Mem!
Cath.
Docks
Reach Rd
Race Course
Zoo
KIDDERPORE
Gdn
Bhawanipore
Library
BALLYGUNGE
ALIPUR
Hazra Rd
Orissa
Tolly's Nala
Dhakuria
Mullick Rd
Trunk Road
Diamond Harbour Rd
Circular Rd
Raja Suboah Rd
BEHALA
TOLLYGUNGE
Race Course
Calcutta Golf Club

0 1 2 3 4 5km

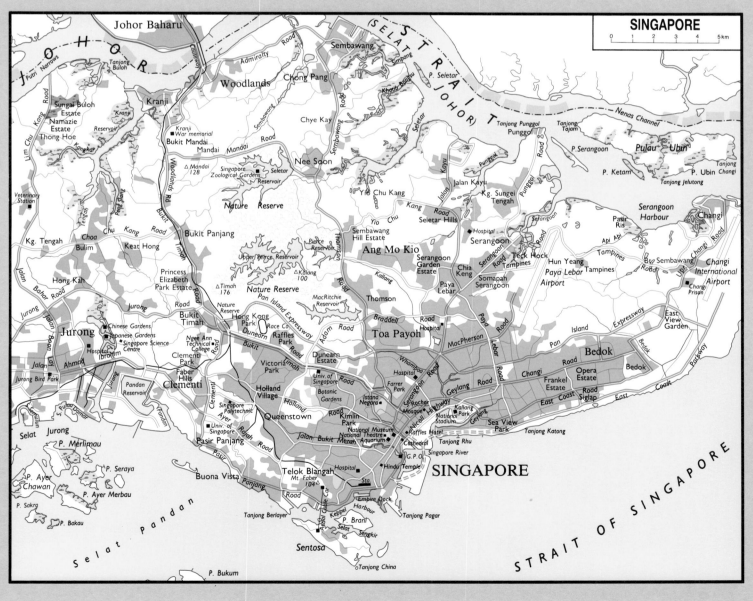

SINGAPORE

0 1 2 3 4 5km

Johor Baharu
JOHOR
(SELAT
STRAIT
P. Putri
Tanjong Narrows
Tanjong Buloh
Admiralty Road
Sembawang
Simpang
P. Seletar
OF
Sungai Buloh Estate
Kranji
Woodlands
Chong Pang
Sembawang Road
Khatib Bongsu
JOHOR)
Namazie Estate
Kranji
Reservoir
Chye Kay
Seletar
Nenas Channel
Thong Hoe
Kongkat
Kranji War memorial
Tanjong Punggol
Tanjong Tajam
Bukit Mandai
Mandai Road
Punggol
Lim Chu Kang Road
Nee Soon
P. Serangoon
Pulau Ubin
Mandai 128
Singapore Zoological Gardens
Seletar Reservoir
Jalan Kayu
P. Ketam
P. Ubin
Tanjong Changi
Veterinary Station
Yio Chu Kang
Kang Road
Kg. Sungei Tengah
Tanjong Jelutong
Peng Siang
Woodlands Rd
Yio Chu
Seletar Hills
Serangoon Harbour
Kg. Tengah
Choa Chu Kang Road
Bukit Panjang
Upper Pierce Reservoir
Pierce Reservoir
Thomson Road
Sembawang Hill Estate
Serangoon
Pasir Ris
Changi
Bulim
Keat Hong
Ang Mo Kio
Serangoon Road
Teck Hock
Hun Yeang
Api Api
Hong Kah
Kalang 100
Nature Reserve
Serangoon Garden Estate
Tampines
Bt. Sembawang Road
Changi International Airport
Princess Elizabeth Park Estate
Timah 176
MacRitchie Reservoir
Chia Keng
Tampines
Jalan Bahar Road
Jurong Road
Nature Reserve
Pan Island Expressway
Thomson
Paya Lebar
Somapah Serangoon
Paya Lebar Airport
Changi Prison
Jurong
Hong Kong Park
Bukit Timah
Race Co
Braddell Road
Island Expressway
East View Garden
Chinese Gardens
Japanese Gardens
Dunearn Road
Toa Payoh
Hospital
Pan
Jalan Boon
Singapore Science Centre
Ngee Ann Technical College
Raffles Park
Adam Road
MacPherson
Bedok
Hospital Ibrahim
Clementi Park
Dunearn Estate
Whampoa
Kallang Road
Bedok
Jalan Ahmad
Faber Hills
Victoria Park
Univ. of Singapore
Hospital
Changi Road
Opera Estate
Jurong Bird Park
Pandan Reservoir
Clementi
Holland Village
Botanic Gardens
Farrer Park
Geylang Road
Frankel Estate
East Coast Road
Ayer Rajah Road
Singapore Polytechnic
Holland Road
Istana Negara
Rochor
Mosque
National Stadium
Kallang Park
Road Siglap
East Coast
S. Pulau Damar
Univ. of Singapore
Queenstown
Nicoll Highway
Geylang
Sea View Park
East Coast Parkway
Selat Jurong
P. Merlimau
Pasir Panjang
Kimlin Park
National Museum
National Theatre
Aquarium
Raffles Hotel
Tanjong Rhu
Tanjong Katong
Jalan Bukit Merah
Cathedral
P. Ayer Chawan
P. Seraya
Buona Vista
Pasir Panjang Road
Hospital
G.P.O.
Singapore River
SINGAPORE
P. Ayer Merbau
Telok Blangah
Mt. Faber 104
Hindu Temple
P. Sakra
Road
Sta.
Keppel Cable Car
P. Bakau
Empire Dock
Keppel Harbour
Tanjong Pagar
Tanjong Berlayer
P. Brani
STRAIT OF SINGAPORE
Selat Sengkir
Sentosa
Selat Pandan
P. Bukum
Tanjong China

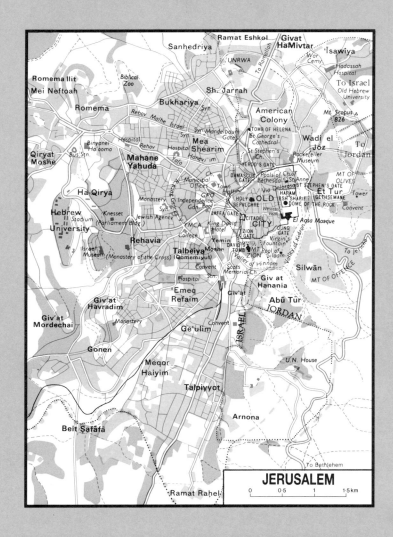

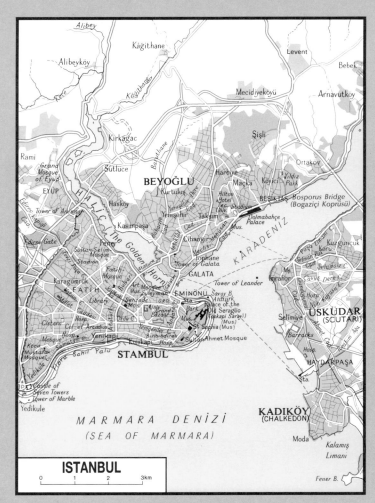

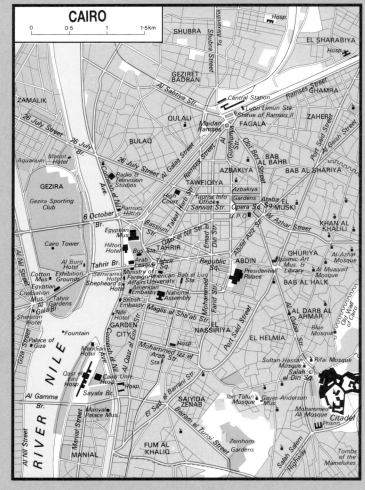

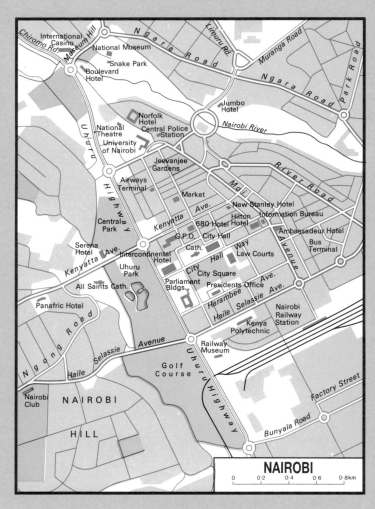

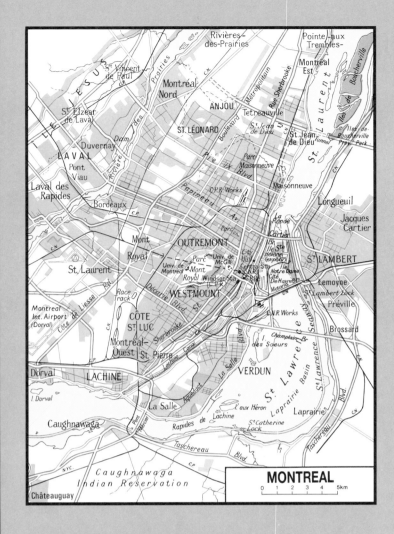

MONTREAL

0 1 2 3 4 5km

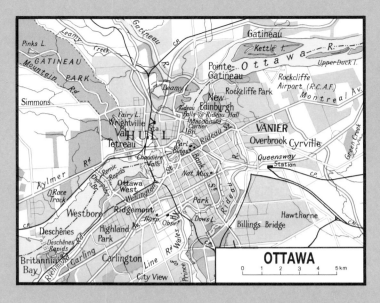

OTTAWA

0 1 2 3 4 5km

TORONTO

0 1 2 3 4 5km

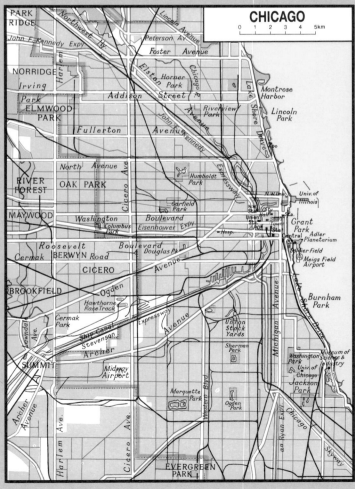

CHICAGO

0 1 2 3 4 5km

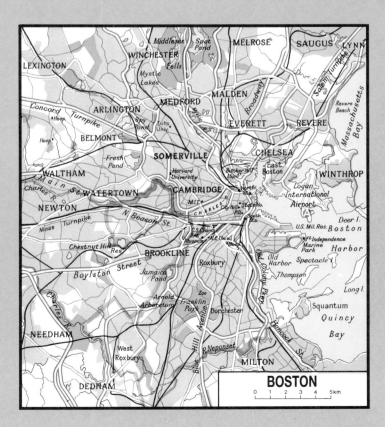

BOSTON

0 1 2 3 4 5km

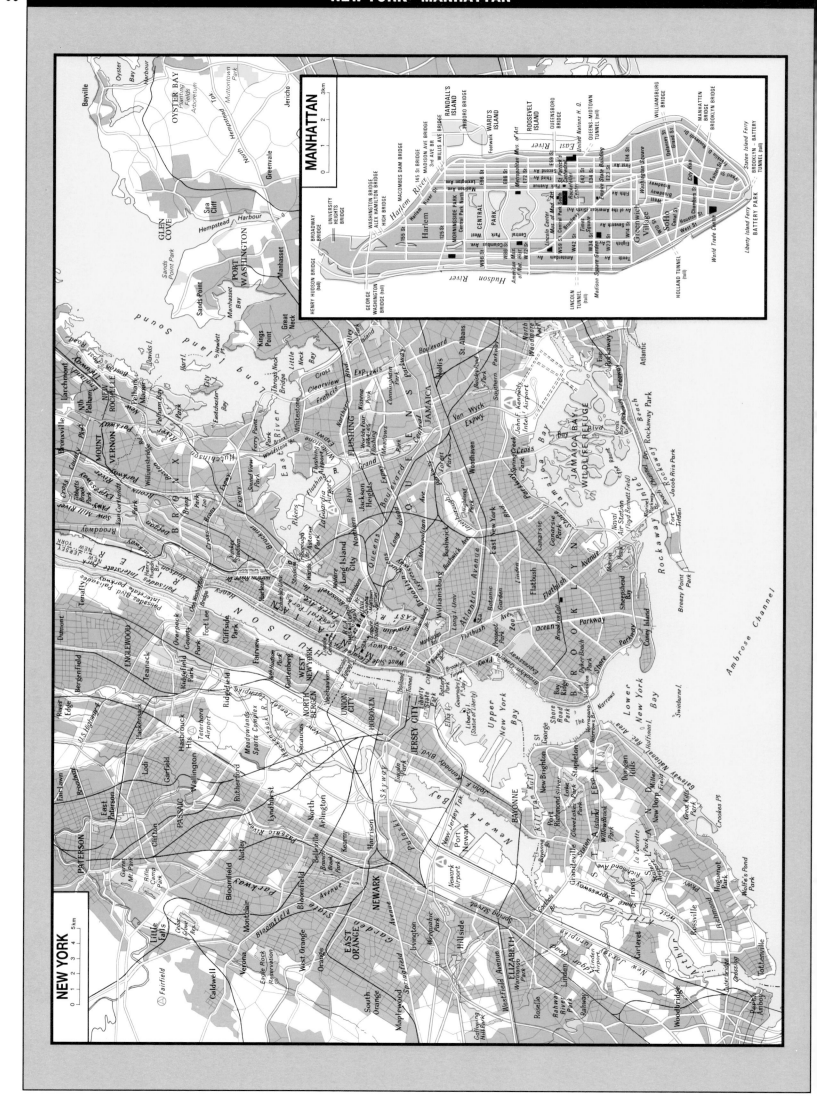

MANHATTAN

3km
2
1
0

BROADWAY BRIDGE

HENRY HUDSON BRIDGE (toll)

UNIVERSITY HEIGHTS BRIDGE

WASHINGTON BRIDGE
ALEX HAMILTON BRIDGE
HIGH BRIDGE

145 St BRIDGE
MACOMBES DAM BRIDGE
MADISON AVE BRIDGE
3rd AVE BR
WILLIS AVE BRIDGE

RANDALL'S ISLAND

TRIBORO BRIDGE

WARD'S ISLAND
Footwalk

Harlem River

Harlem River Dr

155 St
Harlem
125 St

MORNINGSIDE PARK
Central Park North

Metropolitan Mus. of Art

ROOSEVELT ISLAND

East River

QUEENSBORO BRIDGE

UNITED NATIONS H. Q.

QUEENS-MIDTOWN TUNNEL (toll)

WILLIAMSBURG BRIDGE

MANHATTAN BRIDGE
BROOKLYN BRIDGE

CENTRAL PARK
West
Park

Madison Av
Lexington Av
E 96 St
E 86 St
E 72 St
E 59 St
St Patrick's Cathedral
E 42 St
E 34 St
Empire State Building
E 23 St
E 14 St

Grand St
Delancey St
Grand St
Bowery Pell Dr

City Hall
Franklin St

Staten Island Ferry
BROOKLYN — BATTERY TUNNEL (toll)

Columbus Ave
Amsterdam Ave
Central Park West
Rockefeller Center
Lincoln Center
Mus. of Med. Art
Times Square

GEORGE WASHINGTON BRIDGE (toll)

American Mus. of Natural History

Central
Broadway

W 145 St
W 125 St
W 96 St
W 86 St
W 72 St
W 59 St
W 34 St

Fifth Av
Av of the Americas (Sixth Av)
Seventh Av
Eighth Av

Madison Square
Washington Square
Greenwich Village

West
Broadway
Chambers St
West St

SoHo

Houston St
Canal St

World Trade Center

LINCOLN TUNNEL (toll)

Madison Square Garden

W 42 St
W 38 St
W 23 St

Tenth Av

HOLLAND TUNNEL (toll)

Liberty Island Ferry
BATTERY PARK

Pearl St
Franklin D

Hudson River

NEW YORK
5km
4
3
2
1
0

Fairfield

OYSTER BAY
Planting Fields Arboretum

Muttontown Park

Bayville

Oyster Bay

Oyster Bay Harbour

Jericho

Hempstead

North

Greenvale

GLEN COVE

Sea Cliff

Sands Point Park

Sands Point

PORT WASHINGTON

Hempstead Harbour

Manhasset Bay

Manhasset

Kings Point

Great Neck

Long Island Sound

Davids I.

Hart I.

Hewlett Pt.

Little Neck Bay

Whitestone

FLUSHING

Flushing Airport

LARCHMONT

NEW ROCHELLE

Nth Pelham

Pelham

Eastchester Bay

Throgs Neck Bridge

Whitestone Expwy

Ferry Point Park

Whitestone Bridge

Cross Clearview Expwy Lewis

Francis

Kissena Park

Cunningham Park

Boulevard

St. Albans

Hollis

JAMAICA

Van Wyck Expwy

John F. Kennedy (Intercontl.) Airport

North Woodmere Park

Woodmere

Rockaway

Atlantic Beach

JAMAICA BAY WILDLIFE REFUGE

Jacob Riis Park

Rockaway Park

Breezy Point Park

Rockaway Inlet

BRONXVILLE

MOUNT VERNON

BRONX

Bronx Zoo

Van Cortlandt Park

Bronx River Parkway

Hutchinson River Parkway

Williamsbridge

Sound View Park

Rikers I.

LaGuardia Airport

Long Island City

Jackson Heights

Woodhaven

Highland Park

East New York

Canarsie

BROOKLYN

Flatbush

Prospect Park

Flatlands

Sheepshead Bay

Coney Island

Brighton Beach

Ocean Pkwy

Shore Parkway

Lower New York Bay

Breezy Point

Saw Mill River Pkwy

Cross County Pkwy

Yonkers Raceway

Bronx

Yankee Stadium

Shea Stadium

HUDSON RIVER

MANHATTAN

Central Park

Randall's I.

Ward's I.

Roosevelt I.

Long Island Expwy

Queens Blvd

Metropolitan Ave

Bushwick

Williamsburg

Long Island Univ.

Atlantic Avenue

Linden

Botanic Garden

Green-Wood Cemetery

Bay Ridge

Dyker Beach Park

Narrows

Verrazano-Narrows Bridge

Staten Island

Gateway National

Fort Tilden

Broad Channel

Gerritsen Beach

Marine Park

PATERSON

Fair Lawn

East Paterson

Lodi

Garfield

Wallington

PASSAIC

Clifton

North Arlington

Lyndhurst

Rutherford

Nutley

Belleville

Bloomfield

West Orange

Montclair

Verona

EAST ORANGE

Orange

NEWARK

Newark Airport

Irvington

Hillside

ELIZABETH

Linden

Roselle

Rahway

Woodbridge

Perth Amboy

Carteret

Tottenville

Huguenot Park

Wolfe's Pond Park

Great Kills Park

STATEN ISLAND

La Tourette Park

Richmond

Rossville

Crookes Pt.

Arthur Kill

Ambrose Channel

BAYONNE

Kill Van Kull

Port Richmond

New Brighton

Stapleton

Dongan Hills

New Dorp

West Shore Expwy

Newark Bay

JERSEY CITY

HOBOKEN

UNION CITY

NORTH BERGEN

Weehawken

Secaucus

Meadowlands Sports Complex

Teterboro Airport

Hasbrouck Hts.

Hackensack

Teaneck

ENGLEWOOD

Tenafly

Palisades Interstate Parkway

Fort Lee

Cliffside Park

Fairview

Guttenberg

WEST NEW YORK

Upper New York Bay

Governors I.

Ellis I.

Liberty I. (Statue of Liberty)

Liberty State Park

Bergenfield

River Edge

Dumont

Ridgefield Park

Ridgefield

East Rutherford

Garden State Parkway

Branch Brook Park

Harrison

Kearny

Pulaski Skyway

Passaic River

Hackensack River

Little Falls

Cedar Grove

Eagle Rock Reservation

South Orange

Maplewood

West Field Avenue

Rahway River Park

Springfield

Garret Mt. Park

Rifle Camp Park

U.S. Highway 4

Bloomfield Avenue

Morris Turnpike

WASHINGTON

0 1 2 3 4 5km

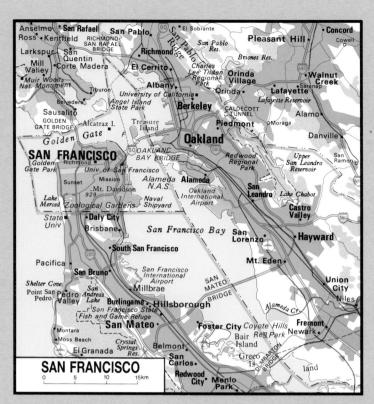

SAN FRANCISCO

0 5 10 15km

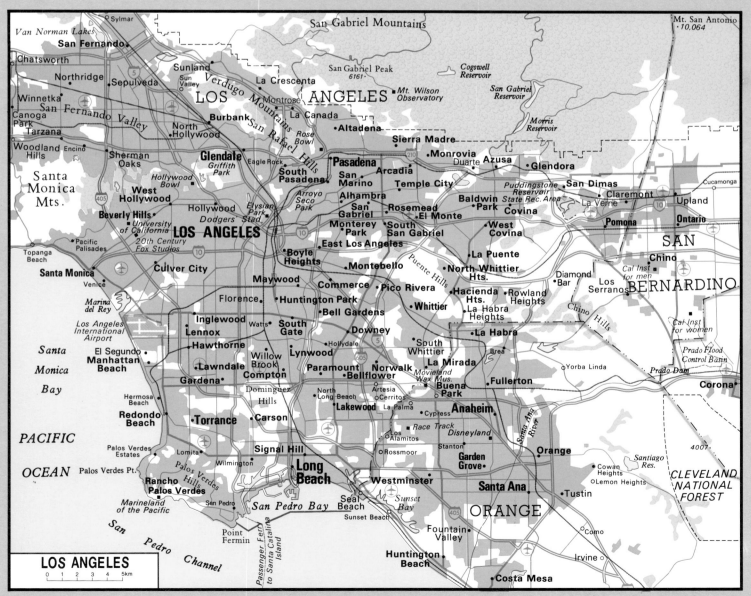

LOS ANGELES

0 1 2 3 4 5km

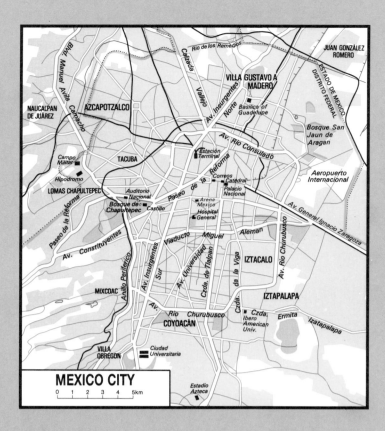

MEXICO CITY

0 1 2 3 4 5km

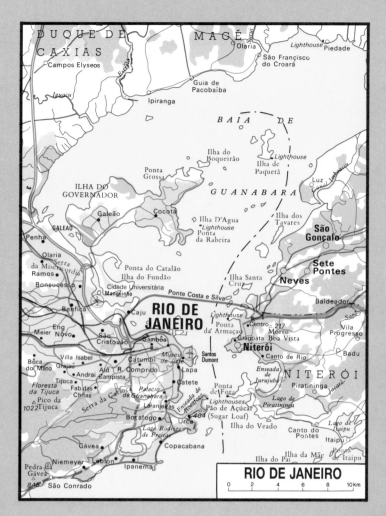

RIO DE JANEIRO

0   2   4   6   8   10km

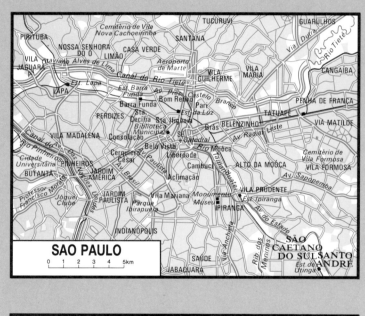

SAO PAULO

0 1 2 3 4 5km

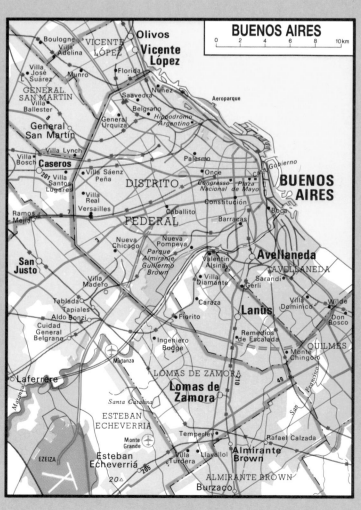

BUENOS AIRES

0   2   4   6   8   10km

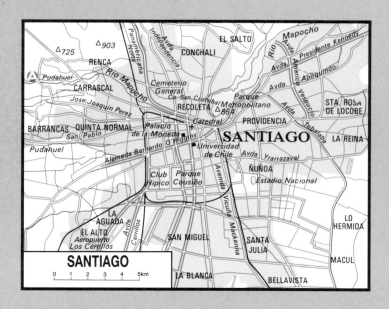

SANTIAGO

0 1 2 3 4 5km

The roman alphabet is used world-wide. Yet the sounds of Latin from which it was inherited were far too few to allow the alphabet to be applied unaltered to the languages of the world. As a result numerous modifications have been made by adding supplementary letters, by changing the original letters or by adding accents or other diacritical signs.

This brief guide is intended to give no more than an indication of the English language equivalents of the more important letters or combinations of letters in the various alphabets used in the Atlas. An English word is added in brackets to illustrate the sound intended.

FRENCH
There are four nasal vowels:
am an aen em en aon   ã
aim ain en eim ein im in   ẽ
om on   õ
um un   ẽũ
ã ẽ õ ẽũ are like a in hart; e in met; o in corn; oo in book pronounced nasally.
au, eau = o (no); é = ay (lay); è, ê, = e (met);
oi oî = wa (wand)
c + a = k; c + e or i = ç = s (sit)
ch = sh (fresh); g + a, o or u = g (got)
g + e or i = j = zh⁺; gn = ni (onion)
gu = g (got); gü = gw (iguana)
ll = l or y; qu = k; th = t
u = between e in few and oo in too

SPANISH
c + a, o or u = k; c + e or i = th (thin) or s (sit)
ch = ch (cheese); g + a, o or u = g (got)
g + e or i = kh*; gu + a, o or u = gw (iguana)
gu + e or i = g (got); j = kh*; ñ = ny (canyon);
ll = y (yes)
qu + a, o or u = kw (quick); qu + e or i =
k (kite)
y = y (yes); z = th (thin) or z depending on dialect

ITALIAN
c + a, o or u = k; c + e or i = ch (cheese)
ch = k
g + a, o or u = g (got); g + e or i = j (jet)
gh = g (got); gli = lli (million)
qu = kw (quick); z = ts or dz

ROMANIAN
ă = a in relative
â = i in ravine
c + a, o or u = k
c + e or i = ch (cheese); ch = k
g + a, o or u = g (got); g + e or i = j (jet)
ş = sh (fresh); ţ = ts (sits)

PORTUGUESE
ã, ãe = French ẽ
õã, õe = French õ
c + a, o or u = k; c + e or i = s
ç = s; ch = sh (fresh)
ih = lli (million)
x = sh (fresh); z = z but = zh when final

GERMAN
ä = e (met); au = ow (down)
äu = oy (boy); c = ts (sits)
ch = kh*; ei, ey = eye (= y in why)
eu = oy (boy); g = g (got)
ie = ie (retrieve); j = y (yes)
ö = oo (book); s = z but s when final
sch = sh (fresh); sp, st = shp, sht
ü = French u; v = f; w = v; z = ts (sits)

DUTCH
aa ee are long vowels
c + e or i or z = s, otherwise k
ij = eye (= y in why)

SCANDINAVIAN
å = aw (law); ä = e (met)
ø = oo (book); øj = oy (boy)
j = y (yes)

ICELANDIC
ð = dh = th (then)
hv = kw; ll = tl; p = th

FINNISH
ay = eye (= y in why)
j = y; y = French u; w = v

HUNGARIAN
a = aw (law); cs = ch (cheese); ccs = chch;
gy = d + y (dew)
j = y; ny = ny (canyon)
s = sh (fresh); ss = shsh
sz = s (sit); ty = t + y (yes)
zs = zh⁺
ai = e (met); av = au or av
dh = th (then); th = th (thin)
kh = kh*; oi = i (ravine)
ou = oo (too)

TURKISH
c = j (jet); ç = ch (cheese)
ö = oo (book); ş = sh
ü = French u
ı and i = i (ravine)

RUSSIAN
ay = a + y (yes)
e = e or ye
ë = yaw; ëy = yoy
ch = ch (cheese); sh = sh (fresh)
sh ch = sh ch (fresh cheese)
ts = ts (sits)
ya = ya (yam); z = z (zoo)
zh = zh (measure)
' = sound of y (yes)
" = silent

OTHER SLAVONIC

§S-C	Pol	Cz		
c	c	c	=	ts (sits)
	ć		=	ts + y (yes)
č	cz	č	=	ch (cheese)
ć			=	t + y (yes)
đ		ď	=	d + y (yes)
		ě	=	e (mother)
h	ch	ch	=	kh*
j	j	j	=	y (yes)
	l		=	w (wood)
nj	ń	ň	=	ny (canyon)
		ř	=	rzh*
š	sz	š	=	sh (fresh)
		ť	=	t + y (yes)
ž	ž, rz, ź	ž	=	zh*

ARABIC
long vowels have a macron (bar), ā
dh = th (then)
h = h (hat); j = (jet)
gh = French r, pronounce as g (got)
kh = kh* q = g (got)
' and ' are best treated as glottal stops
ḍ ḥ ṣ ṭ ẓ = d, h, s, t, z
Note: 1. in Egypt and Sudan g = g (got)
         2. in NW Africa Dj = j (jet)
                ou = w (wadi)

FARSI (IRAN)
Can be read as Arabic above. Stress is on the last syllable.

SOMALI
long vowels are aa, ee, ii, oo, uu
c is silent = glottal stop
dh = th (then)
g = g (got); q = k (kite)
sh = sh (fresh); w = w (wadi)
x = kh*

MALAY – INDONESIAN
As English except
c = ch (cheese)

CHINESE (PINYIN)
q = ch (church); c = ts (sits)
x = hs = h + s

⁺zh = s in measure;
*kh = ch in Scottish loch
     = German ch in achtung

§S-C = Serbo-Croat
 Pol = Polish
 Cz = Czech

A

ABLATION The loss of water from ice and snow surfaces, by melting and run-off, calving of icebergs, evaporation and snow-blowing.

ABRASION The wearing down or away of rocks by friction.

ABSOLUTE HUMIDITY The amount of water vapour in a specified amount of air, frequently expressed as grams of water vapour per kilogram of dry air containing the vapour.

ABYSSAL Usually applied to the very deep parts of the oceans, over 3km below the surface.

ACCRETION The growth of objects by collection of additional material, usually of smaller size. Ice particles in the atmosphere can grow by this process.

ACID PRECIPITATION Rain and snow with a pH of less than 5.6.

ADVECTION Movement of a property in air and water by their motion. Usually applied to horizontal rather than vertical motion.

AEOLIAN Related to winds. Thus aeolian geomorphology is concerned with the processes whereby wind removes, distributes and deposits materials of the earth's surface.

AGGLOMERATE A rock made of small pieces of lava that have been fused by heat.

AGGRADATION The building up of a land surface by deposition of material by wind, water or ice.

AGGREGATE A loose collection of rock fragments.

ALLUVIAL PLAIN A plain, usually at low altitude, made of alluvium.

ANTICYCLONE An extensive region of relatively high atmospheric pressure, usually a few thousand kilometres across, in which the low level winds spiral outwards, clockwise in the northern hemisphere and anticlockwise in the southern hemisphere.

ARCHIPELAGO A sea or lake containing numerous islands, such as the area between Sumatra and the Philippines.

ARTESIAN WELL A well which taps water held under pressure in rocks below the surface. The pressure results in a well water level higher than the highest part of the water-bearing rocks.

ATOLL A coral reef surrounding a lagoon found in the tropical oceans.

AURORA BOREALIS (Northern Lights) Flashing lights in the atmosphere some 400km above polar regions caused by solar particles being trapped in the earth's magnetic field.

AVALANCHE The sudden and rapid movement of ice, snow, earth and rock down a slope.

AZIMUTH Horizontal angle between two directions.

B

BADLANDS Highly dissected landscapes, usually associated with poorly consolidated materials and sparse vegetation cover.

BAR A usually sandy feature, lying parallel to the coast and frequently underwater.

BARCHAN A crescentic sand dune whose horns point in the direction of dune movement.

BAROGRAPH An instrument for recording atmospheric pressure. The output is a graph of pressure changes through time.

BAROMETER An instrument for measuring atmospheric pressure. The reading is either by measuring the height of a column of mercury or by the compression or expansion of a series of vacuum chambers.

BARRIER REEF A coral reef characterized by the presence of a lagoon or body of water between it and the associated coastline.

BASALT A fine-grained and dark coloured igneous rock.

BASE LEVEL The lower limit to the operation of erosional processes generating on land – usually defined with reference to the role of running water. Sea level is the most general form of base level.

BASIN An area of land encompassing the water flow into any specific river channel – hence usually known as a drainage basin.

BATHOLITH A large mass of intrusive igneous rock.

BATHYMETRY Measurement of water depth.

BAUXITE The main ore of aluminium.

BEACH A coastal accumulation of various types of sediment, usually sands and pebbles.

BEAUFORT SCALE A scale of wind speed devised by Admiral Sir Francis Beaufort based on effects of winds on ships. Later modified to include land-based phenomena.

BENCH MARK A reference point used in the measurement of land height in topographic surveying.

BENTHIC Relating to plants, animals and other organisms that inhabit the floors of lakes, seas and oceans.

BERGSCHRUND The crevasse existing at the head of a glacier because of the movement of glacier ice away from the rock wall.

BIGHT A bend in a coast forming an open bay, or the bay itself.

BIOMASS The mass of biological material present per plant or animal, per community or per unit area.

BIOME A mixed community of plants and animals occupying a large area of continental size.

BIOSPHERE The zone at the interface of the earth's surface, ocean and atmosphere where life is found.

BIOTA The entire collection of species or organisms, plants and animals found in a given region.

BISE A cold, dry northerly to north-easterly wind occurring in the mountains of Central Europe in winter.

BLACK EARTH A black soil rich in humus, found extensively in temperate grasslands such as the Russian Steppes.

BLOW HOLE Vertical shaft leading from a sea cave to the surface. Air and water are frequently forced through it by advancing seas.

BORE A large solitary wave which moves up funnel-shaped rivers and estuaries.

BOREAL A descriptive term, usually of climate and forest, to characterize conditions in middle to high latitudes.

BOURNE A river channel on chalk terrain that flows after heavy rain.

BUTTE A small, flat-topped and often steep-sided hill standing isolated on a flat plain. *(see picture below)*

C

CALDERA A depression, usually several kilometres across.

CALVING The breaking away of a mass of ice from a floating glacier or ice shelf to form an iceberg.

CANYON A steep sided valley, usually found in semi-arid and arid areas.

CAPE An area of land jutting out into water, frequently as a peninsula or promontory.

CARDINAL POINTS The four principal compass points, north, east, south and west.

CATARACT A large waterfall over a precipice.

CHINOOK A warm, dry wind that blows down the eastern slopes of the Rocky Mountains of North America.

Above Butte, Monument Valley, Arizona USA. This type of flat-topped, steep sided hill is characteristic of the arid plateau region of the western United States.

CIRQUE OR CORRIE A hollow, open downstream but bounded upstream by a curved, steep headwall, with a gently sloping floor. Found in areas that have been glaciated.

CLIMATE The long-term atmospheric characteristics of a specified area.

CLOUD A collection of a vast number of small water droplets or ice crystals or both in the atmosphere.

COL A pass or saddle between two mountain peaks.

COLD FRONT A zone of strong horizontal temperature gradient in the atmosphere moving such that, for the surface observer, cold air replaces warm.

CONDENSATION The process of formation of liquid water from water vapour.

CONFLUENCE The 'coming together' of material

flows, most usually used in fluids such as the atmosphere and oceans.

CONGLOMERATE   A rock which comprises or contains rounded pebbles more than about 2mm in diameter.

CONTINENTAL DRIFT   The movement of continents relative to each other. (See *Plate Tectonics*)

CONTINENTAL SHELF   A portion of the continental crust below sea level that slopes gently seaward forming an extension of the adjacent coastal plain separated from the deep ocean by the steeply sloping continental slope.

CONTINENTAL SLOPE   Lies on the seaward edge of the continental shelf and slopes steeply to the ocean floor.

CONTOUR   A line on a map that joins points of equal height or equal depth.

CONVECTION CURRENT   A current resulting from convection which is a mode of mass transport within a fluid (especially heat) resulting in movement and mixing of properties of that fluid.

CONVERGENCE   The opposite of divergence which is the outflowing mass of fluid. Hence convergence is the inflowing of such mass.

CORAL REEF   Large structures fringing islands and coastlines consisting mostly of corals and algae.

CORDILLERA   A system of mountain ranges consisting of a number of more or less parallel chains of mountain peaks – such as in the Rocky Mountains.

CRATER   A depression at the top of a volcano where a vent carrying lava and gasses reaches the surface.

CRATON   A continental area that has experienced little internal deformation in the last 600 million years.

CREVASSE   A deep fissure in the surface of a body of ice.

CYCLONE   A region of relatively low atmospheric pressure about 2000 km across around which air rotates anticlockwise in the northern hemisphere and clockwise in the southern.

D

DATUM LEVEL   Something (such as a fixed point or assumed value) used as a basis for calculating or measuring. Frequently a height of ground relative to which other heights are assessed.

DECLINATION   Angular distance north or south from the equator measured along a line of longitude.

DECIDUOUS FOREST   Forest in which the trees shed their leaves at a particular time, season or growth stage. The most common manifestation is the shedding in winter.

DEFLATION   The process whereby the wind removes fine materials from the surface of a beach or desert.

DEGRADATION   The lowering and often flattening of a land surface by erosion.

DELTA   Accumulations of sediment deposited at the mouths of rivers. The Nile and Mississippi deltas are two famous examples.

DENUDATION   The laying bare of underlying rocks or strata by the removal of overlying material.

DEPOSITION   The laying down of material, which, in geomorphological terms, was previously carried by wind, liquid water or ice.

DEPRESSION   See *cyclone*

DESALINIZATION   To take out the salt content of a material. Usually applied to the extraction of salt from sea water to give fresh water.

DESERT   An area in which vegetation cover is sparse or absent and precipitation is low in amount. Deserts can be hot or cold.

DISCHARGE   The volume of flow of fluid in a given time period.

DISSECTED PLATEAU   A relatively flat, high level area of land which has been cut by streams.

DIURNAL   Occurring everyday or having a daily cycle.

DIVERGENCE   A spreading of material. Frequently found in high pressure areas (anticyclones) in the atmosphere where air spirals outwards from the centre.

DOLDRUMS   A zone of light, variable winds and low atmospheric pressure near or slightly north of the equator.

DRAINAGE   The flow of material (usually a fluid) over the earth's surface due to the force of gravity. Most familiarly seen as rivers.

DRIFT ICE   Ice bodies drifting in ocean currents.

DROUGHT   Dryness caused by lack of precipitation, most easily seen in the hot, dry desert areas of the world.

DROWNED VALLEY   A valley which has been filled with water due to a rise of sea level relative to the level with which the river mouth was previously in accord.

DRUMLIN   A depositional landform, usually made of glacially-derived material, which has been streamlined by the passage of overlying ice.

DRY VALLEY   A valley which is seldom, if ever, occupied by a stream channel.

DUNE   An accumulation of sand deposited and shaped by wind.

DUST   Solid particles carried in suspension by the atmosphere.

DYKE   A sheet-like intrusion of igneous rock, usually oriented vertically, which cuts across the structural planes of the host rocks.

E

EARTH PILLAR   A pinnacle of soil or other unconsolidated material that is protected from erosion by the presence of a stone at the top.

EARTHQUAKE   A series of shocks and tremors resulting from the sudden release of pressure along active faults and in areas of volcanic activity.

EBB TIDE   Tide receding to or at its lowest point.

ECLIPSE, LUNAR   The total or partial obscuring of the Moon by the Earth lying on a line between the Moon and the Sun.

ECLIPSE, SOLAR   The total or partial obscuring of the Sun by the Moon lying on a line between the Sun and the Earth.

ECOLOGY   A branch of science that studies the relations of plants and animals with each other and with their non-living environment.

ECOSYSTEM   An entity within which ecological relations operate.

EPICENTRE   The point on the earth's surface which lies directly above the focus of an earthquake.

EQUINOX   The time of year when the sun is directly overhead at noon at the equator.

ERG   A sand desert.

EROSION   The group of processes whereby debris is loosened or dissolved and removed from any part of the earth's surface.

ERRATIC   A rock that has been carried to its present location by a glacier.

ESCARPMENT   A linear land form with one steep side (scarp slope) and one less steep side (dip slope).

ESKER   A sinuous ridge of coarse gravel which has been deposited by a meltwater stream normally flowing underneath a glacier.

ESTUARY   The sections of a river which flow into the sea and are influenced by tidal currents.

EVAPORATION   The diffusion of water vapour into the atmosphere from freely exposed water surfaces.

EXFOLIATION   The weathering of a rock by the peeling off of surface layers.

F

FATHOM   A unit of length equal to six feet, most usually used in measuring depth of water.

FAULT   A crack or fissure in rock, resulting from tectonic movement.

FAUNA   Animals or animal life of an area.

FEN   A low lying area partially covered by water which is characterized by accumulations of peat.

FJORD   A glacially eroded valley whose floor is occupied by the sea.

FIRTH   A sea inlet, particularly in Scotland.

FLORA   Plants or plant life in an area.

FLUVIOGLACIAL   The activity of rivers which are fed by water melted from glaciers.

FOG   An accumulation of water droplets or ice crystals in the atmosphere such that visibility is reduced to 1km or less.

FÖHN WIND   A strong, gusty, warm, down-slope wind which occurs on the lee side of a mountain range.

FOLD   A bend in rock strata resulting from movement of the crustal rocks.

FOOD CHAIN   The transfer of food from one type of organism to another in a sequence.

FORD   A shallow part of a river that allows easy crossing.

FRACTURE   The splitting of material into parts: usually concerned with geological materials.

FRAZIL ICE   Fine spikes of ice in suspension in water, usually associated with the freezing of sea water.

FRONT   A transition zone between air of different density, temperature and humidity.

FROST   A situation resulting from air temperatures falling to 0°C – either in the air (air frost) or at the ground (ground frost).

FUMAROLE   A small, volcanic vent through which hot gasses are emitted.

G

GABBRO   A basic igneous rock, usually coarse grained and dark grey to black in colour.

GEEST   Ancient alluvial sediments which still cover the land surfaces on which they were originally deposited.

GEODESY   The determination of the size and shape of the earth by survey and calculation.

GEOID   The shape of the earth at mean sea level.

GEOLOGY   Science that deals with the nature and origin of the earth's rocks and sediments.

GEOMORPHOLOGY   Science that deals with the nature and origin of landforms of the earth's surface.

GEOSYNCLINE   A very large depression, tens or hundreds of kilometres across and up to ten kilometres deep, the floor of which is built up by sedimentation.

GEYSER   A spring of geothermally heated water that erupts intermittently due to pressures beneath the surface. Old Faithful in Yellowstone National Park, USA, is the most famous example.

GLACIATION   The incursion of ice into (or over) a landscape resulting in a whole suite of glacial processes operating thereupon.

GLACIER   A large body of ice, in a valley or covering a much larger area. The largest are found in polar regions.

GLEN   Valley. Term especially used in Scotland.

GNEISS   A coarse-grained igneous rock that has been metamorphosed.

GONDWANALAND   A large continent which it is thought was split very early in geological time to form parts of Africa, Australia, Antarctica, South America and India.

GORGE   A deep and narrow section of a river valley, usually with very steep sides.

GRAVEL   Loose, rounded fragments of rock.

GREAT CIRCLE   A circle formed on the surface of the earth by the intersection of a plane through the centre of the earth with the surface. Lines of longitude and the Equator are great circles.

GROUND FROST   See *frost*

GROUND WATER   All water (gaseous, liquid or solid) lying below the earth's surface and not chemically combined with the minerals present.

GROYNE   A man-made barrier running across a beach and into the sea; constructed to reduce erosion of the beach by longshore currents.

GULF   A part of the sea that is partly or almost completely enclosed by land.

GULLY   A linear depression worn in the earth by running water after rains.

GUYOT   A flat-topped mountain on the sea floor which does not reach the sea surface.

GYRE   Large circulations of water in the world's oceans, involving the major currents.

H

HAFF   A coastal lagoon separated from the open seas by a sand spit.

HAIL   Solid precipitation which falls as ice particles from cumulonimbus clouds. Contrasts markedly with snow.

HEMISPHERE   Half of the earth, usually thought of in terms of its surface. The most familiar are the northern and southern hemispheres, bounded by the Equator.

HORIZON   Apparent junction of earth and sky.

HORSE LATITUDE   The latitude belts over the oceans at latitudes of 30–35° where winds are predominantly calm or light and weather is often hot and dry.

HOT SPOT   A small area of the earth's crust where an unusually high heat flow is associated with volcanic activity.

HOT SPRING   An emission of hot water at the land surface.

HURRICANE   A severe cyclone occurring in the tropics, characterized by high wind speeds and heavy precipitation.

HYDROLOGICAL CYCLE   The continuous movement of all forms of water (vapour, liquid and solid) on, in and above the earth.

HYDROSPHERE   The earth's water – saline, fresh, gaseous, liquid and solid.

HYGROMETER   A device for measuring the relative humidity of the atmosphere.

HYPSOGRAPHIC CURVE   A generalized profile of the earth and ocean floors which represents the proportions of the area of the surface at various altitudes above or below a datum.

I

ICEBERG   A large floating mass of ice detached from a glacier, usually tens of metres deep and can be several kilometres across.

ICE-CAP   A dome-shaped glacier with a generally outward flow of ice.

ICE FLOE   A piece of floating ice which is not attached to the land and is usually 2–3 metres thick.

ICE SHELF   A floating sheet of ice attached to an embayment in the coast.

IGNEOUS ROCK   Rock formed when molten material solidifies, either within the earth's crust or at the surface.

INSELBERG   A large, residual hill which overlooks a surrounding eroded plain.

INSOLATION   The amount of solar radiation received over a specified area and a specified time.

INTERNATIONAL DATE LINE   An arbitary line, roughly along the 180° longitude line, east and west of which the date differs by one day.

INVERSION (temperature)
An increase of temperature with height.

IRRIGATION   The supply of water to land by artificial means. Usually to improve agricultural productivity.

ISLAND ARC   A chain of islands with an arcuate plan form. The islands are usually volcanic in origin.

ISOBAR   A line drawn on diagrams joining equal values of atmospheric pressure. A particular kind of isopleth.

ISOPLETH   A line drawn on diagrams joining equal values of the plotted element.

ISOSTASY   The condition of balance between the rigid crustal elements of the earth's surface and the underlying, denser and more mobile material.

Above Limestone towers in the world's most spectacular karst region – Li River near Guilin, Guangxi Province, China. The towers are the result of erosional processes.

ISTHMUS   A narrow strip of land which connects two islands or two large land masses.

J

JOINT   A fracture or crack in a rock.

JUNGLE   An area of land overgrown with dense vegetation, usually in the tropics.

K

KAME   An irregular mound of stratified sediment deposited by, in association with stagnant ice.

KARST   Limestone areas which have distinctive landforms such as caves, sinks and frequently a lack of surface water. *(see picture above)*

KELP   A mass of large brown seaweeds.

KETTLE HOLE   An enclosed depression resulting from the melting of buried ice.

KNOT   A measure of speed – one nautical mile per hour (1.15 mi hr^{-1}; 0.85 km hr^{-1}).

KOPJE   A small hill or rock outcrop; term used particularly in South Africa.

KRILL   Small marine animals, resembling shrimps.

L

LACCOLITH   A mass of intrusive rock, usually with a horizontal base and causing the doming of overlying strata.

LAGOON   A shallow pool separated from a larger body of water by a bar or reef.

LANDSAT   An unmanned satellite that carries sensors to record the resources of the earth.

LANDSLIDE   The movement downward under the influence of gravity of a mass of rock debris.

LATERITE   A red clay formed by the weathering of rock that consists especially of compounds of iron and aluminium.

LAURASIA   The northern part of Pangaea, a super-continent thought to have been broken up by continental drift.

LAVA   Molten rock material that emerges from volcanoes and volcanic fissures.

LEACHING   The downward movement of water through soil resulting in the removal of water-soluble materials from upper layers and their accumulation in lower layers.

LEEWARD   To the lee (downwind, downstream) of an obstacle lying in a flow.

LEVEE   A broad, long ridge running parallel and adjacent to a river on its flood-plain.

LIGNITE   A brownish black coal in which the texture of the original wood is distinct.

LITHOSPHERE   The earth's crust and a portion of the upper mantle that together comprise a layer of strength relative to the more easily deformable layer below.

LITTORAL   A coastal region.

LLANOS   An open grassy plain in S. America.

LOAM   A crumbly soil consisting of a mixture of clay, silt and sand.

LOCH   A lake or narrow sea inlet in Scotland.

LOESS   Unconsolidated and frequently unstratified material deposited after transport by wind.

LONGSHORE CURRENT   A current that runs along a coast. It may result in longshore drift, the transport of beach material along the coast.

LOW   See *cyclone*

LUNAR MONTH   The period of time between two successive new moons, being about 29½ days.

M

MAGMA   Fused, molten rock material beneath the earth's crust from which igneous rocks are formed.

MAGNETIC ANOMALIES   Areas with local surface variations in the earth's magnetic field relative to large-scale values.

MAGNETIC FIELD   The field of force exerted by the earth by virtue of its being like a giant magnet. Its most familiar manifestation is in the behaviour of a compass.

MAGNETIC REVERSAL   The reversal of the earth's magnetic field, such that a north-seeking compass points toward the South Pole. Such reversals have occurred in geological time.

MANTLE   The zone within the earth's interior extending from 25 to 70km below the surface to a depth of 2900km.

MAP PROJECTION   A mathematical device for representing a portion of all of the earth's curved surface on a flat surface.

MAP SCALE   A measure of the ratio of distances represented on a map to their true value.

MAQUIS   Scrub vegetation of evergreen shrubs characteristic of the western Mediterranean.

MARL   A fine grained mixture of clay and silt with a high proportion of calcium carbonate.

MASSIF   A large mountainous area, often quite distinct, containing several individual substantial mountains.

MEANDER   A sinuously winding portion of a river channel; also applied to similar forms within larger flows, such as the atmosphere and oceans.

MEAN SEA LEVEL   The level of the sea determined from a mean of the tidal ranges over periods of several months to several years.

METAMORPHIC ROCKS   Rocks in which their composition, structure and texture have been significantly altered by the action of heat and pressure greater than that produced normally by burial.

METEOROLOGY   The study of the workings of the atmosphere.

MILLIBAR   A unit of pressure, most widely used in meteorology. The average pressure exerted by the atmosphere on the surface of the earth is just over 1013 millibars.

MISTRAL   A cold, dry, north or northwest wind affecting the Rhone Valley.

MONSOON   A wind regime with marked seasonal reversal in direction, most famously found in the Indian sub-continent.

MORAINE   A landform resulting from the deposition of till by glaciers, taking on several

distinctive forms depending upon the location and mode of deposition.

N

NADIR   A point that is vertically below the observer.

NASA   National Aeronautics and Space Administration (USA).

NEAP TIDE   A tide of minimum height occurring at the first and third quarter of the moon.

NÉVÉ   Snow that is being compacted into ice, as found in the birth place of glaciers.

NUNATAK   A mountain completely surrounded by an ice cap or ice sheet.

O

OASIS   An area within a desert region where there is sufficient water to sustain animal and plant life throughout the year.

OCEAN BASIN   A large depression in the ocean floor analogous to basins on land.

OCEANIC CRUST   The portion of the earth's surface crust comprising largely sima (silica-magnesia rich rocks) about 5km thick. Underlies most of the world's oceans.

OCEAN RIDGE   A ridge in the ocean floor, sometimes 150 to 1500 km wide and hundreds of metres high.

OCCLUSION   The coming together of warm and cold fronts in cyclones in the latest stages of its evolution.

OROGENESIS   The formation of mountains, such as the Andes and Rocky Mountains. The mechanism is still uncertain but is probably related to plate tectonics.

OUTWASH PLAIN   Stratified material deposited by glacio-fluvial waters beyond the ice margin.

OXBOW LAKE   A lake, usually curved in plan, occupying an abandoned section of meandering river.

P

PACK ICE   Ice formed on sea surface when water temperatures fall to about −2°C and floating free under the influence of currents and wind.

PAMPAS   An extensive, generally grass-covered plain of temperate South America east of the Andes.

PANGAEA   The name given to a postulated continental landmass which split up to produce most of the present northern hemisphere continents.

PASS   A narrow passage over relatively low ground in a mountain range.

PEDIMENT   A smooth, erosional land surface typically sloping from the foot of a high-land area to a local base level.

PELAGIC   The part of an aquatic system that excludes its margins and substrate; it is essentially the main part of the water body.

PENEPLAIN   The supposed end land form resulting from erosional processes wearing down an initially uplifted block.

PENUMBRA   A region of partial darkness in a shadow surrounding the region of total darkness (umbra), such as seen in an eclipse.

PERIHELION The point in its orbit about the sun that a planet is closest to the sun.

PIEDMONT GLACIER A glacier which spreads out into a lobe as it flows onto a lowland.

PILLOW LAVA Lava that has solidified, probably under water, in rounded masses.

PLACER DEPOSIT A sediment, such as in the bed of a stream, which contains particles of valuable minerals.

PLAIN Extensive area of level or rolling treeless country.

PLANKTON Small freshwater and marine organisms that tend to move with water currents and comprise the food of larger and higher order organisms.

PLATE TECTONICS A theory which holds that the earth's surface is divided into several major rigid plates which are in motion with respect to each other and the underlying mantle. Continental drift results from plate motion and earthquakes, volcanoes and mountain-building tend to occur at the plate boundaries.

PLUTONIC ROCK Rock material that has formed at depth where cooling and crystallization have occurred slowly.

POLAR WANDERING The movements of the North and South Poles throughout geological time relative to the positions of the continents.

POLDER A low lying area of land that has been reclaimed from the sea or a lake by artificial means and is kept free of water by pumping.

PRECIPITATION The deposition of water from the atmosphere in liquid and solid form. Rain, snow, hail and dew are the most familiar forms.

PRAIRIE An extensive area of level or rolling, almost treeless grassland in North America.

PRESSURE GRADIENT The change per unit distance of pressure, perhaps most frequently met in atmospheric studies. The cause of winds.

Q

QUARTZ A crystalline mineral consisting of silicon dioxide that is a major constituent of many rocks.

QUICKSAND Water-saturated sand that is semi-liquid and cannot bear the weight of heavy objects.

R

RADAR A device that transmits radio waves and locates objects in the vicinity by analysis of the waves reflected back from them (radio detection and ranging).

RADIATION The transmission of energy in the form of electromagnetic waves and requiring no intervening medium.

RAIN SHADOW An area experiencing relatively low rainfall because of its position on the leeward side of a hill.

RAISED BEACH An emerged shoreline represented by stranded marine deposits and wave cut platforms, usually backed by former cliffs.

RANGE An open region over which livestock may roam and feed, particularly in North America.

RAVINE A narrow, steep sided valley usually formed by running water.

REEF A rocky construction found at or near sea-level; coral reefs are perhaps the most familiar type.

RELATIVE HUMIDITY The amount of water vapour in an air sample relative to the amount the sample could hold if it were saturated at the same temperature; expressed as a percentage.

REMOTE SENSING The observation and measurement of an object without touching it.

RHUMB LINE An imaginary line on the surface of the earth which makes equal oblique angles with all lines of longitude so that it forms a spiral coiling round the poles but never reaching them. This would be the course sailed by a ship following a single compass direction.

RIA An inlet of the sea formed by the flooding of river valleys by rising sea or sinking land. Contrast to fjords which are drowned glacial valleys.

RIFT VALLEY A valley formed when the area between two parallel faults sinks.

RIVER TERRACE A step like land form in the flood plain of rivers due to the river incising further into the plain and leaving remnants of its former flood plain at levels higher than the present level of the river channel.

ROARING FORTIES The area between 40° and 50°S, so called because of the high speeds of the winds occurring there. Sometimes applied to the winds themselves.

RUN-OFF The section of the hydrological cycle connecting precipitation to channel flow.

S

SALINITY The presence of salts in the waters and soils of arid, semi-arid and coastal areas.

SALT-MARSH Vegetated mud-flats found commonly on many low-lying coasts in a wide range of temperate environments.

SANDBANK A large deposit of sand, usually in a river or coastal waters.

SANDSTORM A wind storm driving clouds of sand, most usually in hot, dry deserts.

SAVANNAH A grassland region of the tropics and sub-tropics.

SCHIST Medium to coarse-grained crystalline metamorphic rock.

SEA-FLOOR SPREADING The phenomenon when tectonic plates move apart.

SEAMOUNT A mountain or other area of high relief on the sea-floor which does not reach the surface.

SEASAT A satellite especially designed to sense remotely wind and sea conditions on the oceans.

SEDIMENTARY ROCK Rock composed of the fragments of older rocks which have been eroded and the debris deposited by wind and water, often as distinct strata.

SEISMIC WAVE Wave resulting from the movements of materials in earthquakes.

SEISMOLOGY Science that deals with earthquakes and other vibrations of the earth.

SHALE A compacted sedimentary rock, usually with fine-grained particles.

SHALLOW-FOCUS EARTHQUAKE An earthquake with a focus (or centre) at a shallow level relative to the earth's surface.

SIAL The part of the earth's crust with a composition dominated by minerals rich in silicon and aluminium.

SIDEREAL DAY A period of complete rotation of the earth on its axis, about 23 hours 56 minutes.

SILL A tabular sheet of igneous rock injected along the bedding planes of sedimentary and volcanic formations.

SILT An unconsolidated material of small particles ranging in size from about 2 to 60 micrometres.

SIMA The part of the earth's crust with a composition dominated by minerals rich in silicon and magnesium.

SOIL CREEP The slow movement downslope of soil, usually resulting in thinning of soils on the upper reaches and accumulations on the lower.

SOLIFLUCTION The slow movement downslope of water saturated, seasonally thawed materials.

SOLSTICE The days of maximum declination of the sun measured relative to the equator. When

Above On May 18 1980, Mt St Helens demonstrated a plinian eruption (a kind first described by Pliny the Elder). The apparent smoke cloud is pulverised ash.

the midday sun is overhead at 23½°N it gives the longest day in the northern hemisphere and the shortest day in the southern. The reverse applies when the sun is overhead at 23½°S.

SPIT Usually linear deposits of beach material attached at one end to land and free at the other.

SPRING TIDE A tide of greater than average range occurring at or around the times of the new and full moon.

SQUALL A sudden, violent wind, often associated with rain or hail; frequently occurs under cumulonimbus clouds.

STALACTITE A deposit of calcium carbonate, rather like an icicle, hanging from the roof of a cave.

STALAGMITE A deposit of calcium carbonate growing up from the floor of a cave due to the constant drip of water from the roof.

STANDARD TIME The officially established time, with reference to Greenwich Mean Time, of a region or country.

STEPPE Mid-latitude grasslands with few trees, most typically found in USSR.

STORM SURGE Changes in sea level caused by extreme weather events, notably the winds in storms.

STRAIT A narrow passage joining two large bodies of water.

STRIAE Scratches of a rock surface due to the passage over it of another rock of equal or greater hardness.

SUBDUCTION ZONE An area where the rocks comprising the sea floor are forced beneath continental rocks at a plate margin to be reincorporated in the magma beneath the earth's crust.

SUBSEQUENT RIVER A stream which follows a course determined by the structure of the local bedrock.

SUBSIDENCE Usually applied to the sinking of air in the atmosphere or the downward movement of the earth's surface.

SUBSOIL The layer of weathered material that underlies the surface soil.

SUDD Floating vegetable matter that forms obstructive masses in the upper White Nile.

SUNSPOT Relatively dark regions on the disk of the sun with surface temperature of about 4500K compared to the more normal 6000K of the rest of the surface.

SURGE A sudden excess over the normal value, usually of a flow of material (soil, ice, water).

SWELL A long, perturbation (usually wavelike) of a water surface that continues beyond its cause (eg a strong wind).

T

TAIGA The most northerly coniferous forest of cold temperature regions found in Canada, Alaska and Eurasia.

TECTONIC Concerned with the broad structures of the earth's rocks and the processes of faulting, folding and warping that form them.

TETHYS OCEAN An ocean formed in the Palaeozoic Era which extended from what is now the Mediterranean Sea eastwards as far as South-east Asia.

THERMOCLINE A layer of water or a lake or sea that separates an upper, warmer, oxygen-rich zone from a lower, colder, oxygen-poor zone and in which temperature decreases by 1°C for every metre of increased depth.

THRUST FAULT A low-angle reverse fault.

THUNDERSTORM A cloud in which thunder and lightning occur, usually associated with heavy precipitation and strong winds.

TIDAL BORE A large solitary wave that moves up funnel-shaped rivers and estuaries with the rising tide, especially spring tides.

TIDAL CURRENT The periodic horizontal motions of the sea, generated by the gravitational attraction of the moon and sun, typically of $1ms^{-1}$ on continental shelves.

TIDE The regular movements of the seas due to the gravitational attraction of the moon and sun, most easily observed as changes in coastal sea levels.

TOPOGRAPHY The configuration of a land surface, including its relief and the position of its natural and man-made features.

TOR An exposure of bedrock usually as blocks and boulders, forming an abrupt, steep sided culmination of a more gentle rise to the summits of hills. Famous tors exist on Dartmoor.

TORNADO A violent, localized rotating storm with winds of $100ms^{-1}$ circulating round a funnel cloud some 100m in diameter. Frequent in mid-western USA.

TRADE WIND Winds with an easterly component which blow from the subtropic high pressure areas around 30° toward the equator.

TROPICAL CYCLONE *See hurricane*

TROPOSPHERE The portion of the earth's atmosphere between the earth's surface and a height about 15–20km. This layer contains virtually all the world's weather. Mean temperatures decrease and mean wind speeds increase with height in the troposphere.

TSUNAMI Sea-surface waves caused by submarine earthquakes and volcanic activity. Popularly called tidal waves.

TURBULENCE Chaotic and apparently random fluctuations in fluid flow, familiarly seen in the behaviour of smoke, either from a cigarette, a chimney or a volcano.

TUNDRA Extensive, level, treeless and marshy regions lying polewards of the taiga.

TYPHOON A term used in the Far East to describe tropical cyclones or hurricanes.

U

UMBRA A region of total shadow, especially in an eclipse.

UPWELLING The upward movement of deeper water towards the sea surface.

V

VARVE A sediment bed deposited in a body of water within the course of one year.

VOE An inlet or narrow bay of the Orkney or Shetland Islands.

VOLCANIC ASH Ash emitted from a volcano.

VOLCANO An opening through which magma, molten rock ash or volatiles erupts onto the earth's surface. Also used to describe the landform produced by the erupted material. *(see picture below left)*

W

WADI An ephemeral river channel in deserts.

WARM FRONT An atmospheric front whereby, as it passes over an individual on the ground, warm air replaces cold.

WATERFALL A vertical or very steep descent of water in a stream.

WATERSHED A boundary dividing and separating the areas drained by different rivers.

WATERSPOUT A funnel-shaped, rotating cloud that forms occasionally over water when the atmosphere is very unstable. Akin to tornadoes which occur over land.

WATER TABLE The level below which the ground is wholly and permanently saturated with water.

WAVE HEIGHT The vertical extent of a wave.

WAVE LENGTH The horizontal extent of a wave, most easily seen as the distance along the direction of wave movement between crests or troughs.

WAVE PERIOD The time taken for a complete cycle of the oscillation occurring within a wave.

WAVE VELOCITY The velocity of a wave form, best seen by concentrating on one part of the wave such as its crest or trough.

WEATHERING The alteration by physical, chemical and biological processes of rocks and sediments in the top metres of the earth's crust. So called because this material is exposed to the effects of atmospheric and atmospherically related conditions.

WEATHER ROUTEING Choosing a route for a ship or aeroplane to minimise the deleterious effects of weather.

WESTERLIES Winds with a westerly component occurring between latitudes of about 35° and 60°. The whole regime forms a 'vortex' around each of the poles and forms a major element in world climate.

WHIRLWIND A general term to describe rotating winds of scales up to that of a tornado, usually a result of intense convection over small areas.

WILLY-WILLY Australasian term for a tropical cyclone or hurricane.

WINDSHEAR The variation of speed or direction or both of wind over a distance.

Y

YARDANG A desert landform, usually but not always, of unconsolidated material, shaped by and lying roughly along the direction of the wind.

Z

ZENITH A point that is vertically above the observer: the opposite of nadir.

ZOOPLANKTON One of the three kinds of plankton, including mature representatives of many animal groups such as Protozoa and Crustacea.

ABBREVIATIONS	FULL FORM	ENGLISH FORM
A		
a.d.	an der	on the
Appno	Appennino	mountain range
Aqued.	Aqueduct	aqueduct
Arch.	Archipelago	
	Archipiélago	archipelago
A.S.S.R.	Autonomous Soviet	Autonomous
	Socialist Republic	Soviet
		Socialist Republic
B		
B.	1. Bahía, Baía,	bay
	Baie, Bay, Bucht,	
	Bukhta, Bugt	
	2. Ban	village
	3. Barrage,	dam
	4. Bir, Bîr, Bi'r	well
Bj	Bordj	fort
Bol.	Bol'sh, -oy	big
Br.	1. Branch	branch
	2. Bridge, Brücke	bridge
	3. Burun	cape
Brj	Baraj, -ï	dam
Bu.	Büyük	big
C		
C.	Cabo, Cap, Cape	cape
Can.	Canal	canal
Cat.	Cataract, Catarata	cataract
Cd	Ciudad	town
Ch.	Chott	salt lake
Chan.	Channel	channel
Ck	Creek	creek
Cnia	Colonia	colony
Cnl	Coronel	colonel
Co., Cord.	Cordillera	mountain chain
Cuch.	Cuchillas	hills, ridge
D		
D.	1. Dağ, Dagh, Dağı,	
	Dağları	mountain, range
	2. dake	mountain
	3. Daryācheh	lake
Dj.	Djebel	mountain
Dr.	Doctor	Doctor
E		
E.	East	east
Eil.	Eiland(en)	island(s)
Emb.	Embalse	reservoir
Escarp.	Escarpment	escarpment
Estr.	Estrecho	strait
F		
F.	Firth	estuary
Fj.	2. Fjord, Fjörður	fjord
Ft	Fort	fort
G		
G.	1. Gebel	mountain
	2. Ghedir	well
	3. Göl, Gölü	lake
	4. Golfe, Golfo, Gulf	Gulf
	5. Gora, -gory	mountain, range
	6. Guba	gulf, bay
	7. Gunung	mountain
Gd, Gde	Grand, Grande	grand
Gdor	Gobernador	governor
Geb.	Gebirge	mountain range
Gez.	Gezira	island
Ghub.	Ghubbat	bay
Gl.	Glacier	glacier
Gr.	Grosser	greater
Grl	General	general
Gt, Gtr	Great, Groot, -e,	
	Greater	greater
H		
H.	1. Hawr	lake
	2. Hoch	high
	3. Hora, Hory	mountain(s)
Har.	Harbour, Harbor	harbour
Hd	Head	head
Hg.	Hegy	mountain
Hgts	Heights	heights
Hwy	Highway	highway
I		
I.	Ile, Ilha, Insel,	island
	Isla, Island, Isle	
	Isola,	
	Isole	islands
In.	1. Inner	inner
	2. Inlet	inlet
Is	Iles, Ilhas, Islands,	islands
	Isles, Islas	
Isth.	Isthmus	isthmus
J		
J.	1. Jabal, Jebel,	mountain,
	Jibāl	mountains
	2. Järvi, Jaure, Jezero	lake
	3. Jazira	island
	4. Jökull	glacier
	5. Juan	John
Jct.	Junction	junction

ABBREVIATIONS	FULL FORM	ENGLISH FORM
K		
K.	1. Kaap, Kap, Kapp	cape
	2. kaikyō	channel, strait
	3. Kato	lower
	4. Karang	reef
	5. ko	lake
	6. Kūh(hā)	mountain(s)
	7. Kólpos	gulf
	8. Kopf	peak, hill
	9. Kuala	estuary
Kep.	Kepulauan	islands
Kg	Kampong	village
Kh.	Khawr	wadi, river
Khr.	Khrebet	mountain range
Kör.	Körfez, -i	gulf, bay
Kp.	Kompong	settlement on
		river
L		
L.	1. Lac, Lago, Lagoa,	lake
	Lake, Liman, Limni,	
	Loch, Lough	
	2. Lam	river
Lag.	Lagoon, Laguna,	lagoon
	Lagune, Lagoa	
Ld.	Land	land
Lit.	Little	little
M		
M.	1. Meer	sea, lake
	2. Mys	cape
m	metre, -s	metre(s)
Mal.	Malyy	small
Mf	Massif	mountain group
Mgna	Montagna	mountain
Mgne	Montagne(s)	mountain(s)
Mon.	Monasterio, Monastery	monastery
Mt	Mont, Mount	mountain
Mte	Monte	mountain
Mti	Monti, Munţii	mountains, range
Mtn	Mountain	mountain
Mts	Monts, Mountains,	mountains
	Montañas, Montes	
N		
N.	1. Nam	south
	2. Neu-, Ny-	new
	3. Noord, Nord,	north
	Norte, North, Norra,	
	Nørre	
	4. Nos	cape
Nat.	National	national
Nat. Pk	National Park	national park
Ndr	Nieder	lower
N.E.	North East	north east
Nizh.	Nizhne-, Nizhniy,	lower
	Nizhniye, Nizhnyaya	
Nizm.	Nizmennost'	lowland
N.M.	National Monument	national
		monument
N.O.	NoordOost, Nord-Ost	north east
Nov.	Novaya, Novyy	new
N.P.	National Park	national park
N.W.	North West	north west
O		
O.	1. Old	old
	2. Oost, Ost	east
	3. Ostrov	island
O	1. Öst(er)	east
	2. -øy	island
Or.	Oros(Ori)	mountain(s)
Orm.	Ormos	bay
Ova	Ostrova	islands
Oz.	Ozero, Ozera	lake(s)
P		
P.	1. Pass, Passo	pass
	2. Pic, Pico, Pizzo	peak
	3. Pulau	island
Pass.	Passage	passage
Peg.	Pegunungan	mountains
Pen.	Peninsula, Penisola	peninsula
Per.	Pereval	pass
Pk	1. Park	park
	2. Peak, Pik	peak
Pl.	Planina	mountain range
Pla.	Playa	beach
Plat.	Plateau, Planalto	plateau
Plosk.	Ploskogor'ye	plateau
Pov	Poluostrov	peninsula
Pr.	1. Prince	prince
	2. Proliv	strait
Pres.	Presidente	president
Promy	Promontory	promontory
Pt	1. Petit, -e	small
	2. Point	point
	3. Pont	bridge
Pta	1. Ponta, Punta	point
	2. Puerta	pass
Pte	1. Pointe	point
	2. Ponte, Puente	bridge
Pto	1. Ponto	point
	2. Porto, Puerto	port
Pzo	Pizzo	peak

ABBREVIATIONS	FULL FORM	ENGLISH FORM
Q		
Q.	1. Qal'at	fortress
	2. Qarat	mountain
R		
R.	1. Reka, Rio, Río,	river
	River, Rivière, Rūd,	
	Rzeka	
Ra.	Range	range
Rap.	Rapids	rapids
Rca	Rocca	rock, mountain
Rd	Road	road
Res.	Reserve, Reservation	reserve,
		reservation
Resr	Reservoir	reservoir
Rge	Ridge	ridge
Rly	Railway	railway
R.S.F.S.R.	Russian Soviet	Russian Soviet
	Federated Socialist	Federated Socialist
	Republic	Republic
Rte	Route	route
S		
S.	1. Salar, Salina	salt marsh
	2. San, São	saint
	3. See	sea, lake
	4. seto	strait
	5. sjø	lake
	6. Sør, South, Sud	south
	7. Sungai	river
s.	sur	on
Sa	Serra, Sierra	mountain range
Sab.	Sabkhat	salt flats
Sd	Sound, Sund	sound
S.E.	South East	south east
Seb.	Sebjet, Sebkhat,	salt marsh,
	Sebkra	lagoon
Sev.	Severo-, Severnaya, -nyy	north
Sh.	1. Sha'ib	watercourse
	2. Shaţţ	river-mouth
	3. shima	island
Sp.	Spitze	peak
S.S.R.	Soviet Socialist	Soviet Socialist
	Republic	Republic
St	Saint	saint
Sta	Santa	saint
Ste	Sainte	saint
Sten.	Stenon	pass, strait
Sto	Santo	saint
Str.	Strait	strait
S.W.	South West	south west
T		
T.	1. Tal	valley
	2. Tall, Tell	hill, mountain
	3. Tepe, Tepesi	peak, hill
Talsp.	Talsperre	dam
Tg	Tanjung	cape
Tk	Teluk	bay
Tr.	Trench, Trough	trench, trough
Tun.	Tunnel	tunnel
U		
U.	Uad	wadi
Ug	Ujung	cape
Unt.	Unter	lower
V		
V.	1. Val, Valle	valley
	2. Väster, Vest,	west
	Vester	
	3. Vatn	lake
	4. Ville	town
Va	Villa	town
Vdkhr.	Vodokhranilishche	reservoir
Verkh.	Verkhnyaya	upper
Vol.	Volcán, Volcano,	volcano
	Vulkan	
Vost.	Vostochnyy	eastern
Vozv.	Vozvyshennost'	upland
W		
W.	1. Wadi	wadi
	2. Wald	forest
	3. Wan	gulf, bay
	4. Water	water
	5. Well	well
	6. West	west
Y		
Yuzh.	Yuzhno-, Yuzhnyy	south
Z		
Z	1. Zahrez	intermittent lake
	2. Zaliv	gulf, bay
	3. Zatoka	
Zap.	Zapad-naya, Zapadno-,	western
	Zapadnyy	
Zem.	Zemlya	country, land

Introduction to the index

In the index, the first number refers to the page, and the following letter and
number to the section of the map in which the index entry can be found.
For example, Paris 14C2 means that Paris can be found on page 14 where
column C and row 2 meet.

Abbreviations used in the index

Afghan	Afghanistan	Hung	Hungary	Port	Portugal	Arch	Archipelago
Alb	Albania	Indon	Indonesia	Rom	Romania	B	Bay
Alg	Algeria	Irish Rep	Ireland	S Arabia	Saudi Arabia	C	Cape
Ant	Antarctica	N Ire	Ireland, Northern	Scot	Scotland	Chan	Channel
Arg	Argentina	Leb	Lebanon	Sen	Senegal	Gl	Glacier
Aust	Australia	Lib	Liberia	S Africa	South Africa	I(s)	Island(s)
Bang	Bangladesh	Liech	Liechtenstein	S Yemen	South Yemen	Lg	Lagoon
Belg	Belgium	Lux	Luxembourg	Switz	Switzerland	L	Lake
Bol	Bolivia	Madag	Madagascar	Tanz	Tanzania	Mt(s)	Mountain(s)
Bulg	Bulgaria	Malay	Malaysia	Thai	Thailand	O	Ocean
Cam	Cameroon	Maur	Mauritania	Turk	Turkey	P	Pass
Camb	Cambodia	Mor	Morocco	USSR	Union of Soviet Socialist	Pass	Passage
Can	Canada	Mozam	Mozambique		Republics	Pen	Peninsula
CAR	Central African Republic	Neth	Netherlands	UAE	United Arab Emirates	Plat	Plateau
Czech	Czechoslovakia	NZ	New Zealand	UK	United Kingdom	Pt	Point
Den	Denmark	Nic	Nicaragua	USA	United States of America	Res	Reservoir
Dom Rep	Dominican Republic	Nig	Nigeria	Urug	Uruguay	R	River
E Germ	East Germany	Nor	Norway	Ven	Venezuela	S	Sea
El Sal	El Salvador	Pak	Pakistan	Viet	Vietnam	Sd	Sound
Eng	England	PNG	Papua New Guinea	W Germ	West Germany	Str	Strait
Eq Guinea	Equatorial Guinea	Par	Paraguay	Yugos	Yugoslavia	V	Valley
Eth	Ethiopia	Phil	Philippines	Zim	Zimbabwe		
Fin	Finland	Pol	Poland				

A

Aachen *W Germ*	18B2
Aalsmeer *Neth*	13C1
Aalst *Belg*	13C2
Äänekoski *Fin*	12K6
Aba *China*	31A3
Aba *Nigeria*	48C4
Aba *Zaïre*	50D3
Ābādān *Iran*	41E3
Ābādeh *Iran*	41F3
Abadla *Alg*	48B1
Abaeté *Brazil*	75C2
Abaeté, R *Brazil*	75C2
Abaetetuba *Brazil*	73J4
Abagnar Qi *China*	31D1
Abajo Mts *USA*	59E3
Abakaliki *Nigeria*	48C4
Abakan *USSR*	25L4
Abala *Niger*	48C3
Abalessa *Alg*	48C2
Abancay *Peru*	72D6
Abarqū *Iran*	41F3
Abashiri *Japan*	29E2
Abashiri-wan, B *Japan*	29E2
Abau *PNG*	27H7
Abaya, L *Eth*	50D3
Abbai, R *Eth/Sudan*	50D2
Abbe, L *Eth/Djibouti*	50E2
Abbeville *France*	14C1
Abbeville, Louisiana *USA*	63D3
Abbeville, S Carolina *USA*	67B2
Abbotsford *Can*	58B1
Abbotsford *USA*	64A2
Abbottabad *Pak*	42C2
'Abd al 'Aziz, Jebel, Mt *Syria*	40D2
Abdulino *USSR*	20J5
Abéché *Chad*	50C2
Abengourou *Ivory Coast*	48B4
Åbenrå *Den*	18B1
Abeokuta *Nigeria*	48C4
Abera *Eth*	50D3
Aberaeron *Wales*	7B3
Aberdare *Wales*	7C4
Aberdeen, California *USA*	66C2
Aberdeen, Maryland *USA*	65D3
Aberdeen, Mississippi *USA*	63E2
Aberdeen *S Africa*	47C3

Aberdeen *Scot*	8D3
Aberdeen, S Dakota *USA*	56D2
Aberdeen, Washington *USA*	56A2
Aberdeen L *Can*	54J3
Aberdyfi *Wales*	7B3
Aberfeldy *Scot*	8D3
Aberfoyle *Scot*	8C3
Abergavenny *Wales*	7C4
Aberystwyth *Wales*	7B3
Abez' *USSR*	20L2
Abhā *S Arabia*	50E2
Abhar *Iran*	41E2
Abidjan *Ivory Coast*	48B4
Abilene, Kansas *USA*	61D3
Abilene, Texas *USA*	62C2
Abingdon *Eng*	7D4
Abingdon *USA*	64C3
Abitibi, R *Can*	55K4
Abitibi,L *Can*	55L5
Abkhazian ASSR, Republic *USSR*	21G7
Abohar *India*	42C2
Abomey *Benin*	48C4
Abong Mbang *Cam*	50B3
Abou Deïa *Chad*	50B2
Aboyne *Scot*	8D3
Abqaiq *S Arabia*	41E4
Abrantes *Port*	15A2
Abreojos, Punta, Pt *Mexico*	70A2
Abri *Sudan*	50D1
Abrolhos, Is *Aust*	32A3
Abrolhos, Arquipélago dos *Brazil*	75E2
Absaroka Range, Mts *USA*	56B2
Abū al Abyaḍ, I *UAE*	41F5
Abū 'Ali, I *S Arabia*	41E4
Abu 'Amūd, Wadi *Jordan*	45D3
Abu 'Aweigîla, Well *Egypt*	45C3
Abū Dhabi *UAE*	41F5
Abū el Jurdhān *Jordan*	45C3
Abu Hamed *Sudan*	50D2
Abu Kebir Hihya *Egypt*	45A3
Abunã *Brazil*	72E5
Abunã, R *Bol/Brazil*	72E6
Abu Rûtha, Gebel, Mt *Egypt*	45C4
Abū Sukhayr *Iraq*	41D3

Abu Suweir *Egypt*	45B3
Abu Tarfa, Wadi *Egypt*	45B4
Abut Head, C *NZ*	35B2
Abu Tîg *Egypt*	40B4
Abu'Urug, Well *Sudan*	50D2
Abuye Meda, Mt *Eth*	50D2
Abu Zabad *Sudan*	50C2
Abwong *Sudan*	50D3
Åby *Den*	18B1
Abyei *Sudan*	50C3
Acadia Nat Pk *USA*	65F2
Acámbaro *Mexico*	70B2
Acandí *Colombia*	69B5
Acaponeta *Mexico*	70B2
Acapulco *Mexico*	70B3
Acaraú *Brazil*	73L4
Acarigua *Ven*	72E2
Acatlán *Mexico*	70C3
Accra *Ghana*	48B4
Accrington *Eng*	6C3
Achalpur *India*	42D4
Achao *Chile*	74B6
Achern *W Germ*	13E3
Achill Hd, Pt *Irish Rep*	9A3
Achill I *Irish Rep*	10A3
Achim *W Germ*	13E1
Achinsk *USSR*	25L4
Acireale, *Sicily*	16D3
Ackley *USA*	61E2
Acklins, I *The Bahamas*	69C2
Acobamba *Peru*	72D6
Aconcagua, Mt *Chile*	74B4
Acopiara *Brazil*	73L5
Açores, Is = Azores	
Acre = 'Akko	
Acre, State *Brazil*	72D5
Acton *USA*	66C3
Ada *USA*	63C2
Adaja, R *Spain*	15B1
Adam *Oman*	41G5
Adama *Eth*	50D3
Adamantina *Brazil*	75B3
Adamaoua, Region *Cam/Nig*	50B3
Adamaoua, Massif de l', Mts *Cam*	50B3
Adams *USA*	68D1
Adams,Mt *USA*	56A2
Adam's Bridge *India/Sri Lanka*	44B4
Adam's Peak, Mt *Sri Lanka*	44C4
'Adan = Aden	

Adana *Turk*	21F8
Adapazari *Turk*	21E7
Adare,C *Ant*	76F7
Adavale *Aust*	34B1
Ad Dahna', Region *S Arabia*	41E4
Ad Damman *S Arabia*	41F4
Ad Dawadimi *S Arabia*	41D5
Ad Dibdibah, Region *S Arabia*	41E4
Ad Dilam *S Arabia*	41E5
Ad Dir'iyah *S Arabia*	41E5
Addis Ababa *Eth*	50D3
Ad Diwaniyah *Iraq*	41D3
Ad Duwayd *S Arabia*	40D3
Adel *USA*	61E2
Adelaide *Aust*	32C4
Adelaide *Bahamas*	67C4
Adelaide, Base *Ant*	76G3
Adelaide Pen *Can*	54J3
Adelaide River *Aust*	27G8
Adelanto *USA*	66D3
Aden *S Yemen*	38C4
Aden,G of *Somalia/S. Yemen*	38C4
Aderbissinat *Niger*	48C3
Adhrā' *Syria*	45D2
Adi, I *Indon*	27G7
Adige, R *Italy*	16C1
Adigrat *Eth*	50D2
Adilābād *India*	42D5
Adin *USA*	58B2
Adirondack Mts *USA*	65E2
Adi Ugri *Eth*	50D2
Adıyaman *Turk*	40C2
Adjud *Rom*	17F1
Admiralty I *USA*	54E4
Admiralty Inlet, B *Can*	55K2
Admiralty Is *PNG*	32D1
Adoni *India*	44B2
Adour, R *France*	14B3
Adrar *Alg*	48B2
Adrar, Mts *Alg*	48C2
Adrar, Region *Maur*	48A2
Adrar Soutouf, Region *Mor*	48A2
Adré *Chad*	50C2
Adri *Libya*	49D2
Adrian, Michigan *USA*	64C2
Adrian, Texas *USA*	62B1
Adriatic S *Italy/Yugos*	16C2
Aduwa *Eth*	50D2
Adycha, R *USSR*	25P3

Adzopé *Ivory Coast*	48B4
Adz'va, R *USSR*	20K2
Adz'vavom *USSR*	20K2
Aegean Sea *Greece*	17E3
Afghanistan, Republic *Asia*	38E2
Afgooye *Somalia*	50E3
'Afif *S Arabia*	41D5
Afikpo *Nigeria*	48C4
Åfjord *Nor*	12G6
Aflou *Alg*	48C1
Afmadu *Somalia*	50E3
Afollé, Region *Maur*	48A3
Afton, New York *USA*	68C1
Afton, Wyoming *USA*	58D2
Afula *Israel*	45C2
Afyon *Turk*	21E8
Aga *Egypt*	45A3
Agadem *Niger*	50B2
Agadez *Niger*	48C3
Agadir *Mor*	48B1
Agar *India*	42D4
Agartala *India*	43G4
Agassiz *Can*	58B1
Agboville *Ivory Coast*	48B4
Agdam *USSR*	40E1
Agematsu *Japan*	29C3
Agen *France*	14C3
Agha Jāri *Iran*	41E3
Agnibilékrou *Ivory Coast*	48B4
Agout, R *France*	14C3
Āgra *India*	42D3
Ağri *Turk*	41D2
Agri, R *Italy*	16D2
Agrigento, *Sicily*	16C3
Agrihan, I *Marianas*	26H5
Agrínion *Greece*	17E3
Agropoli *Italy*	16C2
Agryz *USSR*	20J4
Agto *Greenland*	55N3
Agua Clara *Brazil*	75B3
Aguadilla *Puerto Rico*	69D3
Agua Prieta *Mexico*	70B1
Aguaray Guazú *Par*	75A3
Aguascalientes *Mexico*	70B2
Aguas Formosas *Brazil*	75D2
Agueda *Port*	15A1
Aguelhok *Mali*	48C3
Agüenit, Well *Mor*	48A2
Águilas *Spain*	15B2
Aguja, Puerta *Peru*	72B5
Agulhas Basin *Indian O*	36C7
Agulhas,C *S Africa*	51C7

Amazonas **Arikaree**

Amazonas, R *Brazil* 73H4
Amazonas, State *Brazil* 72E4
Ambāla *India* 42D2
Ambalangoda *Sri Lanka* 44C4
Ambalavao *Madag* 51E6
Ambam *Cam* 50B3
Ambanja *Madag* 51E5
Ambarchik *USSR* 25S3
Ambato *Ecuador* 72C4
Ambato-Boeny *Madag* 51E5
Ambatolampy *Madag* 51E5
Ambatondrazaka *Madag* 51E5
Amberg *W Germ* 18C3
Ambergris Cay, I *Belize* 70D3
Ambikāpur *India* 43E4
Ambilobe *Madag* 51E5
Ambleside *Eng* 6C2
Amboasary *Madag* 51E6
Ambodifototra *Madag* 51E5
Ambohimahasoa *Madag* 51E6
Amboina = Ambon
Ambon *Indon* 27F7
Ambositra *Madag* 51E6
Ambovombe *Madag* 51E6
Amboy *USA* 68C2
Amboyna Cay, I *S China Sea* 27E6
Ambre, Montagne d' *Madag* 51E5
Ambriz *Angola* 51B4
Ambrym, I *Vanuatu* 33F2
Am Dam *Chad* 50C2
Amderma *USSR* 24H3
Ameca *Mexico* 70B2
Ameland, I *Neth* 18B2
Amenia *USA* 68D2
American Falls *USA* 58D2
American Falls Res *USA* 58D2
American Fork *USA* 59D2
American Highland, Upland *Ant* 76F10
American Samoa, Is *Pacific O* 37L5
Americus *USA* 67B2
Amersfoort *Neth* 18B2
Amersfoort *S Africa* 47D2
Amery *USA* 61E1
Amery Ice Shelf *Ant* 76G10
Ames *USA* 61E2
Amesbury *USA* 68E1
Amfilokhía *Greece* 17E3
Amfissa *Greece* 17E3
Amga *USSR* 25P3
Amgal, R *USSR* 25P3
Amgu *USSR* 26G2
Amgun', R *USSR* 26G1
Amhara, Region *Eth* 50D2
Amherst *Can* 55M5
Amherst, Massachusetts *USA* 68D1
Amherst, Virginia *USA* 65D3
Amhūr *India* 44B3
Amiata, Monte, Mt *Italy* 16C2
Amiens *France* 14C2
Amino *Japan* 29C3
Amioune *Leb* 45C1
Amirante Is *Indian O* 46K8
Amistad Res *Mexico* 62B3
Amlekhganj *Nepal* 43F3
Amlwch *Wales* 7B3
Amman *Jordan* 40C3
Ammanford *Wales* 7C4
Ämmänsaari *Fin* 12K6
Ammassalik *Greenland* 55P3
Amnyong-dan, C *N Korea* 28A3
Amol *Iran* 41F2
Amorgós, I *Greece* 17F3
Amos *Can* 55L5
Amoy = Xiamen
Ampanihy *Madag* 51E6
Amparo *Brazil* 75C3
Ampasimanolotra *Madag* 51E5
Amposta *Spain* 15C1
Amrāvati *India* 42D4
Amreli *India* 42C4
Amritsar *India* 42C2
Amroha *India* 43K1
Amsterdam *Neth* 18A2
Amsterdam *S Africa* 47E2
Amsterdam *USA* 65E2
Amsterdam, I *Indian O* 36E6
Am Timan *Chad* 50C2
Amudar'ya, R *USSR* 38E1
Amund Ringnes I *Can* 55J2
Amundsen G *Can* 54F2
Amundsen-Scott, Base *Ant* 76E
Amundsen Sea *Ant* 76F4
Amuntai *Indon* 27E7
Amur, R *USSR* 25O4
Amur, R *USSR* 26G1
Anabar, R *USSR* 25N2
Anacapa Is *USA* 66C4
Anaco *Ven* 72F2
Anaconda *USA* 56B2
Anacortes *USA* 58B1
Anadarko *USA* 62C1
Anadyr' *USSR* 25T3
Anadyr', R *USSR* 25T3
Anadyrskiy Zaliv, S *USSR* 25U3
Anadyrskoye Ploskogor'ye, Plat *USSR* 25T3
Anáfi, I *Greece* 17F3
Anagé *Brazil* 75D1
'Anah *Iraq* 40D3
Anaheim *USA* 59C4
Anaimalai Hills *India* 44B3
Anakāpalle *India* 44C2
Analalava *Madag* 51E5
Anambas, Kepulauan, Is *Indon* 27D6
Anamosa *USA* 64A2
Anamur *Turk* 21E8
Anan *Japan* 29B4
Anantapur *India* 44B3
Anantnag *India* 42D2
Anápolis *Brazil* 73J7
Anār *Iran* 41G3
Anārak *Iran* 41F3
Anatahan, I *Pacific O* 27H5
Añatuya *Arg* 74D3
Anbyŏn *N Korea* 28B3
Anchorage *USA* 54D3
Ancohuma, Mt *Bol* 72E7
Ancón *Peru* 72C6
Ancona *Italy* 16C2
Ancram *USA* 68D1
Ancud *Chile* 74B6
Ancud, Golfo de, G *Chile* 74B6
Ancy-le-Franc *France* 13C4
Anda *China* 26F2
Andahuaylas *Peru* 72D6
Åndalsnes *Nor* 12F6
Andalucia, Region *Spain* 15A2
Andalusia *USA* 67A2
Andaman Is *India* 39H4
Andaraí *Brazil* 75D1
Andelot *France* 13C3
Andenes *Nor* 12H5
Andernach *W Germ* 18B2
Anderson, Indiana *USA* 64B2
Anderson, Missouri *USA* 63D1
Anderson, S Carolina *USA* 67B2
Anderson, R *Can* 54F3
Andes, Cordillera de los, Mts *Peru* 72C5
Andhra Pradesh, State *India* 44B2
Andikíthira, I *Greece* 17E3
Andizhan *USSR* 24J5
Andkhui *Afghan* 24H6
Andong *S Korea* 28B3
Andorra, Principality *SW Europe* 15C1
Andorra-La-Vella *Andorra* 15C1
Andover *Eng* 7D4
Andover, New Hampshire *USA* 68E1
Andover, New York *USA* 68B1
Andradina *Brazil* 75B3
Andreapol' *USSR* 19G1
Andreas,C *Cyprus* 40B2
Andrews *USA* 62B2
Andria *Italy* 16D2
Andropov *USSR* 20F4
Ándros, I *Greece* 17E3
Andros, I *The Bahamas* 57F4
Andros Town *Bahamas* 67C4
Androth, I *India* 44A3
Andújar *Spain* 15B2
Andulo *Angola* 51B5
Anéfis *Mali* 48C3
Anécho *Togo* 48C4
Aneityum, I *Vanuatu* 33F3
Angarsk *USSR* 25M4
Ånge *Sweden* 20A3
Angel de la Guarda, I *Mexico* 70A2
Ängelholm *Sweden* 12G7
Angellala Creek, R *Aust* 34C1
Angels Camp *USA* 66B1
Angemuk, Mt *Indon* 27G7
Angers *France* 14B2
Angerville *France* 13B3
Angkor, Hist Site *Camb* 30C3
Anglesey, I *Wales* 10C3
Angleton *USA* 63C3
Angmagssalik = Ammassalik
Angoche *Mozam* 51E5
Angol *Chile* 74B5
Angola, Indiana *USA* 64C2
Angola, Republic *Africa* 46F9
Angola, Republic *Africa* 51B5
Angola Basin *Atlantic O* 52J5
Angoulême *France* 14C2
Angra do Heroismo *Azores* 48A1
Angra dos Reis *Brazil* 75D3
Anguilla, I *Caribbean S* 69E3
Anguilla Cays, Is *Caribbean S* 69B2
Angul *India* 43F4
Angumu *Zaïre* 50C4
Anholt, I *Den* 18C1
Anhua *China* 31C4
Anhui *China* 26F2
Anhui, Province *China* 31D3
Anhumas *Brazil* 75B2
Anhŭng *S Korea* 28A3
Aniak *USA* 54C3
Anicuns *Brazil* 75C2
Animas, R *USA* 62A1
Animas Peak, Mt *USA* 62A2
Anita *USA* 61E2
Aniva, Mys, C *USSR* 26H2
Anizy-le-Château *France* 13B3
Anjou, Region *France* 14B2
Anjouan, I *Comoros* 51E5
Anjozorobe *Madag* 51E5
Anjŭ *N Korea* 28B3
Ankang *China* 31B3
Ankara *Turk* 21E8
Ankaratra, Mt *Madag* 51E5
Ankazoabo *Madag* 51E6
Ankazobe *Madag* 51E5
Ankeny *USA* 61E2
Anklam *E Germ* 18C2
An Loc *Viet* 30D3
Anlong *China* 31B4
Anlu *China* 31C3
Anna *USA* 64B3
'Annaba *Algeria* 16B3
An Nabk *S Arabia* 40C3
An Nabk *Syria* 40C3
An Nafūd, Desert *S Arabia* 40D4
An Najaf *Iraq* 41D3
Annan *Scot* 8D4
Annapolis *USA* 65D3
Annapurna, Mt *Nepal* 43E3
Ann Arbor *USA* 64C2
An Nāsirah *Syria* 45D1
An Nāsiriyah *Iraq* 41E3
Annecy *France* 14D2
An Nhon *Viet* 30D3
Anning *China* 31A5
Anniston *USA* 67A2
Annobon, I *Eq Guinea* 48C4
Annonay *France* 14C2
Annotto Bay *Jamaica* 69J1
Anqing *China* 31D3
Ansai *China* 31B2
Ansbach *W Germ* 18C3
Anse d'Hainault *Haiti* 69C3
Anshan *China* 31E1
Anshun *China* 31B4
Ansley *USA* 60D2
Anson *USA* 62C2
Anson B *Aust* 27F8
Ansongo *Mali* 48C3
Ansonville *Can* 64C1
Ansted *USA* 64C3
Antakya *Turk* 21F8
Antalaha *Madag* 51F5
Antalya *Turk* 21E8
Antalya Körfezi, B *Turk* 21E8
Antananarivo *Madag* 51E5
Antarctic Circle *Ant* 76G1
Antarctic Pen *Ant* 76G3
Antequera *Spain* 15B2
Anthony *USA* 62A2
Anti-Atlas, Mts *Mor* 48B1
Anticosti I *Can* 55M5
Antigo *USA* 64B1
Antigua, I *Caribbean S* 69E3
Anti Lebanon = Sharqi, Jebel esh
Antioch *USA* 59B3
Antipodes Is *NZ* 33G5
Antlers *USA* 63C2
Antofagasta *Chile* 74B2
Antonina *Brazil* 75C4
Antonito *USA* 62A1
Antrim *N Ire* 9C2
Antrim *USA* 68E1
Antrim, County *N Ire* 9C2
Antrim Hills *N Ire* 9C2
Antsirabe *Madag* 51E5
Antsirañana *Madag* 51E5
Antsohiny *Madag* 51E5
Antu *China* 28B2
An Tuc *Viet* 30D3
Antwerp *Belg* 13C2
Antwerpen = Antwerp
An Uaimh *Irish Rep* 9C3
Anui *S Korea* 28A3
Anūpgarh *India* 42C3
Anuradhapura *Sri Lanka* 44C4
Anvers = Antwerp
Anvik *USA* 54B3
Anxi *China* 25L5
Anyang *China* 31C2
A'nyêmaqên Shan, Mts *China* 31A3
Anyuysk *USSR* 25S3
Anzhero-Sudzhensk *USSR* 24K4
Anzio *Italy* 16C2
Aoba, I *Vanuatu* 33F2
Aomori *Japan* 29E2
Aosta *Italy* 16B1
Aouker, Desert Region *Maur* 48B3
Aoulef *Alg* 48C2
Aozou *Chad* 50B1
Apa, R *Brazil/Par* 74E2
Apalachee B *USA* 57E4
Apalachicola *USA* 67B3
Apalachicola B *USA* 67A3
Apaporis, R *Colombia/Brazil* 72D3
Aparecida do Taboado *Brazil* 75B3
Aparri *Phil* 27F5
Apatin *Yugos* 17D1
Apatity *USSR* 20E2
Apatzingan *Mexico* 70B3
Apeldoorn *Neth* 18B2
Apia *Western Samoa* 33H2
Apiaí *Brazil* 75C3
Apoera *Surinam* 73G2
Apollo Bay *Aust* 34B3
Apopka,L *USA* 67B3
Aporé, R *Brazil* 73H7
Apostle Is *USA* 64A1
Appalachian Mts *USA* 57E3
Appennino Abruzzese, Mts *Italy* 16C2
Appennino Ligure, Mts *Italy* 16B2
Appennino Lucano, Mts *Italy* 16D2
Appennino Napoletano, Mts *Italy* 16D2
Appennino Tosco-Emilliano, Mts *Italy* 16C2
Appennino Umbro-Marchigiano, Mts *Italy* 16C2
Appleby *Eng* 6C2
Appleton, Minnesota *USA* 61D1
Appleton, Wisconsin *USA* 64B2
Apsheronskiy Poluostrov Pt *USSR* 21J7
Apucarana *Brazil* 74F2
Apure, R *Ven* 72E2
Apurimac, R *Peru* 72D6
'Aqaba *Jordan* 40C4
'Aqaba,G of *Egypt/S Arabia* 40B4
'Aqaba, Wadi el *Egypt* 45C4
'Aqdā *Iran* 41F3
Aqidauana *Brazil* 73G8
Aquidabán, R *Par* 75A3
Aquidauana *Brazil* 74E2
Aquidauana, R *Brazil* 75A2
Ara *India* 43E3
Arab *USA* 67A2
'Arab al Mulk *Syria* 45C1
'Araba, Wadi *Israel* 45C3
Arabian Basin *Indian O* 36E4
Arabian Sea *S.W. Asia* 38E4
'Arab, Jabal al, Mt *Syria* 45D2
Aracajú *Brazil* 73L6
Aracanguy,Mts de *Par* 75A3
Aracati *Brazil* 73L4
Aracatu *Brazil* 75D1
Araçatuba *Brazil* 73H8
Aracena *Spain* 15A2
Araçuaí *Brazil* 73K7
'Arad *Israel* 45C3
Arad *Rom* 21C6
Arada *Chad* 50C2
'Arādah *UAE* 41F5
Arafura S *Indon/Aust* 32C1
Aragarças *Brazil* 73H7
Aragats, Mt *USSR* 21G7
Aragon, R *Spain* 15B1
Aragón, Region *Spain* 15B1
Araguaçu *Brazil* 75C1
Araguaia, R *Brazil* 73H6
Araguaína *Brazil* 73J5
Araguari *Brazil* 73J7
Araguari, R *Brazil* 75C2
Arai *Japan* 29C3
Araif el Naqa, Gebel, Mt *Egypt* 45C3
Arak *Alg* 48C2
Arāk *Iran* 41E3
Arakan Yoma, Mts *Burma* 30A2
Arakkonam *India* 44B3
Araks, R *USSR/Iran* 41E2
Aral S *USSR* 24G5
Aral'sk *USSR* 24H5
Aranda de Duero *Spain* 15B1
Aran I *Irish Rep* 10B2
Aran Is *Irish Rep* 10B3
Aranjuez *Spain* 15B1
Aranos *Namibia* 47B1
Aransas Pass *USA* 63C3
Arao *Japan* 28B4
Araouane *Mali* 48B3
Arapahoe *USA* 60D2
Arapey, R *Urug* 74E4
Arapiraca *Brazil* 73L5
Araporgas *Brazil* 75B3
Ararangua *Brazil* 74G3
Araraquara *Brazil* 73J8
Araras *Brazil* 75C3
Ararat *Aust* 32D4
Ararat *USSR* 41D2
Ararat, Mt = Büyük Ağrı Dağı
Araruama, Lagoa de *Brazil* 75D3
Ar'ar, Wadi, Watercourse *S Arabia* 40D3
Aras, R *Turk* 41D1
Aras, R *USSR* 21H8
Arato *Japan* 29D3
Arauca, R *Ven* 72E2
Arauea *Colombia* 72D2
Arāvalli Range, Mts *India* 42C3
Arawa *PNG* 33E1
Araxá *Brazil* 73J7
Araxes, R *Iran* 21G8
Arba Minch *Eth* 50D3
Arbatax, Sardinia 16B3
Arbil *Iraq* 21G8
Arbrå *Sweden* 12H6
Arbroath *Scot* 8D3
Arcachon *France* 14B3
Arcade *USA* 68A1
Arcadia *USA* 67B3
Arcata *USA* 58B2
Arc Dome, Mt *USA* 66D1
Archangel *USSR* 20G3
Archbald *USA* 68C2
Arches Nat Pk *USA* 59E3
Arcis-sur-Aube *France* 13C3
Arco *USA* 58D2
Arcos *Brazil* 75C3
Arcos de la Frontera *Spain* 15A2
Arctic Bay *Can* 55K2
Arctic Circle 76C1
Arctic Red, R *Can* 54E3
Arctic Red River *Can* 54E3
Arctic Village *USA* 54D3
Arctowski, Base *Ant* 76G2
Arda, R *Bulg* 17F2
Ardabīl *Iran* 21H8
Ardahan *Turk* 21G7
Årdal *Nor* 12F6
Ardar des Iforas, Upland *Alg/Mali* 48C2
Ardee *Irish Rep* 9C3
Ardekān *Iran* 41F3
Ardennes, Department *France* 13C3
Ardennes, Region *Belg* 18B2
Ardestāh *Iran* 41F3
Ardh es Suwwan, Desert Region *Jordan* 40C3
Ardila, R *Port* 15A2
Ardlethan *Aust* 34C2
Ardmore *USA* 56D3
Ardnamurchan Pt *Scot* 8B3
Ardres *France* 13A2
Ardrishaig *Scot* 8C3
Ardrossan *Scot* 8C4
Arecibo *Puerto Rico* 69D3
Areia Branca *Brazil* 73L4
Arena,Pt *USA* 59B3
Arenberg, Region *W Germ* 13D1
Arendal *Nor* 12F7
Arequipa *Peru* 72D7
Arezzo *Italy* 16C2
Argenta *Italy* 16C2
Argentan *France* 14C2
Argenteuil *France* 13B3
Argentina, Republic *S America* 71D7
Argentine Basin *Atlantic O* 52F7
Argentino, Lago *Arg* 74B8
Argenton-sur-Creuse *France* 14C2
Argeş, R *Rom* 17F2
Arghardab, R *Afghan* 42B2
Argolikós Kólpos, G *Greece* 17E3
Argonne, Region *France* 13C3
Árgos *Greece* 17E3
Argostólion *Greece* 17E3
Arguello,Pt *USA* 66B3
Argus Range, Mts *USA* 66D3
Argyle,L *Aust* 32B2
Argyll *Scot* 8C3
Århus *Den* 18C1
Ariamsvlei *Namibia* 51C6
Aribinda *Burkina* 48B3
Arica *Chile* 74B1
Arifwala *Pak* 42C2
Arihā = Jericho
Arikaree, R *USA* 60C3

Arima Badr Ḥunayn

Arima *Trinidad* 69L1
Arinos *Brazil* 75C2
Arinos, R *Brazil* 73G6
Aripo,Mt *Trinidad* 69L1
Aripuanã *Brazil* 72F5
Aripuanã, R *Brazil* 72F5
Arisaig *Scot* 8C3
'Arîsh, Wadi el *Egypt* 45B3
Arizona, State *USA* 56B3
Årjäng *Sweden* 12G7
Arka *USSR* 25Q4
Arkadak *USSR* 21G5
Arkadelphia *USA* 63D2
Arkaig, L *Scot* 8C3
Arkalyk *USSR* 24H4
Arkansas, R *USA* 57D3
Arkansas, State *USA* 57D3
Arkansas City *USA* 63C1
Arkhipovka *USSR* 29C2
Arkipelag Nordenshelda, Arch *USSR* 25K2
Arklow *Irish Rep* 10B3
Arlanzón, R *Spain* 15B1
Arles *France* 14C3
Arlington, S Dakota *USA* 61D2
Arlington, Texas *USA* 63C2
Arlington, Virginia *USA* 65D3
Arlington, Washington *USA* 58B1
Arlington Heights *USA* 64B2
Arlon *Belg* 18B3
Armageddon = Megiddo
Armagh *N Ire* 9C2
Armagh, County *N Ire* 9C2
Armançon, R *France* 13B4
Armavir *USSR* 21G7
Armenia = Armyanskaya S.S.R.
Armenia *Colombia* 72C3
Armenian SSR, Republic *USSR* 24F5
Armentières *Belgium* 13B2
Armidale *Aust* 32E4
Arnaud, R *Can* 55L3
Arnauti, C *Cyprus* 40B2
Arnett *USA* 62C1
Arnhem *Neth* 18B2
Arnhem,C *Aust* 32C2
Arnhem Land *Aust* 32C2
Arnold *USA* 66B1
Arnprior *Can* 65D1
Arnsberg *W Germ* 13E2
Aroab *Namibia* 47B2
Arolsen *W Germ* 13E2
Arorae, I *Kiribati* 33G1
Arosa *Switz* 16B1
Arpajon *France* 13B3
Arraias *Brazil* 75C1
Arraias, Serra de, Mts *Brazil* 75C1
Ar Ramādī *Iraq* 41D3
Arran, I of *Scot* 8C4
Ar Raqqah *Syria* 40C2
Arras *France* 14C1
Ar Rass *S Arabia* 41D4
Ar Rastan *Syria* 45D1
Arrecife *Canary Is* 48A2
Ar Rifā'i *Iraq* 41E3
Ar Rihāb, Desert Region *Iraq* 41E3
Ar Riyāḍ = Riyadh
Arrochar *Scot* 8C3
Arrojado, R *Brazil* 75C1
Arrowrock Res *USA* 58C2
Arrowtown *NZ* 35A2
Arroyo Grande *USA* 66B3
Ar Ru'ays *Qatar* 41F4
Ar Rustāq *Oman* 41G5
Ar Rutbah *Iraq* 40D3
Ar Ruwayḍah *S Arabia* 41D5
Arsikere *India* 44B3
Arsk *USSR* 20H4
Árta *Greece* 17E3
Artem *USSR* 28C2
Artemovsk *USSR* 25L4
Artemovskiy *USSR* 25N4
Artesia *USA* 56C3
Arthurs P *NZ* 35B2
Artigas *Urug* 74E4
Artillery L *Can* 54H3
Artois, Region *France* 14C1
Artsiz *USSR* 19F3
Arturo Prat, Base *Ant* 76G2
Artvin *Turk* 21G7
Aru *Zaïre* 50D3
Aruanã *Brazil* 73H6
Aruba, I *Caribbean S* 69C4
Aru, Kepulauan, Arch *Indon* 27G7
Arun, R *Nepal* 43F3
Arunāchal Pradesh, Union Territory *India* 43G3
Aruppukkottai *India* 44B4
Arusha *Tanz* 50D4
Aruwimi, R *Zaïre* 50C3
Arvada *USA* 60B3
Arvayheer *Mongolia* 26D2
Arvida *Can* 55L5
Arvidsjaur *Sweden* 12H5
Arvika *Sweden* 12G7
Arvin *USA* 59C3
Arwad, I *Syria* 45C1
Arzamas *USSR* 20G4
Arzew *Alg* 15B2
Asadabad *Afghan* 42C2
Asahi, R *Japan* 29B4
Asahi dake, Mt *Japan* 29E2
Asahikawa *Japan* 29E2
Asan-man, B *S Korea* 28A3
Asansol *India* 43F4
Asawanwah, Well *Libya* 49D2
Asbest *USSR* 20L4
Asbestos Mts *S Africa* 47C2
Asbury Park *USA* 65E2
Ascension, I *Atlantic O* 52H5
Ascensión, B de la *Mexico* 70D3
Aschaffenburg *W Germ* 18B3
Aschersleben *E Germ* 18C2
Ascoli Piceno *Italy* 16C2
Āseb *Eth* 50E2
Asedjrad, Upland *Alg* 48C2
Asela *Eth* 50D3
Åsele *Sweden* 12H6
Asenovgrad *Bulg* 17E2
Asfeld *France* 13C3
Asha *USSR* 20K4
Ashbourne *Eng* 7D3
Ashburn *USA* 67B2
Ashburton *NZ* 33G5
Ashburton, R *Aust* 32A3
Ashdod *Israel* 40B3
Ashdown *USA* 63D2
Asheboro *USA* 67A1
Asheville *USA* 57E3
Ashford *Aust* 34D1
Ashford *Eng* 7E4
Ash Fork *USA* 59D3
Ashibetsu *Japan* 29D2
Ashikaga *Japan* 29D3
Ashizuri-misaki, Pt *Japan* 28B4
Ashkhabad *USSR* 24G6
Ashland, Kansas *USA* 62C1
Ashland, Kentucky *USA* 57E3
Ashland, Montana *USA* 60B1
Ashland, Nebraska *USA* 61D2
Ashland, Ohio *USA* 64C2
Ashland, Oregon *USA* 56A2
Ashland, Virginia *USA* 65D3
Ashland, Wisconsin *USA* 61E1
Ashley *Aust* 34C1
Ashley *USA* 60D1
Ashokan Res *USA* 68C2
Ashqelon *Israel* 45C3
Ash Shabakh *Iraq* 41D3
Ash Sha'm *UAE* 41G4
Ash Sharqāţ *Iraq* 41D2
Ash Shaţrah *Iraq* 41E3
Ash Shiḥr *S Yemen* 38C4
Ash Shumlūl *S Arabia* 41E4
Ashtabula *USA* 64C2
Ashuanipi L *Can* 55M4
Asi, R *Syria* 21F8
Asilah *Mor* 15A2
Asinara, I, Sardinia 16B2
Asino *USSR* 24K4
Asīr, Region *S Arabia* 50E1
Aska *India* 43E5
Aşkale *Turk* 40D2
Askersund *Sweden* 12G7
Asl *Egypt* 45B4
Asmar *Afghan* 42C1
Asmara *Eth* 50D2
Aso *Japan* 28B4
Asosa *Eth* 50D2
Asoteriba, Jebel, Mt *Sudan* 50D1
Aspermont *USA* 62B2
Aspiring,Mt *NZ* 35A2
As Sabkhah *Syria* 40C2
As Salamiyah *S Arabia* 41E5
As Salamiyah *Syria* 40C2
As Salmān *Iraq* 41D3
Assam, State *India* 43G3
As Samāwah *Iraq* 41E3
Aş Şanām, Region *S Arabia* 41F5
Aş Şanamayn *Syria* 45D2
Assen *Neth* 18B2
Assens *Den* 18C1
As Sidrah *Libya* 49D1
Assiniboia *Can* 54H5
Assiniboine,Mt *Can* 54G4
Assis *Brazil* 73H8
Assis Ch *Brazil* 73H8
As Sukhnah *Syria* 40C3
Aş Şumman, Region *S Arabia* 41E5
Assumption, I *Seychelles* 51E4
As Suwaydā' *Syria* 40C3
Aş Şuwayrah *Iraq* 41D3
Astara *USSR* 41E2
Asti *Italy* 16B2
Astipálaia, I *Greece* 17F3
Astorga *Spain* 15A1
Astoria *USA* 56A2
Astrakhan' *USSR* 21H6
Asturias, Region *Spain* 15A1
Asuka, Base *Ant* 76F12
Asunción *Par* 74E3
Asuncion, I *Marianas* 26H5
Aswa, R *Uganda* 50D3
Aswân *Egypt* 40B5
Aswân High Dam *Egypt* 49F2
Asyût *Egypt* 49F2
Atacama, Desierto de, Desert *Chile* 74C2
Atafu, I *Tokelau Is* 33H1
Atā'ita, Jebel el, Mt *Jordan* 45C3
Atakpamé *Togo* 48C4
Atambua *Indon* 27F7
Atangmik *Greenland* 55N3
Ataqa, Gebel, Mt *Egypt* 45B4
Atar *Maur* 48A2
Atascadero *USA* 66B3
Atasu *USSR* 24J5
Atbara *Sudan* 50D2
Atbasar *USSR* 24H4
Atchafalaya B *USA* 57D4
Atchison *USA* 57D3
Atco *USA* 68C3
Atessa *Italy* 16C2
Ath *Belg* 13B2
Athabasca *Can* 54G4
Athabasca, R *Can* 54G4
Athabasca L *Can* 54H4
Athens, Alabama *USA* 67A2
Athens, Georgia *USA* 57E3
Athens *Greece* 17E3
Athens, Ohio *USA* 64C3
Athens, Pennsylvania *USA* 68B2
Athens, Tennessee *USA* 67B1
Athens, Texas *USA* 63C2
Athína = Athens
Athlone *Irish Rep* 10B3
Athna *Cyprus* 45B1
Athol *USA* 68D1
Áthos, Mt *Greece* 17E2
Athy *Irish Rep* 9C3
Ati *Chad* 50B2
Atikoken *Can* 55J5
Atka *USSR* 25R3
Atkarsk *USSR* 21G5
Atkins *USA* 63D1
Atlanta, Georgia *USA* 57E3
Atlanta, Michigan *USA* 64C2
Atlantic *USA* 61D2
Atlantic City *USA* 57F3
Atlantic Highlands *USA* 68C2
Atlantic-Indian Antarctic Basin *Atlantic O* 52H8
Atlantic Indian Ridge *Atlantic O* 52H7
Atlas Mts = Haut Atlas, Moyen Atlas
Atlas Saharien, Mts *Alg* 48C1
Atlin *Can* 54E4
Atlin L *Can* 54E4
'Atlit *Israel* 45C2
Atmore *USA* 57E3
Atofinandrahana *Madag* 51E6
Atoka *USA* 63C2
Atrato, R *Colombia* 72C2
Attaf, Region *UAE* 41F5
Aţ Ţā'if *S Arabia* 50E1
At Tall *Syria* 45D2
Attalla *USA* 67A2
Attawapiskat *Can* 55K4
Attawapiskat, R *Can* 55K4
At Taysiyah, Desert Region *S Arabia* 41D3
Attica, Indiana *USA* 64B2
Attica, New York *USA* 68A1
Attigny *France* 13C3
Attila Line *Cyprus* 45B1
Attleboro, Massachusetts *USA* 65E2
Attopeu *Laos* 30D3
At Tubayq, Upland *S Arabia* 40C4
Atvidaberg *Sweden* 12H7
Atwater *USA* 66B2
Aubagne *France* 14D3
Aube, Department *France* 13C3
Aube, R *France* 13C3
Aubenas *France* 14C3
Auburn, Alabama *USA* 67A2
Auburn, California *USA* 59B3
Auburn, Indiana *USA* 64B2
Auburn, Maine *USA* 65E2
Auburn, Nebraska *USA* 61D2
Auburn, New York *USA* 65D2
Auburn, Washington *USA* 58B1
Auch *France* 14C3
Auckland *NZ* 33G4
Auckland Is *NZ* 37K7
Aude, R *France* 14C3
Auden *Can* 55K4
Audubon *USA* 61E2
Augathella *Aust* 34C1
Aughnacloy *N Ire* 9C2
Aughrabies Falls *S Africa* 47B2
Augsburg *W Germ* 18C3
Augusta *Aust* 32A4
Augusta, Georgia *USA* 57E3
Augusta, Kansas *USA* 63C1
Augusta, Maine *USA* 57G2
Augusta, Montana *USA* 58D1
Augusta, Wisconsin *USA* 64A2
Augustow *Pol* 19E2
Augustus,Mt *Aust* 32A3
Auob, R *Namibia* 47B1
Auraiya *India* 42D3
Aurangābād *India* 42D5
Aurès, Mts *Alg* 48C1
Aurès, Mt de l' *Algeria* 16B3
Aurich *W Germ* 13D1
Aurillac *France* 14C3
Aurora, Colorado *USA* 56C3
Aurora, Illinois *USA* 64B2
Aurora, Indiana *USA* 64C3
Aurora, Mississippi *USA* 63D1
Aurora, Nebraska *USA* 61D2
Aus *Namibia* 47B2
Au Sable *USA* 64C2
Ausert, Well *Mor* 48A2
Auskerry, I *Scot* 8D2
Austin, Minnesota *USA* 57D2
Austin, Nevada *USA* 59C3
Austin, Pennsylvania *USA* 68A2
Austin, Texas *USA* 56D3
Australian Alps, Mts *Aust* 32D4
Austria, Federal Republic *Europe* 28G4
Austria, Republic *Europe* 18C3
Autlán *Mexico* 70B3
Autun *France* 14C2
Auvergne, Region *France* 14C2
Auxerre *France* 14C2
Auxi-le-Château *France* 13A2
Avallon *France* 14C2
Avalon *USA* 66C4
Avalon Pen *Can* 55N5
Avaré *Brazil* 75C3
Ave, R *W Germ* 13E1
Avedat, Hist Site *Israel* 45C3
Aveíro *Brazil* 73G4
Aveiro *Port* 15A1
Avellaneda *Arg* 74E4
Avellino *Italy* 16C2
Avenal *USA* 66B3
Avesnes-sur-Helpe *France* 13B2
Avesta *Sweden* 12H6
Avezzano *Italy* 16C2
Aviemore *Scot* 8D3
Aviemore,L *NZ* 35B2
Avignon *France* 14C3
Avila *Spain* 15B1
Avilés *Spain* 15A1
Avoca, Iowa *USA* 61D2
Avoca, New York *USA* 68B1
Avoca, R *Aust* 34B3
Avon *USA* 68B1
Avon, County *Eng* 7C4
Avon, R, Dorset *Eng* 7D4
Avon, R, Warwick *Eng* 7D3
Avondale *USA* 59D4
Avonmouth *England* 7C4
Avon Park *USA* 67B3
Avre, R *France* 13B3
Avtovac *Yugos* 17D2
A'waj, R *Syria* 45D2
Awaji-shima, I *Japan* 29D4
Awarē *Eth* 50E3
Awarua Pt *NZ* 35A2
Awash *Eth* 50E3
Awash, R *Eth* 50E3
Awa-shima, I *Japan* 29C3
Awatere, R *NZ* 35B2
Awbārī *Libya* 49D2
Aweil *Sudan* 50C3
Awe, Loch, L *Scot* 8C3
Awjilah *Libya* 49E2
Axel *Can* 55J1
Axminster *Eng* 7C4
Ayabe *Japan* 29C3
Ayacucho *Arg* 74E5
Ayacucho *Colombia* 69C5
Ayacucho *Peru* 72D6
Ayaguz *USSR* 24K5
Ayakkum Hu, L *China* 39G2
Ayamonte *Spain* 15A2
Ayan *USSR* 25P4
Ayaviri *Peru* 72D6
Aydin *Turk* 21D8
Áyios Evstrátios, I *Greece* 17F3
Aykhal *USSR* 25N3
Aylesbury *Eng* 7D4
'Ayn al Fijah *Syria* 45D2
Ayn Zālah *Iraq* 40D2
Ayn Zuwayyah, Well *Libya* 49E2
Ayod *Sudan* 50D3
Ayr *Aust* 32D2
Ayr *Scot* 8C4
Ayr, R *Scot* 8C4
Ayre,Pt of, I of Man *British Is* 6B2
Aytos *Bulg* 17F2
Ayutthaya *Thai* 30C3
Ayvacık *Turk* 17F3
Ayvalık *Turk* 17F3
Azamgarh *India* 43E3
Azaouad, Desert Region *Mali* 48B3
Azaouak, Vallée de l' *Niger* 48C3
Azare *Nigeria* 48D3
A'zāz *Syria* 40C2
Azbine = Aïr
Azeffal, Watercourse *Maur* 48A2
Azerbaijan, Republic *USSR* 24F5
Azogues *Ecuador* 72C4
Azopol'ye *USSR* 20H2
Azores, Is *Atlantic O* 46B4
Azoum, R *Chad* 50C2
Azov, S of *USSR* 21F6
Azrou *Mor* 48B1
Aztec *USA* 62A1
Azuero,Pen de *Panama* 72B2
Azul *Arg* 74E5
Azul, Serra, Mts *Brazil* 75B1
Azzaba *Algeria* 16B3
Az-Zabdānī *Syria* 45D2
Aẓ Ẓāhirah, Mts *Oman* 41G5
Az Zilaf *Syria* 40C3
Az Zilfī *S Arabia* 41D4
Az Zubayr *Iraq* 41E3

B

Ba'abda *Leb* 45C2
Ba'albek *Leb* 40C3
Ba'al Hazor, Mt *Israel* 45C3
Baardheere *Somalia* 50E3
Babadag *Rom* 17F2
Babaeski *Turk* 40A1
Babahoyo *Ecuador* 72C4
Bāb al Mandab, Str *Djibouti/S Yemen/ Yemen* 50E2
Babar, Kepulauan, I *Indon* 32B1
Babati *Tanz* 50D4
Babayevo *USSR* 20F4
Babbitt *USA* 61E1
Baberton *USA* 64C2
Babine L *Can* 54F4
Babo *Indon* 32C1
Bābol *Iran* 41F2
Babuyan Is *Phil* 27F5
Bacabal *Brazil* 73J4
Bacan, I *Indon* 27F7
Bacău *Rom* 21D6
Bac Can *Viet* 30D1
Baccarat *France* 13D3
Bacchus Marsh *Aust* 34B3
Bachu *China* 39F2
Back, R *Can* 54J3
Bac Ninh *Viet* 30D1
Bacolod *Phil* 27F5
Bacup *Eng* 6C3
Badagara *India* 44B3
Badain Jaran Shamo, Desert *China* 31A1
Badajoz *Spain* 15A2
Badalona *Spain* 15C1
Badanah *S Arabia* 40D3
Badaohe *China* 28B2
Bad Bergzabern *W Germ* 13E3
Bad Ems *W Germ* 13D2
Baden-Baden *W Germ* 18B3
Badenviller *France* 13D3
Baden-Württemberg, State *W Germ* 18B3
Badgastein *Austria* 18C3
Badger *USA* 66C2
Bad-Godesberg *W Germ* 18B2
Bad Hersfeld *W Germ* 18B2
Bad Honnef *W Germ* 13D2
Badin *Pak* 42B4
Bad Ischl *Austria* 16C1
Badiyat ash Sham, Desert Region *Iraq/ Jordan* 40C3
Bad-Kreuznach *W Germ* 18B3
Badlands, Region *USA* 60C1
Bad Lippspringe *W Germ* 13E2
Bad Nauheim *W Germ* 13E2
Bad Nevenahr-Ahrweiler *W Germ* 13D2
Badr Ḥunayn *S Arabia* 40C5

Bad Ryrmont
Bataan Pen

Bad Ryrmont W Germ 13E2
Bad Tolz W Germ 18C3
Badulla Sri Lanka 44C4
Bad Wildungen W Germ 13E2
Bad Wimpfen W Germ 13E3
Baena Spain 15B2
Bafatá Guinea-Bissau 48A3
Baffin B Can/Greenland 55L2
Baffin B USA 63C3
Baffin I Can 55L2
Bafia Cam 50B3
Bafing, R Mali 48A3
Bafoulabé Mali 48A3
Bafoussam Cam 50B3
Bāfq Iran 41G3
Bafra Burun, Pt Turk 21F7
Bāft Iran 41G4
Bafwasende Zaïre 50C3
Bagaha India 43E3
Bāgalkot India 44B2
Bagamoyo Tanz 51D4
Bagdad USA 59D4
Bagé Brazil 74F4
Baggs USA 60B2
Baghdād Iraq 41D3
Bagherhat Bang 43F4
Bāghin Iran 41G3
Baghlan Afghan 42B1
Bagley USA 61D1
Bagnoa Ivory Coast 48B4
Bagnols-sur-Cèze France 14C3
Bagoé, R Mali 48B3
Bag Tai China 28A2
Baguio Phil 27F5
Bāhādurābād Bang 43F3
Bahamas,The, Is Caribbean S 57F4
Baharampur India 43F4
Bahar Dar Eth 50D2
Baharîya Oasis Egypt 40A4
Bahawalnagar Pak 42C3
Bahawalpur Pak 42C3
Bahawalpur, Division Pak 42C3
Bahia = Salvador
Bahia, State Brazil 73K6
Bahía Blanca Arg 74D5
Bahía, Islas de la Honduras 70D3
Bahia Kino Mexico 56B4
Bahias, Cabo dos Arg 74C6
Bahra el Manzala, L Egypt 45A3
Bahraich India 43E3
Bahrain, Sheikhdom Arabian Pen 38D3
Bahr al Milh, L Iraq 41D3
Bahr Aouk, R Chad/CAR 50C3
Bahrat Lut = Dead S
Bahr el Abiad, R Sudan 50D2
Bahr el Arab, Watercourse Sudan 50C3
Bahr el Azraq, R Sudan 50D2
Bahr el Ghazal, R Sudan 50D3
Bahr el Ghazal, Watercourse Chad 50B2
Bahr Fâqûs, R Egypt 45A3
Baia de Setúbal, B Port 15A2
Baia dos Tigres Angola 51B5
Baia Mare Rom 21C6
Baïbokoum Chad 50B3
Baicheng China 26F2
Baie-Comeau Can 55M5
Baie de St Georges, B Leb 45C2
Baie-du-Poste Can 55L4
Baie St Paul Can 65E1
Baie-Verte Can 55N5
Baihe China 31B3
Bai He, R China 31C3
Ba'ījī Iraq 41D3
Baikal, L USSR 25M4
Baikunthpur India 43E4
Baile Atha Cliath = Dublin
Băileşti Rom 17E2
Bailleul France 13B2
Baima China 31A3
Bainbridge USA 67B2
Baird Mts USA 54B3
Bairin Youqi China 31D1
Bairin Zuoqi China 31D1
Bairnsdale Aust 32D4
Baitadi Nepal 43E3
Baixingt China 28A2
Baja Hung 17D1
Baja California, Pen Mexico 70A1
Baja California, State Mexico 56B3
Baja California Norte, State Mexico 59C4
Baja, Punta, Pt Mexico 70A2
Bakal USSR 20K5
Bakala CAR 50C3
Bakel Sen 48A3
Baker, California USA 59C3
Baker, Montana USA 56C2
Baker, Oregon USA 56B2
Baker USA 54G5
Baker Foreland, Pt Can 55J3
Baker L Can 54J3
Baker Lake Can 54J3
Baker,Mt USA 56A2
Bakersfield USA 56B3
Bakewell Eng 7D3
Bakharden USSR 41G2
Bakhardok USSR 41G2
Bakhmach USSR 21E5
Bakkaflói, B Iceland 12C1
Bako Eth 50D3
Bakouma CAR 50C3
Baku USSR 21H7
Balâ Turk 40B2
Bala Wales 7C3
Balabac, I Phil 27E6
Balabac Str Malaysia/Phil 27E6
Bālaghāt India 43E4
Balaklava Aust 34A2
Balakovo USSR 21H5
Balāngir India 43E4
Balashov USSR 21G5
Balasore India 43F4
Balaton, L Hung 17D1
Balbriggan Irish Rep 9C3
Balcarce Arg 74E5
Balchik Bulg 17F2
Balclutha NZ 33F5
Bald Knob USA 63D1
Baldock Eng 7D4
Baldwin USA 67B2
Baldy Mt USA 58E1
Baldy Peak, Mt USA 56C3
Balearic Is Spain 15C2
Baleia, Ponta da, Pt Brazil 75E2
Baleine, Rivière de la, R Can 55M4
Baler Phil 27F5
Balezino USSR 20J4
Bali, I Indon 32A1
Balıkesir Turk 40A2
Balikh, R Syria/Turk 40C2
Balikpapan Indon 27E7
Baliza Brazil 75B2
Balkh Afghan 42B1
Balkhash USSR 24J5
Balkhash, L USSR 24J5
Ballachulish Scot 8C3
Ballantrae Scot 8C4
Ballantyne Str Can 54G2
Ballāpur India 44B3
Ballarat Aust 32D4
Ballater Scot 8D3
Ballaugh Eng 6B2
Balleny Is Ant 76G7
Ballia India 43E3
Ballina Aust 34D1
Ballina Irish Rep 10B3
Ballinger USA 62C2
Ballinskelligis B Irish Rep 9A4
Ballon d'Alsace, Mt France 13D4
Ballston Spa USA 68D1
Ballycastle N Ire 9C2
Ballyclare N Ire 9D2
Ballycotton B Irish Rep 9C4
Ballyhaunis N Ire 9B3
Ballymena N Ire 9C2
Ballymoney N Ire 9C2
Ballynahinch N Ire 9C2
Ballyshannon Irish Rep 9B2
Ballyteige B Irish Rep 9C3
Balmoral Aust 34B3
Balmorhea USA 62B2
Balombo Angola 51B5
Balonn, R Aust 34C1
Bālotra India 42C3
Balrāmpur India 43E3
Balranald Aust 32D4
Balsas Brazil 73J5
Balsas, R Mexico 70B3
Balta USSR 21D6
Baltic S N Europe 12H7
Baltîm Egypt 40B3
Baltimore USA 57F3
Baluchistan, Region Pak 42B3
Bālurghāt India 43F3
Balykshi USSR 21J6
Bam Iran 41G4
Bama Nig 50B2
Bamako Mali 48B3
Bambari CAR 50C3
Bamberg USA 67B2
Bamberg W Germ 18C3
Bambili Zaïre 50C3
Bambuí Brazil 75C3
Bamenda Cam 50B3
Bamiancheng China 28A2
Bamingui, R CAR 50B3
Bamingui Bangoran National Park CAR 50B3
Bamiyan Afghan 42B2
Banaba, I Kiribati 33F1
Banalia Zaïre 50C3
Banamba Mali 48B3
Bananga, Nicobar Is Indian O 44E4
Ban Aranyaprathet Thai 30C3
Ban Ban Laos 30C2
Ban Betong Thai 30C4
Banbridge N Ire 9C2
Banbury Eng 7D3
Banchory Scot 8D3
Banco Chinchorro, Is Mexico 70D3
Bancroft Can 65D1
Bānda India 43E3
Banda Aceh Indon 27C6
Banda, Kepulauan, Arch Indon 27G7
Bandama, R Ivory Coast 48B4
Bandar 'Abbās Iran 41G4
Bandar Anzalī Iran 21H8
Bandar-e Daylam Iran 41F4
Bandar-e Lengheh Iran 41F4
Bandar-e Māqām Iran 41F4
Bandar-e Rig Iran 41F4
Bandar-e Torkoman Iran 21J8
Bandar Khomeyni Iran 41E3
Bandar Seri Begawan Brunei 27E6
Banda S Indon 27F7
Bandeira, Mt Brazil 75D3
Bandeirantes Brazil 75B1
Banderas, B de Mexico 70B2
Bandiagara Mali 48B3
Bandirma Turk 21D7
Bandolier Kop S Africa 47D1
Bandundu Zaïre 50B4
Bandung Indon 27D7
Baneh Iran 21H8
Banes Cuba 70E2
Banff Scot 8D3
Banff, R Can 54G4
Bangalore India 44B3
Bangassou CAR 50C3
Banggai, Kepulauan, I Indon 32B1
Banggi, I Malay 27E6
Bang Hieng, R Laos 30D2
Bangka, I Indon 27D7
Bangkok Thai 30C3
Bangkok, Bight of, B Thai 30C3
Bangladesh, Republic Asia 39G3
Bangong Co, L China 42D2
Bangor, Maine USA 57G2
Bangor N Ire 9D2
Bangor, Pennsylvania USA 68C2
Bangor Wales 7B3
Bang Saphan Yai Thai 30B3
Bangui CAR 50B3
Bangweulu, L Zambia 51D5
Ban Hat Yai Thai 30C4
Ban Hin Heup Laos 30C2
Ban Houei Sai Laos 30C1
Ban Hua Hin Thai 30B3
Bani, R Mali 48B3
Bani Bangou Niger 48C3
Bani Walid Libya 49D1
Bāniyās Syria 40C2
Banja Luka Yugos 16D2
Banjarmasin Indon 27E7
Banjul The Gambia 48A3
Ban Kantang Thai 30B4
Ban Khemmarat Laos 30D2
Ban Khok Kloi Thai 30B4
Banks I Aust 27H8
Banks I, British Columbia Can 54E4
Banks I, Northwest Territories Can 54F2
Banks Is Vanuatu 33F2
Banks L USA 58C1
Banks Pen NZ 35B2
Banks Str Aust 34C4
Bankura India 43F4
Ban Mae Sariang Thai 30B2
Ban Mae Sot Thai 30B2
Banmauk Burma 43H4
Ban Me Thuot Viet 30D3
Bann, R Irish Rep 9C3
Bann, R N Ire 9C2
Ban Na San Thai 30B4
Bannu Pak 42C2
Ban Pak Neun Laos 30C2
Ban Pak Phanang Thai 30C4
Ban Pu Kroy Camb 30D3
Ban Sai Yok Thai 30B3
Ban Sattahip Thai 30C3
Banská Bystrica Czech 19D3
Bānswāra India 42C4
Ban Tha Kham Thai 30B4
Ban Thateng Laos 30D2
Ban Tha Tum Thai 30C2
Bantry Irish Rep 10B3
Bantry, B Irish Rep 10A3
Banyak, Kepulauan, Is Indon 27C6
Ban Ya Soup Viet 30D3
Banyuwangi Indon 27E7
Banzare Seamount Indian O 36E7
Baoding China 31D2
Baofeng China 31C3
Bao Ha Viet 30C1
Baoji China 31B3
Bao Loc Viet 30D3
Baoshan China 26C4
Baotou China 31C1
Bāpatla India 44C2
Bapaume France 13B2
Bāqir, Jebel, Mt Jordan 45C4
Ba'qūbah Iraq 41D3
Bar Yugos 17D2
Bara Sudan 50D2
Baraawe Somalia 50E3
Bāra Banki India 43E3
Barabash USSR 28C2
Barabinsk USSR 24J4
Barabinskaya Step, Steppe USSR 24J4
Baracaldo Spain 15B1
Baracoa Cuba 69C2
Baradá, R Syria 45D2
Baradine Aust 34C2
Bārāmati India 44A2
Baramula Pak 42C2
Bārān India 42D3
Baranof I USA 54E4
Baranovichi USSR 20D5
Baratta Aust 34A2
Barauni India 43F3
Barbacena Brazil 73K8
Barbados, I Caribbean S 69F4
Barbastro Spain 15C1
Barberton S Africa 47E2
Barbezieux France 14B2
Barbosa Colombia 72D2
Barbuda, I Caribbean S 69E3
Barcaldine Aust 32D3
Barce = Al Marj
Barcellona, Sicily 16D3
Barcelona Spain 15C1
Barcelona Ven 72F1
Barcoo, R Aust 32D3
Bardai Chad 50B1
Bardas Blancas Arg 74C5
Barddhamān India 43F4
Bardejov Czech 19E3
Bardsey, I Wales 7B3
Bardstown USA 64B3
Bareilly India 42D3
Barentsovo More, S = Barents Sea
Barentsøya, I Svalbard 24D2
Barents S USSR 20F1
Barentu Eth 50D2
Barfleur, Pointe de France 14B2
Bargarh India 43E4
Barguzin USSR 25N4
Barguzin, R USSR 25N4
Bar Harbor USA 65F2
Barhi India 43F4
Bari Italy 16D2
Barika Alg 15D2
Barinas Ven 72D2
Baripāda India 43F4
Bârîs Egypt 40B5
Bari Sādri India 42C4
Barisal Bang 43G4
Barisan, Pegunungan, Mts Indon 27D7
Barito, R Indon 27E7
Barjuj, Watercourse Libya 49D2
Barkam China 31A3
Barkley,L USA 64B3
Barkly East S Africa 47D3
Barkly Tableland, Mts Aust 32C2
Bar-le-Duc France 13C3
Barlee,L Aust 32A3
Barlee Range, Mts Aust 32A3
Barletta Italy 16D2
Bārmer India 42C3
Barmera Aust 34B2
Barmouth Wales 7B3
Barnard Castle Eng 6D2
Barnaul USSR 24K4
Barnegat USA 68C3
Barnegat B USA 68C3
Barnesboro USA 68A2
Barnes Icecap Can 55L2
Barnesville, Georgia USA 67B2
Barnesville, Ohio USA 64C3
Barnhart USA 62B2
Barnsley Eng 7D3
Barnstaple Eng 7B4
Baro Nigeria 48C4
Barpeta India 43G3
Barquisimeto Ven 72E1
Barr France 13D3
Barra Brazil 73K6
Barra, I Scot 8B3
Barraba Aust 34D2
Barra da Estiva Brazil 75D1
Barra do Bugres Brazil 75A2
Barra do Garças Brazil 75B2
Barra do Piraí Brazil 75D3
Barra Falsa, Punta de, Pt Mozam 51D6
Barragem de Sobradinho Res Brazil 73K6
Barragem do Castelo do Bode, Res Port 15A2
Barragem do Maranhão Port 15A2
Barra Head, Pt Scot 8B3
Barra Mansa Brazil 73K8
Barranca Peru 72C6
Barrancabermeja Colombia 72D2
Barrancas Ven 72F2
Barranqueras Arg 74E3
Barranquilla Colombia 72D1
Barra,Sound of, Chan Scot 8B3
Barre USA 68D1
Barreiras Brazil 73J6
Barreiro Port 15A2
Barreiros Brazil 73L5
Barren,C Aust 32D5
Barretos Brazil 73J8
Barrie Can 65D2
Barrier Range, Mts Aust 34B2
Barrington,Mt Aust 32E4
Barro Alto Brazil 75C2
Barroloola Aust 27G8
Barron USA 64A1
Barrouallie St Vincent 69N2
Barrow USA 54C2
Barrow, R Irish Rep 10B3
Barrow Creek Aust 32C3
Barrow I Aust 32A3
Barrow-in-Furness Eng 6C2
Barrow,Pt USA 54C2
Barrow Str Can 55J2
Barry Wales 7C4
Barry's Bay Can 65D1
Barryville USA 68C2
Barsi India 44B2
Barsinghausen W Germ 13E1
Barstow USA 56B3
Bar-sur-Aube France 14C2
Bar-sur-Seine France 13C3
Bartica Guyana 73G2
Bartın Turk 40B1
Bartle Frere,Mt Aust 32D2
Bartlesville USA 56D3
Bartlett USA 60D2
Bartolomeu Dias Mozam 51D6
Barton-upon-Humber Eng 6D3
Bartoszyce Pol 19E2
Barú, Mt Panama 72B2
Barwāh India 42D4
Barwāni India 42C4
Barwon, R Aust 34C1
Barysh USSR 20H5
Basalt USA 66C1
Basankusu Zaïre 50B3
Basel = Basle
Basento, R Italy 16D2
Bashi Chan Phil/Taiwan 26F4
Bashkir ASSR, Republic USSR 20J5
Basilan Phil 27F6
Basilan, I Phil 27F6
Basildon Eng 7E4
Basin USA 58E2
Basingstoke Eng 7D4
Basin Region USA 56B2
Baskatong, Réservoir Can 65D1
Basle Switz/France/W Germ 16B1
Basra Iraq 41E3
Bas-Rhin, Department France 13D3
Bassac, R Camb 30D3
Bassano Italy 16C1
Bassar Togo 48C4
Bassas da India, I Mozam Chan 51D6
Bassein Burma 30A2
Basse Terre Guadeloupe 69E3
Bassett USA 60D2
Bassila Benin 48C4
Bass Lake USA 66C2
Bass Str Aust 32D5
Bassum W Germ 13E1
Båstad Sweden 12G7
Bastak Iran 41F4
Basti India 43E3
Bastia, Corsica 16B2
Bastogne Belg 18B3
Bastrop, Louisiana USA 63D2
Bastrop, Texas USA 63C2
Bata Eq Guinea 48C4
Bataan Pen Phil 27F5

Batabanó, G de Bhiwāni

Batabanó, G de *Cuba* 70D2
Batakan *Indon* 27E7
Batāla *India* 42D2
Batang *China* 26C3
Batangafo *CAR* 50B3
Batangas *Phil* 27F5
Batan Is *Phil* 26F4
Batatais *Brazil* 75C3
Batavia *USA* 65D2
Batemans Bay *Aust* 34D3
Batesburg *USA* 67B2
Batesville, Arkansas *USA* 63D1
Batesville, Mississippi *USA* 63E2
Bath *Can* 65F1
Bath *Eng* 7C4
Bath, Maine *USA* 65F2
Bath, New York *USA* 65D2
Batha, R *Chad* 50B2
Bathawana Mt *Can* 64C1
Bathurst *Aust* 32D4
Bathurst *Can* 55M5
Bathurst,C *Can* 54F2
Bathurst I *Aust* 32C2
Bathurst I *Can* 54H2
Bathurst Inlet, B *Can* 54H3
Batié *Burkina* 48B4
Bāţin, Wadi al, Watercourse *Iraq* 41E4
Bāţlāq-e-Gavkhūni, Salt Flat *Iran* 41F3
Batlow *Aust* 34C3
Batman *Turk* 40D2
Batna *Algeria* 16B3
Baton Rouge *USA* 57D3
Batroûn *Leb* 45C1
Battambang *Camb* 30C3
Batticaloa *Sri Lanka* 44C4
Batti Malv, I, Nicobar Is *Indian O* 44E4
Battle *Eng* 7E4
Battle Creek *USA* 57E2
Battle Harbour *Can* 55N4
Battle Mountain *USA* 58C2
Batumi *USSR* 21G7
Batu Pahat *Malay* 30C5
Bat Yam *Israel* 45C2
Baubau *Indon* 32B1
Bauchi *Nigeria* 48C3
Baudette *USA* 61E1
Bauld,C *Can* 55N4
Baunt *USSR* 25N4
Bauru *Brazil* 73J8
Baús *Brazil* 75B2
Bautzen *E Germ* 18C2
Bawean, I *Indon* 27E7
Bawîti *Egypt* 49E2
Bawku *Ghana* 48B3
Bawlake *Burma* 30B2
Bawlen *Aust* 34A2
Baxley *USA* 67B2
Bayamo *Cuba* 70E2
Bayana *India* 43J2
Bayandalay *Mongolia* 31A1
Bayandzürh *Mongolia* 25M5
Bayan Har Shan, Mts *China* 26C3
Bayan Mod *China* 31A1
Bayan Obo *China* 31B1
Bayard, Nebraska *USA* 60C2
Bayard, New Mexico *USA* 62A2
Bayburt *Turk* 40D1
Bay City, Michigan *USA* 57E2
Bay City, Texas *USA* 63C3
Baydaratskaya Guba, B *USSR* 24H3
Baydhabo *Somalia* 50E3
Bayern, State *W Germ* 18C3
Bayeux *France* 14B2
Bayfield *USA* 64A1
Bāyir *Jordan* 40C3
Baykal, Ozero, L = Baikal, L
Baykalskiy Khrebet, Mts *USSR* 26D1
Baykit *USSR* 25L3
Baylik Shan, Mts *China/Mongolia* 25L5
Baymak *USSR* 20K5
Bay Minette *USA* 63E2
Bayonne *France* 14B3
Bayreuth *W Germ* 18C3
Bay St Louis *USA* 63E2
Bay Shore *USA* 65E2
Bays,L of *Can* 65D1
Baytik Shan, Mts *China* 26B2
Bayt Lahm = Bethlehem
Baytown *USA* 63D3
Baza *Spain* 15B2
Bazaliya *USSR* 19F3
Bazar-Dyuzi, Mt *USSR* 21H7
Bazaruto, Ilha *Mozam* 51D6
Bazas *France* 14B3
Bazhong *China* 31B3
Bcharre *Leb* 45D1
Beach *USA* 60C1
Beach Haven *USA* 68C3
Beachy Head *Eng* 7E4
Beacon *USA* 68D2
Bealanana *Madag* 51E5
Bear, R *USA* 58D2
Beardstown *USA* 64A2
Bear I *Barents S* 24C2
Bear L *USA* 58D2
Bear Valley *USA* 66B1
Beata, Cabo, C *Dom Rep* 69C3
Beata, Isla *Dom Rep* 69C3
Beatrice *USA* 56D2
Beatrice, Oilfield *N Sea* 8D2
Beatton River *Can* 54F4
Beatty *USA* 56B3
Beattyville *Can* 65D1
Beauchene Is *Falkland Is* 74E8
Beaudesert *Aust* 34D1
Beaufort *USA* 67B2
Beaufort S *Can/USA* 54D2
Beaufort West *S Africa* 47C3
Beauharnois *Can* 65E1
Beauly *Scot* 8C3
Beaumaris *Wales* 7B3
Beaumont, California *USA* 59C4
Beaumont, Texas *USA* 57D3
Beaune *France* 14C2
Beauvais *France* 14C2
Beaver *USA* 54D3
Beaver, Utah *USA* 59D3
Beaver, R *Can* 54G4
Beaver Creek *Can* 54D3
Beaver Dam, Kentucky *USA* 64B3
Beaver Dam, Wisconsin *USA* 64B2
Beaverhead Mts *USA* 58D1
Beaver I *USA* 64B1
Beaver L *USA* 63D1
Beāwar *India* 42C3
Bebedouro *Brazil* 75C3
Beccles *Eng* 7E3
Bečej *Yugos* 17E1
Béchar *Alg* 48B1
Beckley *USA* 57E3
Beckum *W Germ* 13E2
Bedale *Eng* 6D2
Bederkesa *W Germ* 13E1
Bedford *Eng* 7D3
Bedford, Indiana *USA* 64B3
Bedford, Pennsylvania *USA* 68A3
Bedford, County *Eng* 7D3
Bedford Pt *Grenada* 69M2
Beech Creek *USA* 68B2
Beechey Pt *USA* 54D2
Beechworth *Aust* 34C3
Beenleigh *Aust* 34D1
Beer Menuha *Israel* 45C3
Beer Ora *Israel* 45C4
Beersheba *Israel* 40B3
Be'er Sheva = Beersheba
Be'er Sheva, R *Israel* 45C3
Beeville *USA* 56D4
Befale *Zaïre* 50C3
Befandriana *Madag* 51E5
Bega *Aust* 34C3
Begicheva, Ostrov, I = Bol'shoy Begichev, Ostrov
Begur, C de *Spain* 15C1
Behbehān *Iran* 41F3
Behshahr *Iran* 41F2
Behsud *Afghan* 42B2
Bei'an *China* 26F2
Beihai *China* 31B5
Beijing *China* 31D2
Beiliu *China* 30E1
Beipan Jiang, R *China* 31B4
Beipiao *China* 31E1
Beira = Sofala
Beirut *Leb* 40C3
Bei Shan, Mts *China* 26C2
Beitbridge *Zim* 47E1
Beit ed Dine *Leb* 45C2
Beith *Scot* 8C4
Beit Jala *Israel* 45C3
Beizhen *China* 28A2
Beja *Port* 15A2
Béja *Tunisia* 16B3
Bejaïa *Alg* 15C2
Béjar *Spain* 15A1
Bejestān *Iran* 41G3
Békéscsaba *Hung* 19E3
Bekily *Madag* 51E6
Bela *India* 43E3
Bela *Pak* 42B3
Bel Air *USA* 68B3
Belampalli *India* 44B2
Belang *Indon* 27F6
Belangpidie *Indon* 27C6
Belau = Palau
Béla Vista *Brazil/Par* 75A3
Bela Vista *Mozam* 47E2
Belawan *Indon* 27C6
Belaya, R *USSR* 20K4
Belaya Tserkov' *USSR* 19G3
Belcher Chan *Can* 55J2
Belcher Is *Can* 55L4
Belchiragh *Afghan* 42B1
Belebey *USSR* 20J5
Belém *Brazil* 73J4
Belén *Colombia* 72C3
Belén *Par* 75A3
Belen *USA* 56C3
Bélep., Iles *New Caledonia* 33F2
Belet Uen *Somalia* 50E3
Belezma, Mts de *Algeria* 16B3
Belfast *N Ire* 9C2
Belfast *S Africa* 47E2
Belfast Lough, Estuary *N Ire* 9C2
Belfield *USA* 60C1
Belfodio *Eth* 50D2
Belford *Eng* 6D2
Belfort *France* 14D2
Belgaum *India* 44A2
Belgium, Kingdom *N W Europe* 18A2
Belgorod *USSR* 21F5
Belgorod Dnestrovskiy *USSR* 21E6
Belgrade *USA* 58D1
Belgrade *Yugos* 17E2
Bel Hedan *Libya* 49D2
Belitung, I *Indon* 27D7
Belize *Belize* 70D3
Belize, Republic *Cent America* 70D3
Bel'kovskiy, Ostrov, I *USSR* 25P2
Bellac *France* 14C2
Bella Coola *Can* 54F4
Bellaire *USA* 63C3
Bellary *India* 44B2
Bellata *Aust* 34C1
Bellefonte *USA* 68B2
Belle Fourche *USA* 56C2
Belle Fourche, R *USA* 60C2
Bellegarde *France* 14D2
Belle Glade *USA* 67B3
Belle I *Can* 55N4
Belle-Ile, I *France* 14B2
Belle Isle,Str of *Can* 55N4
Belleville *Can* 55L5
Belleville, Illinois *USA* 64B3
Belleville, Kansas *USA* 61D3
Bellevue, Idaho *USA* 58D2
Bellevue, Iowa *USA* 64A2
Bellevue, Washington *USA* 58B1
Bellingen *Aust* 34D2
Bellingham *Eng* 6C2
Bellingham *USA* 56A2
Bellingshausen, Base *Ant* 76G2
Bellingshausen S *Ant* 76G3
Bellinzona *Switz* 16B1
Bello *Colombia* 72C2
Bellona Reefs *Nouvelle Calédonie* 33E3
Bellota *USA* 66B1
Bellows Falls *USA* 65E2
Bell Pen *Can* 55K3
Belluno *Italy* 16C1
Bell Ville *Arg* 74D4
Belmont *USA* 68B1
Belmonte *Brazil* 73L7
Belmopan *Belize* 70D3
Belogorsk *USSR* 26F1
Beloha *Madag* 51E6
Belo Horizonte *Brazil* 73K7
Beloit, Kansas *USA* 61D3
Beloit, Wisconsin *USA* 57E2
Belomorsk *USSR* 24E3
Beloretsk *USSR* 20K5
Belorussian SSR, Republic *USSR* 20D5
Belo-Tsiribihina *Madag* 51E5
Beloye More, S = White Sea
Beloye Ozero, L *USSR* 20F3
Belozersk *USSR* 20F3
Belper *Eng* 7D3
Belpre *USA* 64C3
Beltana *Aust* 34A2
Belton *USA* 63C2
Bel'tsy *USSR* 19F3
Belukha, Mt *USSR* 24K5
Belush'ye *USSR* 20H2
Belvidere, Illinois *USA* 64B2
Belvidere, New Jersey *USA* 68C2
Belyy, Ostrov, I *USSR* 24J2
Bembe *Angola* 51B4
Bembéréké *Benin* 48C3
Bemidji *USA* 57D2
Bemis *USA* 63E1
Bena Dibele *Zaïre* 50C4
Benalla *Aust* 34C3
Ben Attow, Mt *Scot* 8C3
Benavente *Spain* 15A1
Benbane Hd, Pt *N Ire* 9C2
Benbecula, I *Scot* 8B3
Bencubbin *Aust* 32A4
Bend *USA* 56A2
Ben Dearg, Mt *Scot* 8C3
Bender Beyla *Somalia* 50E3
Bendery *USSR* 19F3
Bendigo *Aust* 32D4
Benešov *Czech* 18C3
Benevento *Italy* 16C2
Bengal,B of *Asia* 39G4
Ben Gardane *Tunisia* 49D1
Bengbu *China* 31D3
Benghāzi *Libya* 49E1
Bengkulu *Indon* 27D7
Benguela *Angola* 51B5
Benha *Egypt* 40B3
Ben Hope, Mt *Scot* 8C2
Beni *Zaïre* 50C3
Béni, R *Bol* 72E6
Beni Abbès *Alg* 48B1
Benicarló *Spain* 15C1
Benidorm *Spain* 15B2
Beni Mansour *Alg* 15C2
Beni Mazâr *Egypt* 49F2
Beni Mellal *Mor* 48B1
Benin, Republic *Africa* 48C4
Benin City *Nigeria* 48C4
Beni-Saf *Alg* 15B2
Beni Suef *Egypt* 49F2
Benkelman *USA* 60C3
Ben Kilbreck, Mt *Scot* 8C2
Ben Lawers, Mt *Scot* 10C2
Ben Macdui, Mt *Scot* 8D3
Ben More *Scot* 8B3
Ben More Assynt, Mt *Scot* 8C2
Benmore,L *NZ* 35B2
Bennetta, Ostrov, I *USSR* 25R2
Ben Nevis, Mt *Scot* 8C3
Bennington *USA* 65E2
Bennt Jbail *Leb* 45C2
Bénoué, R *Cam* 50B3
Bensheim *W Germ* 13E3
Benson, Arizona *USA* 56B3
Benson, Minnesota *USA* 61D1
Benteng *Indon* 27F7
Bentiu *Sudan* 50C3
Bento Gomes, R *Brazil* 75A2
Benton, Arkansas *USA* 63D2
Benton, California *USA* 66C2
Benton, Kentucky *USA* 64B3
Benton Harbor *USA* 64B2
Benue, R *Nigeria* 48C4
Ben Wyvis, Mt *Scot* 8C3
Benxi *China* 31E1
Beograd = Belgrade
Beohāri *India* 43E4
Beppu *Japan* 28C4
Berat *Alb* 17D2
Berau, Teluk, B *Indon* 27G7
Berber *Sudan* 50D2
Berbera *Somalia* 50E2
Berbérati *CAR* 50B3
Berdichev *USSR* 21D6
Berdyansk *USSR* 21F6
Berea *USA* 64C3
Berekum *Ghana* 48B4
Berenda *USA* 66B2
Berenice *Egypt* 40C5
Berens, R *Can* 54J4
Berens River *Can* 54J4
Beresford *USA* 61D2
Berettyóújfalu *Hung* 19E3
Bereza *USSR* 19F2
Berezhany *USSR* 19E3
Berezina, R *USSR* 19F2
Bereznik *USSR* 20G3
Berezniki *USSR* 24G4
Berezovka *USSR* 21E6
Berezovo *USSR* 24H3
Bergama *Turk* 40A2
Bergamo *Italy* 16B1
Bergen *Nor* 12F6
Bergen *USA* 68B1
Bergen op Zoom *Neth* 13C2
Bergerac *France* 14C3
Bergisch-Gladbach *W Germ* 13D2
Berhampur *India* 44C2
Beringa, Ostrov, I *USSR* 25S4
Beringovskiy *USSR* 25U3
Bering S *USA/USSR* 37K2
Bering Str *USA/USSR* 76C6
Berizak *Iran* 41G4
Berja *Spain* 15B2
Berkel, R *Neth/W Germ* 13D1
Berkeley *USA* 56A3
Berkeley Spring *USA* 68A3
Berkhamsted *Eng* 7D4
Berkner I *Ant* 76F2
Berkovitsa *Bulg* 17E2
Berkshire, County *Eng* 7D4
Berkshire Hills *USA* 68D1
Berlin *E Germ* 18C2
Berlin, New Hampshire *USA* 65E2
Bermejo *Bol* 72F8
Bermejo, R *Arg* 74E3
Bermuda, I *Atlantic O* 53M5
Bern = Berne
Bernalillo *USA* 62A1
Bernardo de Irigoyen *Arg* 75B4
Bernardsville *USA* 68C2
Bernburg *E Germ* 18C2
Berne *Switz* 16B1
Berneray, I *Scot* 8B3
Bernier B *Can* 55K2
Berounka, R *Czech* 18C3
Berri *Aust* 34B2
Berriane *Alg* 48C1
Berry, Region *France* 14C2
Berryessa,L *USA* 66A1
Berry Is *The Bahamas* 57F4
Berryville *USA* 68B3
Berseba *Namibia* 47B2
Berthoud P *USA* 60B3
Bertoua *Cam* 50B3
Beru, I *Kiribati* 33G1
Berwick *USA* 65D2
Berwick-upon-Tweed *Eng* 6C2
Berwyn Mts *Wales* 7C3
Besalampy *Madag* 51E5
Besançon *France* 14D2
Beskidy Zachodnie, Mts *Pol* 19E3
Besni *Turk* 40C2
Besor, R *Israel* 45C3
Bessemer, Alabama *USA* 67A2
Bessemer, Michigan *USA* 64B1
Betafo *Madag* 51E5
Betanzos *Spain* 15A1
Bet Guvrin *Israel* 45C3
Bethal *S Africa* 47D2
Bethanie *Namibia* 47B2
Bethany, Missouri *USA* 61E2
Bethany, Oklahoma *USA* 63C1
Bethel, Alaska *USA* 54B3
Bethel, Connecticut *USA* 68D2
Bethel Park *USA* 64C2
Bethesda *USA* 65D3
Bethlehem *Israel* 45C3
Bethlehem *S Africa* 47D2
Bethlehem *USA* 65D2
Bethulie *S Africa* 47D3
Béthune *France* 14C1
Betioky *Madag* 51E6
Betoota *Aust* 34B1
Betou *Congo* 50B3
Betpak Dala, Steppe *USSR* 39E1
Betroka *Madag* 51E6
Betsiamites *Can* 55M5
Bettendorf *USA* 64A2
Bettiah *India* 43E3
Betūl *India* 42D4
Betuwe, Region *Neth* 13C2
Betwa, R *India* 42D3
Betws-y-coed *Wales* 7C3
Betzdorf *W Germ* 13D2
Beverley *Eng* 7D3
Beverly *USA* 68E1
Beverly Hills *USA* 66C3
Bexhill *Eng* 7E4
Bey Dağlari *Turk* 40B2
Beyla *Guinea* 48B4
Beypore *India* 44B3
Beyrouth = Beirut
Beyşehir *Turk* 40B2
Beysehir Gölü, L *Turk* 21E8
Beyt Shean *Israel* 45C2
Bezhetsk *USSR* 20F4
Béziers *France* 14C3
Bezmein *USSR* 41G2
Beznosova *USSR* 26D1
Bhadgaon *Nepal* 43F3
Bhadrāchalam *India* 44C2
Bhadrakh *India* 43F4
Bhadra Res *India* 44B3
Bhadrāvati *India* 44B3
Bhag *Pak* 42B3
Bhāgalpur *India* 43F3
Bhakkar *Pak* 42C2
Bhandāra *India* 42D4
Bharatpur *India* 42D3
Bharūch *India* 42C4
Bhātiāpāra Ghat *Bang* 43F4
Bhatinda *India* 42C2
Bhatkal *India* 44A3
Bhātpāra *India* 43F4
Bhāvnagar *India* 42C4
Bhawānipatna *India* 43E5
Bhera *Pak* 42C2
Bheri, R *Nepal* 43E3
Bhilai *India* 43E4
Bhilwāra *India* 42C3
Bhimavaram *India* 44C2
Bhind *India* 42D3
Bhiwāni *India* 42D3

Bhongir
Boro

Bhongir *India* 44B2
Bhopāl *India* 42D4
Bhubaneshwar *India* 43F4
Bhuj *India* 42B4
Bhusāwal *India* 42D4
Bhutan, Kingdom *Asia* 22F4
Biak, I *Indon* 27G7
Biala Podlaska *Pol* 19E2
Białogard *Pol* 18D2
Bialystok *Pol* 19E2
Biargtangar, C *Iceland* 12A1
Biārjmand *Iran* 41G2
Biarritz *France* 14B3
Biba *Egypt* 40B4
Bibai *Japan* 29E2
Bibala *Angola* 51B5
Biberach *W Germ* 18B3
Bibiani *Ghana* 48B4
Bicaz *Rom* 17F1
Bicester *Eng* 7D4
Bicknell *USA* 59D3
Bida *Nigeria* 48C4
Bidar *India* 44B2
Bidbid *Oman* 41G5
Biddeford *USA* 65E2
Bideford *Eng* 7C6
Bideford B *Eng* 7B4
Bidon 5 *Alg* 48C2
Bié *Angola* 51B5
Biebrza, R *Pol* 19E2
Biel *Switz* 16B1
Bielawa *Pol* 18D2
Bielefeld *W Germ* 18B2
Biella *Italy* 16B1
Bielsk Podlaski *Pol* 19E2
Bien Hoa *Viet* 30D3
Bienville, Lac *Can* 55L4
Biferno, R *Italy* 16C2
Biga *Turk* 40A1
Bigadiç *Turk* 17F3
Big Belt Mts *USA* 58D1
Big Bend Nat Pk *USA* 62B3
Big Black, R *USA* 63E2
Big Blue, R *USA* 61D2
Big Cypress Swamp *USA* 67B3
Big Delta *USA* 54D3
Biggar *Scot* 8D4
Biggar Kindersley *Can* 54H4
Biggenden *Aust* 34D1
Biggleswade *Eng* 7D3
Big Hole, R *USA* 58D1
Bighorn, R *USA* 60B1
Bighorn L *USA* 60B1
Bighorn Mts *USA* 60B2
Bight of Benin, B *W Africa* 48C4
Bight of Biafra, B *Cam* 48C4
Big I *Can* 55L3
Big Lake *USA* 62B2
Bignona *Sen* 48A3
Big Pine *USA* 59C3
Big Pine Key *USA* 67B4
Big Pine Mt *USA* 66C3
Big Rapids *USA* 64B2
Big River *Can* 54H4
Big Sandy *USA* 58D1
Big Sioux, R *USA* 61D2
Big Smokey V *USA* 66D1
Big Spring *USA* 56C3
Big Springs *USA* 60C2
Big Stone City *USA* 61D1
Big Stone Gap *USA* 64C3
Big Sur *USA* 66B2
Big Timber *USA* 58E1
Big Trout L *Can* 55J4
Big Trout Lake *Can* 55K4
Bihać *Yugos* 16D2
Bihār *India* 43F3
Bihār, State *India* 43F4
Biharamulo *Tanz* 50D4
Bihor, Mt *Rom* 21C6
Bijagós, Arquipélago dos Is *Guinea-Bissau* 48A3
Bijāpur *India* 44B2
Bijāpur *India* 44C2
Bijār *Iran* 41E2
Bijauri *Nepal* 43E3
Bijeljina *Yugos* 17D2
Bijie *China* 31B4
Bijnor *India* 42D3
Bijnot *Pak* 42C3
Bikāner *India* 42C3
Bikfaya *Leb* 45C2
Bikin *USSR* 26G2
Bikoro *Zaïre* 50B4
Bilāra *India* 42C3
Bilāspur *India* 42D2
Bilauktaung Range, Mts *Thai/Burma* 30B3
Bilbao *Spain* 15B1
Bilbeis *Egypt* 45A3
Bilé, R *Czech* 18D3
Bileća *Yugos* 17D2
Bilecik *Turk* 40B1
Bili, R *Zaïre* 50C3
Bilibino *USSR* 25S3
Billings *USA* 56C2
Bilma *Niger* 50B2
Biloxi *USA* 57E3
Biltine *Chad* 50C2
Bimini Is *Bahamas* 67C3
Bina-Etawa *India* 42D4
Bindura *Zim* 51D5
Binga *Zim* 51C5
Binga, Mt *Zim/Mozam* 51D5
Bingara *Aust* 34D1
Bingen *W Germ* 18B3
Bingham *USA* 65F1
Binghamton *USA* 57F2
Bingöl *Turk* 40D2
Binhai *China* 31D3
Binibeca, Cabo, C *Spain* 15C2
Bintan, I *Indon* 27D6
Bintulu *Malay* 27E6
Bió Bió, R *Chile* 74B5
Bioko, I *Eq Guinea* 48C4
Bir *India* 44B2
Bîr Abu Husein, Well *Egypt* 49E2
Bi'r al Harash, Well *Libya* 49E2
Birao *CAR* 50C2
Biratnagar *Nepal* 43F3
Birchip *Aust* 34B3
Birch L *USA* 61E1
Birch Mts *Can* 54G4
Bird *Can* 55J4
Birdsville *Aust* 32C3
Birdum *Aust* 32C2
Bîr el 'Agramîya, Well *Egypt* 45A4
Bîr el Duweidâr, Well *Egypt* 45B3
Birganj *Nepal* 43E3
Bîr Gifgâfa, Well *Egypt* 45B3
Bîr Gindali, Well *Egypt* 45A4
Bîr Hasana, Well *Egypt* 45B3
Birigui *Brazil* 75B3
Birin *Syria* 45D1
Birjand *Iran* 41G3
Birkat Qârun, L *Egypt* 40B4
Birkenfeld *W Germ* 13D3
Birkenhead *Eng* 7C3
Bîrlad *Rom* 21D6
Bîr Lahfân, Well *Egypt* 45B3
Birmingham *Eng* 7C3
Birmingham *USA* 57E3
Bîr Misâha, Well *Egypt* 49E2
Bir Moghrein *Maur* 48A2
Birnin-Kebbi *Nigeria* 48C3
Birobidzhan *USSR* 26G2
Birr *Irish Rep* 9C3
Bir Rabalou *Alg* 15C2
Birrie, R *Aust* 34C1
Birsay *Scot* 8D2
Birsk *USSR* 20K4
Bîr Tarfâwi, Well *Egypt* 49E2
Bîr Udelb, Well *Egypt* 45B4
Biryusa, R *USSR* 25L4
Birzăi *USSR* 12J7
Bir Zreigat, Well *Maur* 48B2
Bisalpur *India* 43K1
Bisbee *USA* 59E4
Biscay,B of *France/Spain* 14A2
Biscayne B *USA* 67B3
Bischwiller *France* 13D3
Biscotasi L *Can* 64C1
Bishan *China* 31B4
Bishop *USA* 56B3
Bishop Auckland *Eng* 6D2
Bishops Castle *Eng* 7C3
Bishop's Stortford *Eng* 7E4
Bishrāmpur *India* 43E4
Biskra *Alg* 48C1
Bismarck *USA* 56C2
Bismarck Arch *PNG* 32D1
Bismarck Range, Mts *PNG* 32D1
Bismarck S *PNG* 32D1
Bisotūn *Iran* 41E3
Bissau *Guinea-Bissau* 48A3
Bissett *Can* 57D1
Bistcho L *Can* 54G4
Bistrita, R *Rom* 17F1
Bitam *Gabon* 50B3
Bitburg *W Germ* 18B3
Bitche *France* 13D3
Bitlis *Turk* 40D2
Bitola *Yugos* 17E2
Bitterfeld *E Germ* 18C2
Bitterfontein *S Africa* 47B3
Bitter Lakes *Egypt* 40B3
Bitteroot Range, Mts *USA* 56B2
Biu *Nigeria* 48D3
Biwa-ko, L *Japan* 29D3
Biyo Kaboba *Eth* 50E2
Biysk *USSR* 24K4
Bizerte *Tunisia* 16B3
Bjelovar *Yugos* 16D1
Bj Flye Ste Marie *Alg* 48B2
Bjørnøya, I = Bear I
Black, R *USA* 63D1
Blackall *Aust* 32D3
Black B *Can* 64B1
Blackburn *Eng* 6C3
Blackburn,Mt *USA* 54D3
Black Canyon City *USA* 59D4
Blackduck *USA* 61E1
Black Eagle *USA* 58D1
Blackfoot *USA* 58D2
Blackfoot, R *USA* 58D1
Black Hd, Pt *Irish Rep* 9B3
Black Hills *USA* 54H5
Black Isle, Pen *Scot* 8C3
Blackman's *Barbados* 69Q2
Black Mts *USA* 59D3
Black Mts *Wales* 7C4
Black Nosob, R *Namibia* 47B1
Blackpool *Eng* 6C3
Black River *Jamaica* 69H1
Black River Falls *USA* 64A2
Black Rock Desert *USA* 56B2
Black S *USSR/Europe* 24E5
Blacksburg *USA* 64C3
Black Sugarloaf, Mt *Aust* 34D2
Black Volta, R *W Africa* 48B4
Black Warrior, R *USA* 63E2
Blackwater, R *Eng* 7E4
Blackwater, R *Irish Rep* 10B3
Blackwell *USA* 63C1
Blagoevgrad *Bulg* 17E2
Blagoveshchensk *USSR* 25O4
Blaikiston,Mt *Can* 58D1
Blaine *USA* 58B1
Blair *USA* 61D2
Blair Atholl *Scot* 8D3
Blairgowrie *Scot* 8D3
Blakely *USA* 67C2
Blanca, Bahía, B *Arg* 74D5
Blanca Peak, Mt *USA* 62A1
Blanc, C *Tunisia* 16B3
Blanche, L *Aust* 34A1
Blanc, Mont, Mt *France/Italy* 16B1
Blanco,C *USA* 56A2
Blanc Sablon *Can* 55N4
Blandford Forum *Eng* 7C4
Blanding *USA* 59E3
Blankenberge *Belg* 13B2
Blanquilla, Isla *Ven* 69E4
Blantyre *Malawi* 51D5
Blasket Sd *Irish Rep* 9A3
Blaye *France* 14B2
Blayney *Aust* 34C2
Blenheim *NZ* 33G5
Blida *Alg* 15C2
Blind River *Can* 64C1
Blinman *Aust* 34A2
Block I *USA* 65E2
Block Island Sd *USA* 68E2
Bloemfontein *S Africa* 47D2
Bloemhof *S Africa* 47D2
Bloemhof Dam, Res *S Africa* 47D2
Blommesteinmeer, L *Surinam* 73G3
Blönduós *Iceland* 12A1
Bloomfield, Indiana *USA* 64B3
Bloomfield, Iowa *USA* 61E2
Bloomfield, Nebraska *USA* 61D2
Bloomfield, New Mexico *USA* 62A1
Bloomington, Illinois *USA* 64B2
Bloomington, Indiana *USA* 64B3
Bloomington, Minnesota *USA* 61E2
Bloomsburg *USA* 68B2
Blossburg *USA* 68B2
Blosseville Kyst, Mts *Greenland* 55Q3
Blouberg, Mt *S Africa* 47D1
Bludenz *Austria* 18B3
Bluefield *USA* 57E3
Bluefields *Nic* 72B1
Blue Hill *USA* 60D2
Blue Knob, Mt *USA* 68A2
Blue Mountain Peak, Mt *Jamaica* 69J1
Blue Mt *USA* 68B2
Blue Mts *Aust* 34D2
Blue Mts *USA* 56A2
Blue Mts, The *Jamaica* 69J1
Blue Nile = Abbai
Blue Nile *Ethiopia* = Bahr el Azraq
Blue Nile, R *Sudan* 50D2
Bluenose L *Can* 54G3
Blue Ridge *USA* 67C2
Blue Ridge Mts *USA* 57E3
Blue Stack, Mt *Irish Rep* 9C2
Bluff *NZ* 35A3
Bluff *USA* 59E3
Bluff Knoll, Mt *Aust* 32A4
Blumenau *Brazil* 74G3
Blunt *USA* 60D2
Bly *USA* 58B2
Blyth *Eng* 6D2
Blythe *USA* 56B3
Blytheville *USA* 57E3
Bo *Sierra Leone* 48A4
Boac *Phil* 27F5
Boa Nova *Brazil* 75D1
Boardman *USA* 64C2
Boa Vista *Brazil* 71D3
Boa Vista, I *Cape Verde* 48A4
Bobai *China* 30E1
Bobbili *India* 44C2
Bobo Dioulasso *Burkina* 48B3
Bobrovica *USSR* 19G2
Bobruysk *USSR* 20D5
Boca Chica Key, I *USA* 67B4
Bôca do Acre *Brazil* 72E5
Bocaiúva *Brazil* 75D2
Bocaranga *CAR* 50B3
Boca Raton *USA* 67B3
Bochnia *Pol* 19E3
Bocholt *W Germ* 18B2
Bochum *W Germ* 13D2
Bocoio *Angola* 51B5
Boda *CAR* 50B3
Bodaybo *USSR* 25N4
Bodega Head, Pt *USA* 59B3
Bodélé, Desert Region *Chad* 50B2
Boden *Sweden* 12J5
Boderg, L *Irish Rep* 9C3
Bodhan *India* 44B2
Bodināyakkanūr *India* 44B3
Bodmin *Eng* 7B4
Bodmin Moor, Upland *Eng* 7B4
Bodø *Nor* 12G5
Bodrum *Turk* 17F3
Boende *Zaïre* 50C4
Boffa *Guinea* 48A3
Bogale *Burma* 30B2
Bogalusa *USA* 63E2
Bogan, R *Aust* 34C2
Bogande *Burkina* 48B3
Boğazlıyan *Turk* 40C2
Bogdanovich *USSR* 20L4
Bogda Shan, Mt *China* 26B2
Bogenfels *Namibia* 47B2
Boggabilla *Aust* 34D1
Boggabri *Aust* 34C2
Bognor Regis *Eng* 7D4
Bogong, Mt *Aust* 34C3
Bogor *Indon* 27D7
Bogorodskoye *USSR* 25Q4
Bogotá *Colombia* 72D3
Bogotol *USSR* 25K4
Bogra *Bang* 43F4
Bo Hai, B *China* 31D2
Bohain-en-Vermandois *France* 13B3
Bohai Wan, B *China* 31D2
Bohmer-wald, Upland *W Germ* 18C3
Bohol, I *Phil* 27F6
Bohol S *Phil* 27F6
Boipeba, Ilha de *Brazil* 75E1
Bois, R *Brazil* 75B2
Bois Blanc I *USA* 64C1
Boise *USA* 56B2
Boise City *USA* 62B1
Bois, Lac des *Can* 54F3
Boissevain *Can* 60C1
Bojador,C *Mor* 48A2
Bojeador, C *Phil* 27F5
Bojnūrd *Iran* 41G2
Boké *Guinea* 48A3
Bokhara, R *Aust* 34C1
Boknafjord, Inlet *Nor* 12F7
Boko *Congo* 50B4
Bokor *Camb* 30C3
Bokoro *Chad* 50B2
Bokungu *Zaïre* 50C4
Bol *Chad* 50B2
Bolama *Guinea-Bissau* 48A3
Bolbec *France* 14C2
Bole *Ghana* 48B4
Bolesławiec *Pol* 18D2
Bolgatanga *Ghana* 48B3
Bolgrad *USSR* 21D6
Bolivar, Missouri *USA* 63D1
Bolivar, Tennessee *USA* 63E1
Bolívar, Mt *Ven* 72D2
Bolivia, Republic *S America* 72E7
Bollnäs *Sweden* 12H6
Bollon *Aust* 34C1
Bolobo *Zaïre* 50B4
Bologna *Italy* 16C2
Bologoye *USSR* 20E4
Bolon' *USSR* 26G1
Bolon', Oz, L *USSR* 26G2
Bolsena, L di *Italy* 16C2
Bol'shevik, Ostrov, I *USSR* 25M2
Bol'shezemel'skaya Tundra, Plain *USSR* 20J2
Bol'shoy Anyuy, R *USSR* 25S3
Bol'shoy Begichev, Ostrov, I *USSR* 25N2
Bol'shoy Irgiz, R *USSR* 21H5
Bol'shoy Kamen *USSR* 28C2
Bol'shoy Kavkaz, Mts = Caucasus
Bol'shoy Lyakhovskiy, Ostrov, I *USSR* 25Q2
Bol'shoy Uzen, R *USSR* 21H6
Bolson de Mapimí, Desert *Mexico* 56C4
Bolton *Eng* 7C3
Bolu *Turk* 40B1
Bolungarvik *Iceland* 12A1
Bolus Hd, Pt *Irish Rep* 9A4
Bolvadin *Turk* 40B2
Bolzano *Italy* 16C1
Boma *Zaïre* 50B4
Bombala *Aust* 32D4
Bombay *India* 44A2
Bombetoka, Baie de, B *Madag* 51E5
Bombo *Uganda* 50D3
Bom Despacho *Brazil* 75C2
Bomdila *India* 43G3
Bomi Hills *Lib* 48A4
Bom Jesus da Lapa *Brazil* 73K6
Bomnak *USSR* 25O4
Bomokāndi, R *Zaïre* 50C3
Bomu, R *CAR/Zaïre* 50C3
Bon Air *USA* 65D3
Bonaire, I *Caribbean S* 69D4
Bonanza *Nic* 70D3
Bonavista *Can* 55N5
Bon, C *Tunisia* 16C3
Bondo *Zaïre* 50C3
Bondoukou *Ivory Coast* 48B4
Bône = 'Annaba
Bonesteel *USA* 60D2
Bonfim *Guyana* 73G3
Bongandanga *Zaïre* 50C3
Bongo, Massif des, Upland *CAR* 50C3
Bongor *Chad* 50B2
Bonham *USA* 63C2
Bonifacio, *Corsica* 16B2
Bonifacio,Str of, Chan, *Corsica/Sardinia* 16B2
Bonin Is = Ogasawara Gunto
Bonita Springs *USA* 67B3
Bonito *Brazil* 75A3
Bonn *W Germ* 18B2
Bonners Ferry *USA* 58C1
Bonny *Nigeria* 48C4
Bonthain *Indon* 32A1
Bonthe *Sierra Leone* 48A4
Booaaso *Somalia* 50E2
Booligal *Aust* 34B2
Boonah *Aust* 34D1
Boone, Colorado *USA* 62B1
Boone, Iowa *USA* 61E2
Boone, North Carolina *USA* 67B1
Boonville *USA* 65D2
Boorowa *Aust* 34C2
Boothia,G of *Can* 55J2
Boothia Pen *Can* 55J2
Bootle *Eng* 7C3
Booué *Gabon* 50B4
Bophuthatswana, Self governing homeland *S Africa* 47C2
Boquillas *Mexico* 62B3
Bor *Sudan* 50D3
Bor *Turk* 40B2
Bor *Yugos* 17E2
Borah Peak, Mt *USA* 56B2
Borås *Sweden* 12G7
Borāzjān *Iran* 41F4
Bordeaux *France* 14B3
Borden I *Can* 54G2
Borden Pen *Can* 55K2
Bordentown *USA* 68C2
Borders, Region *Scot* 8D4
Bordertown *Aust* 34B3
Bordj bou Arréidj *Alg* 15C2
Bordj Omar Driss *Alg* 48C2
Borgå = Porvoo
Borgarnes *Iceland* 55Q3
Borger *USA* 56C3
Borgholm *Sweden* 12H7
Borislav *USSR* 19E3
Borisoglebsk *USSR* 21G5
Borisov *USSR* 20D5
Borisovka *USSR* 21F5
Borja *Par* 75A4
Borkou, Desert Region *Chad* 50B2
Borkum, I *W Germ* 13D1
Borlänge *Sweden* 12H6
Borneo, I *Indon/Malaysia* 27E6
Bornholm, I *Den* 12H7
Bornova *Turk* 17F3
Bornu, Region *Nigeria* 48D3
Boro, R *Sudan* 50C3

Borogontsy
Buriram

Borogontsy *USSR* 25P3
Boromo *Burkina* 48B3
Boron *USA* 66D3
Borovichi *USSR* 20E4
Borroloola *Aust* 32C2
Borsa *Rom* 17E1
Borūjen *Iran* 41F3
Borūjerd *Iran* 41E3
Bory Tucholskie, Region *Pol* 18D2
Borzna *USSR* 19G2
Borzya *USSR* 25N4
Bose *China* 31B5
Boshof *S Africa* 47D2
Bosna, R *Yugos* 17D2
Bōsō-hantō, B *Japan* 29D3
Bosporus = Karadeniz Boğazi
Bosquet *Alg* 15C2
Bossangoa *CAR* 50B3
Bossèmbélé *CAR* 50B3
Bossier City *USA* 63D2
Bosten Hu, L *China* 24K5
Boston *Eng* 7D3
Boston *USA* 57F2
Boston Mts *USA* 57D3
Botād *India* 42C4
Botevgrad *Bulg* 17E2
Bothaville *S Africa* 47D2
Bothnia,G of *Fin/Sweden* 20B3
Botletli, R *Botswana* 51C6
Botoşani *Rom* 21D6
Botswana, Republic *Africa* 51C6
Botte Donato, Mt *Italy* 16D3
Bottineau *USA* 60C1
Bottrop *W Germ* 13D2
Botucatu *Brazil* 75C3
Botuporã *Brazil* 75D1
Botwood *Can* 55N5
Bouaké *Ivory Coast* 46D7
Bouar *CAR* 50B3
Bouârfa *Mor* 48B1
Bouca *CAR* 50B3
Boufarik *Alg* 15C2
Bougainville, I *PNG* 33E1
Bougaroun, C *Algeria* 16B3
Bougie = Bejaïa
Bougouni *Mali* 48B3
Bouhalla, Djebel, Mt *Mor* 15A2
Bouillon *France* 13C3
Bouïra *Alg* 15C2
Bou Izakarn *Mor* 48B2
Boulay-Moselle *France* 13D3
Boulder, Colorado *USA* 56C2
Boulder, Montana *USA* 58D1
Boulder City *USA* 56B3
Boulder Creek *USA* 66A2
Boulogne *France* 14C1
Boumba, R *CAR/Cam* 50B3
Bouna *Ivory Coast* 48B4
Boundary Peak, Mt *USA* 56B3
Boundiali *Ivory Coast* 48B4
Bountiful *USA* 58D2
Bounty Is *NZ* 33G5
Bourail *New Caledonia* 33F3
Bourbonne-les-Bains *France* 13C4
Bourem *Mali* 48B3
Bourg *France* 14D2
Bourg de Péage *France* 14D2
Bourges *France* 14C2
Bourg-Madame *France* 14C3
Bourgogne, Region *France* 14C2
Bourke *Aust* 34C2
Bournemouth *Eng* 7D4
Bou Saâda *Alg* 15C2
Bousso *Chad* 50B2
Boutilimit *Maur* 48A3
Bouvet I *Atlantic O* 52J7
Bowbells *USA* 60C1
Bowen *Aust* 32D2
Bowie, Arizona *USA* 59E4
Bowie, Texas *USA* 63C2
Bowland Fells *Eng* 6C3
Bowling Green, Kentucky *USA* 57E3
Bowling Green, Missouri *USA* 63D1
Bowling Green, Ohio *USA* 64C2
Bowling Green, Virginia *USA* 65D3
Bowman *USA* 60C1
Bowmanville *Can* 65D2
Bowna, L *Irish Rep* 9C3
Bowral *Aust* 34D2
Bo Xian *China* 31D3
Boxing *China* 31D2
Boyabat *Turk* 40B1
Boyali *CAR* 50B3
Boyarka *USSR* 19G2
Boyd *Can* 54J4
Boyertown *USA* 68C2
Boyle *Irish Rep* 10B3
Boyne, R *Irish Rep* 9C3
Boynton Beach *USA* 67B3
Boyoma Falls *Zaïre* 50C3
Boysen Res *USA* 58E2
Bozanski Brod *Yugos* 17D1
Bozca Ada, I *Turk* 17F3
Boz Dağlari, Mts *Turk* 17F3
Bozeman *USA* 56B2
Bozen = Bolzano
Bozene *Zaïre* 50B3
Bozoum *CAR* 50B3
Brač, I *Yugos* 16D2
Bracadale, Loch, Inlet *Scot* 8B3
Bracciano, L di *Italy* 16C2
Bracebridge *Can* 65D1
Brach *Libya* 49D2
Bräcke *Sweden* 12H6
Brackettville *USA* 62B3
Bradenton *USA* 67B3
Bradford *Eng* 6D3
Bradford *USA* 68A2
Bradley *USA* 66B3
Brady *USA* 62C2
Brae *Scot* 8E1
Braemar *Scot* 8D3
Braga *Port* 15A1
Bragança *Brazil* 73J4
Bragança *Port* 15A1
Bragança Paulista *Brazil* 75C3
Brahman-Baria *Bang* 43G4
Brāhmani, R *India* 43F4
Brahmaputra, R *India/Bang* 43G3
Brăila *Rom* 21D6
Brainerd *USA* 57D2
Braintree *Eng* 7E4
Brak, R *S Africa* 47C3
Brake *W Germ* 13E1
Brakna, Region *Maur* 48A3
Bralorne *Can* 54F4
Brampton *Can* 65D2
Brampton *Eng* 6C2
Bramsche *W Germ* 13D1
Branco, R *Brazil* 72F3
Brandberg, Mt *Namibia* 51B6
Brandenburg *E Germ* 18C2
Brandfort *S Africa* 47D2
Brandon *Can* 56D2
Brandon *USA* 61D2
Brandvlei *S Africa* 47C3
Brandýs-nad-Laben *Czech* 18C2
Braniewo *Pol* 19D2
Brantford *Can* 57E2
Branxholme *Aust* 34B3
Bras d'Or Lakes *Can* 55M5
Brasiléia *Brazil* 72E6
Brasília *Brazil* 73J7
Brasília de Minas *Brazil* 75D2
Braşov *Rom* 17F1
Bratislava *Czech* 18D3
Bratsk *USSR* 25M4
Bratslav *USSR* 19F3
Brattleboro *USA* 65E2
Braunschweig *W Germ* 18C2
Brava, I *Cape Verde* 48A4
Brawley *USA* 56B3
Bray *Irish Rep* 9C3
Bray I *Can* 55L3
Bray-sur-Seine *France* 13B3
Brazil, Republic *S America* 71E5
Brazil Basin *Atlantic O* 52G5
Brazos, R *USA* 56D3
Brazzaville *Congo* 50B4
Brdy, Upland *Czech* 18C3
Breaksea Sd *NZ* 35A3
Bream B *NZ* 35B1
Brechin *Scot* 8D3
Brecht *Belg* 13C2
Breckenridge, Minnesota *USA* 61D1
Breckenridge, Texas *USA* 62C2
Breckland *Eng* 7E3
Břeclav *Czech* 18D3
Brecon *Wales* 7C4
Brecon Beacons, Mts *Wales* 7C4
Brecon Beacons Nat Pk *Wales* 7B3
Breda *Neth* 18A2
Bredasdorp *S Africa* 47C3
Bredbyn *Sweden* 12H6
Bredy *USSR* 20K5
Breede, R *S Africa* 47B3
Breezewood *USA* 65D2
Breiðafjörður, B *Iceland* 12A1
Breisach *W Germ* 13D3
Bremen *USA* 67A2
Bremen *W Germ* 18B2
Bremerhaven *W Germ* 18B2
Bremerton *USA* 58B1
Bremervörde *W Germ* 13E1
Brendel *USA* 59E3
Brenham *USA* 63C2
Brenner, P *Austria/Italy* 18C3
Brenner, Pass *Austria* 14E2
Brentwood *USA* 66B2
Brescia *Italy* 16C1
Breslau = Wrocław
Bressay, I *Scot* 8E1
Bressuire *France* 14B2
Brest *France* 14B2
Brest *USSR* 19E2
Bretagne, Region *France* 14B2
Breteuil *France* 13B3
Breton Sd *USA* 63E3
Breton Woods *USA* 68C2
Brett,C *NZ* 35B1
Brevard *USA* 67B1
Brewarrina *Aust* 34C1
Brewer *USA* 65F2
Brewster, New York *USA* 68D2
Brewster, Washington *USA* 58C1
Brewton *USA* 67A2
Breyten *S Africa* 47D2
Brezhnev *USSR* 20J4
Brežice *Yugos* 16D1
Bria *CAR* 50C3
Briançon *France* 14D3
Briare *France* 14C2
Bridgend *Wales* 7C4
Bridge of Orchy *Scot* 8C3
Bridgeport, Alabama *USA* 67A2
Bridgeport, California *USA* 59C3
Bridgeport, Connecticut *USA* 65E2
Bridgeport, Nebraska *USA* 60C2
Bridgeport, Texas *USA* 63C2
Bridgeport Res *USA* 66C1
Bridger *USA* 58E1
Bridger Peak *USA* 60B2
Bridgeton *USA* 68C3
Bridgetown *Barbados* 69R3
Bridgewater *Can* 55M5
Bridgewater *USA* 68E2
Bridgwater *Eng* 7C4
Bridgwater B *Eng* 7C4
Bridlington *Eng* 6D2
Bridlington Bay *Eng* 6E3
Bridport *Aust* 34C4
Bridport *Eng* 7C4
Brienne-le-Château *France* 13C3
Briey *France* 13C3
Brig *Switz* 16B1
Brigham City *USA* 56B2
Bright *Aust* 34C3
Brighton *Eng* 7D4
Brilhante, R *Brazil* 75A3
Brilon *W Germ* 13E2
Brindisi *Italy* 17D2
Brinkley *USA* 63D2
Brisbane *Aust* 33E3
Bristol, Connecticut *USA* 65E2
Bristol *Eng* 7C4
Bristol, Pennsylvania *USA* 65E2
Bristol, Rhode Island *USA* 68E2
Bristol, Tennessee *USA* 57E3
Bristol *USA* 64C3
Bristol Chan *Eng/Wales* 7B4
British Columbia, Province *Can* 54F4
British Empire Range, Mts *Can* 55K1
British Mts *Can* 54E3
Brits *S Africa* 47D2
Britstown *S Africa* 47C3
Britton *USA* 61D1
Brive *France* 14C2
Brixham *Eng* 7C4
Brno *Czech* 18D3
Broad, R *USA* 67B2
Broadalbin *USA* 68C1
Broadback, R *Can* 55L4
Broad Bay, Inlet *Scot* 8B2
Broadford *Scot* 8C3
Broad Haven, B *Irish Rep* 9B2
Broadstairs *Eng* 7E4
Broadus *USA* 60B1
Broadwater *USA* 60C2
Brochet *Can* 54H4
Brock I *Can* 54G2
Brockport *USA* 65D2
Brockton *USA* 68E1
Brockville *Can* 65D2
Brockway *USA* 68A2
Brodeur Pen *Can* 55K2
Brodick *Scot* 8C4
Brodnica *Pol* 19D2
Brody *USSR* 21D5
Brokem Haltern *W Germ* 13D2
Broken Bow, Nebraska *USA* 60D2
Broken Bow, Oklahoma *USA* 63D2
Broken Bow L *USA* 63D2
Broken Hill *Aust* 32D4
Bromsgrove *Eng* 7C3
Brønnøysund *Nor* 12G5
Bronx, Borough, New York *USA* 68D2
Brooke's Pt *Phil* 27E6
Brookfield, Missouri *USA* 61E3
Brookfield, Wisconsin *USA* 64B2
Brookhaven *USA* 57D3
Brookings, Oregon *USA* 58B2
Brookings, South Dakota *USA* 56D2
Brookline *USA* 68E1
Brooklyn *USA* 61E2
Brooklyn, Borough, New York *USA* 68D2
Brooklyn Center *USA* 61E1
Brooks *Can* 54G4
Brooks Range, Mts *USA* 54C3
Brooksville *USA* 67B3
Brooloo *Aust* 34D1
Broome *Aust* 32B2
Broom, Loch, Estuary *Scot* 8C3
Brora *Scot* 8D2
Brothers *USA* 58B2
Broughton *Eng* 6C2
Broughty Ferry *Scot* 8D3
Broulkou, Well *Chad* 50B2
Brovary *USSR* 19G2
Browerville *USA* 61E1
Brownfield *USA* 62B2
Brownsville *USA* 56D4
Brownwood *USA* 56D3
Browse I *Aust* 27F8
Bruay-en-Artois *France* 13B2
Bruce,Mt *Aust* 32A3
Bruce Pen *Can* 64C1
Bruchsal *W Germ* 13E3
Bruck an der Mur *Austria* 18D3
Brugge = Bruges
Bruges *Belg* 13B2
Brühl *W Germ* 13D2
Brûk, Wadi el *Egypt* 45B3
Brumado *Brazil* 75D1
Brumath *France* 13D3
Bruneau *USA* 58C2
Bruneau, R *USA* 58C2
Brunei, State *Borneo* 27E6
Brunico *Italy* 16C1
Brunner,L *NZ* 35B2
Brunsbüttel *W Germ* 13E1
Brunswick, Georgia *USA* 57E3
Brunswick, Maine *USA* 65F2
Brunswick, Mississippi *USA* 61E3
Brunswick,Pen de *Chile* 74B8
Bruny I *Aust* 34C4
Brusenets *USSR* 20G3
Brush *USA* 60C2
Brus Laguna *Honduras* 69A3
Brüssel = Brussels
Brussels *Belg* 18A2
Bruxelles = Brussels
Bruyères *France* 13D3
Bryan *USA* 56D3
Bryan,Mt *Aust* 34A2
Bryansk *USSR* 20E5
Bryant *USA* 63D2
Bryce Canyon Nat Pk *USA* 59D3
Brzeg *Pol* 18D2
Būbiyan, I *Kuwait* 41E4
Bubu, R *Tanz* 50D4
Bubye, R *Zim* 47E1
Bucaramanga *Colombia* 72D2
Buchan, Oilfield *N Sea* 8E3
Buchanan *Lib* 48A4
Buchanan,L *USA* 62C2
Buchan Deep *N Sea* 8E3
Buchan G *Can* 55L2
Buchan Ness, Pen *Scot* 10C2
Buchans *Can* 55N5
Bucharest *Rom* 17F2
Buchon,Pt *USA* 66B3
Bückeburg *W Germ* 13E1
Buckeye *USA* 59D4
Buckhaven *Scot* 8D3
Buckie *Scot* 8D3
Buckingham *Eng* 7D3
Bucksport *USA* 65F2
Buco Zau *Congo* 50B4
Bucureşti = Bucharest
Budapest *Hung* 19D3
Budaun *India* 42D3
Bude *Eng* 7B4
Bude *USA* 63D2
Budennovsk *USSR* 21G7
Budhana *India* 43J1
Budhîya, Gebel *Egypt* 45B4
Büdingen *W Germ* 13E2
Budva *Yugos* 17D2
Buéa *Cam* 48C4
Buellton *USA* 66B3
Buenaventura *Colombia* 72C3
Buenaventura *Mexico* 62A3
Buena Vista, Colorado *USA* 60B3
Buena Vista, Virginia *USA* 65D3
Buena Vista L *USA* 66C3
Buenos Aires *Arg* 74E4
Buenos Aires, State *Arg* 74E5
Buenos Aires, Lago *Arg* 74B7
Buffalo, Mississipi *USA* 63D1
Buffalo, New York *USA* 57F2
Buffalo, S Dakota *USA* 60C1
Buffalo, Texas *USA* 63C2
Buffalo, Wyoming *USA* 56C2
Buffalo, R *S Africa* 47E2
Buffalo Hump, Mt *USA* 58C1
Buffalo L *Can* 54G3
Buffalo Narrows *Can* 54H4
Buford *USA* 67B2
Buftea *Rom* 17F2
Bug, R *Pol/USSR* 19E2
Buga *Colombia* 72C3
Bugdayli *USSR* 41F2
Bugrino *USSR* 20H2
Bugulma *USSR* 20J5
Buguruslan *USSR* 20J5
Buḩayrat al Asad, Res *Syria* 40C2
Buhl, Idaho *USA* 58D2
Buhl, Minnesota *USA* 61E1
Builth Wells *Wales* 7C3
Bujumbura *Burundi* 50C4
Buka, I *PNG* 33E1
Bukama *Zaïre* 51C4
Bukavu *Zaïre* 50C4
Bukhara *USSR* 38E2
Bukittinggi *Indon* 27D7
Bukoba *Tanz* 50D4
Bula *Indon* 27G7
Bulan *Phil* 27F5
Bulandshahr *India* 42D3
Bulawayo *Zim* 51C6
Buldan *Turk* 17F3
Buldāna *India* 42D4
Bulgan *Mongolia* 26D2
Bulgaria, Republic *Europe* 17E2
Buller, R *NZ* 35B2
Buller,Mt *Aust* 34C3
Bullfinch *Aust* 32A4
Bulloo, R *Aust* 34B1
Bulloo Downs *Aust* 34B1
Bulloo L *Aust* 34B1
Bull Shoals Res *USA* 63D1
Bulolo *PNG* 32D1
Bultfontein *S Africa* 47D2
Bulu, Gunung, Mt *Indon* 27E6
Bumba *Zaïre* 50C3
Bu Menderes, R *Turk* 21D8
Bumphal Dam *Thai* 30B2
Buna *Kenya* 50D3
Bunbury *Aust* 32A4
Buncrana *Irish Rep* 9C2
Bundaberg *Aust* 33E3
Bundarra *Aust* 34D2
Bünde *W Germ* 13E1
Bündi *India* 42D3
Bungay *Eng* 7E3
Bungil, R *Aust* 34C1
Bungo *Angola* 51B4
Bungo-suidō, Str *Japan* 28B4
Bunguran, I *Indon* 27D6
Bunguran, Kepulauan, I *Indon* 27D6
Bunia *Zaïre* 50D3
Bunker *USA* 63D1
Bunkie *USA* 63D2
Bunnell *USA* 67B3
Buntok *Indon* 27E7
Buol *Indon* 27F6
Buram *Sudan* 50C2
Burang *China* 43E2
Burāq *Syria* 45D2
Buraydah *S Arabia* 41D4
Burbank *USA* 59C4
Burcher *Aust* 34C2
Burco *Somalia* 50E3
Burdur *Turk* 21E8
Burē *Eth* 50D2
Bure, R *Eng* 7E3
Bureinskiy Khrebet, Mts *USSR* 26G1
Bureya *USSR* 26F2
Bûr Fu'ad *Egypt* 45B3
Burg *E Germ* 18C2
Burgas *Bulg* 17F2
Burgaw *USA* 67C2
Burgersdorp *S Africa* 47D3
Burgos *Spain* 15B1
Burgsteinfurt *W Germ* 13D1
Burgsvik *Sweden* 19D1
Burhaniye *Turk* 17F3
Burhānpur *India* 42D4
Buriram *Thai* 30C2

Buritis

Cariacíca

Buritis *Brazil* 75C2
Burketown *Aust* 32C2
Burkina, Republic *W Africa* 48B3
Burks Falls *Can* 65D1
Burley *USA* 56B2
Burlington, Colorado *USA* 60C3
Burlington, Iowa *USA* 57D2
Burlington, New Jersey *USA* 68C2
Burlington, North Carolina *USA* 67C1
Burlington, Vermont *USA* 57F2
Burlington, Washington *USA* 58B1
Burma, Republic *Asia* 39H3
Burnet *USA* 62C2
Burney *USA* 58B2
Burnham *USA* 68B2
Burnham-on-Crouch *Eng* 7E4
Burnie *Aust* 32D5
Burnley *Eng* 6C3
Burns *USA* 58C2
Burns Lake *Can* 54F4
Burqin *China* 24K5
Burra *Aust* 34A2
Burragorang,L *Aust* 34D2
Burray, I *Scot* 8D2
Burren Junction *Aust* 34C2
Burrinjuck Res *Aust* 34C2
Burro, Serranías del, Mts *Mexico* 62B3
Burrow Head, Pt *Scot* 8C4
Burrundie *Aust* 27G8
Bursa *Turk* 21D7
Bur Safâga *Egypt* 40B4
Bûr Saïd = Port Said
Bûr Taufiq *Egypt* 45B4
Burton *USA* 64C2
Burton upon Trent *Eng* 7D3
Burtrask *Sweden* 12J6
Burtundy *Aust* 34B2
Buru, I *Indon* 27F7
Burundi, Republic *Africa* 50C4
Burwell *USA* 60D2
Bury *Eng* 7C3
Buryat ASSR, Republic *USSR* 25N4
Burynshik *USSR* 21J6
Bury St Edmunds *Eng* 7E3
Bushan *China* 28A3
Būshehr *Iran* 41F4
Bushmills *N Ire* 9C2
Busira, R *Zaïre* 50B4
Buskozdroj *Pol* 19E2
Buşrá ash Shām *Syria* 45D2
Bussang *France* 13D4
Busselton *Aust* 32A4
Busto Arsizio *Italy* 16B1
Buta *Zaïre* 50C3
Butare *Rwanda* 50C4
Bute, I *Scot* 8C4
Butha Qi *China* 26F2
Butler *USA* 65D2
Buton, I *Indon* 32B1
Butta *Togo* 48C4
Butte *USA* 56B2
Butterworth *Malay* 30C4
Butterworth *S Africa* 47D3
Butt of Lewis, C *Scot* 10B2
Button Is *Can* 55M3
Buttonwillow *USA* 66C3
Butuan *Phil* 27F6
Buturlinovka *USSR* 21G5
Butwal *Nepal* 43E3
Butzbach *W Germ* 13E2
Buulo Barde *Somalia* 50E3
Buur Hakaba *Somalia* 50E3
Buxton *Eng* 7D3
Buy *USSR* 20G4
Buyant Ovoo *Mongolia* 31B1
Buynaksk *USSR* 21H7
Buyr Nuur, L *Mongolia* 25N5
Büyük Ağrı Dağı, Mt *Turk* 21G8
Büyük Menderes, R *Turk* 40A2
Buzău *Rom* 17F1
Buzău, R *Rom* 17F1
Búzios, Ponta dos, Pt *Brazil* 75D3
Buzuluk *USSR* 20J5
Buzzards B *USA* 68E2
Byala *Bulg* 17F2
Byala Slatina *Bulg* 17E2
Byam Martin, Chan *Can* 54H2
Byam Martin I *Can* 54H2
Byblos, Hist site *Lebanon* 45C1
Bydgoszcz *Pol* 19D2
Byers *USA* 60C3
Bygland *Nor* 12F7
Bykhov *USSR* 19G2
Bylot I *Can* 55L2
Byrock *Aust* 34C2
Byron *USA* 66B2
Byron, C *Aust* 34D1
Bytantay, R *USSR* 25P3
Bytom *Pol* 19D2

C

Caacupú *Par* 74E3
Caaguazú *Par* 75A4
Caála *Angola* 51B5
Caapucú *Par* 75A4
Caarapó *Brazil* 75B3
Caazapá *Par* 74E3
Caballería, Cabo de, C *Spain* 15C1
Caballo Res *USA* 62A2
Cabanatuan *Phil* 27F5
Cabano *Can* 65F1
Cabedelo *Brazil* 73M5
Cabeza del Buey *Spain* 15A2
Cabimas *Ven* 72D1
Cabinda *Angola* 50B4
Cabinda, Province *Angola* 50B4
Cabinet Mts *USA* 58C1
Cabo Frio *Brazil* 75D3
Cabonga,Réservoire *Can* 55L5
Caboolture *Aust* 34D1
Cabora Bassa Dam *Mozam* 51D5
Caborca *Mexico* 70A1
Cabot Str *Can* 55M5
Cabra *Spain* 15B2
Cabral, Serra do, Mts *Brazil* 75D2
Cabreira, Mt *Port* 15A1
Cabrera, I *Spain* 15C2
Cabriel, R *Spain* 15B2
Čačak *Yugos* 17E2
Cacapon, R *USA* 68A3
Cáceres *Brazil* 73G7
Cáceres *Spain* 15A2
Cache, R *USA* 63D1
Cache Creek, R *USA* 66A1
Cache Peak, Mt *USA* 58D2
Cachi *Arg* 74C3
Cachimbo *Brazil* 73G5
Cachimbo, Serra do, Mts *Brazil* 73G5
Cachoeira *Brazil* 73L6
Cachoeira Alta *Brazil* 75B2
Cachoeira de Paulo Afonso, Waterfall *Brazil* 73L5
Cachoeira do Sul *Brazil* 74F4
Cachoeiro de Itapemirim *Brazil* 73K8
Cachuma,L *USA* 66C3
Cacolo *Angola* 51B5
Caconda *Angola* 51B5
Cactus *USA* 62B1
Caçu *Brazil* 75B2
Caculé *Brazil* 75D1
Caculuvar, R *Angola* 51B5
Čadca *Czech* 19D3
Cader Idris, Mt *Wales* 7C3
Cadillac *USA* 57E2
Cádiz *Spain* 15A2
Cádiz, Golfo de, G *Spain* 15A2
Caen *France* 14B2
Caernarfon *Wales* 7B3
Caernarfon B *Wales* 7B3
Caerphilly *Wales* 7C4
Caesarea, Hist Site *Israel* 45C2
Caetité *Brazil* 75D1
Cafayate *Arg* 74C3
Caga Tepe, Mt *Turk* 40B2
Cagayan de Oro *Phil* 27F6
Çagayan Sulu, I *Phil* 27E6
Cagliari, Sardinia 16B3
Cagliari, G di, Sardinia 16B3
Caguas *Puerto Rico* 69D3
Cahaba, R *USA* 67A2
Cahir *Irish Rep* 9C3
Cahore Pt *Irish Rep* 9C3
Cahors *France* 14C3
Caia *Mozam* 51D5
Caiabis, Serra dos, Mts *Brazil* 73G6
Caianda *Angola* 51C5
Caiapó, R *Brazil* 75B2
Caiapônia *Brazil* 75B2
Caiapó, Serra do, Mts *Brazil* 75B2
Caicó *Brazil* 73L5
Caicos Is *Caribbean S* 69C2
Caicos Pass *The Bahamas* 57F4
Cairngorms, Mts *Scot* 8D3
Cairnryan *Scot* 8C4
Cairns *Aust* 32D2
Cairo *Egypt* 40B3
Cairo *USA* 57E3
Caithness *Scot* 8D2
Caiwarro *Aust* 34B1
Cajabamba *Peru* 72C5
Cajamarca *Peru* 72C5
Calabar *Nigeria* 48C4
Calabozo *Ven* 69D5
Calafat *Rom* 17E2
Calafate *Arg* 74B8
Calahorra *Spain* 15B1
Calais *France* 14C1
Calais *USA* 65F1
Calama *Chile* 74C2
Calamar *Colombia* 72D3
Calamian Group, Is *Phil* 27E5
Calang *Indon* 27C6
Calanscio Sand Sea *Libya* 49E2
Calapan *Phil* 27F5
Calarasi *Rom* 17F2
Calatayud *Spain* 15B1
Calaveras Res *USA* 66B2
Calcasieu L *USA* 63D3
Calcutta *India* 43F4
Caldas da Rainha *Port* 15A2
Caldas Novas *Brazil* 73J7
Caldera *Chile* 74B3
Caldwell *USA* 56B2
Caledon *S Africa* 47B3
Caledon, R *S Africa* 47D3
Caledonia, Minnesota *USA* 64A2
Caledonia, New York *USA* 68B1
Caleta Olivia *Arg* 74C7
Calexico *USA* 56B3
Calgary *Can* 54G4
Calhoun *USA* 67B2
Calhoun Falls *USA* 67B2
Cali *Colombia* 72C3
Calicut *India* 44B3
Caliente, California *USA* 66C3
Caliente, Nevada *USA* 56B3
Caliente, New Mexico *USA* 62A1
California, State *USA* 56A3
California Aqueduct *USA* 66C3
California, G de *Mexico* 70A1
Calimera,Pt *India* 44B3
Calipatria *USA* 59C4
Calitzdorp *S Africa* 47C3
Callabonna, R *Aust* 34B1
Callabonna,L *Aust* 34A1
Callander *Can* 65D1
Callander *Scot* 8C3
Callao *Peru* 72C6
Callicoon *USA* 68C2
Caloosahatchee, R *USA* 67B3
Caloundra *Aust* 34D1
Caltanissetta, Sicily 16C3
Caluango *Angola* 51B4
Calulo *Angola* 51B5
Caluquembe *Angola* 51B5
Calvi, Corsica 16B2
Calvinia *S Africa* 47B3
Calw *W Germ* 13E3
Camacari *Brazil* 75E1
Camagüey *Cuba* 70E2
Camagüey,Arch de, Is *Cuba* 70E2
Camamu *Brazil* 75E1
Camaná *Peru* 72D7
Camapuã *Brazil* 75B2
Camargo *Bol* 72E8
Camarillo *USA* 66C3
Camarones *Arg* 74C6
Camas *USA* 58B1
Camaxilo *Angola* 51B4
Cambatela *Angola* 51B4
Cambodia, Republic *S E Asia* 30C3
Camborne *Eng* 7B4
Cambrai *France* 14C1
Cambria *USA* 66B3
Cambrian Mts *Wales* 7C3
Cambridge *Can* 64C2
Cambridge *Eng* 7E3
Cambridge *Jamaica* 69H1
Cambridge, Maryland *USA* 65D3
Cambridge, Massachussets *USA* 65E2
Cambridge, Minnesota *USA* 61E1
Cambridge *NZ* 35C1
Cambridge, Ohio *USA* 64C2
Cambridge, County *Eng* 7D3
Cambridge Bay *Can* 54H3
Cambridge G *Aust* 27F8
Cam Burun, Pt *Turk* 21F7
Camden, Arkansas *USA* 57D3
Camden *Aust* 34D2
Camden, New Jersey *USA* 65E3
Camden, New York *USA* 68C1
Camden, South Carolina *USA* 67B2
Cameron, Missouri *USA* 61E3
Cameron, Texas *USA* 63C2
Cameron I *Can* 54H2
Cameron Mts *NZ* 35A3
Cameroon, Federal Republic *Africa* 50B3
Cameroun, Mt *Cam* 48C4
Cametá *Brazil* 73J4
Camilla *USA* 67B2
Camino *USA* 66B1
Camiri *Bol* 72F8
Camocim *Brazil* 73K4
Camooweal *Aust* 32C2
Camorta, I, Nicobar Is *Indian O* 44E4
Campana, I *Chile* 74A7
Campbell *S Africa* 47C2
Campbell,C *NZ* 35B2
Campbell I *NZ* 37K7
Campbell,Mt *Can* 54E3
Campbellpore *Pak* 42C2
Campbell River *Can* 54F5
Campbellsville *USA* 64B3
Campbellton *Can* 55M5
Campbelltown *Aust* 34D2
Campbeltown *Scot* 8C4
Campeche *Mexico* 70C3
Campeche, B de *Mexico* 70C2
Camperdown *Aust* 34B3
Campina Grande *Brazil* 73L5
Campinas *Brazil* 73J8
Campina Verde *Brazil* 75C2
Camp Nelson *USA* 66C2
Campo *Cam* 48C4
Campobasso *Italy* 16C2
Campo Belo *Brazil* 75C3
Campo Florido *Brazil* 75C2
Campo Gallo *Arg* 74D3
Campo Grande *Brazil* 74F2
Campo Maior *Brazil* 73K4
Campo Mourão *Brazil* 74F2
Campos *Brazil* 75D3
Campos Altos *Brazil* 75C2
Camp Verde *USA* 59D4
Cam Ranh *Viet* 30D3
Camrose *Can* 54G4
Camucuio *Angola* 51B5
Canaan *Tobago* 69K1
Canaan *USA* 68D1
Canacupa *Angola* 51B5
Canada, Dominion *N America* 53F3
Cañada de Gómez *Arg* 74D4
Canadensis *USA* 68C2
Canadian *USA* 62B1
Canadian, R *USA* 56C3
Çanakkale *Turk* 21D7
Canandaigua *USA* 68B1
Canandaigua L *USA* 68B1
Cananea *Mexico* 70A1
Cananeia *Brazil* 75C4
Canarias, Islas = Canary Is
Canary Basin *Atlantic O* 52G3
Canary Is *Atlantic O* 48A2
Canastra, Serra da, Mts *Brazil* 75C3
Canatlán *Mexico* 70B2
Canaveral,C *USA* 57E4
Canavieiras *Brazil* 73L7
Canberra *Aust* 32D4
Canby, California *USA* 58B2
Canby, Minnesota *USA* 61D2
Candala *Somalia* 50E2
Çandarlı Körfezi, B *Turk* 17F3
Candlewood,L *USA* 68D2
Cando *USA* 60D1
Candor *USA* 68B1
Canelones *Urug* 74E4
Caney *USA* 63C1
Cangamba *Angola* 51C5
Cangombe *Angola* 51C5
Cangzhou *China* 31D2
Caniapiscau, R *Can* 55M4
Caniapiscau,L *Can* 55M4
Canicatti, Sicily 16C3
Canindé *Brazil* 73L4
Canisteo *USA* 68B1
Canisteo, R *USA* 68B1
Canjilon *USA* 62A1
Çankırı *Turk* 40B1
Canna, I *Scot* 8B3
Cannanore *India* 44B3
Cannes *France* 14D3
Cannock *Eng* 7C3
Cannonball, R *USA* 60C1
Cann River *Aust* 34C3
Canōas *Brazil* 74F3
Canoinhas *Brazil* 75B4
Canon City *USA* 60B3
Canopus *Aust* 34B2
Canora *Can* 54H4
Canowindra *Aust* 34C2
Cantabria, Region *Spain* 15B1
Cantabrica, Cord, Mts *Spain* 14A3
Canterbury *Eng* 7E4
Canterbury Bight, B *NZ* 35B2
Canterbury Plains *NZ* 35B2
Can Tho *Viet* 30D4
Cantil *USA* 66D3
Canton = Guangzhou
Canton, Mississippi *USA* 63E2
Canton, Missouri *USA* 64A2
Canton, Ohio *USA* 57E2
Canton, Pensylvania *USA* 68B2
Canton, S Dakota *USA* 61D2
Canton, I *Phoenix Is* 33H1
Cantu, Serra do, Mts *Brazil* 75B3
Canyon *USA* 62B2
Canyon City *USA* 58C2
Canyon Ferry L *USA* 58D1
Canyonlands Nat Pk *USA* 59E3
Canyonville *USA* 58B2
Canzar *Angola* 51C4
Cao Bang *Viet* 30D1
Caoshi *China* 28B2
Capanema *Brazil* 73J4
Capão Bonito *Brazil* 75C3
Caparaó, Serra do, Mts *Brazil* 75D3
Capbreton *France* 14B3
Cap Corse, C, Corsica 16B2
Cap de la Hague, C *France* 14B2
Cap-de-la-Madeleine *Can* 65E1
Capdepera *Spain* 15C2
Cape, Cabo etc : *see also individual cape name*
Cape Barren I *Aust* 34C4
Cape Basin *Atlantic O* 52J6
Cape Breton I *Can* 55N5
Cape Coast *Ghana* 48B4
Cape Cod B *USA* 65E2
Cape Fear, R *USA* 67C2
Cape Girardeau *USA* 63E1
Cape Horn *Chile* 74C8
Cape Johnson Depth *Pacific O* 36H4
Capelinha *Brazil* 75D2
Cape Lisburne *USA* 54B3
Capelongo *Angola* 51B5
Cape May *USA* 65E3
Cape Mendocino *USA* 54F5
Capenda Camulemba *Angola* 51B4
Cape Parry *Can* 54F2
Cape Province *S Africa* 47C3
Cape Town *S Africa* 47B3
Cape Verde, Is *Atlantic O* 52G4
Cape Verde Basin *Atlantic O* 52G4
Cape York Pen *Aust* 32D2
Cap-Haïtien *Haiti* 69C3
Capim, R *Brazil* 73J4
Capitán Bado *Par* 75A3
Capitol Reef Nat Pk *USA* 59E3
Capivari, R *Brazil* 75A2
Cappoquin *Irish Rep* 9C3
Cap Pt *St Lucia* 69P2
Capri, I *Italy* 16C2
Caprivi Strip, Region *Namibia* 51C5
Caquetá, R *Colombia* 72D4
Caracal *Rom* 17E2
Caracaraí *Brazil* 72F3
Caracas *Ven* 72E1
Caracol *Brazil* 75A3
Caraguatatuba *Brazil* 75C3
Carahue *Chile* 74B5
Caraí *Brazil* 75D2
Carandaí *Brazil* 75D3
Carandazal *Brazil* 75A2
Carangola *Brazil* 73K8
Caransebeş *Rom* 17E1
Caratasca *Honduras* 69A3
Caratasca, L de, Lg *Honduras* 70D3
Caratinga *Brazil* 75D2
Caravaca de la Cruz *Spain* 15B2
Caravelas *Brazil* 75E2
Carbonara, C, Sardinia 16B3
Carbondale, Illinois *USA* 64B3
Carbondale, Pennsylvania *USA* 68C2
Carbonear *Can* 55N5
Carbonia, Sardinia 16B3
Carcajou *Can* 54G4
Carcar Mts *Somalia* 50E2
Carcassonne *France* 14C3
Carcross *Can* 54E3
Cardamomes, Chaîne des, Mts *Camb* 30C3
Cardenas *Cuba* 70D2
Cardiff *Wales* 7C4
Cardigan *Wales* 7B3
Cardigan B *Wales* 7B3
Cardoso, Ilha do *Brazil* 75C4
Carei *Rom* 17E1
Careiro *Brazil* 73G4
Carey *USA* 64C2
Carhaix-Plouguer *France* 14B2
Carhué *Arg* 74D5
Cariacíca *Brazil* 73K8

Chaura Clyde

Chaura, I, Nicobar Is Indian O 44E4
Chaves Port 15A1
Chaykovskiy USSR 20J4
Cheb Czech 18C2
Cheboksary USSR 24F4
Cheboygan USA 57E2
Chechersk USSR 19G2
Chech'on S Korea 28B3
Checotah USA 63C1
Cheddar Eng 7C4
Cheduba I Burma 30A2
Cheepie Aust 34B1
Chegga Maur 48B2
Chegutu Zim 51D5
Chehalis USA 58B1
Cheju S Korea 28B4
Cheju Do, I S Korea 28B4
Cheju Haehyŏp, Str S Korea 28B4
Chekunda USSR 25P4
Chelan,L USA 58B1
Cheleken USSR 21J8
Chélia, Dj, Mt Algeria 16B3
Cheliff, R Alg 15C2
Chelkar USSR 38D1
Chelm Pol 19E2
Chełmno Pol 19D2
Chelmsford Eng 7E4
Cheltenham Eng 7C4
Chelyabinsk USSR 24H4
Chelyushin, Mys, C USSR 25M2
Chemba Mozam 51D5
Chemung, R USA 68B1
Chenab, R India/Pak 42D2
Chenachen Alg 48B2
Chenango, R USA 68C1
Cheney USA 58C1
Cheney Res USA 63C1
Chengde China 31D1
Chengdu China 31A3
Chengshan Jiao, Pt China 31E2
Chengzitan China 28A3
Chenxi China 31C4
Chen Xian China 31C4
Cheo Xian China 31D3
Chepén Peru 72C5
Chepstow Wales 7C4
Chequamegon B USA 64A1
Cher, R France 14C2
Cheraw USA 67C2
Cherbourg France 14B2
Cherchell Alg 15C2
Cherdyn USSR 20K3
Cheremkhovo USSR 25M4
Cherepovets USSR 20F4
Cherkassy USSR 21E6
Cherkessk USSR 21G7
Chernigov USSR 21E5
Chernobyl USSR 19G2
Chernovtsy USSR 21D6
Chernushka USSR 20K4
Chernyakhovsk USSR 20C5
Chernyye Zemli, Region USSR 21H6
Cherokee, Iowa USA 61D2
Cherokee, Oklahoma USA 62C1
Cherokees,L o'the USA 63D1
Cherrapunji India 43G3
Cherry, I Solomon Is 33F2
Cherskiy USSR 25S3
Cherskogo, Khrebet, Mts USSR 25Q3
Cherven' USSR 20D5
Chervonograd USSR 19E2
Chesapeake USA 65D3
Chesapeake B USA 65D3
Chesham Eng 7D4
Cheshire USA 68D1
Cheshire, County Eng 7C3
Chëshskaya Guba, B USSR 20H2
Chester, California USA 59B2
Chester Eng 7C3
Chester, Illinois USA 64B3
Chester, Massachusets USA 68D1
Chester, Montana USA 58D1
Chester, Pennsylvania USA 65D3
Chester, S Carolina USA 67B2
Chester, Vermont USA 68D1
Chester, R USA 68B3
Chesterfield Eng 7D3
Chesterfield, Îles Nouvelle Calédonie 33E2
Chesterfield Inlet Can 55J3
Chestertown USA 68B3
Chesuncook L USA 65F1
Chetumal Mexico 70D3
Cheviot NZ 35B2
Cheviots, Hills Eng/Scot 10C2
Cheyenne USA 60C2
Cheyenne, R USA 60C2
Cheyenne Wells USA 60C3
Chhapra India 43E3
Chhâtak Bang 43G3
Chhatarpur India 42D4
Chhindwāra India 42D4
Chhukha Bhutan 43F3
Chiange Angola 51B5
Chiang Kham Thai 30C2
Chiang Mai Thai 30B2
Chiayi Taiwan 31E5
Chiba Japan 29E3
Chibia Angola 51B5
Chibougamau Can 55L4
Chiburi-jima, I Japan 28B3
Chibuto Mozam 47E1
Chicago USA 57E2
Chicago Heights USA 64B2
Chichagof I USA 54E4
Chichester Eng 7D4
Chichibu Japan 29C3
Chichi-jima, I Japan 26H4
Chickamauga L USA 57E3
Chickasawhay, R USA 63E2
Chickasha USA 56D3
Chicken USA 54D3
Chiclayo Peru 72B5
Chico USA 56A3
Chico, R Arg 74C6
Chicoa Mozam 51D5
Chicopee USA 65E2
Chicoutimi Can 55L5
Chicualacuala Mozam 51D6
Chidambaram India 44B3
Chidley,C Can 55M3
Chiefland USA 67B3
Chiehn Lib 48B4
Chiengi Zambia 51C4
Chiers, R France 13C3
Chieti Italy 16C2
Chifeng China 31D1
Chifre, Serra do, Mts Brazil 73K7
Chigmit Mts USA 54C2
Chigubo Mozam 47E1
Chihuahua Mexico 70B2
Chihuahua, State Mexico 62A3
Chik Ballāpur India 44B3
Chikmagalūr India 44B3
Chikwawa Malawi 51D5
Chi-kyaw Burma 30A1
Chilakalūrupet India 44C2
Chilaw Sri Lanka 44B4
Childers Aust 34D1
Childress USA 62B2
Chile, Republic 71C6
Chililabombwe Zambia 51C5
Chilka L India 43F5
Chilko L Can 54F4
Chillán Chile 74B5
Chillicothe, Missouri USA 61E3
Chillicothe, Ohio USA 64C3
Chilmari India 43G3
Chiloé, Isla de Chile 74B6
Chilongozi Zambia 51D5
Chiloquin USA 58B2
Chilpancingo Mexico 70C3
Chiltern Hills, Upland Eng 7D4
Chilton USA 64B2
Chilumba Malawi 51D5
Chi-lung = Keelung
Chilwa, L Malawi 51D5
Chimanimani Zim 51D5
Chimay Belg 13C2
Chimbay USSR 24G5
Chimborazo, Mt Ecuador 72C4
Chimbote Peru 72C5
Chimkent USSR 24H5
Chimoio Mozam 51D5
China, Republic Asia 22F4
China Lake USA 66D3
Chinandega Nic 70D3
Chinati Peak, Mt USA 62B3
Chincha Alta Peru 72C6
Chinchilla Aust 34D1
Chinde Mozam 51D5
Chindo S Korea 28A4
Chindwin, R Burma 43G4
Chingola Zambia 51C5
Chinguar Angola 51B5
Chinguetti Maur 48A2
Chinhae S Korea 28B3
Chinhoyi Zim 51D5
Chiniot Pak 42C2
Chinju S Korea 28B3
Chinko, R CAR 50C3
Chino Japan 29C3
Chinsali Zambia 51D5
Chioggia Italy 16C1
Chipata Zambia 51D5
Chipinge Zim 51D6
Chiplūn India 44A2
Chippenham Eng 7C4
Chippewa, R USA 64A1
Chippewa Falls USA 57D2
Chippewa,L USA 64A1
Chipping Norton Eng 7D4
Chipping Sodbury Eng 7C4
Chira, R Peru 72B4
Chirāla India 44C2
Chiredzi Zim 51D6
Chirfa Niger 50B1
Chiricahua Peak, Mt USA 59E4
Chiriquí, G de Panama 70D4
Chiriquí, Lago de Panama 72B2
Chirpan Bulg 17F2
Chirripó Grande, Mt Costa Rica 72B2
Chirundu Zim 51C5
Chisamba Zambia 51C5
Chisholm USA 61E1
Chishui He, R China 31B4
Chisimaio = Kismaayo
Chistopol USSR 20H4
Chita USSR 26E1
Chitado Angola 51B5
Chitembo Angola 51B5
Chitose Japan 29D2
Chitradurga India 44B3
Chitral Pak 42C1
Chitré Panama 72B2
Chittagong Bang 43G4
Chittaurgarh India 42C4
Chittoor India 44B3
Chiume Angola 51C5
Chivilcoy Arg 74D4
Chivu Zim 51D5
Chizu Japan 29B3
Choch'iwŏn S Korea 28A3
Chocontá Colombia 72D2
Ch'o-do, I S Korea 28A4
Choele Choel Arg 74C5
Choiseul, I Solomon Is 33E1
Choix Mexico 70B2
Chojnice Pol 19D2
Chokai-san, Mt Japan 29D3
Choke Mts Eth 50D2
Chokurdakh USSR 25Q2
Cholame USA 66B3
Cholame Creek, R USA 66B3
Cholet France 14B2
Choluteca Honduras 72A1
Choma Zambia 51C5
Chŏmch'ŏn S Korea 28A3
Chomo Yummo, Mt China/India 43F3
Chomutov Czech 18C2
Chona, R USSR 25M3
Ch'ŏnan S Korea 28B3
Chon Buri Thai 30C3
Chonchon N Korea 28A2
Chone Ecuador 72C4
Chones, Archipiélago de las Chile 74B6
Chongdo S Korea 28A3
Ch'ŏngjin N Korea 28B2
Chŏngju N Korea 28B3
Ch'ŏngju S Korea 28B3
Chongoroi Angola 51B5
Chongpyong N Korea 28A3
Chongqing China 31B4
Chŏngsŏn S Korea 28A3
Chŏngŭp S Korea 28B3
Ch'ŏnju S Korea 28B3
Cho Oyu, Mt China/Nepal 43F3
Chopim, R Brazil 75B4
Chorley Eng 6C3
Chortkov USSR 19F3
Ch'ŏrwŏn S Korea 28B3
Chorzow Pol 19D2
Chosan N Korea 28A2
Chōshi Japan 29E3
Choszczno Pol 18D2
Chotanāgpur, Region India 43E4
Choteau USA 58D1
Chott ech Chergui, L Alg 48C1
Chott El Hodna, L Alg 15C2
Chott Melrhir, L Alg 48C1
Chowchilla USA 66B2
Choybalsan Mongolia 25N5
Christchurch Eng 7D4
Christchurch NZ 33G5
Christiana S Africa 47D2
Christian,C Can 55M2
Christianshab Greenland 55N3
Christmas I Indian O 36G5
Chu USSR 24J5
Chu, R USSR 24J5
Chubbuck USA 58D2
Chubut, R Arg 74C6
Chubut, State Arg 74C6
Chudovo USSR 20E4
Chudskoye Ozero, L USSR 24D4
Chugach Mts USA 54D3
Chūgoku-sanchi, Mts Japan 28B3
Chugwater USA 60C2
Chui Urug 74F4
Chukai Malay 30C5
Chukchagirskoye, Oz, L USSR 26G1
Chukotskiy Khrebet, Mts USSR 25T3
Chukotskiy Poluostrov, Pen USSR 25U3
Chu Lai Viet 30D2
Chula Vista USA 59C4
Chulman USSR 26F1
Chulucanas Peru 72B5
Chulumani Bol 72E7
Chulym USSR 24K4
Chulym, R USSR 25K4
Chuma, R USSR 25L4
Chumar India 42D2
Chumikan USSR 25P4
Chumphon Thai 30B3
Ch'unch'ŏn S Korea 28B3
Chunchura India 43F4
Ch'ungju S Korea 28B3
Chungking = Chongqing
Ch'ungmu S Korea 28A4
Chūngsan N Korea 28B3
Chungwa N Korea 28A3
Chunhua China 28C2
Chunya Tanz 51D4
Chunya, R USSR 25M3
Chunyang China 28B2
Ch'unyang S Korea 28A3
Chupara Pt Trinidad 69L1
Chuquicamata Chile 74C2
Chur Switz 16B1
Churāchāndpur India 43G4
Churapcha USSR 25P3
Churchill Can 55J4
Churchill, R, Labrador Can 55M4
Churchill, R, Manitoba Can 55J4
Churchill,C Can 55J4
Churchill Falls Can 55M4
Churchill L Can 54H4
Chūru India 42C3
Chusovoy USSR 20K4
Chuvash ASSR USSR 20H4
Chuxiong China 26D4
Chu Yang Sin, Mt Viet 30D3
Cianorte Brazil 75B3
Ciechanow Pol 19E2
Ciego de Ávila Cuba 70E2
Ciénaga Colombia 72D1
Cienfuegos Cuba 70D2
Cieszyn Pol 19D3
Cieza Spain 15B2
Cihanbeyli Turk 40B2
Cijara, Embalse de, Res Spain 15B2
Cilacap Indon 27D7
Cimarron USA 62B1
Cimarron, R USA 62C1
Cimone, Monte, Mt Italy 16C2
Cîmpina Rom 17F1
Cinca, R Spain 15C1
Cincer, Mt Yugos 16D2
Cincinatti USA 57E3
Cindrelu, Mt Rom 17E1
Cine, R Turk 17F3
Ciney Belg 13C2
Cinto, Monte, Mt, Corsica 16B2
Circle, Alaska USA 54D3
Circle, Montana USA 60B1
Circleville USA 64C3
Cirebon Indon 27D7
Cirencester Eng 7D4
Cisco USA 62C2
Citlaltepetl, Vol Mexico 70C3
Citrusdal S Africa 47B3
Ciudad Acuña Mexico 70B2
Ciudad Bolívar Ven 72F2
Ciudad Camargo Mexico 70B2
Ciudad del Carmen Mexico 70C3
Ciudadela Spain 15C2
Ciudad Guayana Ven 72F2
Ciudad Guzman Mexico 70B3
Ciudad Juárez Mexico 70B1
Ciudad Lerdo Mexico 56C4
Ciudad Madero Mexico 70C2
Ciudad Obregon Mexico 70B2
Ciudad Ojeda Ven 69C4
Ciudad Piar Ven 72F2
Ciudad Real Spain 15B2
Ciudad Rodrigo Spain 15A1
Ciudad Valles Mexico 70C2
Ciudad Victoria Mexico 70C2
Civitavecchia Italy 16C2
Cizre Turk 40D2
Clacton-on-Sea Eng 7E4
Claire,L Can 54G4
Clairton USA 65D2
Clanton USA 67A2
Clanwilliam S Africa 47B3
Clara Irish Rep 9C3
Clare USA 64C2
Claremont USA 65E2
Claremore USA 63C1
Clarence, R Aust 34D1
Clarence, R NZ 35B2
Clarence Str Aust 32C2
Clarendon USA 63D2
Clarenville Can 55N5
Claresholm Can 54G4
Clarinda USA 61D2
Clarion, Iowa USA 61E2
Clarion, Pennsylvania USA 65D2
Clarión, I Mexico 70A3
Clarion, R USA 65D2
Clarion Fracture Zone Pacific O 37M4
Clark Hill Res USA 57E3
Clark Mt USA 59C3
Clark,Pt Can 64C2
Clarksburg USA 64C3
Clarksdale USA 57D3
Clarkston USA 58C1
Clarksville, Arkansas USA 63D1
Clarksville, Tennessee USA 67A1
Claro, R Brazil 75B2
Claromecó Arg 74E5
Clay Center USA 61D3
Claymore, Oilfield N Sea 8E2
Clayton, New Mexico USA 56C3
Clayton, New York USA 65D2
Clear, C Irish Rep 10B3
Clearfield, Pennsylvania USA 68A2
Clearfield, Utah USA 58D2
Clear L USA 59B3
Clear Lake USA 61E2
Clear Lake Res USA 58B2
Clearmont USA 60B2
Clearwater USA 57E4
Clearwater Mts USA 58C1
Cleburne USA 56D3
Cleethorpes Eng 7D3
Clements USA 66B1
Clermont Aust 32D3
Clermont France 13B3
Clermont-en-Argonne France 13C3
Clermont-Ferrand France 14C2
Clervaux Lux 13D2
Cleveland, Mississippi USA 63D2
Cleveland, Ohio USA 57E2
Cleveland, Tennessee USA 67B1
Cleveland, Texas USA 63C2
Cleveland, County Eng 6D2
Clevelândia Brazil 75B4
Cleveland,Mt USA 58D1
Clew B Irish Rep 10B3
Clifton, Arizona USA 59E4
Clifton Aust 34D1
Clifton, New Jersey USA 68C2
Clifton Hills Aust 34A1
Clinch, R USA 67B1
Clinch Mts USA 67B1
Clinton, Arkansas USA 63D1
Clinton Can 54F4
Clinton, Connecticut USA 68D2
Clinton, Iowa USA 64A2
Clinton, Massachusetts USA 68E1
Clinton, Mississippi USA 63D2
Clinton, Missouri USA 63D1
Clinton, N Carolina USA 67C2
Clinton, New Jersey USA 68C2
Clinton, Oklahoma USA 62C1
Clinton-Colden L Can 54H3
Clipperton I Pacific O 70B3
Clitheroe Eng 6C3
Cliza Bol 72E7
Clogher Hd, Pt Irish Rep 9C3
Clonakilty B Irish Rep 9B4
Cloncurry Aust 32D3
Clones Irish Rep 9C3
Clonmel Irish Rep 9C3
Cloppenburg W Germ 13E1
Cloquet USA 57D2
Clorinda Arg 75A4
Cloud Peak, Mt USA 60B2
Cloverdale USA 66A1
Clovis, California USA 66C2
Clovis, New Mexico USA 56C3
Cluj Rom 21C6
Cluj-Napoca Rom 17E1
Clutha, R NZ 35A3
Clwyd, County Wales 7C3
Clwyd, R Wales 7C3
Clyde Can 55M2

Clyde Cranston

Clyde NZ 35A3
Clyde USA 68B1
Clyde, R Scot 8C4
Clydebank Scot 8C4
Coachella USA 59C4
Coahuila, State Mexico 62B3
Coaldale USA 59C3
Coalinga USA 59B3
Coalville Eng 7D3
Coalville USA 58D2
Coaraci Brazil 75E1
Coari, R Brazil 72F5
Coastal Plain USA 67A2
Coast Mts Can 54E4
Coast Ranges, Mts USA 56A2
Coatbridge Scot 8C4
Coatesville USA 68C3
Coaticook Can 65E1
Coats I Can 55K3
Coats Land, Region Ant 76F1
Coatzacoalcas Mexico 70C3
Cobalt Can 55L5
Cobán Guatemala 70C3
Cobar Aust 32D4
Cobargo Aust 34C3
Cobija Bol 72E6
Cobleskill USA 68C1
Cobourg Can 55L5
Cobourg Pen Aust 32C2
Coburg W Germ 18C2
Coca Ecuador 72C4
Cocalinho Brazil 75B1
Cochabamba Bol 72E7
Cochem W Germ 13D2
Cochin India 44B4
Cochrane, Ontario Can 55K5
Cochrane, Lago Arg/Chile 74B7
Cockburn Aust 34B2
Cockermouth Eng 6C2
Cockeysville USA 68B3
Cockpit Country,The Jamaica 69H1
Cockscomb, Mt S Africa 47C3
Coco, R Honduras/Nic 70D3
Cocoa USA 67B3
Cocobeach Eq Guinea 48C4
Coco Channel Andaman Is/Burma 44E3
Coco, Isla del Costa Rica 53K8
Côcos Brazil 75D1
Cocos B Trinidad 69L1
Cocos Is Indian O 36F5
Cocos Ridge Pacific O 37P4
Cod,C USA 57F2
Codfish I NZ 35A3
Cod I Can 55M4
Codi, Sierra del, Mts Spain 15C1
Codó Brazil 73K4
Cody USA 56C2
Coen Aust 27H8
Coesfeld W Germ 18B2
Coeur d'Alene USA 56B2
Coeur d'Alene L USA 58C1
Coevorden Neth 13D1
Coffeyville USA 56D3
Coff's Harbour Aust 34D2
Cofimvaba S Africa 47D3
Coghinas, Lago del, Sardinia 16B2
Cognac France 14B2
Cohocton USA 68B1
Cohocton, R USA 68B1
Cohoes USA 65E2
Cohuna Aust 34B3
Coiba, Isla Panama 72B2
Coihaique Chile 74B7
Coimbatore India 44B3
Coimbra Port 15A1
Cojimies Ecuador 72B3
Cokeville USA 58D2
Colac Aust 32D4
Colatina Brazil 73K7
Colbeck,C Ant 76F6
Colby USA 14B2
Colchester Eng 7E4
Colchester USA 68D2
Coldstream Scot 8D4
Coldwater USA 64C2
Coleman Can 58D1
Coleman, Michigan USA 64C2
Coleman, Texas USA 62C2
Colenso S Africa 47D2
Coleraine N Ire 9C2
Coleridge,L NZ 35B2
Colesberg S Africa 47D3
Coles, Puerta Peru 72D7
Coleville USA 66C1
Colfax, California USA 59B3
Colfax, Louisiana USA 63D2
Colfax, Washington USA 58C1
Colhué Huapí, Lago Arg 74C7
Colima Mexico 70B3
Coll, I Scot 8B3
Collarenebri Aust 34C1
College Park, Georgia USA 67B2
College Park, Washington DC USA 68B3
College Station USA 63C2
Collie Aust 32A4
Collier B Aust 32B2
Collines de l'Artois, Hills France 13A2
Collines de la Thiérache, Hills France 13B3
Collingwood Can 64C2
Collingwood NZ 35B2
Collins, Mississippi USA 63E2
Collins, New York USA 68A1
Collinson Pen Can 54H2
Collinsville Aust 32D3
Collinsville, Illinois USA 64B3
Collinsville, Oklahoma USA 63C1
Colmar France 14D2
Colne Eng 6C3
Colnett, Cabo, C Mexico 56B3
Cologne W Germ 18B2
Colômbia Brazil 75C3
Colombia USA 65D3
Colombia, Republic S America 72D3
Colombo Sri Lanka 44B4
Colón Arg 74E4
Colon Cuba 70D2
Colón Panama 72C2
Colón, Arch. de = Galapagos Is
Colonia Urug 74E4
Colonia Las Heras Arg 74C7
Colonial Heights USA 65D3
Colonsay, I Scot 8B3
Coloradito Ven 69E5
Colorado, R, Buenos Aires Arg 74D5
Colorado, R, Texas USA 56D3
Colorado, R USA/Mexico 56B3
Colorado, State USA 56C3
Colorado City USA 62B2
Colorado Plat USA 56B3
Colorado Springs USA 56C3
Columbia, Maryland USA 68B3
Columbia, Mississippi USA 63E2
Columbia, Missouri USA 57D3
Columbia, Pennsylvania USA 65D2
Columbia, S Carolina USA 57E3
Columbia, Tennessee USA 57E3
Columbia, R USA 56A2
Columbia Falls USA 58D1
Columbia,Mt Can 54G4
Columbia Plat USA 58C1
Columbine,C S Africa 47B3
Columbretes, Islas Spain 15C2
Columbus, Georgia USA 57E3
Columbus, Indiana USA 64B3
Columbus, Mississippi USA 57E3
Columbus, Montana USA 58E1
Columbus, Nebraska USA 56D2
Columbus, New Mexico USA 62A2
Columbus, Ohio USA 57E2
Columbus, Texas USA 63C3
Columbus, Wisconsin USA 64B2
Colville USA 58C1
Colville, R USA 54C3
Colville,C NZ 35C1
Colville L Can 54F3
Colwyn Bay Wales 7C3
Comanche USA 62C2
Comanche Res USA 66B1
Comandante Ferraz, Base Ant 76G2
Comayagua Honduras 70D3
Combeaufontaine France 13C4
Comber N Ire 9D2
Combermere B Burma 43G5
Comeragh Mts Irish Rep 9C3
Comfort USA 62C2
Comilla Bang 43G4
Comitán Mexico 70C3
Commercy France 13C3
Committee B Can 55K3
Como Italy 16B1
Comodoro Rivadavia Arg 74C7
Como, L di Italy 16B1
Comorin,C India 44B4
Comoros, Is, Republic Indian O 51E5
Compiègne France 14C2
Comprida, Ilha Brazil 75C3
Comunidad Valenciana, Region Spain 15B2
Cona China 43G3
Conakry Guinea 48A4
Concarneau France 14B2
Conceiçao da Barra Brazil 75E2
Conceição do Araguaia Brazil 73J5
Conceiçao do Mato Dentro Brazil 75D2
Concepción Arg 74E4
Concepción Brazil/Par 75A3
Concepción Chile 74B5
Concepción Par 74E2
Concepción del Oro Mexico 70B2
Conception B Namibia 47A1
Conception,Pt USA 56A3
Conchas Brazil 75C3
Conchas L USA 62B1
Conchos, R Mexico 56C4
Concord, California USA 59B3
Concord, New Hampshire USA 57F2
Concord, North Carolina USA 67B1
Concordia Arg 74E4
Concordia USA 56D3
Concrete USA 58B1
Condamine Aust 34D1
Condeuba Brazil 75D1
Condobolin Aust 32D4
Condon USA 58B1
Condroz, Mts Belg 13C2
Conecuh, R USA 67A2
Conesus L USA 68B1
Confuso, R Par 75A3
Congleton Eng 7C3
Congo, R W Africa 46F8
Congo, Republic Africa 46F8
Congo,R = Zaire
Coniston Can 64C1
Conneaut USA 64C2
Connecticut, R USA 65E2
Connecticut, State USA 57F2
Connellsville USA 65D2
Connersville USA 64B3
Conn, Lough, L Irish Rep 10B3
Conoble Aust 34B2
Conrad USA 58D1
Conroe USA 63C2
Conselheiro Lafaiete Brazil 75D3
Consett Eng 6D2
Con Son, Is Viet 30D4
Constanţa Rom 21D7
Constantine Algeria 16B3
Constitución Chile 74B5
Contact USA 58D2
Contas, R Brazil 73K6
Contrexéville France 13C3
Contwoyto L Can 54H3
Conway, Arkansas USA 57D3
Conway, New Hampshire USA 65E2
Conway, South Carolina USA 67C2
Conwy Wales 7C3
Conwy, R Wales 7C3
Coober Pedy Aust 32C3
Cookeville USA 67A1
Cook Inlet, B USA 54C3
Cook Is Pacific O 37L5
Cook,Mt NZ 35B2
Cookstown N Ire 9C2
Cook Str NZ 33G5
Cooktown Aust 32D2
Coolabah Aust 34C2
Cooladdi Aust 34C1
Coolah Aust 34C2
Coolamon Aust 34C2
Coolgardie Aust 32B4
Coolidge USA 59D4
Cooma Aust 34C3
Coonabarabran Aust 34C2
Coonambie Aust 34C2
Coonbah Aust 34B2
Coondapoor India 44A3
Coongoola Aust 34C1
Coonoor India 44B3
Cooper Basin Aust 34B1
Cooper Creek, R Aust 34B1
Cooper's Town Bahamas 67C3
Cooperstown, New York USA 68C1
Cooperstown, North Dakota USA 61D1
Coorong,The Aust 34A3
Cooroy Aust 34D1
Coos B USA 58B2
Coos Bay USA 58B2
Cootamundra Aust 32D4
Cootehill Irish Rep 9C2
Cope USA 60C3
Copenhagen Den 18C1
Copiapó Chile 74B3
Copper Center USA 54D3
Copper Cliff Can 64C1
Copper Harbor USA 64B1
Coppermine Can 54G3
Coppermine, R Can 54G3
Coppermine Pt Can 64C1
Coquilhatville = Mbandaka
Coquimbo Chile 74B3
Corabia Rom 17E2
Coral Gables USA 67B3
Coral Harbour Can 55K3
Coral S Aust/PNG 32E2
Coral Sea Basin Pacific O 36J5
Coral Sea Island Territories Aust 32E2
Corangamite,L Aust 34B3
Corantijn, R Guyana/Surinam 73G3
Corbeil-Essonnes France 13B3
Corbin USA 64C3
Corbridge Eng 6D2
Corby Eng 7D3
Corcoran USA 66C2
Corcovado, Golfo, G Chile 74B6
Corcubíon Spain 15A1
Cordele USA 57E3
Cordillera Cantabrica, Mts Spain 15A1
Cordillera Central, Mts Dom Rep/Haiti 69C3
Cordillera de Caaguazú Par 75A4
Cordillera Isabelia, Mts Nic 70D3
Cordillera Occidental, Mts Colombia 72C2
Cordillera Oriental, Mts Colombia 72C3
Cordillo Downs Aust 34B1
Córdoba Arg 74D4
Córdoba Mexico 70C3
Córdoba Spain 15B2
Córdoba, State Arg 74D4
Cordova USA 54D3
Corfu Greece 17D3
Corfu, I Greece 17D3
Coribe Brazil 75D1
Coricudgy,Mt Aust 34D2
Corigliano Calabro Italy 16D3
Coringa Is Aust 32E2
Corinth Greece 17E3
Corinth, Mississippi USA 57E3
Corinth, New York USA 68D1
Corinth, Gulf of Greece 17E3
Corinto Brazil 73K7
Cork Irish Rep 10B3
Çorlu Turk 40A1
Cornel Fabriciano Brazil 73K7
Cornélio Procópio Brazil 75B3
Corner Brook Can 55N5
Corner Inlet, B Aust 34C3
Cornimont France 13D4
Corning USA 65D2
Corno, Monte, Mt Italy 16C2
Cornwall Can 55L5
Cornwall, County Eng 7B4
Cornwall,C Eng 7B4
Cornwall I Can 54H2
Cornwallis I Can 55J2
Coro Ven 72E1
Coroatá Brazil 73K4
Coroico Bol 72E7
Coromandel Brazil 75C2
Coromandel Coast India 44C3
Coromandel Pen NZ 35C1
Coromandel Range, Mts NZ 35C1
Corona, California USA 66D4
Corona, New Mexico USA 62A2
Coronado, B. de Costa Rica 72B2
Coronation G Can 54G3
Coronel Chile 74B5
Coronel Fabriciano Brazil 75D2
Coronel Oviedo Par 74E3
Coronel Pringles Arg 74D5
Coropuna, Mt Peru 72D7
Corowa Aust 34C3
Corps France 14D3
Corpus Christi USA 56D4
Corpus Christi,L USA 63C3
Corraun Pen Irish Rep 9B3
Corregidor, I Phil 27F5
Corrente, R, Bahia Brazil 75D1
Corrente, R, Goias Brazil 75C1
Corrente, R, Mato Grosso Brazil 75B2
Correntina Brazil 75D1
Corrib, Lough, L Irish Rep 10B3
Corrientes Arg 74E3
Corrientes, State Arg 74E3
Corrientes, Cabo, C Colombia 72C2
Corrientes, Cabo, C Mexico 70B2
Corrigan USA 63D2
Corrigin Aust 32A4
Corryong Aust 34C3
Corse = Corsica
Corsewall Pt Scot 8C4
Corsica, I Medit S 16B2
Corsicana USA 56D3
Cort Adelaer, Kap, C Greenland 55O3
Corte, Corsica 16B2
Cortez USA 56C3
Cortina d'Ampezzo Italy 16C1
Cortland USA 65D2
Çoruh, R Turk 21G7
Çorum Turk 21F7
Corumbá Brazil 73G7
Corumbá, R Brazil 75C2
Corumbaiba Brazil 75C2
Corvallis USA 58B2
Corvo, I Azores 48A1
Corwen Wales 7C3
Cosenza Italy 16D3
Cosmoledo Is Seychelles 51E5
Coso Junction USA 66D2
Costa Blanca, Region Spain 15B2
Costa Brava, Region Spain 15C1
Costa Calída, Region Spain 15B2
Costa de Almería, Region Spain 15B2
Costa de la Luz, Region Spain 15A2
Costa del Sol, Region Spain 15B2
Costa Dorada, Region Spain 15C1
Costa Mesa USA 66D4
Costa Rica, Republic Cent America 70D3
Cotabato Phil 27F6
Cotagaita Bol 72E8
Côte d'Azur, Region France 14D3
Côte D'Ivoire = Ivory Coast
Côte-d'Or, Department France 13C4
Côtes de Meuse, Mts France 13C3
Cothi, R Wales 7B4
Cotonou Benin 48C4
Cotopaxi, Mt Ecuador 72C4
Cotswold Hills, Upland Eng 7C4
Cottage Grove USA 58B2
Cottbus E Germ 18C2
Cottonwood USA 59D4
Cotulla USA 62C3
Coudersport USA 68A2
Coulommiers France 13B3
Coulonge, R Can 65D1
Coulterville USA 66B2
Council USA 54B3
Council Bluffs USA 56D2
Coupar Angus Scot 8D3
Courtrai = Kortrijk
Coutances France 14B2
Coventry Eng 7D3
Covilhã Port 15A1
Covington, Georgia USA 67B2
Covington, Kentucky USA 64C3
Covington, Louisiana USA 63D2
Covington, Virginia USA 65D3
Cowal,L Aust 34C2
Cowangie Aust 34B3
Cowansville Can 65E1
Cowdenbeath Scot 8D3
Cowes Aust 34C3
Cowes Eng 7D4
Cowichan L Can 58B1
Cowlitz, R USA 58B1
Cowra Aust 34C2
Coxim Brazil 73H7
Coxim, R Brazil 75B2
Coxsackie USA 68D1
Cox's Bazar Bang 43G4
Coyote USA 66B2
Cozad USA 60D2
Cozumel, Isla de Mexico 70D2
Cracow Aust 34D1
Cracow Pol 19D2
Cradock S Africa 47D3
Craig USA 56C2
Craigavon N Ire 9C2
Crailsheim W Germ 18C3
Craiova Rom 17E2
Cranberry L USA 65E2
Cranbrook Can 54G5
Crane, Oregon USA 58C2
Crane, Texas USA 62B2
Cranston USA 68E2

De Long Mts Dubā

De Long Mts *USA* 54B3
Deloraine *Aust* 34C4
Deloraine *Can* 54H5
Delray Beach *USA* 67B3
Del Rio *USA* 56C4
Delta *USA* 56B3
Delta Res *USA* 68C1
Dembī Dolo *Eth* 50D3
Demer, R *Belg* 13C2
Demidov *USSR* 19G1
Deming *USA* 62A2
Demirköy *Turk* 17F2
Demopolis *USA* 63E2
Dem'yanskoye *USSR* 24H4
Denain *France* 14C1
Denau *USSR* 39E2
Denbigh *Wales* 7C3
Dendermond *Belg* 13C2
Dendi, Mt *Eth* 50D3
Dèndre, R *Belg* 13B2
Dengkou *China* 31B1
Deng Xian *China* 31C3
Den Haag = The Hague
Denham,Mt *Jamaica* 69H1
Den Helder *Neth* 18A2
Denia *Spain* 15C2
Deniliquin *Aust* 32D4
Denio *USA* 58C2
Denison, Iowa *USA* 61D2
Denison, Texas *USA* 56D3
Denizli *Turk* 21D8
Denmark, Kingdom *Europe* 12F7
Denmark Str *Greenland/Iceland* 76C1
Dennery *St Lucia* 69P2
Dennis Head, Pt *Scot* 8D2
Denpasar *Indon* 27E7
Denton, Maryland *USA* 68C3
Denton, Texas *USA* 56D3
D'Entrecasteaux Is *PNG* 32E1
Denver *USA* 56C3
Déo, R *Cam* 50B3
Déo, R *Cam/Nigeria* 48D4
Deoghar *India* 43F4
Deolāli *India* 42C5
Deoria, District *India* 43M2
Deosai Plain *India* 42D1
Depew *USA* 68A1
Deposit *USA* 68C1
Deputatskiy *USSR* 25Q3
De Queen *USA* 63D2
Dera Bugti *Pak* 42B3
Dera Ghazi Khan *Pak* 42C3
Dera Ismail Khan *Pak* 42C2
Derbent *USSR* 21H7
Derby *Aust* 32B2
Derby, Connecticut *USA* 68D2
Derby *Eng* 7D3
Derby, Kansas *USA* 63C1
Derby, County *Eng* 7D3
Dergachi *USSR* 21F5
Derg, Lough, L *Irish Rep* 10B3
De Ridder *USA* 63D2
Derna = Darnah
Derravaragh, L *Irish Rep* 9C3
Derry *USA* 68E1
Derudeb *Sudan* 50D2
De Rust *S Africa* 47C3
De Ruyter *USA* 68C1
Derwent, R *Eng* 6D3
Derwent Bridge *Aust* 34C4
Desaguadero, R *Bol* 72E7
Descanso *Mexico* 59C4
Deschutes, R *USA* 58B2
Desē *Eth* 50D2
Deseado *Arg* 74C7
Deseado, R *Arg* 74C7
Deserta Grande, I *Madeira* 48A1
Desert Center *USA* 59C4
Desert Peak, Mt *USA* 59D2
Desloge *USA* 63D1
Des Moines, Iowa *USA* 57D2
Des Moines, New Mexico *USA* 62B1
Des Moines, R *USA* 61E2
Desna, R *USSR* 21E5
Desolación, I *Chile* 74B8
Des Plaines *USA* 64B2
Dessau *E Germ* 18C2
Destruction Bay *Can* 54E3
Deta *Rom* 17E1
Dete *Zim* 51C5
Detmold *W Germ* 13E2
Detroit *USA* 57E2
Detroit Lakes *USA* 61D1
Det Udom *Thai* 30D3
Deva *Rom* 17E1
Deventer *Neth* 18B2
Deveron, R *Scot* 8D3
Devikot *India* 42C3
Devil Postpile Nat Mon *USA* 66C2
Devils Den *USA* 66C3
Devils Gate, P *USA* 66C1
Devil's Hole, Region *N Sea* 6E1
Devil's Island = Diable, Isla du
Devils L, N Dakota *USA* 60D1
Devils L, Texas *USA* 62B3
Devils Lake *USA* 56D2
Devizes *Eng* 7D4
Devli *India* 42D3
Devoll, R *Alb* 17E2
Devon, County *Eng* 7B4
Devon I *Can* 55J2
Devonport *Aust* 32D5
Dewangiri *Bhutan* 43G3
Dewās *India* 42D4
Dewetsdorp *S Africa* 47D2
Dewey Res *USA* 57E3
De Witt *USA* 63D2
Dewsbury *Eng* 6D3
Dexter, Missouri *USA* 63E1
Dexter, New Mexico *USA* 62B2
Deyang *China* 31A3
Deyhuk *Iran* 41G3
Dezfūl *Iran* 41E3
Dezhou *China* 31D2
Dezh Shāhpūr *Iran* 41E2
Dhab'i, Wadi edh *Jordan* 45D3
Dhahran *S Arabia* 41F4
Dhākā *Bang* 43G4
Dhali *Cyprus* 45B1
Dhamavaram *India* 44B3
Dhamtari *India* 43E4
Dhanbād *India* 43F4
Dhangarhi *Nepal* 43E3
Dhang Range, Mts *Nepal* 43M1
Dhankuta *Nepal* 43F3
Dhār *India* 42D4
Dharmapuri *India* 44B3
Dharmsāla *India* 42D2
Dhar Oualata, Desert Region *Maur* 48B3
Dhaulagiri, Mt *Nepal* 43E3
Dhenkānāl *India* 43F4
Dhībān *Jordan* 45C3
Dhíkti Óri, Mt *Greece* 17F3
Dhodhekánisos = Dodecanese
Dhomokós *Greece* 17E3
Dhone *India* 44B2
Dhoraji *India* 42C4
Dhrāngadhra *India* 42C4
Dhuburi *India* 43F3
Dhule *India* 42C4
Diable, Isle du *French Guiana* 73H2
Diablo,Mt *USA* 66B2
Diablo Range, Mts *USA* 59B3
Diamantina *Brazil* 73K7
Diamantina, R *Aust* 32D3
Diamantino *Brazil* 75A1
Diamond Harbour *India* 43F4
Diamond Springs *USA* 66B1
Diamondville *USA* 58D2
Dibā *UAE* 41G4
Dibaya *Zaïre* 51C4
Dibrugarh *India* 43G3
Dickens *USA* 62B2
Dickinson *USA* 56C2
Dickson *USA* 67A1
Dickson City *USA* 65D2
Dicle, R *Turk* 21G8
Didwāna *India* 42C3
Die Berg, Mt *S Africa* 47E2
Diébougou *Burkina* 48B3
Dieburg *W Germ* 13E3
Diego Ramírez, Islas *Chile* 74C9
Diégo Suarez = Antsirañana
Diekirch *Lux* 13D3
Diéma *Mali* 48B3
Dien Bien Phu *Viet* 30C1
Diepholz *W Germ* 18B2
Dieppe *France* 14C2
Diest *Belg* 13C2
Dieuze *France* 13D3
Diffa *Niger* 48D3
Digboi *India* 43H3
Digby *Can* 55M5
Digne *France* 14D3
Digoin *France* 14C2
Digos *Phil* 27F6
Digul, R *Indon* 32C1
Dihang, R *India/China* 43G3
Dijlah = Tigris
Dijon *France* 14C2
Dik *Chad* 50B3
Dikhil *Djibouti* 50E2
Dīkirnis *Egypt* 45A3
Diksmuide *Belg* 13B2
Dikson *USSR* 24K2
Dilaram *Afghan* 38E2
Dili *Indon* 27F7
Di Linh *Viet* 30D3
Dillenburg *W Germ* 13E2
Dilley *USA* 62C3
Dilling *Sudan* 50C2
Dillingham *USA* 54C4
Dillon *USA* 56B2
Dillsburg *USA* 68B2
Dilolo *Zaïre* 51C5
Dimāpur *India* 43G3
Dimashq = Damascus
Dimbelenge *Zaïre* 50C4
Dimbokro *Ivory Coast* 48B4
Dimitrovgrad *Bulg* 17F2
Dimitrovgrad *USSR* 20H5
Dimona *Israel* 45C3
Dinaget, I *Phil* 27F5
Dinajpur *India* 43F3
Dinan *France* 14B2
Dinant *Belg* 13C2
Dinar *Turk* 40B2
Dinder, R *Sudan* 50D2
Dindigul *India* 44B3
Dingbian *China* 31B2
Dinggyê *China* 43F3
Dingle *Irish Rep* 10A3
Dingle B *Irish Rep* 10A3
Dinguiraye *Guinea* 48A3
Dingwall *Scot* 8C3
Dingxi *China* 31A2
Ding Xian *China* 31D2
Dinh Lap *Viet* 30D1
Dinosaur *USA* 60B2
Dinuba *USA* 66C2
Diouloulou *Sen* 48A3
Diphu *India* 43G3
Dirē Dawa *Eth* 50E3
Dirk Hartog, I *Aust* 32A3
Dirkou *Niger* 50B2
Dirranbandi *Aust* 34C1
Dirri *Somalia* 50E3
Disappointment,C *South Georgia* 74J8
Disappointment,C *USA* 58B1
Disappointment,L *Aust* 32B3
Discovery B *Aust* 34B3
Discovery Reef *S China Sea* 27E5
Discovery Tablemount *Atlantic O* 52J7
Dishna *Egypt* 40B4
Disko *Greenland* 55N3
Disko Bugt, B *Greenland* 55N3
Diskofjord *Greenland* 55N3
Dismal Swamp *USA* 65D3
Disna, R *USSR* 19F1
Disney World *USA* 67B3
Distrito Federal *Brazil* 75C2
Diu *India* 42C4
Divinópolis *Brazil* 73K8
Divnoye *USSR* 21G6
Divriği *Turk* 40C2
Dixon, California *USA* 66B1
Dixon, Illinois *USA* 64B2
Dixon, Montana *USA* 58D1
Dixon Entrance, Sd *Can/USA* 54E4
Diyālā, R *Iraq* 41E3
Diyarbakir *Turk* 21G8
Diz, R *Iran* 41E3
Dja, R *Cam* 50B3
Djado,Plat du *Niger* 50B1
Djambala *Congo* 50B4
Djanet *Alg* 48C2
Djedi, Watercourse *Alg* 48C1
Djelfa *Alg* 48C1
Djéma *CAR* 50C3
Djenné *Mali* 48B3
Djibo *Burkina* 48B3
Djibouti *Djibouti* 50E2
Djibouti, Republic *E Africa* 50E2
Djolu *Zaïre* 50C3
Djougou *Benin* 48C4
Djourab, Erg du, Desert Region *Chad* 50B2
Djugu *Zaïre* 50D3
Djúpivogur *Iceland* 12C2
Djurdjura, Mts *Alg* 15C2
Dmitriya Lapteva, Proliv, Str *USSR* 25P2
Dmitrov *USSR* 20F4
Dnepr, R *USSR* 21E6
Dneprodzerzhinsk *USSR* 21E6
Dnepropetrovsk *USSR* 21F6
Dneprovskaya Nizmennost', Region *USSR* 20D5
Dnestr, R *USSR* 21C6
Dno *USSR* 20E4
Doba *Chad* 50B3
Dobele *USSR* 19E1
Dobo *Indon* 32C1
Doboj *Yugos* 17D2
Dobrush *USSR* 21E5
Doce, R *Brazil* 73K7
Doctor P P Peña *Par* 74D2
Dod *India* 44B3
Doda Betta, Mt *India* 44B3
Dodecanese, Is. *Greece* 17F3
Dodge City *USA* 56C3
Dodgeville *USA* 64A2
Dodoma *Tanz* 50D4
Dog L *Can* 64B1
Dog L *Can* 64C1
Dōgo, I *Japan* 29B3
Dogondoutchi *Niger* 48C3
Doğubayazit *Turk* 41D2
Doha *Qatar* 41F4
Doilungdêqên *China* 43G3
Dokkum *Neth* 13D1
Dokuchayevo, Mys, C *USSR* 29F2
Dolak, I *Indon* 32C1
Doland *USA* 61D2
Dolbeau *Can* 55L5
Dôle *France* 14D2
Dolgellau *Wales* 7C3
Dolgeville *USA* 68C1
Dolgiy, Ostrov, I *USSR* 20K2
Dolo Odo *Eth* 50E3
Dolores *Arg* 74E5
Dolores, R *USA* 60B3
Dolphin and Union Str *Can* 54G3
Dolphin,C *Falkland Is* 74E8
Dom, Mt *Indon* 27G7
Dombarovskiy *USSR* 24G4
Dombås *Nor* 12F6
Dombasle-sur-Meurthe *France* 13D3
Dombóvár *Hung* 17D1
Domfront *France* 14B2
Dominica, I *Caribbean S* 69E3
Dominican Republic *Caribbean S* 69C3
Dominion,C *Can* 55L3
Domino *Can* 55N4
Domna *USSR* 26E1
Domodossola *Italy* 16B1
Domuyo, Vol *Arg* 74B5
Domville,Mt *Aust* 34D1
Don, R *Scot* 8D3
Don, R *USSR* 21G6
Donaghadee *N Ire* 9C2
Donau, R *Austria/W Germ* 18C3
Donaueschingen *W Germ* 13E4
Donauwörth *W Germ* 18C3
Don Benito *Spain* 15A2
Doncaster *Eng* 7D3
Dondo *Angola* 51B4
Dondo *Mozam* 51D5
Dondra Head, C *Sri Lanka* 44C4
Donegal *Irish Rep* 10B3
Donegal, County *Irish Rep* 9C2
Donegal B *Irish Rep* 10B3
Donegal Mts *Irish Rep* 9C2
Donegal Pt *Irish Rep* 9B3
Donetsk *USSR* 21F6
Dong'an *China* 31C4
Dongara *Aust* 32A3
Dongchuan *China* 31A4
Dongfang *China* 30D2
Dongfeng *China* 28B2
Donggala *Indon* 32A1
Donggi Cona, L *China* 26C3
Donggou *China* 28A3
Donghai Dao, I *China* 31C5
Dong He, R *China* 31A1
Dong Hoi *Viet* 30D2
Dong Jiang, R *China* 31C5
Dongliao He, R *China* 28A2
Dongning *China* 28C2
Dongola *Sudan* 50D2
Dongshan *China* 31D5
Dongsha Qundao, I *China* 26E4
Dongsheng *China* 31C2
Dongtai *China* 31E3
Dongting Hu, L *China* 31C4
Dongxing *China* 31B5
Dongzhi *China* 31D3
Doniphan *USA* 63D1
Donji Vakuf *Yugos* 16D2
Dönna, I *Nor* 12G5
Donner P *USA* 59B3
Donnersberg, Mt *W Germ* 13D3
Donnybrook *S Africa* 47D2
Don Pedro Res *USA* 66B2
Doon, Loch, L *Scot* 8C4
Do Qu, R *China* 31A3
Dorbirn *Austria* 14D2
Dorchester *Eng* 7C4
Dorchester,C *Can* 55L3
Dordogne, R *France* 14C2
Dordrecht *Neth* 18A2
Dordrecht *S Africa* 47D3
Dorest Peak, Mt *USA* 68D1
Dori *Burkina* 48B3
Doring, R *S Africa* 47B3
Dorking *Eng* 7D4
Dormans *France* 13B3
Dornbirn *Austria* 18B3
Dornoch *Scot* 8C3
Dornoch Firth, Estuary *Scot* 8D3
Dorotea *Sweden* 12H6
Dorrigo *Aust* 34D2
Dorris *USA* 58B2
Dorset, County *Eng* 7C4
Dorset, Cape *Can* 55L3
Dorsten *W Germ* 13D2
Dortmund *W Germ* 18B2
Doruma *Zaïre* 50C3
Dosatuy *USSR* 25N4
Doshi *Afghan* 42B1
Dos Palos *USA* 66B2
Dosso *Niger* 48C3
Dossor *USSR* 24G5
Dothan *USA* 57E3
Douai *France* 14C1
Douala *Cam* 50A3
Double Island Pt *Aust* 34D1
Double Mountain Fork, R *USA* 62B2
Double Mt *USA* 66C3
Doubs, R *France* 14D2
Doubtful Sd *NZ* 35A3
Douentza *Mali* 48B3
Douglas, Arizona *USA* 56C3
Douglas, Georgia *USA* 67B2
Douglas, I of Man *British Is* 6B2
Douglas *S Africa* 47C2
Douglas, Wyoming *USA* 56C2
Douglas L *USA* 67B1
Doulevant-le-Château *France* 13C2
Doullens *France* 13B2
Dourada, Serra, Mts *Brazil* 75B2
Dourada, Serra, Mts *Brazil* 75C1
Dourados *Brazil* 73H8
Dourados, R *Brazil* 75B3
Dourados, Serra dos, Mts *Brazil* 75B3
Dourdan *France* 13B3
Douro, R *Port* 15A1
Dove, R *Eng* 7D3
Dove Creek *USA* 62A1
Dover, Delaware *USA* 65D3
Dover *Eng* 7E4
Dover, New Hampshire *USA* 65E2
Dover, New Jersey *USA* 68C2
Dover, Ohio *USA* 64C2
Dover,Str of *Eng/France* 7E4
Dovsk *USSR* 19G2
Down, County *N Ire* 9C2
Downingtown *USA* 68C3
Downpatrick *N Ire* 9D2
Downsville *USA* 68C1
Doylestown *USA* 68C2
Dōzen, I *Japan* 28B3
Dozois, Réservoir *Can* 65D1
Dr'aa, Watercourse *Mor* 48A2
Dracena *Brazil* 75B3
Drachten *Neth* 13D1
Dracut *USA* 68E1
Draguignan *France* 14D3
Drake *USA* 60C1
Drakensberg, Mt *S Africa* 47D2
Drake Passage *Atlantic O/Pacific O* 52E7
Dráma *Greece* 17E2
Drammen *Nor* 12G7
Drangajökull, Ice cap *Iceland* 12A1
Drava, R *Yugos* 16D1
Drenthe, Province *Neth* 13D1
Dresden *E Germ* 18C2
Dreux *France* 14C2
Drewsey *USA* 58C2
Driftwood *USA* 68A2
Drin, R *Alb* 17E2
Drina, R *Yugos* 17D2
Drissa, R *USSR* 19F1
Drogheda *Irish Rep* 9C3
Drogobych *USSR* 19E3
Droihead Nua *Irish Rep* 9C3
Droitwich *Eng* 7C3
Dromore *N Ire* 9C2
Dronning Maud Land, Region *Ant* 76F12
Drumheller *Can* 54G4
Drummond *USA* 58D1
Drummond I *USA* 64C1
Drummondville *Can* 65E1
Drumochter Pass *Scot* 8C3
Druskininkai *USSR* 19E2
Druzhina *USSR* 25Q3
Dryberry L *Can* 61E1
Dryden *Can* 55J5
Dryden *USA* 68B1
Dry Harbour Mts *Jamaica* 69H1
Duang, I *Burma* 30B3
Dubā *S Arabia* 40C4

Dubai
Elmira

Dubai *UAE* 41G4
Dubawnt, R *Can* 54H3
Dubawnt L *Can* 54H3
Dubbo *Aust* 32D4
Dublin *Irish Rep* 9C3
Dublin *USA* 67B2
Dublin, County *Irish Rep* 9C3
Dubna *USSR* 20F4
Dubno *USSR* 21D5
Dubois, Idaho *USA* 58D2
Du Bois *USA* 65D2
Dubois, Wyoming *USA* 58E2
Dubossary *USSR* 19F3
Dubrovica *USSR* 19F2
Dubrovnik *Yugos* 17D2
Dubuque *USA* 57D2
Duchesne *USA* 59D2
Duck, R *USA* 67A1
Ducor *USA* 66C3
Dudelange *Lux* 13D3
Dudinka *USSR* 24K3
Dudley *Eng* 7C3
Dudypta, R *USSR* 25L2
Duekoué *Ivory Coast* 48B4
Duero, R *Spain* 15B1
Duff Is *Solomon Is* 33F1
Dufftown *Scot* 8D3
Dugi Otok, I *Yugos* 16C2
Duisburg *W Germ* 18B2
Duiwelskloof *S Africa* 47E1
Dūkan *Iraq* 41E3
Duk Faiwil *Sudan* 50D3
Dukhān *Qatar* 41F4
Dukou *China* 31A4
Dulan *China* 26C3
Dulce, Golfo *Costa Rica* 70D4
Dullabchara *India* 43G4
Dülmen *W Germ* 13D2
Duluth *USA* 57D2
Dulverton *Eng* 7C4
Dūmā *Syria* 45D2
Dumai *Indon* 27D6
Dumas *USA* 56C3
Ḑumayr *Syria* 45D2
Dumbarton *Scot* 8C4
Dumer Rbia *Mor* 48B1
Dumfries *Scot* 8D4
Dumfries and Galloway, Region *Scot* 8C4
Dumka *India* 43F4
Dumoine,L *Can* 65D1
Dumont d'Urville, Base *Ant* 76G8
Dumyat *Egypt* 49F1
Dunărea, R *Rom* 17F2
Dunany Pt *Irish Rep* 9C3
Dunav, R *Bulg* 17E2
Dunav, R *Yugos* 17D1
Dunay *USSR* 28C2
Dunayevtsy *USSR* 19F3
Dunbar *Scot* 8D4
Duncan *USA* 63C2
Duncannon *USA* 68B2
Duncan Pass, Chan *Andaman Is* 44E3
Duncansby Head, Pt *Scot* 8D2
Dundalk *Irish Rep* 9C2
Dundalk *USA* 68B3
Dundalk B *Irish Rep* 9C3
Dundas *Greenland* 55M2
Dundas Pen *Can* 54G2
Dundas Str *Aust* 27G8
Dundee *S Africa* 47E2
Dundee *Scot* 8D3
Dundee *USA* 68B1
Dundoo *Aust* 34B1
Dundrum B *N Ire* 9D2
Dundwa Range, Mts *Nepal* 43M2
Dunedin *NZ* 33G5
Dunedin *USA* 67B3
Dunedoo *Aust* 34C2
Dunfermline *Scot* 8D3
Dungannon *N Ire* 9C2
Dūngarpur *India* 42C4
Dungarvan *Irish Rep* 9C3
Dungeness, Pen *Eng* 7E4
Dungog *Aust* 34D2
Dungu *Zaïre* 50C3
Dungunab *Sudan* 50D1
Dunhua *China* 28B2
Dunhuang *China* 26C2
Dunkeld *Scot* 8D3
Dunkerque = Dunkirk
Dunkirk *France* 13B2
Dunkirk *USA* 57F2
Dunkur *Eth* 50D2
Dunkwa *Ghana* 48B4
Dun Laoghaire *Irish Rep* 10B3
Dunmanus *Irish Rep* 9B4
Dunmore *USA* 68C2
Dunmore Town *The Bahamas* 69B1
Dunn *USA* 67C1
Dunnet Head, Pt *Scot* 8D2
Dunning *USA* 60C2
Dunoon *Scot* 8C4
Duns *Scot* 8D4
Dunseith *USA* 60C1
Dunsmuir *USA* 58B2
Dunstan Mts *NZ* 35A2
Dun-sur-Meuse *France* 13C3
Duolun *China* 31D1
Dupree *USA* 60C1
Duque de Braganca *Angola* 51B4
Du Quoin *USA* 64B3
Dura *Israel* 45C3
Durance, R *France* 14D3
Durand *USA* 64A2
Durango *Mexico* 70B2
Durango *Spain* 15B1
Durango *USA* 56C3
Durant *USA* 56D3
Duraykish *Syria* 45D1
Durazno *Urug* 74E4
Durban *S Africa* 47E2
Duren *W Germ* 13D2
Durg *India* 43E4
Durgapur *India* 43F4
Durham *Eng* 6D2
Durham, N Carolina *USA* 57F3
Durham, New Hampshire *USA* 68E1
Durham, County *Eng* 6D2
Durham Downs *Aust* 34B1
Durmitor, Mt *Yugos* 17D2
Durness *Scot* 8C2
Durrës *Alb* 17D2
Durrie *Aust* 34B1
Dursunbey *Turk* 17F3
D'Urville I *NZ* 35B2
Dushak *USSR* 41H2
Dushan *China* 31B4
Dushanbe *USSR* 39E2
Dushore *USA* 68B2
Dusky Sd *NZ* 35A3
Düsseldorf *W Germ* 18B2
Dutton,Mt *USA* 59D3
Duyun *China* 31B4
Düzce *Turk* 40B1
Dvina, R *USSR* 20D4
Dvinskaya Guba, B *USSR* 20F2
Dwārka *India* 42B4
Dworshak Res *USA* 58C1
Dyer,C *Can* 55M3
Dyersburg *USA* 57E3
Dyfed, County *Wales* 7B3
Dykh Tau, Mt *USSR* 21G7
Dynevor Downs *Aust* 34B1
Dzag *Mongolia* 26C2
Dzamīn Üüd *Mongolia* 26E2
Dzamin Üüd *Mongolia* 25M5
Dzaoudzi, Mayotte *Indian O* 51E5
Dzavhan Gol, R *Mongolia* 26C2
Dzerzhinsk *USSR* 20G4
Dzhalinda *USSR* 25O4
Dzhambul *USSR* 24J5
Dzhankoy *USSR* 21E6
Dzhezkazgan *USSR* 38E1
Dzhilikul' *USSR* 42B1
Dzhugdzhur, Khrebet, Mts *USSR* 25P4
Dzhungarskiy Alatau, Mts *USSR* 24J5
Dzierzoniow *Pol* 18D2
Dzungaria Basin *China* 39G1

E

Eabamet L *Can* 55K4
Eagle, Colorado *USA* 60B3
Eagle Butte *USA* 60C1
Eagle L, California *USA* 58B2
Eagle L, Maine *USA* 65F1
Eagle Lake *USA* 65F1
Eagle Mountain L *USA* 63C2
Eagle Pass *USA* 56C4
Eagle Peak, Mt *USA* 62A2
Eagle Plain *Can* 54E3
Earlimart *USA* 59C3
Earn, R *Scot* 8D3
Earn, Loch, L *Scot* 8C3
Earp *USA* 59D4
Earth *USA* 62B2
Easingwold *Eng* 6D2
Easley *USA* 67B2
East Aurora *USA* 65D2
East B *USA* 63E2
Eastbourne *Eng* 7E4
East Branch Delaware, R *USA* 68C1
East C *NZ* 33G4
East Chicago *USA* 64B2
East China Sea *China/ Japan* 26F3
East Dereham *Eng* 7E3
Easter I *Pacific O* 37O6
Eastern Ghats, Mts *India* 43E5
East Falkland, Is *Falkland Is* 74E8
Eastgate *USA* 59C3
East Germany, Republic *Europe* 18C2
East Grand Forks *USA* 61D1
East Grinstead *Eng* 7D4
Easthampton *USA* 68D1
East Hampton *USA* 68D2
East Kilbride *Scot* 8C4
East Lake *USA* 64B2
Eastleigh *Eng* 7D4
East Liverpool *USA* 64C2
East London *S Africa* 47D3
Eastmain *Can* 55L4
Eastmain, R *Can* 55L4
Eastman *USA* 67B2
East Moline *USA* 64A2
Easton, Maryland *USA* 65D3
Easton, Pennsylvania *USA* 65D2
East Orange *USA* 68C2
East Pacific Ridge *Pacific O* 37O5
East Pacific Rise *Pacific O* 37O4
East Point *USA* 67B2
Eastport *USA* 65F2
East Retford *Eng* 7D3
East Ridge *USA* 67A1
East St Louis *USA* 57D3
East Siberian S *USSR* 25R2
East Sussex, County *Eng* 7E4
Eastville *USA* 65D3
East Walker, R *USA* 66C1
Eatonton *USA* 67B2
Eau Claire *USA* 61E2
Eauripik, I *Pacific O* 27H6
Ebbw Vale *Wales* 7C4
Ebebiyin *Eq Guinea* 50B3
Ebensburg *USA* 68A2
Eberbach *W Germ* 13E3
Eberswalde *E Germ* 18C2
Ebetsu *Japan* 29D2
Ebian *China* 31A4
Ebinur, L *China* 24K5
Eboli *Italy* 16D2
Ebolowa *Cam* 50B3
Ebro, R *Spain* 15B1
Eceabat *Turk* 40A1
Ech Cheliff *Alg* 15C2
Eching *China* 31D2
Echo *USA* 58C1
Echo Bay *Can* 54G3
Echternach *Lux* 13D3
Echuca *Aust* 34B3
Ecija *Spain* 15A2
Eclipse Sd *Can* 55K2
Ecuador, Republic *S America* 72C4
Ēd *Eth* 50E2
Eday, I *Scot* 8D2
Ed Da'ein *Sudan* 50C2
Ed Damer *Sudan* 50D2
Ed Debba *Sudan* 50D2
Eddrachillis B *Scot* 8C2
Ed Dueim *Sudan* 50D2
Eddystone Pt *Aust* 34C4
Ede *Neth* 13C1
Edea *Cam* 50A3
Eden *Aust* 34C3
Eden, Texas *USA* 62C2
Eden, Wyoming *USA* 58E2
Eden, R *Eng* 6C2
Edenburg *S Africa* 47D2
Edendale *NZ* 35A3
Edenderry *Irish Rep* 9C3
Edenkoben *W Germ* 13D3
Eder, R *W Germ* 13E2
Edgeley *USA* 60D1
Edgell I *Can* 55M3
Edgemont *USA* 60C2
Edgeøya, I *Svalbard* 24D2
Edgewood *USA* 68B3
Edh Dhahiriya *Israel* 45C3
Edhessa *Greece* 17E2
Edinburg *USA* 62C3
Edinburgh *Scot* 8D3
Edirne *Turk* 21D7
Edison *USA* 66C3
Edisto, R *USA* 67B2
Edmonds *USA* 58B1
Edmonton *Can* 54G4
Edmore *USA* 60D1
Edmundston *Can* 55M5
Edna *USA* 63C3
Edolo *Italy* 16C1
Edom, Region *Jordan* 45C3
Edremit *Turk* 21D8
Edremit Körfezi, B *Turk* 17F3
Edrengiyn Nuruu, Mts *Mongolia* 26C2
Edson *Can* 54G4
Edward, R *Aust* 34B3
Edward,L *Uganda/Zaïre* 50C4
Edwards *USA* 66D3
Edwards Plat *USA* 56C3
Edwardsville *USA* 64B3
Eeklo *Belg* 13B2
Efate, I *Vanuatu* 33F2
Effingham *USA* 57E3
Egadi,I, Sicily 16C3
Egan Range, Mts *USA* 59D3
Egedesminde *Greenland* 55N3
Egegik *USA* 54C4
Eger *Hung* 19E3
Egersund *Nor* 12F7
Eggegebirge, Mts *W Germ* 13E2
Egg Harbor City *USA* 68C3
Eglinton I *Can* 54G2
Egmont,C *NZ* 35B1
Egmont,Mt *NZ* 35B1
Egremont *Eng* 6C2
Eğridir Gölü, L *Turk* 40B2
Egton *Eng* 6D2
Eguas, R *Brazil* 75C1
Egvekinot *USSR* 25T3
Egypt, Republic *Africa* 49E2
Eibar *Spain* 15B1
Eidsvold *Aust* 34D1
Eifel, Region *W Germ* 13D2
Eigg, I *Scot* 8B3
Eight Degree Chan *Indian O* 39F5
Eighty Mile Beach *Aust* 32B2
Eildon,L *Aust* 34C3
Eindhoven *Neth* 18B2
Ein Yahav *Israel* 45C3
Eisenach *E Germ* 18C2
Eisenerz *Austria* 18C3
Eitorf *W Germ* 13D2
Ejin qi *China* 31A1
Ekalaka *USA* 60C1
Eketahuna *NZ* 35C2
Ekibastuz *USSR* 24J4
Ekimchan *USSR* 25P4
Eksjö *Sweden* 12H7
Ekwan, R *Can* 57E1
El Abbâsa *Egypt* 45A3
El'Alamein *Egypt* 40A3
Elands, R *S Africa* 47D2
Elands Berg, Mt *S Africa* 47C3
El'Arîsh *Egypt* 40B3
Elat *Israel* 40B4
El' Atrun Oasis *Sudan* 50C2
Elaziğ *Turk* 21F8
El Azraq *Jordan* 40C3
Elba, I *Italy* 16C2
El Balyana *Egypt* 49F2
El Banco *Colombia* 72D2
Elbasan *Alb* 17E2
El Baúl *Ven* 69D5
Elbe, R *E Germ/W Germ* 18C2
El Beqa'a, R *Leb* 45D1
Elberta *USA* 64B2
Elbert,Mt *USA* 56C3
Elberton *USA* 67B2
Elbeuf *France* 14C2
Elbistan *Turk* 40C2
Elbląg *Pol* 19D2
El Bolsón *Arg* 74B6
Elbow Lake *USA* 61D1
Elbrus, Mt *USSR* 21G7
Elburz Mts = Reshteh-ye Alborz
El Cajon *USA* 59C4
El Campo *USA* 63C3
El Centro *USA* 59C4
Elche *Spain* 15B2
El Chocón, Embalse, Res *Arg* 74C5
Elda *Spain* 15B2
El-Dar-El-Beida = Casablanca
El'dikan *USSR* 25P3
El Diviso *Colombia* 72C3
El Djouf, Desert Region *Maur* 48B2
Eldon *USA* 63D1
Eldorado *Arg* 75B4
El Dorado, Arkansas *USA* 57D3
Eldorado *Brazil* 75C3
El Dorado, Kansas *USA* 56D3
El Dorado *Mexico* 70B2
Eldorado, Texas *USA* 62B2
El Dorado *Ven* 72F2
Eldoret *Kenya* 50D3
Eldred *USA* 68A2
Elea, C *Cyprus* 45C1
Eleanor,L *USA* 66C1
Electric Peak, Mt *USA* 58D2
El Eglab, Region *Alg* 48B2
Elephant Butte Res *USA* 62A2
Eleşkirt *Turk* 40D2
El Eulma *Algeria* 16B3
Eleuthera, I *The Bahamas* 57F4
El Faiyûm *Egypt* 40B4
El Farsia, Well *Mor* 48B2
El Fasher *Sudan* 50C2
El Fashn *Egypt* 40B4
El Ferrol *Spain* 15A1
El Firdân *Egypt* 45B3
El Fula *Sudan* 50C2
El Gassi *Alg* 48C1
El Geteina *Sudan* 50D2
El Gezira, Region *Sudan* 50D2
El Ghor, V *Israel/Jordan* 45C3
Elgin, Illinois *USA* 57E2
Elgin, N Dakota *USA* 60C1
Elgin *Scot* 8D3
El Gîza *Egypt* 40B3
El Golea *Alg* 48C1
El Golfo de Santa Clara *Mexico* 59D4
Elgon,Mt *Uganda/Kenya* 50D3
El Goran *Eth* 50E3
El Guettara, Well *Mali* 48B2
El Hamurre *Somalia* 50E3
El Hank, Region *Maur* 48B2
El Haricha, Desert Region *Mali* 48B2
El Harra *Egypt* 40A4
El Harrach *Alg* 15C2
El Hawata *Sudan* 50D2
El'Igma, Desert Region *Egypt* 40B4
Elisabethville = Lubumbashi
Elisenvaara *USSR* 12K6
El Iskandarîya = Alexandria
Elista *USSR* 21G6
Elizabeth *Aust* 32C4
Elizabeth *USA* 65E2
Elizabeth B *Namibia* 47B2
Elizabeth City *USA* 57F3
Elizabeth Is *USA* 68E2
Elizabethton, Tennessee *USA* 67B1
Elizabethtown, Kentucky *USA* 64B3
Elizabethtown, N Carolina *USA* 67C2
Elizabethtown, Pennsylvania *USA* 68B2
El Jadida *Mor* 48B1
El Jafr *Jordan* 40C3
El Jafr, L *Jordan* 45D3
El Jebelein *Sudan* 50D2
El Jem *Tunisia* 48D1
Elk *Pol* 19E2
Elk, R, Maryland/Penn *USA* 68C3
Elk, R, W Virginia *USA* 64C3
Elkader *USA* 61E2
El Kala *Algeria* 16B3
El Kamlin *Sudan* 50D2
El Kef *Tunisia* 48C1
Elk Grove *USA* 66B1
El Khalil = Hebron
El Khânka *Egypt* 45A3
El Khârga *Egypt* 40B4
El-Khârga Oasis *Egypt* 40B4
Elkhart *USA* 64B2
El Khenachich, Desert Region *Mali* 48B2
Elkhorn, R *USA* 61D2
Elkhovo *Bulg* 17F2
Elkins *USA* 65D3
Elkland *USA* 68B2
Elk Mt *USA* 60B2
Elko *Can* 58C1
Elko *USA* 56B2
El Kroub *Algeria* 16B3
Elkton *USA* 68C3
El Kûbri *Egypt* 45B3
El Kuntilla *Egypt* 40B3
El Lagowa *Sudan* 50C2
Ellef Ringnes I *Can* 54H2
Ellendale *USA* 60D1
Ellen,Mt *USA* 59D3
Ellensburg *USA* 56A2
Ellenville *USA* 68C2
Ellesmere I *Can* 55K2
Ellesmere,L *NZ* 35B2
Ellesmere Port *Eng* 7C3
Ellicott City *USA* 68B3
Elliot *S Africa* 47D3
Elliot Lake *Can* 55K5
Ellis *USA* 58D2
El Lisān, Pen *Jordan* 45C3
Ellisras *S Africa* 47D1
Ellsworth *USA* 65F2
Ellsworth Land, Region *Ant* 76F3
El Ma'âdi *Egypt* 45A4
El Maghra, L *Egypt* 49E1
El Mahalla el Kubra *Egypt* 40B3
El Mansûra *Egypt* 40B3
El Manzala *Egypt* 45A3
El Matarîya *Egypt* 45A3
El Matarîya *Egypt* 45B3
Elmer *USA* 68C3
El Merejé, Desert Region *Maur/Mali* 48B3
El Milia *Algeria* 16B3
El Mina *Leb* 45C1
El Minya *Egypt* 40B4
Elmira, California *USA* 66B1

Elmira Fatehpur

Elmira, New York *USA* 57F2
El Mirage *USA* 59D4
El Moral *Mexico* 62B3
El Mreiti, Well *Maur* 48B2
Elmshorn *W Germ* 18B2
El Muglad *Sudan* 50C2
El Mzereb, Well *Mali* 48B2
El Obeid *Sudan* 50D2
El Oued *Alg* 48C1
Eloy *USA* 59D4
El Paso *USA* 56C3
El Portal *USA* 59B3
El Porvenir *Mexico* 62A2
El Puerto del Sta Maria *Spain* 15A2
El Qâhira = Cairo
El Qantara *Egypt* 45B3
El Quds = Jerusalem
El Quseima *Egypt* 45C3
El Quwetra *Jordan* 45C4
El Reno *USA* 56D3
Elsa *Can* 54E3
El Saff *Egypt* 45A4
El Sâlhîya *Egypt* 45B3
El Salvador, Republic *Cent America* 70D3
El Sauzal *Mexico* 59C4
El Shallûfa *Egypt* 45B3
El Shatt *Egypt* 45B4
El Simbillâwein *Egypt* 45A3
Elsinore L *USA* 66D4
Elsterwerde *E Germ* 18C2
El Sueco *Mexico* 62A3
El Suweis = Suez
El Tabbin *Egypt* 45A4
El Teleno, Mt *Spain* 15A1
Eltham *NZ* 35B1
El Thamad *Egypt* 45C4
El Tigre *Ven* 72F2
El Tîh, Desert Region *Egypt* 40B4
El Tîna *Egypt* 45B3
Eltopia *USA* 58C1
El Tûr *Egypt* 40B4
Elūru *India* 44C2
Elvas *Port* 15A2
Elvira *Brazil* 72D5
Elvira,C *Can* 54H2
Elwood *USA* 64B2
Ely *Eng* 7E3
Ely, Minnesota *USA* 57D2
Ely, Nevada *USA* 56B3
Elyria *USA* 64C2
El Zarqa *Egypt* 45A3
Emāmrūd *Iran* 41G2
Emām Sāheb *Afghan* 42B1
Eman, R *Sweden* 18D1
Emba *USSR* 21K6
Emba, R *USSR* 21K6
Embalse de Ricobayo, Res = Embalse del Esla
Embarcación *Arg* 74D2
Embarras Portage *Can* 54G4
Embu *Kenya* 50D4
Emden *W Germ* 18B2
Emei *China* 31A4
Emerald *Aust* 32D3
Emeril *Can* 55M4
Emerson *Can* 54J5
Emigrant P *USA* 58C2
Emi Koussi, Mt *Chad* 50B1
Emirdağ *Turk* 40B2
Emmaus *USA* 68C2
Emmen *Neth* 18B2
Emmendingen *W Germ* 13D3
Emmerich *W Germ* 13D2
Emmett *USA* 58C2
Emmitsburg *USA* 68B3
Emory Peak, Mt *USA* 56C4
Empalme *Mexico* 70A2
Empangeni *S Africa* 47E2
Empedrado *Arg* 74E3
Emperor Seamount Chain *Pacific O* 37K2
Emporia, Kansas *USA* 63C1
Emporia, Virginia *USA* 65D3
Emporium *USA* 68A2
Ems, R *W Germ* 18B2
Emu *China* 28B2
Enard B *Scot* 8C2
Encarnación *Par* 74E3
Enchi *Ghana* 48B4
Encinal *USA* 62C3
Encinitas *USA* 66D4
Encruzilhada *Brazil* 75D2
Ende *Indon* 32B1
Enderby Land, Region *Ant* 76G11
Enderlin *USA* 61D1
Endicott *USA* 65D2
Endicott Mts *USA* 54C3
Enfida *Tunisia* 16C3
Enfield *USA* 67C1
Engaño, C *Phil* 27F5
Engaru *Japan* 29D2
En Gedi *Israel* 45C3
Engel's *USSR* 21H5
Enggano, I *Indon* 27D7
England *UK* 10C3
Englee *Can* 55N4
Englehard *USA* 67C1
Englehart *Can* 65D1
Englewood *USA* 60C3
English Channel *Eng/France* 10C3
Enid *USA* 63C1
Eniwa *Japan* 29D2
Enji, Well *Maur* 48B3
Enkhuizen *Neth* 13C1
Enköping *Sweden* 12H7
Enna, Sicily 16C3
En Nahud *Sudan* 50C2
Ennedi, Desert Region *Chad* 50C2
Ennell, L *Irish Rep* 9C3
Enngonia *Aust* 34C1
Enning *USA* 60C2
Ennis *Irish Rep* 10B3
Ennis, Montana *USA* 58D1
Ennis, Texas *USA* 63C2
Enniscorthy *Irish Rep* 9C3
Enniskillen *N Ire* 9C2
Enn Nâqoûra *Leb* 45C2
Enns, R *Austria* 18C3
Enschede *Neth* 12F8
Ensenada *Mexico* 70A1
Enshi *China* 31B3
Ensisheim *France* 13D4
Entebbe *Uganda* 50D4
Enterprise, Alabama *USA* 67A2
Enterprise, Oregon *USA* 58C1
Entre Ríos, State *Arg* 74E4
Enugu *Nigeria* 48C4
Enz, R *W Germ* 13E3
Enzan *Japan* 29C3
Epernay *France* 14C2
Ephesus *Turk* 40A2
Ephraim *USA* 59D3
Ephrata, Pennsylvania *USA* 68B2
Ephrata, Washington *USA* 58C1
Epi, I *Vanuatu* 33F2
Épinal *France* 14D2
Episkopi *Cyprus* 45B1
Episkopi B *Cyprus* 45B1
Epping *Eng* 7E4
Eppingen *W Germ* 13E3
Epsom *Eng* 7D4
Epukiro *Namibia* 47B1
Eqlid *Iran* 41F3
Equator 46D7
Equatorial Guinea, Republic *W Africa* 48C4
Equinox Mt *USA* 68D1
Equinunk *USA* 68C2
Erbach *W Germ* 13E3
Erbeskopf, Mt *W Germ* 13D3
Erciş *Turk* 41D2
Erciyas Dağları, Mt *Turk* 21F8
Erdaobaihe *China* 28B2
Erdao Jiang, R *China* 28B2
Erdene *Mongolia* 31C1
Erdenet *Mongolia* 26D2
Erdi, Desert Region *Chad* 50C2
Erechim *Brazil* 74F3
Ereğli *Turk* 40B1
Ereğli *Turk* 40B2
Erenhot *China* 26E2
Eresma, R *Spain* 15B1
Erft, R *W Germ* 13D2
Erfurt *E Germ* 18C2
Ergani *Turk* 40C2
Erg Chech, Desert Region *Alg/Mali* 48B2
Erg du Ténéré, Desert Region *Niger* 48D3
Ergene, R *Turk* 40A1
Erg Iguidi, Region *Alg/Mauritania* 48B2
Ergli *USSR* 19F1
Erguig, R *Chad* 50B2
Ergun', R *USSR/China* 25N4
Ergun Zuoqi *China* 25O4
Eriba *Sudan* 50D2
Eriboll, Loch, Inlet *Scot* 8C2
Ericht, Loch, L *Scot* 8C3
Erie *USA* 57F2
Erie,L *Can/USA* 57E2
Erimo-misaki, C *Japan* 29D2
Eriskay, I *Scot* 8B3
Eritrea, Region *Eth* 50D2
Erkelenz *W Germ* 13D2
Erlangen *W Germ* 18C3
Erling,L *USA* 63D2
Ermelo *S Africa* 47D2
Ernākulam *India* 44B4
Erne, L *N Ire* 9C2
Erode *India* 44B3
Eromanga *Aust* 34B1
Erongoberg, Mt *Namibia* 47B1
Er Rachida *Mor* 48B1
Er Rahad *Sudan* 50D2
Errego *Mozam* 51D5
Errigal, Mt *Irish Rep* 10B2
Erris Head, Pt *Irish Rep* 10A3
Erromanga, I *Vanuatu* 33F2
Er Roseires *Sudan* 50D2
Er Rummān *Jordan* 45C2
Erskine *USA* 61D1
Erstein *France* 13D3
Erzgebirge, Upland *E Germ* 18C2
Erzincan *Turk* 21F8
Erzurum *Turk* 21G8
Esan-misaki, C *Japan* 29D2
Esashi *Japan* 29D2
Esbjerg *Den* 18B1
Escalante *USA* 59D3
Escalón *Mexico* 56C4
Escanaba *USA* 57E2
Escárcega *Mexico* 70C3
Esch *Lux* 13C3
Escondido *USA* 59C4
Escuinapa *Mexico* 70B2
Escuintla *Guatemala* 70C3
Eséka *Cam* 50B3
Esens *W Germ* 13D1
Esera, R *Spain* 15C1
Eşfahān *Iran* 41F3
Eshowe *S Africa* 47E2
Esh Sharā, Upland *Jordan* 45C3
Esk, R *Scot* 8D4
Eskdale *NZ* 35C1
Eskifjörður *Iceland* 12C1
Eskilstuna *Sweden* 12H7
Eskimo Lakes *Can* 54E3
Eskimo Point *Can* 55J3
Eskişehir *Turk* 21E8
Esla, R *Spain* 15A1
Esla, Embalse del, Res *Spain* 15A1
Esmeralda *Cuba* 69B2
Esmeralda, I *Chile* 74A7
Esmeraldas *Ecuador* 72C3
Espalion *France* 14C3
Espanola *Can* 64C1
Espanola *USA* 62A1
Esperance *Aust* 32B4
Esperanza, Base *Ant* 76G2
Espichel, Cabo, C *Port* 15A2
Espinhaço, Serra do, Mts *Brazil* 75D2
Espírito Santo, State *Brazil* 75D2
Espiritu Santo, I *Vanuatu* 33F2
Espungabera *Mozam* 51D6
Esquel *Arg* 74B6
Esquimalt *Can* 58B1
Es Samrā *Jordan* 45D2
Essaouira *Mor* 48B1
Essen *W Germ* 18B2
Essequibo, R *Guyana* 73G3
Essex, County *Eng* 7E4
Essexville *USA* 64C2
Esslingen *W Germ* 18B3
Essonne, Department *France* 13B3
Essoyes *France* 13C3
Estados, Isla de los *Arg* 74D8
Estância *Brazil* 73L6
Estcourt *S Africa* 47D2
Esteí *Nic* 72A1
Esternay *France* 13B3
Estero B *USA* 66B3
Esteros *Par* 74D2
Estes Park *USA* 60B2
Estevan *Can* 54H5
Estherville *USA* 61E2
Estill *USA* 67B2
Estissac *France* 13B3
Estonian SSR, Republic *USSR* 20C4
Estrella, R *USA* 66B3
Estremoz *Port* 15A2
Esztergom *Hung* 19D3
Etadunna *Aust* 34A1
Etah *Can* 55L2
Etah *India* 43K2
Etam *France* 13C3
Étampes *France* 14C2
Etamunbanie,L *Aust* 34A1
Etāwah *India* 42D3
Ethiopia, Republic *Africa* 50D3
Etive, Loch, Inlet *Scot* 8C3
Etna, Vol, Sicily 16C3
Etosha Nat Pk *Namibia* 51B5
Etosha Pan, Salt L *Namibia* 51B5
Etowah, R *USA* 67B2
Ettelbruck *Lux* 13C3
Eua, I *Tonga* 33H3
Euabalong *Aust* 34C2
Euboea, I *Greece* 17E3
Euclid *USA* 64C2
Eucumbene,L *Aust* 34C3
Eudunda *Aust* 34A2
Eufala L *USA* 63C1
Eufaula *USA* 67A2
Eugene *USA* 56A2
Eugenia, Punta, Pt *Mexico* 70A2
Eulo *Aust* 34C1
Eunice, Louisiana *USA* 63D2
Eunice, New Mexico *USA* 62B2
Eupen *W Germ* 13D2
Euphrates, R *Iraq/Syria* 40D3
Eupora *USA* 63E2
Eure, R *France* 14C2
Eureka, California *USA* 58B2
Eureka *Can* 55K1
Eureka, Montana *USA* 58C1
Eureka, Nevada *USA* 56B3
Eureka, S Dakota *USA* 60D1
Eureka, Utah *USA* 59D3
Eureka Sd *Can* 55K2
Eureka V *USA* 66D2
Euroa *Aust* 34C3
Eurombah, R *Aust* 34C1
Europa, I *Mozam Chan* 51E6
Europoort *Neth* 13C2
Euskirchen *W Germ* 18B2
Eutaw *USA* 63E2
Evans,C *Can* 55K1
Evans,L *Can* 55L4
Evans,Mt, Colorado *USA* 60B3
Evans,Mt, Montana *USA* 58D1
Evans Str *Can* 55K3
Evanston, Illinois *USA* 64B2
Evanston, Wyoming *USA* 56B2
Evansville, Indiana *USA* 57E3
Evansville, Wyoming *USA* 60B2
Evaton *S Africa* 47D2
Everard,L *Aust* 32C4
Everest,Mt *China/Nepal* 39G3
Everett, Pennsylvania *USA* 68A2
Everett, Washington *USA* 56A2
Everett,Mt *USA* 68D1
Everglades,The, Swamp *USA* 57E4
Evergreen *USA* 67A2
Evesham *Eng* 7D3
Evinayong *Eq Guinea* 50B3
Evje *Nor* 12F7
Évora *Port* 15A2
Evoron, Oz, L *USSR* 26G1
Evreux *France* 14C2
Évvoia = Euboea
Ewe, Loch, Inlet *Scot* 8C3
Ewo *Congo* 50B4
Excelsior Mt *USA* 66C1
Excelsior Mts *USA* 66C1
Excelsior Springs *USA* 61E3
Exe, R *Eng* 7C4
Exeter, California *USA* 59C3
Exeter *Eng* 7C4
Exeter, New Hampshire *USA* 65E2
Exmoor *Eng* 7C4
Exmouth *Eng* 7C4
Extremadura, Region *Spain* 15A2
Exuma Sd *The Bahamas* 70E2
Eyasi, L *Tanz* 50D4
Eyemouth *Scot* 8D4
Eyl *Somalia* 50E3
Eyre *Aust* 32B4
Eyre Creek, R *Aust* 32C3
Eyre,L *Aust* 32C3
Eyre Pen *Aust* 32C4
Ezine *Turk* 17F3

F

Faber L *Can* 54G3
Fåborg *Den* 12F7
Fabriano *Italy* 16C2
Fachi *Niger* 50B2
Fada *Chad* 50C2
Fada N'Gourma *Burkina* 48C3
Faddeyevskiy, Ostrov, I *USSR* 25Q2
Faenza *Italy* 16C2
Færingehavn *Greenland* 55N3
Færøerne = Faeroes
Faeroes, Is *N Atlantic Oc* 12D3
Fafa, R *CAR* 50B3
Fafan, R *Eth* 50E3
Făgăras *Rom* 17E1
Fagnes, Region *Belg* 13C2
Faguibine,L *Mali* 48B3
Fahūd *Oman* 41G5
Faiol, I *Azores* 48A1
Fairacres *USA* 62A2
Fairbanks *USA* 54D3
Fairbault *USA* 55J5
Fairborn *USA* 64C3
Fairbury *USA* 56D2
Fairfax *USA* 68B3
Fairfield, California *USA* 59B3
Fairfield, Connecticut *USA* 68D2
Fairfield, Idaho *USA* 58D2
Fairfield, Montana *USA* 58D1
Fairfield, Ohio *USA* 64C3
Fair Head, Pt *N Ire* 9C2
Fair Isle, I *Scot* 10C2
Fairlie *NZ* 35B2
Fairmont, Minnesota *USA* 61E2
Fairmont, W Virginia *USA* 64C3
Fairport *USA* 68B1
Fairview *USA* 62C1
Fairweather,Mt *USA* 54E4
Fais, I *Pacific O* 27H6
Faisalabad *Pak* 42C2
Faith *USA* 60C1
Faither,The, Pen *Scot* 8E1
Fakaofo, I *Tokelau Is* 33H1
Fakenham *Eng* 7E3
Fakfak *Indon* 32C1
Faku *China* 28A2
Falam *Burma* 43G4
Falcon Res *Mexico/USA* 70C2
Falémé, R *Mali/Sen/Guinea* 48A3
Falfurrias *USA* 62C3
Falkenberg *Sweden* 12G7
Falkirk *Scot* 8D4
Falkland Is, Dependency *S Atlantic* 74D8
Falkland Sd *Falkland Is* 74E8
Falköping *Sweden* 12G7
Fallbrook *USA* 66D4
Fallon *USA* 56B3
Fall River *USA* 65E2
Fall River P *USA* 60B2
Falls City *USA* 61D2
Falmouth *Eng* 7B4
Falmouth *Jamaica* 69H1
Falmouth, Maine *USA* 65E2
Falmouth, Massachusetts *USA* 68E2
Falmouth Bay *Eng* 7B4
False B *S Africa* 47B3
Falso,C *Mexico* 70A2
Falster, I *Den* 18C2
Fălticeni *Rom* 17F1
Falun *Sweden* 12H6
Famagusta *Cyprus* 40B2
Famagusta B *Cyprus* 45B1
Famenne, Region *Belg* 13C2
Famoso *USA* 66C3
Fang *Thai* 30B2
Fangak *Sudan* 50D3
Fangliao *Taiwan* 31E5
Fannich, L *Scot* 8C3
Fano *Italy* 16C2
Fâqûs *Egypt* 45A3
Faraday, Base *Ant* 76G3
Faradje *Zaïre* 50C3
Farafangana *Madag* 51E6
Farafra Oasis *Egypt* 49E2
Farah *Afghan* 38E2
Farallon de Medinilla, I *Pacific O* 27H5
Farallon de Pajaros, I *Marianas* 26H4
Faranah *Guinea* 48A3
Farasan Is *S Arabia* 50E2
Faraulep, I *Pacific O* 27H6
Fareham *Eng* 7D4
Farewell,C *Greenland* 55O4
Farewell,C *NZ* 33G5
Farewell Spit, Pt *NZ* 35B2
Fargo *USA* 56D2
Fari'a, R *Israel* 45C2
Faribault *USA* 57D2
Faridpur *Bang* 43F4
Farīmān *Iran* 41G2
Fâriskûr *Egypt* 45A3
Farmington, Maine *USA* 65E2
Farmington, Missouri *USA* 63D1
Farmington, New Hampshire *USA* 68E1
Farmington, New Mexico *USA* 56C3
Farmington, Utah *USA* 58D2
Farmington Res *USA* 66B2
Farne Deep *N Sea* 6D2
Faro *Port* 15A2
Fårö, I *Sweden* 12H7
Farquhar Is *Indian O* 46K9
Farrar, R *Scot* 8C3
Farrell *USA* 64C2
Farrukhabad, District *India* 43K2
Fársala *Greece* 17E3
Fartura, Serra de, Mts *Brazil* 75B4
Farwell *USA* 62B2
Fasā *Iran* 41F4
Fastov *USSR* 21D5
Fatehgarh *India* 43K2
Fatehpur *India* 43E3

Fatima du Sul *Brazil* 73H7
Fauquier *Can* 58C1
Fauresmith *S Africa* 47D2
Fauske *Nor* 12H5
Faversham *Eng* 7E4
Fawn, R *Can* 55K4
Fax, R *Sweden* 12H6
Faxaflói, B *Iceland* 12A2
Faya *Chad* 50B2
Fayette *USA* 63E2
Fayetteville, Arkansas *USA* 57D3
Fayetteville, N Carolina *USA* 57F3
Fayetteville, Tennessee *USA* 67A1
Fâyid *Egypt* 45B3
Faylakah, I *Kuwait* 41E4
Fâzilka *India* 42C2
Fdérik *Maur* 48A2
Fear,C *USA* 57F3
Feather, R *USA* 66B1
Feather Middle Fork, R *USA* 59B3
Fécamp *France* 14C2
Fehmarn, I *W Germ* 18C2
Feia, Lagoa *Brazil* 75D3
Feijó *Brazil* 72D5
Feilai Xai Bei Jiang, R *China* 31C5
Feilding *NZ* 35C2
Feira *Zambia* 51D5
Feira de Santan *Brazil* 73L6
Feke *Turk* 40C2
Feldberg, Mt *W Germ* 13D4
Feldkirch *Austria* 18B3
Felixstowe *Eng* 10D3
Femund, L *Nor* 12G6
Fengcheng *China* 28A2
Fengdu *China* 31B4
Fengjie *China* 31B3
Fengning *China* 31D1
Feng Xian *China* 31B3
Fengzhen *China* 31C1
Fen He, R *China* 31C2
Fenoarivo Atsinanana *Madag* 51E5
Feodosiya *USSR* 21F7
Ferdow *Iran* 41G3
Fère-Champenoise *France* 13B3
Fergana *USSR* 39F1
Fergus Falls *USA* 61D1
Ferkessedougou *Ivory Coast* 48B4
Fermanagh, County *N Ire* 9C2
Fernandina Beach *USA* 67B2
Fernando de Noronha, Isla *Brazil* 73M4
Fernandópolis *Brazil* 75B3
Fernando Poo, I = Bioko
Ferndale *USA* 58B1
Fernie *Can* 58C1
Fernley *USA* 59C3
Ferrara *Italy* 16C2
Ferrat, Cap, C *Alg* 15B2
Ferreñafe *Peru* 72C5
Ferriday *USA* 63D2
Ferrières *France* 13B3
Fès *Mor* 48B1
Festus *USA* 63D1
Feteşti *Rom* 17F2
Fethard *Irish Rep* 9C3
Fethiye *Turk* 40A2
Fetisovo *USSR* 21J7
Fetlar, I *Scot* 8E1
Feuilles, Rivière aux, R *Can* 55L4
Feyzabad *Afghan* 24J6
Ffestiniog *Wales* 7C3
Fianarantsoa *Madag* 51E6
Fiche *Eth* 50D3
Ficksburg *S Africa* 47D2
Fidan, Wadi *Jordan* 45C3
Fier *Alb* 17D2
Fife, Region *Scot* 8D3
Fife Ness, Pen *Scot* 8D3
Figeac *France* 14C3
Figueira da Foz *Port* 15A1
Figueras *Spain* 15C1
Figuig *Mor* 48B1
Fiji, Is *Pacific O* 33G2
Filabres, Sierra de los, Mts *Spain* 15B2
Filadelfia *Par* 73G8
Filey *Eng* 6D2
Filiaşi *Rom* 17E2
Filiatrá *Greece* 17E3
Filicudi, I *Italy* 16C3
Fillmore, California *USA* 59C4
Fillmore, Utah *USA* 59D3
Findhorn, R *Scot* 8C3
Findlay *USA* 57E2
Finger Lakes *USA* 65D2
Fingoè *Mozam* 51D5
Finike *Turk* 21E8

Finisterre, Cabo, C *Spain* 15A1
Finke, R *Aust* 32C3
Finland, Republic *N Europe* 20C3
Finland,G of *N Europe* 12J7
Finlay, R *Can* 54F4
Finlay Forks *Can* 54F4
Finley *Aust* 34C3
Finn, R *Irish Rep* 9C2
Finnsnes *Nor* 12H5
Finschhafen *PNG* 27H7
Finspång *Sweden* 12H7
Finsterwalde *E Germ* 18C2
Fintona *N Ire* 9C2
Fiordland Nat Pk *NZ* 35A3
Fiq *Syria* 45C2
Firat, R *Turk* 21F8
Firebaugh *USA* 66B2
Firenze = Florence
Firozābād *India* 42D3
Firozpur *India* 42C2
Firth of Clyde, Estuary *Scot* 8C4
Firth of Forth, Estuary *Scot* 8D3
Firth of Lorn, Estuary *Scot* 8B3
Firth of Tay, Estuary *Scot* 10C2
Firūzābād *Iran* 41F4
Fish, R *Namibia* 47B2
Fish, R *S Africa* 47C3
Fish Camp *USA* 66C2
Fishers I *USA* 68D2
Fisher Str *Can* 55K3
Fishguard *Wales* 7B4
Fiskenæsset *Greenland* 55N3
Fismes *France* 13B3
Fitchburg *USA* 65E2
Fitful Head, Pt *Scot* 8E2
Fitzgerald *USA* 67B2
Fitzroy, R *Aust* 32B2
Fitzroy Crossing *Aust* 32B2
Fitzwilliam I *Can* 64C1
Fiume = Rijeka
Fizi *Zaïre* 50C4
Flagstaff *S Africa* 47D3
Flagstaff *USA* 56B3
Flagstaff L *USA* 65E1
Flamborough Head, C *Eng* 6D2
Flaming Gorge Res *USA* 56C2
Flamingo, Teluk, B *Indon* 27G7
Flandres, Plaine des *Belg/France* 13B2
Flannan Isles *Scot* 8B2
Flathead L *USA* 56B2
Flat River *USA* 63D1
Flattery,C *Aust* 27H8
Flattery,C *USA* 56A2
Fleetwood *Eng* 6C3
Flekkefjord *Nor* 12F7
Fleming Deep *Pacific O* 26H4
Flemington *USA* 68C2
Flensburg *W Germ* 18B2
Flinders, I *Aust* 32C4
Flinders, I *Aust* 32D5
Flinders, R *Aust* 32D2
Flinders Range, Mts *Aust* 32C4
Flin Flon *Can* 54H4
Flint *USA* 57E2
Flint *Wales* 7C3
Flint, R *USA* 57E3
Flixecourt *France* 13B2
Floodwood *USA* 64A1
Florala *USA* 67A2
Florence, Alabama *USA* 57E3
Florence, Arizona *USA* 59D4
Florence, Colorado *USA* 60B3
Florence *Italy* 16C2
Florence, Kansas *USA* 63C1
Florence, Oregon *USA* 58B2
Florence, S Carolina *USA* 57F3
Florence L *USA* 66C2
Florencia *Colombia* 72C3
Florentine Ameghino, Embalse, Res *Arg* 74C6
Florenville *Belg* 13C3
Flores *Guatemala* 70D3
Flores, I *Azores* 48A1
Flores, I *Indon* 32B1
Flores S *Indon* 27E7
Floriano *Brazil* 73K5
Florianópolis *Brazil* 74G3
Florida *Urug* 74E4
Florida, State *USA* 70D2
Florida B *USA* 67B3
Florida City *USA* 67B3
Florida Is *Solomon Is* 33E1
Florida Keys, Is *USA* 57E4
Florida,Strs of *USA* 57E4
Flórina *Greece* 17E2
Florø *Nor* 12F6
Floydada *USA* 62B2
Fly, R *PNG* 32D1
Focşani *Rom* 17F1

Foggia *Italy* 16D2
Fogo, I *Cape Verde* 48A4
Foix *France* 14C3
Foleyet *Can* 64C1
Foley I *Can* 55L3
Foligno *Italy* 16C2
Folkestone *Eng* 7E4
Folkston *USA* 67B2
Follonica *Italy* 16C2
Folsom *USA* 66B1
Fonda *USA* 68C1
Fond-du-Lac *Can* 54H4
Fond du Lac *USA* 57E2
Fonseca, G de *Honduras* 70D3
Fontainbleau *France* 14C2
Fontenay-le-Comte *France* 14B2
Fonyód *Hung* 17D1
Foochow = Fuzhou
Foraker, Mt *USA* 54C3
Forbach *France* 13D3
Forbes *Aust* 34C2
Forcados *Nigeria* 48C4
Ford City *USA* 66C3
Førde *Nor* 12F6
Fordingbridge *Eng* 7D4
Fords Bridge *Aust* 34C1
Fordyce *USA* 63D2
Forécariah *Guinea* 48A4
Forel,Mt *Greenland* 55P3
Foremost *Can* 58D1
Forest *Can* 64C2
Forest *USA* 63E2
Forest City, Iowa *USA* 61E2
Forest City, Pennsylvania *USA* 68C2
Forest of Dean *Eng* 7C4
Forest Park *USA* 67B2
Forestville *USA* 66A1
Forêt d'Othe *France* 13B3
Forfar *Scot* 8D3
Forgan *USA* 62B1
Forks *USA* 58B1
Forlì *Italy* 16C2
Formby *Eng* 7C3
Formentera, I *Spain* 15C2
Formentor, Cabo, C *Spain* 15C1
Formia *Italy* 16C2
Formigas, I *Azores* 48A1
Formosa = Taiwan
Formosa *Arg* 74E3
Formosa *Brazil* 73J7
Formosa, State *Arg* 74D2
Formosa Channel = Taiwan Str
Formosa, Serra, Mts *Brazil* 73G6
Formoso *Brazil* 75C1
Formoso, R *Brazil* 75C1
Forres *Scot* 8D3
Forrest *Aust* 32B4
Forrest City *USA* 57D3
Forsayth *Aust* 32D2
Forssa *Fin* 12J6
Forster *Aust* 34D2
Forsyth, Missouri *USA* 63D1
Forsyth, Montana *USA* 60B1
Fort Abbas *Pak* 42C3
Fort Albany *Can* 55K4
Fortaleza *Brazil* 73L4
Fort Augustus *Scot* 8C3
Fort Beaufort *S Africa* 47D3
Fort Benton *USA* 58D1
Fort Bragg *USA* 59B3
Fort Cobb Res *USA* 62C1
Fort Collins *USA* 56C2
Fort Coulonge *Can* 65D1
Fort Davis *USA* 62B2
Fort-de-France *Martinique* 69E4
Fort Deposit *USA* 67A2
Fortescue, R *Aust* 32A3
Fort Frances *Can* 55J5
Fort Frances *Can* 57D2
Fort Franklin *Can* 54F3
Fort George *Can* 55L4
Fort Good Hope *Can* 54F3
Fort Grey *Aust* 34B1
Fort Hancock *USA* 62A2
Fort Hope *Can* 55K4
Forties, Oilfield *N Sea* 8F3
Fort Kent *USA* 65F1
Fort Lallemand *Alg* 48C1
Fort Lamy = Ndjamena
Fort Laramie *USA* 60C2
Fort Lauderdale *USA* 57E4
Fort Liard *Can* 54F3
Fort Mackay *Can* 54G4
Fort Macleod *Can* 54G5
Fort McMurray *Can* 54G4
Fort McPherson *Can* 54E3
Fort Madison *USA* 64A2
Fort Morgan *USA* 56C2
Fort Myers *USA* 57E4

Fort Nelson *Can* 54F4
Fort Norman *Can* 54F3
Fort Payne *USA* 67A2
Fort Peck *USA* 60B1
Fort Peck Res *USA* 56C2
Fort Pierce *USA* 57E4
Fort Pierre *USA* 60C2
Fort Plain *USA* 68C1
Fort Providence *Can* 54G3
Fort Resolution *Can* 54G3
Fort Rousset *Congo* 50B4
Fort Rupert *Can* 55L4
Fort St James *Can* 54F4
Fort St John *Can* 54F4
Fort Scott *USA* 63D1
Fort Selkirk *Can* 54E3
Fort Severn *Can* 55K4
Fort Shevchenko *USSR* 21J7
Fort Simpson *Can* 54F3
Fort Smith *Can* 54G3
Fort Smith *USA* 57D3
Fort Smith, Region *Can* 54F3
Fort Stockton *USA* 56C3
Fort Sumner *USA* 62B2
Fort Supply *USA* 62C1
Fortuna, California *USA* 58B2
Fortuna, N Dakota *USA* 60C1
Fort Vermilion *Can* 54G4
Fort Walton Beach *USA* 67A2
Fort Wayne *USA* 57E2
Fort William *Scot* 8C3
Fort Wingate *USA* 62A1
Fort Worth *USA* 56D3
Fort Yukon *USA* 54D3
Foshan *China* 31C5
Fosheim Pen *Can* 55K2
Fosston *USA* 61D1
Fougamou *Gabon* 50B4
Fougères *France* 14B2
Foula *Scot* 8D1
Foulness I *Eng* 7E4
Foulwind,C *NZ* 35B2
Fouman *Cam* 50B3
Foum el Alba, Region *Mali* 48B2
Foumban *Cam* 50B3
Fourmies *France* 14C1
Foúrnoi, I *Greece* 17F3
Fouta Djallon, Mts *Guinea* 48A3
Foveaux Str *NZ* 33F5
Fowey *Eng* 7B4
Fowler *USA* 62B1
Fox, R *USA* 64B2
Foxe Basin, G *Can* 55K3
Foxe Chan *Can* 55K3
Foxe Pen *Can* 55L3
Foxpark *USA* 60B2
Foxton *NZ* 35C2
Foyle, Lough, Estuary *Irish Rep/N Ire* 10B2
Foz do Cuene *Angola* 51B5
Foz do Iguaçu *Brazil* 74F3
Frackville *USA* 68B2
Fraga *Spain* 15C1
Framingham *USA* 68E1
Franca *Brazil* 73J8
France, Republic *Europe* 14C2
France Ville *Gabon* 50B4
Franche Comté, Region *France* 14D2
Francistown *Botswana* 47D1
Francs Peak, Mt *USA* 58E2
Frankenberg *W Germ* 13E2
Frankfort, Indiana *USA* 64B2
Frankfort, Kentucky *USA* 57E3
Frankfort, New York *USA* 68C1
Frankfort *S Africa* 47D2
Frankfurt am Main *W Germ* 18B2
Frankfurt an-der-Oder *E Germ* 18C2
Fränkischer Alb, Upland *W Germ* 18C3
Franklin, Idaho *USA* 58D2
Franklin, Indiana *USA* 64B3
Franklin, Louisiana *USA* 63D3
Franklin, Massachusetts *USA* 68E1
Franklin, N Carolina *USA* 67B1
Franklin, New Hampshire *USA* 68E1
Franklin, New Jersey *USA* 68C2
Franklin, Pennsylvania *USA* 65D2
Franklin, Tennessee *USA* 67A1
Franklin, Virginia *USA* 65D3
Franklin B *Can* 54F2
Franklin D Roosevelt, L *USA* 58C1
Franklin Mts *Can* 54F3
Franklin Str *Can* 54J2
Franklinville *USA* 68A1
Franz Josef Glacier *NZ* 35B2
Franz-Josef-Land = Zemlya Frantsa Josifa

Fraser, R *Can* 54F5
Fraserburg *S Africa* 47C3
Fraserburgh *Scot* 8D3
Fraser I *Aust* 34D1
Frederica *USA* 68C3
Fredericia *Den* 18B1
Frederick, Maryland *USA* 65D3
Frederick, Oklahoma *USA* 62C2
Fredericksburg, Texas *USA* 62C2
Fredericksburg, Virginia *USA* 65D3
Fredericktown *USA* 64A3
Fredericton *Can* 55M5
Frederikshåp *Greenland* 55N3
Frederikshavn *Den* 12G7
Fredonia *USA* 65D2
Fredrikstad *Nor* 12G7
Freehold *USA* 68C2
Freel Peak, Mt *USA* 66C1
Freeman *USA* 61D2
Freeport, Illinois *USA* 64B2
Freeport, Texas *USA* 63C3
Freeport *The Bahamas* 69B1
Freer *USA* 62C3
Freetown *Sierra Leone* 48A4
Freiburg *W Germ* 18B3
Freiburg im Breisgau *W Germ* 13D3
Freistadt *Austria* 18C3
Fremantle *Aust* 32A4
Fremont, California *USA* 66B2
Fremont, Nebraska *USA* 61D2
Fremont, Ohio *USA* 64C2
French Guiana, Dependency *S America* 73H3
Frenchman, R *USA* 60B1
Frenchmans Cap, Mt *Aust* 34C4
French Polynesia, Is *Pacific O* 37M5
Frenda *Alg* 15C2
Fresnillo *Mexico* 70B2
Fresno *USA* 56B3
Fresno, R *USA* 66C2
Fresno Res *USA* 58D1
Freudenstadt *W Germ* 13E3
Frévent *France* 13B2
Freycinet Pen *Aust* 34C4
Fria *Guinea* 48A3
Friant *USA* 66C2
Friant Dam *USA* 66C2
Fribourg *Switz* 16B1
Friedberg *W Germ* 13E2
Friedrichshafen *W Germ* 18B3
Friesland, Province *Neth* 13C1
Frio, R *USA* 62C3
Frio, Cabo, C *Brazil* 75D3
Friona *USA* 62B2
Frobisher B *Can* 55M3
Frobisher Bay *Can* 55M3
Frobisher L *Can* 54H4
Frolovo *USSR* 21G6
Frome *Eng* 7C4
Frome, R *Eng* 7C4
Frome,L *Aust* 32C4
Frontenac *USA* 63D1
Frontera *Mexico* 70C3
Front Royal *USA* 65D3
Frosinone *Italy* 16C2
Fruita *USA* 60B3
Frunze *USSR* 39F1
Fuchuan *China* 31C5
Fuding *China* 31E4
Fuerte, R *Mexico* 70B2
Fuerte Olimpo *Brazil* 75A3
Fuerte Olimpo *Par* 74E2
Fuerteventura, I *Canary Is* 48A2
Fugu *China* 31C2
Fuhai *China* 26B2
Fujairah *UAE* 41G4
Fuji *Japan* 29C3
Fujian, Province *China* 31D4
Fujin *China* 26G2
Fujinomiya *Japan* 29C3
Fuji-san, Mt *Japan* 29D3
Fujisawa *Japan* 29C3
Fuji-Yoshida *Japan* 29C3
Fukang *Japan* 29D2
Fukang *China* 24K5
Fukuchiyama *Japan* 29D3
Fukue *Japan* 28A4
Fukue, I *Japan* 28A4
Fukui *Japan* 29D3
Fukuoka *Japan* 28C4
Fukushima *Japan* 29E3
Fukuyama *Japan* 29C4
Fulda *USA* 61D2
Fulda *W Germ* 18B2
Fulda, R *W Germ* 18B2
Fuling *China* 31B4
Fullarton *Trinidad* 69L1
Fullerton *USA* 66D4
Fulton, Illinois *USA* 64A2

Fulton Głogów

Fulton, Kentucky *USA* 64B3
Fulton, New York *USA* 65D2
Fumay *France* 13C2
Funabashi *Japan* 29D3
Funafuti, I *Tuvalu* 33G1
Funchal *Madeira* 48A1
Fundão *Brazil* 75D2
Fundy,B of *Can* 55M5
Funhalouro *Mozam* 51D6
Funing *China* 31B5
Funing *China* 31D3
Funtua *Nigeria* 48C3
Fuqing *China* 31D4
Furancungo *Mozam* 51D5
Furano *Japan* 29D2
Fūrg *Iran* 41G4
Furnas, Serra das, Mts *Brazil* 75B2
Furneaux Group, Is *Aust* 32D5
Furstenau *W Germ* 13D1
Fürstenwalde *E Germ* 18C2
Fürth *W Germ* 18C3
Furubira *Japan* 29D2
Furukawa *Japan* 29E3
Fury and Hecla St *Can* 55K3
Fushun *China* 28A2
Fushun, Sichuan *China* 31A4
Fusong *China* 28B2
Füssen *W Germ* 18C3
Fu Xian *China* 31E2
Fuxin *China* 31E1
Fuxin *China* 28A2
Fuyang *China* 31D3
Fuyuan, Liaoning *China* 31E1
Fuyuan, Yunnan *China* 31A4
Fuyun *China* 26B2
Fuzhou *China* 31D4
Fuzhoucheng *China* 28A3
Fyn, I *Den* 18C1
Fyne, Loch, Inlet *Scot* 8C3

G

Gaalkacyo *Somalia* 50E3
Gabbs *USA* 59C3
Gabbs Valley Range, Mts *USA* 66C1
Gabela *Angola* 51B5
Gabès, G de *Tunisia* 48D1
Gabilan Range, Mts *USA* 66B2
Gabon, Republic *Africa* 50B4
Gaborone *Botswana* 47D1
Gabriel y Galán, Embalse Res *Spain* 15A1
Gabrovo *Bulg* 17F2
Gach Sārān *Iran* 41F3
Gadag *India* 44B2
Gadsden, Alabama *USA* 67A2
Gadsden, Arizona *USA* 59D4
Gaeta *Italy* 16C2
Gaferut, I *Pacific O* 27H6
Gaffney *USA* 67B1
Gafra, Wadi el *Egypt* 45A3
Gafsa *Tunisia* 48C1
Gagarin *USSR* 20E4
Gagnon *Can* 55M4
Gagra *USSR* 21G7
Gaibanda *Bang* 43F3
Gaimán *Arg* 74C6
Gainesville, Florida *USA* 67B3
Gainesville, Georgia *USA* 67B2
Gainesville, Texas *USA* 63C2
Gainsborough *Eng* 7D3
Gairdner, L *Aust* 32C4
Gairloch *Scot* 8C3
Gaithersburg *USA* 68B3
Gai Xian *China* 28A2
Gajendragarh *India* 44B2
Ga Jiang, R *China* 31D4
Gakarosa, Mt *S Africa* 47C2
Galana, R *Kenya* 50D4
Galapagos Is *Pacific O* 52D5
Gálápagos, Islas = Galapagos Is
Galashiels *Scot* 8D4
Galaţi *Rom* 17F1
Galax *USA* 64C3
Galeana *Mexico* 62A2
Galena, Alaska *USA* 54C3
Galena, Illinois *USA* 64A2
Galena, Kansas *USA* 63D1
Galeota Pt *Trinidad* 69L1
Galera Pt *Trinidad* 69L1
Galesburg *USA* 64A2
Galeton *USA* 68B2
Galich *USSR* 20G4
Galicia, Region *Spain* 15A1
Galilee,S of = Tiberias,L
Galina Pt *Jamaica* 69J1
Gallabat *Sudan* 50D2
Gallatin *USA* 67A1
Gallatin, R *USA* 58D1
Galle *Sri Lanka* 44C4
Gallego *Mexico* 62A3
Gállego, R *Spain* 15B1
Gallinas, Puerta *Colombia* 72D1
Gallipolī = Gelibolu
Gallipoli *Italy* 17D2
Gällivare *Sweden* 20C2
Galloway, District *Scot* 8C4
Galloway,Mull of, C *Scot* 8C4
Gallup *USA* 62A1
Galt *USA* 66B1
Galty Mts *Irish Rep* 9B3
Galveston *USA* 70C2
Galveston B *USA* 57D4
Galway *Irish Rep* 10B3
Galway B *Irish Rep* 10B3
Gamba *China* 43F3
Gambaga *Ghana* 48B3
Gambell *USA* 54A3
Gambia, R *Sen/The Gambia* 48A3
Gambia,The, Republic *Africa* 48A3
Gambier, Îles *Pacific O* 37N6
Gamboma *Congo* 50B4
Gambos *Angola* 51B5
Gampola *Sri Lanka* 44C4
Ganado *USA* 59E3
Ganale Dorya, R *Eth* 50E3
Gananoque *Can* 65D2
Gand = Gent
Ganda *Angola* 51B5
Gandajika *Zaïre* 51C4
Gandak, R *India/Nepal* 43N2
Gandak Dam *Nepal* 43M2
Gandava *Pak* 42B3
Gander *Can* 55N5
Gāndhīdhām *India* 42B4
Gāndhīnagar *India* 42C4
Gāndhi Sāgar, L *India* 42D4
Gandia *Spain* 15B2
Gandu *Brazil* 75E1
Ganga, R = Ganges
Gangānagar *India* 42C3
Gangaw *Burma* 43G4
Gangca *China* 31A2
Gangdise Shan, Mts *China* 39G2
Ganges, R *India* 22F4
Ganges, Mouths of the *Bang/India* 43F4
Gangou *China* 28B2
Gangtok *India* 43F3
Gangu *China* 31B3
Gannett Peak, Mt *USA* 58E2
Ganquan *China* 31B2
Gantsevichi *USSR* 12K8
Ganzhou *China* 31D4
Gao *Mali* 48C3
Gaolan *China* 31A2
Gaoping *China* 31C2
Gaoua *Burkina* 48B3
Gaoual *Guinea* 48A3
Gaoyou Hu, L *China* 31D3
Gaozhou *China* 31C5
Gap *France* 14D3
Gar *China* 42D2
Gara,L *Irish Rep* 9B3
Garah *Aust* 34C1
Garanhuns *Brazil* 73L5
Garberville *USA* 59B2
Garça *Brazil* 75C3
Garcia de Sola, Embalse de, Res *Spain* 15A2
Garcias *Brazil* 75B3
Garda, L di *Italy* 16C1
Garden City *USA* 62B1
Garden Pen *USA* 64B1
Gardez *Afghan* 42B2
Gardiner *USA* 58D1
Gardiners I *USA* 68D2
Gardner *USA* 68E1
Gardner, I *Phoenix Is* 33H1
Gardnerville *USA* 66C1
Gargano, Monte, Mt *Italy* 16D2
Gargano, Prom. del *Italy* 16D2
Garhākota *India* 42D4
Garhmuktesar *India* 43K1
Gari *USSR* 20L4
Garies *S Africa* 47B3
Garissa *Kenya* 50D4
Garland *USA* 63C2
Garmisch-Partenkirchen *W Germ* 18C3
Garmsar *Iran* 41F2
Garnett *USA* 63C1
Garnett Peak, Mt *USA* 56B2
Garonne, R *France* 14C3
Garoua *Cam* 49D4
Garoua Boulai *Cam* 49D4
Garrison *USA* 60C1
Garron Pt *N Ire* 9D2
Garry, R *Scot* 8C3
Garry L *Can* 54H3
Garwa *India* 43E4
Gary *USA* 64B2
Garyarsa *China* 39G2
Garza-Little Elm, Res *USA* 63C2
Gasan Kuli *USSR* 41F2
Gascogne, Region *France* 14B3
Gasconade, R *USA* 63D1
Gascoyne, R *Aust* 32A3
Gashaka *Nig* 50B3
Gashua *Nigeria* 48D3
Gaspé *Can* 57G2
Gaspé,C *Can* 57G2
Gaspé Pen *Can* 57G2
Gastonia *USA* 67B1
Gaston,L *USA* 67C1
Gata, C *Cyprus* 45B1
Gata, Cabo de, C *Spain* 15B2
Gatchina *USSR* 20D4
Gatehouse of Fleet *Scot* 8C4
Gateshead *Eng* 6D2
Gatesville *USA* 63C2
Gâtinais, Region *France* 13B3
Gatineau *Can* 65D1
Gatineau, R *Can* 65D1
Gatlinburg *USA* 67B1
Gatton *Aust* 34D1
Gaua, I *Vanuatu* 33F2
Gauhāti *India* 43G3
Gauja, R *USSR* 19E1
Gauri Phanta *India* 43E3
Gávdhos, I *Greece* 17E4
Gavião, R *Brazil* 75D1
Gaviota *USA* 66B3
Gävle *Sweden* 12H6
Gawler Ranges, Mts *Aust* 32C4
Gaxun Nur, L *China* 31A1
Gaya *India* 43E4
Gaya *Niger* 48C3
Gaya *Nigeria* 48C3
Gaya He, R *China* 28B2
Gaylord *USA* 64C1
Gayndah *Aust* 34D1
Gayny *USSR* 20J3
Gaysin *USSR* 19F3
Gaza *Israel* 40B3
Gaziantep *Turk* 40C2
Gbaringa *Lib* 48B4
Gbbès *Tunisia* 48D1
Gdańsk *Pol* 19D2
Gdańsk,G of *Pol* 19D2
Gdov *USSR* 12K7
Gdynia *Pol* 19D2
Gebel el Galâla el Baharîya, Desert *Egypt* 45A4
Gedaref *Sudan* 50D2
Gediz, R *Turk* 17F3
Gedser *Den* 18C2
Geel *Belg* 13C2
Geelong *Aust* 34B3
Geeveston *Aust* 34C4
Geidam *Nigeria* 48D3
Geilenkirchen *W Germ* 13D2
Geita *Tanz* 50D4
Gejiu *China* 31A5
Gela *Italy* 16C3
Geladī *Eth* 50E3
Geldern *W Germ* 13D2
Gelibolu *Turk* 17F2
Gelidonya Burun *Turk* 40B2
Gelnhausen *W Germ* 13E2
Gelsenkirchen *W Germ* 13D2
Gelting *W Germ* 12F8
Gemas *Malay* 30C5
Gembloux *Belg* 13C2
Gemena *Zaïre* 50B3
Gemerek *Turk* 40C2
Gemlik *Turk* 40A1
Gemona *Italy* 16C1
Gemsbok Nat Pk *Botswana* 47C2
Geneina *Sudan* 50C2
General Alvear *Arg* 74C5
General Belgrano, Base *Ant* 76F2
General Bernardo O'Higgins, Base *Ant* 76G2
General Carrera, Lago *Chile* 74B7
General Eugenio A Garay *Par* 74D2
General Grant Grove Section, Region *USA* 66C2
General Manuel Belgrano, Mt *Arg* 74C3
General Pico *Arg* 74D5
General Roca *Arg* 74C5
General Santos *Phil* 27F6
Genesee, R *USA* 65D2
Geneseo *USA* 65D2
Geneva, Nebraska *USA* 61D2
Geneva, New York *USA* 68B1
Geneva *Switz* 16B1
Geneva,L of = Léman, L
Genève = Geneva
Genil, R *Spain* 15B2
Gennargentu, Monti del, Mt, *Sardinia* 16B2
Genoa *Aust* 34C3
Genoa *Italy* 16B2
Genova = Genoa
Genova, G di *Italy* 16B2
Gent *Belg* 13B2
Genteng *Indon* 27D7
Genthin *E Germ* 18C2
Geokchay *USSR* 21H7
George *S Africa* 47C3
George, R *Can* 55M4
George,L *Aust* 34C2
George,L, Florida *USA* 67B3
George,L, New York *USA* 65E2
George Sd *NZ* 35A2
George Town *Aust* 34C4
Georgetown, California *USA* 66B1
Georgetown, Delaware *USA* 65D3
Georgetown *Guyana* 73G2
Georgetown, Kentucky *USA* 64C3
George Town *Malay* 30C4
Georgetown *St Vincent* 69N2
Georgetown, S Carolina *USA* 67C2
Georgetown, Texas *USA* 63C2
Georgetown *The Gambia* 48A3
George V Land, Region *Ant* 76G8
George West *USA* 62C3
Georgia, State *USA* 67B2
Georgian B *Can* 64C1
Georgian SSR, Republic *USSR* 24F5
Georgia, Str of *Can* 54F5
Georgina, R *Aust* 32C3
Georgiu-Dezh *USSR* 21F5
Georgiyevsk *USSR* 21G7
Georg von Neumayer, Base *Ant* 76F1
Gera *E Germ* 18C2
Geraardsbergen *Belg* 13B2
Geral de Goiás, Serra, Mts *Brazil* 75C1
Geraldine *NZ* 35B2
Geral do Paraná, Serra, Mts *Brazil* 75C2
Geraldton *Aust* 32A3
Geraldton *Can* 57E2
Geral, Serra, Mts, Bahia *Brazil* 75D2
Geral, Serra, Mts, Paraná *Brazil* 75B4
Gerar, R *Israel* 45C3
Gérardmer *France* 13D3
Gerdine,Mt *USA* 54C3
Gerik *Malay* 30C4
Gering *USA* 60C2
Gerlachovsky, Mt *Pol* 21C6
Germiston *S Africa* 47D2
Gerolstein *W Germ* 13D2
Gerona *Spain* 15C1
Geseke *W Germ* 13E2
Gestro, R *Eth* 50E3
Getafe *Spain* 15B1
Gettysburg, Pennsylvania *USA* 68B3
Gettysburg, S Dakota *USA* 60D1
Gevaş *Turk* 41D2
Gevgeliija *Yugos* 17E2
Ghabāghib *Syria* 45D2
Ghadaf, Wadi el *Jordan* 45D3
Ghadamis *Libya* 48C1
Ghaem Shahr *Iran* 41F2
Ghāghara, R *India* 43E3
Ghaghara, R *India* 43L2
Ghana, Republic *Africa* 48B4
Ghanzi *Botswana* 47C1
Ghardaïa *Alg* 48C1
Gharyān *Libya* 49D1
Ghāt *Libya* 49D2
Ghazaouet *Alg* 15B2
Ghāziābād *India* 42D3
Ghazni *Afghan* 42B2
Gheorge Gheorgiu-Dej *Rom* 17F1
Gheorgheni *Rom* 17F1
Ghudāf, Wadi al, Watercourse *Iraq* 40D3
Gialo *Libya* 49E2
Giamame *Somalia* 50E3
Giarre, *Sicily* 16D3
Gibbon *USA* 60D2
Gibeon *Namibia* 47B2
Gibraltar, Colony *SW Europe* 15A2
Gibraltar, Pt *Eng* 7E7
Gibraltar,Str of *Africa/Spain* 15A2
Gibson Desert *Aust* 32B3
Gibsons *Can* 58B1
Giddalūr *India* 44B2
Giddi, Gebel el, Mt *Egypt* 45B3
Giddi Pass *Egypt* 45B3
Giddolē *Eth* 50D3
Gien *France* 13B4
Giessen *W Germ* 18B2
Gifford *Scot* 8D4
Gifford *USA* 67B3
Gifu *Japan* 29D3
Gigha, I *Scot* 8C4
Giglio, I *Italy* 16C2
Gijón *Spain* 15A1
Gila, R *USA* 59D4
Gila Bend *USA* 59D4
Gila Bend Mts *USA* 59D4
Gilbert, R *Aust* 32D2
Gilbert Is *Pacific O* 33G1
Gildford *USA* 58D1
Gilé *Mozam* 51D5
Gilead, Region *Jordan* 45C2
Gilf Kebir Plat *Egypt* 49E2
Gilgandra *Aust* 34C2
Gilgit *Pak* 42C1
Gilgit, R *Pak* 42C1
Gilgunnia *Aust* 34C2
Gillam *Can* 55J4
Gillette *USA* 60B2
Gillingham *Eng* 7E4
Gills Rock *USA* 64B1
Gilman *USA* 64B2
Gilroy *USA* 66B2
Gimie, Mont *St Lucia* 69P2
Gineifa *Egypt* 45B3
Gingindlovu *S Africa* 47E2
Ginir *Eth* 50E3
Gióna, Mt *Greece* 17E3
Gippsland, Mts *Aust* 34C3
Girard *USA* 64C2
Girardot *Colombia* 72D3
Girdle Ness, Pen *Scot* 8D3
Giresun *Turk* 40C1
Girga *Egypt* 40B4
Gīr Hills *India* 42C4
Giri, R *Zaïre* 50B3
Girīdīh *India* 43F4
Girishk *Afghan* 42A2
Giromagny *France* 13D4
Gironde, R *France* 14B2
Girvan *Scot* 8C4
Gisborne *NZ* 35C1
Gitega *Burundi* 50C4
Giuba,R = Juba,R
Giurgiu *Rom* 17F2
Givet *France* 13C2
Gizhiga *USSR* 25S3
Gizycko *Pol* 19E2
Gjirokastër *Alb* 17E2
Gjoatlaven *Can* 54J3
Gjøvik *Nor* 12G6
Glace Bay *Can* 55M5
Glacier Peak, Mt *USA* 58B1
Glacier Str *Can* 55K2
Gladstone, Queensland *Aust* 32E3
Gladstone, S Aust *Aust* 34A2
Gladstone, Tasmania *Aust* 34C4
Gladstone *USA* 64B1
Glâma, Mt *Iceland* 12A1
Glåma, R *Nor* 12G6
Glan, R *W Germ* 13D3
Glasco *USA* 61D3
Glasgow, Kentucky *USA* 64B3
Glasgow, Montana *USA* 60B1
Glasgow *Scot* 8C4
Glassboro *USA* 68C3
Glass Mt *USA* 66C2
Glastonbury *Eng* 7C4
Glazov *USSR* 20J4
Gleisdorf *Austria* 18D3
Glen Afton *NZ* 35C1
Glenarm *N Ire* 9D2
Glen Burnie *USA* 68B3
Glencoe *S Africa* 47E2
Glendale, Arizona *USA* 59D4
Glendale, California *USA* 66C3
Glendive *USA* 60C1
Glendo Res *USA* 60C2
Glengad Hd,Pt *Irish Rep* 9C2
Glen Innes *Aust* 34D1
Glenluce *Scot* 8C4
Glenmorgan *Aust* 34C1
Glenreagh *Aust* 34D2
Glen Rock *USA* 68B3
Glen Rose *USA* 63C2
Glenrothes *Scot* 8D3
Glens Falls *USA* 68D1
Glenwood, Arkansas *USA* 63D2
Glenwood, Minnesota *USA* 61D1
Glenwood, New Mexico *USA* 62A2
Glenwood Springs *USA* 60B3
Glidden *USA* 64A1
Glittertind, Mt *Nor* 12F6
Gliwice *Pol* 19D2
Globe *USA* 59D4
Głogów *Pol* 18D2

Glomfjord **Groom**

Glomfjord *Nor* 12G5
Glorieuses, Isles *Madag* 51E5
Glossop *Eng* 7C3
Gloucester *Aust* 34D2
Gloucester *Eng* 7C4
Gloucester *USA* 68E1
Gloucester, County *Eng* 7C4
Gloversville *USA* 68C1
Glubokoye *USSR* 19F1
Glückstadt *W Germ* 13E1
Glukhov *USSR* 21E5
Gmünd *Austria* 18D3
Gmunden *Austria* 18C3
Gniezno *Pol* 19D2
Goa, Daman and Diu, Union Territory *India* 44A2
Goageb *Namibia* 47B2
Goālpāra *India* 43G3
Goba *Eth* 50D3
Gobabis *Namibia* 47B1
Gobi, Desert *China/ Mongolia* 31B1
Gobo *Japan* 29C4
Gobza, R *USSR* 19G1
Gochas *Namibia* 47B1
Godalming *Eng* 7D4
Godāvari, R *India* 44C2
Goddard,Mt *USA* 66C2
Goderich *Can* 64C2
Godhavn *Greenland* 55N3
Godhra *India* 42C4
Gods L *Can* 57D1
Godthåb *Greenland* 55N3
Godwin Austen, Mt = K2
Goffstown *USA* 68E1
Gogama *Can* 64C1
Gohfeld *W Germ* 13E1
Goiandira *Brazil* 75C2
Goianésia *Brazil* 75C2
Goiânia *Brazil* 71F5
Goiás *Brazil* 75B2
Goiás, State *Brazil* 73J6
Goio-Erê *Brazil* 75B3
Gojab, R *Eth* 50D3
Gökçeada, I *Turk* 17F2
Gökova Körfezi, B *Turk* 17F3
Goksu, R *Turk* 21F8
Göksun *Turk* 40C2
Golāghāt *India* 43G3
Gola, I *Irish Rep* 9B2
Gölbaşı *Turk* 40C2
Gol'chikha *USSR* 24K2
Golconda *USA* 58C2
Gold *USA* 68B2
Gold Beach *USA* 58B2
Gold Coast *Aust* 34D1
Golden B *NZ* 35B2
Goldendale *USA* 58B1
Golden Gate, Chan *USA* 66A2
Golden Meadow *USA* 63D3
Goldfield *USA* 59C3
Gold Point *USA* 66D2
Goldsboro *USA* 67C1
Goldthwaite *USA* 62C2
Goleniów *Pol* 18C2
Goleta *USA* 66C3
Golmud *China* 26C3
Gololcha *Eth* 50E3
Golovnino *USSR* 29F2
Goma *Zaïre* 50C4
Gomati *India* 43L2
Gombe *Nigeria* 48D3
Gomel *USSR* 19G2
Gomera, I *Canary Is* 48A2
Gómez Palacio *Mexico* 70B2
Gonam, R *USSR* 25O4
Gonâve, Isla de la *Cuba* 69C3
Gonbad-e Kāvūs *Iran* 41G2
Gonda *India* 43E3
Gondal *India* 42C4
Gonder *Eth* 50D2
Gondia *India* 43E4
Gönen *Turk* 40A1
Gonen, R *Turk* 17F3
Gongga Shan, Mt *China* 31A4
Gonghe *China* 31A2
Gongogi, R *Brazil* 75D1
Gongola, R *Nigeria* 48D3
Gonzales, California *USA* 66B2
Gonzales, Texas *USA* 63C3
Good Hope,C of *S Africa* 47B3
Gooding *USA* 58D2
Goodland *USA* 60C3
Goodooga, R *Aust* 34C1
Goole *Eng* 7D3
Goolgowi *Aust* 34C2
Goolwa *Aust* 34A3
Goomalling *Aust* 32A4
Goombalie *Aust* 34C2
Goomeri *Aust* 34D1
Goondiwindi *Aust* 34D1
Goose Bay *Can* 55N4
Goose Creek *USA* 67C2
Goose L *USA* 58B2
Gooty *India* 44B2
Goraka *PNG* 32D1
Gorakhpur *India* 43E3
Gora Koyp, Mt *USSR* 20K3
Gora Munku Sardyk, Mt *USSR/Mongolia* 25L4
Gora Narodnaya, Mt *USSR* 20K3
Gora Pay-Yer, Mt *USSR* 20L2
Gora Telpos-Iz, Mt *USSR* 20K3
Goražde *Yugos* 17D2
Gordon *USA* 54D2
Gordonsville *USA* 65D3
Goré *Chad* 50B3
Gore *Eth* 50D3
Gore *NZ* 35A3
Gore Topko, Mt *USSR* 25P4
Gorey *Irish Rep* 9C3
Gorgān *Iran* 41F2
Gorinchem *Neth* 13C2
Goris *USSR* 41E2
Gorizia *Italy* 16C1
Gorki, Belorusskaya S.S. R. *USSR* 19G2
Gorki, Rossiyskaya S.F.S. R. *USSR* 20M2
Gor'kiy *USSR* 24F4
Gor'kovskoye Vodokhranilishche, Res *USSR* 20G4
Gorleston *Eng* 7E3
Görlitz *E Germ* 18C2
Gorlovka *USSR* 21F6
Gorman *USA* 66C3
Gorna Orjahovica *Bulg* 17F2
Gorno-Altaysk *USSR* 26B1
Gornozavodsk *USSR* 26H2
Goro Denezhkin Kamen', Mt *USSR* 20K3
Gorodets *USSR* 20G4
Gorodnya *USSR* 19G2
Gorodok, Belorusskaya S.S.R. *USSR* 19G1
Gorodok, Ukrainskaya S. S.R. *USSR* 19E3
Gorodok, Ukrainskaya S. S.R. *USSR* 19F3
Goroka *PNG* 27H7
Gorongosa *Mozam* 51D5
Gorontalo *Indon* 27F6
Goro Yurma, Mt *USSR* 20L4
Gorutuba, R *Brazil* 75D2
Goryachinsk *USSR* 25M4
Gory Akkyr, Upland *USSR* 21J7
Gory Byrranga, Mts *USSR* 25L2
Goryn', R *USSR* 19F3
Gory Putorana, Mts *USSR* 25L3
Góry Świetokrzyskie, Upland *Pol* 19E2
Gory Tel'pos-iz, Mt *USSR* 24G3
Gorzów Wielkopolski *Pol* 12H8
Goshen *USA* 66C2
Goshogawara *Japan* 29E2
Gospić *Yugos* 16D2
Gosport *Eng* 7D4
Gostivar *Yugos* 17E2
Gostynin *Pol* 19D2
Göteborg *Sweden* 12G7
Gotel Mts *Nig* 50B3
Gothenburg *USA* 60C2
Gotland, I *Sweden* 12H7
Gotō-rettō, Is *Japan* 28B4
Gotska Sandön, I *Sweden* 12H7
Gōtsu *Japan* 28C4
Göttingen *W Germ* 18B2
Gottwaldov *Czech* 19D3
Goubangzi *China* 28A2
Gouda *Neth* 13C2
Goudoumaria *Niger* 50B2
Gough I *Atlantic O* 52H7
Gouin, Réservoire *Can* 55L5
Goulburn *Aust* 34C2
Goumbou *Mali* 48B3
Goundam *Mali* 48B3
Gouré *Niger* 50B2
Gourma Rharous *Mali* 48B3
Gouro *Chad* 50B2
Govenlock *Can* 58E1
Gove Pen *Aust* 27G8
Goverla, Mt *USSR* 21C6
Governador Valadares *Brazil* 75D2
Govind Ballabh Paht Sāgar, L *India* 43E4
Gowārān *Afghan* 42B3
Gower *Wales* 7B4
Goya *Arg* 74E3
Goz-Beïda *Chad* 50C2
Gozo, I *Malta* 16C3
Goz Regeb *Sudan* 50D2
Graaff-Reinet *S Africa* 47C3
Gracefield *Can* 65D1
Gracias à Dios, Cabo *Honduras* 69A4
Grafton *Aust* 33E3
Grafton, N Dakota *USA* 61D1
Grafton, W Virginia *USA* 64C3
Graham I *Can* 54E4
Graham,Mt *USA* 59E4
Grahamstown *S Africa* 47D3
Grajaú *Brazil* 73J5
Grajewo *Pol* 19E2
Grámmos, Mt *Alb/ Greece* 17E2
Grampian, Mts *Scot* 8C3
Grampian, Region *Scot* 8D3
Granada *Colombia* 72D3
Granada *Nic* 72A1
Granada *Spain* 15B2
Granby *Can* 65E1
Granby *USA* 60B2
Gran Canaria, I *Canary Is* 48A2
Gran Chaco, Region *Arg* 74D3
Grand, R, Michigan *USA* 64B2
Grand, R, Missouri *USA* 61E2
Grand B *Dominica* 69Q2
Grand Bahama, I *The Bahamas* 57F4
Grand Ballon, Mt *France* 13D4
Grand Bank *Can* 55N5
Grand Banks *Atlantic O* 52F2
Grand Bassam *Ivory Coast* 48B4
Grand Canyon *USA* 59D3
Grand Canyon Nat Pk *USA* 59D3
Grand Cayman, I, Cayman Is *Caribbean S* 69A3
Grand Coulee *USA* 58C1
Grande, R, Bahia *Brazil* 73K6
Grande, R, Minas Gerais/São Paulo *Brazil* 75C2
Grande, Bahía, B *Arg* 74C8
Grande Comore, I *Comoros* 51E5
Grande, Ilha *Brazil* 75D3
Grande Prairie *USA* 63C2
Grand Erg de Bilma, Desert Region *Niger* 50B2
Grand Erg Occidental, Desert *Alg* 48C1
Grand Erg Oriental, Desert *Alg* 48C2
Grande Rivière de la Baleine, R *Can* 55L4
Grande Ronde, R *USA* 58C1
Gran Desierto *USA* 59D4
Grand Falls, New Brunswick *Can* 55M5
Grand Falls, Newfoundland *Can* 55N5
Grand Forks *Can* 58C1
Grand Forks *USA* 61D1
Grand Gorge *USA* 68C1
Grand Haven *USA* 64B2
Grand Island *USA* 60D2
Grand Isle *USA* 63E2
Grand Junction *USA* 60B3
Grand L *USA* 63D3
Grand Marais *USA* 64A1
Grand Mère *Can* 65E1
Grândola *Port* 15A2
Grand Prairie *Can* 54G4
Grand Rapids *Can* 54J4
Grand Rapids, Michigan *USA* 64B2
Grand Rapids, Minnesota *USA* 64A1
Grand St Bernard, Col du, P *Italy/Switz* 16B1
Grand Teton, Mt *USA* 56B2
Grand Teton Nat Pk *USA* 58D2
Grand Valley *USA* 60B3
Grangeville *USA* 58C1
Granite Peak, Mt, Montana *USA* 58E1
Granite Peak, Mt, Utah *USA* 59D2
Granollérs *Spain* 15C1
Gran Paradiso, Mt *Italy* 16B1
Grantham *Eng* 7D3
Grant,Mt *USA* 66C1
Grantown-on-Spey *Scot* 8D3
Grants *USA* 62A1
Grants Pass *USA* 58B2
Granville *France* 14B2
Granville *USA* 68D1
Granville L *Can* 54H4
Grão Mogol *Brazil* 75D2
Grapevine *USA* 66C3
Grapevine Mts *USA* 66D2
Graskop *S Africa* 47E1
Gras, Lac de *Can* 54G3
Grasse *France* 14D3
Grassington *Eng* 6D2
Grassrange *USA* 58E1
Grass Valley *USA* 59B3
Gravatai *Brazil* 74F4
Gravelbourg *Can* 54H5
Gravelines *France* 13B2
Gravelotte *S Africa* 51D6
Gravenhurst *Can* 65D2
Grave Peak, Mt *USA* 58D1
Gravesend *Aust* 34D1
Gravesend *Eng* 7E4
Grays Harbour, B *USA* 58B1
Grays L *USA* 58D2
Grayson *USA* 64C3
Grayville *USA* 64B3
Graz *Austria* 18D3
Great, R *Jamaica* 69H1
Great Abaco, I *The Bahamas* 57F4
Great Australian Bight, G *Aust* 32B4
Great B, New Hampshire *USA* 68E1
Great B, New Jersey *USA* 68C3
Great Bahama Bank *The Bahamas* 70E2
Great Barrier I *NZ* 35C1
Great Barrier Reef, Is *Aust* 32D2
Great Barrington *USA* 68D1
Great Basin *USA* 59C2
Great Bear L *Can* 54F3
Great Bend *USA* 62C1
Great Bitter L *Egypt* 45B3
Great Cacapon *USA* 68A3
Great Coco I *Burma* 44E3
Great Dividing Range, Mts *Aust* 32D3
Great Driffield *Eng* 6D2
Great Egg Harbor, B *USA* 68C3
Greater Antarctica, Region *Ant* 76F10
Greater Antilles, Is *Caribbean S* 69B2
Greater London, Metropolitan County *Eng* 7D4
Greater Manchester, Metropolitan County *Eng* 7C3
Great Exuma, I *The Bahamas* 70E2
Great Falls *USA* 58D1
Great Fish, R *S Africa* 47D3
Great Glen, V *Scot* 8C3
Great Himalayan Range, Mts *Asia* 43F3
Great Inagua, I *The Bahamas* 57F4
Great Karoo, Mts *S Africa* 47C3
Great Kei, R *S Africa* 47D3
Great L *Aust* 34C4
Great Malvern *Eng* 7C3
Great Namaland, Region *Namibia* 51B6
Great Nicobar, I *Indian O* 44E4
Great Ormes Head, C *Wales* 7C3
Great Pt *USA* 68E2
Great Ragged, I *The Bahamas* 57F4
Great Ruaha, R *Tanz* 51D4
Great Sacandaga L *USA* 65E2
Great Salt L *USA* 58D2
Great Salt Lake Desert *USA* 58D2
Great Sand Sea *Libya/ Egypt* 49E2
Great Sandy Desert *Aust* 32B3
Great Sandy Desert *USA* 56A2
Great Sandy I = Fraser I
Great Slave L *Can* 54G3
Great Smoky Mts *USA* 67B1
Great Smoky Mts Nat Pk *USA* 67B1
Great South B *USA* 68D2
Great Tafelberg, Mt *S Africa* 47C3
Great Victoria Desert *Aust* 32B3
Great Wall *China* 31B2
Great Yarmouth *Eng* 7E3
Gréboun, Mont *Niger* 48C2
Greco, C *Cyprus* 45C1
Gredos, Sierra de, Mts *Spain* 15A1
Greece *USA* 65D2
Greece, Republic *Europe* 17E3
Greeley *USA* 60C2
Greely Fjord *Can* 55K1
Greem Bell, Ostrov, I *USSR* 24H1
Green, R, Kentucky *USA* 64B3
Green, R, Utah *USA* 59D3
Green B *USA* 64B1
Green Bay *USA* 64B2
Greencastle, Indiana *USA* 64B3
Greencastle, Pennsylvania *USA* 68B3
Greene *USA* 68C1
Greeneville *USA* 67B1
Greenfield, California *USA* 66B2
Greenfield, California *USA* 66C3
Greenfield, Massachusetts *USA* 68D1
Greenfield, Wisconsin *USA* 64B2
Greenland, Dependency *N Atlantic O* 55O2
Greenland, I *Atlantic O* 52F1
Greenland Basin *Greenland S* 52H1
Greenland Sea *Greenland* 76B1
Greenlaw *Scot* 8D4
Greenock *Scot* 8C4
Greenport *USA* 68D2
Green River, Utah *USA* 59D3
Green River, Wyoming *USA* 58E2
Greensboro, Maryland *USA* 68C3
Greensboro, N Carolina *USA* 67C1
Greensburg, Kansas *USA* 62C1
Greensburg, Kentucky *USA* 64B3
Greensburg, Pennsylvania *USA* 65D2
Greenstone Pt *Scot* 8C3
Greenup *USA* 64B3
Green Valley *USA* 59D4
Greenville, Alabama *USA* 67A2
Greenville *Lib* 48B4
Greenville, Mississippi *USA* 63D2
Greenville, N Carolina *USA* 67C1
Greenville, N Hampshire *USA* 68E1
Greenville, Ohio *USA* 64C2
Greenville, S Carolina *USA* 67B2
Greenville, Texas *USA* 63C2
Greenville, Florida *USA* 67B2
Greenville,C *Aust* 27H8
Greenwich *Eng* 7E4
Greenwich *USA* 68D2
Greenwood, Delaware *USA* 68C3
Greenwood, Mississippi *USA* 63D2
Greenwood, S Carolina *USA* 67B2
Greers Ferry L *USA* 63D1
Gregory *USA* 60D2
Gregory,L *Aust* 34A1
Gregory Range, Mts *Aust* 32D2
Greifswald *E Germ* 18C2
Gremikha *USSR* 20F2
Grenå *Den* 12G7
Grenada *USA* 63E2
Grenada, I *Caribbean S* 69E4
Grenadines,The, Is *Caribbean S* 69E4
Grenfell *Aust* 34C2
Grenoble *France* 14D2
Grenville *Grenada* 69M2
Grenville,C *Aust* 32D2
Gresham *USA* 58B1
Gretna *USA* 63D3
Grey, R *NZ* 35B2
Greybull *USA* 58E2
Grey Is *Can* 55N4
Greylock,Mt *USA* 68D1
Greymouth *NZ* 35B2
Grey Range, Mts *Aust* 32D3
Greystones *Irish Rep* 9C3
Greytown *S Africa* 47E2
Griffin *USA* 67B2
Griffith *Aust* 34C2
Grim,C *Aust* 32D5
Grimsby *Can* 65D2
Grimsby *Eng* 7D3
Grimsey, I *Iceland* 12B1
Grimstad *Nor* 12F7
Grinnell *USA* 61E2
Grinnell Pen *Can* 55J2
Grise Fjord *Can* 55K2
Griva *USSR* 20J3
Grobina *USSR* 12J7
Groblersdal *S Africa* 47D2
Grodno *USSR* 19E2
Gromati, R *India* 43E3
Gronan *W Germ* 13D1
Groningen *Neth* 18B2
Groningen, Province *Neth* 13D1
Groom *USA* 62B1

Groot Harrisburg

Groot, R S Africa 47C3
Groote Eylandt, I Aust 32C2
Grootfontein Namibia 51B5
Groot-Karasberge, Mts Namibia 47B2
Groot Laagte, R Botswana/Namibia 47C1
Groot Vloer, Salt L S Africa 47C2
Gros Islet St Lucia 69P2
Grosser Feldberg, Mt W Germ 13E2
Grosseto Italy 16C2
Gross-Gerau W Germ 13E3
Grossglockner, Mt Austria 18C3
Gros Ventre Range, Mts USA 58D2
Groton USA 61D1
Groundhog, R Can 64C1
Grove Hill USA 63E2
Groveland USA 66B2
Grover City USA 66B3
Groveton USA 65E2
Groznyy USSR 21H7
Grudziadz Pol 19D2
Grünau Namibia 47B2
Grutness Scot 8E2
Gryazi USSR 21G5
Gryazovets USSR 20F4
Grytviken South Georgia 74J8
Guacanayabo, G de Cuba 69B2
Guaçuí Brazil 75D3
Guadalajara Mexico 70B2
Guadalajara Spain 15B1
Guadalcanal, I Solomon Is 33E1
Guadalimar, R Spain 15B2
Guadalope, R Spain 15B1
Guadalqivir, R Spain 15B2
Guadalupe Mexico 70B2
Guadalupe USA 66B3
Guadalupe, I Mexico 53G6
Guadalupe, R USA 62C3
Guadalupe Mtns Nat Pk USA 62B2
Guadalupe Peak, Mt USA 62B2
Guadalupe, Sierra de, Mts Spain 15A2
Guadarrama, Sierra de, Mts Spain 15B1
Guadeloupe, I Caribbean S 69E3
Guadian, R Spain 15B2
Guadiana, R Port 15A2
Guadiana, R Spain 15B2
Guadix Spain 15B2
Guaíra Brazil 75B3
Guajará Mirim Brazil 72E6
Guajira,Pen de Colombia 72D1
Guajiri, Península de la Colombia 69C4
Gualaceo Ecuador 72C4
Guam, I Pacific O 27H5
Guaminí Arg 74D5
Gua Musang Malay 30C5
Guanabacoa Cuba 69A2
Guanambi Brazil 75D1
Guanare Ven 72E2
Guandi China 28B2
Guane Cuba 70D2
Guangdong, Province China 31C5
Guanghan China 31A3
Guanghua China 31C3
Guangmao Shan, Mt China 31A4
Guangnan China 31A5
Guangxi, Province China 31B5
Guangyuan China 31B3
Guangze China 31D4
Guangzhou China 31C5
Guanhães Brazil 75D2
Guania, R Colombia/Ven 72E3
Guanipa, R Ven 69E5
Guantánamo Cuba 69B2
Guanting Shuiku, Res China 31D1
Guan Xian China 31A3
Guapá Colombia 72C2
Guaporé, R Bol/Brazil 72F6
Guaquí Bol 72E7
Guará, R Brazil 75D1
Guaranda Ecuador 72C4
Guarapuava Brazil 75B4
Guaraqueçaba Brazil 75C4
Guara, Sierra de, Mts Spain 15B1
Guaratinguetá Brazil 75C3
Guaratuba, B Brazil 75C4
Guarda Port 15A1
Guardafui,C Somalia 50E2
Guarda Mor Brazil 75C2
Guasave Mexico 56C4
Guatemala Guatemala 70C3
Guatemala, Republic Cent America 70C3
Guaviare, R Colombia 72D3
Guaxupé Brazil 75C3
Guayaguayare Trinidad 69L1
Guayaquil Ecuador 72B4
Guayaquil, Golfo de Ecuador 72B4
Guaymas Mexico 70A2
Guba Eth 50D3
Guba Zaïre 51C5
Guba Buorkhaya, B USSR 25P2
Guban, Region Somalia 50E3
Gubin Pol 18C2
Gudar, Sierra de, Mts Spain 15B1
Güdür India 44B3
Guebwiller France 13D4
Guelma Algeria 16B3
Guelph Can 64C2
Guelta Zemmur Mor 48A2
Guéréda Chad 50C2
Guéret France 14C2
Guernsey USA 60C2
Guernsey, I Channel Is 14B2
Gughe, Mt Eth 50D3
Gugigu China 25O4
Guguan, I Pacific O 27H5
Guider Cam 49D4
Guidong China 31C4
Guiglo Ivory Coast 48B4
Guijá Mozam 47E1
Gui Jiang, R China 31C5
Guildford Eng 7D4
Guilin China 31C4
Guinan China 31A2
Guinda USA 66A1
Guinea, Republic Africa 48A3
Guinea Basin Atlantic O 52H4
Guinea-Bissau, Republic Africa 48A3
Guinea,G of W Africa 48C4
Güines Cuba 69A2
Guir, Well Mali 48B3
Guiratinga Brazil 75B2
Güiria Ven 72F1
Guisborough Eng 6D2
Guise France 13B3
Guiuan Phil 27F5
Gui Xian China 31B5
Guiyang China 31B4
Guizhou, Province China 31B4
Gujarāt, State India 42C4
Gujranwala Pak 42C2
Gujrat Pak 42C2
Gulargambone Aust 34C2
Gulbarga India 44B2
Gulbene USSR 19F1
Guledagudda India 44B2
Gulfport USA 63E2
Gulf,The S W Asia 38D3
Gulgong Aust 34C2
Gulin China 31B4
Güllük Körfezi, B Turk 17F3
Gulu Uganda 50D3
Guluguba Aust 34C1
Gumel Nigeria 48C3
Gumla India 43E4
Gummersbach W Germ 13D2
Gümüşhane Turk 40C1
Guna India 42D4
Guna, Mt Eth 50D2
Gundagai Aust 34C3
Gungu Zaïre 50B4
Gunnbjørn Fjeld, Mt Greenland 55Q3
Gunnedah Aust 34D2
Gunnison USA 60B3
Gunnison, R USA 60B3
Guntakal India 44B2
Guntersville USA 67A2
Guntersville L USA 67A2
Guntūr India 44C2
Gunung Batu Puteh, Mt Malay 30C5
Gunung Tahan, Mt Malay 30C5
Gunza Angola 51B5
Guoyang China 31D3
Gurdāspur India 42D2
Gurgaon India 42D3
Guri, Embalse de, Res Ven 72F2
Gurkha Nepal 43E3
Gürün Turk 40C2
Gurupi, R Brazil 73J4
Guruve Zim 51D5
Gurvan Sayhan Uul, Upland Mongolia 31A1
Gur'yev USSR 21J6
Gusau Nigeria 48C3
Gusev USSR 19E2
Gushan China 28A3
Gus' Khrustalnyy USSR 20G4
Gustav Holm, Kap, C Greenland 55P3
Gustavus USA 54E4
Gustine USA 66B2
Guston USA 57E3
Gütersloh W Germ 18B2
Guthrie, Kentucky USA 64B3
Guthrie, Oklahoma USA 63C1
Guthrie, Texas USA 62B2
Guttenberg USA 61E2
Guyana, Republic S America 73G3
Guyana Basin Atlantic O 52F4
Guyang China 31C1
Guyenne, Region France 14B3
Guymon USA 62B1
Guyra Aust 34D2
Guyuan China 31B2
Guzmán, Laguna, L Mexico 62A2
Gwa Burma 43G5
Gwabegar Aust 34C2
Gwadar Pak 38E3
Gwalior India 42D3
Gwanda Zim 47D1
Gwane Zaïre 50C3
Gwent, County Wales 7C4
Gweru Zim 51C5
Gwydir, R Aust 34C1
Gwynedd Wales 7C3
Gyangzê China 43F3
Gyaring Hu, L China 26C3
Gydanskiy Poluostrov, Pen USSR 24J2
Gyirong China 43F3
Gyldenløves Fjord Greenland 55O3
Gympie Aust 34D1
Gyöngyös Hung 19D3
Györ Hung 19D3

H

Ha'apai Group, Is Tonga 33H2
Haapajärvi Fin 12K6
Haapsalu USSR 20C4
Haarlem Neth 18A2
Haarstrang, Region W Germ 13D2
Habana, La = Havana
Habiganj Bang 43G4
Hachijō-jima, I Japan 29D4
Hachiman Japan 29C3
Hachinohe Japan 29E2
Hachioji Japan 29C3
Hackettstown USA 68C2
Hack,Mt, Mt Aust 34A2
Haddington Scot 8D4
Haddon Corner Aust 34B1
Haddon Downs Aust 34B1
Hadejia Nigeria 48D3
Hadejia, R Nigeria 48C3
Hadera Israel 45C2
Haderslev Den 18B1
Hadiboh Socotra 38D4
Hadley B Can 54H2
Hadong S Korea 28A3
Hadong Vietnam 31B5
Ḩaḑramawt, Region S Yemen 38C4
Hadsund Den 18C1
Haeju N Korea 28B3
Haeju-man, B N Korea 28A3
Haenam S Korea 28A4
Hafar al Bātin S Arabia 41E4
Haffners Bjerg, Mt Greenland 55M2
Hafizabad Pak 42C2
Hāflong India 43G3
Hafnarfjörður Iceland 12A2
Hagen W Germ 18B2
Hagerstown USA 68B3
Hagi Japan 28B4
Ha Giang Vietnam 31A5
Hagondange France 13D3
Haguenan France 13D3
Hagunia, Well Mor 48A2
Haha-jima, I Japan 26H4
Hah Xil Hu, L China 26C3
Haicheng China 28A2
Hai Duong Viet 30D1
Haifa Israel 45C2
Haifa,B of Israel 45C2
Hai He, R China 31D2
Haikang China 31C5
Haikou China 30E1
Hā'il S Arabia 40D4
Hailākāndi India 43G4
Hailar China 25N5
Hailong China 28B2
Hailun China 26F2
Hailuoto, I Fin 12J5
Hainan, I China 30D2
Haines USA 54E4
Haines Junction Can 54E3
Hainfeld Austria 18D3
Haiphong Vietnam 31B5
Haisgai China 28A2
Haiti, Republic Caribbean S 69C3
Haiwee Res USA 66D2
Haiya Sudan 50D2
Haiyan China 31A2
Haiyuan China 31B2
Hajdúböszörmény Hung 19E3
Hajiki-saki, Pt Japan 29C3
Haka Burma 43G4
Hakalau Hawaiian Is 66E5
Hakkâri Turk 41D2
Hakodate Japan 29E2
Hakui Japan 29C3
Haku-san, Mt Japan 29C3
Ḩalab = Aleppo
Halabja Iraq 41E2
Halaib Egypt 50D1
Halâl, Gebel, Mt Egypt 45B3
Halba Leb 45D1
Halberstadt E Germ 18C2
Halden Nor 12G7
Haldia India 43F4
Haldwāni India 42D3
Halifax Can 55M5
Halifax Eng 6D3
Halifax USA 65D3
Halimah, Jabal, Mt Leb/Syria 45D1
Halkirk Scot 8D2
Halla-san, Mt S Korea 28A4
Hall Basin, Sd Can 55M1
Hall Beach Can 55K3
Halle Belg 13C2
Halle E Germ 18C2
Halley, Base Ant 76F1
Halleybury Can 65D1
Halliday USA 60C1
Hallingdal, R Nor 12F6
Hallock USA 61D1
Hall Pen Can 55M3
Hall's Creek Aust 32B2
Hallstead USA 68C2
Halmahera, Is Indon 27F6
Halmstad Sweden 12G7
Halq el Qued Tunisia 16C3
Haltern W Germ 18B2
Halti, Mt Fin/Nor 20C2
Halti, Mt Nor 12J5
Haltwhistle Eng 8D4
Halul, I Qatar 41F4
Haluza, Hist Site Israel 45C3
Hamada Japan 28B4
Hamada de Tinrhert, Desert Region Alg 48C2
Hamada du Dra, Upland Alg 48B2
Hamadān Iran 41E3
Hamada Tounassine, Region Alg 48B2
Ḩamāh Syria 21F8
Hamamatsu Japan 29C4
Hamar Nor 12G6
Hamâta, Gebel, Mt Egypt 40C5
Hama-Tombetsu Japan 29D1
Hambantota Sri Lanka 44C4
Hamburg, Arkansas USA 63D2
Hamburg, Iowa USA 61D2
Hamburg, New York USA 68A1
Hamburg, Pennsylvania USA 68C2
Hamburg W Germ 18B2
Hamden USA 68D2
Hämeenlinna Fin 12J6
Hameln W Germ 13E1
Hamersley Range, Mts Aust 32A3
Hamgyong Sanmaek, Mts N Korea 28B2
Hamhŭng N Korea 28B3
Hami China 26C2
Ḩamidiyah Syria 45C1
Hamilton, Alabama USA 63E2
Hamilton Aust 34B3
Hamilton Can 65D2
Hamilton, Montana USA 58D1
Hamilton, New York USA 68C1
Hamilton NZ 35C1
Hamilton, Ohio USA 64C3
Hamilton Scot 8C4
Hamilton Inlet, B Can 55N4
Hamilton,Mt USA 66B2
Hamina Fin 12K6
Hamirpur India 43E3
Hamju N Korea 28A3
Hamm W Germ 18B2
Hammādāh al Hamrā, Upland Libya 49D2
Hammamet Tunisia 16C3
Hammamet, Golfe de Tunisia 16C3
Hammerdal Sweden 12H6
Hammerfest Nor 12J4
Hammond, Illinois USA 64B2
Hammond, Louisiana USA 63D2
Hammond, Montana USA 60C1
Hammonton USA 68C3
Hampden NZ 35B3
Hampshire, County Eng 7D4
Hampton, Arkansas USA 63D2
Hampton, Iowa USA 61E2
Hampton, New Hampshire USA 68E1
Hampton, Virginia USA 65D3
Hāmūn-e-Jāz-Mūriān, L Iran 38D3
Hamun-i-Lora, Salt L Pak 42B3
Han, R S Korea 28A3
Hana Hawaiian Is 66E5
Hanalei Hawaiian Is 66E5
Hanamaki Japan 29E3
Hanau W Germ 13E2
Hancheng China 31C2
Hanchuan China 31C3
Hancock, Maryland USA 65D3
Hancock, Michigan USA 64B1
Hancock, New York USA 68C2
Handa Japan 29C4
Handa, I Scot 8C2
Handan China 31C2
Handeni Tanz 50D4
Hanford USA 66C2
Hanggin Qi China 31B2
Hangö Fin 12J7
Hangzhou China 31E3
Hangzhou Wan, B China 31E3
Hankinson USA 61D1
Hanksville USA 59D3
Hanmer Springs NZ 35B2
Hanna Can 54G4
Hannibal USA 61E3
Hannover W Germ 18B2
Hanöbukten, B Sweden 12G7
Hanoi Viet 30D1
Hanover S Africa 47C3
Hanover USA 68B3
Hanover, I Chile 74B8
Han Shui, R China 31C3
Hānsi India 42D3
Hantay Mongolia 26D2
Hanzhong China 31B3
Hāora India 43F4
Haparanda Sweden 12J5
Hapch'on S Korea 28A3
Hāpoli India 43G3
Hapur India 43J1
Ḩaql S Arabia 40C4
Ḩaradh S Arabia 41E5
Harad, Jebel el, Mt Jordan 45C4
Hara Fanna Eth 50E3
Haramachi Japan 29D3
Harare Zim 51D5
Harazé Chad 50C2
Harbin China 26F2
Harbor Beach USA 64C2
Harda India 42D4
Hardangerfjord, Inlet Nor 12F6
Härdenberg Neth 13D1
Harderwijk Neth 13C1
Hardin USA 60B1
Hardoi India 43L2
Hardt, Region W Germ 13D3
Hardy USA 63D1
Hareidin, Wadi Egypt 45C3
Härer Eth 50E3
Hargeysa Somalia 50E3
Har Hakippa, Mt Israel 45C3
Harhu, L China 26C3
Hari, R Indon 27D7
Harima-nada, B Japan 29B4
Harlan USA 64C3
Harlech Wales 7B3
Harlem USA 58E1
Harleston Eng 7E3
Harlingen Neth 18B2
Harlingen USA 63C3
Harlow Eng 7E4
Harlowtown USA 58E1
Har Meron, Mt Israel 45C2
Harney Basin USA 58C2
Harney L USA 58C2
Härnösand Sweden 12H6
Harper Lib 48B4
Harper L USA 66D3
Harpers Ferry USA 65D3
Harpstedt W Germ 13E1
Har Ramon, Mt Israel 45C3
Harrāt al 'Uwayrid, Region S Arabia 40C4
Ḩarrāt Kishb, Region S Arabia 40D5
Harricanaw, R Can 55L4
Harriman USA 67B1
Harriman Res USA 68D1
Harrington USA 68C3
Harrington Harbour Can 55N4
Harris, District Scot 8B3
Harrisburg, Illinois USA 64B3

Harrisburg Hønefoss

Harrisburg, Pennsylvania *USA* 68B2
Harrismith *S Africa* 47D2
Harrison *USA* 63D1
Harrisonburg *USA* 65D3
Harrison,C *Can* 55N4
Harrisonville *USA* 61E3
Harris,Sound of, Chan *Scot* 8B3
Harrisville *USA* 64C2
Harrogate *Eng* 6D2
Har Saggi, Mt *Israel* 45C3
Ḩarsīr, Wadi al *Syria* 45D2
Harstad *Nor* 12H5
Hartao *China* 28A2
Hartbees, R *S Africa* 47C2
Hårteigen, Mt *Nor* 12F6
Hartford, Connecticut *USA* 68D2
Hartford, Michigan *USA* 64B2
Hartford, S Dakota *USA* 61D2
Hartkjølen, Mt *Nor* 12G6
Hartland *Can* 65F1
Hartland *Eng* 7B4
Hartland Pt *Eng* 7B4
Hartlepool *Eng* 6D2
Hartley *USA* 62B1
Hartselle *USA* 67A2
Hartshorne *USA* 63C2
Hartwell Res *USA* 67B2
Hartz, R *S Africa* 47C2
Hārūn, Jebel, Mt *Jordan* 45C3
Har Us Nuur, L *Mongolia* 25L5
Harut, R *Afghan* 38E2
Harvard,Mt *USA* 60B3
Harvey *USA* 60C1
Harwich *Eng* 7E4
Haryāna, State *India* 42D3
Hāsā *Jordan* 45C3
Hasana, Wadi *Egypt* 45B3
Hāsā, Wadi el *Jordan* 45C3
Hāsbaiya *Leb* 45C2
Hase, R *W Germ* 13E1
Haselünne *W Germ* 13D1
Hashimoto *Japan* 29C4
Hashtpar *Iran* 41E2
Hashtrūd *Iran* 41E2
Haskell *USA* 62C2
Haslemere *Eng* 7D4
Hassan *India* 44B3
Hasselt *Belg* 18B2
Hassi Inifel *Alg* 48C2
Hassi Mdakane, Well *Alg* 48B2
Hassi Messaoud *Alg* 48C1
Hässleholm *Sweden* 12G7
Hastings *Aust* 34C3
Hastings *Eng* 7E4
Hastings, Minnesota *USA* 61E2
Hastings, Nebraska *USA* 56D2
Hastings *NZ* 35C1
Hatchie, R *USA* 63E1
Hatfield *Aust* 34B2
Hāthras *India* 42D3
Ha Tinh *Viet* 30D2
Hattah *Aust* 34B2
Hatteras,C *USA* 57F3
Hattiesburg *USA* 63E2
Hatvan *Hung* 19D3
Hau Bon *Viet* 30D3
Haud, Region *Eth* 50E3
Haugesund *Nor* 12F7
Hauhungaroa Range, Mts *NZ* 35C1
Hauraki G *NZ* 35B1
Hauroko,L *NZ* 35A3
Haut Atlas, Mts *Mor* 48B1
Haute Kotto, Region *CAR* 50C3
Haute-Marne, Department *France* 13C3
Haute-Saône, Department *France* 13D4
Hautes Fagnes, Mts *Belg/W Germ* 13C2
Haut, Isle au *USA* 65F2
Hautmont *France* 13C2
Haut-Rhin, Department *France* 13D4
Hauz Qala *Afghan* 42A2
Havana *Cuba* 70D2
Havana *USA* 64A2
Havankulam *Sri Lanka* 44B4
Havasu L *USA* 59D4
Havelock *USA* 67C2
Havelock North *NZ* 35C1
Haverhill *Eng* 7E3
Haverhill *USA* 68E1
Hāveri *India* 44B3
Haverstraw *USA* 68D2
Havlíčkův Brod *Czech* 18D3
Havre *USA* 58E1
Havre de Grace *USA* 68B3
Havre-St-Pierre *Can* 55M4
Havsa *Turk* 17F2
Hawaii, Is, State *Pacific O* 66E5
Hawaii Volcanoes Nat Pk *Hawaiian Is* 66E5
Hawea,L *NZ* 35A2
Hawera *NZ* 35B1
Hawi *Hawaiian Is* 66E5
Hawick *Scot* 8D4
Hawkdun Range, Mts *NZ* 35A2
Hawke B *NZ* 35C1
Hawke,C *Aust* 34D2
Hawker *Aust* 34A2
Hawley *USA* 68C2
Hawng Luk *Burma* 30B1
Hawr al Habbaniyah, L *Iraq* 41D3
Hawr al Hammár, L *Iraq* 41E3
Ḩawrān, Wadi, R *Iraq* 40D3
Hawthorne *USA* 66C1
Hay *Aust* 34B2
Hay *Eng* 7C3
Hay, R *Can* 54G3
Hayange *France* 13C3
Haycock *USA* 54B3
Hayden, Arizona *USA* 59D4
Hayden, Colorado *USA* 60B2
Hayes, R *Can* 55J4
Hayes Halvø, Region *Greenland* 55M2
Hayes, Mt *USA* 54D3
Hayle *Eng* 7B4
Hayling, I *Eng* 7D4
Haymarket *USA* 68B3
Hay River *Can* 54G3
Hays *USA* 60D3
Haysville *USA* 63C1
Hayward, California *USA* 66A2
Hayward, Wisconsin *USA* 64A1
Haywards Heath *Eng* 7D4
Hazarajat, Region *Afghan* 42A2
Hazard *USA* 64C3
Hazārībāg *India* 43F4
Hazebrouck *France* 13B2
Hazelhurst *USA* 63D2
Hazelton *Can* 54F4
Hazen B *USA* 54B3
Hazen L *Can* 55L1
Hazen Str *Can* 54G2
Hazeva *Israel* 45C3
Hazleton *USA* 68C2
Healdsburg *USA* 66A1
Healesville *Aust* 34C3
Heard I *Indian O* 36E7
Hearne *USA* 63C2
Hearst *Can* 57E2
Heart, R *USA* 60C1
Hebbronville *USA* 62C3
Hebei, Province *China* 31D2
Hebel *Aust* 34C1
Heber City *USA* 58D2
Hebgen L *USA* 58D2
Hebi *China* 31C2
Hebian *China* 31C2
Hebron *Can* 55M4
Hebron *Israel* 45C3
Hebron, N. Dakota *USA* 60C1
Hebron, Nebraska *USA* 61D2
Hecate Str *Can* 54E4
Hechi *China* 31B5
Hechingen *W Germ* 13E3
Hecla and Griper B *Can* 54G2
Hector,Mt *NZ* 35C2
Hede *Sweden* 12G6
Hedemora *Sweden* 12H6
He Devil Mt *USA* 58C1
Heerenveen *Neth* 18B2
Heerlen *Neth* 13C2
Hefa = Haifa
Hefei *China* 31D3
Hefeng *China* 31B4
Hegang *China* 26G2
Hegura-jima, I *Japan* 29C3
Heho *Burma* 30B1
Heiburg I *Can* 55J2
Heidan, R *Jordan* 45C3
Heide *W Germ* 18B2
Heidelberg, Cape Province *S Africa* 47C3
Heidelberg, Transvaal *S Africa* 47D2
Heidelberg *W Germ* 18B3
Heidenheim *W Germ* 18C3
Heihe *China* 25O4
Heilbron *S Africa* 47D2
Heilbronn *W Germ* 18B3
Heiligenstadt *E Germ* 18C2
Heinola *Fin* 12K6
Heishan *China* 28A2
Hejiang *China* 31B4
Hekla, Mt *Iceland* 55R3
Hekou *Viet* 30C1
Hekou Yaozou Zizhixian *China* 31A5
Helan *China* 31B2
Helan Shan, Mt *China* 31B2
Helena, Arkansas *USA* 63D2
Helena, Montana *USA* 58D1
Helendale *USA* 66D3
Helen Reef *Pacific O* 27G6
Helensburgh *Scot* 8C3
Heliopolis *Egypt* 45A3
Helleh, R *Iran* 41F4
Hellín *Spain* 15B2
Hells Canyon, R *USA* 58C1
Hellweg, Region *W Germ* 13D2
Helm *USA* 66B2
Helmand, R *Iran/Afghan* 38E2
Helmeringhausen *Namibia* 47B2
Helmond *Neth* 13C2
Helmsdale *Scot* 8D2
Helodrano Antongila, B *Madag* 51F5
Helong *China* 28B2
Helsingborg *Sweden* 12G7
Helsingfors = Helsinki
Helsingør *Den* 18C1
Helsinki *Fin* 12J6
Helston *Eng* 7B4
Helvick Hd, Pt *Irish Rep* 9C3
Helwân *Egypt* 40B4
Hemel Hempstead *Eng* 7D4
Hempstead *USA* 63C2
Hemse *Sweden* 12H7
Henan *China* 31A3
Henan, Province *China* 31C3
Hen and Chickens Is *NZ* 35B1
Henashi-zaki, C *Japan* 29C2
Henderson, Kentucky *USA* 64B3
Henderson, N. Carolina *USA* 67C1
Henderson, Nevada *USA* 59D3
Henderson, Texas *USA* 63D2
Hendersonville, N. Carolina *USA* 67B1
Hendersonville, Tennessee *USA* 67A1
Hendrik Verwoerd Dam *S Africa* 47D3
Hengchun *Taiwan* 31E5
Hengduan Shan, Mts *China* 26C4
Hengelo *Neth* 18B2
Hengshan *China* 31B2
Hengshui *China* 31D2
Heng Xian *China* 30D1
Hengyang *China* 31C4
Henhoaha, Nicobar Is 30A4
Henley-on-Thames *Eng* 7D4
Henlopen,C *USA* 68C3
Henniker *USA* 68E1
Henrietta *USA* 62C2
Henrietta Maria,C *Can* 55K4
Henrieville *USA* 59D3
Henryetta *USA* 63C1
Henry Kater Pen *Can* 55M3
Henties Bay *Namibia* 47A1
Hentiyn Nuruu, Mts *Mongolia* 26D2
Henzada *Burma* 30B2
Hepu *China* 31B5
Herat *Afghan* 38E2
Herbert *Can* 54H4
Herbertville *NZ* 35C2
Herborn *W Germ* 13E2
Heredia *Costa Rica* 69A4
Hereford *Eng* 7C3
Hereford *USA* 62B2
Hereford & Worcester, County *Eng* 7C3
Herentals *Belg* 13C2
Herford *W Germ* 13E1
Herington *USA* 61D3
Heriot *NZ* 35A3
Herkimer *USA* 68C1
Herma Ness, Pen *Scot* 8E1
Hermanus *S Africa* 47B3
Hermidale *Aust* 34C2
Hermitage *NZ* 35B2
Hermit Is *PNG* 32D1
Hermon, Mt *Leb/Syria* 45C2
Hermosillo *Mexico* 70A2
Hernandarias *Par* 75B4
Herndon *USA* 68B2
Herne *W Germ* 13D2
Herne Bay *Eng* 7E4
Herning *Den* 18B1
Herowābad *Iran* 41E2
Herradura *Arg* 75A4
Herrera del Duque *Spain* 15B2
Hershey *USA* 68B2
Hertford *Eng* 7D4
Hertford, County *Eng* 7D4
Herzliyya *Israel* 45C2
Hesbaye, Region *Belg* 13C2
Hesdin *France* 13A2
Heshui *China* 31B2
Hesperia *USA* 66D3
Hessen, State *W Germ* 18B2
Hetch Hetchy Res *USA* 66C2
Hettinger *USA* 60C1
Heuts Plateaux *Mor/Alg* 48B1
Hewett, Oilfield *N Sea* 7E3
Hexham *Eng* 6C2
He Xian *China* 31C5
Heysham *Eng* 6C2
Heystekrand *S Africa* 47D2
Heyuan *China* 31C5
Heywood *Aust* 34B3
Heze *China* 31D2
Hialeah *USA* 67B3
Hibbing *USA* 61E1
Hickory *USA* 67B1
Hicks Bay *NZ* 35C1
Hicks,Pt *Aust* 34C3
Hico *USA* 63C2
Hidaka-sammyaku, Mts *Japan* 29D2
Hidalgo del Parral *Mexico* 70B2
Hidrolândia *Brazil* 75C2
Hierro, I *Canary Is* 48A2
Higashine *Japan* 29D3
Higashi-suidō, Str *Japan* 28B4
Higāyib, Wadi el *Egypt* 45B3
High Desert *USA* 58B2
High Island *USA* 63D3
Highland *USA* 66D3
Highland, Region *Scot* 8C3
Highlander, Oilfield *N Sea* 8E2
Highland Peak, Mt *USA* 66C1
Highlands Falls *USA* 68C2
High Point *USA* 67B1
High Prairie *Can* 54G4
High River *Can* 54G4
High Springs *USA* 67B3
Hightstown *USA* 68C2
High Wycombe *Eng* 7D4
Hiiumaa, I *USSR* 12J7
Hijaz, Region *S Arabia* 40C4
Hikigawa *Japan* 29C4
Hiko *USA* 59C3
Hikone *Japan* 29C3
Hikurangi *NZ* 35B1
Hildago del Parral *Mexico* 56C4
Hildesheim *W Germ* 18B2
Hillaby,Mt *Barbados* 69R2
Hill City *USA* 60D3
Hillerød *Den* 18C1
Hillsboro, N. Dakota *USA* 61D1
Hillsboro, New Hampshire *USA* 68E1
Hillsboro, New Mexico *USA* 62A2
Hillsboro, Ohio *USA* 64C3
Hillsboro, Oregon *USA* 58B1
Hillsboro, Texas *USA* 63C2
Hillston *Aust* 34C2
Hillsville *USA* 64C3
Hillswick *Scot* 8E1
Hilo *Hawaiian Is* 66E5
Hilpsford, Pt *Eng* 6C2
Hilton *USA* 68B1
Hilvan *Turk* 40C2
Hilversum *Neth* 18B2
Himāchal Pradesh, State *India* 42D2
Himalaya = Great Himalayan Range
Himalaya, Mts *Asia* 39G3
Himalchuli, Mt *Nepal* 43N1
Himatnagar *India* 42C4
Himeji *Japan* 29C4
Himi *Japan* 29D3
Ḩimş *Syria* 45D1
Hinckley *Eng* 7D3
Hinckley, Minnesota *USA* 61E1
Hinckley Res *USA* 68C1
Hindaun *India* 42D3
Hindu Kush, Mts *Afghan* 42B1
Hindupur *India* 44B3
Hines Creek *Can* 54G4
Hinganghāt *India* 42D4
Hingol, R *Pak* 42B3
Hingoli *India* 42D5
Hinkley *USA* 66D3
Hinnøya, I *Nor* 12H5
Hinsdale *USA* 68D1
Hinton *USA* 62C1
Hirado *Japan* 28A4
Hirado-shima, I *Japan* 28A4
Hirakud Res *India* 43E4
Hirfanli Baraji, Res *Turk* 40B2
Hirihar *India* 44B3
Hiroo *Japan* 29D2
Hirosaki *Japan* 29E2
Hiroshima *Japan* 28C4
Hirson *France* 13C3
Hirşova *Rom* 17F2
Hirtshals *Den* 18B1
Hisār *India* 42D3
Hispaniola, I *Caribbean S* 69C3
Ḩisyah *Syria* 45D1
Hit *Iraq* 40D3
Hitachi *Japan* 29E3
Hitachi-Ota *Japan* 29D3
Hitchin *Eng* 7D4
Hitoyoshi *Japan* 28C4
Hitra, I *Nor* 12F6
Hiuchi-nada, B *Japan* 29B4
Hiwasa *Japan* 29B4
Hiyon, R *Israel* 45C3
Hjørring *Den* 18B1
Hka, R *Burma* 30B1
Ho *Ghana* 48C4
Hoa Binh *Viet* 30D1
Hoa Da *Viet* 30D3
Hobart *Aust* 34C4
Hobart *USA* 62C2
Hobbs *USA* 62B2
Hobro *Den* 18B1
Hobyo *Somalia* 50E3
Ho Chi Minh City *Viet* 30D3
Hochkonig, Mt *Austria* 18C3
Hochon *N Korea* 28A2
Hockenheim *W Germ* 13E3
Hodeida = Al Ḩudaydah
Hódmezö'hely *Hung* 17E1
Hodna, Monts du *Alg* 15C2
Hodonin *Czech* 18D3
Hoek van Holland *Neth* 13C2
Hoengsŏng *S Korea* 28A3
Hoeryŏng *N Korea* 28B2
Hoeyang *N Korea* 28A3
Hof *W Germ* 18C2
Höfn *Iceland* 55R3
Hofsjökull, Mts *Iceland* 12B2
Hōfu *Japan* 28C4
Hoggar, Upland *Alg* 48C2
Hohe Acht, Mt *W Germ* 13D2
Hohes Gras, Mts *W Germ* 13E2
Hohhot *China* 31C1
Hoh Sai Hu, L *China* 26C3
Hoh Xil Shan, Mts *China* 39G2
Hoima *Uganda* 50D3
Hojāi *India* 43G3
Hojo *Japan* 28B4
Hokianga Harbour, B *NZ* 35B1
Hokitika *NZ* 35B2
Hokkaidō, I *Japan* 26H2
Hokmābād *Iran* 41G2
Hokota *Japan* 29D3
Holbeach *Eng* 7E3
Holbrook *Aust* 34C3
Holbrook *USA* 59D4
Holden *USA* 59D3
Holdenville *USA* 63C1
Holdrege *USA* 60D2
Hole Narsipur *India* 44B3
Holetown *Barbados* 69Q2
Holguín *Cuba* 69B2
Hollabrunn *Austria* 18D3
Holland *USA* 64B2
Hollidaysburg *USA* 68A2
Hollis *USA* 62C2
Hollister *USA* 66B2
Holly Springs *USA* 63E2
Hollywood, California *USA* 66C3
Hollywood, Florida *USA* 67B3
Holman Island *Can* 54G2
Holmsund *Sweden* 12J6
Holon *Israel* 45C2
Holstebro *Den* 18B1
Holstein *USA* 61D2
Holsteinborg *Greenland* 55N3
Holston, R *USA* 67B1
Holt *USA* 64C2
Holton *USA* 61D3
Holy Cross *USA* 54C3
Holyhead *Wales* 7B3
Holy I *Eng* 6D3
Holy I *Wales* 7B3
Holyoke, Colorado *USA* 60C2
Holyoke, Massachusetts *USA* 68D1
Holywood *N Ire* 9D2
Holzminden *W Germ* 13E2
Homalin *Burma* 43G4
Homburg *W Germ* 13E2
Home B *Can* 55M3
Homer, Louisiana *USA* 63D2
Homer *USA* 54C4
Homer Tunnel *NZ* 35A2
Homerville *USA* 67B2
Homestead *USA* 67B3
Homewood *USA* 67A2
Homnābād *India* 44B2
Homoine *Mozam* 51D6
Homs = Al Khums
Homs = Ḩimş
Homs *Syria* 29J5
Hondeklip B *S Africa* 47B3
Hondo, New Mexico *USA* 62A2
Hondo, Texas *USA* 62C3
Hondo, R *Mexico* 70D3
Honduras, Republic *Cent America* 70D3
Honduras,G of *Honduras* 70D3
Hønefoss *Nor* 12G6

Honesdale Ingersoll

Honesdale USA 68C2
Honey L USA 59B2
Hong, R = Nui Con Voi
Hong, R Viet 30C1
Hon Gai Viet 30D1
Hongchŏn S Korea 28A3
Hongguo China 31A4
Hong Hu, L China 31C4
Honghui China 31B2
Hongjiang China 31C4
Hong Kong, Colony S E Asia 31C5
Hongor Mongolia 26E2
Hongshui He, R China 31B5
Hongsong S Korea 28A3
Hongwon N Korea 28A3
Hongyuan China 31A3
Hongze Hu, L China 31D3
Honiara Solomon Is 33E1
Honiton Eng 7C4
Honjō Japan 29D3
Hon Khoai, I Camb 30C4
Hon Lan, I Viet 30D3
Honnigsvåg Nor 12K4
Honningsvåg Nor 20D1
Honokaa Hawaiian Is 66E5
Honolulu Hawaiian Is 66E5
Hon Panjang, I Viet 30C4
Honshū, I Japan 26G3
Hood,Mt USA 58B1
Hood River USA 58B1
Hoogeveen Neth 13D1
Hooker USA 62B1
Hook Head, C Irish Rep 9C3
Hoonah USA 54E4
Hooper Bay USA 54B3
Hoopstad S Africa 47D2
Hoorn Neth 18A2
Hoosick Falls USA 68D1
Hoover Dam USA 56B3
Hope, Arkansas USA 63D2
Hopedale Can 55M4
Hopen, I Svalbard 24D2
Hopes Advance,C Can 55M3
Hopetoun Aust 34B3
Hopetown S Africa 47C2
Hopewell, Pennsylvania USA 68A2
Hopewell, Virginia USA 65D3
Hopkinsville USA 64B3
Hoquiam USA 58B1
Horasan Turk 40D2
Horb W Germ 13E3
Hordiyo Somalia 50E2
Hörh Uul, Mt Mongolia 31B1
Horizon Depth Pacific O 37L6
Hormuz,Str of Oman/Iran 41G4
Horn Austria 18D3
Horn, C Iceland 55Q3
Hornavan, L Sweden 12H5
Hornbeck USA 63D2
Hornbrook USA 58B2
Hornby NZ 35B2
Horncastle Eng 7D3
Hornell USA 68B1
Hornepayne Can 55K5
Horn I USA 63E2
Horn, Îles de Pacific O 33H2
Horn Mts Can 54F3
Hornos, Cabo de, C Chile 74C9
Hornsea Eng 6D3
Horqin Zuoyi Houqi China 28A2
Horqueta Par 74E2
Horseheads USA 68B1
Horsens Den 18C1
Horseshoe Bay Can 58B1
Horseshoe Bend USA 58C2
Horsham Aust 34B3
Horsham Eng 7D4
Horten Nor 12G7
Horton, R Can 54F3
Hose Mts Borneo 27E6
Hoshangābād India 42D4
Hoshiārpur India 42D2
Hosington USA 62C1
Hospet India 44B2
Hoste, I Chile 74C9
Hotan China 39F2
Hotazel S Africa 47C2
Hot Springs, Arkansas USA 63D2
Hot Springs, S. Dakota USA 60C2
Hottah L Can 54G3
Hotte, Massif de la, Mts Haiti 69C3
Hottentot Pt Namibia 47A2
Houghton USA 64B1
Houlton USA 65F1
Houma China 31C2
Houma USA 63D3
Hourn, Loch, Inlet Scot 8C3
Housatonic, R USA 68D2
Houston, Mississippi USA 63E2
Houston, Texas USA 63C3
Houtman, Is Aust 32A3
Houtzdale USA 68A2
Hovd Mongolia 26C2
Hövsgol Nuur, L Mongolia 26D1
Howard Aust 34D1
Howard City USA 64B2
Howa, Wadi, Watercourse Sudan/Chad 50C2
Howe,C Aust 34C3
Howe Sd Can 58B1
Howick S Africa 47E2
Howland USA 65F1
Howth Irish Rep 9C3
Höxter W Germ 13E2
Hoy, I Scot 8D2
Høyanger Nor 12F6
Hoyt Lakes USA 61E1
Hradec-Králové Czech 18D2
Hranice Czech 19D3
Hron, R Czech 19D3
Hsinchu Taiwan 31E5
Hsipaw Burma 30B1
Hsüeh Shan, Mt Taiwan 31E5
Huab, R Namibia 47A1
Huachi China 31B2
Huacho Peru 72C6
Huade China 31C1
Huadian China 28B2
Huaibei China 31D3
Huaibin China 31D3
Huaide China 28A2
Huaidezhen China 28A2
Huai He, R China 31D3
Huaihua China 31C4
Huaiji China 31C5
Huainan China 31D3
Hualapai Peak, Mt USA 59D3
Hualien Taiwan 26F4
Huallaga, R Peru 72C5
Huallanca Peru 72C5
Huamachuco Peru 72C5
Huambo Angola 51B5
Huanay Bol 72E7
Huancabamba Peru 72C5
Huancavelica Peru 72C6
Huancayo Peru 72C6
Huangchuan China 31D3
Huang Hai = Yellow S
Huang He, R China 31D2
Huangling China 31B2
Huangliu China 30D2
Huangnihe China 28B2
Huangpi China 31C3
Huangshi China 31D3
Huangyan China 31E4
Huanren China 28B2
Huánuco Peru 72C5
Huanuni Bol 74C1
Huan Xian China 31B2
Huaráz Peru 72C5
Huarmey Peru 72C6
Huascarán, Mt Peru 72C5
Huasco Chile 74B3
Hua Xian China 31C2
Huayapan, R Mexico 70B2
Hubei, Province China 31C3
Hubli India 44B2
Huch'ang N Korea 28B2
Hucknell Torkard Eng 7D3
Huddersfield Eng 7D3
Hude W Germ 13E1
Hudiksvall Sweden 12H6
Hudson, Florida USA 67B3
Hudson, Michigan USA 64C2
Hudson, New York USA 68D1
Hudson, R USA 68D1
Hudson B Can 55K4
Hudson Bay Can 54H4
Hudson Falls USA 68D1
Hudson Str Can 55L3
Hue Viet 30D2
Huelva Spain 15A2
Húercal Overa Spain 15B2
Huesca Spain 15B1
Hughenden Aust 32D3
Hughes USA 54C3
Hugli, R India 43F4
Hugo USA 63C2
Hugoton USA 62B1
Hui'an China 31D4
Huiarau Range, Mts NZ 35C1
Huib Hochplato, Plat Namibia 47B2
Hüich'on N Korea 28B2
Huila, Mt Colombia 72C3
Huilai China 31D5
Huili China 31A4
Huinan China 28B2
Huixtla Mexico 70C3
Huize China 31A4
Huizhou China 31C5
Ḩulayfah S Arabia 40D4
Hulin China 26G2
Hull Can 65D1
Hull Eng 6D3
Hull, I Phoenix Is 33H1
Hultsfred Sweden 18D1
Hulun Nur, L China 25N5
Humaitá Brazil 72F5
Humansdorp S Africa 47C3
Humber, R Eng 7D3
Humberside, County Eng 6D3
Humboldt Can 54H4
Humboldt, Iowa USA 61E2
Humboldt, Tennessee USA 63E1
Humboldt, R USA 58C2
Humboldt B USA 58B2
Humboldt Gletscher, Gl Greenland 55M2
Humboldt L USA 59C3
Humeburn Aust 34C1
Hume,L Aust 34C3
Hümmling, Hill W Germ 13D1
Humpata Angola 51B5
Humphreys USA 66C2
Humphreys,Mt, California USA 66C2
Humphreys Peak, Mt, Arizona USA 59D3
Húnaflóri, B Iceland 12A1
Hunan, Province China 31C4
Hunchun China 28C2
Hunedoara Rom 17E1
Hungary, Republic Europe 19D3
Hungerford Aust 34B1
Hüngnam N Korea 28B3
Hungry Horse Res USA 58D1
Hunjiang China 28B2
Hunsberge, Mts Namibia 47B2
Hunsrück, Mts W Germ 13D3
Hunstanton Eng 7E3
Hunte, R W Germ 13E1
Hunter, R Aust 34D2
Hunter Is Aust 34C4
Huntingburg USA 64B3
Huntingdon Eng 7D3
Huntingdon, Indiana USA 64B2
Huntingdon, Pennsylvania USA 68A2
Huntington USA 64C3
Huntington Beach USA 66C4
Huntington L USA 66C2
Huntly NZ 35C1
Huntly Scot 8D3
Hunt, Mt Can 54F3
Huntsville, Alabama USA 67A2
Huntsville Can 65D1
Huntsville, Texas USA 63C2
Huong Khe Viet 30D2
Huon Peninsula PNG 27H7
Huonville Aust 34C4
Hurd,C Can 64C1
Hure Qi China 28A2
Hurghada Egypt 40B4
Hurley USA 64A1
Huron, California USA 66B2
Huron, S. Dakota USA 61D2
Huron,L Can/USA 64C1
Hurunui, R NZ 35B2
Hurup, Ostrov, I USSR 25Q5
Húsavík Iceland 12B1
Huşi Rom 17F1
Huskvarna Sweden 12G7
Husn Jordan 45C2
Husum W Germ 18B2
Hutchinson USA 56D3
Hutton,Mt Aust 34C1
Hutuo He, R China 31D2
Huy Belg 13C2
Huzhu China 31A2
Hvar, I Yugos 16D2
Hwadae N Korea 28A2
Hwange Zim 51C5
Hwange Nat Pk Zim 51C5
Hwapyong N Korea 28A2
Hyannis, Massachusetts USA 68E2
Hyannis, Nebraska USA 60C2
Hyargas Nuur, L Mongolia 26C2
Hydaburg USA 54E4
Hyde Park USA 68D2
Hyderābād India 44B2
Hyderabad Pak 42B3
Hyères France 14D3
Hyères, Iles d', Is France 14D3
Hyesan N Korea 28B2
Hyndman USA 68A3
Hyndman Peak, Mt USA 56B2
Hyrynsalmi Fin 20D3
Hythe Eng 7E4
Hyvinkää Fin 12J6

I

Iaçu Brazil 73K6
Ialomiţa, R Rom 17F2
Iaşi Rom 17F1
Ibadan Nigeria 48C4
Ibagué Colombia 72C3
Ibar, R Yugos 17E2
Ibarra Ecuador 72C3
Ibbenbüren W Germ 13D1
Ibiá Brazil 75C2
Ibicaraí Brazil 75E1
Ibicuí, R Brazil 74E3
Ibicuy Arg 74E4
Ibiza Spain 15C2
Ibiza, I Spain 15C2
Ibo Mozam 51E5
Ibotirama Brazil 73K6
Ibra, Wadi, Watercourse Sudan 50C2
'Ibri Oman 41G5
Ica Peru 72C6
Içá, R Brazil 72E4
Içana Brazil 72E3
Iceland, Republic N Atlantic O 12A1
Icha USSR 25R4
Ichalkaranji India 44A2
Ichinomiya Japan 29C3
Ichinosek Japan 29E3
Icy C USA 54B2
Idabell USA 63D2
Ida Grove USA 61D2
Idaho, State USA 58D2
Idaho City USA 58C2
Idaho Falls USA 58D2
Idaho Springs USA 60B3
Idalion, Hist Site Cyprus 45B1
Idanha USA 58B2
Idar Oberstein W Germ 13D3
Idehan Marzūg, Desert Libya 49D2
Idehan Ubari, Desert Libya 49D2
Idelès Alg 48C2
Ideriym Gol, R Mongolia 26C2
Idfu Egypt 40B5
Ídhi Óros, Mt Greece 17E3
Ídhra, I Greece 17E3
Idiofa Zaïre 50B4
Idlib Syria 40C2
Idritsa USSR 12K7
Idutywa S Africa 47D3
Ieper Belg 13B2
Ierápetra Greece 17F3
Ifakara Tanz 51D4
Ifalik, I Pacific O 27H6
Ifanadiana Madag 51E6
Ife Nigeria 48C4
Iférouane Niger 48C3
Igan Malay 27E6
Igarapava Brazil 75C3
Igarka USSR 24K3
Igatimi Par 75A3
Igdir Iran 41E2
Iggesund Sweden 12H6
Iglesias, Sardinia 16B3
Igloolik Can 55K3
Ignace Can 57D2
Iğneada Burun, Pt Turk 40A1
Ignil-Izane Alg 48C1
Ignoitijala Andaman Is 44E3
Igoumenítsa Greece 17E3
Igra USSR 20J4
Igrim USSR 20L3
Iguaçu, Quedas do, Falls Arg/Brazil 74F3
Iguala Mexico 70C3
Iguape Brazil 74G2
Iguatama Brazil 75C3
Iguatemi Brazil 75B3
Iguatemi, R Brazil 75A3
Iguatu Brazil 73L5
Iguéla Gabon 50A4
Ihosy Madag 51E6
Iida Japan 29D3
Iide-san, Mt Japan 29C3
Iisalmi Fin 12K6
Iizuka Japan 28B4
Ijebu Nigeria 48C4
Ijmuiden Neth 13C1
Ijssel, R Neth 13C1
Ijsselmeer, S Neth 18B2
Ikaría, I Greece 17F3
Ikeda Japan 29E2
Ikela Zaïre 50C4
Ikhtiman Bulg 17E2
Iki, I Japan 28A4
Ikopa, R Madag 51E5
Ilagan Phil 27F5
Ilām Iran 41E3
Ilanskiy USSR 26C1
Ilebo Zaïre 50C4
Île de France, Region France 14C2
Ile d'Orleans Can 65E1
Ilek, R USSR 21K5
Ilfracombe Eng 7B4
Ilgaz Dağları, Mts Turk 40B1
Ilha do Bananal, Region Brazil 73H6
Ilha Grande, B de Brazil 75D3
Ilha Grande ou Sete Quedas, I Brazil 75B3
Ilha Solteira Dam Brazil 75B3
Ilhéus Brazil 73L6
Iliamna L USA 54C4
Ilim, R USSR 26D1
Il'inskiy USSR 26H2
Iliodhrómia, I Greece 17E3
Ilion USA 68C1
Ilkley Eng 6D3
Illapel Chile 74B4
Illéla Niger 48C3
Illinois, R USA 64A3
Illinois, State USA 64B2
Illizi Alg 48C2
Il'men, Ozero, L USSR 20E4
Ilo Peru 72D7
Iloilo Phil 27F5
Ilomantsi Fin 12L6
Ilorin Nigeria 48C4
Il'yino USSR 19G1
Imabari Japan 28B4
Imaichi Japan 29C3
Imari Japan 28A4
Imatra Fin 20D3
Imbituba Brazil 74G3
Imbituva Brazil 75B4
Imi Eth 50E3
Imjin, R N Korea 28A3
Imlay USA 58C2
Imola Italy 16C2
Imperatriz Brazil 73J5
Imperia Italy 16B2
Imperial USA 60C2
Imperial V USA 59C4
Impfondo Congo 50B3
Imphāl India 43G4
Ina Japan 29C3
In Afaleleh, Well Alg 48C2
Inamba-jima, I Japan 29C4
In Amenas Alg 48C2
Inaraña Madag 51F5
Inari Fin 12K5
Inarijärvi, L Fin 12K5
Inawashiro-ko, L Japan 29D3
In Belbel Alg 48C2
Ince Burun, Pt Turk 21F7
Incekum Burun, Pt Turk 40B2
Inchnadamph Scot 8C2
Inch'on S Korea 28B3
Indaal, Loch, Inlet Scot 8B4
In Dagouber, Well Mali 48B2
Indaiá, R Brazil 75C2
Indals, R Sweden 12H6
Independence, California USA 66C2
Independence, Iowa USA 61E2
Independence, Kansas USA 63C1
Independence, Missouri USA 61E3
Independence Mts USA 58C2
Inderborskiy USSR 21J6
India, Federal Republic Asia 39F3
Indiana USA 65D2
Indiana, State USA 64B2
Indian-Antarctic Basin Indian O 36F7
Indian-Antarctic Ridge Indian O 36F7
Indianapolis USA 64B3
Indian Desert = Thar Desert
Indian Harbour Can 55N4
Indian O 36E5
Indianola, Iowa USA 61E2
Indianola, Mississippi USA 63D2
Indianópolis Brazil 75C2
Indian Springs USA 59C3
Indiga USSR 20H2
Indigirka, R USSR 25Q3
Indo-China, Region S E Asia 30D2
Indonesia, Republic S E Asia 27F7
Indore India 42D4
Indre, R France 14C2
Indus, R Pak 42B3
Indus, Mouths of the Pak 42B4
In Ebeggi, Well Alg 48C2
Inebolu Turk 21E7
In Ecker Alg 48C2
Inegöl Turk 40A1
In Ezzane Alg 48D2
Infantta, C S Africa 47C3
Infiernillo, Pico del, Mt Mexico 70B3
Ingal Niger 48C3
Ingersoll Can 64C2

Ingham

Ji'an

Ingham *Aust* **32D2**
Inglefield Land, Region *Can* **55M2**
Inglewood *NZ* **35B1**
Inglewood, Queensland *Aust* **34D1**
Inglewood *USA* **66C4**
Inglewood, Victoria *Aust* **34B3**
Ingólfshöfði, I *Iceland* **12B2**
Ingolstadt *W Germ* **18C3**
Ingrāj Bāzār *India* **43F4**
In Guezzam, Well *Alg* **48C3**
Inhaca, I *Mozam* **47E2**
Inhaca Pen *Mozam* **47E2**
Inhambane *Mozam* **51D6**
Inharrime *Mozam* **51D6**
Inhumas *Brazil* **75C2**
Inirida, R *Colombia* **72E3**
Inishowen, District *Irish Rep* **9C2**
Inishtrahull Sd *Irish Rep* **9C2**
Injune *Aust* **34C1**
Innamincka *Aust* **34B1**
Innerleithen *Scot* **8D4**
Inner Mongolia Aut. Region *China* **31B1**
Innisfail *Aust* **32D2**
Innsbruck *Austria* **18C3**
Inongo *Zaïre* **50B4**
Inowrocław *Pol* **19D2**
In Salah *Alg* **48C2**
Insil *S Korea* **28A3**
Inta *USSR* **20K2**
Interlaken *Switz* **16B1**
International Date Line **33H3**
International Falls *USA* **61E1**
Inubo-saki, C *Japan* **29D3**
Inukjuac *Can* **55L4**
Inuvik *Can* **54E3**
Inuvik, Region *Can* **54E3**
Inveraray *Scot* **8C3**
Inverbervie *Scot* **8D3**
Invercargill *NZ* **35A3**
Inverell *Aust* **34D1**
Invergordon *Scot* **8C3**
Inverness *Scot* **8C3**
Inverurie *Scot* **8D3**
Investigator Str *Aust* **32C4**
Inya *USSR* **26B1**
Inya, R *USSR* **25Q3**
Inyanga *Zim* **51D5**
Inyokern *USA* **66D3**
Inyo Mts *USA* **66C2**
Inzia, R *Zaïre* **50B4**
Ioánnina *Greece* **17E3**
Iola *USA* **63C1**
Iona, I *Scot* **8B3**
Iôna Nat Pk *Angola* **51B5**
Ione *USA* **58C1**
Ionian Is. *Greece* **17E3**
Ionian S *Greece/Italy* **17D3**
Iónioi Nísoi, Is = Ionian Is
Íos, I *Greece* **17F3**
Iosser *USSR* **20J3**
Iowa, R *USA* **61E2**
Iowa, State *USA* **61E2**
Iowa City *USA* **64A2**
Iowa Falls *USA* **61E2**
Ipameri *Brazil* **75C2**
Ipanema *Brazil* **75D2**
Ipatovo *USSR* **21G6**
Ipiales *Colombia* **72C3**
Ipiaú *Brazil* **75E1**
Ipiranga *Brazil* **75B4**
Ipoh *Malay* **30C5**
Iporá *Brazil* **73H7**
Ipsala *Turk* **17F2**
Ipswich *Aust* **34D1**
Ipswich *Eng* **7E3**
Ipswich *USA* **68E1**
Iput, R *USSR* **19G2**
Iquape *Brazil* **75C3**
Iquique *Chile* **74B2**
Iquitos *Peru* **72D4**
Iráklion *Greece* **17F3**
Iran, Republic *S W Asia* **38D2**
Irapuato *Mexico* **70B2**
Iraq, Republic *S W Asia* **40D3**
Irati *Brazil* **75B4**
Irāwan, Watercourse *Libya* **49D2**
Irbid *Jordan* **45C2**
Irbit *USSR* **20L4**
Ireland, Republic of *NW Europe* **10B3**
Ireng, R *Guyana* **73G3**
Iri *S Korea* **28B3**
Irian Jaya, Province *Indon* **27G7**
Iriba *Chad* **50C2**
Iringa *Tanz* **51D4**
Iriomote, I, Ryukyu Is *Japan* **26F4**
Iriona *Honduras* **69A3**
Iriri, R *Brazil* **73H5**
Irish S *Eng/Ire* **10B3**
Irkutsk *USSR* **25M4**
Iron Knob *Aust* **32C4**
Iron Mountain *USA* **64B1**
Iron Range *Aust* **32D2**
Iron River *USA* **64B1**
Irontown *USA* **64C3**
Ironwood *USA* **64A1**
Iroquois Falls *Can* **57E2**
Iro-zaki, C *Japan* **29C4**
Irrawaddy, R *Burma* **30B2**
Irrawaddy, Mouths of the *Burma* **30A2**
Irtysh, R *USSR* **24H4**
Irún *Spain* **15B1**
Irvine *Scot* **8C4**
Irvine, R *Scot* **8C4**
Irving *USA* **63C2**
Isabella Res *USA* **66C3**
Isachsen *Can* **54H2**
Isachsen, C *Can* **54H2**
Ísafjörður *Iceland* **55Q3**
Isahaya *Japan* **28C4**
Isangi *Zaïre* **50C3**
Isbister *Scot* **8E1**
Ischia, I *Italy* **16C2**
Ise *Japan* **29C4**
Iserlohn *W Germ* **13D2**
Isernia *Italy* **16C2**
Ise-wan, B *Japan* **29C4**
Isfahan = Esfahan
Ishigaki, I, Ryukyu Is *Japan* **26F4**
Ishikari, R *Japan* **29E2**
Ishikari-wan, B *Japan* **29E2**
Ishim *USSR* **24H4**
Ishim, R *USSR* **24H4**
Ishinomaki *Japan* **29E3**
Ishioka *Japan* **29D3**
Ishkashim *Afghan* **42C1**
Ishpeming *USA* **64B1**
Isil'kul' *USSR* **24J4**
Isiolo *Kenya* **50D3**
Isiro *Zaïre* **50C3**
Iskenderun *Turk* **40C2**
Iskenderun Körfezi, B *Turk* **40C2**
İskilip *Turk* **40B1**
Iskitim *USSR* **24K4**
Iskur, R *Bulg* **17E2**
Islamabad *Pak* **42C2**
Islamorada *USA* **67B4**
Island L *Can* **57D1**
Island Magee *N Ire* **9D2**
Island Park *USA* **58D2**
Islands, B of *NZ* **35B1**
Islas Baleares = Balearic Is
Islas Malvinas = Falkland Is
Islay, I *Scot* **8B4**
Isle, Island, Isola etc : *see also individual island name*
Isle, R *France* **14C2**
Isle of Wight, County *Eng* **7D4**
Isle Royale Nat Pk *USA* **64B1**
Isles of Scilly *Eng* **7A5**
Isleton *USA* **66B1**
Ismâ'ilîya *Egypt* **40B3**
Isna *Egypt* **40B4**
Isoanala *Madag* **51E6**
Isoka *Zambia* **51D5**
Isola de Correnti, C, Sicily **16D3**
Isosaki *Japan* **29C3**
İsparta *Turk* **40B2**
Israel, Republic *S W Asia* **45C2**
Isser, R *Alg* **15C2**
Issoire *France* **14C2**
Issoudun *France* **14C2**
Issyk Kul', Ozero, L *USSR* **39F1**
İstanbul *Turk* **40A1**
Istiáia *Greece* **17E3**
Istokpoga, L *USA* **67B3**
Istra, Pen *Yugos* **16C1**
Itaberai *Brazil* **75C2**
Itabira *Brazil* **75D2**
Itabirito *Brazil* **75D3**
Itabuna *Brazil* **75E1**
Itacaré *Brazil* **75E1**
Itacoatiara *Brazil* **73G4**
Itacurubí del Rosario *Par* **75A3**
Itaguari, R *Brazil* **75C1**
Itagui *Colombia* **72C2**
Itaituba *Brazil* **73G4**
Itajaí *Brazil* **74G3**
Itajuba *Brazil* **75C3**
Italy, Republic *Europe* **16C2**
Itamaraju *Brazil* **75E2**
Itamarandiba *Brazil* **75D2**
Itambacuri *Brazil* **75D2**
Itambé *Brazil* **75D2**
Itambé, Mt *Brazil* **75D2**
Itānagar *India* **43G3**
Itanhaém *Brazil* **75C3**
Itanhém *Brazil* **75D2**
Itanhém, R *Brazil* **75D2**
Itaobím *Brazil* **75D2**
Itapaci *Brazil* **75C1**
Itapecerica *Brazil* **75C3**
Itaperuna *Brazil* **75D3**
Itapetinga *Brazil* **73K7**
Itapetininga *Brazil* **75C3**
Itapeva *Brazil* **75C3**
Itapipoca *Brazil* **73L4**
Itapuranga *Brazil* **75C2**
Itaqui *Brazil* **74E3**
Itarantim *Brazil* **75D2**
Itararé *Brazil* **75C3**
Itararé, R *Brazil* **75C3**
Itaúna *Brazil* **75D3**
Iténez, R *Bol/Brazil* **72F6**
Ithaca *USA* **65D2**
Ithrīyat, Jebel, Mt *Jordan* **45D3**
Itimbiri, R *Zaïre* **50C3**
Itinga *Brazil* **75D2**
Itiquira, R *Brazil* **75A2**
Itivdleq *Greenland* **55N3**
Ito *Japan* **29C4**
Itoigawa *Japan* **29D3**
Itonomas, R *Bol* **72F6**
Itu *Brazil* **75C3**
Ituberá *Brazil* **75E1**
Ituiutaba *Brazil* **75C2**
Itumbiara *Brazil* **75C2**
Iturama *Brazil* **75B2**
Iturbe *Arg* **74C2**
Iturup, I *USSR* **26H2**
Itzehoe *W Germ* **18B2**
Iul'tin *USSR* **25U3**
Ivacevichi *USSR* **19F2**
Ivai, R *Brazil* **75B3**
Ivalo *Fin* **12K5**
Ivangrad *Yugos* **17D2**
Ivanhoe *Aust* **34B2**
Ivano-Frankovsk *USSR* **19E3**
Ivanovo *USSR* **20G4**
Ivdel' *USSR* **20L3**
Ivindo, R *Gabon* **50B3**
Ivinhema *Brazil* **75B3**
Ivinhema, R *Brazil* **75B3**
Ivohibe *Madag* **51E6**
Ivongo Soanierana *Madag* **51E5**
Ivory Coast, Republic *Africa* **48B4**
Ivrea *Italy* **16B1**
Ivujivik *Can* **55L3**
Iwaki *Japan* **29E3**
Iwaki, R *Japan* **29D2**
Iwaki-san, Mt *Japan* **29D2**
Iwakuni *Japan* **28C4**
Iwamizawa *Japan* **29D2**
Iwanai *Japan* **29E2**
Iwo *Nigeria* **48C4**
Iwo Jima, I *Japan* **26H4**
Ixtepec *Mexico* **70C3**
Iyo *Japan* **28B4**
Iyo-nada, B *Japan* **28B4**
Izhevsk *USSR* **24G4**
Izhma *USSR* **20J2**
Izhma, R *USSR* **20J2**
Izkī *Oman* **41G5**
Izmail *USSR* **19F3**
İzmir *Turk* **40A2**
Izmir Körfezi, B *Turk* **17F3**
İzmit *Turk* **40A1**
İznik *Turk* **40A1**
Iznik Golü, L *Turk* **17F2**
Izra' *Syria* **45D2**
Izuhara *Japan* **28A4**
Izumi-sano *Japan* **29C4**
Izumo *Japan* **28B3**

J

Jabal az Zannah *UAE* **41F5**
Jabalpur *India* **43E4**
Jabal Shammar, Region *S Arabia* **40D4**
Jablah *Syria* **45C1**
Jablonec nad Nisou *Czech* **18D2**
Jaboatão *Brazil* **73L5**
Jaboticabal *Brazil* **75C3**
Jaca *Spain* **15B1**
Jacareacanga *Brazil* **73G5**
Jacarezinho *Brazil* **73H8**
Jacarie *Brazil* **75C3**
Jáchal *Arg* **74C4**
Jaciara *Brazil* **75B2**
Jacinto *Brazil* **75D2**
Jackman Station *USA* **65E1**
Jacksboro *USA* **62C2**
Jacks Mt *USA* **68B2**
Jackson, Alabama *USA* **67A2**
Jackson *Aust* **34C1**
Jackson, California *USA* **66B1**
Jackson, Michigan *USA* **64C2**
Jackson, Minnesota *USA* **61E2**
Jackson, Mississippi *USA* **63D2**
Jackson, Missouri *USA* **64B3**
Jackson, Ohio *USA* **64C3**
Jackson, Tennessee *USA* **63E2**
Jackson, Wyoming *USA* **58D2**
Jackson, C *NZ* **35B2**
Jackson Head, Pt *NZ* **35A2**
Jackson L *USA* **58D2**
Jacksonville, Arkansas *USA* **63D2**
Jacksonville, Florida *USA* **67B2**
Jacksonville, Illinois *USA* **64A3**
Jacksonville, N Carolina *USA* **67C2**
Jacksonville, Texas *USA* **63C2**
Jacksonville Beach *USA* **67B2**
Jacmel *Haiti* **69C3**
Jacobabad *Pak* **42B3**
Jacobina *Brazil* **73K6**
Jadotville = Likasi
Jaén *Peru* **72C5**
Jaén *Spain* **15B2**
Jaffa = Tel Aviv-Yafo
Jaffa, C *Aust* **34A3**
Jaffna *Sri Lanka* **44B4**
Jaffrey *USA* **68D1**
Jagannathganj Ghat *Bang* **43F4**
Jagdalpur *India* **44C2**
Jagin, R *Iran* **41G4**
Jagtial *India* **44B2**
Jaguaquara *Brazil* **75E1**
Jaguarão, R *Urug/Brazil* **74F4**
Jaguariaiva *Brazil* **75C3**
Jahan Dāgh, Mt *Iran* **21H8**
Jahrom *Iran* **41F4**
Jainca *China* **31A2**
Jaipur *India* **42D3**
Jaisalmer *India* **42C3**
Jajarm *Iran* **41G2**
Jajce *Yugos* **16D2**
Jakarta *Indon* **27D7**
Jakobshavn *Greenland* **55N3**
Jakobstad *Fin* **12J6**
Jal *USA* **62B2**
Jalalabad *Afghan* **42C2**
Jalapa *Mexico* **70C3**
Jales *Brazil* **75B3**
Jaleswar *Nepal* **43F3**
Jalgaon *India* **42D4**
Jalingo *Nigeria* **48D4**
Jālna *India* **42D5**
Jalón, R *Spain* **15B1**
Jalo Oasis *Libya* **49E2**
Jālor *India* **42C3**
Jalpāiguri *India* **43F3**
Jama *Ecuador* **72B4**
Jamaica, I *Caribbean S* **69B3**
Jamaica Chan *Jamaica/Haiti* **69B3**
Jamalpur *Bang* **43F4**
Jambi *Indon* **27D7**
Jambusar *India* **42C4**
James, R, N. Dakota *USA* **60D1**
James, R, Virginia *USA* **65D3**
James B *Can* **55K4**
Jamestown *Aust* **34A2**
Jamestown, N. Dakota *USA* **60D1**
Jamestown, New York *USA* **65D2**
Jamestown, Rhode Island *USA* **68E2**
Jamestown *S Africa* **47D3**
Jamestown *USA* **54J5**
Jamkhandi *India* **44B2**
Jammu *India* **42C2**
Jammu and Kashmir, State *India* **42D2**
Jāmnagar *India* **42B4**
Jampur *Pak* **42C3**
Jämsä *Fin* **20C3**
Jamshedpur *India* **43F4**
Janab, Wadi el *Jordan* **45D3**
Janakpur *Nepal* **43F3**
Janaúba *Brazil* **75D2**
Jandaq *Iran* **41F3**
Jandowae *Aust* **34D1**
Janesville *USA* **64B2**
Jan Mayen, I *Norwegian S* **76B1**
Januária *Brazil* **75D2**
Jaora *India* **42D4**
Japan, S of *Japan* **26G3**
Japan Trench *Pacific O* **36J3**
Japurá, R *Brazil* **72E4**
Jarābulus *Syria* **40C2**
Jaraguá *Brazil* **75C2**
Jaraguari *Brazil* **75B3**
Jarama, R *Spain* **15B1**
Jarash *Jordan* **45C2**
Jardim *Brazil* **75A3**
Jardines de la Reina, Is *Cuba* **69B2**
Jargalant = Hovd
Jari, R *Brazil* **73H3**
Jaria Jhānjail *Bang* **43G3**
Jarny *France* **13C3**
Jarocin *Pol* **18D2**
Jarosław *Pol* **19E2**
Järpen *Sweden* **12G6**
Jartai *China* **31B2**
Jasdan *India* **42C4**
Jasikan *Ghana* **48C4**
Jāsk *Iran* **41G4**
Jasło *Pol* **19E3**
Jason Is *Falkland Is* **74D8**
Jasper, Alabama *USA* **63E2**
Jasper, Arkansas *USA* **63D1**
Jasper *Can* **54G4**
Jasper, Florida *USA* **67B2**
Jasper, Indiana *USA* **64B3**
Jasper, Texas *USA* **63D2**
Jastrowie *Pol* **18D2**
Jataí *Brazil* **75B2**
Játiva *Spain* **15B2**
Jatobá *Brazil* **73J4**
Jau *Brazil* **75C3**
Jauja *Peru* **72C6**
Jaunpur *India* **43E3**
Javadi Hills *India* **44B3**
Javari, R = Yavari
Java S *Indon* **27D7**
Java Trench *Indon* **32A2**
Java, I *Indon* **27D7**
Jawa = Java
Jaya, Pk *Indon* **27G7**
Jayapura *Indon* **27H7**
Jayrūd *Syria* **45D2**
Jeanerette *USA* **63D3**
Jebba *Nigeria* **48C4**
Jebel Abyad, Desert Region *Sudan* **50C2**
Jebel esh Sheikh = Hermon, Mt
Jedburgh *Scot* **8D4**
Jedda = Jiddah
Jedrzejów *Pol* **19E2**
Jefferson, Iowa *USA* **61E2**
Jefferson, Texas *USA* **63D2**
Jefferson, R *USA* **58D1**
Jefferson City *USA* **57D3**
Jefferson, Mt *USA* **56B3**
Jeffersonville *USA* **64B3**
Jeib, Wadi el *Israel/Jordan* **45C3**
Jejui-Guazú, R *Par* **75A3**
Jekabpils *USSR* **20D4**
Jelena Gora *Pol* **18D2**
Jelgava *USSR* **20C4**
Jember *Indon* **27E7**
Jemez Pueblo *USA* **62A1**
Jena *E Germ* **18C2**
Jendouba *Tunisia* **16B3**
Jenin *Israel* **45C2**
Jennings *USA* **63D2**
Jensen Nunatakker, Mt *Greenland* **55O3**
Jens Munk, I *Can* **55K3**
Jeparit *Aust* **34B3**
Jequié *Brazil* **73L6**
Jequitai, R *Brazil* **75D2**
Jequitinhonha *Brazil* **75D2**
Jequitinhonha, R *Brazil* **73K7**
Jerba, I de *Tunisia* **48D1**
Jerez de la Frontera *Spain* **15A2**
Jerez de los Caballeros *Spain* **15A2**
Jericho *Israel* **45C3**
Jerilderie *Aust* **34C3**
Jerome *USA* **58D2**
Jersey, I *Channel Is* **14B2**
Jersey City *USA* **57F2**
Jersey Shore *USA* **65D2**
Jerseyville *USA* **64A3**
Jerusalem *Israel* **40C3**
Jervis B *Aust* **34D3**
Jesenice *Yugos* **16C1**
Jeseniky, Upland *Czech* **18D2**
Jessore *Bang* **43F4**
Jesup *USA* **57E3**
Jetmore *USA* **62C1**
Jever *W Germ* **13D1**
Jewett City *USA* **68E2**
Jeypore *India* **44C2**
Jezerce, Mt *Alb* **17D2**
Jezioro Mamry, L *Pol* **19E2**
Jezioro Śniardwy, L *Pol* **19E2**
Jezzine *Leb* **45C2**
Jhābua *India* **42C4**
Jhālāwār *India* **42D4**
Jhang Maghiana *Pak* **42C2**
Jhānsi *India* **42D3**
Jhārsuguda *India* **43E4**
Jhelum *Pak* **42C2**
Jhelum, R *Pak* **42C2**
Jhunjhunūn *India* **42D3**
Jialing Jiang, R *China* **31B3**
Jiamusi *China* **26G2**
Ji'an *China* **28B2**
Ji'an, Jiangxi *China* **31C4**

Jiande *China* 31D4
Jiang'an *China* 31B4
Jiangbiancun *China* 31D4
Jiangcheng *China* 31A5
Jiangmen *China* 31C5
Jiangsu, Province *China* 31D3
Jiangxi, Province *China* 31C4
Jiangyou *China* 31A3
Jianping *China* 31D1
Jianshui *China* 31A5
Jian Xi, R *China* 31D4
Jianyang *China* 31D4
Jiaohe *China* 28B2
Jiaonan *China* 31E2
Jiao Xian *China* 31E2
Jiaozhou Wan, B *China* 31E2
Jiaozuo *China* 31C2
Jiaxiang *China* 31E3
Jiayuguan *China* 26C3
Jibão, Serra do, Mts *Brazil* 75C2
Jiddah *S Arabia* 50D1
Jieshou *China* 31D3
Jiexiu *China* 31C2
Jigzhi *China* 31A3
Jihlava *Czech* 18D3
Jijel *Algeria* 16B3
Jilib *Somalia* 50E3
Jilin *China* 28B2
Jilin, Province *China* 28B2
Jiloca, R *Spain* 15B1
Jima *Eth* 50D3
Jiménez, Coahuila *Mexico* 62B3
Jinan *China* 31D2
Jind *India* 42D3
Jingbian *China* 31B2
Jingdezhen *China* 31D4
Jinghong *China* 30C1
Jingmen *China* 31C3
Jingning *China* 31B2
Jing Xian *China* 31B4
Jingyu *China* 28B2
Jinhua *China* 31D4
Jining *Nei Mongol China* 31C1
Jining, Shandong *China* 31D2
Jinja *Uganda* 50D3
Jinping *China* 30C1
Jinsha Jiang, R *China* 31A4
Jinshi *China* 31C4
Jinxi *China* 31E1
Jin Xian *China* 31E2
Jinzhou *China* 31E1
Jiparaná, R *Brazil* 72F5
Jipijapa *Ecuador* 72B4
Jiroft *Iran* 41G4
Jishou *China* 31B4
Jisr ash Shughūr *Syria* 40C2
Jiu, R *Rom* 17E2
Jiujiang *China* 31D4
Jiuling Shan, Hills *China* 31C4
Jiulong *China* 31A4
Jiulong Jiang, R *China* 31D4
Jixi *China* 26G2
Jiza *Jordan* 45C3
Jīzān *S Arabia* 50E2
Joal *Sen* 48A3
João Monlevade *Brazil* 75D2
João Pessoa *Brazil* 73M5
João Pinheiro *Brazil* 73J7
Jodhpur *India* 42C3
Joensuu *Fin* 12K6
Joeuf *France* 13C3
Jogbani *India* 43F3
Jog Falls *India* 44A3
Johannesburg *S Africa* 47D2
Johannesburg *USA* 59C3
Johan Pen *Can* 55L2
John Day *USA* 58C2
John Day, R *USA* 58B1
John H Kerr L *USA* 57F3
John H. Kerr Res *USA* 65D3
John Martin Res *USA* 62B1
John o'Groats *Scot* 8D2
John Redmond Res *USA* 63C1
Johnsonburg *USA* 68A2
Johnson City, New York *USA* 68C1
Johnson City, Tennessee *USA* 67B1
Johnston *USA* 67B2
Johnston Pt *St Vincent* 69N2
Johnstown, New York *USA* 68C1
Johnstown, Pennsylvania *USA* 65D2
Johor Bharu *Malay* 30C5
Joigny *France* 14C2
Joinville *Brazil* 74G3
Joinville *France* 13C3
Jok, R *USSR* 20J5
Jokkmokk *Sweden* 12H5
Jolfa *Iran* 21H8
Joliet *USA* 57E2
Joliette *Can* 55L5
Jolo *Phil* 27F6
Jolo, I *Phil* 27F6

Joma, Mt *China* 39H2
Jonava *USSR* 19E1
Jonē *China* 31A3
Jonesboro, Arkansas *USA* 57D3
Jonesboro, Louisiana *USA* 63D2
Jones Sd *Can* 55K2
Joniškis *USSR* 19E1
Jönköping *Sweden* 12G7
Jonquière *Can* 65E1
Joplin *USA* 57D3
Jordan, Montana *USA* 60B1
Jordan, New York *USA* 68B1
Jordan, Kingdom *S W Asia* 40C3
Jordan, R *Israel* 45C2
Jordan Valley *USA* 58C2
Jordão, R *Brazil* 75B4
Jorhāt *India* 43G3
Jörn *Sweden* 20C2
Jørpeland *Nor* 12F7
Jos *Nigeria* 48C3
Joseph Bonaparte G *Aust* 32B2
Joseph City *USA* 59D3
Joseph, Lac *Can* 55M4
Jotunheimen, Mt *Nor* 24B3
Jouai'ya *Leb* 45C2
Jounié *Leb* 45C2
Jowai *India* 43G3
Jowhar *Somalia* 50E3
Juan de Fuca,Str of *Can/USA* 54F5
Juan de Nova, I *Mozam Chan* 51E5
Juan Fernández, Islas *Pacific O* 72Q
Juàzeiro *Brazil* 73K5
Juàzeiro do Norte *Brazil* 73L5
Juba *Sudan* 50D3
Juba, R *Somalia* 50E3
Jubail *Leb* 45C1
Jubany, Base *Ant* 76G2
Jubbah *S Arabia* 40D4
Júcar, R *Spain* 15B2
Judenburg *Austria* 18C3
Juist, I *W Germ* 13D1
Juiz de Fora *Brazil* 73K8
Jujuy, State *Arg* 74C2
Julesburg *USA* 60C2
Juli *Peru* 72E7
Juliaca *Peru* 72D7
Julianatop, Mt *Surinam* 73G3
Julianehåb *Greenland* 55O3
Jülich *W Germ* 13D2
Jullundur *India* 42D2
Jumla *Nepal* 43E3
Jum Suwwāna, Mt *Jordan* 45C3
Jūnāgadh *India* 42C4
Junan *China* 31D2
Junction, Texas *USA* 62C2
Junction, Utah *USA* 59D3
Junction City *USA* 56D3
Jundiaí *Brazil* 74G2
Juneau *USA* 54E4
Junee *Aust* 32D4
June Lake *USA* 66C2
Jungfrau, Mt *Switz* 16B1
Juniata, R *USA* 68B2
Junín *Arg* 74D4
Junipero Serra Peak, Mt *USA* 66B2
Junlian *China* 31A4
Juparanã, Lagoa *Brazil* 75D2
Juquiá *Brazil* 74G2
Jur, R *Sudan* 50C3
Jura, I *Scot* 8C4
Jura, Mts *France* 14D2
Jura,Sound of, Chan *Scot* 8C3
Jurf ed Darāwish *Jordan* 45C3
Jurga *USSR* 24K4
Jūrmala *USSR* 20C4
Juruá, R *Brazil* 72E4
Juruena, R *Brazil* 73G6
Jūsīyah *Syria* 45D1
Jutaí, R *Brazil* 72E4
Juticalpa *Honduras* 70D3
Jutland, Pen = Jylland
Juventud, Isla de la *Cuba* 69A2
Jūymand *Iran* 41G3
Jylland, Pen *Den* 18B1
Jyväskyla *Fin* 12K6

K

K2, Mt *China/India* 39F2
Kaakhka *USSR* 41G2
Kaapmuiden *S Africa* 47E2
Kabaena *Indon* 27F7
Kabaena, I *Indon* 32B1
Kabala *Sierra Leone* 48A4
Kabale *Uganda* 50D4
Kabalo *Zaïre* 50C4

Kabambare *Zaïre* 50C4
Kabarole *Uganda* 50D3
Kabinakagami L *Can* 64C1
Kabinda *Zaïre* 50C4
Kabir, R *Syria* 45C1
Kabir Kuh, Mts *Iran* 41E3
Kabompo *Zambia* 51C5
Kabompo, R *Zambia* 51C5
Kabongo *Zaïre* 51C4
Kabul *Afghan* 42B2
Kachchh,G of *India* 42B4
Kachkanar *USSR* 20K4
Kachug *USSR* 25M4
Kadan, I *Burma* 30B3
Kadi *India* 42C4
Kadinhanı *Turk* 40B2
Kadiri *India* 44B3
Kadiyevka *USSR* 21F6
Kadoka *USA* 60C2
Kadoma *China* 51C5
Kadugli *Sudan* 50C2
Kaduna *Nigeria* 48C3
Kaduna, R *Nigeria* 48C3
Kadūr *India* 44B3
Kadusam, Mt *China* 43H3
Kadzherom *USSR* 20K3
Kaechon *N Korea* 28A3
Kaédi *Maur* 48A3
Kaena Pt *Hawaiian Is* 66E5
Kaesŏng *N Korea* 28B3
Kafanchan *Nigeria* 48C4
Kaffrine *Sen* 48A3
Kafr Behum *Syria* 45D1
Kafr Sa'd *Egypt* 45A3
Kafr Saqv *Egypt* 45A3
Kafrün Bashūr *Syria* 45D1
Kafue *Zambia* 51C5
Kafue, R *Zambia* 51C5
Kafue Nat Pk *Zambia* 51C5
Kaga *Japan* 29D3
Kagan *USSR* 24H6
Kağizman *Turk* 21G7
Kagul *USSR* 19F3
Kahama *Tanz* 50D4
Kahan *Pak* 42B3
Kahemba *Zaïre* 51B4
Kahler Asten, Mt *W Germ* 13E2
Kahnūj *Iran* 41G4
Kahoka *USA* 64A2
Kahoolawe, I *Hawaiian Is* 66E5
Kahramanmaraş *Turk* 40C2
Kahuku Pt *Hawaiian Is* 66E5
Kahului *Hawaiian Is* 66E5
Kaiapoi *NZ* 35B2
Kaibab Plat *USA* 59D3
Kaieteur Falls *Guyana* 73G2
Kaifeng *China* 31C3
Kai, Kepulauan, Arch *Indon* 27G7
Kaikohe *NZ* 35B1
Kaikoura *NZ* 33G5
Kaikoura Pen *NZ* 35B2
Kaikoura Range, Mts *NZ* 35B2
Kaili *China* 31B4
Kailu *China* 28A2
Kailua *Hawaii* 66E5
Kailua, Oahu *Hawaiian Is* 66E5
Kaimana *Indon* 27G7
Kaimenawa Mts *NZ* 35C1
Kainan *Japan* 29C4
Kainji Res *Nigeria* 48C3
Kaipara Harbour, B *NZ* 35B1
Kaiping *China* 31C5
Kairouan *Tunisia* 16C3
Kaiser Peak, Mt *USA* 66C2
Kaiserslautern *W Germ* 14D2
Kaishantun *China* 28B2
Kaisiadorys *USSR* 19E2
Kaitaia *NZ* 35B1
Kaitangata *NZ* 35A3
Kaithal *India* 42D3
Kaiwi Chan *Hawaiian Is* 66E5
Kai Xian *China* 31B3
Kaiyuan, Liaoning *China* 28A2
Kaiyuan, Yunnan *China* 31A5
Kajaani *Fin* 12K6
Kajaki *Afghan* 42B2
Kaka *Sudan* 50D2
Kajiado *Kenya* 50D4
Kajrān *Afghan* 42B2
Kaka *Sudan* 50D2
Kakabeka Falls *Can* 64B1
Kakamega *Kenya* 50D3
Kake *Japan* 28B4
Kakhovskoye Vodokhranilishche, Res *USSR* 24E5
Kāki *Iran* 41F4
Kākināda *India* 44C2
Kakogawa *Japan* 29B4
Kaktovik *USA* 54D2
Kakuda *Japan* 29D3
Kalaat Khasba *Tunisia* 16B3
Kalabáka *Greece* 17E3
Kalabo *Zambia* 51C5
Kandi *Benin* 48C3

Kalach *USSR* 21G5
Kalach-na-Donu *USSR* 21G6
Kaladan, R *Burma/India* 43G4
Ka Lae, C *Hawaiian Is* 66E5
Kalahari Desert *Botswana* 51C6
Kalahari Gemsbok Nat Pk *S Africa* 47C2
Kalajoki *Fin* 20C3
Kalakan *USSR* 25N4
Kalakepen *Indon* 27C6
Kalam *Pak* 42C1
Kálamai *Greece* 17E3
Kalamazoo *USA* 57E2
Kalapana *Hawaiian Is* 66E5
Kalarash *USSR* 19F3
Kalat *Pak* 42B3
Kalaupapa *Hawaiian Is* 66E5
Kalecik *Turk* 40B1
Kalémié *Zaïre* 50C4
Kalevala *USSR* 20E2
Kalewa *Burma* 43G4
Kalgoorlie *Aust* 32B4
Kali, R *India/Nepal* 43E3
Kalima *Zaïre* 50C4
Kalimantan, Terr *Indon* 27E7
Kálimnos, I *Greece* 17F3
Kālimpang *India* 43F3
Kali Nadi, R *India* 43K1
Kaliningrad *USSR* 12J8
Kalinin *USSR* 20F4
Kaliningrad *USSR* 20B5
Kalinkovichi *USSR* 21D5
Kalinovka *USSR* 19F3
Kalispell *USA* 56B2
Kalisz *Pol* 19D2
Kaliua *Tanz* 50D4
Kalix, R *Sweden* 12J5
Kalkfeld *Namibia* 51B6
Kalkfontein *Botswana* 47C1
Kallavesi, L *Fin* 12K6
Kallonis Kólpos, B *Greece* 17F3
Kalmar *Sweden* 12H7
Kalmyk ASSR, Republic *USSR* 21H6
Kalomo *Zambia* 51C5
Kalona *USA* 64A2
Kalpeni, I *India* 44A3
Kālpi *India* 42D3
Kaluga *USSR* 20F5
Kalundborg *Den* 12G7
Kalush *USSR* 19E3
Kalyān *India* 44A2
Kalyandurg *India* 44B3
Kalyazin *USSR* 20F4
Kama, R *USSR* 20J3
Kamaishi *Japan* 29E3
Kamalia *Pak* 42C2
Kamanjab *Namibia* 51B5
Kamara *China* 25O4
Kamat, Mt *India/China* 42D2
Kambam *India* 44B4
Kambarka *USSR* 20J4
Kambia *Sierra Leone* 48A4
Kamchatka, Pen *USSR* 25S4
Kamenets Podolskiy *USSR* 19F3
Kamenka *USSR* 20G5
Kamen-na-Obi *USSR* 24K4
Kamenskoya *USSR* 25S3
Kamensk-Ural'skiy *USSR* 20L4
Kamieskroon *S Africa* 47B3
Kamilukuak L *Can* 54H3
Kamina *Zaïre* 51C4
Kaminak L *Can* 55J3
Kaminoyama *Japan* 29D3
Kamloops *Can* 54F4
Kamo *USSR* 41E1
Kamogawa *Japan* 29D3
Kampala *Uganda* 50D3
Kampar *Malay* 30C5
Kampen *Neth* 18B2
Kamphaeng Phet *Thai* 30B2
Kampot *Camb* 30C3
Kampuchea = Cambodia
Kamskoye Vodokhranilishche, Res *USSR* 20K4
Kamyama *Japan* 29C3
Kanazawa *Japan* 29D3
Kanab *USA* 59D3
Kananga *Zaïre* 50C4
Kanash *USSR* 20H4
Kanayama *Japan* 29C3
Kanchipuram *India* 44B3
Kandagan *Indon* 27E7
Kandahar *Afghan* 42B2
Kandalaksha *USSR* 24E3
Kandalakshskaya Guba, B *USSR* 12L5
Kandel, Mt *W Germ* 13D3

Kandos *Aust* 34C2
Kandy *Sri Lanka* 44C4
Kane *USA* 65D2
Kane Basin, B *Can* 55L1
Kanem, Desert Region *Chad* 50B2
Kaneohe *Hawaiian Is* 66E5
Kanevka *USSR* 20F2
Kang *Botswana* 47C1
Kangaba *Mali* 48B3
Kangal *Turk* 40C2
Kangâmiut *Greenland* 55N3
Kangān *Iran* 41F4
Kangar *Malay* 30C4
Kangaroo I *Aust* 32C4
Kangatsiaq *Greenland* 55N3
Kangavar *Iran* 41E3
Kangbao *China* 31C1
Kangchenjunga, Mt *Nepal/China* 39G3
Kangding *China* 31A4
Kangean, Is *Indon* 32A1
Kangerdlugssuaq, B *Greenland* 55P3
Kangerdlugssuatsaiq, B *Greenland* 55P3
Kangetet *Kenya* 50D3
Kanggye *N Korea* 28B2
Kanghwa *S Korea* 28B3
Kangiqsualujjuaq *Can* 55M4
Kangiqsujuak *Can* 55L3
Kangirsuk *Can* 55L3
Kangnŭng *S Korea* 28B3
Kango *Gabon* 50B3
Kangping *China* 28A2
Kangto, Mt *China/India* 26C4
Kang Xian *China* 31B3
Kaniama *Zaïre* 51C4
Kani Giri *India* 44B2
Kanin Nos, Pt *USSR* 24F3
Kanin, Poluostrov, Pen *USSR* 20G2
Kankaanpää *Fin* 12J6
Kankakee *USA* 64B2
Kankakee, R *USA* 64B2
Kankan *Guinea* 48B3
Känker *India* 43E4
Kannapolis *USA* 67B1
Kanniyákumari *India* 44B4
Kano *Nigeria* 48C3
Kanorado *USA* 60C3
Känpur *India* 43E3
Kansas, R *USA* 61D3
Kansas, State *USA* 56D3
Kansas City *USA* 57D3
Kanshi *China* 31D5
Kansk *USSR* 26C1
Kansŏng *S Korea* 28A3
Kantchari *Burkina* 48C3
Kanté *Togo* 48C4
Kanthi *India* 43F4
Kantishna *USA* 54C3
Kanturk *Irish Rep* 9B3
Kanye *Botswana* 47D1
Kaoka Veld, Plain *Namibia* 51B5
Kaolack *Sen* 48A3
Kaoma *Zambia* 51C5
Kapaa *Hawaiian Is* 66E5
Kapaau *Hawaiian Is* 66E5
Kapanga *Zaïre* 51C4
Kapellskär *Sweden* 12H7
Kap Farvel = Farewell, C
Kapiri *Zambia* 51C5
Kaplan *USA* 63D2
Kaplice *Czech* 18C3
Kapoe *Thai* 30B4
Kapona *Zaïre* 51C4
Kaposvár *Hung* 17D1
Kapsan *N Korea* 28A2
Kapsukas *USSR* 20C5
Kapuas, R *Indon* 27E6
Kapunda *Aust* 34A2
Kapurthala *India* 42D2
Kapuskasing *Can* 55K5
Kapuskasing, R *Can* 64C1
Kaputar, Mt *Aust* 34D2
Kapydzhik, Mt *USSR* 21H8
Kapyŏng *S Korea* 28A3
Kara, R *USSR* 21G8
Karabük *Turk* 40B1
Karacabey *Turk* 17F2
Karachi *Pak* 42B4
Karād *India* 44A2
Kara Dağları, Mt *Turk* 21F7
Karadeniz Boğazi, Str *Turk* 21D7
Karaftit *USSR* 26E1
Karaganda *USSR* 24J5
Karagayly *USSR* 24J5
Karaginskiy, Ostrov, I *USSR* 25S4
Kāraikāl *India* 44B3
Karaj *Iran* 41F2
Karak *Jordan* 40C3

Karakalpak ASSR — Kiffa

Karakalpak ASSR, Republic USSR 24G5
Karakax He, R China 42D1
Karakelong, I Indon 27F6
Karakoram, Mts India 42D1
Karakoram P India/China 42D1
Karakoro, Watercourse Maur/Mali 48A3
Karakumy, Desert USSR 24G6
Karama Jordan 45C3
Karaman Turk 21E8
Karamay China 24K5
Karamea NZ 35B2
Karamea Bight, B NZ 35B2
Kāranja India 42D4
Karanlik, R Turk 21E8
Karapınar Turk 40B2
Kara S USSR 24J2
Karasburg Namibia 47B2
Karasjok Nor 12K5
Karasuk USSR 24J4
Karataş Turk 40C2
Kara Tau, Mts USSR 24H5
Karathuri Burma 30B3
Karatsu Japan 28B4
Karaul USSR 24K2
Karavostasi Cyprus 45B1
Karāz Iran 41F4
Karbalā' Iraq 41D3
Karcag Hung 19E3
Kardhítsa Greece 17E3
Karelian ASSR, Republic USSR 20E3
Karen Andaman Is 44E3
Karepino USSR 20K3
Karesvando Sweden 12J5
Karet, Desert Region Maur 48B2
Kargasok USSR 24K4
Kargopol' USSR 20F3
Kari Nigeria 48D3
Kariba Zim 51C5
Kariba Dam Zambia/Zim 51C5
Kariba, L Zambia/Zim 51C5
Karibib Namibia 47B1
Karima Sudan 50D2
Karimata, I Indon 27D7
Karimganj India 43G4
Karīmnagar India 44B2
Karin Somalia 50E2
Karis Fin 12J6
Karisimbe, Mt Zaïre 50C4
Káristos Greece 17E3
Kārkal India 44A3
Karkar, I PNG 27H7
Karkheh, R Iran 41E3
Karkinitskiy Zaliv, B USSR 21E6
Karlik Shan, Mt China 25L5
Karlino Pol 18D2
Karl Marx Stadt E Germ 18C2
Karlobag Yugos 16D2
Karlovac Yugos 16D1
Karlovo Bulg 17E2
Karlovy Vary Czech 18C2
Karlshamn Sweden 12G7
Karlskoga Sweden 12G7
Karlskrona Sweden 12H7
Karlsruhe W Germ 18B3
Karlstad Sweden 12G7
Karlstad USA 61D1
Karluk USA 54C4
Karnafuli Res Bang 43G4
Karnāl India 42D3
Karnātaka, State India 44A2
Karnobat Bulg 17F2
Karoi Zim 51C5
Karonga Malawi 51D4
Karora Sudan 50D2
Kárpathos, I Greece 17F3
Karrats Fjord Greenland 55N2
Karree Berge, Mts S Africa 47C3
Kars Turk 21G7
Karsakpay USSR 24H5
Kārsava USSR 19F1
Karshi USSR 38E2
Karskiye Vorota, Proliv, Str USSR 24G2
Karstula Fin 12J6
Kartaba Leb 45C1
Kartal Turk 17F2
Kartaly USSR 20L5
Karthaus USA 68A2
Kārūn, R Iran 41E3
Karwa India 43E3
Kārwār India 44A3
Karymskoye USSR 26E1
Kasai, R Zaïre 50B4
Kasaji Zaïre 51C5
Kasama Zambia 51D5
Kasanga Tanz 51D4
Kāsaragod India 44A3
Kasba L Can 54H3
Kasempa Zambia 51C5
Kasenga Zaïre 51C5
Kasese Uganda 50D3
Kasganj India 43K2
Kāshān Iran 41F3
Kashi China 39F2
Kashima Japan 28B4
Kāshipur India 42D3
Kashiwazaki Japan 29D3
Kāshmar Iran 41G2
Kashmir, State India 22E4
Kasimov USSR 20G5
Kaskaskia, R USA 64B3
Kaskinen Fin 12J6
Kasli USSR 20L4
Kaslo Can 54G5
Kasongo Zaïre 50C4
Kasongo-Lunda Zaïre 51B4
Kásos, I Greece 17F3
Kaspiyskiy USSR 21H6
Kassala Sudan 50D2
Kassel W Germ 18B2
Kasserine Tunisia 48C1
Kassinga Angola 51B5
Kastamonu Turk 40B1
Kastélli Greece 17E3
Kastellorizon, I Greece 40A2
Kastoría Greece 17E2
Kástron Greece 17F3
Kasugai Japan 29D3
Kasumi Japan 29B3
Kasungu Malawi 51D5
Kasur Pak 42C2
Kataba Zambia 51C5
Katahdin,Mt USA 65F1
Katako-kombe Zaïre 50C4
Katalla USA 54D3
Katangli USSR 25Q4
Katanning Aust 32A4
Katchall, I, Nicobar Is Indian O 44E4
Kateríni Greece 17E2
Kates Needle, Mt Can/USA 54E4
Katharîna, Gebel, Mt Egypt 40B4
Katherine Aust 32C2
Kāthiāwār, Pen India 42C4
Kathib el Henu, hill Egypt 45B3
Kathmandu Nepal 43F3
Kathua India 42D2
Katihār India 43F3
Katima Mulilo Namibia 51C5
Katiola Ivory Coast 48B4
Katmai,Mt USA 54C4
Katni India 43E4
Katoomba Aust 34D2
Katowice Pol 19D2
Katrineholm Sweden 12H7
Katrine, Loch, L Scot 8C3
Katsina Nigeria 48C3
Katsina, R Cam/Nigeria 48C4
Katsina Ala Nigeria 48C4
Katsuta Japan 29D3
Katsuura Japan 29D3
Katsuyama Japan 29C3
Kattakurgan USSR 24H5
Kattegat, Str Den/Sweden 12G7
Katzenbuckel, Mt W Germ 13E3
Kauai, I Hawaiian Is 66E5
Kauai Chan Hawaiian Is 66E5
Kaulakahi Chan Hawaiian Is 66E5
Kaunakakai Hawaiian Is 66E5
Kaunas USSR 20C5
Kaura Namoda Nigeria 48C3
Kautokeino Nor 12J5
Kavadarci Yugos 17E2
Kavajë Alb 17D2
Kavali India 44B3
Kaválla Greece 17E2
Kāvda India 42B4
Kavieng PNG 32E1
Kawagoe Japan 29C3
Kawaguchi Japan 29C3
Kawaihae Hawaiian Is 66E5
Kawakawa NZ 35B1
Kawambwa Zambia 51C4
Kawardha India 43E4
Kawartha Lakes Can 65D2
Kawasaki Japan 29D3
Kaweah, R USA 66C2
Kawerau NZ 35C1
Kawhia NZ 35B1
Kaya Burkina 48B3
Kayan, R Indon 27E6
Kāyankulam India 44B4
Kaycee USA 60B2
Kayenta USA 59D3
Kayes Mali 48A3
Kayseri Turk 21F8
Kazach'ye USSR 25P2
Kazakh USSR 41E1
Kazakh SSR, Republic USSR 24G5
Kazan' USSR 20H4
Kazanlük Bulg 17F2
Kazan Retto, Is Japan 26H4
Kazatin USSR 19F3
Kazbek, Mt USSR 21G7
Kāzerūn Iran 41F4
Kazhim USSR 20J3
Kazi Magomed USSR 41E1
Kazincbarcika Hung 19E3
Kazym, R USSR 20M3
Kazymskaya USSR 20M3
Kéa, I Greece 17E3
Keady N Ire 9C2
Kealaikahiki Chan Hawaiian Is 66E5
Kearney USA 56D2
Kearny USA 59D4
Keban Baraji, Res Turk 40C2
Kébémer Sen 48A3
Kebili Tunisia 48C1
Kebir, R Leb/Syria 45D1
Kebnekaise, Mt Sweden 12H5
Kecskemét Hung 19D3
Kedainiai USSR 19E1
Kedgwick Can 65F1
Kediri Indon 27E7
Kédougou Sen 48A3
Kedva USSR 20J3
Keele Pk, Mt Can 54E3
Keeler USA 59C3
Keeling Is Indian O 27C8
Keelung Taiwan 26F4
Keene, California USA 66C3
Keene, New Hampshire USA 65E2
Keetmanshoop Namibia 47B2
Keewanee USA 64B2
Keewatin USA 64A1
Keewatin, Region Can 55J3
Kefallinía, I Greece 17E3
Kefar Sava Israel 45C2
Keffi Nigeria 48C4
Keflavík Iceland 55Q3
Keg River Can 54G4
Kehsi Mansam Burma 30B1
Keita Niger 48C3
Keith Aust 34B3
Keith Scot 8D3
Keith Arm, B Can 54F3
Keithley Eng 6C3
Kekertuk Can 55M3
Kekri India 42D3
Kelang Malay 30C5
Kelantan, R Malay 30C4
Kelibia Tunisia 16C3
Kelif USSR 42B1
Kelkit, R Turk 40C1
Kellé Congo 50B4
Kellett,C Can 54F2
Kellogg USA 58C1
Kelloselka Fin 24D3
Kells Irish Rep 33B9
Kells Range, Hills Scot 8C4
Kelme USSR 19E1
Kelowna Can 54G5
Kelsey Bay Can 54F4
Kelso Scot 8D4
Kelso USA 58B1
Kem' USSR 24E3
Kem', R USSR 20E3
Ke Macina Mali 48B3
Kemerovo USSR 24K4
Kemi Fin 12J5
Kemi, R Fin 12K5
Kemijärvi Fin 12K5
Kemmerer USA 58D2
Kempen, Region Belg 13C2
Kemp,L USA 62C2
Kemps Bay The Bahamas 69B2
Kempsey Aust 34D2
Kempten W Germ 18C3
Kempt,L Can 65E1
Kenai USA 54C3
Kenai Pen USA 54C3
Kenamuke Swamp Sudan 50D3
Kendal Eng 6C2
Kendall Aust 34D2
Kendari Indon 32B1
Kendawangan Indon 27E7
Kendrāpāra India 43F4
Kendrick USA 58C1
Kenedy USA 63C3
Kenema Sierra Leone 48A4
Kenge Zaïre 50B4
Kengtung Burma 30B1
Kenhardt S Africa 47C2
Kéniéba Mali 48A3
Kenitra Mor 48B1
Kenmare USA 60C1
Kenna USA 62B2
Kennebec, R USA 65F1
Kennebunk USA 68E1
Kenner USA 63D3
Kennett USA 63E1
Kennett Square USA 68C3
Kennewick USA 58C1
Kenny Dam Can 54F4
Kenora Can 55J5
Kenosha USA 57E2
Kent, Texas USA 62B2
Kent, Washington USA 58B1
Kent, County Eng 7E4
Kentland USA 64B2
Kenton USA 64C2
Kent Pen Can 54H3
Kentucky, R USA 64C3
Kentucky, State USA 57E3
Kentucky L USA 57E3
Kentwood, Louisiana USA 63D2
Kentwood, Michigan USA 64B2
Kenya, Republic Africa 50D3
Kenya,Mt Kenya 50D4
Keokuk USA 64A2
Keonchi India 43E4
Keonjhargarh India 43F4
Kepno Pol 19D2
Kerala, State India 44B3
Kerang Aust 34B3
Kerava Fin 12K6
Kerch' USSR 21F6
Kerchem'ya USSR 20J3
Kerema PNG 32D1
Keremeos Can 58C1
Keren Eth 50D2
Kerguelen, Is Indian O 36E7
Kerguelen Ridge Indian O 36E7
Kericho Kenya 50D4
Kerinci, Mt Indon 27D7
Kerio, R Kenya 50D3
Kerkenna, Îles Tunisia 48D1
Kerki USSR 38E2
Kérkira = Corfu
Kermadec Is Pacific O 33H3
Kermadec Trench Pacific O 33H4
Kermān Iran 41G3
Kerman USA 66B2
Kermānshāh Iran 41E3
Kermit USA 62B2
Kern, R USA 59C3
Kernville USA 66C3
Keros USSR 20J3
Kerrville USA 62C2
Kerry Hd Irish Rep 9B3
Kershaw USA 67B2
Kerulen, R Mongolia 25N5
Kerzaz Alg 48B2
Keşan Turk 17F2
Kesariya India 43N2
Kesennuma Japan 29E3
Kesir Dağları, Mt Turk 21G7
Kestenga USSR 12L5
Keswick Eng 6C2
Kéta Ghana 48C4
Ketapang Indon 27E7
Ketchikan USA 54E4
Keti Bandar Pak 42B4
Kętrzyn Pol 19E2
Kettering Eng 7D3
Kettering USA 64C3
Kettle, R Can 58C1
Kettleman City USA 66C2
Kettle River Range, Mts USA 58C1
Kettlestone B Can 55L3
Keuka L USA 68B1
Kevir-i-Namak, Salt Flat Iran 41G3
Kewaunee USA 64B2
Keweenaw B USA 64B1
Keweenaw Pen USA 64B1
Key Harbour Can 64C1
Key Largo USA 67B3
Key West USA 57E4
Kezhma USSR 25M4
Khabab Syria 45D2
Khabarovsk USSR 26G2
Khabūr, al, R Syria 21G8
Khairpur Pak 42B3
Khairpur, Division Pak 42B3
Khakhea Botswana 47C1
Khalig el Tîna, B Egypt 45B3
Khalīj Maşīrah, G Oman 38D4
Khálki, I Greece 17F3
Khalkidhíki, Pen Greece 17E2
Khalkís Greece 17E3
Khal'mer-Yu USSR 20L2
Khalturin USSR 20H4
Khambhāt,G of India 42C4
Khāmgaon India 42D4
Kham Keut Laos 30C2
Khammam India 44C2
Khamsa Egypt 45B3
Khamseh, Mts Iran 41E2
Khan, R Laos 30C2
Khanabad Afghan 42B1
Khānaqīn Iraq 41E3
Khandwa India 42D4
Khanewal Pak 42C2
Khan ez Zabib Jordan 45D3
Khanh Hung Viet 30D4
Khaniá Greece 17E3
Khanka, Oz, L USSR 26G2
Khanpur Pak 42C3
Khān Shaykhūn Syria 45D1
Khanty-Mansiysk USSR 24H3
Khan Yunis Israel 45C3
Khapalu India 42D1
Khapcheranga USSR 26E2
Kharabali USSR 21H6
Kharagpur India 43F4
Kharan Pak 42B3
Khārān, R Iran 41G4
Kharānaq Iran 41F3
Khārg, I Iran 41F4
Khârga Oasis Egypt 49F2
Khargon India 42D4
Kharîm, Gebel, Mt Egypt 45B3
Khar'kov USSR 21F6
Kharlovka USSR 20F2
Kharmanli Bulg 17F2
Kharovsk USSR 20G4
Khartoum Sudan 50D2
Khartoum North Sudan 50D2
Khasan USSR 28C2
Khashm el Girba Sudan 50D2
Khasi-Jaintia Hills India 43G3
Khaskovo Bulg 17F2
Khatanga USSR 25M2
Khatangskiy Zaliv, Estuary USSR 25N2
Khatyrka USSR 25T3
Khawsa Burma 30B3
Khaybar S Arabia 40C4
Khazzan an-Nasr, L Egypt 40B5
Khe Bo Viet 30C2
Khed Brahma India 42C4
Khemis Alg 15C2
Khenchela Algeria 16B3
Kheri, District India 43L1
Kherrata Alg 15D2
Kherson USSR 21E6
Khilok USSR 25N4
Khíos Greece 17F3
Khíos, I Greece 17F3
Khmel'nitskiy USSR 21D6
Khodorov USSR 19E3
Kholm Afghan 42B1
Kholm USSR 19G1
Khōmas Hochland, Mts Namibia 47B1
Khong Laos 30D3
Khonj Iran 41F4
Khor USSR 26G2
Khōr Duwayhin, B UAE 41F5
Khorog USSR 42C1
Khorramābad Iran 41E3
Khorramshahr Iran 41E3
Khosf Iran 41G3
Khost Pak 42B2
Khotin USSR 21D6
Khoyniki USSR 21E5
Khrebet Kopet Dag, Mts USSR/Iran 41G2
Khrebet Pay-khoy, Mts USSR 20L2
Khrysokhou B Cyprus 45B1
Khulga, R USSR 20L3
Khulna Bang 43F4
Khunjerāb P China/India 42D1
Khunsar Iran 41F3
Khurays S Arabia 41E4
Khurda India 43F4
Khurja India 42D3
Khushab Pak 42C2
Khushniyah Syria 45C2
Khush Shah, Wadi el Jordan 45D4
Khust USSR 19E3
Khuwei Sudan 50C2
Khuzdar Pak 42B3
Khvalynsk USSR 21H5
Khvor Iran 41G3
Khvormūj Iran 41F4
Khvoy Iran 21G8
Khwaja Muhammad Ra, Mts Afghan 42C1
Khyber P Afghan/Pak 42C2
Kiambi Zaïre 51C4
Kiamichi, R USA 63C2
Kibangou Congo 50B4
Kibaya Tanz 50D4
Kibombo Zaïre 50C4
Kibondo Tanz 50D4
Kibungu Rwanda 50D4
Kicevo Yugos 17E2
Kicking Horse P Can 54G4
Kidal Mali 48C3
Kidderminster Eng 7C3
Kidira Sen 48A3
Kidnappers,C NZ 35C1
Kiel W Germ 18C2
Kielce Pol 19E2
Kielder Res Eng 6C2
Kieler Bucht, B W Germ 18C2
Kiev USSR 21E5
Kifab USSR 38E2
Kiffa Maur 48A3

Kigali **Ko Way**

Kigali *Rwanda* **50D4**
Kigoma *Tanz* **50C4**
Kiholo *Hawaiian Is* **66E5**
Kii-sanchi, Mts *Japan* **29C4**
Kii-suid, Str *Japan* **29C4**
Kikhchik *USSR* **25R4**
Kikinda *Yugos* **17E1**
Kikládhes = Cyclades
Kikon *PNG* **32D1**
Kikonai *Japan* **29D2**
Kikori *PNG* **27H7**
Kikwit *Zaïre* **50B4**
Kilauea Crater, Vol *Hawaiian Is* **66E5**
Kilbrannan Sd *Scot* **8C4**
Kilbuck Mts *USA* **54C3**
Kilchu *N Korea* **28B2**
Kilcoy *Aust* **34D1**
Kildare *Irish Rep* **9C3**
Kildare, County *Irish Rep* **9C3**
Kilgore *USA* **63D2**
Kilifi *Kenya* **50E4**
Kilimanjaro, Mt *Tanz* **50D4**
Kilindoni *Tanz* **51D4**
Kilis *Turk* **40C2**
Kiliya *USSR* **19F3**
Kilkeel *N Ire* **9D2**
Kilkenny *Irish Rep* **9C3**
Kilkenny, County *Irish Rep* **9C3**
Kilkís *Greece* **17E2**
Killarney *Aust* **34D1**
Killarney *Irish Rep* **10B3**
Killeen *USA* **63C2**
Killin *Scot* **8C3**
Killíni, Mt *Greece* **17E3**
Killorglin *Irish Rep* **9B3**
Killyleagh *N Ire* **9D2**
Kilmarnock *Scot* **8C4**
Kil'mez *USSR* **20J4**
Kilmichael Pt *Irish Rep* **9C3**
Kilosa *Tanz* **51D4**
Kilrush *Irish Rep* **10B3**
Kilsyth *Scot* **8C4**
Kilwa *Zaïre* **51C4**
Kilwa Kisiwani *Tanz* **51D4**
Kilwa Kivinje *Tanz* **51D4**
Kimball *USA* **60C2**
Kimberley *Can* **54G5**
Kimberley *S Africa* **47C2**
Kimberley Plat *Aust* **32B2**
Kimch'aek *N Korea* **28B2**
Kimch'ŏn *S Korea* **28B3**
Kimhae *S Korea* **28A3**
Kími *Greece* **17E3**
Kimje *S Korea* **28A3**
Kimry *USSR* **20F4**
Kimwha *N Korea* **28A3**
Kinabalu, Mt *Malay* **27E6**
Kinbrace *Scot* **8D2**
Kincardine *Can* **64C2**
Kinder *USA* **63D2**
Kindia *Guinea* **48A3**
Kindu *Zaïre* **50C4**
Kinel' *USSR* **20J5**
Kineshma *USSR* **20G4**
Kingaroy *Aust* **34D1**
King City *USA* **59B3**
Kingcome Inlet *Can* **54F4**
Kingfisher *USA* **63C1**
King George I *Ant* **76H4**
King George Is *Can* **55L4**
King I *Aust* **32D5**
Kingissepp *USSR* **20C4**
King Leopold Range, Mts *Aust* **32B2**
Kingman *USA* **56B3**
Kingombe *Zaïre* **50C4**
Kingsburg *USA* **66C2**
Kings Canyon Nat Pk *USA* **59C3**
King Sd *Aust* **32B2**
Kingsford *USA* **64B1**
Kingsland *USA* **67B2**
King's Lynn *Eng* **7E3**
Kingsmill Group, Is *Kiribati* **33G1**
Kings Park *USA* **68D2**
Kings Peak, Mt *USA* **56B2**
Kingsport *USA* **67B1**
Kingston *Aust* **32C4**
Kingston *Can* **55L5**
Kingston *Jamaica* **70E3**
Kingston, New York *USA* **65E2**
Kingston *NZ* **35A3**
Kingston, Pennsylvania *USA* **68C2**
Kingstown *St Vincent* **69N2**
Kingsville *USA* **56D4**
Kington *Eng* **7C3**
Kingussie *Scot* **8C3**
King William I *Can* **54J3**
King William's Town *S Africa* **47D3**
Kinkala *Congo* **50B4**
Kinna *Sweden* **12G7**
Kinnairds Head, Pt *Scot* **8D3**
Kinomoto *Japan* **29C3**
Kinross *Scot* **8D3**
Kinshasa *Zaïre* **50B4**
Kinsley *USA* **62C1**
Kinston *USA* **67C1**
Kintap *Indon* **27E7**
Kintyre, Pen *Scot* **8C4**
Kinyeti, Mt *Sudan* **50D3**
Kiparissía *Greece* **17E3**
Kiparissiakós Kólpos, G *Greece* **17E3**
Kipawa,L *Can* **65D1**
Kipili *Tanz* **51D4**
Kippure, Mt *Irish Rep* **9C3**
Kipushi *Zaïre* **51C5**
Kirensk *USSR* **25M4**
Kirghiz SSR, Republic *USSR* **24J5**
Kirgizskiy Khrebet, Mts *USSR* **39F1**
Kiri *Zaïre* **50B4**
Kiribati, Is., Republic *Pacific O* **33G1**
Kırıkkale *Turk* **40B2**
Kirishi *USSR* **20E4**
Kirithar Range, Mts *Pak* **42B3**
Kirkağaç *Turk* **17F3**
Kirk Bulāg Dāgh, Mt *Iran* **21H8**
Kirkby *Eng* **6C2**
Kirkcaldy *Scot* **8D3**
Kirkcudbright *Scot* **8C4**
Kirkenes *Nor* **12K5**
Kirkham *Eng* **6C3**
Kirkland Lake *Can* **55K5**
Kırklareli *Turk* **40A1**
Kirkoswald *Eng* **6C2**
Kirkpatrick,Mt *Ant* **76E7**
Kirksville *USA* **57D2**
Kirkūk *Iraq* **41D2**
Kirkwall *Scot* **8D2**
Kirkwood *S Africa* **47D3**
Kirkwood *USA* **61E3**
Kirov *USSR* **20E5**
Kirov *USSR* **20H4**
Kirovabad *USSR* **21H7**
Kirovakan *USSR* **41D1**
Kirovgrad *USSR* **20K4**
Kirovograd *USSR* **21E6**
Kirovsk *USSR* **20E2**
Kirovskiy, Kamchatka *USSR* **25R4**
Kirriemuir *Scot* **8D3**
Kirs *USSR* **20J4**
Kirşehir *Turk* **40B2**
Kiruna *Sweden* **18C2**
Kiryū *Japan* **29C3**
Kisangani *Zaïre* **50C3**
Kisarazu *Japan* **29C3**
Kishanganj *India* **43F3**
Kishangarh *India* **42C3**
Kishinev *USSR* **21D6**
Kishiwada *Japan* **29C4**
Kisii *Kenya* **50D4**
Kisiju *Tanz* **51D4**
Kiskunfélegyháza *Hung* **17D1**
Kiskunhalas *Hung* **19D3**
Kislovodsk *USSR* **24F5**
Kismaayo *Somalia* **50E4**
Kiso-sammyaku, Mts *Japan* **29C3**
Kissidougou *Guinea* **48B4**
Kissimmee,L *USA* **67B3**
Kisumu *Kenya* **50D4**
Kisvárda *Hung* **19E3**
Kita *Mali* **48B3**
Kitab *USSR* **24H6**
Kitakami *Japan* **29D3**
Kitakami, R *Japan* **29D3**
Kitakata *Japan* **29D3**
Kita-Kyūshū *Japan* **28C4**
Kitale *Kenya* **50D3**
Kitalo, I *Japan* **26H4**
Kitami *Japan* **29E2**
Kitami-Esashi *Japan* **29D2**
Kit Carson *USA* **60C3**
Kitchener *Can* **55K5**
Kitgum *Uganda* **50D3**
Kíthira, I *Greece* **17E3**
Kíthnos, I *Greece* **17E3**
Kiti, C *Cyprus* **45B1**
Kitikmeot, Region *Can* **54G2**
Kitimat *Can* **54F4**
Kitinen, R *Fin* **12K5**
Kitsuki *Japan* **28B4**
Kittanning *USA* **65D2**
Kittery *USA* **65E2**
Kittilä *Fin* **12J5**
Kitty Hawk *USA* **67C1**
Kitunda *Tanz* **51D4**
Kitwe *Zambia* **51C5**
Kitzbühel *Austria* **18C3**
Kitzingen *W Germ* **18C3**
Kiumbi *Zaïre* **50C4**
Kivalina *USA* **54B3**
Kivercy *USSR* **19F2**
Kivu,L *Zaïre/Rwanda* **50C4**
Kiwalik *USA* **54B3**
Kiyev = Kiev
Kiyevskoye Vodokhranilishche, Res *USSR* **19G2**
Kizel *USSR* **20K4**
Kizema *USSR* **20G3**
Kizil, R *Turk* **40C2**
Kizyl'-Arvat *USSR* **38D2**
Kizyl-Atrek *USSR* **21J8**
Kladno *Czech* **18C2**
Klagenfurt *Austria* **18C3**
Klaipėda *USSR* **20C4**
Klamath, R *USA* **56A2**
Klamath Falls *USA* **56A2**
Klamath Mts *USA* **58B2**
Klatovy *Czech* **18C3**
Kleiat *Leb* **45C1**
Kleinsee *S Africa* **47B2**
Klerksdorp *S Africa* **47D2**
Kletnya *USSR* **19G2**
Kleve *W Germ* **13D2**
Klimovichi *USSR* **19G2**
Klin *USSR* **20F4**
Klintehamn *Sweden* **19D1**
Klintsy *USSR* **21E5**
Klipplaat *S Africa* **47C3**
Ključ *Yugos* **16D2**
Kłodzko *Pol* **18D2**
Klondike Plat *Can/USA* **54D3**
Klosterneuburg *Austria* **18D3**
Kluczbork *Pol* **19D2**
Knaresborough *Eng* **6D2**
Knighton *Wales* **7C3**
Knin *Yugos* **16D2**
Knob,C *Aust* **32A4**
Knockmealdown Mts *Irish Rep* **9B3**
Knokke-Heist *Belg* **13B2**
Knox Coast *Ant* **76G9**
Knoxville, Iowa *USA* **61E2**
Knoxville, Tennessee *USA* **57E3**
Knud Rasmussens Land, Region *Greenland* **55Q3**
Knutsford *Eng* **7C3**
Knysna *S Africa* **47C3**
Kobberminebugt, B *Greenland* **55O3**
Kōbe *Japan* **29D4**
København = Copenhagen
Koblenz *W Germ* **18B2**
Kobrin *USSR* **20C5**
Kobroör, I *Indon* **27G7**
Kobuk, R *USA* **54B3**
Kočani *Yugos* **17E2**
Kŏch'ang *S Korea* **28A3**
Ko Chang, I *Thai* **30C3**
Koch Bihār *India* **43F3**
Koch I *Can* **55L3**
Kōchi *Japan* **29C4**
Kodiak *USA* **54C4**
Kodiak I. *USA* **54C4**
Kodikkarai *India* **44B3**
Kodok *Sudan* **50D3**
Kodomari-misaki, C *Japan* **29D2**
Kodyma *USSR* **19F3**
Koehn L *USA* **66D3**
Koes *Namibia* **47B2**
Koffiefontein *S Africa* **47D2**
Koforidua *Ghana* **48B4**
Kofu *Japan* **29D3**
Koga *Japan* **29C3**
Køge *Den* **12G7**
Kohat *Pak* **42C2**
Koh-i-Baba, Mts *Afghan* **42B2**
Koh-i-Hisar, Mts *Afghan* **42B1**
Koh-i-Khurd, Mt *Afghan* **42B2**
Kohima *India* **43G3**
Koh-i-Mazar, Mt *Afghan* **42B2**
Kohlu *Pak* **42B3**
Kohtla Järve *USSR* **20D4**
Kohung *S Korea* **28A4**
Kohyon *S Korea* **28A4**
Koide *Japan* **29C3**
Koihoa, Nicobar Is **30A4**
Koin *N Korea* **28A2**
Kōje Do, I *S Korea* **28B4**
Ko-jima, I *Japan* **29C2**
Kokchetav *USSR* **24H4**
Kokemäki, L *Fin* **12J6**
Kokkola *Fin* **12J6**
Kokoda *PNG* **32D1**
Kokomo *USA* **64B2**
Kokonau *Indon* **27G7**
Kokpekty *USSR* **26B2**
Koksan *N Korea* **28A3**
Koksoak, R *Can* **55M4**
Koksŏng *S Korea* **28A3**
Kokstad *S Africa* **47D3**
Ko Kut, I *Thai* **30C3**
Kola *USSR* **20E2**
Kolaka *Indon* **27F7**
Ko Lanta, I *Thai* **30B4**
Kolār *India* **44B3**
Kolār Gold Fields *India* **44B3**
Kolda *Sen* **48A3**
Kolding *Den* **12F7**
Kolguyev, Ostrov, I *USSR* **20H2**
Kolhāpur *India* **44A2**
Kolín *Czech* **18D2**
Köln = Cologne
Koło *Pol* **19D2**
Koloa *Hawaiian Is* **66E5**
Kołobrzeg *Pol* **18D2**
Kolokani *Mali* **48B3**
Kolomna *USSR* **20F4**
Kolomyya *USSR* **21D6**
Kolpakovskiy *USSR* **25R4**
Kolpashevo *USSR* **24K4**
Kólpos Merabéllou, B *Greece* **17F3**
Kólpos Singitikós, G *Greece* **17E2**
Kólpos Strimonikós, G *Greece* **17E2**
Kólpos Toronaíos, G *Greece* **17E2**
Kol'skiy Poluostrov, Pen *USSR* **20F2**
Kolva, R *USSR* **20K2**
Kolvereid *Nor* **12G6**
Kolwezi *Zaïre* **51C5**
Kolyma, R *USSR* **25R3**
Kolymskaya Nizmennost', Lowland *USSR* **25R3**
Kolymskoye Nagor'ye, Mts *USSR* **25S3**
Kom, Mt *Bulg/Yugos* **17E2**
Koma *Eth* **50D3**
Koma *Japan* **29D3**
Komadugu Gana, R *Nigeria* **48D3**
Komaga take, Mt *Japan* **29D2**
Komandorskiye Ostrova, Is *USSR* **25S4**
Komárno *Czech* **19D3**
Komati, R *S Africa/ Swaziland* **47E2**
Komati Poort *S Africa* **47E2**
Komatsu *Japan* **29D3**
Komatsushima *Japan* **29B4**
Komi ASSR, Republic *USSR* **24G3**
Kommunar *USSR* **26B1**
Komodo, I *Indon* **27E7**
Komoran, I *Indon* **27G7**
Komoro *Japan* **29C3**
Komotiní *Greece* **17F2**
Kompasberg, Mt *S Africa* **47C3**
Kompong Cham *Camb* **30D3**
Kompong Chhnang *Camb* **30C3**
Kompong Som *Camb* **30C3**
Kompong Thom *Camb* **30D3**
Kompong Trabek *Camb* **30D3**
Komrat *USSR* **19F3**
Komsberg, Mts *S Africa* **47C3**
Komsomolets, Ostrov, I *USSR* **25L1**
Komsomol'skiy *USSR* **20L2**
Komsomol'sk na Amure *USSR* **25P4**
Konda, R *USSR* **24H4**
Kondagaon *India* **43E5**
Kondoa *Tanz* **50D4**
Kondopoga *USSR* **20E3**
Kondukür *India* **44B2**
Konevo *USSR* **20F3**
Kong Christian IX Land, Region *Greenland* **55P3**
Kong Frederik VI Kyst, Mts *Greenland* **55O3**
Kongju *S Korea* **28A3**
Kong Karls Land, Is *Svalbard* **24D2**
Kongolo *Zaïre* **50C4**
Kongsberg *Nor* **12F7**
Kongsvinger *Nor* **12G6**
Königsberg = Kaliningrad
Konin *Pol* **19D2**
Konjic *Yugos* **17D2**
Konosha *USSR* **20G3**
Konosu *Japan* **29C3**
Konotop *USSR* **21E5**
Końskie *Pol* **19E2**
Konstanz *W Germ* **18B3**
Kontagora *Nigeria* **48C3**
Kontum *Viet* **30D3**
Konya *Turk* **21E8**
Kootenay L *Can* **58C1**
Kopargaon *India* **42C5**
Kópasker *Iceland* **55R3**
Kópavogur *Iceland* **12A2**
Koper *Yugos* **16C1**
Kopet Dag, Mts *Iran/ USSR* **38D2**
Kopeysk *USSR* **20L4**
Ko Phangan, I *Thai* **30C4**
Ko Phuket, I *Thai* **30B4**
Köping *Sweden* **12H7**
Kopo-ri *S Korea* **28A3**
Koppal *India* **44B2**
Koprivnica *Yugos* **16D1**
Korangi *Pak* **42B4**
Koraput *India* **44C2**
Korba *India* **43E4**
Korbach *W Germ* **18B2**
Korçë *Alb* **17E2**
Korčula, I *Yugos* **16D2**
Korea B *China/Korea* **31E2**
Korea, North, Republic *Asia* **28B2**
Korea, South, Republic *Asia* **28B3**
Korea Strait *Japan/ Korea* **26F3**
Korec *USSR* **19F2**
Korf *USSR* **25S3**
Körğlu Tepesi, Mt *Turk* **40B1**
Korhogo *Ivory Coast* **48B4**
Kori Creek *India* **42B4**
Kórinthos = Corinth
Kōriyama *Japan* **29E3**
Korkino *USSR* **20L5**
Korkodon *USSR* **25R3**
Korkodon, R *USSR* **25R3**
Korkuteli *Turk* **40B2**
Korla *China* **39G1**
Kormakiti, C *Cyprus* **45B1**
Kornat, I *Yugos* **16D2**
Köroğlu Tepesi, Mt *Turk* **21E7**
Korogwe *Tanz* **50D4**
Koroit *Aust* **34B3**
Koror, Palau *Pacific O* **27G6**
Körös, R *Hung* **19E3**
Korosten *USSR* **21D5**
Korostyshev *USSR* **19F2**
Koro Toro *Chad* **50B2**
Korsakov *USSR* **26H2**
Korsør *Den* **12G7**
Kortkeros *USSR* **20J3**
Kortrijk *Belg* **18A2**
Koryakskoye Nagor'ye, Mts *USSR* **25S3**
Koryong *S Korea* **28A3**
Kós, I *Greece* **17F3**
Ko Samui, I *Thai* **30C4**
Kosan *N Korea* **28A3**
Kościerzyna *Pol* **19D2**
Kosciusko *USA* **63E2**
Kosciusko, Mt *Aust* **32D4**
Kosi *India* **43J2**
Kosi, R *India* **43K1**
Košice *Czech* **19E3**
Kosma, R *USSR* **20J2**
Kosŏng *N Korea* **28B3**
Kossou, L *Ivory Coast* **48B4**
Koster *S Africa* **47D2**
Kosti *Sudan* **50D2**
Kostopol' *USSR* **19F2**
Kostroma *USSR* **20G4**
Kostrzyn *Pol* **18C2**
Kos'yu, R *USSR* **20K2**
Koszalin *Pol* **12H8**
Kota *India* **42D3**
Kota Bharu *Malay* **30C4**
Kot Addu *Pak* **42C2**
Kota Kinabalu *Malay* **27E6**
Kotapad *India* **44C2**
Kotel'nich *USSR* **20H4**
Kotel'nikovo *USSR* **21G6**
Kotel'nyy, Ostrov, I *USSR* **25P2**
Kotka *Fin* **12K6**
Kotlas *USSR* **20H3**
Kotlik *USA* **54B3**
Kotor *Yugos* **17D2**
Kotovsk *USSR* **21D6**
Kotri *Pak* **42B3**
Kottagüdem *India* **44C2**
Kottayam *India* **44B4**
Kotto, R *CAR* **50C3**
Kottūru *India* **44B3**
Kotuy, R *USSR* **25L3**
Kotzebue *USA* **54B3**
Kotzebue Sd *USA* **54B3**
Kouandé *Benin* **48C3**
Kouango *CAR* **50C3**
Koudougou *Burkina* **48B3**
Kougaberge, Mts *S Africa* **47C3**
Koulamoutou *Gabon* **50B4**
Koulikoro *Mali* **48B3**
Koupéla *Burkina* **48B3**
Kourou *French Guiana* **73H2**
Kouroussa *Guinea* **48B3**
Kousséri *Cam* **50B2**
Kouvola *Fin* **12K6**
Kovdor *USSR* **20D2**
Kovel *USSR* **21C5**
Kovno = Kaunas
Kovrov *USSR* **20G4**
Kovylkino *USSR* **20G5**
Kovzha, R *USSR* **20F3**
Ko Way, I *Thai* **30C4**

Kowloon **La'nga Co**

Kowloon Hong Kong 31C5
Kowŏn N Korea 28A3
Kowt-e-Ashrow Afghan 42B2
Köycegğiz Turk 40A2
Koyda USSR 20G2
Koyna Res India 44A2
Koynas USSR 20H3
Koyukuk USA 54C3
Kozan Turk 40C2
Kozańi Greece 17E2
Kozhikode = Calicut
Kozhim USSR 20K2
Koz'modemyansk USSR 20H4
Kōzu-shima, I Japan 29C4
Kpalimé Togo 48C4
Kraai, R S Africa 47D3
Kragerø Nor 12F7
Kragujevac Yugos 17E2
Kra,Isthmus of Burma/ Malay 30B3
Krak des Chevaliers, Hist Site Syria 45D1
Kraków = Cracow
Kraljevo Yugos 17E2
Kramatorsk USSR 21F6
Kramfors Sweden 12H6
Kranj Yugos 16C1
Krasavino USSR 20H3
Krasino USSR 24G2
Kraskino USSR 28C2
Kraśnik Pol 19E2
Krasnoarmeysk USSR 21H5
Krasnodar USSR 21F7
Krasnokamsk USSR 20K4
Krasnotur'insk USSR 20L4
Krasnoufimsk USSR 20K4
Krasnousol'skiy USSR 20K5
Krasnovishersk USSR 20K3
Krasnovodsk USSR 21J7
Krasnoyarsk USSR 25L4
Krasnystaw Pol 19E2
Krasnyy Kut USSR 21H5
Krasnyy Luch USSR 21F6
Krasnyy Yar USSR 21H6
Kratie Camb 30D3
Kraulshavn Greenland 55N2
Krefeld W Germ 18B2
Kremenchug USSR 21E6
Kremenchugskoye Vodokhranilische, Res USSR 21E6
Kremenets USSR 19F2
Kremming USA 60B2
Kribi Cam 48C4
Krichev USSR 20E5
Krishna, R India 44B2
Krishnagiri India 44B3
Krishnanagar India 43F4
Kristiansand Nor 12F7
Kristianstad Sweden 12G7
Kristiansund Nor 24B3
Kristiinankaupunki Fin 12J6
Kristinehamn Sweden 12G7
Kríti = Crete
Krivoy Rog USSR 21E6
Krk, I Yugos 16C1
Krokodil, R S Africa 47D1
Kronotskaya Sopka, Mt USSR 25S4
Kronotskiy, Mys, C USSR 25S4
Kronprins Frederik Bjerge, Mts Greenland 55P3
Kronshtadt USSR 12K7
Kroonstad S Africa 47D2
Kropotkin USSR 21G6
Kruger Nat Pk S Africa 47E1
Krugersdorp S Africa 47D2
Kruje Alb 17D2
Krung Thep = Bangkok
Krupki USSR 19F2
Kruševac Yugos 17E2
Krustpils USSR 12K7
Krym = Crimea
Krym, Pen USSR 24E5
Krymsk USSR 21F7
Krzyz Pol 18D2
Ksar El Boukhari Alg 15C2
Ksar-el-Kebir Mor 15A2
Ksour, Mts des Alg 48C1
Kuala Indon 27C6
Kuala Dungun Malay 30C5
Kuala Kerai Malay 30C4
Kuala Kubu Baharu Malay 30C5
Kuala Lipis Malay 30C5
Kuala Lumpur Malay 30C5
Kuala Trengganu Malay 30C4
Kuandang Indon 27F6
Kuandian China 28A2
Kuantan Malay 30C5
Kuba USSR 21H7
Kubor, Mt PNG 27H7
Kuching Malay 27E6
Kudat Malay 27E6
Kudymkar USSR 20J4
Kufstein Austria 18C3
Kuh Duren, Upland Iran 41G3
Kūh-e Dinar, Mt Iran 41F3
Kūh-e-Hazār Masjed, Mts Iran 41G2
Kūh-e Jebāl Barez, Mts Iran 41G4
Kūh-e Karkas, Mts Iran 41F3
Kūh-e Laleh Zar, Mt Iran 41G4
Kūh-e Sahand, Mt Iran 41E2
Kuh-e-Taftān, Mt Iran 38E3
Kūhhaye Alvand, Mts Iran 21H9
Kūhhaye Sabalan, Mts Iran 21H8
Kūhhā-ye Zāgros, Mts Iran 41E3
Kuhmo Fin 12K6
Kūhpāyeh Iran 41F3
Kūhpāyeh, Mt Iran 41G3
Kūh-ye Bashākerd, Mts Iran 41G4
Kūh-ye Sabalan, Mt Iran 41E2
Kuibis Namibia 47B2
Kuiseb, R Namibia 47B1
Kujang N Korea 28A3
Kuji Japan 29E2
Kuju-san, Mt Japan 28B4
Kukës Alb 17E2
Kukup Malay 30C5
Kūl, R Iran 41G4
Kula Turk 17F3
Kulakshi USSR 21K6
Kulal,Mt Kenya 50D3
Kulata Bulg 17E2
Kuldīga USSR 20C4
Kulov, R USSR 20G2
Kul'sary USSR 21J6
Kulu India 42D2
Kulu Turk 40B2
Kulunda USSR 24J4
Kulwin Aust 34B2
Kuma, R USSR 21H7
Kumagaya Japan 29C3
Kumai Indon 27E7
Kumak USSR 21L5
Kumamoto Japan 28C4
Kumano Japan 29C4
Kumanovo Yugos 17E2
Kumasi Ghana 48B4
Kumba Cam 48C4
Kumbakonam India 44B3
Kūmch'ŏn N Korea 28A3
Kumertau USSR 20K5
Kumgang N Korea 28A3
Kumla Sweden 12H7
Kŭmnyŏng S Korea 28A4
Kŭmo-do, I S Korea 28A4
Kumta India 44A3
Kumüx China 39G1
Kumwha S Korea 28B3
Kunar, R Afghan 42C2
Kunashir, Ostrov, I USSR 29F2
Kunda USSR 12K7
Kundla India 42C4
Kunduz Afghan 42B1
Kunene, R = Cunene R
Kungsbacka Sweden 12G7
Kungur USSR 20K4
Kunhing Burma 30B1
Kunlun Shan, Mts China 39G2
Kunming China 31A4
Kunovat, R USSR 20M3
Kunsan S Korea 28B3
Kuopio Fin 12K6
Kupa, R Yugos 16D1
Kupang Indon 32B2
Kupiano PNG 32D2
Kupreanof I USA 54E4
Kupyansk USSR 21F6
Kuqa China 39G1
Kura, R USSR 21H8
Kurabe Japan 29C3
Kurashiki Japan 29C4
Kurayoshi Japan 29B3
Kurdistan, Region Iran 41E2
Kŭrdzhali Bulg 17F2
Kure Japan 28C4
Kureyka, R USSR 25L3
Kurgan USSR 24H4
Kurikka Fin 12J6
Kuril Is USSR 25Q5
Kuril'skiye Ostrova, Is = Kuril Is
Kuril Trench Pacific O 36J2
Kurinskaya Kosa, Sand Spit USSR 21H8
Kurnool India 44B2
Kuroishi Japan 29D2
Kuroiso Japan 29D3
Kurow NZ 35B2
Kurri Kurri Aust 34D2
Kursk USSR 21F5
Kurskiy Zaliv, Lg USSR 19E1
Kuruktag, R China 26B2
Kuruman S Africa 47C2
Kuruman, R S Africa 47C2
Kurume Japan 28C4
Kurunegala Sri Lanka 44C3
Kurunktag, R China 24K5
Kur'ya USSR 20K3
Kusa USSR 20K4
Kuşadasi Körfezi, B Turk 17F3
Kus Golü, L Turk 17F2
Kushimoto Japan 29D4
Kushiro Japan 29E2
Kushka USSR 38E2
Kushtia Bang 43F4
Kushum, R USSR 21J5
Kushva USSR 24H4
Kuskokwim, R USA 54B3
Kuskokwim Mts USA 54C3
Kusma Nepal 43E3
Kusŏng N Korea 28B3
Kustanay USSR 24H4
Kuta, R Indon 27E7
Kütahya Turk 21D8
Kutaisi USSR 21G7
Kutchan Japan 29D2
Kutcharo-ko, L Japan 29E2
Kutná Hora Czech 18D3
Kutno Pol 19D2
Kutu Zaïre 50B4
Kutubdia I Bang 43G4
Kutum Sudan 50C2
Kuujjuaq Can 55M4
Kuusamo Fin 12K5
Kuvandyk USSR 21K5
Kuvbyshev USSR 29L3
Kuwait Kuwait 41E4
Kuwait, Sheikhdom S W Asia 38C3
Kuwana Japan 29C3
Kuybyshev USSR 24G4
Kuybyshev USSR 24J4
Kuybyshevskoye Vodokhranilishche, Res USSR 20H5
Kuyto, Ozero, L USSR 20E2
Kuytun USSR 25M4
Kuzey Anadolu Dağları, Mts Turk 21F7
Kuzomen USSR 20F2
Kvænangen, Sd Nor 20C2
Kvigtind, Mt Nor 12G5
Kvikkjokk Sweden 20B2
Kwale Kenya 50D4
Kwangju S Korea 28B3
Kwango, R Zaïre 50B4
Kwangyang S Korea 28A3
Kwanmo-bong, Mt N Korea 28A2
Kwekwe Zim 51C5
Kwidzyn Pol 19D2
Kwigillingok USA 54B4
Kwoka, Mt Indon 27G7
Kyabram Aust 34C3
Kyaikkami Burma 30B2
Kyaikto Burma 30B2
Kyakhta USSR 26D1
Kyaukme Burma 30B1
Kyauk-padaung Burma 30B1
Kyaukpyu Burma 30A2
Kychema USSR 20G2
Kyle of Lochalsh Scot 10B2
Kyll, R W Germ 13D2
Kyneton Aust 34B3
Kyoga, L Uganda 50D3
Kyogle Aust 34D1
Kyŏngju S Korea 28B3
Kyongsang Sanmaek, Mts S Korea 28A3
Kyŏngsŏng N Korea 28A2
Kyōto Japan 29D3
Kyrenia Cyprus 45B1
Kyrta USSR 20K3
Kyshtym USSR 24H4
Kythrea Cyprus 45B1
Kyūshū, I Japan 28B4
Kyushu-Palau Ridge Pacific O 36H4
Kyustendil Bulg 17E2
Kyusyur USSR 25O2
Kyzyl USSR 26C1
Kyzylkum, Desert USSR 24H5
Kzyl Orda USSR 24H5

L

Laas Caanood Somalia 50E3
Laasphe W Germ 13E2
Laas Qoray Somalia 50E2
La Asunción Ven 72F1
La Barge USA 58D2
Labé Guinea 48A3
Labe, R Czech 18D2
Labelle Can 65E1
La Belle USA 67B3
Labinsk USSR 21G7
Laboué Leb 45D1
Labrador, Region Can 55M4
Labrador City Can 55M4
Labrador S Can/ Greenland 55N4
Lábrea Brazil 72F5
Labuk B Malay 27E6
Labutta Burma 30A2
Labytnangi USSR 20M2
La Capelle France 13B2
Laccadive Is = Lakshadweep
Laccadive Is India 39F4
La Ceiba Honduras 70D3
Lacepede B Aust 34A3
La Châtre France 14C2
Lachish, Hist Site Israel 45C3
Lachlan, R Aust 32D4
La Chorrera Panama 72C2
Lachute Can 65E1
Lackawanna USA 65D2
Lac la Biche Can 54G4
Lac L'eau Claire Can 55L4
Lac Mégantic Can 65E1
Lacombe Can 54G4
Laconia USA 65E2
La Coruña Spain 15A1
La Crosse USA 57D2
La Cruces USA 56C3
La Cygne USA 63D1
Ladākh Range, Mts India 42D2
Ladd Reef S China Sea 27E6
Ladnun India 42C3
Ladoga, L USSR 20E3
Ladong China 31B5
Ladozhskoye Oz, L = Ladoga, L
Lady Ann Str Can 55K2
Lady Barron Aust 34C4
Ladybrand S Africa 47D2
Ladysmith S Africa 47D2
Ladysmith USA 64A1
Lae PNG 32D1
Laem Ngop Thai 30C3
Laesø, I Den 18C1
Lafayette, Colorado USA 60B3
Lafayette, Indiana USA 57E2
Lafayette, Louisiana USA 57D3
La Fère France 13B3
La-Ferté-sous-Jouarre France 13B3
Lafia Nigeria 48C4
Lafiagi Nigeria 48C4
La Flèche France 14B2
La Galite, I Tunisia 16B3
Lagan, R Sweden 18C1
Lagarto Brazil 73L6
Laggan, L Scot 8C3
Laghouat Alg 48C1
Lago Agrio Ecuador 72C4
Lagos Nigeria 48C4
Lagos Port 15A2
Lagos de Moreno Mexico 70B2
La Grande USA 56B2
La Grande Rivière, R Can 55L4
Lagrange Aust 32B2
La Grange, Georgia USA 57E3
La Grange, Kentucky USA 64B3
La Grange, N Carolina USA 67C1
La Grange, Texas USA 63C3
La Gran Sabana, Mts Ven 72F2
Laguna USA 62A2
Laguna Beach USA 59C4
Laguna Seca Mexico 56C4
Lagusha N Korea 28B2
Lahad Datu Malay 27E6
Lāhijān Iran 41F2
Lahn, R W Germ 13D2
Lahnstein W Germ 13D2
Lahore Pak 42C2
Lahr W Germ 13D3
Lahti Fin 12K6
Lai Chad 50B3
Laibin China 31B5
Lai Chau Viet 30C1
Laignes France 13C4
Laihia Fin 12J6
Laingsburg S Africa 47C3
Lairg Scot 8C2
Laiyang China 31E2
Laizhou Wan, B China 31D2
Laja, Lago de la Chile 74B5
Lajes Brazil 74F3
La Jolla USA 66D4
La Junta USA 56C3
Lake Andes USA 60D2
Lake Cargelligo Aust 34C2
Lake Charles USA 57D3
Lake City, Florida USA 67B2
Lake City, Minnesota USA 61E2
Lake City, S Carolina USA 67C2
Lake District, Region Eng 6C2
Lake Elsinore USA 66D4
Lake Eyre Basin Aust 32C3
Lakefield Can 65D2
Lake Geneva USA 64B2
Lake George USA 68D1
Lake Harbour Can 55M3
Lake Havasu City USA 59D4
Lake Hughes USA 66C3
Lakehurst USA 68C2
Lake Isabella USA 66C3
Lake Jackson USA 63C3
Lakeland USA 67B3
Lake of the Woods Can 55J5
Lake Oswego USA 58B1
Lakeport USA 59B3
Lake Providence USA 63D2
Lake Pukaki NZ 35B2
Lakes Entrance Aust 34C3
Lakeshore USA 66C2
Lake Stewart Aust 34B1
Lake Traverse Can 65D1
Lakeview USA 56A2
Lakeview Mt Can 58B1
Lake Village USA 63D2
Lake Wales USA 67B3
Lakewood, California USA 66C4
Lakewood, Colorado USA 60B3
Lakewood, New Jersey USA 68C2
Lakewood, Ohio USA 64C2
Lake Worth USA 67B3
Lakhimpur India 43E3
Lakhpat India 42B4
Lakin USA 62B1
Lakki Pak 42C2
Lakonikós Kólpos, G Greece 17E3
Lakota Ivory Coast 48B4
Laksefjord, Inlet Nor 12K4
Lakselv Nor 12K4
Lakshadweep, Is, Union Territory India 44A3
La Libertad Ecuador 72B4
La Linea Spain 15A2
Lalitpur India 42D4
La Loche Can 54H4
La Louvière Belg 13C2
La Luz Nic 69A4
La Malbaie Can 55L5
Lamar, Colorado USA 56C3
Lamar, Missouri USA 63D1
La Marque USA 63C3
Lambaréné Gabon 50B4
Lambayeque Peru 72B5
Lambert Glacier Ant 76F10
Lamberts Bay S Africa 47B3
Lambertville USA 68C2
Lambton,C Can 54F2
Lam Chi, R Thai 30C2
Lamego Port 15A1
La Merced Peru 72C6
Lamesa USA 62B2
La Mesa USA 59C4
Lamía Greece 17E3
Lammermuir Hills Scot 8D4
Lammhult Sweden 12G7
Lamoni USA 61E2
Lamont, California USA 66C3
Lamont, Wyoming USA 60B2
Lamotrek, I Pacific O 27H6
Lamotte-Beuvron France 13B4
La Moure USA 60D1
Lampasas USA 62C2
Lampeter Wales 7B3
Lamu Kenya 50E4
Lanai, I Hawaiian Is 66E5
Lanai City Hawaiian Is 66E5
Lanao, L Phil 27F6
Lanark Scot 8D4
Lanbi, I Burma 30B3
Lancang, R China 30C1
Lancashire, County Eng 6C3
Lancaster, California USA 59C4
Lancaster Eng 6C2
Lancaster, Missouri USA 61E2
Lancaster, New Hampshire USA 65E2
Lancaster, New York USA 68A1
Lancaster, Ohio USA 64C3
Lancaster, Pennsylvania USA 57F3
Lancaster, S Carolina USA 67B2
Lancaster Sd Can 55K2
Landan W Germ 13E3
Landeck Austria 18C3
Lander USA 56C2
Landes, Les, Region France 14B3
Landrum USA 67B1
Landsberg W Germ 18C3
Lands End, C Can 54F2
Land's End, Pt Eng 7B4
Landshut W Germ 18C3
Låndskrona Sweden 12G7
Lanett USA 67A2
La'nga Co, L China 43E2

Linhares

Lushoto

Linhares *Brazil* 73L7
Linhe *China* 31B1
Linjiang *China* 28B2
Linjiatai *China* 28A2
Linköping *Sweden* 12H7
Linnhe, Loch, Inlet *Scot* 8C3
Linqing *China* 31D2
Lins *Brazil* 75C3
Lintao *China* 31A2
Linton *USA* 60C1
Linxi *China* 26E2
Linxia *China* 31A2
Linz *Austria* 18C3
Lion, Golfe du, G *France* 14C3
Lipari, I *Italy* 16C3
Lipari, Isole, Is *Italy* 16C3
Lipetsk *USSR* 21F5
Lipova *Rom* 17E1
Lippe, R *W Germ* 18B2
Lippstadt *W Germ* 13E2
Lira *Uganda* 50D3
Liranga *Congo* 50B4
Lisala *Zaïre* 50C3
Lisboa = Lisbon
Lisbon *Port* 15A2
Lisbon *USA* 61D1
Lisburn *N Ire* 9C2
Lishui *China* 31D4
Li Shui, R *China* 31C4
Lisichansk *USSR* 21F6
Lisieux *France* 14C2
L'Isle-Adam *France* 13B3
Lismore *Aust* 33E3
Lismore *Irish Rep* 9C3
Litang *China* 31B5
Litāni, R *Leb* 45C2
Litani, R *Surinam* 73H3
Litchfield, Illinois *USA* 64B3
Litchfield, Minnesota *USA* 61E1
Lithgow *Aust* 32E4
Lithuanian SSR, Republic *USSR* 20C4
Lititz *USA* 68B2
Litovko *USSR* 26G2
Little, R *USA* 63C2
Little Abaco, I *The Bahamas* 57F4
Little Andaman, I *Andaman Is* 44E3
Little Bahama Bank *Bahamas* 67C3
Little Barrier I *NZ* 35C1
Little Belt Mts *USA* 58D1
Little Bitter L *Egypt* 45B3
Little Cayman, I, Cayman Is *Caribbean S* 70D3
Little Egg Harbor, B *USA* 68C3
Little Falls, Minnesota *USA* 61E1
Little Falls, New York *USA* 68C1
Littlefield *USA* 62B2
Littlefork *USA* 61E1
Little Fork, R *USA* 61E1
Little Halibut Bank, Sandbank *Scot* 8E2
Littlehampton *Eng* 7D4
Little Inagua, I *The Bahamas* 69C2
Little Karoo, Mts *S Africa* 47C3
Little Lake *USA* 66D3
Little Missouri, R *USA* 60C1
Little Nicobar, I, Nicobar Is 30A4
Little Rock *USA* 57D3
Littlerock *USA* 66D3
Littlestown *USA* 68B3
Littleton, Colorado *USA* 60B3
Littleton, New Hampshire *USA* 65E2
Liuhe *China* 28B2
Liupan Shan, Upland *China* 31B2
Liuzhou *China* 31B5
Livanátais *Greece* 17E3
Līvāni *USSR* 19F1
Live Oak *USA* 67B2
Livermore *USA* 59B3
Livermore,Mt *USA* 62B2
Liverpool *Can* 55M5
Liverpool *Eng* 7C3
Liverpool B *Can* 54E2
Liverpool B *Eng* 7C3
Liverpool,C *Can* 55L2
Liverpool Range, Mts *Aust* 34D2
Livingston, Montana *USA* 56B2
Livingston, Tennessee *USA* 67A1
Livingston, Texas *USA* 63D2
Livingstone *Scot* 8D4
Livingstone *Zambia* 51C5
Livingston,L *USA* 63C2
Livno *Yugos* 16D2
Livny *USSR* 21F5
Livonia *USA* 64C2
Livorno *Italy* 16C2
Livramento do Brumado *Brazil* 75D1
Liwale *Tanz* 51D4
Lizard Pt *Eng* 7B5
Ljubljana *Yugos* 16C1
Ljungan, R *Sweden* 12G6
Ljungby *Sweden* 12G7
Ljusdal *Sweden* 12H6
Ljusnan, R *Sweden* 20B3
Llandeilo *Wales* 7C4
Llandovery *Wales* 7C4
Llandrindod Wells *Wales* 7C3
Llandudno *Wales* 7C3
Llanelli *Wales* 7D4
Llangollen *Wales* 7C3
Llano *USA* 62C2
Llano, R *USA* 62C2
Llano Estacado, Plat *USA* 56C3
Llanos, Region *Colombia/Ven* 72D2
Llanos de Chiquitos, Region *Bol* 72F7
Llantrisant *Wales* 7C4
Llanwrst *Wales* 7C3
Llerena *Spain* 15A2
Lleyn, Pen *Wales* 7B3
Llimsk *USSR* 25M4
Llin, R *USSR* 25M4
Lloyd George,Mt *Can* 54F4
Lloydminster *Can* 54H4
Llullaillaco, Mt *Arg/Chile* 74C2
Loa, R *Chile* 74C2
Loange, R *Zaïre* 50B4
Lobatse *Botswana* 47D2
Lobaye, R *CAR* 50B3
Lobito *Angola* 51B5
Lochboisdale *Scot* 8B3
Lochearnhead *Scot* 8C3
Loches *France* 14C2
Lochgoilhead *Scot* 8C3
Lochinver *Scot* 8C2
Lochmaben *Scot* 8D4
Lochmaddy *Scot* 8B3
Lochnagar, Mt *Scot* 8D3
Loch Ness *Scot* 8C3
Lochsa, R *USA* 58C1
Lochy, Loch, L *Scot* 8C3
Lockerbie *Scot* 8D4
Lock Haven *USA* 65D2
Lockport *USA* 65D2
Loc Ninh *Viet* 30D3
Locri *Italy* 16D3
Lod *Israel* 45C3
Loddon, R *Aust* 34B3
Lodeynoye Pole *USSR* 20E3
Lodge Grass *USA* 58E1
Lodhran *Pak* 42C3
Lodi *Italy* 16B1
Lodi *USA* 59B3
Lodja *Zaïre* 50C4
Lodwar *Kenya* 50D3
Łódź *Pol* 19D2
Loeriesfontein *S Africa* 47B3
Lofoten, Is *Nor* 12G5
Loftus *Eng* 6D2
Logan, New Mexico *USA* 62B1
Logan, Utah *USA* 56B2
Logan,Mt *Can* 54D3
Logansport, Indiana *USA* 64B2
Logansport, Louisiana *USA* 15D3
Loganton *USA* 68B2
Logone, R *Chad/Cam* 50B2
Logroño *Spain* 14B3
Lohardaga *India* 43E4
Lohja *Fin* 12J6
Loikaw *Burma* 30B2
Loimaa *Fin* 12J6
Loing, R *France* 13B3
Loir, R *France* 14C2
Loire, R *France* 14C2
Loiret, Department *France* 13B4
Loja *Ecuador* 72C4
Loja *Spain* 15B2
Lokan Tekojärvi, Res *Fin* 12K5
Lokeren *Belg* 13B2
Lokialaki, G, Mt *Indon* 27F7
Lokitaung *Kenya* 50D3
Loknya *USSR* 19F1
Lokolo, R *Zaïre* 50C4
Lokoro, R *Zaïre* 50C4
Loks Land, I *Can* 55M3
Lolland, I *Den* 18C2
Lolo P *USA* 58D1
Lom *Bulg* 17E2
Lomami, R *Zaïre* 51C4
Loma Mts *Guinea/Sierra Leone* 48A4
Lomblen, I *Indon* 27F7
Lombok, I *Indon* 27E7
Lomé *Togo* 48C4
Lomela *Zaïre* 50C4
Lomela, R *Zaïre* 50C4
Lomond, Loch, L *Scot* 8C3
Lomonosov *USSR* 20D4
Lompoc *USA* 59B4
Łomża *Pol* 19E2
Lonāvale *India* 44A2
Loncoche *Chile* 74B5
London *Can* 55K5
London *Eng* 7D4
London *USA* 64C3
Londonderry *N Ire* 9C2
Londonderry, County *N Ire* 9C2
Londonderry, I *Chile* 74B9
Londonderry,C *Aust* 32B2
Londres *Arg* 74C3
Londrina *Brazil* 73H8
Londrina *Brazil* 74F2
Lone Mt *USA* 66D1
Lone Pine *USA* 66C2
Long, I *PNG* 27H7
Long, I *The Bahamas* 57F4
Longa, Proliv, Str *USSR* 25T2
Long B *Jamaica* 69H2
Long B *USA* 67C2
Long Beach, California *USA* 56B3
Long Beach, New York *USA* 65E2
Long Branch *USA* 65E2
Longchuan *China* 31D5
Long Creek *USA* 58C2
Long Eaton *Eng* 7D3
Longford *Aust* 34C4
Longford *Irish Rep* 9C3
Longford, County *Irish Rep* 9C3
Long Forties, Region *N Sea* 8E3
Longgang Shan, Mts *China* 28B2
Longhua *China* 31D1
Long I *Bahamas* 57F4
Long I *Can* 55L4
Long I *PNG* 32D1
Long I *USA* 57F2
Long Island Sd *USA* 68D2
Longjing *China* 28B2
Long L *Can* 64B1
Long L *USA* 60C1
Longlac *Can* 55K4
Longlin *China* 31B5
Long, Loch, Inlet *Scot* 8C3
Long Melford *Eng* 7E3
Longmont *USA* 56C2
Longny *France* 13C3
Long Prairie *USA* 61E1
Longreach *Aust* 32D3
Longshou Shan, Upland *China* 31A2
Longs Peak, Mt *USA* 60B2
Long Sutton *Eng* 7E3
Longtown *Eng* 6C2
Longueuil *Can* 65E1
Longuyon *France* 13C3
Longview, Texas *USA* 57D3
Longview, Washington *USA* 56A2
Longwy *France* 14D2
Longxi *China* 31A3
Long Xuyen *Viet* 30D3
Longyan *China* 31D4
Longzhou *China* 31B5
Löningen *W Germ* 13D1
Lonquimay *Chile* 74B5
Lons-le-Saunier *France* 14D2
Looe *Eng* 7B4
Lookout,C *USA* 57F3
Loolmalasin, Mt *Tanz* 50D4
Lopatka, Mys, C *USSR* 25R4
Lop Buri *Thai* 30C3
Lop Nur, L *China* 26C2
Lora del Rio *Spain* 15A2
Lorain *USA* 57E2
Loralai *Pak* 42B2
Lorca *Spain* 15B2
Lordegān *Iran* 41F3
Lord Howe, I *Aust* 33E4
Lord Howe Rise *Pacific O* 37K6
Lord Mayor B *Can* 55J3
Lordsburg *USA* 56C3
Lorena *Brazil* 75C3
Lorient *France* 14B2
Lorne *Aust* 34B3
Lörrach *W Germ* 18B3
Lorraine, Region *France* 13C3
Los Alamos *USA* 56C3
Los Angeles *Chile* 74B5
Los Angeles *USA* 56B3
Los Angeles Aqueduct *USA* 66C3
Los Banos *USA* 59B3
Los Gatos *USA* 59B3
Lošinj, I *Yugos* 16C2
Los Lagos *Chile* 74B5
Los Lunas *USA* 62A2
Los Mochis *Mexico* 70B2
Los Olivos *USA* 66B3
Los Roques, Islas *Ven* 72E1
Lossie, R *Scot* 8D3
Lossiemouth *Scot* 8D3
Los Testigos, Is *Ven* 69E4
Lost Hills *USA* 66C3
Lost Trail P *USA* 58D1
Los Vilos *Chile* 74B4
Lot, R *France* 14C3
Lothian, Region *Scot* 8D4
Lotikipi Plain *Sudan/Kenya* 50D3
Loto *Zaïre* 50C4
Lotsane, R *Botswana* 47D1
Lotta, R *Fin USSR* 12K5
Loudéac *France* 14B2
Louga *Sen* 48A3
Loughborough *Eng* 7D3
Lougheed I *Can* 54H2
Louisa *USA* 64C3
Louisa Reef *S China Sea* 27E6
Louisiade Arch *PNG* 33E2
Louisiana, State *USA* 57D3
Louis Trichardt *S Africa* 47D1
Louisville, Georgia *USA* 67B2
Louisville, Kentucky *USA* 57E3
Louisville, Mississippi *USA* 63E2
Loukhi *USSR* 20E2
Loup, R *USA* 61D2
Lourdes *France* 14B3
Lourenço Marques = Maputo
Louth *Aust* 34C2
Louth *Eng* 7D3
Louth, County *Irish Rep* 9C3
Louvain = Leuven
Louviers *France* 14C2
Lovat, R *USSR* 20E4
Lovech *Bulg* 17E2
Loveland *USA* 60B2
Loveland P *USA* 60B3
Lovell *USA* 58E2
Lovelock *USA* 59C2
Lóvere *Italy* 16C1
Lovington *USA* 62B2
Lovozero *USSR* 20F2
Low,C *Can* 55K3
Lowell, Massachusetts *USA* 57F2
Lowell, Oregon *USA* 58B2
Lowell *USA* 68E1
Lower Arrow L *Can* 58C1
Lower Hutt *NZ* 35B2
Lower Lake *USA* 66A1
Lower Red L *USA* 61D1
Lower Seal,L *Can* 55L4
Lowestoft *Eng* 7E3
Łowicz *Pol* 19D2
Loxton *Aust* 34B2
Loxton *S Africa* 47C3
Loyalsock Creek, R *USA* 68B2
Loyalty Is, *New Caledonia* 33F3
Loznica *Yugos* 17D2
Lozva, R *USSR* 24H3
Luacano *Angola* 51C5
Luachimo *Angola* 51C4
Lualaba, R *Zaïre* 50C4
Luampa *Zambia* 51C5
Luân *Angola* 51C5
Lu'an *China* 31D3
Luanda *Angola* 51B4
Luando, R *Angola* 51B5
Luanginga, R *Angola* 51C5
Luang Namtha *Laos* 30C1
Luang Prabang *Laos* 30C2
Luangue, R *Angola* 51B4
Luangwa, R *Zambia* 51D5
Luan He, R *China* 31D1
Luanping *China* 31D1
Luanshya *Zambia* 51C5
Luapula, R *Zaïre* 51C5
Luarca *Spain* 15A1
Lubalo *Angola* 51B4
L'uban *USSR* 19F2
Lubango *Angola* 51B5
Lubbock *USA* 56C3
Lübeck *W Germ* 18C2
Lubefu *Zaïre* 50C4
Lubefu, R *Zaïre* 50C4
Lubero *Zaïre* 50C3
Lubilash, R *Zaïre* 51C4
Lublin *Pol* 19E2
Lubny *USSR* 21E5
Lubudi *Zaïre* 51C4
Lubudi, R *Zaïre* 51C4
Lubuklinggau *Indon* 27D7
Lubumbashi *Zaïre* 51C5
Lubutu *Zaïre* 50C4
Lucas *Brazil* 75A1
Lucaya *Bahamas* 67C3
Lucca *Italy* 16C2
Luce B *Scot* 8C4
Lucedale *USA* 63E2
Lucenec *Czech* 19D3
Lucerne = Luzern
Lucero *Mexico* 62A2
Luchuan *China* 31C5
Lucia *USA* 66B2
Luckenwalde *E Germ* 18C2
Luckhoff *S Africa* 47C2
Lucknow *India* 43E3
Lucusse *Angola* 51C5
Lüda *China* 31E2
Lüdenscheid *W Germ* 13D2
Lüderitz *Namibia* 47B2
Ludhiana *India* 42D2
Ludington *USA* 64B2
Ludlow, California *USA* 59C4
Ludlow *Eng* 7C3
Ludlow, Vermont *USA* 68D1
Ludogorie, Upland *Bulg* 17F2
Ludowici *USA* 67B2
Luduş *Rom* 17E1
Ludvika *Sweden* 12H6
Ludwigsburg *W Germ* 18B3
Ludwigshafen *W Germ* 18B3
Ludwigslust *E Germ* 18C2
Luebo *Zaïre* 50C4
Luema, R *Zaïre* 50C4
Luembe, R *Angola* 51C4
Luena *Angola* 51B5
Luene, R *Angola* 51C5
Lüeyang *China* 31B3
Lufeng *China* 31D5
Lufkin *USA* 57D3
Luga *USSR* 20D4
Luga, R *USSR* 20D4
Lugano *Switz* 16B1
Lugela *Mozam* 51D5
Lugenda, R *Mozam* 51D5
Lugnaquillia, Mt *Irish Rep* 9C3
Lugo *Spain* 15A1
Lugoj *Rom* 17E1
Luhfi, Wadi *Jordan* 45D2
Luhuo *China* 31A3
Lui, R *Angola* 51B4
Luiana *Angola* 51C5
Luiana, R *Angola* 51C5
Luichow Peninsula = Leizhou Bandao
Luiro, R *Fin* 20D2
Luishia *Zaïre* 51C5
Luixi *China* 26C4
Luiza *Zaïre* 51C4
Lujiang *China* 31D3
Lukenie, R *Zaïre* 50B4
Lukeville *USA* 59D4
Luki *USSR* 24E4
Lukolela *Zaïre* 50B4
Łuków *Pol* 19E2
Lukuga, R *Zaïre* 50C4
Lukulu *Zambia* 51C5
Lule, R *Sweden* 20C2
Luleå *Sweden* 12J5
Lüleburgaz *Turk* 17F2
Lüliang Shan, Mts *China* 31C2
Luling *USA* 63C3
Lulonga, R *Zaïre* 50C3
Luluabourg = Kananga
Lumbala *Angola* 51C5
Lumberton *USA* 57F3
Lumbovka *USSR* 20G2
Lumding *India* 43G3
Lumeje *Angola* 51C5
Lumsden *NZ* 35A3
Lund *Sweden* 12G7
Lundazi *Zambia* 51D5
Lundi, R *Zim* 51D6
Lundy, I *Eng* 7B4
Lüneburg *W Germ* 18C2
Lunéville *France* 13D3
Lunga, R *Zambia* 51C5
Lunglei *India* 43G4
Lungue Bungo, R *Angola* 51B5
Luninec *USSR* 19F2
Luning *USA* 66C1
Luobomo *Congo* 50B4
Luocheng *China* 31B5
Luoding *China* 31C5
Luohe *China* 31C3
Luo He, R, Henan *China* 31C3
Luo He, R, Shaanxi *China* 31B2
Luoxiao Shan, Hills *China* 31C4
Luoyang *China* 31C3
Luozi *Zaïre* 50B4
Lupane *Zim* 51C5
Lupilichi *Mozam* 51D5
Lu Qu, R = Tao He
Luque *Par* 74E3
Lure *France* 13D4
Lurgan *N Ire* 9C2
Lurio, R *Mozam* 51D5
Luristan, Region *Iran* 41E3
Lusaka *Zambia* 51C5
Lusambo *Zaïre* 50C4
Lushnjë *Alb* 17D2
Lushoto *Tanz* 50D4

Lushui
Mandsaur

Lushui China 26C4
Lüshun China 31E2
Lusk USA 60C2
Luton Eng 7D4
Lutsk USSR 21D5
Luuq Somalia 50E3
Luverne USA 61D2
Luvua, R Zaïre 51C4
Luwegu, R Tanz 51D4
Luwingu Zambia 51D5
Luwuk Indon 27F7
Luxembourg Lux 14D2
Luxembourg, Grand Duchy N W Europe 13D3
Luxeuil-les-Bains France 13D4
Luxi China 31A5
Luxor Egypt 49F2
Luza USSR 20H3
Luza, R USSR 20H3
Luzern Switz 16B1
Luzerne USA 68D1
Luzhai China 31B5
Luzhi China 31B4
Luzhou China 31B4
Luziânia Brazil 75C2
Luzon, I Phil 27F5
Luzon Str Phil 27F5
L'vov USSR 19E3
Lybster Scot 8D2
Lycksele Sweden 12H6
Lydd Eng 7E4
Lydenburg S Africa 51C6
Lyell,Mt USA 56B3
Lykens USA 68B2
Lyman USA 58D2
Lyme B Eng 7C4
Lyme Regis Eng 7C4
Lymington Eng 7D4
Lynchburg USA 57F3
Lyndhurst Aust 34A2
Lynn USA 65E2
Lynn Haven USA 67A2
Lynn Lake Can 54H4
Lynton Eng 7C4
Lynx L Can 54H3
Lyon France 14C2
Lyons, Georgia USA 67B2
Lyons, New York USA 68B1
Lyons, R Aust 32A3
Lys'va USSR 20K4
Lytham St Anne's Eng 6C3
Lyttelton NZ 35B2
Lytton USA 66A1
Lyubeshov USSR 19F2
Lyublino USSR 20F4

M

Ma, R Laos/Viet 30C1
Ma'agan Jordan 45C2
Ma'alot Tarshiha Israel 45C2
Ma'an Jordan 40C3
Ma'anshan China 31D3
Ma'arrat an Nu'man Syria 45D1
Maas, R Neth 18B2
Maaseik Belg 13C2
Maastricht Belg 18B2
Mabalane Mozam 47E1
Mabaruma Guyana 73G2
Mablethorpe Eng 7E3
Mabote Mozam 51D6
Mabrita USSR 19E2
Macaé Brazil 75D3
McAlester USA 56D3
McAllen USA 56D4
Macaloge Mozam 51D5
Macapá Brazil 73H3
Macarani Brazil 75D2
Macas Ecuador 72C4
Macaú Brazil 73L5
Macau, Dependency S E Asia 31C5
Macaúbas Brazil 75D1
McCall USA 58C2
McCamey USA 62B2
McCammon USA 58D2
Macclesfield Eng 7C3
McClintock B Can 55K1
McClintock Chan Can 54H2
McClure USA 68B2
McClure,L USA 66B2
McClure Str Can 54G2
McComb USA 63D2
McConaughy,L USA 60C2
McConnellsburg USA 68B3
McCook USA 56C2
Macculloch,C Can 55L2
McDame Can 54F4
McDermitt USA 58C2
McDonald Peak, Mt USA 58D1
Macdonnell Ranges, Mts Aust 32C3
MacDuff Scot 8D3
Macedo de Cavaleiros Port 15A1
Maceió Brazil 73L5
Macenta Guinea 48B4
Macerata Italy 16C2
McGehee USA 63D2
McGill USA 59D3
McGrath USA 54C3
McGuire,Mt USA 58D1
Machado Brazil 75C3
Machaíla Mozam 51D6
Machakos Kenya 50D4
Machala Ecuador 72C4
Machaze Mozam 51D6
Mācherla India 44B2
Machgharab Leb 45C2
Machias USA 65F2
Machilipatnam India 44C2
Machiques Ven 72D1
Machu-Picchu, Hist Site Peru 72D6
Machynlleth Wales 7C3
Macia Mozam 51D6
Macias Nguema, I = Bioko
McIntosh USA 60C1
MacIntyre, R Aust 34C1
Mack USA 60B3
Mackay Aust 32D3
Mackay USA 58D2
Mackay,L Aust 32B3
McKean, I Phoenix Is 33H1
McKeesport USA 65D2
Mackenzie, R Can 54F3
Mackenzie B Can 54E3
Mackenzie King I Can 54G2
Mackenzie Mts Can 54E3
Mackinac,Str of USA 64C1
Mackinaw City USA 64C1
McKinley, Mt USA 54C3
McKinney USA 63C2
Mackinson Inlet, B Can 55L2
McKittrick USA 66C3
Macksville Aust 34D2
McLaughlin USA 60C1
Maclean Aust 34D1
Maclear S Africa 47D3
McLennan Can 54G4
McLeod B Can 54G3
McLeod,L Aust 32A3
McLoughlin,Mt USA 58B2
Macmillan, R Can 54E3
McMillan,L USA 62B2
McMinnville, Oregon USA 58B1
McMinnville, Tennessee USA 67A1
McMurdo, Base Ant 76F7
McNary USA 59E4
Macomb USA 64A2
Macomer, Sardinia 16B2
Macomia Mozam 51D5
Mâcon France 14C2
Macon, Georgia USA 57E3
Macon, Missouri USA 61E3
Macondo Angola 51C5
McPherson USA 63C1
Macquarie, R Aust 34C2
Macquarie Harbour, B Aust 34C4
Macquarie Is Aust 36J7
Macquarie,L Aust 34D2
McRae USA 67B2
Mac Robertson Land, Region Ant 76F11
McTavish Arm, B Can 54G3
McVicar Arm, B Can 54F3
Mādabā Jordan 45C3
Madadi, Well Chad 50C2
Madagascar, I Indian O 46J9
Madagascar Basin Indian O 36D6
Madama Niger 50B1
Madang PNG 32D1
Madaoua Niger 48C3
Madaripur Bang 43G4
Madau USSR 41F2
Madawaska, R Can 65D1
Madeira, I Atlantic O 48A1
Madeira, R Brazil 72F5
M'adel USSR 19F2
Madelia USA 61E2
Madera Mexico 70B2
Madera USA 59B3
Madgaon India 44A2
Madhubani India 43F3
Madhya Pradesh, State India 43E4
Madikeri India 44B3
Madimba Zaïre 50B4
Madingo Kayes Congo 50B4
Madingou Congo 50B4
Madison, Indiana USA 57E3
Madison, Minnesota USA 61D1
Madison, Nebraska USA 61D2
Madison, S Dakota USA 61D2
Madison, Wisconsin USA 57E2
Madison, R USA 58D1
Madisonville, Kentucky USA 64B3
Madisonville, Texas USA 63C2
Mado Gashi Kenya 50D3
Madras India 44C3
Madras USA 58B2
Madre de Dios, I Chile 74A8
Madre de Dios, R Bol 72E6
Madre, Laguna Mexico 70C2
Madre, Laguna USA 63C3
Madrid Spain 15B1
Madridejos Spain 15B2
Madura, I Indon 27E7
Madurai India 44B4
Maebashi Japan 29C3
Mae Khlong, R Thai 30B3
Mae Luang, R Thai 30B4
Mae Nam Mun, R Thai 30C2
Mae Nam Ping, R Thai 30B2
Maengsan N Korea 28A3
Maevatanana Madag 51E5
Maewo, I Vanuatu 33F2
Mafeteng Lesotho 47D2
Maffra Aust 34C3
Mafia I Tanz 51D4
Mafikeng S Africa 47D2
Mafra Brazil 74G3
Mafraq Jordan 40C3
Magadan USSR 25Q4
Magallanes, Estrecho de, Str Chile 74B8
Magangué Colombia 72D2
Magdalena Mexico 56B3
Magdalena USA 62A2
Magdalena, R Colombia 72D2
Magdalena, Bahía Mexico 70A2
Magdalena, Isla Mexico 70A2
Magdalen Is Can 55M5
Magdeburg E Germ 18C2
Magé Brazil 73K8
Maggiore, L Italy 16B1
Maghâgha Egypt 40B4
Maghâra, Gebel, Mt Egypt 45B3
Maghera N Ire 9C2
Magherafelt N Ire 9C2
Maglie Italy 17D2
Magnitogorsk USSR 20K5
Magnolia USA 63D2
Magoé Mozam 51D5
Magog Can 65E1
Magruder Mt USA 66D2
Maguarinho, Cabo, C Brazil 73J4
Magude Mozam 47E2
Maguse River Can 55J3
Magwe Burma 30B1
Mahābād Iran 21H8
Mahabharat Range, Mts Nepal 43F3
Mahād India 44A2
Mahadeo Hills India 42D4
Mahaffey USA 68A2
Mahajamba, Baie de, B Madag 51E5
Mahajanga Madag 51E5
Mahalapye Botswana 47D1
Mahānadi, R India 43E4
Mahanoro Madag 51E5
Mahanoy City USA 68B2
Mahārāshtra, State India 44A2
Mahāsamund India 43E4
Maha Sarakham Thai 30C2
Mahavavy, R Madag 51E5
Mahbubnagar India 44B2
Mahdia Tunisia 48D1
Mahe India 44B3
Mahenge Tanz 51D4
Mahesana India 42C4
Mahia Pen NZ 35C1
Mahnomen USA 61D1
Mahoba India 42D3
Mahón Spain 15C2
Mahrès Tunisia 48D1
Mahuva India 42C4
Maicao Colombia 72D1
Maidenhead Eng 7D4
Maidstone Eng 7E4
Maiduguri Nig 50B2
Maihar India 43E4
Maijdi Bang 43G4
Maikala Range, Mts India 43E4
Maimana Afghan 42A1
Main Chan Can 64C1
Mai-Ndombe, L Zaïre 50B4
Maine, State USA 57G2
Mainland, I Scot 8D2
Mainpuri India 42D3
Maintirano Madag 51E5
Mainz W Germ 18B2
Maio, I Cape Verde 48A4
Maipó, Vol Arg/Chile 74C4
Maiquetía Ven 72E1
Mairābari India 43G3
Maiskhal I Bang 43G4
Maitland, New South Wales Aust 32E4
Maíz, Isla del Caribbean S 70D3
Maizuru Japan 29D3
Majene Indon 32A1
Majes, R Peru 72D7
Maji Eth 50D3
Majia He, R China 31D2
Majorca, I, Balearic Is Spain 15C2
Majunga = Mahajanga
Makale Eth 50D2
Makale Indon 27E7
Makalu, Mt China/Nepal 43F3
Makanza Zaïre 50B3
Makarikha USSR 20K2
Makarska Yugos 16D2
Makaryev USSR 20G4
Makassar = Ujung Pandang
Makassar Str Indon 27E7
Makat USSR 21J6
Makeni Sierra Leone 48A4
Makerwaard, Polder Neth 13C1
Makeyevka USSR 21F6
Makgadikgadi, Salt Pan Botswana 51C6
Makhachkala USSR 21H7
Makharadze USSR 40D1
Makindu Kenya 50D4
Makkah = Mecca
Makkovik Can 55N4
Makó Hung 19E3
Makokou Gabon 50B3
Makorako,Mt NZ 35C1
Makoua Congo 50B3
Makrana India 42C3
Makran Coast Range, Mts Pak 42A3
Makthar Tunisia 16B3
Maku Iran 21G8
Makumbi Zaïre 50C4
Makurdi Nigeria 48C4
Malabar Coast India 44B3
Malabo Eq Guinea 48C4
Malacca = Melaka
Malacca,Str of S E Asia 30C5
Malad City USA 58D2
Málaga Colombia 72D2
Málaga Spain 15B2
Malaga USA 62B2
Malaimbandy Madag 51E6
Malaita, I Solomon Is 33F1
Malakal Sudan 50D3
Malakand Pak 42C2
Malanbang Phil 27F6
Malang Indon 27E7
Malanje Angola 51B4
Malanville Benin 48C3
Mal Anyuy, R USSR 25S3
Mälaren, L Sweden 12H7
Malartic Can 65D1
Malatya Turk 21F8
Malawi, Republic Africa 51D5
Malawi,L = Nyasa,L
Malayer Iran 41E3
Malaysia, Federation S E Asia 27D6
Malazgirt Turk 40D2
Malbork Pol 19D2
Malchin E Germ 18C2
Malden USA 63E1
Maldives, Is Indian O 39F5
Maldives Ridge Indian O 36E4
Maldon Eng 7E4
Maldonado Urug 74F4
Malegaon India 42C4
Malé Karpaty, Upland Czech 18D3
Malekula, I Vanuatu 33F2
Malema Mozam 51D5
Malen'ga USSR 20F3
Malesherbes France 13B3
Malestan Afghan 42B2
Malgomaj, L Sweden 12H5
Malgomaj, R Sweden 20B3
Malha, Well Sudan 50C2
Malheur L USA 58C2
Mali, Republic Africa 48B3
Mali Kyun, I Burma 30B3
Malin USSR 19F2
Malinau Indon 27E6
Malindi Kenya 50E4
Malines = Mechelen
Malin Head, Pt Irish Rep 10B2
Malkapur India 42D4
Malkara Turk 17F2
Malko Tŭrnovo Bulg 17F2
Mallaig Scot 8C3
Mallawi Egypt 49F2
Mallorca, I = Majorca
Malm Nor 12G6
Malmberget Sweden 12J5
Malmédy W Germ 13D2
Malmesbury Eng 7C4
Malmesbury S Africa 47B3
Malmö Sweden 12G7
Malmyzh USSR 20J4
Malone USA 65E2
Maloti Mts Lesotho 47D2
Måloy Nor 12F6
Malozemel'skaya Tundra, Plain USSR 20J2
Malpelo, I Colombia 71B3
Malpura India 42D3
Malta, Idaho USA 58D2
Malta, Montana USA 56C2
Malta, I and Republic Medit S 16C3
Malta Chan Italy/Malta 16C3
Maltahöhe Namibia 47B1
Malton Eng 6D2
Ma'lula, Jabal, Mt Syria 45D2
Malung Sweden 12G6
Malvan India 44A2
Malvern USA 63D2
Malvérnia Mozam 47E1
Malvinas, Islas = Falkland Is
Malwa Plat India 42D4
Malyy Kavkaz, Mts USSR 24F5
Malyy Lyakhovskiy, Ostrov, I USSR 25Q2
Malyy Taymyr, Ostrov, I USSR 25M2
Malyy Uzen', R USSR 21H6
Mama USSR 25N4
Mamadysh USSR 20J4
Mambasa Zaïre 50C3
Mamberamo, R Aust 32C1
Mamberamo, R Indon 27G7
Mambéré, R CAR 50B3
Mamfé Cam 48C4
Mammoth USA 59D4
Mammoth Cave Nat Pk USA 64B3
Mammoth Pool Res USA 66C2
Mamoré, R Bol/Brazil 72E6
Mamou Guinea 48A3
Mampikony Madag 51E5
Mampong Ghana 48B4
Mamshit, Hist Site Israel 45C3
Mamuju Indon 27E7
Mamuno Botswana 47C1
Man Ivory Coast 48B4
Mana Hawaiian Is 66E5
Manabo Madag 51E6
Manacapuru Brazil 72F4
Manacor Spain 15C2
Manado Indon 27F6
Managua Nic 72A1
Managua, L de Nic 70D3
Manakara Madag 51E6
Manam, I PNG 32D1
Mananara Madag 51E5
Mananjary Madag 51E6
Manapouri NZ 35A3
Manapouri,L NZ 35A3
Manas China 39G1
Manas, R Bhutan 43G3
Manas Hu, L China 24K5
Manaslu, Mt Nepal 43E3
Manasquan USA 68C2
Manaus Brazil 73G4
Manavgat Turk 21E8
Manbij Syria 40C2
Man,Calf of, I, I of Man British Is 6B2
Mancelona USA 64B2
Mancheral India 44B2
Manchester, Connecticut USA 65E2
Manchester Eng 7C3
Manchester, Kentucky USA 64C3
Manchester, New Hampshire USA 57F2
Manchester, Pennsylvania USA 68B2
Manchester, Tennessee USA 67A1
Manchester, Vermont USA 68D1
Manchuria, Division China 26F2
Mand, R Iran 41F4
Manda Tanz 51D5
Mandaguari Brazil 75B3
Mandal Nor 12F7
Mandala, Peak, Mt Indon 27G7
Mandalay Burma 30B1
Mandalgovĭ Mongolia 26D2
Mandal Ovoo Mongolia 31A1
Mandan USA 56C2
Mandera Eth 50E3
Mandeville Jamaica 69H1
Mandi India 42D2
Mandimba Mozam 51D5
Mandiore, Lagoa Brazil 75A2
Mandla India 43E4
Mandritsara Madag 51E5
Mandsaur India 42D4

Manduria
Mazār

Manduria *Italy* 17D2
Māndvi *India* 42B4
Mandya *India* 44B3
Manendragarh *India* 43E4
Manevichi *USSR* 19F2
Manfalût *Egypt* 40B4
Manfredonia *Italy* 16D2
Manga *Brazil* 75D1
Manga, Desert Region *Niger* 50B2
Mangakino *NZ* 35C1
Mangalia *Rom* 17F2
Mangalmé *Chad* 50C2
Mangalore *India* 44A3
Mangin Range, Mts *Burma* 43H4
Mangnai *China* 26C3
Mango *Togo* 48C3
Mangoche *Malawi* 51D5
Mangoky, R *Madag* 51E6
Mangole, I *Indon* 27F7
Māngral *India* 42B4
Mangueirinha *Brazil* 75B4
Mangui *China* 25O4
Mangum *USA* 62C2
Manhattan *USA* 56D3
Manhica *Mozam* 47E2
Manhuacu *Brazil* 73K8
Mania, R *Madag* 51E5
Manica *Mozam* 51D5
Manicouagan, R *Can* 55M5
Manicouagan Res *Can* 55M4
Manifah *S Arabia* 41E4
Manila *Phil* 27F5
Manila *USA* 58E2
Manilla *Aust* 34D2
Maninian *Ivory Coast* 48B3
Manipur, R *Burma/India* 43G4
Manipur, State *India* 43G4
Manisa *Turk* 21D8
Man,Isle of *Irish S* 10C3
Manistee *USA* 64B2
Manistee, R *USA* 64B2
Manistique *USA* 64B1
Manitoba, Province *Can* 54J4
Manitoba,L *Can* 54J4
Manitou *Can* 60D1
Manitou Is *USA* 64B1
Manitoulin, I *Can* 55K5
Manitou Springs *USA* 60C3
Manitowik L *Can* 64C1
Manitowoc *USA* 64B2
Maniwaki *Can* 65D1
Manizales *Colombia* 72C2
Manja *Madag* 51E6
Manjimup *Aust* 32A4
Mānjra, R *India* 44B2
Mankato *USA* 57D2
Mankono *Ivory Coast* 48B4
Manly *NZ* 35B1
Manmād *India* 42C4
Mannahill *Aust* 34A2
Mannar *Sri Lanka* 44B4
Mannār,G of *India* 44B4
Mannārgudi *India* 44B3
Mannheim *W Germ* 18B3
Manning *USA* 67B2
Mannum *Aust* 34A2
Mano *Sierra Leone* 48A4
Manokwari *Indon* 32C1
Manono *Zaïre* 51C4
Manoron *Burma* 30B3
Manouane, Lac *Can* 55L4
Mano-wan, B *Japan* 29C3
Manp'o *N Korea* 28B2
Mānsa *India* 42D2
Mansa *Zambia* 51C5
Mansel I *Can* 55K3
Mansfield, Arkansas *USA* 63D1
Mansfield *Aust* 34C3
Mansfield *Eng* 7D3
Mansfield, Louisiana *USA* 63D2
Mansfield, Massachusetts *USA* 68E1
Mansfield, Ohio *USA* 57E2
Mansfield, Pennsylvania *USA* 65D2
Manso, R *Brazil* 75B2
Mansyu Deep *Pacific O* 27H5
Manta *Ecuador* 72B4
Mantap-san, Mt *N Korea* 28A2
Mantaro, R *Peru* 72C6
Manteca *USA* 66B2
Manteo *USA* 67C1
Mantes *France* 14C2
Manti *USA* 59D3
Mantiqueira, Serra da, Mts *Brazil* 75C3
Mantova *Italy* 16C1
Mäntta *Fin* 12J6
Mantua = Mantova
Manturovo *USSR* 20G4
Manuel Benavides *Mexico* 62B3
Manuel Ribas *Brazil* 75B3
Manukan *Phil* 27F6
Manukau *NZ* 33G4
Manus, I *Pacific O* 27H7
Manzanares *Spain* 15B2
Manzanillo *Cuba* 70E2
Manzanillo *Mexico* 70B3
Manzhouli *China* 25N5
Manzil *Jordan* 45D3
Manzini *Swaziland* 51D6
Mao *Chad* 50B2
Maoke, Pegunungan, Mts *Indon* 27G7
Maomao Shan, Mt *China* 31A2
Maoming *China* 31C5
Mapai *Mozam* 51D6
Mapam Yumco, L *China* 43E2
Mapia, Is *Pacific O* 27G6
Maple Creek *Can* 54H5
Mapulanguene *Mozam* 47E1
Maputo *Mozam* 47E2
Maputo, R *Mozam* 47E2
Maputo, Baia de, B *Mozam* 47E2
Ma Qu = Huang He
Maqu *China* 31A3
Maquan He, R *China* 43F3
Maquela do Zombo *Angola* 50B4
Maquinchao *Arg* 74C6
Marabá *Brazil* 73J5
Maracaibo *Ven* 72D1
Maracaibo, Lago de *Ven* 72D2
Maracá, Ilha de, I *Brazil* 73H3
Maracaju *Brazil* 75A3
Maracaju, Serra de, Mts *Brazil* 75A3
Máracás *Brazil* 75D1
Maracay *Ven* 72E1
Marādah *Libya* 49D2
Maradi *Niger* 48C3
Marāgheh *Iran* 21H8
Marajó, Baia de, B *Brazil* 73J4
Marajó, Ilha de, I *Brazil* 73H4
Marajó, Isla de *Brazil* 71F4
Marakech *Mor* 28E5
Maralal *Kenya* 50D3
Maramasike, I *Solomon Is* 33F1
Maramba = Livingstone
Marana *USA* 59D4
Marand *Iran* 21H8
Maranhão, R *Brazil* 75C1
Maranhão, State *Brazil* 73J4
Maranoa, R *Aust* 34C1
Marañón, R *Peru* 72C4
Maras *Turk* 21F8
Marathon *Can* 55K5
Marathon, Florida *USA* 67B4
Marathon, New York *USA* 68B1
Marathon, Texas *USA* 62B2
Maraú *Brazil* 75E1
Marawi *Phil* 27F6
Marbella *Spain* 15B2
Marble Bar *Aust* 32A3
Marble Canyon *USA* 59D3
Marble Hall *S Africa* 47D2
Marblehead *USA* 68E1
Marburg *W Germ* 18B2
Mar Cantabrico = Biscay, B of
Marca, Punta da, Pt *Angola* 51B5
Marche *Belg* 18B2
Marche-en-Famenne *Belg* 13C2
Marchena *Spain* 15A2
Mar Chiquita, Lagoa, L *Arg* 74D4
Marco *USA* 67B3
Marcy,Mt *USA* 65E2
Mardan *Pak* 42C2
Mar del Plata *Arg* 74E5
Mardin *Turk* 21G8
Maré, I *New Caledonia* 33F3
Mareb, R *Eth* 50D2
Mareeba *Aust* 27H8
Maree, Loch, L *Scot* 8C3
Marfa *USA* 62B2
Margaretville *USA* 68C1
Margarita, Isla *Ven* 69E4
Margarita, Islas de *Ven* 72F1
Margaritovo *USSR* 29C2
Margate *Eng* 7E4
Marghita *Rom* 17E1
Maria I *Aust* 34C4
Marianas, Is *Pacific O* 27H5
Mariana Trench *Pacific O* 36J4
Mariani *India* 43G3
Marianna, Arkansas *USA* 63D2
Marianna, Florida *USA* 67A2
Mari ASSR, Republic *USSR* 20H4
Mariato, Puerta *Panama* 72B2
Maria Van Diemen,C *NZ* 57G4
Mariazell *Austria* 18D3
Maribor *Yugos* 16D1
Marico, R *Botswana/S Africa* 47D1
Maricopa *USA* 66C3
Maridi *Sudan* 50C3
Marie Byrd Land, Region *Ant* 76F5
Marie Galante, I *Caribbean S* 69E3
Mariehamn *Fin* 12H6
Mariembourg *Belg* 13C2
Marienburg *Surinam* 73H2
Mariental *Namibia* 47B1
Mariestad *Sweden* 12G7
Marietta, Georgia *USA* 67B2
Marietta, Ohio *USA* 64C3
Marietta, Oklahoma *USA* 63C2
Marigot *Dominica* 69Q2
Marília *Brazil* 74G2
Marimba *Angola* 51B4
Marinette *USA* 57E2
Maringá *Brazil* 74F2
Maringa, R *Zaïre* 50C3
Marion, Arkansas *USA* 63D1
Marion, Illinois *USA* 64B3
Marion, Indiana *USA* 57E2
Marion, Ohio *USA* 57E2
Marion, S Carolina *USA* 67C2
Marion,L *USA* 57E3
Marion Reef *Aust* 33E2
Mariposa *USA* 59C3
Mariposa, R *USA* 66B2
Mariposa Res *USA* 66B2
Marista, R *Bulg* 21D7
Marjayoun *Leb* 45C2
Marjina Gorki *USSR* 19F2
Marka *Jordan* 45C3
Marka *Somalia* 50E3
Markaryd *Sweden* 18C1
Market Drayton *Eng* 7C3
Market Harborough *Eng* 7D3
Market Weighton *Eng* 6D3
Markham,Mt *Ant* 76E7
Markleeville *USA* 66C1
Markovo *USSR* 25S3
Marlboro, Massachusetts *USA* 68E1
Marlboro, New Hampshire *USA* 68D1
Marlborough *Aust* 32D3
Marlborough *Eng* 7D4
Marle *France* 13B3
Marlin *USA* 63C2
Marlow *USA* 68D1
Marmande *France* 14C3
Marmara Adasi, I *Turk* 17F2
Marmara,S of *Turk* 40A1
Marmaris *Turk* 17F3
Marmarth *USA* 60C1
Marmet *USA* 64C3
Marmion L *Can* 61E1
Marmolada, Mt *Italy* 16C1
Marne, Department *France* 13C3
Marne, R *France* 13B3
Maro *Chad* 50B3
Maroantsetra *Madag* 51E5
Marondera *Zim* 51D5
Maroni, R *French Guiana* 73H3
Maroochydore *Aust* 34D1
Maroua *Cam* 50B2
Marovoay *Madag* 51E5
Marquesas Keys, Is *USA* 57E4
Marquette *USA* 57E2
Marquises, Îles *Pacific O* 37N5
Marra, R *Aust* 34C2
Marracuene *Mozam* 47E2
Marra, Jebel, Mt *Sudan* 50C2
Marrakech *Mor* 48B1
Marree *Aust* 32C3
Marrero *USA* 63D3
Marromeu *Mozam* 51D5
Marrupa *Mozam* 51D5
Marsa Alam *Egypt* 40B4
Marsabit *Kenya* 50D3
Marsa Fatma *Eth* 50E2
Marsala, Sicily 16C3
Marsberg *W Germ* 13E2
Marseilles *France* 14D3
Mar, Serra do, Mts *Brazil* 75D3
Marshall, Illinois *USA* 64B3
Marshall, Michigan *USA* 64C2
Marshall, Minnesota *USA* 61D2
Marshall, Missouri *USA* 61E3
Marshall, Texas *USA* 57D3
Marshall, Virginia *USA* 68B3
Marshall Is *Pacific O* 37K4
Marshalltown *USA* 61E2
Marshfield, Missouri *USA* 63D1
Marshfield, Wisconsin *USA* 64A2
Marsh Harbour *The Bahamas* 69B1
Marsh I *USA* 63D3
Martaban,G of *Burma* 30B2
Martha's Vineyard, I *USA* 65E2
Martigny *Switz* 14D2
Martigues *France* 14D3
Martin *Czech* 19D3
Martin, S Dakota *USA* 60C2
Martin, Tennessee *USA* 63E1
Martinborough *NZ* 35C2
Martinique, I *Caribbean S* 69E4
Martin,L *USA* 67A2
Martinsburg *USA* 65D3
Martins Ferry *USA* 64C2
Martinsville *USA* 65D3
Martin Vaz, I *Atlantic O* 52G6
Marton *NZ* 35C2
Martos *Spain* 15B2
Martre, Lac la *Can* 54G3
Maruf *Afghan* 42B2
Marugame *Japan* 29B4
Marvine,Mt, Mt *USA* 59D3
Mārwār *India* 42C3
Mary *USSR* 24H6
Maryborough, Queensland *Aust* 33E3
Maryborough, Victoria *Aust* 34B3
Mary Henry,Mt *Can* 54F4
Maryland, State *USA* 57F3
Maryport *Eng* 6C2
Marysville, California *USA* 59B3
Marysville, Kansas *USA* 61D3
Marysville, Washington *USA* 58B1
Maryville, Iowa *USA* 57D2
Maryville, Missouri *USA* 61D2
Maryville, Tennessee *USA* 67B1
Marzuq *Libya* 49D2
Masabb Dumyât, C *Egypt* 45A3
Masada = Mezada
Mas'adah *Syria* 45C2
Masai Steppe, Upland *Tanz* 50D4
Masaka *Uganda* 50D4
Masally *USSR* 41E2
Masan *S Korea* 28B3
Masasi *Tanz* 51D5
Masaya *Nic* 70D3
Masbate *Phil* 27F5
Masbate, I *Phil* 27F5
Mascara *Alg* 15C2
Mascarene Ridge *Indian O* 36D5
Mascote *Brazil* 75E2
Maseru *Lesotho* 47D2
Mashaki *Afghan* 42B2
Mashhad *Iran* 41G2
Masi-Manimba *Zaïre* 50B4
Masindi *Uganda* 50D3
Maşirah, I *Oman* 38D3
Masisi *Zaïre* 50C4
Masjed Soleyman *Iran* 41E3
Masoala, C *Madag* 51F5
Mason, Nevada *USA* 66C1
Mason, Texas *USA* 62C2
Mason City *USA* 57D2
Masqat = Muscat
Massa *Italy* 16C2
Massachusetts, State *USA* 57F2
Massachusetts B *USA* 65E2
Massakori *Chad* 50B2
Massangena *Mozam* 51D6
Massawa = Mits'iwa
Massena *USA* 65E2
Massénya *Chad* 50B2
Massey *Can* 64C1
Massif Central, Mts *France* 14C2
Massif de l'Isalo, Upland *Madag* 51E6
Massif du Tsaratanana, Mts *Madag* 51E5
Massillon *USA* 64C2
Massina, Region *Mali* 48B3
Massinga *Mozam* 51D6
Massingir *Mozam* 47E1
Masteksay *USSR* 21J6
Masterton *NZ* 33G5
Masuda *Japan* 28C4
Maşyaf *Syria* 40C2
Matachewan *Can* 64C1
Matachie *Mexico* 62A3
Matadi *Zaïre* 50B4
Matagalpa *Nic* 72A1
Matagami *Can* 55L5
Matagorda B *USA* 56D4
Matagorda I *USA* 63C3
Matakana I *NZ* 35C1
Matala *Angola* 51B5
Matale *Sri Lanka* 44C4
Matam *Sen* 48A3
Matameye *Niger* 48C3
Matamoros *Mexico* 70C2
Ma'tan as Sarra, Well *Libya* 49E2
Matane *Can* 55M5
Matanzas *Cuba* 70D2
Matapedia, R *Can* 65F1
Matara *Sri Lanka* 44C4
Mataram *Indon* 32A1
Matarani *Peru* 72D7
Mataripe *Brazil* 75E1
Mataró *Spain* 15C1
Matatiele *S Africa* 47D3
Mataura *NZ* 35A3
Matehuala *Mexico* 70B2
Matelot *Trinidad* 69L1
Matera *Italy* 16D2
Mátészalka *Hung* 19E3
Mateur *Tunisia* 16B3
Mather *USA* 66C2
Matheson *Can* 64C1
Mathis *USA* 63C3
Mathura *India* 42D3
Matlock *Eng* 7D3
Mato Grosso, State *Brazil* 73G6
Mato Grosso do Sul, State *Brazil* 73G7
Matola *Mozam* 47E2
Matrûh *Egypt* 49E1
Matsue *Japan* 28C3
Matsumae *Japan* 29E2
Matsumoto *Japan* 29D3
Matsusaka *Japan* 29D4
Matsuyama *Japan* 28C4
Mattagami, R *Can* 55K5
Mattawa *Can* 65D1
Matterhorn, Mt *Italy/Switz* 16B1
Matterhorn, Mt *USA* 58C2
Matthew Town *The Bahamas* 69C2
Mattituck *USA* 68D2
Mattoon *USA* 64B3
Matun *Afghan* 42B2
Matura B *Trinidad* 69L1
Maturín *Ven* 72F2
Mau *India* 43E3
Maúa *Mozam* 51D5
Maubeuge *France* 14C1
Maude *Aust* 34B2
Maud Seamount *Atlantic O* 52J8
Maug Is *Marianas* 26H4
Maui, I *Hawaiian Is* 66E5
Maumee *USA* 64C2
Maumee, R *USA* 64C2
Maun *Botswana* 51C5
Mauna Kea, Vol *Hawaiian Is* 66E5
Mauna Loa, Vol *Hawaiian Is* 66E5
Maunoir,L *Can* 54F3
Mauriac *France* 14C2
Mauritania, Republic *Africa* 48A2
Mauritius, I *Indian O* 46K10
Mauston *USA* 64A2
Mavinga *Angola* 51C5
Mavue *Mozam* 47E1
Mawlaik *Burma* 43G4
Mawson, Base *Ant* 76G10
Max *USA* 60C1
Maxaila *Mozam* 47E1
Maya, I *Indon* 27D7
Maya, R *USSR* 25P4
Mayadin *Syria* 40D2
Mayaguana, I *The Bahamas* 57F4
Mayagüez *Puerto Rico* 69D3
Mayahi *Niger* 48C3
Mayama *Congo* 50B4
Mayamey *Iran* 41G2
Maybole *Scot* 8C4
May,C *USA* 57F3
Maydena *Aust* 34C4
Mayen *W Germ* 13D2
Mayenne *France* 14B2
Mayer *USA* 59D4
Mayfield *USA* 64B3
Mayhill *USA* 62A2
Maykop *USSR* 21F7
Maymyo *Burma* 30B1
Mayo *Can* 54E3
Mayo *USA* 68B3
Mayor, Mt *Spain* 15C2
Mayor I *NZ* 35C1
Mayor P Lagerenza *Par* 74D1
Mayotte, I *Indian O* 51E5
May Pen *Jamaica* 69H2
May Point,C *USA* 68C3
Mays Landing *USA* 68C3
Maysville *USA* 64C3
Mayumba *Gabon* 50B4
Mayville *USA* 61D1
Maywood *USA* 60C2
Mazabuka *Zambia* 51C5
Mazar *China* 42D1
Mazar *Jordan* 45C3

Mazara del Vallo Minnesota

Mazara del Vallo, Sicily 16C3
Mazar-i-Sharif *Afghan* 42B1
Mazarrón, Golfo de, G *Spain* 15B2
Mazatlán *Mexico* 70B2
Mazeikiai *USSR* 20C4
Mazra *Jordan* 45C3
Mbabane *Swaziland* 51D6
Mbaïki *CAR* 50B3
Mbala *Zambia* 51D4
Mbalabala *Zim* 51C6
Mbale *Uganda* 50D3
Mbalmayo *Cam* 50B3
Mbam, R *Cam* 50B3
Mbamba Bay *Tanz* 51D5
Mbandaka *Zaïre* 50B3
Mbanza Congo *Angola* 50B4
Mbanza-Ngungu *Zaïre* 50B4
Mbarara *Uganda* 50D4
M'Bari, R *CAR* 50C3
Mbèndza *Congo* 50B3
Mbére, R *Cam/CAR/ Chad* 50B3
Mbeya *Tanz* 51D4
Mbinda *Congo* 50B4
Mbout *Maur* 48A3
Mbuji-Mayi *Zaïre* 50C4
Mbulu *Tanz* 50D4
Mcherrah, Region *Alg* 48B2
Mchinji *Malawi* 51D5
Mdrak *Viet* 30D3
Meade *USA* 62B1
Mead,L *USA* 56B3
Meadow Lake *Can* 54H4
Meadville *USA* 64C2
Me-akan dake, Mt *Japan* 29D2
Mealy Mts *Can* 55N4
Meandarra *Aust* 34C1
Meander River *Can* 54G4
Meath *Irish Rep* 9C3
Meaux *France* 14C2
Mecca *S Arabia* 50E1
Mecca *USA* 59C4
Mechanicville *USA* 68D1
Mechelen *Belg* 18A2
Mecheria *Alg* 48B1
Mecklenburger Bucht, B *E Germ* 18C2
Meconta *Mozam* 51D5
Mecuburi *Mozam* 51D5
Mecufi *Mozam* 51E5
Mecula *Mozam* 51D5
Medan *Indon* 27C6
Médanosa, Puerta, Pt *Arg* 74C7
Médéa *Alg* 15C2
Medellín *Colombia* 72C2
Medemblik *Neth* 13C1
Medenine *Tunisia* 48D1
Medford *USA* 56A2
Medgidia *Rom* 17F2
Mediaş *Rom* 17E1
Medical Lake *USA* 58C1
Medicine Bow *USA* 60B2
Medicine Bow Mts *USA* 60B2
Medicine Bow Peak, Mt *USA* 60B2
Medicine Hat *Can* 54G5
Medicine Lodge *USA* 62C1
Medina *Brazil* 75D2
Medina, N Dakota *USA* 60D1
Medina, New York *USA* 68A1
Medina *S Arabia* 40C5
Medinaceli *Spain* 15B1
Medina del Campo *Spain* 15A1
Medina de Rioseco *Spain* 15A1
Medina L *USA* 62C3
Medinipur *India* 43F4
Mediterranean *S Europe* 46E4
Medjerda, R *Tunisia/Alg* 16B3
Medjerda, Mts de la *Tunisia/Alg* 16B3
Mednogorsk *USSR* 21K5
Mednyy, Ostrov, I *USSR* 25S4
Mêdog *China* 43H3
Medouneu *Gabon* 50B3
Medvedista, R *USSR* 21G5
Medvezh'i Ova, Is *USSR* 25S2
Medvezh'yegorsk *USSR* 24E3
Meekatharra *Aust* 32A3
Meeker *USA* 60B2
Meerut *India* 42D3
Meeteetse *USA* 58E2
Mega *Eth* 50D3
Megalópolis *Greece* 17E3
Mégara *Greece* 17E3
Meghālaya, State *India* 43G3
Meghna, R *Bang* 43G4
Megiddo, Hist Site *Israel* 45C2
Mehekar *India* 42D4
Mehndawal *India* 43M2
Mehrān, R *Iran* 41F4
Mehriz *Iran* 41F3
Meia Ponte, R *Brazil* 75C2
Meiganga *Cam* 50B3
Meiktila *Burma* 30B1
Meishan *China* 31A4
Meissen *E Germ* 18C2
Mei Xian *China* 31D5
Meizhou *China* 31D5
Mejillones *Chile* 72D8
Mekambo *Gabon* 50B3
Meknès *Mor* 48B1
Mekong, R *Camb* 30D3
Mekong, Mouths of the *Viet* 30D4
Mekrou, R *Benin* 48C3
Melaka *Malay* 30C5
Melanesia, Region *Pacific O* 36J5
Melbourne *Aust* 32D4
Melbourne *USA* 57E4
Melchor Muźguiz *Mexico* 56C4
Meleuz *USSR* 20K5
Melfi *Chad* 50B2
Melfort *Can* 54H4
Melilla *N W Africa* 15B2
Melimoyu, Mt *Chile* 74B6
Melita *Can* 60C1
Melitopol' *USSR* 21F6
Melle *W Germ* 13E1
Mellégue, R *Tunisia/Alg* 16B3
Melmoth *S Africa* 47E2
Melo *Urug* 74F4
Melo, R *Brazil* 75A3
Melones Res *USA* 66B2
Melrose *Scot* 8D4
Melrose *USA* 61E1
Melton Mowbray *Eng* 7D3
Melun *France* 14C2
Melville *Can* 54H4
Melville Bugt, B *Greenland* 55M2
Melville,C *Dominica* 69Q2
Melville Hills *Can* 54F3
Melville I *Aust* 32C2
Melville I *Can* 54G2
Melville,L *Can* 55N4
Melville Pen *Can* 55K3
Memba *Mozam* 51E5
Memboro *Indon* 32A1
Memmingen *W Germ* 18C3
Memphis, Tennessee *USA* 57E3
Memphis, Texas *USA* 62B2
Mena *USA* 63D2
Mena *USSR* 19G2
Menai Str *Wales* 7B3
Ménaka *Mali* 48C3
Menasha *USA* 64B2
Mendawai, R *Indon* 27E7
Mende *France* 14C3
Mendebo Mts *Eth* 50D3
Mendi *PNG* 32D1
Mendip Hills, Upland *Eng* 7C4
Mendocino,C *USA* 58B2
Mendocino Seascarp *Pacific O* 37M3
Mendota, California *USA* 66B2
Mendota, Illinois *USA* 64B2
Mendoza *Arg* 74C4
Mendoza, State *Arg* 74C5
Menemen *Turk* 17F3
Menen *Belg* 13B2
Mengcheng *China* 31D3
Menghai *China* 30B1
Mengla *China* 31A5
Menglian *China* 30B1
Mengzi *China* 31A5
Menindee *Aust* 32D4
Menindee L *Aust* 34B2
Meningie *Aust* 34A3
Menominee *USA* 64B1
Menomonee Falls *USA* 64B2
Menomonie *USA* 64A2
Menongue *Angola* 51B5
Menorca, I = Minorca
Mentawi, Kepulauan, Is *Indon* 27C7
Mentmore *USA* 62A1
Mentok *Indon* 27D7
Mentor *USA* 64C2
Menyapa, Mt *Indon* 27E6
Menyuan *China* 31A2
Menzel *Tunisia* 16B3
Menzelinsk *USSR* 20J4
Meppel *Neth* 13D1
Meppen *W Germ* 18B2
Mequinenza, Embalse de Res *Spain* 15B1
Meramec, R *USA* 63D1
Merano *Italy* 16C1
Meratus, Pegunungan, Mts *Indon* 27E7
Merauke *Indon* 32D1
Merced *USA* 56A3
Merced, R *USA* 66B2
Mercedario, Mt *Arg* 74B4
Mercedes, Buenos Aires *Arg* 74E4
Mercedes, Corrientes *Arg* 74E3
Mercedes, San Luis *Arg* 74C4
Mercedes *Urug* 74E4
Mercury B *NZ* 35C1
Mercury Is *NZ* 35C1
Mercy B *Can* 54F2
Mercy,C *Can* 55M3
Meredith,L *USA* 62B1
Meregh *Somalia* 50E3
Mergui *Burma* 30B3
Mergui Arch *Burma* 30B3
Mérida *Mexico* 70D2
Mérida *Spain* 15A2
Mérida *Ven* 72D2
Mérida, Cordillera de *Ven* 72D2
Meridian *USA* 57E3
Merimbula *Aust* 34C3
Meringur *Aust* 34B2
Merir, I *Pacific O* 27G6
Merkel *USA* 62B2
Merowe *Sudan* 50D2
Merredin *Aust* 32A4
Merrick, Mt *Scot* 8C4
Merrill *USA* 64B1
Merrillville *USA* 64B2
Merrimack, R *USA* 68E1
Merriman *USA* 60C2
Merritt Island *USA* 67B3
Merriwa *Aust* 34D2
Mersea, I *Eng* 7E4
Mers el Kebir *Alg* 15B2
Mersey, R *Eng* 7C3
Merseyside, Metropolitan County *Eng* 7C3
Mersin *Turk* 21E8
Mersing *Malay* 30C5
Merta *India* 42C3
Merthyr Tydfil *Wales* 7C4
Mertola *Port* 15A2
Méru *France* 13B3
Meru, Mt *Tanz* 50D4
Merzifon *Turk* 21F7
Merzig *W Germ* 13D3
Mesa *USA* 56B3
Mesa Verde Nat Pk *USA* 62A1
Meschede *W Germ* 13E2
Mescit Dağ, Mt *Turk* 40D1
Meshra Er Req *Sudan* 50C3
Mesolóngion *Greece* 17E3
Mesquite, Nevada *USA* 59D3
Mesquite, Texas *USA* 63C2
Messalo, R *Mozam* 51D5
Messina *S Africa* 47D1
Messina, Sicily 16D3
Messina, Stretto de, Str *Italy/Sicily* 16D3
Messíni *Greece* 17E3
Messiniakós Kólpos, G *Greece* 17E3
Mesta, R = Néstos
Mesta, R *Bulg* 17E2
Mestre *Italy* 16C1
Meta, R *Colombia/Ven* 72D3
Meta, R *USSR* 20E4
Meta Incognito Pen *Can* 55M3
Metairie *USA* 63D3
Metaline Falls *USA* 58C1
Metán *Arg* 74D3
Metangula *Mozam* 51D5
Metaponto *Italy* 16D2
Methil *Scot* 8D3
Methuen *USA* 68E1
Methven *NZ* 35B2
Metlakatla *USA* 54E4
Metropolis *USA* 64B3
Mettur *India* 44B3
Metz *France* 14D2
Meulaboh *Indon* 27C6
Meurthe, R *France* 13D3
Meurthe-et-Moselle, Department *France* 13D3
Meuse, Department *France* 13C3
Meuse, R *Belg* 13C2
Meuse, R *France* 14D2
Mexborough *Eng* 7D3
Mexia *USA* 63C2
Mexicali *Mexico* 70A1
Mexican Hat *USA* 59E3
México *Mexico* 70C3
Mexico *USA* 61E3
Mexico, Federal Republic *Cent America* 70B2
Mexico,G of *Cent America* 70C2
Meymaneh *Afghan* 24H6
Mezada, Hist Site *Israel* 45C3
Mezen' *USSR* 24F3
Mezen', R *USSR* 20H3
Mézenc, Mount *France* 14C3
Mezha, R *USSR* 19G1
Mezhdusharskiy, Ostrov, I *USSR* 24G2
Mhow *India* 42D4
Miami, Arizona *USA* 59D4
Miami, Florida *USA* 57E4
Miami, Oklahoma *USA* 63D1
Miami Beach *USA* 57E4
Miandowab *Iran* 21H8
Miandrivazo *Madag* 51E5
Mianeh *Iran* 21H8
Mianwali *Pak* 42C2
Mianyang *China* 31A3
Mianyang *China* 31C3
Mianzhu *China* 31A3
Miaodao Qundao, Arch *China* 31E2
Miao Ling, Upland *China* 31B4
Miass *USSR* 20L5
Michalovce *Czech* 19E3
Michel *Can* 58D1
Miches *Dom Rep* 69D3
Michigan, State *USA* 57E2
Michigan City *USA* 64B2
Michigan,L *USA* 57E2
Michipicoten *Can* 64C1
Michipicoten I *Can* 55K5
Michurin *Bulg* 17F2
Michurinsk *USSR* 21G5
Micronesia, Is *Pacific O* 27H6
Micronesia, Region *Pacific O* 36J4
Mid Atlantic Ridge *Atlantic O* 52F4
Middelburg, Cape Province *S Africa* 47C3
Middelburg *Neth* 13B2
Middelburg, Transvaal *S Africa* 47D2
Middle Alkali L *USA* 58B2
Middle America Trench *Pacific O* 37O4
Middle Andaman, I *Indian O* 44E3
Middleboro *USA* 68E2
Middleburg, Pennsylvania *USA* 68B2
Middleburg, Virginia *USA* 68B3
Middleburgh *USA* 68C1
Middlebury *USA* 65E2
Middlesboro *USA* 57E3
Middlesbrough *Eng* 6D2
Middletown, Connecticut *USA* 68D2
Middletown, Delaware *USA* 68C3
Middletown, New York *USA* 65E2
Middletown, Ohio *USA* 64C3
Middletown, Pennsylvania *USA* 68B2
Middleville *USA* 68C1
Middlewich *Eng* 7C3
Midelt *Mor* 48B1
Mid Glamorgan, County *Wales* 7C4
Midi *Yemen* 50E2
Mid Indian Basin *Indian O* 36E5
Mid Indian Ridge *Indian O* 36E5
Midland *Can* 55L5
Midland, Michigan *USA* 64C2
Midland, Texas *USA* 56C3
Midleton *Irish Rep* 9B4
Midongy Atsimo *Madag* 51E6
Mid Pacific Mts *Pacific O* 37K4
Midvale *USA* 58C2
Midway Is *Pacific O* 37L3
Midwest *USA* 60B2
Midwest City *USA* 63C1
Midyat *Turk* 40D2
Midžor, Mt *Yugos* 17E2
Mielec *Pol* 19E2
Miercurea-Ciuc *Rom* 17F1
Mieres *Spain* 15A1
Mifflintown *USA* 68B2
Migennes *France* 13B4
Mihara *Japan* 28B4
Mikhaylovgrad *Bulg* 17E2
Mikhaylovka *USSR* 21G5
Mikhaylovka *USSR* 28C2
Mikhaylovskiy *USSR* 24J4
Mikhrot Timna *Israel* 45C4
Mikkeli *Fin* 12K6
Míkonos, I *Greece* 17F3
Mikulov *Czech* 18D3
Mikumi *Tanz* 51D4
Mikun *USSR* 20J3
Mikuni-sammyaku, Mts *Japan* 29D3
Mikura-jima, I *Japan* 29C4
Milaca *USA* 61E1
Milagro *Ecuador* 72C4
Milan *Italy* 16B1
Milan *USA* 63E1
Milange *Mozam* 51D5
Milano = Milan
Milas *Turk* 21D8
Milbank *USA* 61D1
Mildura *Aust* 32D4
Mile *China* 31A5
Mileh Tharthār, L *Iraq* 41D3
Miles *Aust* 32E3
Miles City *USA* 56C2
Miletto, Monte, Mt *Italy* 16C2
Milford, Connecticut *USA* 68D2
Milford, Delaware *USA* 65D3
Milford, Nebraska *USA* 61D2
Milford, New Hampshire *USA* 68E1
Milford, Pennsylvania *USA* 68C2
Milford, Utah *USA* 59D3
Milford Haven *Wales* 7B4
Milford Haven, Sd *Wales* 7B4
Milford L *USA* 61D3
Milford Sd *NZ* 35A2
Miliana *Alg* 15C2
Milk, R *Can/USA* 54G4
Milk, R *USA* 60B1
Mil'kovo *USSR* 25R4
Milk, Wadi el, Watercourse *Sudan* 50C2
Millau *France* 14C3
Millbrook *USA* 68D2
Milledgeville *USA* 67B2
Mille Lacs L *USA* 61E1
Mille Lacs, Lac des *Can* 61E1
Miller *USA* 60D2
Millerovo *USSR* 21G6
Millersburg *USA* 68B2
Millers Falls *USA* 68D1
Millerton *USA* 68D2
Millerton L *USA* 66C2
Millford, Massachusetts *USA* 65E2
Millicent *Aust* 34B3
Millington *USA* 63E1
Millinocket *USA* 65F1
Millmerran *Aust* 34D1
Millom *Eng* 6C2
Millport *Scot* 8C4
Millstreet *Irish Rep* 9B3
Milltown *Can* 65F1
Milltown *USA* 58D1
Mill Valley *USA* 66A2
Millville *USA* 65E3
Milne Land, I *Greenland* 55Q2
Milolii *Hawaiian Is* 66E5
Mílos, I *Greece* 17E3
Milparinka *Aust* 32D3
Milroy *USA* 68B2
Milton, Florida *USA* 67A2
Milton *NZ* 35A3
Milton, Pennsylvania *USA* 68B2
Milton Keynes *Eng* 7D3
Milwaukee *USA* 57E2
Mimmaya *Japan* 29D2
Mina *USA* 66C1
Mina, R *Alg* 15C2
Mina' al Aḥmadi *Kuwait* 41E4
Mīnab *Iran* 41G4
Minas *Urug* 74E4
Minas Gerais, State *Brazil* 73J7
Minas Novas *Brazil* 75D2
Minatitlán *Mexico* 70C3
Minbu *Burma* 30A1
Minbya *Burma* 30A1
Minch,Little, Sd *Scot* 8B3
Minch,North, Sd *Scot* 8B2
Minch,The, Sd *Scot* 10B2
Mindanao, I *Phil* 27F6
Minden, Louisiana *USA* 63D2
Minden, Nevada *USA* 66C1
Minden *W Germ* 18B2
Mindona L *Aust* 34B2
Mindoro, I *Phil* 27F5
Mindoro Str *Phil* 27F5
Minehead *Eng* 7C4
Mineiros *Brazil* 73H7
Mineola *USA* 63C2
Mineral Wells *USA* 62C2
Minersville *USA* 68B2
Mingary *Aust* 34B2
Mingechaurskoye Vodokhranilische, Res *USSR* 21H7
Mingulay, I *Scot* 8B3
Minhe *China* 31A2
Minicoy, I *India* 44A4
Min Jiang, R, Fujian *China* 31D4
Min Jiang, R, Sichuan *China* 31A4
Minkler *USA* 66C2
Minlaton *Aust* 34A2
Minle *China* 31A2
Minna *Nigeria* 48C4
Minneapolis *USA* 57D2
Minnedosa *Can* 54J4
Minnesota, R *USA* 61D2

Minnesota Mosquito

Minnesota, State USA 57D2
Miño, R Spain 15A1
Minorca, I Spain 15C1
Minot USA 56C2
Minqin China 31A2
Min Shan, Upland China 31A3
Minsk USSR 20D5
Minsk Mazowiecki Pol 19E2
Minto Inlet, B Can 54G2
Minto,L Can 55L4
Minturn USA 60B3
Minusinsk USSR 26C1
Min Xian China 31A3
Minya el Qamn Egypt 45A3
Miquelon Can 55N5
Mirage L USA 66D3
Mirah, Wadi al, Watercourse Iraq/S Arabia 40D3
Miraj India 44A2
Miramar Arg 74E5
Miram Shah Pak 42B2
Miranda Brazil 75A3
Miranda, R Brazil 75A2
Miranda de Ebro Spain 15B1
Mirante, Serra do, Mts Brazil 75B3
Mir Bachchen Küt Afghan 42B2
Mirecourt France 13C3
Miri Malay 27E6
Mirik,C Maur 48A3
Mirim, Lagoa, L Brazil/Urug 74F4
Mirnoye USSR 25K3
Mirnyy USSR 25N3
Mirnyy, Base Ant 76G9
Mironovka USSR 19G3
Mirpur Pak 42C2
Mirpur Khas Pak 42B3
Mirtoan S Greece 17E3
Miryang S Korea 28B3
Mirzāpur India 43E3
Misgar Pak 42C1
Mishawaka USA 64B2
Mi-shima, I Japan 28B4
Mishmi Hills India 43H3
Misima, I PNG 33E2
Misiones, State Arg 74F3
Miskolc Hung 19E3
Mismīyah Syria 45D2
Misoöl, I Indon 27G7
Misrātah Libya 49D1
Missinaibi, R Can 55K5
Missinaibi L Can 64C1
Mission, S Dakota USA 60C2
Mission, Texas USA 62C3
Mission City Can 58B1
Mississauga Can 65D2
Mississippi, R USA 57D3
Mississippi, State USA 57D3
Mississippi Delta USA 63E3
Missoula USA 56B2
Missour Mor 48B1
Missouri, R USA 57D2
Missouri, State USA 57D3
Missouri Valley USA 61D2
Mistassini,L Can 57F1
Misti, Mt Peru 72D7
Mitchell Aust 34C1
Mitchell USA 56D2
Mitchell, R Aust 32D2
Mitchell,Mt USA 57E3
Mitchell River Aust 27H8
Mît el Nasâra Egypt 45A3
Mît Ghamr Egypt 45A3
Mithankot Pak 42C3
Mitilíni Greece 17F3
Mitla Pass Egypt 45B3
Mito Japan 29E3
Mitre, I Solomon Is 33G2
Mits'iwa Eth 50D2
Mittel Land Kanal W Germ 13D1
Mitú Colombia 72D3
Mitumba, Chaine des, Mts Zaïre 51C4
Mitumbar Mts Zaïre 50C4
Mitwaba Zaïre 51C4
Mitzic Gabon 50B3
Miura Japan 29C3
Mi Xian China 31C3
Miyake, I Japan 26G3
Miyake-jima, I Japan 29C4
Miyako Japan 29E3
Miyako, I, Ryukyu Is Japan 26F4
Miyazu Japan 29C3
Miyoshi Japan 28C4
Miyun China 31D1
Miyun Shuiku, Res China 31D1
Mi-zaki, Pt Japan 29D2
Mizan Teferi Eth 50D3
Mizdah Libya 49D1
Mizil Rom 17F1
Mizo Hills India 43G4
Mizoram, Union Territory India 43G4
Mizpe Ramon Israel 45C3
Mizusawa Japan 29E3
Mjölby Sweden 12H7
Mkushi Zambia 51C5
Mkuzi S Africa 47E2
Mladá Boleslav Czech 18C2
Mlawa Pol 19E2
Mljet, I Yugos 17D2
Mmabatho S Africa 47D2
Moa, R Sierra Leone 48A4
Moab USA 56C3
Moab, Region Jordan 45C3
Moamba Mozam 47E2
Moanda Congo 50B4
Moanda Gabon 50B4
Moate Irish Rep 9C3
Moba Zaïre 51C4
Mobara Japan 29D3
Mobaye CAR 50C3
Mobayi Zaïre 50C3
Moberly USA 57D3
Mobile USA 57E3
Mobile B USA 57E3
Mobile Pt USA 63E2
Mobridge USA 56C2
Moçambique Mozam 51E5
Moçâmedes = Namibe
Moc Chau Viet 30C1
Mocha = Al Mukhā
Mochudi Botswana 47D1
Mocimboa da Praia Mozam 51E5
Mocoa Colombia 72C3
Mococa Brazil 75C3
Mocuba Mozam 51D5
Modder, R S Africa 47D2
Modena Italy 16C2
Moder, R France 13D3
Modesto USA 56A3
Modesto Res USA 66B2
Modica, Sicily 16C3
Mödling Austria 18D3
Moffat Scot 8D4
Moga India 42D2
Mogadishu Somalia 50E3
Mogi das Cruzes Brazil 75C3
Mogilev USSR 19G2
Mogilev Podol'skiy USSR 21D6
Mogi-Mirim Brazil 75C3
Mogincual Mozam 51E5
Mogocha USSR 26E1
Mogochin USSR 24K4
Mogol, R S Africa 47D1
Moguer Spain 15A2
Mohaka, R NZ 35C1
Mohale's Hoek Lesotho 47D3
Mohall USA 60C1
Mohammadia Alg 15C2
Mohanganj Bang 43G4
Mohave,L USA 59D3
Mohawk USA 68C1
Mohawk, R USA 65E2
Mohéli, I Comoros 51E5
Mohoro Tanz 51D4
Mointy USSR 24J5
Mo i Rana Nor 12G5
Moissac France 14C3
Mojave USA 59C3
Mojave, R USA 66D3
Mojave Desert USA 56B3
Mokama India 43F3
Mokau, R NZ 35B1
Mokelumne, R USA 66B1
Mokelumne Aqueduct USA 66B1
Mokelumne Hill USA 66B1
Mokhotlong Lesotho 47D2
Moknine Tunisia 16C3
Mokokchūng India 43G3
Mokolo Cam 50B2
Mokp'o S Korea 28B4
Moksha, R USSR 20G5
Moláoi Greece 17E3
Mold Wales 7C3
Moldavian SSR, Republic USSR 21D6
Molde Nor 12F6
Moldoveanu, Mt Rom 17E1
Molepolole Botswana 47D1
Molesheim France 13D3
Molfetta Italy 16D2
Mollendo Peru 72D7
Molodechno USSR 20D5
Molodezhnaya, Base Ant 76G11
Molokai, I Hawaiian Is 66E5
Moloma, R USSR 20H4
Molong Aust 34C2
Molopo, R Botswana/S Africa 47C2
Molounddu Cam 50B3
Molson L Can 56D1
Molucca S Indon 32B1
Moluccas, Is Indon 27F7
Moma Mozam 51D5
Mombaça Brazil 73K5
Mombasa Kenya 50D4
Mombetsu Japan 29D2
Mombuca, Serra da, Mts Brazil 75B2
Mompono Zaïre 50C3
Mon, I Den 18C2
Monach Is Scot 8B3
Monaco, Principality Europe 14D3
Monadhliath Mts Scot 8C3
Monaghan Irish Rep 9C2
Monaghan, County Irish Rep 9C2
Monahans USA 62B2
Mona Pass Caribbean S 69D3
Monarch P USA 60B3
Monashee Mts Can 54G4
Monastereven Irish Rep 10B3
Monastir Tunisia 16C3
Monbetsu Japan 29D2
Monção Brazil 73J4
Monchegorsk USSR 12L5
Mönchen-gladbach W Germ 18B2
Monclova Mexico 70B2
Moncton Can 55M5
Mondego, R Port 15A1
Mondovi Italy 16B2
Moneague Jamaica 69H1
Monessen USA 65D2
Monett USA 63D1
Monfalcone Italy 16C1
Monforte de Lemos Spain 15A1
Monga Zaïre 50C3
Mongala, R Zaïre 50C3
Mongalla Sudan 50D3
Mong Cai Viet 30D1
Mongo Chad 50B2
Mongolia, Republic Asia 26C2
Mongu Zambia 51C5
Mönhhaan Mongolia 25N5
Moniaive Scot 8D4
Monitor Range, Mts USA 59C3
Monkoto Zaïre 50C4
Monmouth USA 64A2
Monmouth Wales 7C4
Mono, R Togo/Benin 48C4
Mono L USA 59C3
Monopoli Italy 17D2
Monreal del Campo Spain 15B1
Monroe, Louisiana USA 63D2
Monroe, Michigan USA 64C2
Monroe, N Carolina USA 67B2
Monroe, Washington USA 58B1
Monroe, Wisconsin USA 64B2
Monroe City USA 61E3
Monrovia Lib 48A4
Monrovia USA 66D3
Mons Belg 18A2
Monson USA 68D1
Mont, Monte : see also individual mt. name
Montagu S Africa 47C3
Montague I USA 54D4
Montaigu France 14B2
Montallo, Mt Italy 16D3
Montana, State USA 56B2
Montañas de León, Mts Spain 15A1
Montargis France 14C2
Montauban France 14C3
Montauk USA 65E2
Montauk Pt USA 65E2
Montbard France 13C4
Montbéliard France 14D2
Mont Blanc France/Italy 16B1
Montblanc Spain 15C1
Montceau-les-Mines France 14C2
Mont Cenis, Col du, P France/Italy 16B1
Montceny, Mt Spain 15C1
Montcornet France 13C3
Mont-de-Marsin France 14B3
Montdidier France 14C2
Monteagudo Bol 72F7
Monte Alegre Brazil 73H4
Monte Azul Brazil 75D2
Montebello Can 65D1
Monte Bello Is Aust 32A3
Monte Carlo Monaco 14D3
Monte Carmelo Brazil 75C2
Montecristi Dom Rep 69C3
Montecristo, I Italy 16C2
Montego Bay Jamaica 69H1
Montélimar France 14C3
Montelindo, R Par 75A3
Montemorelos Mexico 70C2
Montemor-o-Novo Port 15A2
Montenegro, Region Yugos 17D2
Montepuez Mozam 51D5
Montereau-Faut-Yonne France 13B3
Monterey, California USA 56A3
Monterey, Virginia USA 65D3
Monterey B USA 56A3
Montería Colombia 72C2
Montero Bol 72F7
Monterrey Mexico 70B2
Montes Claros Brazil 73K7
Montes de Toledo, Mts Spain 15B2
Montevideo Urug 74E4
Montevideo USA 61D2
Monte Vista USA 62A1
Montezuma USA 62B1
Montezuma Peak, Mt USA 66D2
Montgomery, Alabama USA 57E3
Montgomery, Pennsylvania USA 68B2
Montgomery Wales 7C3
Montgomery P USA 66C2
Monthermé France 13C3
Monticello, Arkansas USA 63D2
Monticello, Iowa USA 64A2
Monticello, Minnesota USA 61E1
Monticello, New York USA 68C2
Monticello, Utah USA 56C3
Montier-en-Der France 13C3
Mont-Laurier Can 55L5
Montluçon France 14C2
Montmagny Can 55L5
Montmédy France 13C3
Montmirail France 13B3
Montmorency Can 65E1
Montoro Spain 15B2
Montoursville USA 68B2
Montpelier, Idaho USA 58D2
Montpelier, Ohio USA 64C2
Montpelier, Vermont USA 57F2
Montpellier France 14C3
Montréal Can 55L5
Montreuil France 14C1
Montreux Switz 16B1
Montrose, Colorado USA 56C3
Montrose, Pennsylvania USA 68C2
Montrose Scot 10C2
Montrose, Oilfield N Sea 8F3
Mont-St-Michel France 14B2
Montserrat, I Caribbean S 69E3
Monument V USA 56B3
Monveda Zaïre 50C3
Monywa Burma 30B1
Monza Italy 16B1
Monze Zambia 51C5
Mooi, R S Africa 47E2
Mooi River S Africa 47D2
Moomba Aust 34B1
Moonbi Range, Mts Aust 34D2
Moonda L Aust 34B1
Moonie Aust 34D1
Moonie, R Aust 34C1
Moonta Aust 34A2
Moora Aust 32A4
Mooraberree Aust 34B1
Moorcroft USA 60C2
Moore,L Aust 32A3
Moorfoot Hills Scot 8D4
Moorhead USA 56D2
Moorpark USA 66C3
Moorreesburg S Africa 47B3
Moose, R Can 55K4
Moosehead L USA 65F1
Moose Jaw Can 54H4
Moose Lake USA 61E1
Moosomin Can 54H4
Moosonee Can 55K4
Moosup USA 68E2
Mopeia Mozam 51D5
Mopti Mali 48B3
Moquegua Peru 72D7
Mora Sweden 12G6
Mora USA 61E1
Moradabad India 42D3
Morada Nova Brazil 73L5
Morada Nova de Minas Brazil 75C2
Morafenobe Madag 51E5
Moramanga Madag 51E5
Moran USA 58D2
Morant Bay Jamaica 69J2
Morant Pt Jamaica 69J2
Morar, Loch, L Scot 8C3
Moratuwa Sri Lanka 44B4
Morava, R Austria/Czech 18D3
Morava, R Yugos 17E2
Moraveh Tappeh Iran 41G2
Moray Firth, Estuary Scot 10C2
Morbi India 42C4
Mor Dağ, Mt Turk 41D2
Morden Can 54J5
Mordovian ASSR, Republic USSR 20G5
Moreau, R USA 60C1
Morecambe Eng 7C2
Morecambe B Eng 7C2
Moree Aust 32D3
Morehead USA 64C3
Morehead City USA 67C2
Morelia Mexico 70B3
Morena India 42D3
Morena, Sierra, Mts Spain 15A2
Moresby I Can 54E4
Moreton I Aust 34D1
Moreuil France 13B3
Morgan City USA 63D3
Morgan Hill USA 66B2
Morgan,Mt USA 66C2
Morganton USA 67B1
Morgantown USA 65D3
Morgenzon S Africa 47D2
Morhange France 13D3
Mori Japan 29E2
Moriah Tobago 69K1
Moriarty USA 62A2
Morioka Japan 29E3
Morisset Aust 34D2
Morkoka, R USSR 25N3
Morlaix France 14B2
Morne Diablotin, Mt Dominica 69Q2
Morney Aust 34B1
Mornington, I Aust 32C2
Moro Pak 42B3
Morobe PNG 32D1
Morocco, Kingdom Africa 48B1
Moro G Phil 27F6
Morogoro Tanz 51D4
Morombe Madag 51E6
Morón Cuba 69B2
Morondava Madag 51E6
Moron de la Frontera Spain 15A2
Moroni Comoros 51E5
Morotai, I Indon 27F6
Moroto Uganda 50D3
Morozovsk USSR 21G6
Morpeth Eng 6D2
Morphou Cyprus 45B1
Morphou B Cyprus 45B1
Morrill USA 60C2
Morrilton USA 63D1
Morrinhos Brazil 75C2
Morrinsville NZ 35C1
Morris Can 61D1
Morris USA 61D1
Morristown, New Jersey USA 68C2
Morristown, New York USA 65D2
Morristown, Tennessee USA 67B1
Morrisville, New York USA 68C1
Morrisville, Pennsylvania USA 68C2
Morro Bay USA 66B3
Morrumbala Mozam 51D5
Morrumbene Mozam 51D6
Morshansk USSR 20G5
Mortes, R = Manso
Mortes, R, Mato Grosso Brazil 73H6
Mortes, R, Minas Gerais Brazil 75D3
Mortlake Aust 34B3
Morton USA 62B2
Moruga Trinidad 69L1
Moruya Aust 34D3
Morven Aust 34C1
Morvern, Pen Scot 8C3
Morwell Aust 34C3
Mosbach W Germ 13E3
Moscos Is Burma 30B3
Moscow, Idaho USA 58C1
Moscow, Pennsylvania USA 68C2
Moscow USSR 24E4
Mosel, R W Germ 18B2
Moselebe, R Botswana 47C2
Moselle, Department France 13D3
Moselle, R France 13D3
Moses Lake USA 58C1
Mosgiel NZ 35B3
Moshi Tanz 50D4
Mosinee USA 64B2
Mosjøen Nor 12G5
Moskal'vo USSR 25Q4
Moskva = Moscow
Mosquero USA 62B1
Mosquito, R Brazil 75D2

Namsos Nicoya,Pen de

Namsos *Nor* 12G6
Namton *Burma* 30B1
Namtsy *USSR* 25O3
Namuno *Mozam* 51D5
Namur *Belg* 13C2
Namutoni *Namibia* 51B5
Nanaimo *Can* 56A2
Nanam *N Korea* 28B2
Nanango *Aust* 34D1
Nanao *Japan* 29D3
Nanatsu-jima, I *Japan* 29C3
Nanbu *China* 31B3
Nanchang *China* 31D4
Nanchong *China* 31B3
Nancowry, I, Nicobar Is *Indian O* 44E4
Nancy *France* 14D2
Nanda Devi, Mt *India* 43E2
Nānded *India* 44B2
Nandewar Range, Mts *Aust* 34D2
Nandurbār *India* 42C4
Nandyāl *India* 44B2
Nanga Eboko *Cam* 50B3
Nanga Parbat, Mt *Pak* 42C1
Nangapinoh *Indon* 27E7
Nangis *France* 13B3
Nangnim *N Korea* 28A2
Nangnim Sanmaek, Mts *N Korea* 28B2
Nang Xian *China* 43G3
Nanjangūd *India* 44B3
Nanjing *China* 31D3
Nanking = Nanjing
Nankoku *Japan* 29B4
Nan Ling, Region *China* 31C4
Nanliu, R *China* 30D1
Nanning *China* 31B5
Nanortalik *Greenland* 55O3
Nanpan Jiang, R *China* 31A5
Nānpāra *India* 43E3
Nanping *China* 31D4
Nanping *China* 28B2
Nansen Sd *Can* 55J1
Nanshan, I *S China Sea* 27E5
Nansio *Tanz* 50D4
Nantes *France* 14B2
Nanticoke *USA* 68C2
Nantong *China* 31E3
Nantucket *USA* 68E2
Nantucket I *USA* 68E2
Nantucket Sd *USA* 68E2
Nantwich *Eng* 7C3
Nanumanga, I *Tuvalu* 33G1
Nanumea, I *Tuvalu* 33G1
Nanuque *Brazil* 75D2
Nanyang *China* 31C3
Nanyang Hu, L *China* 31D2
Nanyuki *Kenya* 50D3
Nanzamu *China* 28A2
Nao, Cabo de la, C *Spain* 15C2
Naoetsu *Japan* 29D3
Naokot *Pak* 42B4
Napa *USA* 66A1
Napanee *Can* 65D2
Napas *USSR* 24K4
Napassoq *Greenland* 55N3
Nape *Laos* 30D2
Napier *NZ* 35C1
Naples, Florida *USA* 67B3
Naples *Italy* 16C2
Naples, New York *USA* 68B1
Naples, Texas *USA* 63D2
Napo *China* 31B5
Napo, R *Ecuador/Peru* 72D4
Napoleon *USA* 60D1
Napoli = Naples
Naqadeh *Iran* 41E2
Naqb Ishtar *Jordan* 45C3
Nara *Japan* 29C4
Nara *Mali* 48B3
Naracoorte *Aust* 32D4
Narasarāopet *India* 44B2
Narathiwat *Thai* 30C4
Narayanganj *Bang* 43G4
Nārāyenpet *India* 44B2
Narbonne *France* 14C3
Narcondam, I *Indian O* 30A3
Narendranagar *India* 42D2
Nares Str *Can* 55L2
Narew, R *Pol* 19E2
Narhong *China* 28B2
Narita *Japan* 29D3
Narmada, R *India* 42C4
Nārnaul *India* 42D3
Naro Fominsk *USSR* 20F4
Narok *Kenya* 50D4
Narovl'a *USSR* 19F2
Narowal *Pak* 42C2
Narrabri *Aust* 32D4
Narran, R *Aust* 34C1
Narrandera *Aust* 34C2
Narran L *Aust* 34C1
Narrogin *Aust* 32A4
Narromine *Aust* 34C2
Narrows *USA* 64C3
Narrowsburg *USA* 68C2
Narsimhapur *India* 42D4
Narsipatnam *India* 44C2
Narssalik *Greenland* 55O3
Narssaq *Greenland* 55O3
Narssarssuaq *Greenland* 55O3
Narubis *Namibia* 47B2
Narugo *Japan* 29D3
Naruto *Japan* 29B4
Narva *USSR* 20D4
Narvik *Nor* 12H5
Narwana *India* 42D3
Nar'yan Mar *USSR* 20J2
Narylico *Aust* 34B1
Naryn *USSR* 24J5
Nasarawa *Nigeria* 48C4
Nasca Ridge *Pacific O* 52D6
Nashua *USA* 68E1
Nashville, Arkansas *USA* 63D2
Nashville, Tennessee *USA* 67A1
Našice *Yugos* 17D1
Nasik *India* 42C4
Nasir *Sudan* 50D3
Nassau *The Bahamas* 69B1
Nassau *USA* 68D1
Nasser,L *Egypt* 49F2
Nässjö *Sweden* 12G7
Nastapoka Is *Can* 55L4
Nata *Botswana* 51C6
Natal *Brazil* 73L5
Natal *Indon* 27C6
Natal, Province *S Africa* 47E2
Natal Basin *Indian O* 36C6
Natanz *Iran* 41F3
Natashquan *Can* 55M4
Natashquan, R *Can* 55M4
Natchez *USA* 63D2
Natchitoches *USA* 63D2
Nathalia *Aust* 34C3
Nathorsts Land, Region *Greenland* 55Q2
National City *USA* 59C4
Natori *Japan* 29D3
Natron, L *Tanz* 50D4
Natrun, Wadi el, Watercourse *Egypt* 40A3
Naturaliste,C *Aust* 32A4
Nauen *E Germ* 18C2
Naugatuck *USA* 68D2
Naumburg *E Germ* 18C2
Naur *Jordan* 45C3
Nauru, I, Republic *Pacific O* 33F1
Naushki *USSR* 25M4
Naute Dam, Res *Namibia* 47B2
Navajo Res *USA* 56C3
Navalmoral de la Mata *Spain* 15A2
Navarin, Mys, C *USSR* 25T3
Navarino, I *Chile* 74C9
Navarra, Province *Spain* 15B1
Navasota *USA* 63C2
Navasota, R *USA* 63C2
Naver, L *Scot* 8C2
Navia, R *Spain* 15A1
Naviraí *Brazil* 75B3
Navlakhi *India* 42C4
Navlya *USSR* 21E5
Navojoa *Mexico* 70B2
Návpaktos *Greece* 17E3
Návplion *Greece* 17E3
Navsāri *India* 42C4
Nawá *Syria* 45D2
Nawabshah *Pak* 42B3
Nawāda *India* 43F4
Nawah *Afghan* 42B2
Naxi *China* 31B4
Náxos, I *Greece* 17F3
Nay Band *Iran* 41F4
Nay Band *Iran* 41G3
Nayoro *Japan* 29E2
Nazaré *Brazil* 75E1
Nazareth *Israel* 45C2
Nazca *Peru* 72D6
Nazilli *Turk* 40A2
Nazimovo *USSR* 25L4
Nazwá' *Oman* 41G5
Nazyvayevsk *USSR* 24J4
Ndalatando *Angola* 51B4
Ndélé *CAR* 50C3
Ndendé *Gabon* 50B4
Ndende, I *Solomon Is* 33F2
Ndjamena *Chad* 50B2
Ndjolé *Gabon* 50B4
Ndola *Zambia* 51C5
Neabul *Aust* 34C1
Neagh, Lough, L *N Ire* 10B3
Neápolis *Greece* 17E3
Neath *Wales* 7C4
Nebine, R *Aust* 34C1
Nebit Dag *USSR* 24G6
Nebraska, State *USA* 56C2
Nebraska City *USA* 61D2
Nebrodi, Monti, Mts, Sicily 16C3
Neches, R *USA* 63C2
Necochea *Arg* 74E5
Nêdong *China* 43G3
Needham Market *Eng* 7E3
Needles *USA* 59D4
Needles, Pt *Eng* 7D4
Neenah *USA* 64B2
Neepawa *Can* 54J4
Neerpelt *Belg* 13C2
Neftelensk *USSR* 25M4
Negele *Eth* 50D3
Negev, Desert *Israel* 45C3
Negla, R *Par* 75A3
Negolu, Mt *Rom* 21C6
Negombo *Sri Lanka* 44B4
Negrais,C *Burma* 30A2
Negritos *Peru* 72B4
Negro, R, Amazonas *Brazil* 72F4
Negro, R *Arg* 74D5
Negro, R, Mato Grosso do Sul *Brazil* 75A2
Negro, R *Par* 75A3
Negro, R *Urug/Brazil* 74F4
Negro, Cap, C *Mor* 15A2
Negros, I *Phil* 27F6
Negru Vodă *Rom* 17F2
Neijiang *China* 31B4
Neillsville *USA* 64A2
Nei Mongol Zizhiqu = Inner Mongolia Aut. Region
Neiva *Colombia* 72C3
Nejo *Eth* 50D3
Nelidovo *USSR* 20E4
Neligh *USA* 61D2
Nellore *India* 44B3
Nel'ma *USSR* 26G2
Nelson *Can* 54G5
Nelson *Eng* 6C3
Nelson *NZ* 35B2
Nelson,C *Aust* 34B3
Nelspruit *S Africa* 47E2
Néma *Maur* 48B3
Nemagt Uul, Mt *Mongolia* 31A1
Neman, R *USSR* 19E1
Nementcha, Mts Des *Algeria* 16B3
Nemira, Mt *Rom* 17F1
Nemours *France* 13B3
Nemuro *Japan* 29F2
Nemuro-kaikyo, Str *USSR/Japan* 29F2
Nen, R *China* 25O5
Nenagh *Irish Rep* 10B3
Nenana *USA* 54D3
Nene, R *Eng* 7D3
Nenjiang *China* 26F2
Neodesha *USA* 63C1
Neosho *USA* 63D1
Nepa *USSR* 25M4
Nepal, Kingdom *Asia* 39G3
Nepalganj *Nepal* 43E3
Nephi *USA* 59D3
Neqarot, R *Israel* 45C3
Nerchinsk *USSR* 26E1
Neretva, R *Yugos* 17D2
Nero Deep *Pacific O* 27H5
Nes' *USSR* 20G2
Neskaupstaur *Iceland* 12C1
Nesle *France* 13B3
Ness City *USA* 62C1
Ness, Loch, L *Scot* 8C3
Néstos, R *Greece* 17E2
Netanya *Israel* 45C2
Netcong *USA* 68C2
Netherlands, Kingdom *Europe* 18B2
Netherlands Antilles, Is *Caribbean S* 53M7
Netrakona *Bang* 43G4
Nettilling L *Can* 55L3
Neubrandenburg *E Germ* 18C2
Neuchâtel *Switz* 16B1
Neufchâteau *Belg* 13C3
Neufchâteau *France* 13C3
Neufchâtel *France* 14C2
Neumünster *W Germ* 18B2
Neunkirchen *Austria* 16D1
Neunkirchen *W Germ* 13D3
Neuquén *Arg* 74C5
Neuquén, R *Arg* 74C5
Neuquén, State *Arg* 74B5
Neuruppin *E Germ* 18C2
Neuse, R *USA* 67C1
Neuss *W Germ* 13D2
Neustadt *W Germ* 18C2
Neustadt an der Weinstrasse *W Germ* 13E3
Neustadt a R *W Germ* 13E1
Neustadt im Schwarzwald *W Germ* 13E4
Neustrelitz *E Germ* 18C2
Neuwerk, I *W Germ* 13E1
Neuwied *W Germ* 13D2
Nevada *USA* 63D1
Nevada, State *USA* 56B3
Nevada, Sierra, Mts *Spain* 15B2
Nevatim *Israel* 45C3
Nevel' *USSR* 20D4
Nevers *France* 14C2
Nevertire *Aust* 34C2
Nevis, I *Caribbean S* 69E3
Nevis, R *USSR* 19F2
Nevşehir *Turk* 40B2
Nev'yansk *USSR* 20L4
New, R *USA* 64C3
Newala *Tanz* 51D5
New Albany, Indiana *USA* 64B3
New Albany, Mississippi *USA* 63E2
New Amsterdam *Guyana* 73G2
New Angledool *Aust* 34C1
Newark, Delaware *USA* 65D3
Newark, New Jersey *USA* 57F2
Newark, New York *USA* 68B1
Newark, Ohio *USA* 64C2
Newark-upon-Trent *Eng* 7D3
New Bedford *USA* 65E2
Newberg *USA* 58B1
New Bern *USA* 67C1
Newberry *USA* 67B2
New Bethesda *S Africa* 47C3
New Bight *The Bahamas* 69B2
New Boston *USA* 64C3
New Braunfels *USA* 62C3
New Britain *USA* 68D2
New Britain, I *PNG* 32E1
New Britain Trench *PNG* 32E1
New Brunswick *USA* 68C2
New Brunswick, Province *Can* 55M5
Newburgh *USA* 68C2
Newbury *Eng* 7D4
Newburyport *USA* 68E1
New Caledonia, I *S W Pacific O* 33F3
New Canaan *USA* 68D2
Newcastle *Aust* 34D2
New Castle, Indiana *USA* 64B3
Newcastle *N Ire* 9D2
New Castle, Pennsylvania *USA* 64C2
Newcastle *S Africa* 47D2
Newcastle, Wyoming *USA* 60C2
New Castleton *Scot* 8D4
Newcastle under Lyme *Eng* 7C3
Newcastle upon Tyne *Eng* 6D2
Newcastle Waters *Aust* 32C2
New Cuyama *USA* 66C3
New Delhi *India* 42D3
New England Range, Mts *Aust* 34D2
Newfane *USA* 68A1
New Forest,The *Eng* 7D4
Newfoundland, I *Can* 55N5
Newfoundland, Province *Can* 55M4
Newfoundland Basin *Atlantic O* 52F2
New Franklin *USA* 61E3
New Galloway *Scot* 8C4
New Georgia, I *Solomon Is* 33E1
New Glasgow *Can* 55M5
New Guinea, I *S E Asia* 32D1
Newhall *USA* 66C3
New Hampshire, State *USA* 57F2
New Hampton *USA* 61E2
New Hanover *S Africa* 47E2
New Hanover, I *PNG* 32E1
Newhaven *Eng* 7E4
New Haven *USA* 65E2
New Hebrides Trench *Pacific O* 33F3
New Iberia *USA* 63D2
New Ireland, I *PNG* 32E1
New Jersey, State *USA* 57F2
Newkirk *USA* 62B2
New Liskeard *Can* 55L5
New London *USA* 68D2
Newman *Aust* 32A3
Newman *USA* 66B2
Newmarket *Eng* 7E3
New Market *USA* 65D3
New Meadows *USA* 58C2
New Mexico, State *USA* 56C3
New Milford, Connecticut *USA* 68D2
New Milford, New York *USA* 68C2
Newnan *USA* 67B2
New Norfolk *Aust* 34C4
New Orleans *USA* 57D3
New Paltz *USA* 68C2
New Philadelphia *USA* 64C2
New Plymouth *NZ* 35B1
Newport, Arkansas *USA* 63D1
Newport *Eng* 7D4
Newport, Kentucky *USA* 64C3
Newport, New Hampshire *USA* 68D1
Newport, Oregon *USA* 58B2
Newport, Pennsylvania *USA* 68B2
Newport, Rhode Island *USA* 65E2
Newport, Vermont *USA* 65E2
Newport *Wales* 7C4
Newport, Washington *USA* 58C1
Newport Beach *USA* 66D4
Newport News *USA* 57F3
New Providence, I *The Bahamas* 69B1
Newquay *Eng* 7B4
New Quay *Wales* 7B3
New Quebec Crater *Can* 55L3
New Radnor *Wales* 7C3
New Romney *Eng* 7E4
New Ross *Irish Rep* 9C3
Newry *N Ire* 9C2
New Siberian Is = Novosibirskye Ostrova
New Smyrna Beach *USA* 67B3
New South Wales, State *Aust* 32D4
Newton, Iowa *USA* 61E2
Newton, Kansas *USA* 63C1
Newton, Massachusetts *USA* 68E1
Newton, Mississippi *USA* 63E2
Newton, New York *USA* 68C2
Newtonabbey *N Ire* 9D2
Newton Abbot *Eng* 7C4
Newton Stewart *N Ire* 9C2
Newton Stewart *Scot* 8C4
New Town *USA* 60C1
Newtown *Wales* 7C3
Newtownards *N Ire* 9D2
New Ulm *USA* 61E2
Newville *USA* 68B2
New Westminster *Can* 54F5
New York *USA* 57F2
New York, State *USA* 57F2
New Zealand, Dominion *SW Pacific O* 33G5
New Zealand Plat *Pacific O* 37K7
Neya *USSR* 20G4
Neyrız *Iran* 41F4
Neyshabur *Iran* 41G2
Nezeto *Angola* 51B4
Nezhin *USSR* 21E5
Ngabé *Congo* 50B4
Ngami, L *Botswana* 51C6
Ngaoundéré *Cam* 49D4
Ngape *Burma* 30A1
Ngaruawahia *NZ* 35C1
Ngaruroro, R *NZ* 35C1
Ngauruhoe,Mt *NZ* 35C1
Ngo *Congo* 50B4
Ngoc Linh, Mt *Viet* 30D2
Ngoko, R *Cam/Congo/CAR* 50B3
Ngoring Hu, L *China* 26C3
Ngorongoro Crater *Tanz* 50D4
N'Gounié, R *Gabon* 50B4
Nguigmi *Niger* 50B2
Ngulu, I *Pacific O* 27G6
Nguru *Nigeria* 48D3
Nha Trang *Viet* 30D3
Nhecolândia *Brazil* 75A2
Nhill *Aust* 34B3
Nhlangano *Swaziland* 47E2
Nhommarath *Laos* 30D2
Nhulunbuy *Aust* 32C2
Niafounké *Mali* 48B3
Niagara *USA* 64B1
Niagara Falls *Can* 65D2
Niagara Falls *USA* 65D2
Niah *Malay* 27E6
Niakaramandougou *Ivory Coast* 48B4
Niamey *Niger* 48C3
Niangara *Zaïre* 50C3
Nia Nia *Zaïre* 50C3
Niapa, Mt *Indon* 27E6
Nias, I *Indon* 27C6
Nicaragua, Republic *Cent America* 70D3
Nicaragua, L de *Nic* 70D3
Nicastro *Italy* 16D3
Nice *France* 14D3
Nicholl's Town *The Bahamas* 69B1
Nicholson *USA* 68C2
Nicobar Is *India* 39H5
Nicosia *Cyprus* 45B1
Nicoya, Golfo de *Costa Rica* 72A2
Nicoya,Pen de *Costa Rica* 70D3

Nidd Nyssa

Nidd, R *Eng* 6D2
Nidda, R *W Germ* 13E2
Nidzica *Pol* 19E2
Niederbronn *France* 13D3
Niedersachsen, State *W Germ* 18B2
Niemba *Zaïre* 50C4
Nienburg *W Germ* 18B2
Niers, R *W Germ* 13D2
Niete,Mt *Lib* 48B4
Nieuw Amsterdam *Surinam* 73G2
Nieuw Nickerie *Surinam* 73G2
Nieuwoudtville *S Africa* 47B3
Nieuwpoort *Belg* 13B2
Niğde *Turk* 40B2
Niger, R *W Africa* 48B3
Niger, Republic *Africa* 48C3
Nigeria, Federal Republic *Africa* 48C4
Niger, Mouths of the *Nig* 48C4
Nighasan *India* 43L1
Nighthawk L *Can* 64C1
Nigríta *Greece* 17E2
Nihommatsu *Japan* 29D3
Niigata *Japan* 29D3
Niihama *Japan* 29C4
Nii-jima, I *Japan* 29C4
Niimi *Japan* 29B4
Niitsu *Japan* 29D3
Nijil *Jordan* 45C3
Nijmegen *Neth* 18B2
Nikel' *USSR* 20E2
Nikki *Benin* 48C4
Nikko *Japan* 29D3
Nikolayev *USSR* 21E6
Nikolayevsk *USSR* 21H6
Nikolayevsk-na-Amure *USSR* 25Q4
Nikol'sk, Penza *USSR* 20H5
Nikol'sk, RSFSR *USSR* 20H4
Nikopol *USSR* 21E6
Niksar *Turk* 40C1
Nikšić *Yugos* 17D2
Nikunau, I *Kiribati* 33G1
Nila, I *Indon* 27F7
Nile, R *N E Africa* 38B3
Niles *USA* 64B2
Nilgiri Hills *India* 44B3
Nimach *India* 42C4
Nîmes *France* 14C3
Nimmitabel *Aust* 34C3
Nimule *Sudan* 50D3
Nine Degree Chan *Indian O* 39F5
Ninety-East Ridge *Indian O* 36F5
Ninety Mile Beach *Aust* 34C3
Ningde *China* 31D4
Ningdu *China* 31D4
Ningjing Shan, Mts *China* 26C3
Ningming *China* 30D1
Ningnan *China* 31A4
Ningxia, Province *China* 31B2
Ning Xian *China* 31B2
Ninh Binh *Vietnam* 31B5
Ninigo Is *PNG* 32D1
Nioaque *Brazil* 75A3
Niobrara, R *USA* 60C2
Niobrara, R *USA* 56D2
Nioki *Zaïre* 50B4
Nioro du Sahel *Mali* 48B3
Niort *France* 14B2
Nipawin *Can* 54H4
Nipigon *Can* 55K5
Nipigon B *Can* 64B1
Nipigon,L *Can* 55K5
Nipissing, L *Can* 55K5
Nipissing,L *Can* 64C1
Nipomo *USA* 66B3
Nipton *USA* 59C3
Niquelândia *Brazil* 75C1
Nirmal *India* 44B2
Nirmāli *India* 43F3
Niš *Yugos* 17E2
Nişāb *S Yemen* 38C4
Nishino-shima, I *Japan* 26H4
Nishino-shima, I *Japan* 28B3
Nishi-suidō, Str *S Korea* 28A4
Nishiwaki *Japan* 29B4
Nissan Is *PNG* 33E1
Nitchequon *Can* 55L4
Niterói *Brazil* 73K8
Nith, R *Scot* 8D4
Nitra *Czech* 19D3
Nitro *USA* 64C3
Niue, I *Pacific O* 33J2
Niulakita, I *Tuvalu* 33G2
Niut, Mt *Indon* 27E6
Niutao, I *Tuvalu* 33G1
Niuzhuang *China* 28A2
Nivelles *Belg* 13C2
Nivernais, Region *France* 14C2
Nivskiy *USSR* 12L5
Nizāmābād *India* 44B2
Nizana, Hist Site *Israel* 45C3
Nizhneudinsk *USSR* 26C1
Nizhniye Sergi *USSR* 20K4
Nizhniy Lomov *USSR* 20G5
Nizhniy Odes *USSR* 20J3
Nizhniy Tagil *USSR* 24G4
Nizhnyaya, R *USSR* 25L3
Nizhnyaya Zolotitsa *USSR* 20G2
Nizip *Turk* 40C2
Njarðvik *Iceland* 12C1
Njoko, R *Zambia* 51C5
Njombe *Tanz* 51D4
Nkambé *Cam* 50B3
Nkhata Bay *Malawi* 51D5
Nkongsamba *Cam* 50B3
N'Konni *Niger* 48C3
Noakhali *Bang* 43G4
Noatak *USA* 54B3
Noatak, R *USA* 54B3
Nobeoka *Japan* 28C4
Noboribetsu *Japan* 29D2
Nobres *Brazil* 75A1
Nocona *USA* 63C2
Nogales, Sonora *Mexico* 70A1
Nogales *USA* 59D4
Nogata *Japan* 28B4
Nogent-en-Bassigny *France* 13C3
Nogent-sur-Seine *France* 13B3
Noginsk *USSR* 20F4
Nohar *India* 42C3
Noheji *Japan* 29D2
Noirmoutier, Ile de, I *France* 14B2
Nojane *Botswana* 47C1
Nojima-zaki, C *Japan* 29C4
Nola *CAR* 50B3
Nolinsk *USSR* 20H4
Nomans Land, I *USA* 68E2
Nome *USA* 54B3
Nomeny *France* 13D3
Nomgon *Mongolia* 31B1
Nomo-saki, Pt *Japan* 28A4
Nonacho L *Can* 54H3
Nong Khai *Thai* 30C2
Nongoma *S Africa* 47E2
Nonouti, I *Kiribati* 33G1
Nonsan *S Korea* 28A3
Noord Holland, Province *Neth* 13C1
Noordoewer *Namibia* 47B2
Noordoost Polder *Neth* 13C1
Noordzeekanal *Neth* 13C1
Noorvik *USA* 54B3
Noqui *Angola* 50B4
Noranda *Can* 55L5
Nord, Department *France* 13B2
Nordaustlandet, I *Svalbard* 24D2
Norden *W Germ* 13D1
Nordenham *W Germ* 13E1
Norderney, I *W Germ* 13D1
Nordfjord, Inlet *Nor* 12F6
Nordfriesische, Is *W Germ* 12F8
Nordhausen *E Germ* 18C2
Nordhorn *W Germ* 13D1
Nordrhein Westfalen, State *W Germ* 18B2
Nordkapp, C *Nor* 12J4
Nordre Strømfyord, Fyord *Greenland* 55N3
Nord Storfjället, Mt *Sweden* 12G5
Nordvik *USSR* 25N2
Nore, R *Irish Rep* 9C3
Norfolk, Nebraska *USA* 61D2
Norfolk, Virginia *USA* 65D3
Norfolk, County *Eng* 7E3
Norfolk I *Pacific O* 33F3
Norfolk I Ridge *Pacific O* 37K6
Norfolk L *USA* 63D1
Noril'sk *USSR* 25K3
Normal *USA* 64B2
Norman *USA* 63C1
Normandie, Region *France* 14B2
Norman,L *USA* 67B1
Normanton *Aust* 32D2
Norman Wells *Can* 54F3
Norra Storfjället, Mt *Sweden* 20B2
Norris L *USA* 67B1
Norristown *USA* 65D2
Norrköping *Sweden* 12H7
Norrsundet *Sweden* 12H6
Norrtälje *Sweden* 12H7
Norseman *Aust* 32B4
Norsk *USSR* 26G1
Nortelândia *Brazil* 75A1
Northallerton *Eng* 6D2
Northam *Aust* 32A4
Northam *S Africa* 47D2
North American Basin *Atlantic O* 52E3
Northampton *Aust* 32A3
Northampton *Eng* 7D3
Northampton *USA* 65E2
Northampton, County *Eng* 7D3
North Andaman, I *Indian O* 44E3
North Arm, B *Can* 54G3
North Augusta *USA* 67B2
North Aulatsivik, I *Can* 55M4
North Battleford *Can* 54H4
North Bay *Can* 55L5
North Bend *USA* 58B2
North Berwick *Scot* 8D3
North Berwick *USA* 68E1
North,C *Can* 55M5
North Canadian, R *USA* 62B1
North Carolina, State *USA* 57E3
North Cascades Nat Pk *USA* 58B1
North Chan *Can* 64C1
North Chan *Ire/Scot* 6B2
North Dakota, State *USA* 56C2
North Downs *Eng* 7E4
North East *USA* 65D2
North East Atlantic Basin *Atlantic O* 52H2
Northeast C *USA* 54B3
Northern Ireland *UK* 10B3
Northern Light L *Can/USA* 61E1
Northern Marianas, Is *Pacific O* 27H5
Northern Range, Mts *Trinidad* 69L1
Northern Territory *Aust* 32C2
North Esk, R *Scot* 8D3
Northfield, Massachusetts *USA* 68D1
Northfield, Minnesota *USA* 61E2
North Foreland *Eng* 7E4
North I *NZ* 35B1
North Korea, Republic *SE Asia* 28B3
North Land = Severnaya Zemlya
North Little Rock *USA* 63D2
North Loup, R *USA* 60C2
North Magnetic Pole *Can* 76B4
North Miami *USA* 67B3
North Miami Beach *USA* 67B3
North Palisade, Mt *USA* 66C2
North Platte *USA* 60C2
North Platte, R *USA* 56C2
North Pole *Arctic* 76A
North Pt *Barbados* 69R3
North Pt *USA* 64C1
North Raccoon, R *USA* 61E2
North Rona, I *Scot* 10B2
North Ronaldsay, I *Scot* 8D2
North Scotia Ridge *Atlantic O* 52F7
North Sea *N W Europe* 10D2
North Sentinel, I *Andaman Is* 44E3
North Slope, Region *USA* 54D3
North Stradbroke I *Aust* 34D1
North Syracuse *USA* 68B1
North Taranaki Bight, B *NZ* 35B1
North Tonawanda *USA* 68A1
North Truchas Peak, Mt *USA* 56C3
North Uist, I *Scot* 8B3
Northumberland, County *Eng* 6C2
Northumberland Is *Aust* 32E3
Northumberland Str *Can* 55M5
North Vancouver *Can* 58B1
Northville *USA* 68C1
North Walsham *Eng* 7E3
Northway *USA* 54D3
North West C *Aust* 32A3
North West Frontier Province *Pak* 42C2
North West River *Can* 55M4
North West Territories *Can* 54G3
Northwood *USA* 61D1
North York Moors *Eng* 6D2
North Yorkshire, County *Eng* 6D2
Norton, R *USA* 60D3
Norton Sd *USA* 54B3
Norvegia,C *Ant* 76F1
Norwalk, Connecticut *USA* 68D2
Norwalk, Ohio *USA* 64C2
Norway, Kingdom *Europe* 12F6
Norway House *Can* 54J4
Norwegian B *Can* 55J2
Norwegian Basin *Norwegian S* 52H1
Norwegian S *N W Europe* 24B3
Norwich, Connecticut *USA* 68D2
Norwich *Eng* 7E3
Norwich, New York *USA* 68C1
Norwood, Massachusetts *USA* 68E1
Norwood, Ohio *USA* 64C3
Nos Emine, C *Bulg* 17F2
Noshiro *Japan* 29E2
Nos Kaliakra, C *Bulg* 17F2
Nosob, R *Namibia* 47B1
Nosovaya *USSR* 20J2
Nosovka *USSR* 19G2
Noss, I *Scot* 8E1
Noss Head, Pt *Scot* 8D2
Nosy Barren, I *Madag* 51E5
Nosy Bé, I *Madag* 51E5
Nosy Boraha, I *Madag* 51F5
Nosy Varika *Madag* 51E6
Notéc, R *Pol* 18D2
Notikewin *Can* 54G4
Noto *Italy* 16D3
Notodden *Nor* 12F7
Noto-hanto, Pen *Japan* 29C3
Notre Dame B *Can* 55N5
Notsé *Togo* 48C4
Nottingham *Eng* 7D3
Nottingham, County *Eng* 7D3
Nottingham, I *Can* 55L3
Nottingham Island *Can* 55L3
Nouadhibou *Maur* 48A2
Nouakchott *Maur* 48A3
Nouméa *New Caledonia* 33F3
Nouna *Burkina* 48B3
Noup Head, Pt *Scot* 8D2
Noupoort *S Africa* 47C3
Nouvelle-France, Cap de, C *Can* 55L3
Nova América *Brazil* 75C2
Nova Caipemba *Angola* 51B4
Nova Chaves *Angola* 51C5
Nova Esperança *Brazil* 75B3
Nova Friburgo *Brazil* 75D3
Nova Gaia *Angola* 51B5
Nova Granada *Brazil* 75C3
Nova Horizonte *Brazil* 75C3
Nova Lima *Brazil* 75D3
Nova Lisboa = Huambo
Nova Londrina *Brazil* 75B3
Nova Mambone *Mozam* 51D6
Novara *Italy* 16B1
Nova Roma *Brazil* 75C1
Nova Russas *Brazil* 73K4
Nova Scotia, Province *Can* 55M5
Novato *USA* 66A1
Nova Venécia *Brazil* 75D2
Novaya Kakhovka *USSR* 21E6
Novaya Sibir, Ostrov, I *USSR* 25R2
Novaya Zemlya, I *USSR* 24G2
Nova Zagora *Bulg* 17F2
Nové Zámky *Czech* 17D1
Novgorod *USSR* 20E4
Novi Ligure *Italy* 16B2
Novi Pazar *Bulg* 17F2
Novi Pazar *Yugos* 17E2
Novi Sad *Yugos* 17D1
Novoalekseyevka *USSR* 21K5
Novoanninskiy *USSR* 21G5
Novocherkassk *USSR* 21F6
Novodvinsk *USSR* 20G3
Novograd Volynskiy *USSR* 21D5
Novogrudok *USSR* 19F2
Novo Hamburgo *Brazil* 74F3
Novokazalinsk *USSR* 24H5
Novokuznetsk *USSR* 24K4
Novolazarevskaya, Base *Ant* 76F12
Novo Mesto *Yugos* 16D1
Novomirgorod *USSR* 19G3
Novomoskovsk *USSR* 20F5
Novo Redondo = Sumbe
Novorossiysk *USSR* 21F7
Novorybnoye *USSR* 25M2
Novosibirsk *USSR* 24K4
Novosibirskye Ostrova, Is *USSR* 25P2
Novotroitsk *USSR* 21K5
Novo Uzensk *USSR* 21H5
Novovolynsk *USSR* 19E2
Novo Vyatsk *USSR* 20H4
Novozybkov *USSR* 21E5
Novvy Port *USSR* 24J3
Novy Dwór Mazowiecki *Pol* 19E2
Novyy Lyalya *USSR* 20L4
Novyy Port *USSR* 20N2
Novyy Uzen *USSR* 21J7
Nowa Sól *Pol* 18D2
Nowata *USA* 63C1
Nowgong *India* 43G3
Nowra *Aust* 34D2
Now Shahr *Iran* 41F2
Nowshera *Pak* 42C2
Nowy Sącz *Pol* 19E3
Noyon *France* 13B3
Nozay *France* 14B2
Nsawam *Ghana* 48B4
Nuanetsi *Zim* 47E1
Nuba Mts *Sudan* 50D2
Nubian Desert *Sudan* 50D1
Nueces, R *USA* 56D4
Nueltin L *Can* 54J3
Nü'erhe *China* 28A2
Nueva Casas Grandes *Mexico* 70B1
Nueva Germania *Par* 75A3
Nueva Gerona *Cuba* 69A2
Nueva Laredo *Mexico* 56C4
Nueva Rosita *Mexico* 70B2
Nuevitas *Cuba* 69B2
Nuevo Casas Grandes *Mexico* 70B1
Nuevo Laredo *Mexico* 70C2
Nugaal, Region *Somalia* 50E3
Nûgâtsiaq *Greenland* 55N2
Nûgussuaq, I *Greenland* 55N2
Nûgussuaq, Pen *Greenland* 55N2
Nui, I *Tuvalu* 33G1
Nui Con Voi, R *Vietnam* 31A5
Nuits *France* 13C4
Nukhayb *Iraq* 40D3
Nukufetau, I *Tuvalu* 33G1
Nukulaelae, I *Tuvalu* 33G1
Nukunon, I *Tokelau Is* 33H1
Nukus *USSR* 24G5
Nulato *USA* 54C3
Nullarbor Plain *Aust* 32B4
Numan *Nigeria* 48D4
Numata *Japan* 29C3
Numatinna, R *Sudan* 50C3
Numazu *Japan* 29D3
Numfoor, I *Indon* 27G7
Numurkah *Aust* 34C3
Nunda *USA* 68A1
Nuneaton *Eng* 7D3
Nunkun, Mt *India* 42D2
Nuoro, Sicily 16B2
Nurabad *Iran* 41F3
Nuriootpa *Aust* 34A2
Nuristan, Region *Afghan* 42C1
Nurlat *USSR* 20J5
Nurmes *Fin* 12K6
Nürnberg *W Germ* 18C3
Nurri,Mt *Aust* 34C2
Nusaybin *Turk* 40D2
Nuşayrıyah, Jabalan, Mts *Syria* 45D1
Nushki *Pak* 42B3
Nutak *Can* 55M4
Nuuk = Godthåb
Nuwakot *Nepal* 43E3
Nuwara-Eliya *Sri Lanka* 44C4
Nuweveldreeks, Mts *S Africa* 47C3
Nuyukjuak *Can* 55L3
Nyac *USA* 54C3
Nyack *USA* 68D2
Nyahururu Falls *Kenya* 50D3
Nyah West *Aust* 34B3
Nyainqentanglha Shan, Mts, Tibet *China* 26C3
Nyakabindi *Tanz* 50D4
Nyaksimvol' *USSR* 20L3
Nyala *Sudan* 50C2
Nyalam *China* 43F3
Nyamlell *Sudan* 50C3
Nyanda *Zim* 51D6
Nyandoma *USSR* 20G3
Nyanga, R *Gabon* 50B4
Nyasa, L *Malawi/Mozam* 51D5
Nyaunglebin *Burma* 30B2
Nyazepetrovsk *USSR* 20K4
Nyborg *Den* 12G7
Nybro *Sweden* 12H7
Nyda *USSR* 24J3
Nyeboes Land, Region *Can* 55M1
Nyeri *Kenya* 50D4
Nyimba *Zambia* 51D5
Nyingchi *China* 39H2
Nyíregyháza *Hung* 19E3
Nyiru,Mt *Kenya* 50D3
Nykarleby *Fin* 12J6
Nykøbing *Den* 12F7
Nykøbing *Den* 12G8
Nyköping *Sweden* 12H7
Nyl, R *S Africa* 47D1
Nylstroom *S Africa* 47D1
Nymagee *Aust* 34C2
Nynäshamn *Sweden* 12H7
Nyngan *Aust* 34C2
Nyong, R *Cam* 50B3
Nyongwol *S Korea* 28A3
Nyongwon *N Korea* 28A3
Nyons *France* 14D3
Nysa *Pol* 18D2
Nyssa *USA* 58C2

Nyukhcha

Otaru

Nyukhcha USSR 20H3
Nyukzha, R USSR 26F1
Nyurba USSR 25N3
Nzega Tanz 50D4
Nzérékoré Guinea 48B4

O

Oacoma USA 60D2
Oahe,L USA 60C2
Oahu, I Hawaiian Is 66E5
Oakbank Aust 34B2
Oakdale USA 66B2
Oakes USA 61D1
Oakey Aust 34D1
Oakland, California USA 59B3
Oakland, Nebraska USA 61D2
Oakland, Oregon USA 58B2
Oakland City USA 64B3
Oak Lawn USA 64B2
Oakley, California USA 66B2
Oakley, Kansas USA 60C3
Oak Ridge USA 67B1
Oakridge USA 58B2
Oakville Can 65D2
Oamaru NZ 35B3
Oasis, California USA 66D2
Oasis, Nevada USA 58D2
Oates Land, Region Ant 76F7
Oatlands Aust 34C4
Oaxaca Mexico 70C3
Ob', R USSR 24J3
Obama Japan 29C3
Oban NZ 35A3
Oban Scot 8C3
Obanazawa Japan 29D3
Oberhausen W Germ 13D2
Oberlin USA 60C3
Obernburg W Germ 13E3
Obi, I Indon 27F7
Obidos Brazil 73G4
Obihiro Japan 29E2
Obluch'ye USSR 26G2
Obo CAR 50C3
Obock Djibouti 50E2
Oborniki Pol 18D2
Oboyan' USSR 21F5
O'Brien USA 58B2
Obshchiy Syrt, Mts USSR 21J5
Obskaya Guba, B USSR 24J2
Obuasi Ghana 48B4
Ocala USA 67B3
Ocaña Colombia 72D2
Ocaña Spain 15B2
Ocean City, Maryland USA 65D3
Ocean City, New Jersey USA 68C3
Ocean Falls Can 54F4
Ocean I = Banaba
Oceano USA 66B3
Oceanside USA 66D4
Ocean Springs USA 63E2
Ocher USSR 20J4
Ochil Hills Scot 8D3
Ochlockonee, R USA 67B2
Ocho Rios Jamaica 69H1
Ocmulgee, R USA 67B2
Oconee, R USA 67B2
Oconto USA 64B2
Ocotlán Mexico 70B2
Oda Ghana 48B4
Oda Japan 28B3
Ódáðahraun Region Iceland 12B2
Ŏdaejin N Korea 28A2
Oda, Jebel, Mt Sudan 50D1
Odate Japan 29E2
Odawara Japan 29D3
Odda Nor 12F6
Ode Nigeria 48C4
Odem USA 63C3
Odemira Port 15A2
Ödemiş Turk 17F3
Odendaalsrus S Africa 47D2
Odense Den 12G7
Oder, R E Germ/Pol 18C2
Odessa, Texas USA 62B2
Odessa USSR 21E6
Odessa, Washington USA 58C1
Odienné Ivory Coast 48B4
Odra = Oder
Odra, R Pol 19D2
Oeiras Brazil 73K5
Oelrichs USA 60C2
Oelwein USA 61E2
Ofanto, R Italy 16D2
Ofaqim Israel 45C3
Offaly, County Irish Rep 9C3
Offenbach W Germ 13E2
Offenburg W Germ 13D3
Ofunato Japan 29D3
Oga Japan 29D3
Ogaden, Region Eth 50E3
Ōgaki Japan 29D3
Ogallala USA 60C2
Ogasawara Gunto, Is Japan 26H4
Ogbomosho Nigeria 48C4
Ogden, Iowa USA 61E2
Ogden, Utah USA 58D2
Ogdensburg USA 65D2
Ogeechee, R USA 67B2
Ogilvie Mts Can 54E3
Oglethorpe,Mt USA 67B2
Ogoja Nigeria 48C4
Ogre USSR 19E1
Oguilet Khenachich, Well Mali 48B2
Ogulin Yugos 16D1
Ogunquit USA 68E1
Ogurchinskiy, Ostrov, I USSR 21J8
Ohai NZ 35A3
Ohakune NZ 35C1
Ohanet Alg 48C2
Ōhata Japan 29D2
Ohau,L NZ 35A2
O'Higgins, Lago Chile 74B7
Ohio, R USA 64B3
Ohio, State USA 57E2
Ohm, R W Germ 13E2
Ohopoho Namibia 51B5
Ohre, R Czech 18C2
Ohrid Yugos 17E2
Ohridsko Jezero, L Alb/Yugos 17E2
Ohura NZ 35B1
Oiapoque French Guiana 73H3
Oil City USA 65D2
Oildale USA 66C3
Oise, Department France 13B3
Oise, R France 14C2
Ōita Japan 28C4
Ojai USA 66C3
Ojinaga Mexico 70B2
Ojiya Japan 29C3
Ojos del Salado, Mt Arg 74C3
Oka, R USSR 20F5
Okahandja Namibia 47B1
Okanagan Falls Can 58C1
Okanogan USA 58C1
Okanogan, R USA 58C1
Okanogan Range, Mts Can/USA 58B1
Okara Pak 42C2
Okasise Namibia 47B1
Okavango, R Angola/Namibia 51B5
Okavango Delta, Marsh Botswana 51C5
Okaya Japan 29D3
Okayama Japan 29C4
Okazaki Japan 29C4
Okeechobee USA 67B3
Okeechobee,L USA 67B3
Okefenokee Swamp USA 67B2
Okene Nigeria 48C4
Okha India 42B4
Okhaldunga Nepal 43F3
Okhotsk USSR 25Q4
Okhotsk, S of USSR 26H1
Okinawa, I Japan 26F4
Okinawa gunto, Arch Japan 26F4
Oki-shotō, Is Japan 28C3
Okkang-dong N Korea 28A2
Oklahoma, State USA 56D3
Oklahoma City USA 63C1
Okmulgee USA 63C1
Okoja Nigeria 48C4
Okombahe Namibia 47B1
Okondja Gabon 50B4
Okoppe Japan 29D2
Okoyo Congo 50B4
Okpara, R Benin/Nigeria 48C4
Okstindan, Mt Nor 20A2
Oktyabr'sk USSR 21K6
Oktyabr'skiy, Bashkirskaya USSR 20J5
Oktyabr'skiy, Kamchatka USSR 26J1
Oktyabr'skoye USSR 20M3
Oktyabrskoy Revolyutsii, Ostrov, I USSR 25L2
Oktyabr'ya, imeni 11 Letnyaya USSR 25N4
Okushiri-tō Japan 29D2
Okwa, R Botswana 47C1
Olafsjorður Iceland 12B1
Olancha USA 66D2
Olancha Peak, Mt USA 66C2
Öland, I Sweden 12H7
Olary Aust 34B2
Olathe USA 61E3
Olavarría Arg 74D5
Olbia, Sicily 16B2
Olcott USA 68A1
Old Crow Can 54E3
Oldenburg, Niedersachsen W Germ 18B2
Oldenburg, Schleswig-Holstein W Germ 18C2
Old Forge USA 68C2
Oldham Eng 7C3
Old Head of Kinsale, C Irish Rep 10B3
Old Lyme USA 68D2
Oldmeldrum Scot 8D3
Olds Can 54G4
Old Town USA 65F2
Olean USA 68A1
Olekma, R USSR 25O4
Olekminsk USSR 25N3
Olenegorsk USSR 20E2
Olenek USSR 25N3
Olenek, R USSR 25O2
Olevsk USSR 19F2
Ol'ga USSR 29D2
Olifants, R, Cape Province S Africa 47C3
Olifants, R Namibia 47B1
Olifants, R, Transvaal S Africa 47E1
Olifantshoek S Africa 47C2
Ólimbos, Mt Greece 17E2
Olímpia Brazil 75C3
Olinda Brazil 73M5
Olivares, Mt Arg/Chile 74C4
Oliveira Brazil 75D3
Olivia USA 61E2
Ollagüe Chile 74C2
Ollagüe, Vol Bol 74C2
Ollerton Eng 7D3
Olney, Illinois USA 64B3
Olney, Texas USA 62C2
Olochi USSR 26F1
Olofström Sweden 12G7
Olombo Congo 50B4
Olomouc Czech 18D3
Olonets USSR 20E3
Oloron-Ste-Marie France 14B3
Olovyannaya USSR 26E1
Olpe W Germ 13D2
Olsztyn Pol 19E2
Olten Switz 16B1
Oltul, R Rom 17E2
Olympia USA 58B1
Olympic Nat Pk USA 58B1
Olympus, Mt = Ólimbos
Olympus,Mt Cyprus 45B1
Olympus,Mt USA 58B1
Olyutorskiy, Mys, C USSR 25T4
Omachi Japan 29C3
Omae-zaki, C Japan 29C4
Omagh N Ire 9C2
Omaha USA 61D2
Omak USA 58C1
Oman, Sultanate Arabian Pen 38D4
Oman,G of UAE 38D3
Omaruru Namibia 47B1
Omaruru, R Namibia 47A1
Oma-saki, C Japan 29D2
Omboué Gabon 50A4
Omdurman Sudan 50D2
Om Hager Eth 50D2
Ōminato Japan 29D2
Omineca Mts Can 54F4
Omiya Japan 29C3
Ommanney B Can 54H2
Omo, R Eth 50D3
Omodeo, L, Sardinia 16B2
Omolon, R USSR 25R3
Omoloy, R USSR 25P3
Omono, R Japan 29D3
Omsk USSR 24J4
Ōmu Japan 29D2
Omura Japan 28C4
Omuramba Eiseb, R Botswana 47C1
Ōmuta Japan 28C4
Omutninsk USSR 20J4
Onalaska USA 64A2
Onancock USA 65D3
Onandausi India 43K1
Onaping L Can 64C1
Onawa USA 61D2
Oncócua Angola 51B5
Ondangua Namibia 51B5
Ondava, R Czech 19E3
Ondo Nigeria 48C4
Öndörhaan Mongolia 26E2
One and Half Degree Chan Indian O 39F5
Onega USSR 24E3
Onega, R USSR 20F3
Onega, L USSR 20F3
Oneida USA 68C1
Oneida L USA 68B1
O'Neill USA 60D2
Onekotan, I, Kuril Is USSR 26J2
Onema Zaïre 50C4
Oneonta USA 68C1
Onezhskaya Guba, B USSR 20F2
Onezhskoye, Oz, L = Onega, L
Ongers, R S Africa 47C3
Ongiva Angola 51B5
Ongjin N Korea 28B3
Ongniud Qi China 31D1
Ongole India 44C2
Onilahy, R Madag 51E6
Onitsha Nigeria 48C4
Onjüül Mongolia 26D2
Ono Japan 29C3
Onohara-jima, I Japan 29C4
Onomichi Japan 29C4
Onotoa, I Kiribati 33G1
Onslow Aust 32A3
Onslow B USA 67C2
Ontake-san, Mt Japan 29C3
Ontario, California USA 66D3
Ontario, Oregon USA 58C2
Ontario, Province Can 55J4
Ontario,L Can/USA 65D2
Onteniente Spain 15B2
Ontong Java Atoll Solomom Is 33E1
Onyang S Korea 28A3
Onyx USA 66C3
Oodnadatta Aust 32C3
Ooldea Aust 32C4
Oologah L USA 63C1
Oostelijk Flevoland, Polder Neth 13C1
Oostende Belg 13B2
Oosterschelde, Estuary Neth 13B2
Ootacamund India 44B3
Opala USSR 25R4
Opala Zaïre 50C4
Opanake Sri Lanka 44C4
Oparino USSR 20H4
Opava Czech 19D3
Opelika USA 67A2
Opelousas USA 63D2
Opheim USA 60B1
Opochka USSR 19F1
Opole Pol 19D2
Oporto Port 15A1
Opotiki NZ 35C1
Opp USA 67A2
Oppdal Nor 12F6
Opunake NZ 35B1
Oradea Rom 17E1
Öræfajökull, Mts Iceland 12B2
Orai India 42D3
Oran Alg 15B2
Orán Arg 72F8
Orang N Korea 28A2
Orange Aust 34C2
Orange, California USA 66D4
Orange France 14C3
Orange, Texas USA 63D2
Orange, R S Africa 47B2
Orangeburg USA 67B2
Orange, Cabo, C Brazil 73H3
Orange City USA 61D2
Orange Free State, Province S Africa 47D2
Orange Park USA 67B2
Orangeville Can 64C2
Oranienburg E Germ 18C2
Oranjemund Namibia 47B2
Orapa Botswana 47D1
Oras Phil 27F5
Orăştie Rom 17E1
Oravita Rom 17E1
Orbetello Italy 16C2
Orbisonia USA 68B2
Orbost Aust 34C3
Orchies France 13B2
Orcutt USA 66B3
Ord USA 60D2
Ord, R Aust 32B2
Orderville USA 59D3
Ord,Mt Aust 32B2
Ordos, Desert China 25M6
Ordu Turk 40C1
Ordway USA 62B1
Ordzhonikidze USSR 21G7
Örebro Sweden 12H7
Oregon USA 64C2
Oregon, State USA 56A2
Oregon City USA 58B1
Öregrund Sweden 12H6
Orekhovo Zuyevo USSR 20F4
Orel USSR 21F5
Orem USA 59D2
Orenburg USSR 21J5
Orense Spain 15A1
Oresund, Str Den/Sweden 18C1
Oreti, R NZ 35A3
Orgeyev USSR 19F3
Orhaneli, R Turk 17F3
Orhon Gol, R Mongolia 26D2
Orientos Aust 34B1
Orihuela Spain 15B2
Orillia Can 65D2
Orinoco, R Ven 72F2
Oriskany Falls USA 68C1
Orissa, State India 43E4
Oristano, Sicily 16B3
Oristano, G.di, Sardinia 16B3
Orivesi, L Fin 12K6
Oriximiná Brazil 73G4
Orizaba Mexico 70C3
Orizona Brazil 75C2
Orkney, Is, Region Scot 8D2
Orlândia Brazil 75C3
Orlando USA 67B3
Orléanais, Region France 14C2
Orléans France 14C2
Orleans USA 68E2
Orlik USSR 25L4
Ormond Beach USA 67B3
Ormskirk Eng 7C3
Ornain, R France 13C3
Orne, R France 14B2
Örnsköldsvik Sweden 12H6
Oro N Korea 28A2
Orocué Colombia 72D3
Orofino USA 58C1
Oron Israel 45C3
Oronsay, I Scot 8B3
Orontes = Asi
Orosháza Hung 19E3
Orotukan USSR 25R3
Oroville, California USA 59B3
Oroville, Washington USA 58C1
Orsha USSR 19G2
Orsk USSR 24G4
Ørsta Nor 12F6
Orthez France 14B3
Ortigueira Spain 15A1
Ortles, Mt Italy 14E2
Ortoire, R Trinidad 69L1
Ortonville USA 61D1
Orulgan, Khrebet, Mts USSR 25O3
Oruro Bol 72E7
Orwell, R Eng 7E3
Osa USSR 20K4
Osage, Iowa USA 61E2
Osage, Wyoming USA 60C2
Osage, R USA 63D1
Osaka Japan 29D4
Osa,Pen de Costa Rica 70D4
Osceola, Arkansas USA 63E1
Osceola, Iowa USA 61E2
Osgood Mts USA 58C2
Oshamambe Japan 29D2
Oshawa Can 65D2
O-shima, I Japan 29C2
Oshkosh, Nebraska USA 60C2
Oshkosh USA 55K5
Oshkosh, Wisconsin USA 64B2
Oshnovīyeh Iran 21H8
Oshogbo Nigeria 48C4
Oshwe Zaïre 50B4
Osijek Yugos 17D1
Osinniki USSR 24K5
Osipovichi USSR 19F2
Oskaloosa USA 61E2
Oskarshamn Sweden 20B4
Oslo Nor 12G6
Osmaniye Turk 40C2
Osnabrück W Germ 18B2
Osorno Chile 74B6
Osorno Spain 15B1
Osoyoos Can 58C1
Ossa,Mt Aust 32D5
Osseo USA 64A2
Ossining USA 68D2
Ossora USSR 25S4
Ostashkov USSR 20E4
Oste, R W Germ 13E1
Ostend = Oostende
Østerdalen, V Nor 12G6
Osterholz-Scharmbeck W Germ 13E1
Östersund Sweden 12G6
Ostfriesland, Region W Germ 13D1
Östhammär Sweden 12H6
Ostia Italy 16C2
Ostrava Czech 19D3
Ostróda Pol 19D2
Ostrołeka Pol 19E2
Ostrov USSR 20D4
Ostrów Pol 19D2
Ostrowiec Pol 19E2
Ostrów Mazowiecka Pol 19E2
Osuna Spain 15A2
Oswego USA 68B1
Oswego, R USA 68B1
Oswestry Eng 7C3
Oświęcim Pol 19D3
Ota Japan 29C3
Otago Pen NZ 35B3
Otaki NZ 35C2
Otaru Japan 29E2

Pathfinder Res

Pittsfield

Pathfinder Res *USA* 60B2
Patiāla *India* 42D2
Pativilca *Peru* 72C6
Pátmos, I *Greece* 17F3
Patna *India* 43F3
Patnos *Turk* 40D2
Patomskoye Nagor'ye, Upland *USSR* 25N4
Patos *Brazil* 73L5
Patos de Minas *Brazil* 75C2
Patos, Lagoa dos, Lg *Brazil* 74F4
Pátrai *Greece* 17E3
Patrasuy *USSR* 20L3
Patrocínio *Brazil* 75C2
Patta I *Kenya* 50E4
Pattani *Thai* 30C4
Pattaya *Thai* 30C3
Patterson, California *USA* 66B2
Patterson, Louisiana *USA* 63D3
Patterson Mt *USA* 66C2
Patton *USA* 68A2
Patu *Brazil* 73L5
Patuakhali *Bang* 43G4
Patuca, R *Honduras* 70D3
Pau *France* 14B3
Paulatuk *Can* 54F3
Paulistana *Brazil* 73K5
Paulpietersburg *S Africa* 47E2
Pauls Valley *USA* 63C2
Paungde *Burma* 30B2
Pauri *India* 42D2
Pavão *Brazil* 75D2
Pavia *Italy* 16B1
Pavlodar *USSR* 24J4
Pavlovich *USSR* 25O4
Pavlovka *USSR* 20K4
Pavlovo *USSR* 20G4
Pavlovsk *USSR* 21G5
Pawhuska *USA* 63C1
Paw Paw *USA* 68A3
Pawtucket *USA* 68E2
Paxton *USA* 60C2
Payette *USA* 58C2
Payne,L *Can* 55L4
Paynesville *USA* 61E1
Paysandú *Urug* 74E4
Pazardzhik *Bulg* 17E2
Peace, R *Can* 54G4
Peace, R *USA* 67B3
Peach Springs *USA* 59D3
Peak District Nat Pk *Eng* 7D3
Peaked Mt *USA* 65F1
Peak Hill *Aust* 34C2
Peak,The, Mt *Eng* 7D3
Peale,Mt *USA* 59E3
Pearl, R *USA* 63D2
Pearl City *Hawaiian Is* 66E5
Pearl Harbor *Hawaiian Is* 66E5
Pearsall *USA* 62C3
Pearston *S Africa* 47D3
Peary Chan *Can* 54H2
Pebane *Mozam* 51D5
Peć *Yugos* 17E2
Peçanha *Brazil* 75D2
Pecan Island *USA* 63D3
Pechenga *USSR* 12L5
Pechora *USSR* 20K2
Pechora, R *USSR* 20J2
Pechorskaya Guba, G *USSR* 20J2
Pechorskoye More, S *USSR* 20J2
Pecoraro, Mt *Italy* 16D3
Pecos *USA* 62B2
Pecos, R *USA* 62B2
Pécs *Hung* 19D3
Pedhoulas *Cyprus* 45B1
Pedra Azul *Brazil* 75D2
Pedregulho *Brazil* 75C3
Pedro Cays, Is *Caribbean S* 69B3
Pedro de Valdivia *Chile* 74C2
Pedro Gomes *Brazil* 75B2
Pedro Juan Caballero *Par* 75A3
Pedro,Pt *Sri Lanka* 44C4
Peebinga *Aust* 34B2
Peebles *Scot* 8D4
Pee Dee, R *USA* 67C2
Peekskill *USA* 68D2
Peel, I of Man *British Is* 6B2
Peel, R *Can* 54E3
Peel Sd *Can* 54J2
Pefos = Paphos
Peg Arfak, Mt *Indon* 27G7
Pegasus B *NZ* 35B2
Pegu *Burma* 30B2
Pegunungan Maoke, Mts *Indon* 32C1
Pegu Yoma, Mts *Burma* 30B2
Pehuajó *Arg* 74D5
Peixe, R, Mato Grosso *Brazil* 75B1
Peixe, R, São Paulo *Brazil* 75B3
Pei Xian *China* 31D3
Pekan *Malay* 30C5
Pekanbaru *Indon* 27D6
Pekin *USA* 64B2
Peking = Beijing
Pelabohan Kelang *Malay* 30C5
Pelat, Mont *France* 14D3
Peleaga, Mt *Rom* 17E1
Peleduy *USSR* 25N4
Pelee I *Can* 64C2
Peleng, I *Indon* 32B1
Pelican L *USA* 61E1
Pelican Pt *S Africa* 47A1
Pello *Fin* 12J5
Pelly Bay *Can* 55J3
Pelly Mts *Can* 54E3
Pelotas *Brazil* 74F4
Pelotas, R *Brazil* 74F3
Pelusium, Hist Site *Egypt* 45B3
Pelvoux, Massif du, Mts *France* 14D2
Pelym, R *USSR* 20L3
Pemba *Mozam* 51E5
Pemba, Baiá de, B *Mozam* 51E5
Pemba I *Tanz* 50D4
Pembina *USA* 61D1
Pembroke *Can* 65D1
Pembroke *USA* 67B2
Pembroke *Wales* 7B4
Penacook *USA* 68E1
Penápolis *Brazil* 75B3
Peñarroya *Spain* 15A2
Peñarroya, Mt *Spain* 15B1
Penarth *Wales* 7C4
Peñas, Cabo de, C *Spain* 15A1
Penas, Golfo de, G *Chile* 74B7
Peña Trevinca, Mt *Spain* 15A1
Pende, R *Chad/CAR* 50B3
Pendleton *USA* 58C1
Pend Oreille, R *USA* 58C1
Penedo *Brazil* 73L6
Penganga, R *India* 42D5
Pengho Lieh Tao, Is *Taiwan* 31D5
Penglai *China* 31E2
Pengshui *China* 31B4
Penicuik *Scot* 8D4
Peninsular Malaysia *Malay* 30C5
Penistone *Eng* 7D3
Penner, R *India* 44B3
Pennine Chain, Mts *Eng* 6C2
Penns Grove *USA* 68C3
Pennsylvania, State *USA* 57F2
Penn Yan *USA* 68B1
Penny Highlands, Mts *Can* 55M3
Penobscot, R *USA* 65F1
Penobscot B *USA* 65F2
Penola *Aust* 34B3
Penong *Aust* 32C4
Penonomé *Panama* 69A5
Penrith *Eng* 6C2
Pensacola *USA* 63E2
Pensacola Mts *Ant* 76E2
Pentecost, I *Vanuatu* 33F2
Penticton *Can* 54G5
Pentland Firth, Chan *Scot* 8D2
Pentland Hills *Scot* 8D4
Pen-y-ghent, Mt *Eng* 6C2
Penza *USSR* 20H5
Penzance *Eng* 7B4
Penzhina, R *USSR* 25S3
Penzhinskaya Guba, B *USSR* 25S3
Peoria *USA* 64B2
Perak, R *Malay* 30C5
Perdido, R *Brazil* 75A3
Pereira *Colombia* 72C3
Pereira Barreto *Brazil* 75B3
Perelazovskiy *USSR* 21G6
Pereyaslav *USSR* 19G2
Pergamino *Arg* 74D4
Perge *Turk* 40B2
Peribonca, R *Can* 55L4
Périgueux *France* 14C2
Perlas, Archipiélago de las *Panama* 72C2
Perlas, Laguna de *Nic* 69A4
Perm' *USSR* 20K4
Pernambuco = Recife
Pernambuco, State *Brazil* 73L5
Pernik *Bulg* 17E2
Péronne *France* 13B3
Perpignan *France* 14C3
Perris *USA* 66D4
Perry, Florida *USA* 67B2
Perry, Georgia *USA* 67B2
Perry, New York *USA* 68A1
Perry, Oklahoma *USA* 63C1
Perry River *Can* 54H3
Perrysburg *USA* 64C2
Perryton *USA* 62B1
Perryville, Missouri *USA* 63E1
Persia = Iran
Persian Gulf = The Gulf
Perth *Aust* 32A4
Perth *Can* 65D2
Perth *Scot* 8D3
Perth Amboy *USA* 68C2
Peru *USA* 64B2
Peru, Republic *S America* 72D6
Peru Basin *Pacific O* 37P5
Peru-Chile Trench *Pacific O* 52E6
Perugia *Italy* 16C2
Perušic *Yugos* 16D2
Pervari *Turk* 40D2
Pervomaysk, RSFSR *USSR* 20G5
Pervomaysk, Ukraine SSR *USSR* 21E6
Pervoural'sk *USSR* 20K4
Pesaro *Italy* 16C2
Pescadero *USA* 66A2
Pescadores = Pengho Lieh Tao
Pescara *Italy* 16C2
Peshawar *Pak* 42C2
Peshkopi *Alb* 17E2
Peshtigo *USA* 64B1
Pestovo *USSR* 20F4
Petacalco, B de *Mexico* 70B3
Petah Tiqwa *Israel* 45C2
Petaluma *USA* 59B3
Pétange *Lux* 13C3
Petauke *Zambia* 51D5
Petenwell L *USA* 64B2
Peterborough *Aust* 34A2
Peterborough *Can* 65D2
Peterborough *Eng* 7D3
Peterborough *USA* 68E1
Peterhead *Scot* 8E3
Petermann Gletscher, Gl *Greenland* 55M1
Petermann Range, Mts *Aust* 32B3
Peteroa, Vol *Arg/Chile* 74B5
Peter 1 Øy, I *Ant* 76G4
Petersburg *USA* 54E4
Petersburg, Virginia *USA* 65D3
Petersfield *Eng* 7D4
Petite Kabylie, Hills *Algeria* 16B3
Petit Mècatina, Rivière du, R *Can* 55M4
Petlād *India* 42C4
Peto *Mexico* 70D2
Petoskey *USA* 64C1
Petra, Hist Site *Jordan* 45C3
Petra, Ostrova, Is *USSR* 25N2
Petra Velikogo, Zaliv, B *USSR* 28C2
Petrified Forest Nat Pk *USA* 59E3
Petrolina *Brazil* 73K5
Petropavlovsk *USSR* 24H4
Petropavlovsk-Kamchatskiy *USSR* 26J1
Petrópolis *Brazil* 75D3
Petrovsk *USSR* 21H5
Petrovsk Zabakal'skiy *USSR* 25M4
Petrovsk Zabaykal'skiy *USSR* 26D1
Petrozavodsk *USSR* 20E3
Petrusburg *S Africa* 47D2
Petrus Steyn *S Africa* 47D2
Petrusville *S Africa* 47C3
Pevek *USSR* 25T3
Peza, R *USSR* 20H2
Pfälzer Wald, Region *W Germ* 13E2
Pforzheim *W Germ* 18B3
Phagwara *India* 42D2
Phalaborwa *S Africa* 47E1
Phalodi *India* 42C3
Phalsbourg *France* 13D3
Phaltan *India* 44A2
Phangnga *Thai* 30B4
Phanom Dang, Mts *Camb/Thai* 30C3
Phan Rang *Viet* 30D3
Phan Thiet *Viet* 30D3
Pharr *USA* 62C3
Phelps L *USA* 67C1
Phenix City *USA* 67A2
Phet Buri *Thai* 30B3
Phiafay *Laos* 30D3
Philadelphia, Mississippi *USA* 63E2
Philadelphia, Pennsylvania *USA* 68C2
Philip *USA* 60C2
Philippeville = Skikda
Philippeville *Belg* 13C2
Philippine S *Pacific O* 27F5
Philippines, Republic *S E Asia* 27F5
Philippine Trench *Pacific O* 36H4
Philippolis *S Africa* 47D3
Philipsburg, Montana *USA* 58D1
Philipsburg, Pennsylvania *USA* 65D2
Philip Smith Mts *USA* 54D3
Philipstown *S Africa* 47C3
Phillips B *Can* 55K1
Phillipsburg, Kansas *USA* 60D3
Phillipsburg, New Jersey *USA* 68C2
Philpots Pen *Can* 55K2
Phnom Penh *Camb* 30C3
Phoenix, Arizona *USA* 59D4
Phoenix, New York *USA* 68B1
Phoenix Is *Pacific O* 33H1
Phoenixville *USA* 68C2
Phong Saly *Laos* 30C1
Phu Bia, Mt *Laos* 30C2
Phu Cuong *Viet* 30D3
Phuket *Thai* 30B4
Phulbani *India* 43E4
Phu Miang, Mt *Thai* 30C2
Phu Set, Mt *Laos* 30D2
Phu Tho *Viet* 30D1
Phu Vinh *Viet* 30D4
Piacenza *Italy* 16B1
Pialba *Aust* 34D1
Pian, R *Aust* 34C2
Pianosa, I *Italy* 16C2
Pianosa, I *Italy* 16D2
Piaseczno *Pol* 19E2
Piatã *Brazil* 75D1
Piatra-Neamţ *Rom* 17F1
Piauí, State *Brazil* 73K5
Piave, R *Italy* 16C1
Pibor, R *Sudan* 50D3
Pibor Post *Sudan* 50D3
Picardie, Region *France* 13B3
Picayune *USA* 63E2
Pichilemu *Chile* 74B4
Pickering *Eng* 6D2
Pickle Lake *Can* 55J4
Pico, I *Azores* 48A1
Pico Bolivar, Mt *Ven* 69C5
Pico de Almanzor, Mt *Spain* 15A1
Pico de Aneto, Mt *Spain* 15C1
Pico Duarte, Mt *Dom Rep* 69C3
Picos *Brazil* 73K5
Picos de Europa, Mt *Spain* 15B1
Picton *Aust* 34D2
Picton *NZ* 35B2
Pic Toussidé, Mt *Chad* 50B1
Piedade *Brazil* 75C3
Piedra *USA* 66C2
Piedras Blancas,Pt *USA* 66B3
Piedras Negras *Mexico* 70B2
Pie I *Can* 64B1
Pieksämäki *Fin* 12K6
Pielinen, L *Fin* 12K6
Pienaar's River *S Africa* 47D2
Pierre *USA* 60C2
Piešťany *Czech* 19D3
Pietermaritzburg *S Africa* 47E2
Pietersburg *S Africa* 47D1
Piet Retief *S Africa* 47E2
Pietrosul, Mt *Rom* 17F1
Pigailoe, I *Pacific O* 27H6
Piggott *USA* 63D1
Pihyŏn *N Korea* 28A3
Pikangikum L *Can* 55J4
Pikes Peak *USA* 60B3
Piketberg *S Africa* 47B3
Pikeville *USA* 64C3
Pikiutaleq *Greenland* 55O3
Pik Kommunizma, Mt *USSR* 39F2
Pikounda *Congo* 50B3
Pik Pobedy, Mt *China/USSR* 39G1
Piła *Pol* 18D2
Pilar *Par* 74E3
Pilcomayo, R *Arg/Par/Bol* 74D2
Pilgrim's Rest *S Africa* 47E1
Pilibhit *India* 42D3
Pilica, R *Pol* 19D2
Pillar,C *Aust* 34C4
Pilões, Serra dos, Mts *Brazil* 75C2
Pílos *Greece* 17E3
Pilot Knob, Mt *USA* 58C1
Pilot Peak, Mt *USA* 66D1
Pilottown *USA* 63E3
Pimenta *Brazil* 73G4
Pinang, I *Malay* 30C4
Pinar del Rio *Cuba* 69A2
Pinche *Belg* 13C2
Pindaré, R *Brazil* 73J4
Píndhos, Mts *Greece* 17E3
Pine Bluff *USA* 63D2
Pine Bluffs *USA* 60C2
Pine City *USA* 61E1
Pine Creek *Aust* 32C2
Pine Creek, R *USA* 68B2
Pinecrest *USA* 66C1
Pinedale, California *USA* 66C2
Pinedale, Wyoming *USA* 58E2
Pine Flat Res *USA* 66C2
Pinega *USSR* 20G3
Pinega, R *USSR* 20H3
Pine Grove *USA* 68B2
Pine Hills *USA* 67B3
Pinehurst *USA* 67C1
Pine I *USA* 67B3
Pineland *USA* 63D2
Pinellas Park *USA* 67B3
Pine Mt *USA* 66B3
Pine Point *Can* 54G3
Pine Ridge *USA* 60C2
Pines,L. o'the *USA* 63D2
Pineville *USA* 63D2
Pingdingshan *China* 31C3
Pingguo *China* 31B5
Pingliang *China* 31B2
Pingluo *China* 31B2
Pingtan Dao, I *China* 31D4
Pingtung *Taiwan* 31E5
Pingwu *China* 31A3
Pingxiang, Guangxi *China* 31B5
Pingxiang, Jiangxi *China* 31C4
Pinheiro *Brazil* 73J4
Pini, I *Indon* 27C6
Piniós, R *Greece* 17E3
Pinjarra *Aust* 32A4
Pinnacles Nat. Mon. *USA* 66B2
Pinnaroo *Aust* 34B3
Pinos,I de = Juventud, Isla de la
Pinos,Mt *USA* 66C3
Pinos,Pt *USA* 59B3
Pinrang *Indon* 27E7
Pins, Île des *New Caledonia* 33F3
Pinsk *USSR* 21D5
Pinyug *USSR* 20H3
Pioche *USA* 59D3
Piombino *Italy* 16C2
Pioneer Mts *USA* 58D1
Pioner, Ostrov, I *USSR* 25K2
Pionerskiy *USSR* 20L3
Piotrków Trybunalski *Pol* 19D2
Piper, Oilfield *N Sea* 8F2
Piper Peak, Mt *USA* 66D2
Pipestone *USA* 61D2
Pipmuacan, Rés *Can* 57F2
Pipmudcan, Res *Can* 55M4
Piqua *USA* 64C2
Piquiri, R *Brazil* 75B4
Piracanjuba *Brazil* 75C2
Piracicaba *Brazil* 75C3
Piraçununga *Brazil* 75C3
Piraí do Sul *Brazil* 75C3
Piraiévs *Greece* 17E3
Pirajuí *Brazil* 75C3
Piranhas *Brazil* 75B2
Pirapora *Brazil* 75D2
Pirenópolis *Brazil* 75C2
Pires do Rio *Brazil* 75C2
Pírgos *Greece* 17E3
Pirineos, Mts *Spain/France* 14B3
Piripiri *Brazil* 73K4
Pirmasens *W Germ* 13D3
Pirot *Yugos* 17E2
Pir Panjāl Range, Mts *Pak* 42C2
Piru *Indon* 27F7
Piru Creek, R *USA* 66C3
Pisa *Italy* 16C2
Pisco *Peru* 72C6
Piseco *USA* 68C1
Písek *Czech* 18C3
Pishin *Pak* 42B2
Pismo Beach *USA* 66B3
Pissis, Mt *Arg* 74C3
Pistoia *Italy* 16C2
Pisuerga, R *Spain* 15B1
Pit, R *USA* 58B2
Pitalito *Colombia* 72C3
Pitanga *Brazil* 74F2
Pitcairn, I *Pacific O* 37N6
Pite, R *Sweden* 12H5
Piteå *Sweden* 12J5
Piteşti *Rom* 17E2
Pit Gorodok *USSR* 25L4
Pithiviers *France* 13B3
Pitkyaranta *USSR* 20E3
Pitlochry *Scot* 8D3
Pitlyar *USSR* 20M2
Pitt, I *NZ* 33H5
Pitt I *Can* 54F4
Pittsburg, California *USA* 66B1
Pittsburg, Kansas *USA* 63D1
Pittsburgh *USA* 65D2
Pittsfield, Illinois *USA* 64A3

Pittsfield Princeton

Pittsfield, Massachusetts USA 68D1
Pittston USA 68C2
Pittsworth Aust 34D1
Piura Peru 72B5
Piute Peak, Mt USA 66C3
Piuthan Nepal 43E3
Pixley USA 66C3
Pjórsá, R Iceland 12B2
Placentia B Can 55N5
Placerville USA 66B1
Plaine Lorraine, Region France 13C3
Plains USA 62B1
Plainview, Nebraska USA 61D2
Plainview, Texas USA 62B2
Planada USA 66B2
Planalto de Mato Grosso Plat Brazil 73H7
Planalto do Borborema, Plat Brazil 73L5
Planet Deep PNG 33E1
Plankinton USA 60D2
Plano USA 63C2
Plantation USA 67B3
Plant City USA 67B3
Plasencia Spain 15A1
Plast USSR 20L5
Plastun USSR 26G2
Plata, Río de la Arg/Urug 74E5
Plateau Lorrain France 13D2
Plato Colombia 69C5
Platres Cyprus 45B1
Platte USA 60D2
Platte, R USA 60C2
Platteville USA 64A2
Plattsburgh USA 65E2
Plattsmouth USA 61D2
Plauen E Germ 18C2
Plavsk USSR 20F5
Playas Ecuador 72B4
Pleasanton, California USA 66B2
Pleasanton, Texas USA 62C3
Pleasantville USA 68C3
Pleasure Ridge Park USA 64B3
Pleiku Viet 30D3
Plenty,B of NZ 35C1
Plentywood USA 60C1
Plesetsk USSR 20F3
Pleszew Pol 19D2
Pletipi,L Can 55L4
Pleven Bulg 17E2
Plevlja Yugos 17D2
Ploče Yugos 17D2
Płock Pol 19D2
Ploërmel France 14B2
Ploieşti Rom 17F2
Plombières-les-Bains France 13D4
Płońsk Pol 20C5
Plovdiv Bulg 17E2
Plummer USA 58C1
Plumtree Zim 51C6
Plymouth, California USA 66B1
Plymouth Eng 7B4
Plymouth, Indiana USA 64B2
Plymouth, Massachusetts USA 68E2
Plymouth, Pennsylvania USA 68C2
Plymouth B USA 68E2
Plymouth Sd Eng 7B4
Plynlimon, Mt Wales 7C3
Plzeň Czech 18C3
Pniewy Pol 18D2
Po Burkina 48B3
Po, R Italy 16C2
Pobé Benin 48C4
Pobedino USSR 26H2
Pocatello USA 54G5
Pochinok USSR 19G2
Poções Brazil 75D1
Pocomoke City USA 65D3
Poconé Brazil 75A2
Poços de Caldas Brazil 75C3
Podkamennaya Tunguska, R USSR 25L3
Podol'sk USSR 20F4
Podol'skaya Vozvyshennost', Upland USSR 19F3
Podporozh'ye USSR 20E3
Podyuga USSR 20G3
Pofadder S Africa 47B2
Poghdar Afghan 42A2
P'ohang S Korea 28B3
Poinsett,C Ant 76G9
Point Aust 34C2
Pointe-à-Pitre Guadeloupe 69E3
Pointe Noire Congo 50B4
Point Fairy Aust 34B3
Point Fortin Trinidad 69L1
Point Hope USA 54B3
Point L Can 54G3
Point Lay USA 54B3
Point Pleasant, New Jersey USA 68C2
Point Pleasant, W Virginia USA 64C3
Poitiers France 14C2
Poitou, Region France 14B2
Poix France 13A3
Pokaran India 42C3
Pokataroo Aust 34C1
Pokhara Nepal 43E3
Pokrovsk USSR 25O3
Polacca USA 59D3
Poland USA 68C1
Poland, Republic Europe 19D2
Polatlı Turk 40B2
Poli Cam 49D4
Policastro, G di Italy 16D3
Polillo Is Phil 27F5
Poliny Osipenko USSR 25P4
Polis Cyprus 45B1
Políyiros Greece 17E2
Pollāchi India 44B3
Pollino, Monte, Mt Italy 16D3
Polonnye USSR 19F2
Polotsk USSR 19F1
Polson USA 58D1
Poltava USSR 21E6
Pölten Austria 16D1
Polunochoye USSR 20K3
Poluostrov Mangyshlak, Pen USSR 21J7
Poluostrov Rybachiy, Pen USSR 12L5
Polvadera USA 62A2
Polyarnyy, Murmansk USSR 20E2
Polyarnyy, Yakutskaya USSR 25Q2
Polyarnyy Ural, Mts USSR 20L2
Polynesia, Region Pacific O 37L4
Pomabamba Peru 72C5
Pomba, R Brazil 75D3
Pomeroy N Ire 9C2
Pomona USA 66D3
Pomona Res USA 61D3
Pompano Beach USA 67B3
Pompton Lakes USA 68C2
Ponca City USA 63C1
Ponce Puerto Rico 69D3
Ponce de Leon B USA 67B3
Pondicherry India 44B3
Pond Inlet Can 55L2
Ponferrada Spain 15A1
Pongara, Pte Eq Guinea 48C4
Pongo, R Sudan 50C3
Pongola, R S Africa 47E2
Ponnāni India 44B3
Ponnyadoung Range, Mts Burma 43G4
Ponoy USSR 24F3
Ponoy, R USSR 20G2
Pons France 14B2
Ponta Delgada Azores 48A1
Ponta Grossa Brazil 75B4
Pontal Brazil 75C3
Pont-à-Mousson France 13C3
Ponta Pora Brazil 75A3
Pontarlier France 14D2
Pontchartrain,L USA 63D2
Ponte de Pedra Brazil 75A1
Pontedera Italy 16C2
Pontefract Eng 7D3
Ponte Leccia, Corsica 16B2
Pontevedra Spain 15A1
Pontiac, Illinois USA 64B2
Pontiac, Michigan USA 64C2
Pontianak Indon 27D7
Pontivy France 14B2
Pontoise France 13B3
Pontotoc USA 63E2
Pont-sur-Yonne France 13B3
Pontypool Wales 7C4
Pontypridd Wales 7C4
Ponziane, I Italy 16C2
Poole Eng 7D4
Poona = Pune
Pooncarie Aust 34B2
Poopelloe,L Aust 34B2
Poopó, Lago Bol 72E7
Poorman USA 54C3
Popayán Colombia 72C3
Poperinge Belg 13B2
Popilta L Aust 34B2
Poplar USA 60B1
Poplar Bluff USA 63D1
Poplarville USA 63E2
Popocatepetl, Vol Mexico 70C3
Popokabaka Zaïre 50B4
Popondetta PNG 27H7
Popovo Bulg 17F2
Porangatu Brazil 75C1
Porbandar India 42B4
Porcos, R Brazil 75C1
Porcupine, R USA/Can 54D3
Poreč Yugos 16C1
Porecatu Brazil 75B3
Pori Fin 12J6
Porirua NZ 35B2
Porjus Sweden 12H5
Porlamar Venezuela 69E4
Poronaysk USSR 26H2
Porosozero USSR 20E3
Porsangen, Inlet Nor 12K4
Porsgrunn Nor 12F7
Portadown N Ire 9C2
Portaferry N Ire 9D2
Portage USA 64B2
Portal USA 60C1
Port Alberni Can 54F5
Portalegre Port 15A2
Portales USA 62B2
Port Alfred S Africa 47D3
Port Alice Can 54F4
Port Allegany USA 68A2
Port Allen USA 63D2
Port Angeles USA 58B1
Port Antonio Jamaica 69B3
Portarlington Irish Rep 9C3
Port Arthur USA 63D3
Port Askaig Scot 8B4
Port Augusta Aust 32C4
Port-au-Prince Haiti 69C3
Port Austin USA 64C2
Port Blair Andaman Is 44E3
Port Campbell Aust 34B3
Port Canning India 43F4
Port Cartier Can 55M5
Port Chalmers NZ 35B3
Port Charlotte USA 67B3
Port Chester USA 68D2
Port Clinton USA 64C2
Port Colborne Can 65D2
Port Davey, B Aust 34C4
Port-de-Paix Haiti 69C3
Port Dickson Malay 30C5
Port Edward S Africa 47E3
Porteirinha Brazil 75D2
Port Elgin Can 64C2
Port Elizabeth S Africa 47D3
Port Ellen Scot 8B4
Port Erin, I of Man British Is 6B2
Porter Pt St Vincent 69N2
Porterville USA 66C2
Port Fairy Aust 32D4
Port Gentil Gabon 50A4
Port Gibson USA 63D2
Port Hammond Can 58B1
Port Harcourt Nigeria 48C4
Port Hardy Can 54F4
Port Hawkesbury Can 55M5
Porthcawl Wales 7C4
Port Hedland Aust 32A3
Porthmadog Wales 7B3
Port Hope Simpson Can 55N4
Port Hueneme USA 66C3
Port Huron USA 64C2
Portimão Port 15A2
Port Jackson, B Aust 34D2
Port Jefferson USA 68D2
Port Jervis USA 68C2
Port Kembla Aust 34D2
Portland Eng 7C4
Portland, Indiana USA 64C2
Portland, Maine USA 65E2
Portland, New South Wales Aust 34C2
Portland, Oregon USA 58B1
Portland, Victoria Aust 34B3
Portland Bight, B Jamaica 69H2
Portland Bill, Pt Eng 7C4
Portland,C Aust 34C4
Portland I NZ 35C1
Portland Pt Jamaica 69H2
Port Laoise Irish Rep 9C3
Port Lavaca USA 63C3
Port Lincoln Aust 32C4
Port Loko Sierra Leone 48A4
Port Louis Mauritius 51F6
Port MacDonnell Aust 34B3
Port Macquarie Aust 34D2
Port Matilda USA 68A2
Port Moresby PNG 32D1
Port Nolloth S Africa 47B2
Port Norris USA 68C3
Porto = Oporto
Pôrto Alegre Brazil 74F4
Porto Alexandre Angola 51B5
Porto Armuelles Panama 69A5
Pôrto Artur Brazil 75A1
Pôrto 15 de Novembro Brazil 75B3
Pôrto dos Meinacos Brazil 75B1
Pôrto E Cunha Brazil 74F2
Pôrto Esperança Brazil 75A2
Portoferraio Italy 16C2
Port of Spain Trinidad 69L1
Pôrto Jofre Brazil 75A2
Pôrto Mendez Brazil 75B3
Pôrto Murtinho Brazil 75A3
Porto Novo Benin 48C4
Port Orchard USA 58B1
Port Orford USA 58B2
Pôrto Santa Helena Brazil 75B3
Porto Santo, I Madeira 48A1
Pôrto São José Brazil 75B3
Pôrto Seguro Brazil 73L7
Porto Torres, Sardinia 16B2
Pôrto União Brazil 75B4
Porto Vecchio, Corsica 16B2
Pôrto Velho Brazil 72F5
Portpatrick Scot 8C4
Port Pegasus, B NZ 35A3
Port Phillip B Aust 34B3
Port Pirie Aust 34A2
Portree Scot 8B3
Port Renfrew Can 58B1
Port Royal Jamaica 69J2
Port Royal Sd USA 67B2
Portrush N Ire 9C2
Port Said Egypt 45B3
Port St Joe USA 67A3
Port St Johns S Africa 47D3
Port Saunders Can 55N4
Port Shepstone S Africa 47E3
Portsmouth Dominica 69Q2
Portsmouth Eng 7D4
Portsmouth, New Hampshire USA 68E1
Portsmouth, Ohio USA 64C3
Portsmouth, Virginia USA 65D3
Port Stephens, B Aust 34D2
Portstewart N Ire 9C2
Port Sudan Sudan 50D2
Port Sulphur USA 63E3
Porttipahdan Tekojärvi, Res Fin 12K5
Portugal, Republic Europe 15A2
Portumna Irish Rep 9B3
Portville USA 68A1
Port Washington USA 64B2
Port Weld Malay 30C5
Porvenir Bol 72E6
Porvoo Fin 12K6
Posadas Arg 74E3
Posadas Spain 15A2
Posht-e Badam Iran 41G3
Poso Indon 27F7
Posŏng S Korea 28A4
Pos Poluy USSR 20M2
Posse Brazil 75C1
Post USA 62B2
Postavy USSR 19F1
Poste-de-la-Baleine Can 55L4
Postmasburg S Africa 47C2
Postojna Yugos 16C1
Pos'yet USSR 28C2
Potchefstroom S Africa 47D2
Poteau USA 63D1
Potenza Italy 16D2
Potgietersrus S Africa 47D1
Poth USA 62C3
Poti USSR 21G7
Potiskum Nigeria 48D3
Potlatch USA 58C1
Potloer, Mt S Africa 47C3
Pot Mt USA 58C1
Potomac, R USA 65D3
Potosí Bol 72E7
Potrerillos Chile 74C3
Potsdam E Germ 18C2
Potter USA 60C2
Pottstown USA 68C2
Pottsville USA 68B2
Poughkeepsie USA 68D2
Pouso Alegre Brazil 75C3
Poverty B NZ 35C1
Povonets USSR 20F3
Povorino USSR 21G5
Povungnituk Can 55L4
Powder, R USA 60B1
Powder River USA 60B2
Powell USA 58E2
Powell Creek Aust 32C2
Powell,L USA 59D3
Powell River Can 54F5
Powys, County Wales 7C3
Poxoréo Brazil 75B2
Poyang Hu, L China 31D4
Pozantı Turk 40C2
Poza Rica Mexico 70C2
Poznań Pol 18D2
Pozo Colorado Par 74E2
Pozzuoli Italy 16C2
Pra, R Ghana 48B4
Prachin Buri Thai 30C3
Prachuap Khiri Khan Thai 30B3
Praděd, Mt Czech 18D2
Pradelles France 14C3
Prado Brazil 75E2
Prague Czech 18C2
Praha = Prague
Praia Cape Verde 48A4
Praia Rica Brazil 75A1
Prainha Brazil 72F5
Prairie Dog Town Fork, R USA 62B2
Prairie du Chien USA 64A2
Prairie Village USA 61E3
Prakhon Chai Thai 30C3
Prata Brazil 75C2
Prata, R Brazil 75C2
Prates, I = Dongsha Qundao
Prato Italy 16C2
Prattsville USA 68C1
Prattville USA 67A2
Prawle Pt Eng 14B1
Predivinsk USSR 25L4
Predporozhnyy USSR 25Q3
Pregolyu, R USSR 19E2
Prek Kak Camb 30D3
Prentice USA 64A1
Prenzlau E Germ 18C2
Preparis I Burma 44E3
Přerov Czech 18D3
Prescott, Arizona USA 59D4
Prescott, Arkansas USA 63D2
Prescott Can 65D2
Presho USA 60C2
Presidencia Roque Sáenz Peña Arg 74D3
Presidente Epitácio Brazil 75B3
Presidente Murtinho Brazil 75B2
Presidente Prudente Brazil 75B3
Presidenté Vargas Brazil 73H8
Presidente Venceslau Brazil 75B3
Presidio USA 62B3
Prešov Czech 19E3
Presque Isle USA 65F1
Preston Eng 6C3
Preston, Idaho USA 56B2
Preston, Minnesota USA 61E2
Preston, Missouri USA 63D1
Prestwick Scot 8C4
Prêto Brazil 73J8
Prêto, R Brazil 75C2
Pretoria S Africa 47D2
Préveza Greece 17E3
Prey Veng Camb 30D3
Price USA 59D3
Prichard USA 63E2
Prichernomorskaya Nizmennost', Lowland USSR 21E6
Prickly Pt Grenada 69M2
Pridneprovskaya Vozvyshennost', Upland USSR 19F3
Priekule USSR 19E1
Prieska S Africa 47C2
Priest L USA 58C1
Priest River USA 58C1
Prikaspiyskaya Nizmennost', Region USSR 21H6
Prilep Yugos 17E2
Priluki USSR 21E5
Primavera, Base Ant 76G3
Primorsk USSR 12K6
Primorsko-Akhtarsk USSR 21F6
Prince Albert Can 54H4
Prince Albert S Africa 47C3
Prince Albert,C Can 54F2
Prince Albert Pen Can 54G2
Prince Albert Sd Can 54G2
Prince Charles I Can 55L3
Prince Charles Mts Ant 76F10
Prince Edward I Can 55M5
Prince Edward Is Indian O 36C7
Prince George Can 54F4
Prince Gustaf Adolf, S Can 54H2
Prince of Wales I Aust 27H8
Prince of Wales I Can 54H2
Prince of Wales I USA 54E4
Prince of Wales Str Can 54G2
Prince Patrick I Can 54F2
Prince Regent Inlet, Str Can 55J2
Prince Rupert Can 54E4
Princess Charlotte B Aust 32D2
Princes Town Trinidad 69L1
Princeton Can 54F5
Princeton, Illinois USA 64B2
Princeton, Kentucky USA 64B3
Princeton, Missouri USA 61E2
Princeton, New Jersey USA 68C2

Princeton **Ramsey**

Princeton, W Virginia USA 64C3
Prince William Sd USA 54D3
Príncipe, I Sao Tome & Principe 48C4
Prineville USA 58B2
Prins Christian Sund Greenland 55O3
Prinsesse Astrid Kyst, Region Ant 76F12
Prinsesse Ragnhild Kyst, Region Ant 76F12
Prins Karls Forland, I Svalbard 24C2
Prinzapolca Nic 70D3
Priozersk USSR 20E3
Pripyat', R USSR 19F2
Prispansko Jezero, L Yugos 17E2
Priština Yugos 17E2
Pritzwalk E Germ 18C2
Privolzhskaya Vozvyshennost', Upland USSR 20G5
Prizren Yugos 17E2
Probolinggo Indon 27E7
Proctor USA 61E1
Proddatūr India 44B3
Progreso Mexico 70D2
Project City USA 58B2
Prokhladnyy USSR 21G7
Prokop'yevsk USSR 24K4
Proletarskaya USSR 21G6
Prome Burma 43H5
Promissão Brazil 75A2
Pronya, R USSR 19G2
Propriá Brazil 73L6
Proserpine Aust 32D3
Prospect, New York USA 68C1
Prospect, Oregon USA 58B2
Prostějov Czech 18D3
Prøven Greenland 55N2
Provence, Region France 14D3
Providence USA 68E2
Providencia, Isla de Caribbean S 69A4
Provideniya USSR 25U3
Provincetown USA 68E1
Provins France 13B3
Provo USA 59D2
Provost Can 54G4
Prudentópolis Brazil 75B4
Prudhoe Bay USA 54D2
Prudhoe Land Greenland 55M2
Pruszkow Pol 19E2
Prut, R USSR 19F3
Prutul, R Romania 21D6
Pruzhany USSR 19E2
Pryor USA 63C1
Przemys'l Pol 19E3
Psará, I Greece 17F3
Pskov USSR 20D4
Ptich, R USSR 19F2
Ptolemaïs Greece 17E2
Puan S Korea 28A3
Pucallpa Peru 72D5
Pucheng China 31D4
Pudasjärvi Fin 12K5
Pudozh USSR 20F3
Pudukkottai India 44B3
Puebla Mexico 70C3
Puebla de Sanabria Spain 15A1
Puebla de Trives Spain 15A1
Pueblo USA 62B1
Puerta do Calcanhar, Pt Brazil 73L5
Puerta do Oro, Pt S Africa 47E2
Puerto Adela Brazil 75B3
Puerto Aisén Chile 74B7
Puerto Armuelles Panama 70D4
Puerto Artur Brazil 73G6
Puerto Asis Colombia 72C3
Puerto Ayacucho Ven 72E2
Puerto Barrios Guatemala 70D3
Puerto Berrio Colombia 72D2
Puerto Cabello Ven 72E1
Puerto Cabezas Nic 70D3
Puerto Carreño Colombia 72E2
Puerto Casado Brazil 75A3
Puerto Cooper Brazil 75A3
Puerto Cortés Costa Rica 70D4
Puerto Cortés Honduras 70D3
Puerto del Rosario Canary Is 48A2
Puerto E. Cunha Brazil 73H8
Puerto Fijo Ven 72D1
Puerto Franco Brazil 73J5
Puerto Guaraní Brazil 75A3
Puerto Heath Bol 72E6
Puerto Juárez Mexico 70D2
Puerto la Cruz Ven 72F1
Puertollano Spain 15B2
Puerto López Colombia 69C4
Puerto Madryn Arg 74D6
Puerto Maldonado Peru 72E6
Puerto Montt Chile 74B6
Puerto Murtinho Brazil 73G8
Puerto Natales Chile 74B8
Puerto Peñasco Mexico 70A1
Puerto Pinasco Brazil 75A3
Puerto Pirámides Arg 74D6
Puerto Plata Dom Rep 69C3
Puerto Presidente Stroessner Brazil 74F3
Puerto Princesa Phil 27E6
Puerto Rico Colombia 72C3
Puerto Rico, I Caribbean S 69D3
Puerto Rico Trench Caribbean S 69D3
Puerto Santana Brazil 73H4
Puerto Sastre Brazil 75A3
Puerto Suárez Bol 74E1
Puerto Vallarta Mexico 70B2
Puerto Varas Chile 74B6
Puerto Villarroel Bol 72F7
Pugachev USSR 21H5
Pūgal India 42C3
Puigcerdá Spain 15C1
Pujŏn N Korea 28A2
Pujŏn Res N Korea 28A2
Pukaki,L. L NZ 35B2
Pukchin N Korea 28A2
Pukch'ŏng N Korea 28B2
Pukekohe NZ 35B1
Puketeraki Range, Mts NZ 35B2
Puksoozero USSR 20G3
Pula Yugos 16C2
Pulaski, New York USA 65D2
Pulaski, Tennessee USA 67A1
Pulaski, Virginia USA 64C3
Pulau Kolepom, I Indon 27G7
Pulau Pulau Batu, Is Indon 27C7
Pulau Pulau Macan-Kepulauan = Takabonerate
Pulawy Pol 19E2
Pulicat L India 44C3
Pul-i-Khumri Afghan 42B1
Puliyangudi India 44B4
Pullman USA 58C1
Pulo Anna, I Pacific O 27G6
Pulozero USSR 12L5
Pułtusk Pol 19E2
Puna de Atacama Arg 74C3
Puná, Isla Ecuador 72B4
Punakha Bhutan 43F3
Pūnch Pak 42C2
Punda Milia S Africa 47E1
Pune India 44A2
Pungsan N Korea 28A2
Pungso N Korea 28A2
Punia Zaïre 50C4
Punitaqui Chile 74B4
Punjab, Province Pak 42C2
Punjab, State India 42D2
Puno Peru 72D7
Punta Alta Arg 74D5
Punta Arenas Chile 74B8
Punta Banda, Cabo, C Mexico 59C4
Punta del Este Urug 74F4
Punta Gorda Belize 70D3
Punta Gorda USA 67B3
Puntarenas Costa Rica 72B1
Puqi China 31C4
Purace, Vol Colombia 72C3
Purcell USA 63C1
Purgatoire, R USA 62B1
Puri India 43F5
Pūrna India 44B2
Pūrnia India 43F3
Pursat Camb 30C3
Purus, R Brazil 72F4
Purvis USA 63E2
Purwokerto Indon 27D7
Puryŏng N Korea 28B2
Pusad India 42D5
Pusan S Korea 28B3
Pushkin USSR 20E4
Pushlakhta USSR 20F3
Pustoshka USSR 19F1
Putao Burma 43H3
Putaruru NZ 35C1
Putian China 31D4
Puting, Tanjung, C Indon 27E7
Putnam USA 68E2
Putney USA 68D1
Puttalam Sri Lanka 44B4
Puttgarden W Germ 18C2
Putumayo, R Ecuador/Col/Peru 72C4
Putussiban Indon 27E6
Puulavesi, L Fin 12K6
Puyallup USA 58B1
Puysegur Pt NZ 35A3
Pweto Zaïre 51C4
Pwllheli Wales 7B3
Pyal'ma USSR 20F3
Pyaozero, L USSR 20E2
Pyapon Burma 30B2
Pyasina, R USSR 25K2
Pyatigorsk USSR 21G7
Pyhäselkä, L Fin 12K6
Pyinmana Burma 30B2
Pyŏktong N Korea 28A2
Pyonggang N Korea 28A3
Pyŏnggok-dong S Korea 28A3
P'yŏngsan N Korea 28A3
P'yŏngt'aek S Korea 28A3
P'yŏngyang N Korea 28B3
Pyramid Hill Aust 34B3
Pyramid L USA 59C2
Pyramid,Mt NZ 35A2
Pyrénées, Mts France/Spain 14B3
Pytalovo USSR 19F1
Pyu Burma 30B2

Q

Qa'ash Shubyk, Wadi Jordan 45D4
Qabatiya Israel 45C2
Qa'el Hafira, Mud Flats Jordan 45D3
Qa'el Jinz, Mud Flats Jordan 45D3
Qagssimiut Greenland 55O3
Qaidam Pendi, Salt Flat China 26C3
Qa Khanna, Salt Marsh Jordan 45D2
Qala'en Nahl Sudan 50D2
Qalat Afghan 42B2
Qal'at al Ḩişn Syria 45D1
Qal'at al Marqab, Hist Site Syria 45C1
Qal'at Bishah S Arabia 50E2
Qal'at Sālih Iraq 41E3
Qamdo, Tibet China 26C3
Qaqortoq = Julianehåb
Qara Egypt 49E2
Qardho Somalia 50E3
Qareh Dagh, Mts Iran 21H8
Qaryat al Ulya S Arabia 41E4
Qasr ed Deir, Jebel, Mt Jordan 45C3
Qasr el Kharana Jordan 45D3
Qāşr e Shīrīn Iran 41E3
Qasr Farâfra Egypt 49E2
Qaţanā Syria 45D2
Qatar, Emirate Arabian Pen 41F4
Qatim, Jebel, Mt Jordan 45C4
Qatrāna Jordan 45D3
Qattâra Depression Egypt 49E2
Qāyen Iran 41G3
Qazvīn Iran 41F2
Qena Egypt 40B4
Qeqertarsuaq = Godhavn
Qeqertarsuaq = Julianehåb
Qeydar Iran 41E2
Qeys, I Iran 41F4
Qezel Owzan, R Iran 21H8
Qeziot Israel 45C3
Qian Jiang, R China 31B5
Qian Shan, Upland China 31E1
Qidong China 31E3
Qijiang China 31B4
Qijiaojing China 26C2
Qila Saifullah Pak 42B2
Qilian China 31A2
Qilian Shan China 26C3
Qilian Shan, Mts China 25L6
Qin'an China 31B3
Qingdao China 31E2
Qingduizi China 28A3
Qinghai, Province China 31A2
Qinghai Hu, L China 31A2
Qingjiang, Jiangsu China 31D3
Qingjiang, Jiangxi China 31D4
Qing Jiang, R China 31B3
Qingshuihe China 31C2
Qingshui He, R China 31B2
Qingtongxia China 31B2
Qingyang China 31B2
Qingyuan China 28A2
Qingyuan, Zhejiang China 31D4
Qing Zang, Upland China 39G2
Qingzhou China 31B5
Qinhuangdao China 31D2
Qin Ling, Mts China 31B3
Qinzhou China 30D1
Qionghai China 30E2
Qionglai Shan, Upland China 31A3
Qiongzhou Haixia, Str China 30D1
Qiqihar China 26F2
Qîraîya, Wadi Egypt 45C3
Qiryat Ata Israel 45C2
Qiryat Gat Israel 45C3
Qiryat Shemona Israel 45C2
Qiryat Yam Israel 45C2
Qishon, R Israel 45C2
Qitai China 25K5
Qiyang China 31C4
Qog Qi China 31B1
Qolleh-ye-Damavand, Mt Iran 21J8
Qom Iran 41F3
Qomisheh Iran 41F3
Qomolangma Feng, Mt = Everest,Mt
Qornet es Saouda, Mt Leb 45D1
Qôrnoq Greenland 55N3
Qorveh Iran 41E2
Qotbabad Iran 41G4
Qotur, R Iran 21H8
Quabbin Res USA 68D1
Quaggablat S Africa 47C2
Quakenbrück W Germ 13D1
Quakertown USA 68C2
Quam Phu Quoc, I Viet 30C3
Quanah USA 62C2
Quang Ngai Viet 30D2
Quang Tri Viet 30D2
Quan Long Viet 30D4
Quanzhou, Fujian China 31D5
Quanzhou, Guangxi China 31C4
Qu' Appelle, R Can 54H4
Quartzsite USA 59D4
Quchan Iran 41G2
Queanbeyan Aust 34C3
Québec Can 65E1
Quebec, Province Can 55L4
Quebra-Anzol, R Brazil 75C2
Quedas do Iguaçu, Falls Arg/Brazil 74F3
Queen Anne USA 68B3
Queen Charlotte Is Can 54E4
Queen Charlotte Sd Can 54F4
Queen Charlotte Str Can 54F4
Queen Elizabeth Is Can 54H1
Queen Mary Land, Region Ant 76F9
Queen Maud G Can 54H3
Queen Maud Mts Ant 76E6
Queens, Borough, New York USA 68D2
Queen's Ch Aust 27F8
Queenscliff Aust 34B3
Queensland, State Aust 32D3
Queenstown Aust 34C4
Queenstown NZ 35A3
Queenstown S Africa 47D3
Queenstown USA 68B3
Quela Angola 51B4
Quelimane Mozam 51D5
Quemado USA 62A2
Querétaro Mexico 70B2
Quetta Pak 42B2
Quezaltenango Guatemala 70C3
Quezon City Phil 27F5
Quibala Angola 51B5
Quibaxe Angola 51B4
Quibdó Colombia 72C2
Quiberon France 14B2
Quicama Nat Pk Angola 51B4
Quiindy Par 75A4
Quillabamba Peru 72D6
Quillacollo Bol 72E7
Quillan France 14C3
Quill Lakes Can 54H4
Quillota Chile 74B4
Quilon India 44B4
Quilpie Aust 34B1
Quimbele Angola 51B4
Quimper France 14B2
Quimperlé France 14B2
Quincy, California USA 59B3
Quincy, Illinois USA 64A3
Quincy, Massachusetts USA 68E1
Qui Nhon Viet 30D3
Quintanar de la Orden Spain 15B2
Quirima Angola 51B5
Quirindi Aust 34D2
Quissanga Mozam 51E5
Quissico Mozam 51D6
Quito Ecuador 72C4
Quixadá Brazil 73L4
Qujing China 31A4
Qumbu S Africa 47D3
Quorn Aust 32C4
Qus Egypt 40B4
Quseir Egypt 40B4
Qutdligssat Greenland 55N3
Quthing = Moyeni
Qu Xian, Sichuan China 31B3
Qu Xian, Zhejiang China 31D4
Quynh Luu Viet 30D2
Quzhou China 31C2
Qūzū China 43G3

R

Raahe Fin 12J6
Raasay, I Scot 8B3
Raasay,Sound of, Chan Scot 8B3
Rab, I Yugos 16C2
Raba Indon 27E7
Rába, R Hung 18D3
Rabat Mor 48B1
Rabaul PNG 32E1
Rabba Jordan 45C3
Rabigh S Arabia 40C5
Race,C Can 55N5
Race Pt USA 68E1
Rachaya Leb 45C2
Rachel, Mt W Germ 18C3
Rach Gia Viet 30D3
Racine USA 64B2
Rădăuţi Rom 19F3
Radcliff USA 64B3
Radford USA 64C3
Radhanpur India 42C4
Radix,Pt Trinidad 69L1
Radom Pol 19E2
Radomsko Pol 19D2
Radomyshl' USSR 19F2
Radstad Austria 18C3
Radviliškis USSR 19E1
Rae Can 54G3
Rae Bareli India 43E3
Rae Isthmus Can 55K3
Rae L Can 54G3
Raetihi NZ 35C1
Rafaela Arg 74D4
Rafah Egypt 45C3
Rafai CAR 50C3
Rafha S Arabia 41D3
Rafsanjan Iran 41G3
Raga Sudan 50C3
Ragged Pt Barbados 69Q2
Raguba Libya 49D2
Ragusa, Sicily 16C3
Rahad, R Sudan 50D2
Rahimyar Khan Pak 42C3
Rahjerd Iran 41F3
Raichur India 44B2
Raigarh India 43E4
Rainbow Aust 34B3
Rainbow City USA 67A2
Rainier USA 58B1
Rainier,Mt USA 58B1
Rainy, R Can/USA 61E1
Rainy L Can 55J5
Rainy L Can/USA 61E1
Rainy River Can 61E1
Raipur India 43E4
Rājahmundry India 44C2
Rajang, R Malay 27E6
Rajanpur Pak 42C3
Rājapālaiyam India 44B4
Rajasthan, State India 42C3
Rajgarh, Madhya Pradesh India 42D4
Rājgarh, Rajasthan India 42D3
Rājkot India 42C4
Rajmahal Hills India 43F4
Raj Nandgaon India 43E4
Rājpīpla India 42C4
Rajshahi Bang 43F4
Rajur India 42D4
Rakaia, R NZ 35B2
Raka Zangbo, R China 39G3
Rakhov USSR 19E3
Rakhshan, R Pak 42A3
Rakops Botswana 47C1
Rakov USSR 19F2
Raleigh USA 67C1
Ram Jordan 45C4
Rama Israel 45C2
Ramalho, Serra do, Mts Brazil 75D1
Ramallah Israel 45C3
Ramanathapuram India 44B4
Ramapo Deep Pacific O 26H3
Ramat Gan Israel 45C2
Rambervillers France 13D3
Rambouillet France 14C2
Ramgarh, Bihar India 43F4
Ramgarh, Rajasthan India 42C3
Ramhormoz Iran 41E3
Ram, Jebel, Mt Jordan 45C4
Ramla Israel 45C3
Ramona USA 59C4
Rampur India 42D3
Rampura India 42D4
Ramree I Burma 43G5
Ramsar Iran 21J8
Ramsey, I of Man British Is 6B2

Ramsey Rockport

Ramsey *USA* 68C2
Ramsey I *Wales* 7B4
Ramsgate *Eng* 7E4
Ramtha *Jordan* 45D2
Ramu, R *PNG* 32D1
Ranau *Malay* 27E6
Rancagua *Chile* 74B4
Ranchester *USA* 60B2
Rānchi *India* 43F4
Rānchi Plat *India* 43E4
Ranco, Lago *Chile* 74B6
Randers *Den* 12F7
Randfontein *S Africa* 47D2
Randolph, Vermont *USA* 65E2
Randsburg *USA* 66D3
Ranfurly *NZ* 35B3
Rangamati *Bang* 43G4
Rangely *USA* 60B2
Rangiora *NZ* 35B2
Rangitaiki, R *NZ* 35C1
Rangitata, R *NZ* 35B2
Rangitikei, R *NZ* 35C1
Rangoon *Burma* 30B2
Rangpur *Bang* 43F3
Rānībennur *India* 44B3
Ranier,Mt *USA* 56A2
Rānīganj *India* 43F4
Rankins Springs *Aust* 34C2
Ranklin Inlet *Can* 55J3
Rannoch, Loch, L *Scot* 8C3
Rann of Kachchh, Flood Area *India* 42B4
Ranong *Thai* 30B4
Rantauparapat *Indon* 27C6
Rantekombola, G, Mt *Indon* 27F7
Rantoul *USA* 64B2
Ranuro, R *Brazil* 75B1
Raon-l'Etape *France* 13D3
Raoul, I *Pacific O* 33H3
Rapallo *Italy* 16B2
Raper,C *Can* 55M3
Rapid City *USA* 60C2
Rapid River *USA* 64B1
Rappahannock, R *USA* 65D3
Rapti, R *India* 43M2
Raritan B *USA* 68C2
Ras Abû Dâra, C *Egypt* 40C5
Ra's Abu Madd, C *S Arabia* 40C5
Ras Abu Shagara, C *Sudan* 50D1
Ra's al 'Ayn *Syria* 40D2
Ras al Khaimah *UAE* 41G4
Ra's al Madrakah, C *Oman* 38D4
Ras Andadda, C *Eth* 50E2
Ra's az Zawr, C *S Arabia* 41E4
Râs Banâs, C *Egypt* 40C5
Râs Burûn, C *Egypt* 45B3
Ras Dashan, Mt *Eth* 50D2
Ra's-e Barkan, Pt *Iran* 41E3
Râs el Barr, C *Egypt* 45A3
Ras El Hadid *Algeria* 16B3
Râs el Kenâyis, Pt *Egypt* 40A3
Râs el Nafas, Mt *Egypt* 45C4
Râs el Sudr, C *Egypt* 45B4
Ras en Naqb, Upland *Jordan* 45C4
Ra's Fartak, C *S Yemen* 38D4
Râs Ghârib *Egypt* 40B4
Rashad *Sudan* 50D2
Rashādīya *Jordan* 45C3
Rashîd *Egypt* 40B3
Rasht *Iran* 41E2
Ra's ibn Hāni', C *Syria* 45C1
Ras Khanzira, C *Somalia* 50E2
Ras Koh, Mt *Pak* 42B3
Râs Matarma, C *Egypt* 45B4
Râs Muhammad, C *Egypt* 40B4
Ras Nouadhibou, C *Maur/Mor* 48A2
Rasshua, I, Kuril Is *USSR* 26J2
Rasskazovo *USSR* 21G5
Ra's Tanāqib, C *S Arabia* 41E4
Ra's Tannūrah *S Arabia* 41F4
Rastatt *W Germ* 18B3
Ras Uarc, C = Tres Forcas, Cabo
Ras Um Seisabān, Mt *Jordan* 45C4
Ras Xaafuun, C *Somalia* 50E2
Ratangarh *India* 42C3
Rat Buri *Thai* 30B3
Rāth *India* 42D3
Rathenow *E Germ* 18C2
Rathfriland *N Ire* 9C2
Rathlin I *N Ire* 9C2
Rathmelton *Irish Rep* 9C2
Ratiyah, Wadi *Jordan* 45D4
Ratlām *India* 42C4
Ratnāgiri *India* 44A2
Ratnapura *Sri Lanka* 44C4
Ratno *USSR* 19E2
Raton *USA* 62B1
Rättvik *Sweden* 12H6
Raukumara Range, Mts *NZ* 35C1
Raul Soares *Brazil* 75D3
Rauma *Fin* 12J6
Raurkela *India* 43E4
Ravānsar *Iran* 41E3
Rāvar *Iran* 41G3
Rava Russkaya *USSR* 19E2
Ravena *USA* 68D1
Ravenna *Italy* 16C2
Ravensburg *W Germ* 18B3
Ravenshoe *Aust* 32D2
Ravi, R *Pak* 42C2
Ravn Kap, C *Greenland* 55Q3
Rawalpindi *Pak* 42C2
Rawāndiz *Iraq* 41D2
Rawicz *Pol* 18D2
Rawlinna *Aust* 32B4
Rawlins *USA* 56C2
Rawson *Arg* 74D6
Rawtenstall *Eng* 6C3
Rāyadurg *India* 44B3
Rāyagada *India* 44C2
Rayak *Leb* 45D2
Ray,C *Can* 55N5
Rāyen *Iran* 41G4
Raymond, California *USA* 66C2
Raymond *Can* 58D1
Raymond, New Hampshire *USA* 68E1
Raymond, Washington *USA* 58B1
Raymond Terrace *Aust* 34D2
Raymondville *USA* 63C3
Razan *Iran* 41E2
Razdel'naya *USSR* 19G3
Razdol'noye *USSR* 28C2
Razgrad *Bulg* 17F2
Razim, L *Rom* 17F2
Reading *Eng* 7D4
Reading *USA* 68C2
Read Island *Can* 54G3
Readsboro *USA* 68D1
Rebiana, Well *Libya* 49E2
Rebiana Sand Sea *Libya* 49E2
Reboly *USSR* 12L6
Rebun-tō, I *Japan* 29E1
Recherche,Arch of the, Is *Aust* 32B4
Rechitsa *USSR* 19G2
Recife *Brazil* 73M5
Recife,C *S Africa* 47D3
Recifes da Pedra Grande Arch *Brazil* 75E2
Récifs d'Entrecasteaux *New Caledonia* 33F2
Recklinghausen *W Germ* 13D2
Reconquista *Arg* 74E3
Red, R *Can/USA* 61D1
Red, R *USA* 63D2
Redang, I *Malay* 30C4
Red Bank, New Jersey *USA* 68C2
Red Bank, Tennessee *USA* 67A1
Red Bluff *USA* 59B2
Red Bluff L *USA* 62B2
Redcar *Eng* 6D2
Redcliffe *Aust* 34D1
Red Cliffs *Aust* 34B2
Red Cloud *USA* 60D2
Red Deer *Can* 54G4
Red Deer, R *Can* 54G4
Redding *USA* 58B2
Redditch *Eng* 7D3
Redfield *USA* 60D2
Redhill *Eng* 7D4
Red Hills *USA* 62C1
Red L *USA* 57D2
Red Lake *Can* 55J4
Red Lake, R *USA* 61D1
Redlands *USA* 66D3
Red Lion *USA* 68B3
Red Lodge *USA* 58E1
Redmond *USA* 58B2
Red Mountain *USA* 66D3
Red Oak *USA* 61D2
Redon *France* 14B2
Redondo Beach *USA* 66C4
Red River Delta *Vietnam* 31B5
Redruth *Eng* 7B4
Red Sea *Africa/Arabian Pen* 38B3
Redwater *Can* 54G4
Red Wing *USA* 61E2
Redwood City *USA* 66A2
Redwood Falls *USA* 61D2
Reed City *USA* 64B2
Reedley *USA* 66C2
Reedsport *USA* 58B2
Reedville *USA* 65D3
Reefton *NZ* 35B2
Ree, Lough, L *Irish Rep* 10B3
Reeth *Eng* 6D2
Refahiye *Turk* 40C2
Refugio *USA* 63C3
Regência *Brazil* 75E2
Regensburg *W Germ* 18C3
Reggane *Alg* 48C2
Reggio di Calabria *Italy* 16D3
Reggio nell'Emilia *Italy* 16C2
Reghin *Rom* 17E1
Regina *Can* 54H4
Registan, Region *Afghan* 42A2
Rehoboth *Namibia* 47B1
Rehoboth Beach *USA* 65D3
Rehovot *Israel* 45C3
Reidsville *USA* 67C1
Reigate *Eng* 7D4
Ré, Ile de, I *France* 14B2
Reims *France* 13B3
Reina Adelaida, Archipiélago de la *Chile* 74B8
Reinbeck *USA* 61E2
Reindeer L *Can* 54H4
Reinosa *Spain* 15B1
Reisterstown *USA* 68B3
Reitz *S Africa* 47D2
Reliance *Can* 54H3
Reliance *USA* 58E2
Relizane *Alg* 15C2
Remarkable,Mt *Aust* 34A2
Rembang *Indon* 27E7
Remiremont *France* 13D3
Remscheid *W Germ* 13D2
Remsen *USA* 68C1
Rena *Nor* 12G6
Rend L *USA* 64B3
Rendsburg *W Germ* 18B2
Renfrew *Can* 65D1
Renfrew *Scot* 8C4
Rengat *Indon* 27D7
Reni *USSR* 19F3
Renk *Sudan* 50D2
Renland, Pen *Greenland* 55Q2
Renmark *Aust* 34B2
Rennell, I *Solomon Is* 33F2
Rennes *France* 14B2
Reno *USA* 59C3
Reno, R *Italy* 16C2
Renovo *USA* 68B2
Rensselaer *USA* 68D1
Renton *USA* 58B1
Reo *Indon* 27F7
Repki *USSR* 19G2
Reprêsa de Furnas, Dam *Brazil* 75C3
Reprêsa Três Marias, Dam *Brazil* 75C2
Republic *USA* 58C1
Republican, R *USA* 60D2
Repulse Bay *Can* 55K3
Reshteh-ye Alborz, Mts *Iran* 41F2
Reshui *China* 31A2
Resistencia *Arg* 74E3
Reşiţa *Rom* 17E1
Resolute *Can* 55J2
Resolution I *NZ* 35A3
Resolution Island *Can* 55M3
Ressano Garcia *Mozam* 47E2
Rethel *France* 13C3
Réthimnon *Greece* 17E3
Réunion, I *Indian O* 36D6
Reus *Spain* 15C1
Reutlingen *W Germ* 13E3
Revda *USSR* 20L4
Revelstoke *Can* 54G4
Revigny-sur-Ornain *France* 13C3
Revillagigedo, Is *Mexico* 70A3
Revilla Gigedo, Islas *Pacific O* 37O4
Revin *France* 13C3
Revivim *Israel* 45C3
Rewa *India* 43E4
Rewāri *India* 42D3
Rexburg *USA* 58D2
Reykjavik *Iceland* 12A2
Reynosa *Mexico* 70C2
Rezé *France* 14B2
Rezekne *USSR* 19F1
Rezh *USSR* 20L4
Rhayader *Wales* 7C3
Rhazir *Leb* 45C1
Rheda Wiedenbrück *W Germ* 13E2
Rhein, R *W Europe* 18B2
Rheine *W Germ* 18B2
Rheinland Pfalz, Region *W Germ* 14D2
Rhine, R = Rhein
Rhinebeck *USA* 68D2
Rhinelander *USA* 64B1
Rhode Island, State *USA* 65E2
Rhode Island Sd *USA* 68E2
Rhodes *Greece* 17F3
Rhodes, I *Greece* 17F3
Rhodes Drift, Ford *S Africa/Botswana* 47D1
Rhodes Peak, Mt *USA* 58D1
Rhondda *Wales* 7C4
Rhône, R *France* 14C3
Rhyl *Wales* 7C3
Riachão do Jacuipe *Brazil* 73L6
Riacho de Santana *Brazil* 75D1
Ria de Arosa, B *Spain* 15A1
Ria de Betanzos, B *Spain* 15A1
Ria de Corcubion, B *Spain* 15A1
Ria de Lage, B *Spain* 15A1
Ria de Sta Marta, B *Spain* 15A1
Ria de Vigo, B *Spain* 15A1
Riāsi *Pak* 42C2
Riau, Kepulauan, Is *Indon* 27D6
Ribadeo *Spain* 15A1
Ribas do Rio Pardo *Brazil* 75B3
Ribauè *Mozam* 51D5
Ribble, R *Eng* 6C3
Ribeira *Brazil* 75C3
Ribeirão Prêto *Brazil* 75C3
Riberalta *Bol* 72E6
Rice L *Can* 65D2
Rice Lake *USA* 64A1
Richard's Bay *S Africa* 47E2
Richardson *USA* 63C2
Richardson Mts *Can* 54E3
Richfield *USA* 59D3
Richfield Springs *USA* 68C1
Richgrove *USA* 66C3
Richland *USA* 58C1
Richlands *USA* 64C3
Richmond, California *USA* 66A2
Richmond, Cape Province *S Africa* 47C3
Richmond *Eng* 6D2
Richmond, Kentucky *USA* 64C3
Richmond, Natal *S Africa* 47E2
Richmond, New South Wales *Aust* 34D2
Richmond *NZ* 35B2
Richmond, Queensland *Aust* 32D3
Richmond, Virginia *USA* 65D3
Richmond Range, Mts *NZ* 35B2
Richmondville *USA* 68C1
Rickmansworth *Eng* 7D4
Rideau Lakes *Can* 65D2
Ridgeland *USA* 67B2
Ridgway *USA* 68A2
Riecito *Ven* 69D4
Riesa *E Germ* 18C2
Riesco, I *Chile* 74B8
Riet, R *S Africa* 47C2
Rieti *Italy* 16C2
Rif, Mts *Mor* 15B2
Rif, R *Mor* 48B1
Rifle *USA* 60B3
Riga *USSR* 19E1
Riga,G of *USSR* 20C4
Rigby *USA* 58D2
Riggins *USA* 58C1
Rigolet *Can* 55N4
Riihimaki *Fin* 12J6
Rijeka *Yugos* 16C1
Rikuzen-Tanaka *Japan* 29D3
Rimbo *Sweden* 12H7
Rimini *Italy* 16C2
Rîmnicu Sărat *Rom* 17F1
Rimnicu Vîlcea *Rom* 21C6
Rimouski *Can* 57G2
Ringkøbing *Den* 12F7
Rinjani, Mt *Indon* 27E7
Rinns Point *Scot* 8B4
Rinteln *W Germ* 13E1
Riobamba *Ecuador* 72C4
Rio Benito *Eq Guinea* 48C4
Rio Branco *Brazil* 72E5
Rio Branco do Sul *Brazil* 75C4
Rio Bravo *Mexico* 62C3
Rio Bravo del Norte, R *Mexico/USA* 70B1
Rio Brilhante *Brazil* 75B3
Rio Claro *Brazil* 75C3
Rio Claro *Trinidad* 69L1
Ríocuarto *Arg* 74D4
Rio de Janeiro *Brazil* 75D3
Rio de Janeiro, State *Brazil* 75D3
Rio de Oro, Bahia de, B *Mor* 48A2
Río Gallegos *Arg* 74C8
Río Grande *Arg* 74C8
Rio Grande *Brazil* 74F4
Rio Grande *Nic* 69A4
Rio Grande, R *Mexico/USA* 70B2
Rio Grande, R *Nic* 70D3
Rio Grande City *USA* 62C3
Rio Grande de Santiago, R *Mexico* 70B2
Rio Grande do Norte, State *Brazil* 73L5
Rio Grande Do Sul, State *Brazil* 74F3
Rio Grande Rise *Atlantic O* 52G6
Ríohacha *Colombia* 72D1
Ríohacha *Colombia* 69C4
Riom *France* 14C2
Rio Mulatos *Bol* 72E7
Rio Negro *Brazil* 75C4
Río Negro, State *Arg* 74C5
Rio Negro, Embalse de, Res *Urug* 74E4
Rio Pardo *Brazil* 74F3
Rio Turbio *Arg* 74B8
Rio Verde *Brazil* 75B2
Rio Verde de Mato Grosso *Brazil* 75B2
Ripley *Eng* 7D3
Ripley, Ohio *USA* 64C3
Ripley, Tennessee *USA* 63E1
Ripley, West Virginia *USA* 64C3
Ripon *Eng* 6D2
Ripon *USA* 66B2
Rishiri-tō, I *Japan* 29E1
Rishon le Zion *Israel* 45C3
Rising Sun *USA* 68B3
Risør *Nor* 12F7
Ritchie's Arch, Is *Andaman Is* 44E3
Ritenbenk *Greenland* 55N2
Ritter,Mt *USA* 66C2
Ritzville *USA* 58C1
Rivadavia *Chile* 74B3
Rivas *Nic* 72A1
Rivera *Urug* 74E4
Riverbank *USA* 66B2
River Cess *Lib* 48B4
Riverdale *USA* 66C2
Riverhead *USA* 68D2
Riverina, Region *Aust* 34B3
Riversdale *NZ* 35A3
Riversdale *S Africa* 47C3
Riverside *USA* 66D4
Riverton *NZ* 35A3
Riverton *USA* 58E2
Riviera Beach *USA* 67B3
Riviére-du-Loup *Can* 65F1
Riwon *N Korea* 28A2
Riyadh *S Arabia* 41E5
Rize *Turk* 40D1
Rizhao *China* 31D2
Rizhskiy Zaliv = Riga,G of
Rizokaipaso *Cyprus* 45C1
Rizzuto, C *Italy* 16D3
Rjukan *Nor* 12F7
Roag, Loch, Inlet *Scot* 8B2
Roanes Pen *Can* 55K2
Roanne *France* 14C2
Roanoke, Alabama *USA* 67A2
Roanoke, Virginia *USA* 65D3
Roanoke, R *USA* 65D3
Roanoke Rapids *USA* 67C1
Roan Plat *USA* 59D3
Roberts *USA* 58D2
Roberts Creek Mt *USA* 59C3
Robertsfors *Sweden* 12J6
Robert S Kerr Res *USA* 63D1
Robertson *S Africa* 47B3
Robertsport *Lib* 48A4
Roberval *Can* 55L5
Robin Hood's Bay *Eng* 6D2
Robinvale *Aust* 34B2
Robstown *USA* 63C3
Roca, Cabo de, C *Port* 15A2
Roca Partida, I *Mexico* 70A3
Rocas, I *Brazil* 73M4
Rocha *Urug* 74F4
Rochdale *Eng* 7C3
Rochedo *Brazil* 75B2
Rochefort *France* 14B2
Rochelle *USA* 64B2
Rocher River *Can* 54G3
Rochester *Aust* 34B3
Rochester *Can* 55L5
Rochester *Eng* 7E4
Rochester, Minnesota *USA* 61E2
Rochester, New Hampshire *USA* 68E1
Rochester, New York *USA* 68B1
Rock, R *USA* 64B2
Rockall, I *UK* 52H2
Rockford *USA* 64B2
Rock Hill *USA* 67B2
Rockingham *USA* 67C2
Rock Island *USA* 64A2
Rockland *USA* 64B1
Rocklands Res *Aust* 34B3
Rockledge *USA* 67B3
Rockport *USA* 63C3

Rock Rapids

St-Hubert

Rock Rapids *USA* 61D2
Rock River *USA* 60B2
Rock Springs, Montana *USA* 60B1
Rocksprings, Texas *USA* 62B2
Rock Springs, Wyoming *USA* 58E2
Rocks Pt *NZ* 35B2
Rock,The *Aust* 34C3
Rockville, Connecticut *USA* 68D2
Rockville, Indiana *USA* 64B3
Rockville, Maryland *USA* 68B3
Rockwood *USA* 65F1
Rocky Ford *USA* 62B1
Rocky Island L *Can* 64C1
Rocky Mount *USA* 67C1
Rocky Mountain Nat Pk *USA* 60B2
Rocky Mts *Can/USA* 56B1
Rødbyhavn *Den* 18C2
Rodez *France* 14C3
Ródhos = Rhodes
Rodi Garganico *Italy* 16D2
Rodopi Planina, Mts *Bulg* 17E2
Roebourne *Aust* 32A3
Roedtan *S Africa* 47D1
Roer, R *Neth* 13D2
Roermond *Neth* 13C2
Roeselare *Belg* 13B2
Roes Welcome Sd *Can* 55K3
Rog *USSR* 26G2
Rogachev *USSR* 19F2
Rogaguado, Lago *Bol* 72E6
Rogers *USA* 63D1
Rogers City *USA* 64C1
Rogers L *USA* 66D3
Rogers,Mt *USA* 64C3
Rogerson *USA* 58D2
Roggeveldberge, Mts *S Africa* 47B3
Rogue, R *USA* 58B2
Rohri *Pak* 42B3
Rohtak *India* 42D3
Roja *USSR* 19E1
Rojo, Cabo, C *Mexico* 70C2
Rolândia *Brazil* 75B3
Rolla *USA* 63D1
Rollins *USA* 58D1
Roma = Rome
Roma *Aust* 34C1
Romain,C *USA* 67C2
Roman *Rom* 17F1
Romanche Gap *Atlantic O* 52H5
Romang, I *Indon* 27F7
Romania, Republic *E Europe* 21C6
Romano,C *USA* 67B3
Romans-sur-Isère *France* 14D2
Romblon *Phil* 27F5
Rome, Georgia *USA* 67A2
Rome *Italy* 16C2
Rome, New York *USA* 68C1
Rome *USA* 65D2
Romilly-sur-Seine *France* 14C2
Romney *USA* 65D3
Romny *USSR* 21E5
Rømø, I *Den* 18B1
Romoratin *France* 14C2
Rona, I *Scot* 8C3
Ronay, I *Scot* 8B3
Roncador, Serra do, Mts *Brazil* 75B1
Ronda *Spain* 15A2
Ronda, Sierra de, Mts *Spain* 15A2
Rondônia *Brazil* 72F6
Rondônia, State *Brazil* 72F6
Rondonópolis *Brazil* 75B2
Rong'an *China* 31B4
Rongchang *China* 31B4
Rongcheng *China* 31E2
Ronge, Lac la *Can* 54H4
Rongjiang *China* 31B4
Rong Jiang, R *China* 31B4
Rongklang Range, Mts *Burma* 30A1
Rønne *Den* 12G7
Ronneby *Sweden* 12H7
Ronne Ice Shelf *Ant* 76F2
Ronse *Belg* 13B2
Roodeschool *Neth* 13D1
Roof Butte, Mt *USA* 56C3
Roorkee *India* 42D3
Roosendaal *Neth* 13C2
Roosevelt *USA* 59D2
Roosevelt I *Ant* 76E6
Root, R *USA* 61E2
Roper, R *Aust* 32C2
Rora Head, Pt *Scot* 8D2
Roraima, Mt *Ven/Brazil/Guyana* 72F2
Roraima, State *Brazil* 72F3
Røros *Nor* 20A3
Rørvik *Nor* 12G6
Ros' R *USSR* 19G3
Rosalie *Dominica* 69Q2
Rosamond *USA* 66C3
Rosamond L *USA* 66C3
Rosario *Arg* 74D4
Rosário *Brazil* 73K4
Rosario *Par* 75A3
Rosário Oeste *Brazil* 75A1
Roscoe *USA* 68C2
Roscoff *France* 14B2
Roscommon *Irish Rep* 10B3
Roscrea *Irish Rep* 9C3
Roseau *Dominica* 69Q2
Rosebery *Aust* 34C4
Rosebud *USA* 60B1
Roseburg *USA* 58B2
Rosenberg *USA* 63C3
Rosenheim *W Germ* 18C3
Rosetown *Can* 54H4
Roseville *USA* 66B1
Roskilde *Den* 12G7
Roslavl' *USSR* 20E5
Roslyatino *USSR* 20G4
Roşorii de Vede *Rom* 17E2
Ross *NZ* 35B2
Rossano *Italy* 16D3
Rossan Pt *Irish Rep* 10B3
Ross Barnett Res *USA* 63E2
Rosseau L *Can* 65D1
Rossel, I *PNG* 33E2
Ross Ice Shelf *Ant* 76E6
Ross L *USA* 58B1
Rosslare *Irish Rep* 9C3
Ross,Mt *NZ* 35C2
Rosso *Maur* 48A3
Rosso, C, Corsica 16B2
Ross-on-Wye *Eng* 7C4
Rossosh *USSR* 21F5
Ross River *Can* 54E3
Ross S *Ant* 76F6
Rostâq *Iran* 41F4
Rostock *E Germ* 18C2
Rostov *USSR* 20F4
Rostov-na-Donu *USSR* 21F6
Roswell, Georgia *USA* 67B2
Roswell, New Mexico *USA* 62B2
Rota, I *Pacific O* 27H5
Rote, I *Indon* 27F8
Rotenburg, Niedersachsen *W Germ* 18B2
Rothaar-Geb, Region *W Germ* 13E2
Rothbury *Eng* 6D2
Rothera, Base *Ant* 76G3
Rotherham *Eng* 7D3
Rothesay *Scot* 8C4
Rothes-on-Spey *Scot* 8D3
Roto *Aust* 34C2
Rotoiti,L *NZ* 35B2
Rotoroa,L *NZ* 35B2
Rotorua *NZ* 35C1
Rotorua,L *NZ* 35C1
Rottenburg *W Germ* 13E3
Rotterdam *Neth* 18A2
Rottweil *W Germ* 13E3
Rotuma, I *Fiji* 33G2
Roubaix *France* 13B2
Rouen *France* 14C2
Rough, Oilfield *N Sea* 6E3
Roulers = Roeselare
Round I *Mauritius* 51F6
Round Mountain *USA* 66D1
Round Mt *Aust* 34D2
Roundup *USA* 58E1
Rousay, I *Scot* 8D2
Roussillon, Region *France* 14C3
Rouxville *S Africa* 47D3
Rouyn *Can* 65D1
Rovaniemi *Fin* 12K5
Rovereto *Italy* 16C1
Rovigo *Italy* 16C1
Rovinj *Yugos* 16C1
Rovno *USSR* 21D5
Row'ān *Iran* 41E2
Rowena *Aust* 34C1
Rowley I *Can* 55L3
Rowley Shoals *Aust* 32A2
Roxas *Phil* 27F5
Roxboro *USA* 67C1
Roxburgh *NZ* 35A3
Roy *USA* 58E1
Royal Canal *Irish Rep* 9C3
Royale, Isle *USA* 64B1
Royal Leamington Spa *Eng* 7D3
Royal Oak *USA* 64C2
Royal Tunbridge Wells *Eng* 7E4
Royan *France* 14B2
Roye *France* 13B3
Royston *Eng* 7D3
Rožňava *Czech* 19E3
Rozoy *France* 13B3
Rtishchevo *USSR* 21G5
Ruabon *Wales* 7C3
Ruaha Nat Pk *Tanz* 51D4
Ruahine Range, Mts *NZ* 35C1
Ruapehu,Mt *NZ* 35C1
Rub' al Khālī, Desert *S Arabia* 38C4
Rubha Hunish, C *Scot* 8B3
Rubha Réidh, Pt *Scot* 8C3
Rubinéia *Brazil* 75B3
Rubtsovsk *USSR* 24K4
Ruby *USA* 54C3
Ruby Mts *USA* 59C2
Rudan *Iran* 41G4
Rudanli *India* 43L2
Rūdbār *Iran* 41E2
Rudnaya *USSR* 29F2
Rudnaya Pristan' *USSR* 26G2
Rudnya *USSR* 19G2
Rudoka Planina, Mt *Yugos* 17E2
Rudol'fa, Ostrov, I *USSR* 24G1
Rudong *China* 31E3
Rudyard *USA* 64C1
Ruffec *France* 14C2
Rufiji, R *Tanz* 51D4
Rufino *Arg* 74D4
Rufisque *Sen* 48A3
Rufunsa *Zambia* 51C5
Rugby *Eng* 7D3
Rugby *USA* 60C1
Rügen, I *E Germ* 12G8
Ruhr, R *W Germ* 13D2
Ruijin *China* 31D4
Rujen, Mt *Bulg/Yugos* 17E2
Rukwa, L *Tanz* 51D4
Rum, I *Scot* 8B3
Ruma *Yugos* 17D1
Rumāh *S Arabia* 41E4
Rumbek *Sudan* 50C3
Rum Cay, I *The Bahamas* 69C2
Rumford *USA* 65E2
Rum Jungle *Aust* 32C2
Rumoi *Japan* 29D2
Rumphi *Malawi* 51D5
Runanga *NZ* 35B2
Runaway,C *NZ* 35C1
Runcorn *Eng* 7C3
Rundu *Namibia* 51B5
Rungwa *Tanz* 51D4
Rungwa, R *Tanz* 51D4
Rungwe, Mt *Tanz* 51D4
Ruoqiang *China* 39G2
Ruo Shui, R *China* 26D2
Rupea *Rom* 17F1
Rupert *USA* 58D2
Rupert, R *Can* 55L4
Rur, R *W Germ* 13D2
Rurrenabaque *Bol* 72E6
Rusape *Zim* 51D5
Ruse *Bulg* 17F2
Rushville, Illinois *USA* 64A2
Rushville, Nebraska *USA* 60C2
Rushworth *Aust* 34B3
Rusk *USA* 63C2
Ruskin *USA* 67B3
Russell *NZ* 35B1
Russell *USA* 60D3
Russellville, Alabama *USA* 63E2
Russellville, Arkansas *USA* 63D1
Russellville, Kentucky *USA* 64B3
Russian, R *USA* 59B3
Russian S.F.S.R., Republic *USSR* 20E4
Russkaya, Base *Ant* 76F5
Russkiy, Ostrov, I *USSR* 25L2
Rustavi *USSR* 41E1
Rustenburg *S Africa* 47D2
Ruston *USA* 63D2
Rutana *Burundi* 50C4
Ruteng *Indon* 27F7
Rutenga *Zim* 47E1
Ruth *USA* 59C3
Rüthen *W Germ* 13E2
Rutland *USA* 65E2
Rutland, I *Andaman Is* 44E3
Rutog *China* 42D2
Ruvu = Pangani
Ruvuma, R *Tanz/Mozam* 51E5
Ruweila, Wadi *Jordan* 45D4
Ruwenzori Range, Mts *Uganda/Zaïre* 50D3
Ruya, R *Zim* 51D5
Ružomberok *Czech* 19D3
Rwanda, Republic *Africa* 50C4
Ryan, L *Scot* 8C4
Ryazan' *USSR* 20F5
Ryazhsk *USSR* 20G5
Rybinskoye Vodokhranilishche, Res *USSR* 20F4
Rybnitsa *USSR* 19F3
Ryde *Eng* 7D4
Rye *Eng* 7E4
Rye Patch Res *USA* 58C2
Ryl'sk *USSR* 21E5
Ryn Peski, Desert *USSR* 21H6
Ryoju *S Korea* 28A3
Ryōtsu *Japan* 29D3
Ryskany *USSR* 19F3
Ryūkyū Is *Japan* 26F4
Rzeszów *Pol* 19E2
Rzhev *USSR* 20E4

S

Sa'ādatābād *Iran* 41F3
Saad el Aali, Dam *Egypt* 40B5
Saale, R *E Germ* 18C2
Saar, R *W Germ* 13D3
Saarbrücken *W Germ* 13D3
Saarburg *W Germ* 13D3
Saaremaa, I *USSR* 12J7
Saarland, State *W Germ* 13D3
Saarlouis *W Germ* 13D3
Saba'a *Egypt* 45B3
Šabac *Yugos* 17D2
Sabadell *Spain* 15C1
Sabae *Japan* 29C3
Sabah, State *Malay* 27E6
Sabanalarga *Colombia* 69C4
Sabang *Indon* 27C6
Sabari, R *India* 44C2
Sabastiya *Israel* 45C2
Sabaya *Bol* 72E7
Sab'Bi'ār *Syria* 40C3
Sabhā *Jordan* 45D2
Sabhā *Libya* 49D2
Sabi, R *Zim* 51D6
Sabie, R *S Africa* 47E2
Sabinas *Mexico* 70B2
Sabinas Hidalgo *Mexico* 70B2
Sabine, R *USA* 63C2
Sabine L *USA* 63D3
Sabkhat Maţţi, Salt Marsh *UAE* 41F5
Sabkhet el Bardawîl, Lg *Egypt* 45B3
Sable,C *Can* 55M5
Sable,C *USA* 67B3
Sable I *Can* 55M5
Şabyā *S Arabia* 50E2
Sabzevār *Iran* 41G2
Sacajawea Peak *USA* 58C1
Sacandaga Res *USA* 68C1
Sac City *USA* 61E2
Sachigo, R *Can* 57D1
Sach'on *S Korea* 28A3
Sachs Harbour *Can* 54F2
Saco, Maine *USA* 65E2
Saco, Montana *USA* 60B1
Sacramento *USA* 66B1
Sacramento, R *USA* 66B1
Sacramento, V *USA* 59B2
Sacramento Mts *USA* 62A2
Şa'dah *Yemen* 50E2
Sadanski *Bulg* 17E2
Sadiya *India* 43H3
Sado, R *Port* 15A2
Sado-shima, I *Japan* 29D3
Sādri *India* 42C3
Safad = Zefat
Safed Koh, Mts *Afghan* 42A2
Säffle *Sweden* 12G7
Safford *USA* 59E4
Saffron Walden *Eng* 7E3
Safi *Jordan* 40C3
Safi *Mor* 48B1
Şāfītā *Syria* 45D1
Safonovo *USSR* 19G1
Safwān *Iraq* 41E3
Saga *China* 43F3
Saga *Japan* 28B4
Sagaing *Burma* 30B1
Sagami-nada, B *Japan* 29C4
Sāgar *India* 42D4
Sag Harbor *USA* 68D2
Saginaw *USA* 64C2
Saginaw B *USA* 64C2
Saglek B *Can* 55M4
Sagŏ-ri *S Korea* 28A3
Saguache *USA* 62A1
Sagua de Tánamo *Cuba* 69B2
Sagua la Grande *Cuba* 69B2
Saguenay, R *Can* 57F2
Saguia el Hamra, Watercourse *Mor* 48A2
Sagunto *Spain* 15B2
Sahāb *Jordan* 45D3
Sahagún *Spain* 15A1
Sahara, Desert *N Africa* 48C2
Sahāranpur *India* 42D3
Sahaswan *India* 43K1
Saheira, Wadi el *Egypt* 45B4
Sahiwal *Pak* 42C2
Şaḩrā al Hijārah, Desert Region *Iraq* 41D3
Sahra esh Sharqiya, Desert Region *Egypt* 40B4
Sahuayo *Mexico* 70B2
Sahyūn, Hist Site *Syria* 45D1
Saibai I *Aust* 32D1
Saïda = Sidon
Sa'īdābād *Iran* 41G4
Saïdia *Mor* 15B2
Saidpur *Bang* 43F3
Saidu *Pak* 42C2
Saigō *Japan* 29B3
Saigon = Ho Chi Minh City
Saiha *India* 43G4
Saihan Tal *China* 26E2
Saijo *Japan* 29B4
Saiki *Japan* 28C4
Saimaa, L *Fin* 12K6
St Abb's Head, Pt *Scot* 8D4
St Albans *Eng* 7D4
St Albans, Vermont *USA* 65E2
St Albans, West Virginia *USA* 64C3
St Albans Head, C *Eng* 7C4
St Amand-les-Eaux *France* 13B2
St Amand-Mont Rond *France* 14C2
St Andrew B *USA* 67A3
St Andrews *Scot* 8D3
St Andrew Sd *USA* 67B2
Ste Anne *Can* 61D1
Ste Anne de Beaupré *Can* 65E1
St Ann's Bay *Jamaica* 69H1
St Anthony *Can* 55N4
St Anthony *USA* 58D2
St Arnaud *Aust* 34B3
St Augustin, Baie de, B *Madag* 51E6
St Augustine *USA* 67B3
St Austell *Eng* 7B4
St Austell Bay *Eng* 7B4
St-Avold *France* 13D3
St Bees Head, Pt *Eng* 6C2
St Brides B *Wales* 7B4
St-Brieuc *France* 14B2
St Catharines *Can* 65D2
St Catherine,Mt *Grenada* 69M2
St Catherines I *USA* 67B2
St Catherines Pt *Eng* 7D4
St-Chamond *France* 14C2
St Charles, Idaho *USA* 58D2
St Charles, Missouri *USA* 61E3
St Clair *USA* 64C2
St Clair,L *Can/USA* 64C2
St Clair Shores *USA* 64C2
St Claude *France* 14D2
St Cloud *USA* 61E1
St Croix, I *Caribbean S* 69E3
St Croix, R *Can/USA* 65F1
St Croix, R *USA* 64A1
St Croix Falls *USA* 64A1
St Davids Head, Pt *Wales* 7B4
St Denis *France* 13B3
St Denis *Réunion* 51F6
St-Dié *France* 13D3
St-Dizier *France* 13C3
St Elias, Mt *USA* 54D3
St Elias Mts *Can* 54E3
Saintes *France* 14B2
St-Étienne *France* 14C2
St-Félicien *Can* 65E1
St Florent, G de, Corsica 16B2
St Florent, Golfo de *Corse* 14D3
St-Florentin *France* 13B3
St Francis *USA* 60C3
St Francis, R *USA* 63D1
St Francis B *S Africa* 47C3
St Francis,C *S Africa* 47C3
St Gallen *Switz* 16B1
St-Gaudens *France* 14C3
St George *Aust* 34C1
St George, South Carolina *USA* 67B2
St George, Utah *USA* 59D3
St George I, Florida *USA* 67B3
St Georgen im Schwarzwald *W Germ* 13E3
St George,Pt *USA* 58B2
St-Georges *Can* 65E1
St George's *Grenada* 69M2
St George's Chan *Irish Rep/Wales* 7A4
St George's Chan *PNG* 33E1
St Gotthard, Pass *Switz* 16B1
St Govans Head, Pt *Wales* 7B4
St Helena *USA* 66A1
St Helena, I *Atlantic O* 52H5
St Helena B *S Africa* 47B3
St Helena Sd *USA* 67B2
St Helens *Aust* 34C4
St Helens *Eng* 7C3
St Helens *USA* 58B1
St Helens,Mt *USA* 58B1
St Helier, Jersey *Channel Is.* 14B2
St-Hubert *Belg* 13C2

St-Hyacinthe **San Rafael Mts**

St-Hyacinthe *Can* 55L5
St Ignace *USA* 64C1
St Ignace I *Can* 64B1
St Ives, Cambs *Eng* 7D3
St Ives, Cornwall *Eng* 7B4
St James, Minnesota *USA* 61E2
St James, Missouri *USA* 63D1
St James, C *Can* 54E4
St-Jean *Can* 65E1
St Jean-d'Angely *France* 14B2
St-Jean,L *Can* 65E1
St-Jérôme *Can* 65E1
St Joe, R *USA* 58C1
Saint John *Can* 55M5
St John, R *USA/Can* 65F1
St Johns, Arizona *USA* 59E4
St John's *Can* 55N5
St Johns, Michigan *USA* 64C2
St Johns, R *USA* 67B3
St Johnsbury *USA* 65E2
St John's Chapel *Eng* 6C2
St John's Pt *N Ire* 9D2
St Johnsville *USA* 68C1
St-Joseph *Can* 65E1
St Joseph, Louisiana *USA* 63D2
St Joseph, Michigan *USA* 64B2
St Joseph, Missouri *USA* 61E3
St Joseph *Trinidad* 69L1
St Joseph, R *USA* 64C2
St Joseph I *Can* 64C1
St Joseph I *USA* 63C3
St Joseph,L *Can* 55J4
St-Junien *France* 14C2
St-Just-en-Chaussée *France* 13B3
St Kilda, I *Scot* 8A3
St Kitts, I *Caribbean S* 69E3
St Lawrence, R *Can* 55M5
Saint Lawrence,G of *Can* 55M5
St Lawrence I *USA* 54B3
St Lawrence Seaway *Can/USA* 65D2
St Leonard *Can* 65F1
St Leonards *Eng* 7E4
St-Lô *France* 14B2
St-Louis *Sen* 48A3
St Louis *USA* 64A3
St-Loup-sur-Semouse *France* 13D4
St Lucia, I *Caribbean S* 69E4
St Lucia,L *S Africa* 47E2
St Magnus B *Scot* 8E1
St-Malo *France* 14B2
St-Malo, Golfe de, B *France* 14B2
Ste-Marie-aux-Mines *France* 13D3
St Maries *USA* 58C1
St Martin, I *Caribbean S* 69E3
St Mary,Mt *PNG* 32D1
St Mary Peak, Mt *Aust* 34A2
St Marys *Aust* 34C4
St Marys *USA* 65D2
St Marys, I *Eng* 7A5
St Marys, R *USA* 67B2
Saint Mathias Group, Is *PNG* 32E1
St Maurice, R *Can* 65E1
Ste-Menehould *France* 13C3
St Michael *USA* 54B3
St Michaels *USA* 68B3
St-Mihiel *France* 13C3
St Moritz *Switz* 16B1
St-Nazaire *France* 14B2
St Neots *Eng* 7D3
St-Niklaas *Belg* 13C2
St-Omer *France* 13B2
St-Pascal *Can* 65F1
St Paul *Can* 54G4
St Paul, Minnesota *USA* 61E2
St Paul, Nebraska *USA* 60D2
St Paul, I *Indian O* 36E6
St Paul, R *Lib* 48A4
St Peter *USA* 61E2
St Petersburg *USA* 67B3
St Pierre *Can* 55N5
St Pierre,L *Can* 65E1
St-Pol-sur-Ternoise *France* 13B2
St Pölten *Austria* 18D3
St-Quentin *France* 13B3
St Raphaël *France* 14D3
St-Siméon *Can* 65F1
St Simons I *USA* 67B2
St Stephen *USA* 67B2
St Thomas *Can* 64C2
St Tropez *France* 14D3
St Truiden *Belg* 13C2
St Vincent *USA* 61D1
St Vincent, I *Caribbean S* 69E4
St Vincent,G *Aust* 34A2
St-Vith *W Germ* 13D2
St Wendel *W Germ* 13D3
Saipan, I *Pacific O* 27H5
Saiydabad *Afghan* 42B2
Sajama, Mt *Bol* 72E7
Sak, R *S Africa* 47C3
Sakai *Japan* 29D4
Sakaidi *Japan* 29B4
Sakaiminato *Japan* 28B3
Sakākah *S Arabia* 40D4
Sakakawea,L *USA* 60C1
Sakami,L *Can* 57F1
Sakania *Zaïre* 51C5
Sakaraha *Madag* 51E6
Sakarya, R *Turk* 21E7
Sakasleja *USSR* 19E1
Sakata *Japan* 29D3
Sakété *Benin* 48C4
Sakhalin, I *USSR* 26H1
Sakishima guntō, Is *Japan* 26F4
Sakrivier *S Africa* 47C3
Sal, I *Cape Verde* 48A4
Sal, R *USSR* 21G6
Sala *Sweden* 12H7
Salada, Laguna, L *Mexico* 59C4
Salado, R, Sante Fe *Arg* 74D3
Salaga *Ghana* 48B4
Sala Hintoun *Camb* 30C3
Salal *Chad* 50B2
Şalālah *Oman* 38D4
Salamanca *Spain* 15A1
Salamanca *USA* 68A1
Salamat, R *Chad* 50B3
Salamaua *PNG* 27H7
Salamis, Hist Site *Cyprus* 45B1
Salangen *Nor* 12H5
Salar de Arizaro, Salt Pan *Arg* 74C2
Salar de Atacama, Salt Pan *Chile* 74C2
Salar de Coipasa, Salt Pan *Bol* 72E7
Salar de Uyuni, Salt Pan *Bol* 72E8
Salavat *USSR* 20K5
Salawati, I *Indon* 32C1
Sala y Gómez, I *Pacific O* 37O6
Salbris *France* 14C2
Saldanha *S Africa* 47B3
Saldus *USSR* 19E1
Sale *Aust* 34C3
Salekhard *USSR* 20M2
Salem, Illinois *USA* 64B3
Salem *India* 44B3
Salem, Massachusetts *USA* 68E1
Salem, New Jersey *USA* 68C3
Salem, New York *USA* 68D1
Salem, Oregon *USA* 58B2
Salem, Virginia *USA* 64C3
Sälen *Sweden* 12G6
Salerno *Italy* 16C2
Salford *Eng* 7C3
Salgótarján *Hung* 17D1
Salgótarján *Hung* 19D3
Salgueiro *Brazil* 73L5
Salida *USA* 60B3
Salihli *Turk* 17F3
Salima *Malawi* 51D5
Salina, Kansas *USA* 61D3
Salina, Utah *USA* 59D3
Salina, I *Italy* 16C3
Salina Cruz *Mexico* 70C3
Salinas *Brazil* 75D2
Salinas *USA* 66B2
Salinas, R *USA* 66B2
Salinas, Cabo de, C *Spain* 15C2
Salinas Grandes, Salt Pans *Arg* 74D3
Salinas Peak, Mt *USA* 62A2
Saline, R, Arkansas *USA* 63D2
Saline, R, Kansas *USA* 60C3
Salines,Pt *Grenada* 69M2
Saline V *USA* 66D2
Salinópolis *Brazil* 73J4
Salisbury = Harare
Salisbury *Eng* 7D4
Salisbury, Maryland *USA* 65D3
Salisbury, North Carolina *USA* 67B1
Salisbury I *Can* 55L3
Salisbury Plain *Eng* 7D4
Şalkhad *Syria* 45D2
Salla•*Fin* 12K5
Sallisaw *USA* 63D1
Salluit *Can* 55L3
Sallyana *Nepal* 43E3
Salmas *Iran* 41D2
Salmi *USSR* 12L6
Salmo *Can* 58C1
Salmon *USA* 58D1
Salmon, R *USA* 58C1
Salmon Arm *Can* 54G4
Salmon River Mts *USA* 58C1
Salo *Fin* 12J6
Salon-de-Provence *France* 14D3
Salonica = Thessaloníki
Salonta *Rom* 17E1
Salpausselkä, Region *Fin* 12K6
Sal'sk *USSR* 21G6
Salt *Jordan* 45C2
Salt, R *S Africa* 47C3
Salt, R *USA* 59D4
Salta *Arg* 74C2
Salta, State *Arg* 74C2
Saltash *Eng* 7B4
Saltee, I *Irish Rep* 9C3
Saltillo *Mexico* 70B2
Salt Lake City *USA* 58D2
Salto Angostura, Waterfall *Colombia* 72D3
Salto da Divisa *Brazil* 75E2
Salto das Sete Quedas *Brazil* 75B3
Salto del Angel, Waterfall *Ven* 72F2
Salto del Guaíra, Waterfall *Brazil* 74E2
Salto Grande, Waterfall *Colombia* 72D4
Salton S *USA* 59C4
Saltos do Iguaçu, Waterfall *Arg* 75B4
Salto Tacuarembó *Urug* 74E4
Salt Range, Mts *Pak* 42C2
Salt River *Jamaica* 69H2
Saluda *USA* 67B2
Sālūr *India* 44C2
Salvador *Brazil* 73L6
Salvador,L *USA* 63D3
Salwah *Qatar* 41F5
Salween, R *Burma* 30B1
Sal'yany *USSR* 21H8
Salyersville *USA* 64C3
Salzburg *Austria* 18C3
Salzgitter *W Germ* 18C2
Salzwedel *E Germ* 18C2
Samagaltay *USSR* 26C1
Samaná *Dom Rep* 69D3
Samandaği *Turk* 40C2
Samangan *Afghan* 42B1
Samani *Japan* 29D2
Samannûd *Egypt* 45A3
Samar, I *Phil* 27F5
Samarai *PNG* 32E2
Samarinda *Indon* 27E7
Samarkand *USSR* 39E2
Sāmarr' *Iraq* 41D3
Sambalpur *India* 43E4
Sambas *Indon* 27D6
Sambava *Madag* 51F5
Sambhal *India* 42D3
Sambor *USSR* 19E3
Sambre, R *France* 13B2
Samch'ŏk *S Korea* 28B3
Samch'ŏnp'o *S Korea* 28A4
Samdŭng *N Korea* 28A3
Same *Tanz* 50D4
Samfya *Zambia* 51C5
Samka *Burma* 30B1
Sam Neua *Laos* 30C1
Samoan Is *Pacific O* 33H2
Sámos, I *Greece* 17F3
Samothráki, I *Greece* 17F2
Sampit *Indon* 27E7
Sam Rayburn Res *USA* 63D2
Samrong *Camb* 30C3
Samsø, I *Den* 18C1
Samsu *N Korea* 28A2
Samsun *Turk* 40C1
San *Mali* 48B3
San, R *Camb* 30D3
San, R *Pol* 19E2
San'ā *Yemen* 50E2
Sanaga, R *Cam* 50B3
San Agustín *Arg* 74C4
San Ambrosia, Isla *Pacific O* 52D6
Sanandaj *Iran* 41E2
San Andreas *USA* 66B1
San Andres, Isla de *Caribbean S* 69A4
San Andres Mts *USA* 62A2
San Andrés Tuxtla *Mexico* 70C3
San Angelo *USA* 62B2
San Antioco, Sardinia 16B3
San Antioco, I, Sardinia 16B3
San Antonia, Pt *Mexico* 56B4
San Antonio *Chile* 74B4
San Antonio, New Mexico *USA* 62A2
San Antonio, Texas *USA* 62C3
San Antonio, R, California *USA* 66B2
San Antonio, R, Texas *USA* 63C3
San Antonio Abad *Spain* 15C2
San Antonio,C *Cuba* 70D2
San Antonio, Cabo, C *Cuba* 69A2
San Antonio de Bravo *Mexico* 62B2
San Antonio de los Banos *Cuba* 69A2
San Antonio,Mt *USA* 66D3
San Antonio Oeste *Arg* 74D6
San Antonio Res *USA* 66B3
San Ardo *USA* 66B2
Sanāwad *India* 42D4
San Benedicto, I *Mexico* 70A3
San Benito *USA* 63C3
San Benito, R *USA* 66B2
San Benito Mt *USA* 66B2
San Bernardino *USA* 66D3
San Bernardo *Chile* 74B4
San Bernardo Mts *USA* 59C4
San Blas,C *USA* 67A3
San Blas, Puerta, Pt *Panama* 70E4
San Borja *Brazil* 74E3
San Carlos *Chile* 74B5
San Carlos *Nic* 72B1
San Carlos *USA* 59D4
San Carlos de Bariloche *Arg* 74B6
Sanchursk *USSR* 20H4
San Clemente *USA* 66D4
San Clemente I *USA* 59C4
San Cristóbal *Mexico* 70C3
San Cristóbal *Ven* 72D2
San Cristobal, I *Solomon Is* 33F2
Sancti Spíritus *Cuba* 70E2
Sancy, Puy de, Mt *France* 14C2
Sand, R *S Africa* 47D1
Sanda, I *Scot* 8C4
Sandakan *Malay* 27E6
Sanday, I *Scot* 8D2
Sanderson *USA* 62B2
Sandgate *Eng* 7E4
San Diego *USA* 59C4
San Diego, Cabo *Arg* 74C8
Sandikli *Turk* 40B2
Sandīla *India* 43E3
Sandnes *Nor* 12F7
Sandnessjøen *Nor* 12G5
Sandoa *Zaïre* 51C4
Sandomierz *Pol* 19E2
Sandoway *Burma* 43G5
Sandown *Eng* 7D4
Sandoy, I *Faeroes* 12D3
Sandpoint *USA* 58C1
Sand Springs *USA* 63C1
Sandstone *Aust* 32A3
Sandstone *USA* 61E1
Sandu *China* 31C4
Sandusky *USA* 64C2
Sandviken *Sweden* 12H6
Sandwich *USA* 68E2
Sandy L *Can* 55J4
San Estanislao *Par* 75A3
San Felipe, Baja Cal *Mexico* 56B3
San Felipe *Chile* 74B4
San Felipe *Ven* 69D4
San Felíu de Guixols *Spain* 15C1
San Felix, Isla *Pacific O* 52D6
San Fernando *Chile* 74B4
San Fernando *Phil* 27F5
San Fernando *Spain* 15A2
San Fernando *Trinidad* 69L2
San Fernando *USA* 66C3
San Fernando *Ven* 72E2
Sanford, Florida *USA* 67B3
Sanford, Maine *USA* 65E2
Sanford, N Carolina *USA* 67C1
Sanford *USA* 57E4
Sanford, Mt *USA* 54D3
San Francisco *Arg* 74D4
San Francisco *Dom Rep* 69C3
San Francisco *USA* 66A2
San Francisco B *USA* 66A2
San Francisco del Oro *Mexico* 70B2
San Gabriel Mts *USA* 66D3
Sangamner *India* 42C5
Sangamon, R *USA* 64B3
Sangar *USSR* 25O3
Sangāreddi *India* 44B2
Sanger *USA* 66C2
Sanggan He, R *China* 31C2
Sanggau *Indon* 27E6
Sangha, R *Congo* 50B3
Sanghar *Pak* 42B3
Sangir, I *Indon* 27F6
Sangir, Kepulauan, Is *Indon* 27F6
Sangkhla Buri *Thai* 30B3
Sangkulirang *Indon* 27E6
Sāngli *India* 44A2
Sangmélima *Cam* 50B3
San Gorgonio Mt *USA* 56B3
Sangre de Cristo Mts *USA* 62A1
San Gregorio *USA* 66A2
Sangrūr *India* 42D2
Sangutane, R *Mozam* 47E1
San Ignacio *Arg* 74E3
San Jacinto *Colombia* 72D2
San Jacinto Peak, Mt *USA* 59C4
Sanjiangkou *China* 28A2
Sanjō *Japan* 29D3
San João del Rei *Brazil* 74H2
San Joaquin, R *USA* 66B2
San Joaquin Valley *USA* 66B2
San Jon *USA* 62B1
San Jorge, Golfo, G *Arg* 74C7
San Jorge, Golfo de, G *Spain* 15C1
San José *Costa Rica* 72B1
San José *Guatemala* 70C3
San Jose *USA* 66B2
San José, I *Mexico* 56B4
San José de Chiquitos *Bol* 72F7
San José del Cabo *Mexico* 56C4
San José do Rio Prêto *Brazil* 74G2
San Joseé del Cabo *Mexico* 70B2
Sanju *S Korea* 28A3
San Juan *Arg* 74C4
San Juan *Puerto Rico* 69D3
San Juan *Trinidad* 69L1
San Juan *Ven* 72E2
San Juan, Mt *Cuba* 69B2
San Juan, R, California *USA* 66B3
San Juan, R *Costa Rica/Nic* 70D3
San Juan, R, Utah *USA* 59D3
San Juan, State *Arg* 74C4
San Juan Bautista *Par* 74E3
San Juan Bautista *USA* 66B2
San Juan del Norte *Nic* 70D3
San Juan de los Cayos *Ven* 69D4
San Juan del Sur *Nic* 70D3
San Juan Is *USA* 58B1
San Juan Mts *USA* 62A1
San Julián *Arg* 74C7
Sankuru, R *Zaïre* 50C4
San Leandro *USA* 66A2
San Lorenzo *Ecuador* 72C3
San Lorenzo, Cabo, C *Ecuador* 72B4
San Lorenzo de Escorial *Spain* 15B1
San Lucas *USA* 66B2
San Luis *Arg* 74C4
San Luis *USA* 59D4
San Luis, State *Arg* 74C4
San Luis Canal *USA* 66B2
San Luis Obispo *USA* 66B3
San Luis Obispo B *USA* 66B3
San Luis Potosí *Mexico* 70B2
San Luis Res *USA* 66B2
Sanluri, Sardinia 16B3
San Maigualida, Mts *Ven* 72E2
San Marcos *USA* 63C3
San Martin, Base *Ant* 76G3
San Martin, Lago *Arg/Chile* 74B7
San Mateo *USA* 66A2
San Matías *Bolivia* 73G7
San Matías, Golfo, G *Arg* 74D6
Sanmenxia *China* 31C3
San Miguel *El Salvador* 70D3
San Miguel *USA* 66B3
San Miguel, I *USA* 66B3
San Miguel de Tucumán *Arg* 74C3
San Miguel d'Oeste *Brazil* 74F3
Sanming *China* 31D4
San Nicolas *Arg* 74D4
San Nicolas, I *USA* 56B3
Sannieshof *S Africa* 47D2
Sanniquellie *Lib* 48B4
Sanok *Pol* 19E3
San Onofore *Colombia* 69B5
San Onofre *USA* 66D4
San Pablo *Phil* 27F5
San Pablo B *USA* 66A1
San Pédro *Ivory Coast* 48B4
San Pedro, Jujuy *Arg* 74D2
San Pedro *Par* 74E2
San Pedro, R *USA* 59D4
San Pedro Chan *USA* 66C4
San Pedro de los Colonias *Mexico* 56C4
San Pedro Sula *Honduras* 70D3
San Pietro, I, Sardinia 16B3
Sanquar *Scot* 8D4
San Quintin *Mexico* 70A1
San Rafael *Arg* 74C4
San Rafael *USA* 66A2
San Rafael Mts *USA* 66C3

San Remo

Selvas

San Remo *Italy* 16B2
San Saba, R *USA* 62C2
San Salvador *El Salvador* 71B2
San Salvador, I *The Bahamas* 69C2
San Salvador de Jujuy *Arg* 74C2
San Sebastián *Spain* 15B1
San Severo *Italy* 16D2
San Simeon *USA* 66B3
Santa Ana *Bol* 72E7
Santa Ana *Guatemala* 70C3
Santa Ana *USA* 66D4
Santa Ana Mts *USA* 66D4
Santa Anna *USA* 62C2
Santa Barbara *Mexico* 70B2
Santa Barbara *USA* 66C3
Santa Barbara, I *USA* 66C4
Santa Barbara Chan *USA* 66B3
Santa Barbara Res *USA* 66C3
Santa Catalina, I *USA* 66C4
Santa Catalina,G of *USA* 66C4
Santa Catarina, State *Brazil* 74F3
Santa Catarina, Isla de *Brazil* 74G3
Santa Clara *Cuba* 69B2
Santa Clara *USA* 66B2
Santa Clara, R *USA* 66C3
Santa Cruz *Arg* 74C8
Santa Cruz *Bol* 72F7
Santa Cruz *Phil* 27F5
Santa Cruz *USA* 66A2
Santa Cruz, I *USA* 66C4
Santa Cruz, R *USA* 59D4
Santa Cruz, State *Arg* 74B7
Santa Cruz Cabrália *Brazil* 75E2
Santa Cruz Chan *USA* 66C3
Santa Cruz de la Palma *Canary Is* 48A2
Santa Cruz del Sur *Cuba* 69B2
Santa Cruz de Tenerife *Canary Is* 48A2
Santa Cruz do Cuando *Angola* 51C5
Santa Cruz do Rio Pardo *Brazil* 75C3
Santa Cruz Is *Solomon Is* 33F2
Santa Cruz Mts *USA* 66A2
Santa Elena *Ven* 72F3
Santa Fe *Arg* 74D4
Santa Fe *USA* 62A1
Santa Fe, State *Arg* 74D3
Santa Helena de Goiás *Brazil* 75B2
Santai *China* 31B3
Santa Inés, I *Chile* 74B8
Santa Isabel, I *Solomon Is* 33E1
Santa Lucia Range, Mts *USA* 66B2
Santa Luzia, I *Cape Verde* 48A4
Santa Margarita *USA* 66B3
Santa Margarita, R *USA* 66D4
Santa Margarita, Isla *Mexico* 70A2
Santa Maria *Brazil* 74F3
Santa Maria *USA* 66B3
Santa Maria, I *Azores* 48A1
Santa María, R, Chihuahua *Mexico* 62A2
Santa Maria, Cabo de, C *Mozam* 47E2
Santa Maria da Vitória *Brazil* 75D1
Santa Maria di Leuca, Capo, C *Italy* 17D3
Santa María Laguna de, L *Mexico* 62A2
Santa Marta *Colombia* 69C4
Santa Marta, Sierra Nevada de, Mts *Colombia* 72D1
Santa Monica *USA* 66C3
Santa Monica B *USA* 66C4
Santana *Brazil* 75D1
Santana do Livramento *Brazil* 74E4
Santander *Colombia* 72C3
Santander *Spain* 15B1
Santañy *Spain* 15C2
Santa Paula *USA* 66C3
Santa Quitéria *Brazil* 73K4
Santarém *Brazil* 73H4
Santarém *Port* 15A2
Santa Rita do Araguaia *Brazil* 75B2
Santa Rosa *Arg* 74D5
Santa Rosa, California *USA* 66A1
Santa Rosa *Honduras* 70D3
Santa Rosa, New Mexico *USA* 62B2
Santa Rosa, I *USA* 66B3
Santa Rosalía *Mexico* 70A2
Santa Rosa Range, Mts *USA* 58C2
Santa Talhada *Brazil* 73L5
Santa Teresa *Brazil* 75D2
Santa Teresa di Gallura, Sardinia 16B2
Santa Ynez, R *USA* 66B3
Santa Ynez Mts *USA* 66B3
Santee, R *USA* 67C2
Santiago *Chile* 74B4
Santiago *Dom Rep* 69C3
Santiago *Panama* 72B2
Santiago, R *Peru* 72C4
Santiago de Compostela *Spain* 15A1
Santiago de Cuba *Cuba* 69B2
Santiago del Estero *Arg* 74D3
Santiago del Estero, State *Arg* 74D3
Santiago Peak, Mt *USA* 66D4
Santo *Vanuatu* 33F2
Santo Amaro, Ilha *Brazil* 75C3
Santo Anastacátio *Brazil* 75B3
Santo Angelo *Brazil* 74F3
Santo Antão, I *Cape Verde* 48A4
Santo Antônio da Platina *Brazil* 75B3
Santo Antônio de Jesus *Brazil* 75E1
Santo Antônio do Leverger *Brazil* 75A2
Santo Domingo *Dom Rep* 69D3
Santos *Brazil* 75C3
Santos Dumont *Brazil* 75D3
Santo Tomas *Mexico* 59C4
Santo Tomé *Arg* 74E3
San Valentin, Mt *Chile* 74B7
San Vito, C, *Sicily* 16C3
Sanyuanpu *China* 28B2
Sanza Pomba *Angola* 51B4
São Carlos *Brazil* 75C3
São Domingos *Brazil* 75C1
São Félix, Mato Grosso *Brazil* 73H5
São Fidélis *Brazil* 75D3
São Francisco *Brazil* 75D2
São Francisco, R *Brazil* 73L5
São Francisco do Sul *Brazil* 74G3
São Francisco, Ilha de *Brazil* 75C4
São Gotardo *Brazil* 75C2
Sao Hill *Tanz* 51D4
São Jerônimo, Serra de, Mts *Brazil* 75A2
São João da Barra *Brazil* 75D3
São João da Boa Vista *Brazil* 75C3
São João d'Aliança *Brazil* 75C1
São João da Ponte *Brazil* 75D2
São João del Rei *Brazil* 75D3
São João do Paraíso *Brazil* 75D2
São Joaquim da Barra *Brazil* 75C3
São Jorge, I *Azores* 48A1
São José do Rio Prêto *Brazil* 75C3
São José dos Campos *Brazil* 75C3
São José dos Pinhais *Brazil* 75C4
São Lourenço, R *Brazil* 75A2
São Luís *Brazil* 73K4
São Marcos, R *Brazil* 75C2
São Marcos, Baia de, B *Brazil* 73K4
São Maria do Suaçui *Brazil* 75D2
São Mateus *Brazil* 75E2
São Mateus, R *Brazil* 75D2
São Miguel, I *Azores* 48A1
São Miguel de Araguaia *Brazil* 75B1
Saône, R *France* 14C2
São Nicolau, I *Cape Verde* 48A4
São Onofre, R *Brazil* 75D1
São Paulo *Brazil* 75C3
São Paulo, State *Brazil* 75B3
São Pedro e São Paulo, Is *Atlantic O* 71H3
São Raimundo Nonato *Brazil* 73K5
São Romão *Brazil* 75C2
São Sebastia do Paraíso *Brazil* 75C3
São Sebastião, Ilha de *Brazil* 75C3
São Simão, Goias *Brazil* 75B2
São Simão, São Paulo *Brazil* 75C3
São Tiago, I *Cape Verde* 48A4
São Tomé, I *W Africa* 48C4
São Tomé and Principe, Republic *W Africa* 48C4
São Tomé, Cabo de, C *Brazil* 75D3
Saoura, Watercourse *Alg* 48B2
Saouriuiná, R *Brazil* 75A1
São Vicente *Brazil* 75C3
São Vicente, Cabo de, C *Port* 15A2
São Vincente, I *Cape Verde* 48A4
Sápai *Greece* 17F2
Sapele *Nigeria* 48C4
Sapporo *Japan* 29E2
Sapri *Italy* 16D2
Sapulpa *USA* 63C1
Saqqez *Iran* 41E2
Sarāb *Iran* 21H8
Sarajevo *Yugos* 17D2
Saraktash *USSR* 21K5
Sarala *USSR* 25K4
Saranac Lake *USA* 65E2
Sarandë *Alb* 17E3
Saranpaul' *USSR* 20L3
Saransk *USSR* 20H5
Sarapul *USSR* 20J4
Sarasota *USA* 67B3
Sarata *USSR* 17F1
Saratoga *USA* 60B2
Saratoga Springs *USA* 68D1
Saratov *USSR* 21H5
Saratovskoye Vodokhranilishche, Res *USSR* 21H5
Saravane *Laos* 30D2
Sarawak, State *Malay* 27E6
Saraykoy *Turk* 40A2
Sardalas *Libya* 49D2
Sar Dasht *Iran* 41E2
Sardegna = Sardinia
Sardinia, I *Medit S* 16B2
Sarektjåkkå, Mt *Sweden* 12H5
Sargodha *Pak* 42C2
Sarh *Chad* 50B3
Sarhro, Jbel, Mt *Mor* 48B1
Sārī *Iran* 41F2
Sarida, R *Israel* 45C2
Sarigan, I *Pacific O* 27H5
Sarıkamış *Turk* 40D1
Sarina *Aust* 32D3
Sar-i-Pul *Afghan* 42B1
Sarir *Libya* 49E2
Sarir Tibesti, Desert *Libya* 49D2
Sariwŏn *N Korea* 28B3
Sark, I *Channel Is* 14B2
Şarkışla *Turk* 40C2
Sarmi *Indon* 27G7
Sarmiento *Arg* 74C7
Särna *Sweden* 12G6
Sarnia *Can* 64C2
Sarny *USSR* 19F2
Sarobi *Afghan* 42B2
Saronikós Kólpos, G *Greece* 17E3
Saros Körfezi, B *Turk* 17F2
Saroto *USSR* 20M2
Sarpsborg *Nor* 12G7
Sarqaq *Greenland* 55N2
Sarralbe *France* 13D3
Sarrebourg *France* 13D3
Sarreguemines *France* 13D3
Sarre-Union *France* 13D3
Sarrion *Spain* 15B1
Sartanahu *Pak* 42B3
Sartène, *Corsica* 16B2
Sarthe, R *France* 14B2
Sārūt, R *Syria* 45D1
Sarykamys *USSR* 21J6
Sarysu, R *USSR* 24H5
Sasarām *India* 43E4
Sasebo *Japan* 28B4
Saskatchewan, Province *Can* 54H4
Saskatchewan, R *Can* 54H4
Saskatoon *Can* 54H4
Saskylakh *USSR* 25N2
Sasolburg *S Africa* 47D2
Sasovo *USSR* 20G5
Sassandra *Ivory Coast* 48B4
Sassandra, R *Ivory Coast* 48B4
Sassari, *Sardinia* 16B2
Sassnitz *E Germ* 18C2
Sasuna *Japan* 28A4
Sātāra *India* 44A2
Satellite B *Can* 54G2
Säter *Sweden* 12H6
Satilla, R *USA* 67B2
Satka *USSR* 20K4
Satluj, R *India* 42D2
Satna *India* 43E4
Sātpura Range, Mts *India* 42C4
Satu Mare *Rom* 21C6
Sauðárkrókur *Iceland* 12B1
Sauda *Nor* 12F7
Saudi Arabia, Kingdom *Arabian Pen* 38C3
Sauer, R *W Germ/Lux* 13D3
Sauerland, Region *W Germ* 13D2
Saugatuck *USA* 64B2
Saugerties *USA* 68D1
Sauk Center *USA* 61E1
Sauk City *USA* 64B2
Sault Ste Marie *Can* 64C1
Sault Ste Marie *USA* 64C1
Saumlaki *Indon* 27G7
Saumur *France* 14B2
Saurimo *Angola* 51C4
Sauteurs *Grenada* 69M2
Sava, R *Yugos* 17D2
Savai'i, I *Western Samoa* 33H2
Savalou *Benin* 48C4
Savannah, Georgia *USA* 67B2
Savannah, Tennessee *USA* 63E1
Savannah, R *USA* 67B2
Savannakhet *Laos* 30C2
Savanna la Mar *Jamaica* 69G1
Savant Lake *Can* 55J4
Savé *Benin* 48C4
Save, R *Mozam* 51D6
Sāveh *Iran* 41F3
Saverne *France* 13D3
Savigny *France* 13B3
Savinskiy *USSR* 20F3
Savoie, Region *France* 14D2
Savona *Italy* 16B2
Savonlinna *Fin* 12K6
Savoonga *USA* 54A3
Savu, I *Indon* 32B2
Savukoski *Fin* 12K5
Savu S *Indon* 27F7
Saw *Burma* 30A1
Sawai Mādhopur *India* 42D3
Sawankhalok *Thai* 30C2
Sawara *Japan* 29D3
Sawatch Mts *USA* 60B3
Sawdā', Jabal as, Mts *Libya* 49D2
Sawknah *Libya* 49D2
Sawtooth Range, Mts *USA* 58C2
Sawu, I *Indon* 27F8
Saxmundham *Eng* 7E3
Saxton *USA* 68A2
Say *Niger* 48C3
Sayghan *Afghan* 42B1
Sayhandulaan *Mongolia* 31B1
Sayhūt *S Yemen* 38D4
Saykhin *USSR* 21H6
Saynshand *Mongolia* 26D2
Sayre, Oklahoma *USA* 62C1
Sayre, Pennsylvania *USA* 68B2
Say-Utes *USSR* 21J7
Sayville *USA* 68D2
Sázava, R *Czech* 18C3
Sbisseb, R *Alg* 15C2
Scafell Pike, Mt *Eng* 6C2
Scalloway *Scot* 8E1
Scalpay, I *Scot* 8C3
Scapa Flow, Sd *Scot* 8D2
Scarborough *Can* 65D2
Scarborough *Eng* 6D2
Scarborough *Tobago* 69K1
Scarp, I *Scot* 8B2
Schaffhausen *Switz* 16B1
Schärding *Austria* 18C3
Scharhörn, I *W Germ* 13E1
Scharteberg, Mt *W Germ* 13D2
Schefferville *Can* 55M4
Schelde, R *Belg* 13B2
Schell Creek Range, Mts *USA* 59D3
Schenectady *USA* 68D1
Schertz *USA* 62C3
Schiedam *Neth* 13C2
Schiermonnikoog, I *Neth* 13D1
Schleiden *W Germ* 13D2
Schleswig *W Germ* 18B2
Schleswig Holstein, State *W Germ* 18B2
Schoharie *USA* 68C1
Schouten Is *PNG* 32D1
Schramberg *W Germ* 13E3
Schreiber *Can* 55K5
Schull *Irish Rep* 9B4
Schurz *USA* 59C3
Schuykill Haven *USA* 68B2
Schuylkill, R *USA* 68C2
Schwabische Alb, Upland *W Germ* 18B3
Schwaner, Pegunungan, Mts *Indon* 27E7
Schwarzrand, Mts *Namibia* 47B2
Schwarzwald, Mts *W Germ* 13E3
Schweinfurt *W Germ* 18C2
Schweizer Reneke *S Africa* 47D2
Schwerin *E Germ* 18C2
Schwyz *Switz* 16B1
Sciacca *Italy* 16C3
Scilly, Isles of *Eng* 7A5
Scioto, R *USA* 64C3
Scobey *USA* 60B1
Scone *Aust* 34D2
Scoresby Sd *Greenland* 55Q2
Scotia Sea *Atlantic O* 52F7
Scotland *U K* 8C3
Scott, Base *Ant* 76F7
Scottburgh *S Africa* 47E3
Scott City *USA* 62B1
Scott I *Ant* 76G6
Scott Inlet, B *Can* 55L2
Scott,Mt *USA* 58B2
Scott Reef *Timor S* 32B2
Scottsbluff *USA* 60C2
Scottsboro *USA* 67A2
Scottsdale *Aust* 34C4
Scottsdale *USA* 59D4
Scranton *USA* 68C2
Scribner *USA* 61D2
Scunthorpe *Eng* 7D3
Scutari = Shkodër
Seacow, R *S Africa* 47C3
Seaford *Eng* 7E4
Seal, R *Can* 54J4
Sea Lake *Aust* 34B3
Searchlight *USA* 59D3
Searcy *USA* 63D1
Searles *USA* 66D3
Seaside, California *USA* 66B2
Seaside, Oregon *USA* 58B1
Seaside Park *USA* 68C3
Seattle *USA* 58B1
Sebago L *USA* 65E2
Sebastian Vizcaino, B *Mexico* 70A2
Sebastopol *USA* 66A1
Sebderaf *Eth* 50D2
Sebez *USSR* 19F1
Seboomook L *USA* 65F1
Sebring *USA* 67B3
Secretary I *NZ* 35A3
Sedalia *USA* 61E3
Sedan *France* 13C3
Sedbergh *Eng* 6C2
Seddonville *NZ* 35B2
Sede Boqer *Israel* 45C3
Sederot *Israel* 45C3
Sédhiou *Sen* 48A3
Sedom *Israel* 45C3
Sedona *USA* 59D4
Seeheim *Namibia* 47B2
Seelig,Mt *Ant* 76E4
Sefton,Mt *NZ* 35B2
Segamat *Malay* 30C5
Segezha *USSR* 20E3
Segorbe *Spain* 15B2
Ségou *Mali* 48B3
Segovia = Coco
Segovia *Spain* 15B1
Segre, R *Spain* 15C1
Séguéla *Ivory Coast* 48B4
Seguin *USA* 63C3
Segura, R *Spain* 15B2
Segura, Sierra de, Mts *Spain* 15B2
Sehwan *Pak* 42B3
Seiling *USA* 62C1
Seille, R *France* 13D3
Seinäjoki *Fin* 12J6
Seine, R *Can* 61E1
Seine, R *France* 13C4
Seine-et-Marne, Department *France* 13B3
Sekenke *Tanz* 50D4
Sekondi *Ghana* 48B4
Selah *USA* 58B1
Selaru, I *Indon* 27G7
Selatan, I *Indon* 27D6
Selat Dampier, Str *Indon* 27G7
Selat Lombok, Chan *Indon* 27E7
Selat Sunda, Str *Indon* 27D7
Selat Wetar, Chan *Indon* 27F7
Selawik *USA* 54C3
Selayar, I *Indon* 32B1
Selby *Eng* 6D3
Selby *USA* 60C1
Selçuk *Turk* 17F3
Selebi Pikwe *Botswana* 47D1
Selennyakh, R *USSR* 25Q3
Selestat *France* 13D3
Selfoss *Iceland* 55Q3
Selfridge *USA* 60C1
Selima Oasis *Sudan* 50C1
Selizharovo *USSR* 19G1
Selkirk *Can* 54J4
Selkirk *Scot* 8D4
Selkirk Mts *Can/USA* 54G4
Selma, Alabama *USA* 67A2
Selma, California *USA* 66C2
Selmer *USA* 63E1
Selouane *Mor* 15B2
Selvas, Region *Brazil* 72D5

Selvegens, Ilhas
Silver Spring

Selvegens, Ilhas, Is *Atlantic O* **48A2**
Selway, R *USA* **58C1**
Selwyn *Aust* **32D3**
Selwyn Mts *Can* **54E3**
Semarang *Indon* **27E7**
Semenov *USSR* **20G4**
Semiluki *USSR* **21F5**
Seminoe Res *USA* **60B2**
Seminole, Oklahoma *USA* **63C1**
Seminole, Texas *USA* **62B2**
Seminole,L *USA* **67B2**
Semipalatinsk *USSR* **24K4**
Semirom *Iran* **41F3**
Semnān *Iran* **41F2**
Semois, R *Belg* **13C3**
Sena Madureira *Brazil* **72E5**
Senanga *Zambia* **51C5**
Senatobia *USA* **63E2**
Sendai *Japan* **29E3**
Sendwha *India* **42D4**
Seneca Falls *USA* **68B1**
Seneca L *USA* **68B1**
Senecu *Mexico* **62A2**
Sénégal, R *Maur/Sen* **48A3**
Senegal, Republic *Africa* **48A3**
Senekal *S Africa* **47D2**
Senhor do Bonfim *Brazil* **73L6**
Senigallia *Italy* **16C2**
Senj *Yugos* **16D2**
Senkaku Gunto, Is *Japan* **26F4**
Senlis *France* **13B3**
Sennar *Sudan* **50D2**
Senneterre *Can* **55L5**
Senones *France* **13D3**
Sens *France* **13B3**
Senta *Yugos* **17D1**
Sentery *Zaïre* **50C4**
Seoni *India* **42D4**
Seoul *S Korea* **28B3**
Separation Pt *NZ* **35B2**
Sepetiba, B de *Brazil* **75D3**
Sepik, R *PNG* **27H7**
Sep'o *N Korea* **28A3**
Sepone *Laos* **30D2**
Sepotuba, R *Brazil* **75A2**
Sept-Iles *Can* **55M4**
Séquédine *Niger* **50B1**
Sequoia Nat Pk *USA* **66C2**
Serai *Syria* **45C1**
Seram, I *Indon* **27F7**
Seram Sea *Indon* **27F7**
Serbia, Region *Yugos* **17D2**
Serdobsk *USSR* **21G5**
Serein, R *France* **13B4**
Seremban *Malay* **30C5**
Serengeti Nat Pk *Tanz* **50D4**
Serenje *Zambia* **51D5**
Seret, R *USSR* **19F3**
Sergach *USSR* **20H4**
Sergeyevka *USSR* **28C2**
Sergino *USSR* **24H3**
Sergipe, State *Brazil* **73L6**
Seria *Brunei* **27E6**
Serian *Malay* **27E6**
Sérifos, I *Greece* **17E3**
Serir Calanscio, Desert *Libya* **49E2**
Sermaize-les-Bains *France* **13C3**
Sermata, I *Indon* **32B1**
Sermilik, Fjord *Greenland* **55P3**
Sernovodsk *USSR* **20J5**
Serov *USSR* **24H4**
Serowe *Botswana* **47D1**
Serpa *Port* **15A2**
Serpukhov *USSR* **20F5**
Serra da Estrela, Mts *Port* **15A1**
Serra do Navio *Brazil* **73H3**
Sérrai *Greece* **17E2**
Serrana Bank, Is *Caribbean S* **70D3**
Serraná de Cuenca, Mts *Spain* **15B1**
Serranópolis *Brazil* **75B2**
Serrat, C *Tunisia* **16B3**
Serre, R *France* **13B3**
Serrinha *Brazil* **73L6**
Serro *Brazil* **75D2**
Sersou, Plateau du *Alg* **15C2**
Sertanópolis *Brazil* **75B3**
Sêrtar *China* **31A3**
Serule *Botswana* **47D1**
Sesfontein *Namibia* **51B5**
Sesheke *Zambia* **51C5**
Setana *Japan* **29D2**
Sète *France* **14C3**
Sete Lagoas *Brazil* **75D2**
Sétif *Alg* **15C2**
Seto *Japan* **29C3**
Seto Naikai, S *Japan* **28B4**
Settat *Mor* **48B1**
Settle *Eng* **6C2**
Setúbal *Port* **15A2**
Seul, Lac *Can* **55J4**
Sevan, Ozero, L *USSR* **21H7**
Sevastopol' *USSR* **21E7**
Sevenoaks *Eng* **7E4**
Severn, R *Can* **55K4**
Severn, R *Eng* **7C3**
Severnaya Dvina, R *USSR* **20G3**
Severnaya Zemlya, I *USSR* **25M1**
Severnyy Sos'va, R *USSR* **20L3**
Severnyy Ural, Mts *USSR* **20K3**
Severo Baykal'skoye Nagor'ye, Mts *USSR* **25M4**
Severo Donets, R *USSR* **21F6**
Severodvinsk *USSR* **20F3**
Severo Sos'va, R *USSR* **24H3**
Severoural'sk *USSR* **20L3**
Sevier, R *USA* **59D3**
Sevier Desert *USA* **59D3**
Sevier L *USA* **59D3**
Sevilla = Seville
Seville *Spain* **15A2**
Sevlievo *Bulg* **17F2**
Sewa, R *Sierra Leone* **48A4**
Seward, Nebraska *USA* **61D2**
Seward *USA* **54D3**
Seward Pen *USA* **54B3**
Seychelles, Is, Republic *Indian O* **46K8**
Seyhan, R *Turk* **40C2**
Seyðisfjorður *Iceland* **12C1**
Seym, R *USSR* **21F5**
Seymchan *USSR* **25R3**
Seymour *Aust* **34C3**
Seymour, Connecticut *USA* **68D2**
Seymour, Indiana *USA* **64B3**
Seymour, Texas *USA* **62C2**
Sézanne *France* **13B3**
Sfax *Tunisia* **48D1**
Sfînto Gheorghe *Rom* **17F1**
's-Gravenhage = The Hague
Sgúrr na Lapaich,, Mt *Scot* **8C3**
Shaanxi, Province *China* **31B3**
Shabeelle, R *Eth/Somalia* **50E3**
Shabunda *Zaïre* **50C4**
Shache *China* **39F2**
Shackleton Ice Shelf *Ant* **76G9**
Shadadkot *Pak* **42B3**
Shādhām, R *Iran* **41F3**
Shafter *USA* **66C3**
Shaftesbury *Eng* **7C4**
Shagang *China* **28A2**
Shag Rocks, Is *South Georgia* **74J8**
Shāhābād *India* **44B2**
Shāhābād *Iran* **41E3**
Shahbā *Syria* **45D2**
Shahdāb *Iran* **41G3**
Shahdol *India* **43E4**
Shāhin Dezh *Iran* **41E2**
Shāh Kūh, Mt *Iran* **41G3**
Shahr-e Bābak *Iran* **41G3**
Shahresa = Qomisheh
Shahr Kord *Iran* **41F3**
Shahsavār *Iran* **21J8**
Shaim *USSR* **20L3**
Sha'īra, Gebel, Mt *Egypt* **45C4**
Sha'it, Wadi, Watercourse *Egypt* **40B5**
Shājahānpur *India* **42D3**
Shājāpur *India* **42D4**
Shakhty *USSR* **21G6**
Shakhun'ya *USSR* **20H4**
Shaki *Nigeria* **48C4**
Shakopee *USA* **61E2**
Shakotan-misaki, C *Japan* **29D2**
Shamary *USSR* **20K4**
Shambe *Sudan* **50D3**
Shamokin *USA* **68B2**
Shamrock *USA* **62B1**
Shandaken *USA* **68C1**
Shandon *USA* **66B3**
Shandong, Province *China* **31D2**
Shangchuan Dao, I *China* **31C5**
Shangdu *China* **31C1**
Shanghai *China* **31E3**
Shangnan *China* **31C3**
Shangombo *Zambia* **51C5**
Shangqiu *China* **31D3**
Shangrao *China* **31D4**
Shangsi *China* **31B5**
Shang Xian *China* **31C3**
Shanklin *Eng* **7D4**
Shannon, R *Irish Rep* **9B3**
Shansonggang *China* **28B2**
Shantarskiye Ostrova, I *USSR* **26G1**
Shantou *China* **31D5**
Shanxi, Province *China* **31C2**
Shan Xian *China* **31D3**
Shaoguan *China* **31C5**
Shaoxing *China* **31E4**
Shaoyang *China* **31C4**
Shapinsay, I *Scot* **8D2**
Shaqqā *Syria* **45D2**
Shaqra' *S Arabia* **41E4**
Shari *Japan* **29D2**
Sharifābād *Iran* **41G2**
Sharjah *UAE* **41G4**
Shark B *Aust* **32A3**
Sharlauk *USSR* **41G2**
Sharon,Plain of *Israel* **45C2**
Sharpsburg *USA* **68B3**
Sharqi, Jebel esh, Mts *Leb/Syria* **40C3**
Sharya *USSR* **20H4**
Shashamenē *Eth* **50D3**
Shashani, R *Zim* **47D1**
Shashe, R *Botswana* **47D1**
Shashi *China* **31C3**
Shasta L *USA* **58B2**
Shasta,Mt *USA* **58B2**
Shaṭḥah at Taḥta *Syria* **45D1**
Shaṭṭ al Gharraf, R *Iraq* **41E3**
Shaubak *Jordan* **45C3**
Shaver L *USA* **66C2**
Shawangunk Mt *USA* **68C2**
Shawano *USA* **64B2**
Shawinigan *Can* **65E1**
Shawnee, Oklahoma *USA* **63C1**
Shawnee, Wyoming *USA* **60B2**
Sha Xian *China* **31D4**
Shay Gap *Aust* **32B3**
Shaykh Miskin *Syria* **45D2**
Shaykh 'Uthman *S Yemen* **50E2**
Shchigry *USSR* **21F5**
Shchors *USSR* **21E5**
Shchuchinsk *USSR* **24J4**
Shebele, R *Eth* **50E3**
Sheboygan *USA* **64B2**
Shebshi Mts *Nig* **50B3**
Sheelin, L *Irish Rep* **9C3**
Sheep Haven, Estuary *Irish Rep* **9C2**
Sheerness *Eng* **7E4**
Shefar'am *Israel* **45C2**
Sheffield, Alabama *USA* **63E2**
Sheffield *Eng* **7D3**
Sheffield, Texas *USA* **62B2**
Sheil, Loch, L *Scot* **8C3**
Shekhupura *Pak* **42C2**
Shelagskiy, Mys, C *USSR* **25T2**
Shelburne Falls *USA* **68D1**
Shelby, Michigan *USA* **64B2**
Shelby, Montana *USA* **58D1**
Shelby, N Carolina *USA* **67B1**
Shelbyville, Indiana *USA* **64B3**
Shelbyville, Tennessee *USA* **67A1**
Sheldon *USA* **61D2**
Shelikof Str *USA* **54C4**
Shelley *USA* **58D2**
Shellharbour *Aust* **34D2**
Shelter Pt *NZ* **35A3**
Shelton *USA* **58B1**
Shemakha *USSR* **41E1**
Shenandoah *USA* **61D2**
Shenandoah, R *USA* **65D3**
Shenandoah Nat Pk *USA* **65D3**
Shendam *Nigeria* **48C4**
Shendi *Sudan* **50D2**
Shenkursk *USSR* **20G3**
Shenmu *China* **31C2**
Shenyang *China* **31E1**
Shenzhen *China* **31C5**
Sheopur *India* **42D3**
Shepetovka *USSR* **19F2**
Shepherdstown *USA* **68B3**
Shepparton *Aust* **34C3**
Sheppey, I *Eng* **7E4**
Sherard,C *Can* **55K2**
Sherborne *Eng* **7C4**
Sherbro I *Sierra Leone* **48A4**
Sherbrooke *Can* **65E1**
Sherburne *USA* **68C1**
Shergarh *India* **42C3**
Sheridan, Arkansas *USA* **63D2**
Sheridan, Wyoming *USA* **60B2**
Sheringham *Eng* **7E3**
Sherman *USA* **63C2**
's-Hertogenbosch *Neth* **18B2**
Shetland, Is *Scot* **10C1**
Shevchenko *USSR* **21J7**
Sheyenne *USA* **60D1**
Sheyenne, R *USA* **60D1**
Sheyk Sho'eyb, I *Iran* **41F4**
Shiant, Sd of *Scot* **8B3**
Shiashkotan, I, Kuril Is *USSR* **26J2**
Shibarghan *Afghan* **42B1**
Shibata *Japan* **29D3**
Shibetsu *Japan* **29D2**
Shibîn el Kom *Egypt* **49F1**
Shibîn el Qanâtir *Egypt* **45A3**
Shibukawa *Japan* **29C3**
Shickshinny *USA* **68B2**
Shidao *China* **28A3**
Shijiazhuang *China* **31C2**
Shikarpur *Pak* **42B3**
Shikoku, I *Japan* **26G3**
Shikoku-sanchi, Mts *Japan* **29B4**
Shikotan, I *USSR* **26H2**
Shikotsu-ko, L *Japan* **29D2**
Shilega *USSR* **20G3**
Shiliguri *India* **43F3**
Shilka *USSR* **26E1**
Shilka, R *USSR* **26E1**
Shillington *USA* **68C2**
Shillong *India* **43G3**
Shilovo *USSR* **20G5**
Shimabara *Japan* **28B4**
Shimada *Japan* **29C4**
Shimanovsk *USSR* **26F1**
Shimizu *Japan* **29D3**
Shimoda *Japan* **29C4**
Shimoga *India* **44B3**
Shimonoseki *Japan* **28C4**
Shinano, R *Japan* **29C3**
Shināş *Oman* **41G5**
Shindand *Afghan* **38E2**
Shinglehouse *USA* **68A2**
Shingū *Japan* **29D4**
Shinjō *Japan* **29D3**
Shin, Loch, L *Scot* **8C2**
Shinminato *Japan* **29D3**
Shinshār *Syria* **45D1**
Shinyanga *Tanz* **50D4**
Shiogama *Japan* **29E3**
Shiono-misaki, C *Japan* **29C4**
Shiping *China* **31A5**
Shippensburg *USA* **68B2**
Shiprock *USA* **62A1**
Shiquan *China* **31B3**
Shirakawa *Japan* **29D3**
Shirani-san, Mt *Japan* **29C3**
Shīraz *Iran* **41F4**
Shirbîn *Egypt* **45A3**
Shiretoko-misaki, C *Japan* **29F2**
Shiriya-saki, C *Japan* **29D2**
Shīr Kūh, Mt *Iran* **41F3**
Shirotori *Japan* **29C3**
Shirvān *Iran* **41G2**
Shishmaref *USA* **54B3**
Shitanjing *China* **31B2**
Shively *USA* **64B3**
Shivpuri *India* **42D3**
Shivta, Hist Site *Israel* **45C3**
Shivwits Plat *USA* **59D3**
Shiwa Ngandu *Zambia* **51D5**
Shiyan *China* **31C3**
Shizuishan *China* **31B2**
Shizuoka *Japan* **29C3**
Shkodër *Alb* **17D2**
Shkov *USSR* **19G2**
Shmidta, Ostrov, I *USSR* **25L1**
Shoalhaven, R *Aust* **34D2**
Shobara *Japan* **28B4**
Shoranur *India* **44B3**
Shorāpur *India* **44B2**
Shoshone, California *USA* **59C3**
Shoshone, Idaho *USA* **58D2**
Shoshone, R *USA* **58E2**
Shoshone L *USA* **58D2**
Shoshone Mts *USA* **56B3**
Shoshoni *USA* **58E2**
Shostka *USSR* **21E5**
Show Low *USA* **59D4**
Shreveport *USA* **63D2**
Shrewsbury *Eng* **7C3**
Shropshire, County *Eng* **7C3**
Shuangliao *China* **31E1**
Shuangyang *China* **28B2**
Shuangyashan *China* **26G2**
Shubar-Kuduk *USSR* **21K6**
Shuga *USSR* **20N2**
Shu He, R *China* **31D2**
Shuicheng *China* **31A4**
Shujaabad *Pak* **42C3**
Shujālpur *India* **42D4**
Shule He, R *China* **26C2**
Shumen *Bulg* **17F2**
Shumerlya *USSR* **20H4**
Shuncheng *China* **31D4**
Shungnak *USA* **54C3**
Shuo Xian *China* **31C2**
Shurugwi *Zim* **51C5**
Shuya *USSR* **20G4**
Shwebo *Burma* **30B1**
Shwegyin *Burma* **30B2**
Siah Koh, Mts *Afghan* **42A2**
Sialkot *Pak* **42C2**
Sian = Xi'an
Siargao, I *Phil* **27F6**
Siaton *Phil* **27F6**
Šiauliai *USSR* **19E1**
Sibay *USSR* **24G4**
Sibayi L *S Africa* **47E2**
Šibenik *Yugos* **16D2**
Siberia *USSR* **25L5**
Siberut, I *Indon* **27C7**
Sibi *Pak* **42B3**
Sibirskoye *USSR* **26D1**
Sibiti *Congo* **50B4**
Sibiti, R *Tanz* **50D4**
Sibiu *Rom* **17E1**
Sibley *USA* **61D2**
Sibolga *Indon* **27C6**
Sibsāgar *India* **43G3**
Sibu *Malay* **27E6**
Sibut *CAR* **50B3**
Sichuan, Province *China* **31A3**
Sicilia = Sicily
Sicilian Chan *Italy/Tunisia* **16C3**
Sicily, I *Medit S* **16C3**
Sicuani *Peru* **72D6**
Siddhapur *India* **42C4**
Siddipet *India* **44B2**
Sidhi *India* **43E4**
Sidi Barrani *Egypt* **49E1**
Sidi-bel-Abbès *Alg* **15B2**
Sidlaw Hills *Scot* **8D3**
Sidley,Mt *Ant* **76F5**
Sidmouth *Eng* **7C4**
Sidney *Can* **58B1**
Sidney, Montana *USA* **60C1**
Sidney, Nebraska *USA* **60C2**
Sidney, New York *USA* **68C1**
Sidney, Ohio *USA* **64C2**
Sidney Lanier,L *USA* **67B2**
Sidon *Leb* **45C2**
Sidrolândia *Brazil* **75B3**
Siedlce *Pol* **19E2**
Sieg, R *W Germ* **13D2**
Siegburg *W Germ* **13D2**
Siegen *W Germ* **13D2**
Siem Reap *Camb* **30C3**
Siena *Italy* **16C2**
Sierpc *Pol* **19D2**
Sierra Blanca *USA* **62A2**
Sierra de los Alamitos, Mts *Mexico* **70B2**
Sierra Leone, Republic *Africa* **48A4**
Sierra Leone,C *Sierra Leone* **48A4**
Sierra Madre del Sur *Mexico* **70B3**
Sierra Madre Mts *USA* **66B3**
Sierra Madre Occidental, Mts *Mexico* **70B2**
Sierra Madre Oriental, Mts *Mexico* **70B2**
Sierra Mojada *Mexico* **56C4**
Sierra Nevada, Mts *USA* **59B3**
Sierra Vista *USA* **59D4**
Siete Puntas, R *Par* **75A3**
Sífnos, I *Greece* **17E3**
Sig *Alg* **15B2**
Sig *USSR* **20E2**
Sighet *Rom* **19E3**
Sighisoara *Rom* **17E1**
Siglufjörður *Iceland* **12B1**
Siguatepeque *Honduras* **72A1**
Sigüenza *Spain* **15B1**
Siguiri *Guinea* **48B3**
Sihora *India* **42D4**
Siirt *Turk* **40D2**
Sikandarabad *India* **43J1**
Sikar *India* **42D3**
Sikaram, Mt *Afghan* **42B2**
Sikasso *Mali* **48B3**
Sikeston *USA* **63E1**
Sikhote-Alin', Mts *USSR* **26G2**
Síkinos, I *Greece* **17F3**
Sikionía *Greece* **17E3**
Sikkim, State *India* **43F3**
Siktyakh *USSR* **25O2**
Sil, R *Spain* **15A1**
Silchar *India* **43G4**
Silet *Alg* **48C2**
Silgarhi *Nepal* **43E3**
Silifke *Turk* **40B2**
Şilinfah *Syria* **45D1**
Siling Co, L *China* **39G2**
Silistra *Bulg* **17F2**
Siljan, L *Sweden* **20A3**
Silkeborg *Den* **12F7**
Silloth *Eng* **6C2**
Siloam Springs *USA* **63D1**
Silsbee *USA* **63D2**
Siltou, Well *Chad* **50B2**
Šilute *USSR* **19E1**
Silvan *Turk* **40D2**
Silvania *Brazil* **75C2**
Silvassa *India* **42C4**
Silver Bay *USA* **61E1**
Silver City, Nevada *USA* **59C3**
Silver City, New Mexico *USA* **62A2**
Silver Lake *USA* **58B2**
Silver Peak Range, Mts *USA* **66D2**
Silver Spring *USA* **68B3**

Silverton South Saskatchewan

Silverton *Aust* 34B2
Silverton *USA* 62A1
Simanggang *Malay* 27E6
Simao *China* 30C1
Simard,L *Can* 65D1
Simareh, R *Iran* 41E3
Simav *Turk* 17F3
Simav, R *Turk* 17F3
Simcoe,L *Can* 65D2
Simeulue, I *Indon* 27C6
Simferopol' *USSR* 21E7
Sími, I *Greece* 17F3
Simikot *Nepal* 43E3
Simla *India* 42D2
Simla *USA* 60C3
Simmern *W Germ* 13D2
Simmler *USA* 66C3
Simonstown *S Africa* 47B3
Simplon, Mt *Switz* 14D2
Simplon, Pass *Switz/Italy* 16B1
Simpson,C *USA* 54C2
Simpson Desert *Aust* 32C3
Simpson Pen *Can* 55K3
Simrishamn *Sweden* 12G7
Simushir, I, Kuril Is *USSR* 26J2
Sinadogo *Somalia* 50E3
Sinai, Pen *Egypt* 40B4
Sincelejo *Colombia* 72C2
Sinclair,L *USA* 67B2
Sincora, Serra do, Mts *Brazil* 75D1
Sind, Province *Pak* 42B3
Sind, R *India* 42D3
Sindirği *Turk* 17F3
Sindri *India* 43F4
Sines *Port* 15A2
Sines, Cabo de, C *Port* 15A2
Singa *Sudan* 50D2
Singapore, Republic *S E Asia* 30C5
Singapore,Str of *S E Asia* 30C5
Singaraja *Indon* 27E7
Singen *W Germ* 13E4
Singida *Tanz* 50D4
Singkaling Hkamti *Burma* 43H3
Singkawang *Indon* 27D6
Singkep, I *Indon* 27D7
Singleton *Aust* 34D2
Singu *Burma* 30B1
Singuédeze, R *Mozam* 47E1
Sin'gye *N Korea* 28A3
Sinhŭng *N Korea* 28A2
Siniscola, Sardinia 16B2
Sinjár *Iraq* 40D2
Sinkai Hills, Mts *Afghan* 42B2
Sinkat *Sudan* 50D2
Sinkiang, Autonomous Region *China* 39G1
Sinkobabad *India* 43K2
Sinnamary *French Guiana* 73H2
Sinn Bishr, Gebel, Mt *Egypt* 45B4
Sinnyong *S Korea* 28A3
Sinop *Turk* 40C1
Sinpa *N Korea* 28A2
Sinp'o *N Korea* 28A2
Sinp'yong *N Korea* 28A3
Sintana *Rom* 17E1
Sintang *Indon* 27E6
Sinton *USA* 63C3
Sintra *Port* 15A2
Sinú, R *Colombia* 72C2
Sinŭiju *N Korea* 28A2
Siófok *Hung* 19D3
Sion *Switz* 16B1
Sioux City *USA* 61D2
Sioux Falls *USA* 61D2
Siparia *Trinidad* 69L1
Siping *China* 28A2
Siple, Base *Ant* 76F3
Siple I *Ant* 76F5
Sipora, I *Indon* 27C7
Sipsey, R *USA* 63E2
Sîq, Wadi el *Egypt* 45B4
Sira *India* 44B3
Siracusa = Syracuse
Sirajganj *Bang* 43F4
Şir Bani Yās, I *UAE* 41F5
Sir Edward Pellew Group Is *Aust* 32C2
Siret, R *Rom* 17F1
Sirhān, Wādi as, V *Jordan/S Arabia* 40C3
Şirnak *Turk* 40D2
Sirohi *India* 42C4
Sironcha *India* 44C2
Sironj *India* 42D4
Síros, I *Greece* 17E3
Sirretta Peak, Mt *USA* 66C3
Sirri, I *Iran* 41F4
Sirsa *India* 42C3
Sirsi *India* 44A3
Sirt *Libya* 49D1
Sirte Desert *Libya* 49D1
Sirte,G of *Libya* 49D1
Sirvan, R *Iran* 21H9
Sisak *Yugos* 16D1
Sisaket *Thai* 30C2
Sisophon *Camb* 30C3
Sisquoc *USA* 66B3
Sisquoc, R *USA* 66C3
Sisseton *USA* 61D1
Sissonne *France* 13B3
Sisteron *France* 14D3
Sistig Khem *USSR* 25L4
Sitāpur *India* 43E3
Sitía *Greece* 17F3
Sítio d'Abadia *Brazil* 75C1
Sitka *USA* 54E4
Sittang, R *Burma* 30B2
Sittard *Neth* 13C2
Sittwe *Burma* 43G4
Sivas *Turk* 40C2
Siverek *Turk* 40C2
Sivrihisar *Turk* 40B2
Sivuchiy, Mys, C *USSR* 25S4
Siwa *Egypt* 49E2
Siwalik Range, Mts *India* 42D2
Siwalik Range, Mts *Nepal* 43E3
Siya *USSR* 20G3
Siyang *China* 31D3
Sjaelland, I *Den* 18C1
Skagen *Den* 12G7
Skagerrak, Str *Den/Nor* 12F7
Skagit, R *USA* 58B1
Skagit Mt *Can* 58B1
Skagway *USA* 54E4
Skaneateles *USA* 68B1
Skaneateles L *USA* 68B1
Skara *Sweden* 12G7
Skarzysko-Kamienna *Pol* 19E2
Skeena, R *Can* 54F4
Skeene Mts *Can* 54F4
Skeenjek, R *USA* 54D3
Skegness *Eng* 7E3
Skellefte, R *Sweden* 20B2
Skellefteå *Sweden* 12J6
Skerries *Irish Rep* 9C3
Skíathos, I *Greece* 17E3
Skidegate *Can* 54E4
Skiemiewice *Pol* 19E2
Skien *Nor* 12F7
Skikda *Algeria* 16B3
Skipton *Eng* 6D3
Skíros, I *Greece* 17E3
Skive *Den* 12F7
Skjern *Den* 18B1
Skjoldungen *Greenland* 55O3
Skokie *USA* 64B2
Skópelos, I *Greece* 17E3
Skopje *Yugos* 17E2
Skövde *Sweden* 12G7
Skovorodino *USSR* 25O4
Skowhegan *USA* 65F2
Skukuza *S Africa* 47E1
Skwentna *USA* 54C3
Skwierzyna *Pol* 18D2
Skye, I *Scot* 10B2
Slagelse *Den* 12G7
Slamet, Mt *Indon* 27D7
Slaney, R *Irish Rep* 9C3
Slatina *Rom* 17E2
Slave, R *Can* 54G3
Slavgorod, Belorusskaya *USSR* 19G2
Slavgorod, Rossiyskaya *USSR* 24J4
Slavuta *USSR* 19F2
Slavyansk *USSR* 21F6
Sławno *Pol* 18D2
Sleaford *Eng* 7D3
Sleat,Sound of, Chan *Scot* 8C3
Sleetmute *USA* 54C3
Slidell *USA* 63E2
Slide Mt *USA* 68C2
Slieve Aughty Mts *Irish Rep* 9B3
Slieve Bloom, Mts *Irish Rep* 9C3
Sligo *Irish Rep* 10B3
Sligo B *Irish Rep* 10B3
Sliven *Bulg* 17F2
Sloan *USA* 59C3
Slobozia *Rom* 17F2
Slonim *USSR* 19F2
Slough *Eng* 7D4
Slough, R *USA* 66B2
Slovensko, Region *Czech* 19D3
Słubice *Pol* 18C2
Sluch', R *USSR* 19F2
Słupsk *Pol* 18D2
Slutsk *USSR* 19F2
Slutsk, R *USSR* 19F2
Slyne Head, Pt *Irish Rep* 10A3
Slyudvanka *USSR* 25M4
Smallwood Res *Can* 55M4
Smara *Mor* 48A2
Smederevo *Yugos* 17E2
Smederevska Palanka *Yugos* 17E2
Smela *USSR* 21E6
Smethport *USA* 68A2
Smith *USA* 66C1
Smith Arm, B *Can* 54F3
Smithers *Can* 54F4
Smithfield, N Carolina *USA* 67C1
Smithfield *S Africa* 47D3
Smithfield, Utah *USA* 58D2
Smith I *Can* 55L3
Smiths Falls *Can* 65D2
Smithton *Aust* 34C4
Smoky, R *USA* 60C3
Smoky C *Aust* 34D2
Smoky Hills *USA* 60D3
Smoky Mts *USA* 58D2
Smøla, I *Nor* 12F6
Smolensk *USSR* 20E5
Smólikas, Mt *Greece* 17E2
Smolyan *Bulg* 17E2
Smorgon' *USSR* 19F2
Smyrna = İzmir
Smyrna, Delaware *USA* 68C3
Smyrna, Georgia *USA* 67B2
Snæfell, Mt *Iceland* 12B2
Snaefell, Mt, I of Man *British Is* 6B2
Snake, R *USA* 58C1
Snake River Canyon *USA* 56B2
Snake River Plain *USA* 58D2
Snares Is *NZ* 33F5
Sneek *Neth* 18B2
Snelling *USA* 66B2
Sněžka, Mt *Czech/Pol* 18D2
Snizort, Loch, Inlet *Scot* 8B3
Snøhetta, Mt *Nor* 12F6
Snohomish *USA* 58B1
Snoqualmie P *USA* 58B1
Snoul *Camb* 30D3
Snowdon, Mt *Wales* 7B3
Snowdonia Nat Pk *Wales* 7B3
Snowdrift *Can* 54G3
Snowflake *USA* 59D4
Snow Lake *Can* 54H4
Snow Shoe *USA* 68B2
Snowtown *Aust* 34A2
Snowville *USA* 58D2
Snowy Mts *Aust* 34C3
Snyder *USA* 62B2
Soan Kundo, Is *S Korea* 28B4
Soay, I *Scot* 8B3
Sobaek Sanmaek, Mts *S Korea* 28A3
Sobat, R *Sudan* 50D3
Sobral *Brazil* 73K4
Sochaczew *Pol* 19E2
Sochi *USSR* 21F7
Söch'on *S Korea* 28A3
Société, Îles de la *Pacific O* 37M5
Socorro *USA* 62A2
Socorro, I *Mexico* 70A3
Socotra, I *S Yemen* 38D4
Soda L *USA* 66C3
Sodankylä *Fin* 12K5
Soda Springs *USA* 58D2
Soddo *Eth* 50D3
Söderhamn *Sweden* 12H6
Södertälje *Sweden* 12H7
Sodiri *Sudan* 50C2
Sodus Point *USA* 68B1
Soest *W Germ* 13E2
Sofala *Mozam* 51D5
Sofia *Bulg* 17E2
Sofiya = Sofia
Sofporog *USSR* 20E2
Sofu Gan, I *Japan* 26H4
Sogamoso *Colombia* 72D2
Sognefjorden, Inlet *Nor* 12F6
Sōgwi-ri *S Korea* 28A4
Sog Xian *China* 39H2
Sohâg *Egypt* 40B4
Sohano *PNG* 33E1
Soignies *Belg* 13B2
Soissons *France* 13B3
Sojat *India* 42C3
Sokcho *S Korea* 28A3
Söke *Turk* 40A2
Sokłka *Pol* 19E2
Sokodé *Togo* 48C4
Sokol *USSR* 20F4
Sokolo *Mali* 48B3
Søkongens Øy, I *Greenland* 55Q3
Sokota *Eth* 50D2
Sokoto *Nigeria* 48C3
Sokoto, R *Nigeria* 48C3
Solander I *NZ* 35A3
Solāpur *India* 44B2
Soledad *Colombia* 69C4
Soledad *USA* 66B2
Solent, Sd *Eng* 7D4
Solesmes *France* 13B2
Soligorsk *USSR* 19F2
Solikamsk *USSR* 20K4
Sol'Iletsk *USSR* 24G4
Solimões *Peru* 72D4
Solingen *W Germ* 13D2
Solitaire *Namibia* 47B1
Sollefteå *Sweden* 12H6
Sol'Iletsk *USSR* 21J5
Solok *Indon* 27D7
Solomon Is *Pacific O* 33E1
Solon Springs *USA* 64A1
Solovetskiye, Ostrova, I *USSR* 20F2
Soltau *W Germ* 12F8
Solvang *USA* 66B3
Solvay *USA* 68B1
Solway Firth, Estuary *Eng/Scot* 8D4
Solwezi *Zambia* 51C5
Sōma *Japan* 29D3
Soma *Turk* 17F3
Somalia, Republic *E Africa* 38C5
Somali Basin *Indian O* 36D4
Sombor *Yugos* 17D1
Sombrero Chan, Nicobar Is *Indian O* 44E4
Somerset *Aust* 32D2
Somerset, Kentucky *USA* 64C3
Somerset, Massachusetts *USA* 68E2
Somerset, Pennsylvania *USA* 65D2
Somerset, County *Eng* 7C4
Somerset East *S Africa* 47D3
Somerset I *Can* 55J2
Somerset Res *USA* 68D1
Somers Point *USA* 68C3
Somersworth *USA* 68E1
Somerville *USA* 68C2
Somerville Res *USA* 63C2
Someş, R *Rom* 17E1
Somme, Department *France* 13B3
Somme, R *France* 13B3
Sommesous *France* 13C3
Somoto *Nic* 72A1
Son, R *India* 43E4
Sŏnch'ŏn *N Korea* 28A3
Sondags, R *S Africa* 47D3
Sønderborg *Den* 12F8
Søndre Strømfjord *Greenland* 55N3
Søndre Upernavik *Greenland* 55N2
Sondrio *Italy* 14D2
Song Ba, R *Viet* 30D3
Song Cau *Viet* 30D3
Sŏngch'on *N Korea* 28A3
Songea *Tanz* 51D5
Songgan *N Korea* 28A2
Songhua, R *China* 26F2
Songjiang *China* 31E3
Songjŏng *S Korea* 28A3
Songkhla *Thai* 30C4
Sông Pahang, R *Malay* 30C5
Songpan *China* 31A3
Sŏngsan-ni *S Korea* 28A4
Sonid Youqi *China* 31C1
Sonipat *India* 42D3
Son La *Viet* 30C1
Sonmiani *Pak* 42B3
Sonmiani Bay *Pak* 42B3
Sonoita *Mexico* 59D4
Sonoma *USA* 66A1
Sonora, California *USA* 66B2
Sonora, Texas *USA* 62B2
Sonora, R *Mexico* 70A2
Sonora, State *Mexico* 59D4
Sonoran Desert *USA* 56B3
Sonora P *USA* 66C1
Sonsonate *El Salvador* 70D3
Sonsorol, I *Pacific O* 27G6
Soo Canals *Can/USA* 57E2
Sopot *Pol* 19D2
Sopron *Hung* 18D3
Soquel *USA* 66B2
Sora *Italy* 16C2
Sored, R *Israel* 45C3
Sorel *Can* 65E1
Sorell *Aust* 34C4
Sorgun *Turk* 40C2
Soria *Spain* 15B1
Sørkapp, I *Barents S* 24C2
Sørkjosen *Nor* 12J5
Sor Mertvyy Kultuk, Plain *USSR* 21J6
Sorocaba *Brazil* 75C3
Sorochinsk *USSR* 20J5
Soroki *USSR* 19F3
Sorol, I *Pacific O* 27H6
Soroma-ko, L *Japan* 29D2
Sorong *Indon* 27G7
Soroti *Uganda* 50D3
Sørøya, I *Nor* 12J4
Sorrento *Italy* 16C2
Sorsatunturi, Mt *Fin* 12K5
Sorsele *Sweden* 12H5
Sorsele *Sweden* 20B2
Sortavala *USSR* 20E3
Sŏsan *S Korea* 28B3
Sosnowiec *Pol* 19D2
Sos'va *USSR* 24H4
Souanké *Congo* 50B3
Soubré *Ivory Coast* 48B4
Souderton *USA* 68C2
Soufrière *St Lucia* 69P2
Soufrière, Mt *St Vincent* 69N2
Souillac *France* 14C3
Souk Ahras *Algeria* 16B3
Sŏul = Seoul
Soummam, R *Alg* 15C2
Sour = Tyre
Sources,Mt aux *Lesotho* 47D2
Souris *Can* 60C1
Souris, R *Can/USA* 60C1
Sousa *Brazil* 73L5
Sousse *Tunisia* 16C3
South Africa, Republic *Africa* 51C7
Southampton *Can* 64C2
Southampton *Eng* 7D4
Southampton *USA* 68D2
Southampton I *Can* 55K3
South Andaman, I *Indian O* 44E3
South Aulatsivik I *Can* 55M4
South Australia, State *Aust* 32C3
South Australian Basin *Indian O* 36H6
Southaven *USA* 63E2
South Baldy, Mt *USA* 62A2
South Bay *USA* 67B3
South Baymouth *Can* 64C1
South Bend, Indiana *USA* 64B2
South Bend, Washington *USA* 58B1
South Boston *USA* 65D3
Southbridge *USA* 68E1
South Cape = Ka Lae
South Carolina, State *USA* 57E3
South China S *S E Asia* 27E5
South Dakota, State *USA* 56C2
South Deerfield *USA* 68D1
South Downs *Eng* 7D4
South East C *Aust* 34C4
South East Pacific Basin *Pacific O* 37O7
Southend *Can* 54H4
Southend-on-Sea *Eng* 7E4
Southern Alps, Mts *NZ* 35A2
Southern Cross *Aust* 32A4
Southern Indian L *Can* 54J4
Southern Pines *USA* 67C1
Southfield *Jamaica* 69H2
South Fiji Basin *Pacific O* 37K6
South Foreland, Pt *Eng* 7E4
South Fork *USA* 62A1
South Fork, R, California *USA* 66B1
South Fork American, R *USA* 66B1
South Fork Kern, R *USA* 66C3
South Georgia, I *S Atlantic O* 71G9
South Glamorgan, County *Wales* 7C4
South Haven *USA* 64B2
South Henik L *Can* 54J3
South Hill *USA* 65D3
South Honshu Ridge *Pacific O* 36J3
South I *NZ* 35A2
Southington *USA* 68D2
South Korea, Republic *S Korea* 28B3
South Lake Tahoe *USA* 59B3
South Madagascar Ridge *Indian O* 36D6
South Magnetic Pole *Ant* 76G8
South Miami *USA* 67B3
South Mt *USA* 68B3
South Nahanni, R *Can* 54F3
South Negril Pt *Jamaica* 69G1
South Orkney Is *Atlantic O* 52F8
South Pacific O 71B5
South Platte, R *USA* 60C2
South Pole *Ant* 76E
South Porcupine *Can* 64C1
Southport *Eng* 7C3
South Pt *Barbados* 69Q2
South River *USA* 68C2
South Ronaldsay, I *Scot* 8D2
South Sandwich Trench *Atlantic O* 52G7
South San Francisco *USA* 66A2
South Saskatchewan, R *Can* 54H4

South Shields **Swains I**

South Shields *Eng* 6D2
South Taranaki Bight, B *NZ* 35B1
South Uist, I *Scot* 8B3
South West Africa = Namibia
South West C *Aust* 32D5
South West Indian Ridge *Indian O* 36D6
South West Pacific Basin *Pacific O* 37M6
South West Peru Ridge *Pacific O* 52D5
Southwold *Eng* 7E3
South Yemen, Republic *Arabian Pen* 38C4
South Yorkshire, County *Eng* 7D3
Soutpansberg, Mts *S Africa* 47D1
Sovetsk, RSFSR *USSR* 19E1
Sovetsk, RSFSR *USSR* 20H4
Sovetskaya Gavan' *USSR* 26G2
Sovetskiy *USSR* 20L3
Sōya-misaki, C *Japan* 29D1
Soyo Congo *Angola* 51B4
Sozh, R *USSR* 19G2
Spa *Belg* 13C2
Spain, Kingdom *S.W. Europe* 15
Spalato = Split
Spalding *Eng* 7D3
Spanish, R *Can* 64C1
Spanish Fork *USA* 59D2
Spanish Town *Jamaica* 69J1
Sparks *USA* 59C3
Sparta *USA* 64A2
Spartanburg *USA* 67B2
Spartí *Greece* 17E3
Spartivento, C *Italy* 16D3
Spassk *USSR* 26G2
Spearfish *USA* 60C2
Spearman *USA* 62B1
Speightstown *Barbados* 69R2
Spenard *USA* 54D3
Spence Bay *Can* 55J3
Spencer, Indiana *USA* 64B3
Spencer, Iowa *USA* 61D2
Spencer G *Aust* 32C4
Spencer I *Can* 55L3
Spenser Mts *NZ* 35B2
Sperrin Mts *N Ire* 9C2
Spey, R *Scot* 8D3
Speyer *W Germ* 18B3
Speyside *Tobago* 69K1
Spirit Lake *USA* 58C1
Spirit River *Can* 54G4
Spitsbergen, I *Svalbard* 24C2
Spitsbergen, Is = Svalbard
Spittal *Austria* 18C3
Spjekeroog, I *W Germ* 13D1
Spjelkavik *Nor* 12F6
Split *Yugos* 16D2
Spokane *USA* 58C1
Spooner *USA* 64A1
Sporádhes, Is = Dodecanese
Spratly, I *S China Sea* 27E6
Spratly Is *S China Sea* 27E6
Spray *USA* 58C2
Spree, R *E Germ* 18C2
Springbok *S Africa* 47B2
Springdale *USA* 63D1
Springer *USA* 62B1
Springerville *USA* 59E4
Springfield, Colorado *USA* 62B1
Springfield, Illinois *USA* 64B3
Springfield, Massachusetts *USA* 68D1
Springfield, Minnesota *USA* 61E2
Springfield, Missouri *USA* 63D1
Springfield, Ohio *USA* 64C3
Springfield, Oregon *USA* 58B2
Springfield, Tennessee *USA* 67A1
Springfield, Vermont *USA* 65E2
Springfontein *S Africa* 47D3
Spring Mts *USA* 59C3
Springs *S Africa* 47D2
Springville, New York *USA* 68A1
Springville, Utah *USA* 59D2
Springwater *USA* 68B1
Spruce Mt *USA* 58D2
Spurn Head, C *Eng* 7E3
Spuzzum *Can* 58B1
Squillace, G di *Italy* 16D3
Sredinnyy Khrebet, Mts *USSR* 25S4
Srednekolymsk *USSR* 25R3
Sredne-Russkaya Vozvyshennost', Upland *USSR* 20F5
Sredne Sibirskoye Ploskogorye, *USSR* 25M3
Sredniy Ural, Mts *USSR* 20K4
Srepok, R *Camb* 30D3
Sretensk *USSR* 26E1
Sre Umbell *Camb* 30C3
Srikākulam *India* 44C2
Sri Kālahasti *India* 44B3
Sri Lanka, Republic *S Asia* 39G5
Srinagar *Pak* 42C2
Srivardhan *India* 44A2
Sroda *Pol* 18D2
Stack Skerry, I *Scot* 8C2
Stade *W Germ* 13E1
Stadthagen *W Germ* 13E1
Staffa, I *Scot* 8B3
Stafford *Eng* 7C3
Stafford, County *Eng* 7C3
Stafford Springs *USA* 68D2
Stalingrad = Volgograd
Stallberg, Mt *S Africa* 47B3
Stallworthy,C *Can* 55J1
Stalowa Wola *Pol* 19E2
Stamford, Connecticut *USA* 68D2
Stamford *Eng* 7D3
Stamford, New York *USA* 68C1
Stamford, Texas *USA* 62C2
Stampriet *Namibia* 47B1
Standerton *S Africa* 47D2
Standish *USA* 64C2
Stanford *USA* 58D1
Stanger *S Africa* 47E2
Stanhope *Eng* 6C2
Stanislaus, R *USA* 66B2
Stanke Dimitrov *Bulg* 17E2
Stanley *Aust* 34C4
Stanley *Falkland Is* 74E8
Stanley, Idaho *USA* 58D2
Stanley, N Dakota *USA* 60C1
Stanley Res *India* 44B3
Stanleyville = Kisangani
Stann Creek *Belize* 70D3
Stanovoy Khrebet, Mts *USSR* 26F1
Stanthorpe *Aust* 34D1
Stanton Banks, Sand-bank *Scot* 8A3
Stapleton *USA* 60C2
Starachowice *Pol* 19E2
Stara Planiná, Mts *Bulg* 17E2
Staraya Russa *USSR* 20E4
Stara Zagora *Bulg* 17F2
Stargard *Pol* 18D2
Starkville *USA* 63E2
Starnberg *W Germ* 18C3
Starogard Gdański *Pol* 19D2
Starokonstantinov *USSR* 19F3
Start Pt *Eng* 7C4
Staryy Oskol *USSR* 21F5
State College *USA* 68B2
Staten I *USA* 68C2
Statesboro *USA* 67B2
Statesville *USA* 67B1
Staunton *USA* 65D3
Stavanger *Nor* 12F7
Stavelot *Belg* 13C2
Stavoren *Neth* 13C1
Stavropol' *USSR* 21G6
Stawell *Aust* 34B3
Stayton *USA* 58B2
Steamboat Springs *USA* 60B2
Steelton *USA* 68B2
Steens Mt *USA* 58C2
Steenstrups Gletscher, Gl *Greenland* 55N2
Steenwijk *Neth* 13D1
Stefansson I *Can* 54H2
Stegi *Swaziland* 47E2
Steinback *Can* 61D1
Steinkjer *Nor* 12G6
Steinkjer *Nor* 20A3
Steinkopf *S Africa* 47B2
Stella *S Africa* 47C2
Stellenbosch *S Africa* 47B3
Stenay *France* 13C3
Stendal *E Germ* 18C2
Stepanakert *USSR* 21H8
Stephen *USA* 61D1
Stephens,C *NZ* 35B2
Stephens Creek *Aust* 34B2
Stephenson *USA* 64B1
Stephenville *Can* 55N5
Stephenville *USA* 62C2
Sterkstroom *S Africa* 47D3
Sterling, Colorado *USA* 60C2
Sterling, Illinois *USA* 64B2
Sterling, Kansas *USA* 62C1
Sterling, N Dakota *USA* 60C1
Sterling City *USA* 62B2
Sterling Heights *USA* 64C2
Sterlitamak *USSR* 20K5
Stettler *Can* 54G4
Steubenville *USA* 64C2
Stevenage *Eng* 7D4
Stevens Point *USA* 64B2
Stevens Village *USA* 54D3
Stewart *Can* 54F4
Stewart *USA* 59C3
Stewart, R *Can* 54E3
Stewart I *NZ* 35A3
Stewart Is *Solomon Is* 33F1
Stewarton *Scot* 8C4
Stewart River *Can* 54E3
Stewartstown *USA* 68B3
Stewartville *USA* 61E2
Steynsburg *S Africa* 47D3
Steyr *Austria* 18C3
Steytlerville *S Africa* 47C3
Stikine, R *Can* 54F4
Stillwater, Minnesota *USA* 61E1
Stillwater, Oklahoma *USA* 63C1
Stillwater Range, Mts *USA* 59C3
Stinnett *USA* 62B1
Stirling *Aust* 34A2
Stirling *Scot* 8D3
Stjørdal *Nor* 12G6
Stockach *W Germ* 13E4
Stockbridge *USA* 68D1
Stockerau *Austria* 18D3
Stockholm *Sweden* 12H7
Stockport *Eng* 7C3
Stockton, California *USA* 66B2
Stockton *Eng* 6D2
Stockton, Kansas *USA* 60D3
Stockton L *USA* 63D1
Stoke-on-Trent *Eng* 7C3
Stokmarknes *Nor* 12G5
Stolbovoy, Ostrov, I *USSR* 25P2
Stolbtsy *USSR* 12K8
Stolin *USSR* 19F2
Stone *Eng* 7C3
Stone Harbor *USA* 68C3
Stonehaven *Scot* 8D3
Stonewall *USA* 63C2
Stony Stratford *Eng* 7D3
Storavan, L *Sweden* 12H5
Støren *Nor* 12G6
Storm B *Aust* 34C4
Storm Lake *USA* 61D2
Stornoway *Scot* 8B2
Storozhinets *USSR* 19F3
Storrs *USA* 68D2
Storsjön, L *Sweden* 12G6
Storuman *Sweden* 12H5
Story *USA* 60B2
Stoughton *USA* 68E1
Stour, R *Eng* 7E4
Stourbridge *Eng* 7C3
Stourport *Eng* 7C3
Stowmarket *Eng* 7E3
Strabane *N Ire* 9C2
Strahan *Aust* 34C4
Stralsund *E Germ* 18C2
Strand *S Africa* 47B3
Stranda *Nor* 12F6
Strangford Lough, L *Irish Rep* 9D2
Strängnäs *Sweden* 12H7
Stranraer *Scot* 8C4
Strasbourg *France* 14D2
Strasburg *USA* 65D3
Stratford, California *USA* 66C2
Stratford *Can* 64C2
Stratford, Connecticut *USA* 68D2
Stratford *NZ* 35B1
Stratford, Texas *USA* 62B1
Stratford-on-Avon *Eng* 7D3
Strathalbyn *Aust* 34A3
Strathclyde, Region *Scot* 8C4
Stratton *USA* 65E1
Streator *USA* 64B2
Stroma, I *Scot* 8D2
Stromboli, I *Italy* 16D3
Stromness *Scot* 8D2
Stromsburg *USA* 61D2
Stromsund *Sweden* 12H6
Ströms Vattudal, L *Sweden* 12G6
Stronsay, I *Scot* 8D2
Stroud *Eng* 7C4
Stroudsburg *USA* 68C2
Struma, R *Bulg* 17E2
Strumble Head, Pt *Wales* 7B3
Strumica *Yugos* 17E2
Stryy *USSR* 19E3
Stryy, R *USSR* 19E3
Strzelecki Creek, R *Aust* 34B1
Stuart, Florida *USA* 67B3
Stuart, Nebraska *USA* 60D2
Stuart L *Can* 54F4
Stubice *Pol* 12G8
Stung Sen, R *Camb* 30D3
Stung Treng *Camb* 30D3
Stura, R *Italy* 16B2
Sturge I *Ant* 76G7
Sturgeon Bay *USA* 64B2
Sturgeon Falls *Can* 65D1
Sturgis, Kentucky *USA* 64B3
Sturgis, Michigan *USA* 64B2
Sturgis, S Dakota *USA* 60C2
Sturt Creek, R *Aust* 32B2
Sturt Desert *Aust* 34B1
Stutterheim *S Africa* 47D3
Stuttgart *USA* 63D2
Stuttgart *W Germ* 18B3
Stykkishólmur *Iceland* 12A1
Styr', R *USSR* 19F2
Suaçuí Grande, R *Brazil* 75D2
Suakin *Sudan* 50D2
Suan *N Korea* 28A3
Suao *Taiwan* 31E5
Subotica *Yugos* 17D1
Suceava *Rom* 21D6
Sucre *Bol* 72E7
Sucuriú, R *Brazil* 75B2
Sudan, Republic *Africa* 50C2
Sudbury *Can* 64C1
Sudbury *Eng* 7E3
Sudd, Swamp *Sudan* 50C3
Suddie *Guyana* 73G2
Sudr *Egypt* 45B4
Sue, R *Sudan* 50C3
Suez *Egypt* 40B4
Suez Canal *Egypt* 40B3
Suez,G of *Egypt* 40B4
Suffern *USA* 68C2
Suffolk *USA* 65D3
Suffolk, County *Eng* 7E3
Sugarloaf Mt *USA* 65E2
Sugarloaf Pt *Aust* 34D2
Sugoy, R *USSR* 25R3
Suḩar *Oman* 41G5
Sühbaatar *Mongolia* 26D1
Sui *Pak* 42B3
Suide *China* 31C2
Suifen He, R *China* 28C2
Suihua *China* 26F2
Suining *China* 31B3
Suippes *France* 13C3
Suir, R *Irish Rep* 10B3
Sui Xian *China* 31C3
Suizhong *China* 31E1
Sujāngarh *India* 42C3
Sukadana *Indon* 27D7
Sukagawa *Japan* 29E3
Sukai Hu, L *China* 26C3
Sukch'ŏn *N Korea* 28B3
Sukhinichi *USSR* 20F5
Sukhona, R *USSR* 20G4
Sukhumi *USSR* 21G7
Sukkertoppen *Greenland* 55N3
Sukkertoppen Isflade, Ice field *Greenland* 55N3
Sukkozero *USSR* 12L6
Sukkur *Pak* 42B3
Sukma *India* 44C2
Sukses *Namibia* 51B6
Sukumo *Japan* 28B4
Sula, R *USSR* 21F5
Sulaiman Range, Mts *Pak* 42B3
Sula, Kepulauan, I *Indon* 32B1
Sula Sgeir, I *Scot* 8B2
Sulawesi, Is *Indon* 27E7
Sulaymānīyah *Iraq* 41E2
Sule Skerry, I *Scot* 8C2
Sulina *Rom* 17F1
Sulingen *W Germ* 13E1
Sulitjelma *Nor* 12H5
Sullana *Peru* 72B4
Sullivan *USA* 63D1
Sully-sur-Loire *France* 13B4
Sulmona *Italy* 16C2
Sulphur, Louisiana *USA* 63D2
Sulphur, Oklahoma *USA* 63C2
Sulphur Springs *USA* 63C2
Sultan Dağlari, Mts *Turk* 21E8
Sultānpur *India* 43E3
Sulu Arch, Is *Phil* 27F6
Sulu S *Phil* 27E6
Sulz *W Germ* 13E3
Sumampa *Arg* 74D3
Sumatera, I *Indon* 27C6
Sumba, I *Indon* 27E8
Sumbawa, I *Indon* 27E7
Sumbawa Besar *Indon* 27E7
Sumbawanga *Tanz* 51D4
Sumbe *Angola* 51B5
Sumburgh Head, Pt *Scot* 8E2
Sumesar Ra, Mts *Nepal* 43N2
Sumgait *USSR* 21H7
Sumisu, I *Japan* 26H3
Summit Lake *Can* 54F4
Summit Mt *USA* 59C3
Sumner,L *NZ* 35B2
Sumoto *Japan* 29B4
Sumter *USA* 67B2
Sumy *USSR* 21E5
Sun, R *USA* 58D1
Sunagawa *Japan* 29D2
Sunan *N Korea* 28A3
Sunart, Loch, Inlet *Scot* 8C3
Sunbury *USA* 68B2
Sunch'ŏn *N Korea* 28B3
Sunch'ŏn *S Korea* 28B4
Sundance *USA* 60C2
Sundargarh *India* 43E4
Sunderbans, Swamp *India/Bang* 43F4
Sunderland *Eng* 6D2
Sundridge *Can* 65D1
Sundsvall *Sweden* 12H6
Sunnyside *USA* 58C1
Sunnyvale *USA* 59B3
Sun Prairie *USA* 64B2
Suntar *USSR* 25N3
Sun Valley *USA* 58D2
Sunyani *Ghana* 48B4
Suojarvi *USSR* 20E3
Suo-nada, B *Japan* 28B4
Suonenjoki *Fin* 12K6
Supaul *India* 43F3
Superior, Arizona *USA* 59D4
Superior, Nebraska *USA* 61D2
Superior, Wisconsin *USA* 64A1
Superior,L *Can/USA* 64B1
Suphan Buri *Thai* 30C3
Süphan Daǧ, Mt *Turk* 40D2
Supiori, I *Indon* 27G7
Sūq ash Suyukh *Iraq* 41E3
Şuqaylibiyah *Syria* 45D1
Suqian *China* 31D3
Suqutra = Socotra
Sur *Oman* 38D3
Sura, R *USSR* 20H5
Surabaya *Indon* 27E7
Suraga-wan, B *Japan* 29C4
Surakarta *Indon* 27E7
Şuran *Syria* 45D1
Surat *Aust* 34C1
Surat *India* 42C4
Suratgarh *India* 42C3
Surat Thani *Thai* 30B4
Surendranagar *India* 42C4
Surf City *USA* 68C3
Surgut *USSR* 24J3
Suriapet *India* 44B2
Surigao *Phil* 27F6
Surin *Thai* 30C3
Surinam, Republic *S America* 73G3
Sur,Pt *USA* 66B2
Surrey, County *Eng* 7D4
Surtsey, I *Iceland* 12A2
Susa *Italy* 16B1
Susa *Japan* 28B4
Susaki *Japan* 29B4
Susanville *USA* 59B2
Susquehanna *USA* 68C2
Susquehanna, R *USA* 68B3
Sussex *USA* 68C2
Sussex West *Eng* 7D4
Sutherland *S Africa* 47C3
Sutherland *USA* 60C2
Sutlej, R *Pak* 42C2
Sutter Creek *USA* 59B3
Sutton *USA* 64C3
Suttsu *Japan* 29D2
Suwa *Japan* 29D3
Suwalki *Pol* 19E2
Suwannee, R *USA* 67B3
Suweilih *Jordan* 45C2
Suwŏn *S Korea* 28B3
Su Xian *China* 31D3
Suzaka *Japan* 29C3
Suzhou *China* 31E3
Suzu *Japan* 29D3
Suzuka *Japan* 29C4
Suzu-misaki, C *Japan* 29C3
Svalbard, Is *Barents S* 24C2
Svalyava *USSR* 19E3
Svartenhuk Halvø, Region *Greenland* 55N2
Svartisen, Mt *Nor* 12G5
Svay Rieng *Camb* 30D3
Sveg *Sweden* 12G6
Svendborg *Den* 12G7
Sverdlovsk *USSR* 24H4
Sverdrup Chan *Can* 55J1
Sverdrup Is *Can* 54H2
Svetlaya *USSR* 26G2
Svetlogorsk *USSR* 19E2
Svetogorsk *USSR* 12K6
Svetozarevo *Yugos* 17E2
Svilengrad *Bulg* 17F2
Svir' *USSR* 19F2
Svir', R *USSR* 20E3
Svitavy *Czech* 18D3
Svobodnyy *USSR* 26F1
Svolvær *Nor* 12G5
Swaffam *Eng* 7E3
Swain Reefs *Aust* 33E3
Swainsboro *USA* 67B2
Swains I *American Samoa* 33H2

Swakop Tejon P

Swakop, R Namibia 47B1
Swakopmund Namibia 47A1
Swale, R Eng 6D2
Swallow Reef S China Sea 27E6
Swāmihalli India 44B3
Swan, I Honduras 70D3
Swanage Eng 7D4
Swan Hill Aust 34B3
Swan I Caribbean S 69A3
Swan River Can 54H4
Swansea Wales 7C4
Swansea B Wales 7C4
Swartberge, Mts S Africa 47C3
Swartruggens S Africa 47D2
Swatow = Shantou
Swaziland, Kingdom S Africa 47E2
Sweden, Kingdom N Europe 12G7
Sweet Home USA 58B2
Sweetwater USA 62B2
Sweetwater, R USA 60B2
Swellendam S Africa 47C3
Świdnica Pol 18D2
Swidwin Pol 18D2
Świebodzin Pol 18D2
Swiecie Pol 19D2
Swift Current Can 54H4
Swilly, Lough, Estuary Irish Rep 9C2
Swindon Eng 7D4
Świnoujście Pol 18C2
Switzerland Europe 14D2
Swords Irish Rep 9C3
Syang Nepal 43M1
Sybil Pt Irish Rep 9A3
Sydney Aust 34D2
Syktyvkar USSR 20H3
Sylacauga USA 67A2
Sylarna, Mt Sweden 12G6
Sylhet Bang 43G4
Sylt, I W Germ 18B1
Sylvania USA 64C2
Syowa, Base Ant 76G11
Syracuse Italy 16D3
Syracuse, Kansas USA 62B1
Syracuse, New York USA 68B1
Syracuse USA 65D2
Syrdar'ya, R USSR 24H5
Syria, Republic S W Asia 40C2
Sysert' USSR 20L4
Syzran' USSR 20H5
Szczecin Pol 18C2
Szczecinek Pol 18D2
Szczytno Pol 19E2
Szeged Hung 19E3
Székesfehérvar Hung 19D3
Szekszárd Hung 19D3
Szolnok Hung 19D3
Szombathely Hung 18D3
Szprotawa Pol 18D2

T

Tabankulu S Africa 47D3
Tabar Is PNG 32E1
Tabarka Tunisia 16B3
Tabas Iran 41G3
Tabatinga Brazil 72E4
Tabelbala Alg 48B2
Tabeng Camb 30C3
Taber Can 54G5
Table Mt S Africa 47B3
Table Rock Res USA 63D1
Tábor Czech 18C3
Tabora Tanz 50D4
Tabory USSR 20L4
Tabou Ivory Coast 48B4
Tabriz Iran 41E2
Tabūk S Arabia 40C4
Tacheng China 39G1
Tacloban Phil 27F5
Tacna Peru 72D7
Tacna USA 59D4
Tacoma USA 56A2
Taconic Range USA 68D1
Tacuatí Par 75A3
Tademait, Plateau du Alg 48C2
Tadjoura Djibouti 50E2
Tadoussac Can 65F1
Tādpatri India 44B3
Tadzhik SSR, Republic USSR 39E2
Taebaek Sanmaek, Mts N Korea/S Korea 28B3
T'aech'ŏn N Korea 28B3
Taech'on S Korea 28A3
Taedasa-Do N Korea 28A3
Taedong, R N Korea 28A3
Taegang-got, Pen N Korea 28A3
Taegu S Korea 28B3
Taehung N Korea 28A2
Taejŏn S Korea 28B3
Tafalla Spain 15B1
Tafasaset, Watercourse Alg 48C2
Taff, R Wales 7C4
Tafila Jordan 45C3
Taft USA 66C3
Taganrog USSR 21F6
Tagant, Region Maur 48A3
Taguenout Hagguerete, Well Mali 48B2
Tagula, I PNG 33E2
Tagus = Tejo
Tahat, Mt Alg 48C2
Tahiti, I Pacific O 37M5
Tahlequah USA 63C1
Tahoe City USA 59B3
Tahoe,L USA 59B3
Tahoka USA 62B2
Tahoua Niger 48C3
Tahta Egypt 40B4
Tahuna Indon 27F6
Tai'an China 28A2
Taibai Shan, Mt China 31B3
Taibus Qi China 31D1
Taichung Taiwan 31E5
Taieri, R NZ 35B3
Taihang Shan, Upland China 31C2
Taihape NZ 35C1
Tai Hu, L China 31E3
Taiki Japan 29D2
Tailem Bend Aust 34A3
Tain Scot 8C3
Tainan Taiwan 31E5
Taiobeiras Brazil 75D2
Taipei Taiwan 31E5
Taiping Malay 30C5
Taira Japan 29D3
Taisha Japan 28B3
Taitao,Pen de Chile 74B7
Taitung Taiwan 31E5
Taivalkoski Fin 12K5
Taiwan, Republic 26F4
Taiwan Str China/Taiwan 31D5
Taiyiba Jordan 45C3
Taiyuan China 31C2
Taizhou China 31D3
Ta'izz Yemen 50E2
Tajo, R Spain 15B1
Tak Thai 30B2
Takabonerate, Kepulauan Is Indon 32B1
Takada Japan 29D3
Takahashi Japan 29B4
Takaka NZ 35B2
Takamatsu Japan 29C4
Takaoka Japan 29D3
Takapuna NZ 35B1
Takasaki Japan 29D3
Takayama Japan 29C3
Takefu Japan 29D3
Takeo Camb 30C3
Takeo Japan 28B4
Take-shima = Tok-do
Takestān Iran 41E2
Taketa Japan 28B4
Takikawa Japan 29D2
Takingeun Indon 27C6
Takinoue Japan 29D2
Takiyvak L Can 54G3
Takkaze, R Eth 50D2
Takoradi Ghana 48B4
Talagang Pak 42C2
Talaimannar Sri Lanka 44B4
Talak, Desert Region Niger 48C3
Talara Peru 72B4
Talasea PNG 32E1
Talata Egypt 45B3
Talaud, Kepulauan, Is Indon 27F6
Talavera de la Reina Spain 15B2
Talca Chile 74B5
Talcahuano Chile 74B5
Tālcher India 43F4
Taldy Kurgan USSR 39F1
Taliabu, I Indon 27F7
Taligan Afghan 42B1
Tali Post Sudan 50D3
Taliwang Indon 27E7
Talkeetna USA 54D3
Talkha Egypt 45A3
Talladega USA 67A2
Tall 'Afar Iraq 40D2
Tallahassee USA 67B2
Tall Bisah Syria 45D1
Tallinn USSR 20C4
Tall Kalakh Syria 40C3
Tallulah USA 63D2
Tal'menka USSR 26B1
Tal'noye USSR 21E6
Talpaki USSR 19E2
Taltal Chile 74B3
Talwood Aust 34C1
Tama USA 61E2
Tamabo Ra, Mts Borneo 27E6
Tamale Ghana 48B4
Tamano Japan 29C4
Tamanrasset Alg 48C2
Tamanrasset, Watercourse Alg 48C2
Tamaqua USA 68C2
Tamar, R Eng 7B4
Tamatave = Toamasina
Tambacounda Sen 48A3
Tambov USSR 21G5
Tambre, R Spain 15A1
Tambura Sudan 50C3
Tamchaket Maur 48A3
Tamega, R Port 15A1
Tamiahua, L de, Lg Mexico 70C2
Tamil Nadu, State India 44B3
Tamis, R Rom 17E1
Tam Ky Viet 30D2
Tampa USA 67B3
Tampa B USA 67B3
Tampere Fin 12J6
Tampico Mexico 70C2
Tamsagbulag Mongolia 26E2
Tamsui Taiwan 26F4
Tamu Burma 43G4
Tamworth Aust 34D2
Tamworth Eng 7D3
Tana Nor 20D1
Tana, R Fin/Nor 12K5
Tana, R Kenya 50E4
Tanabe Japan 29C4
Tanafjord, Inlet Nor 12K4
Tanahgrogot Indon 27E7
Tanahmerah Indon 27G7
Tana, L Eth 50D2
Tanana USA 54C3
Tanana, R USA 54C3
Tananarive = Antananarivo
Tanch'ŏn N Korea 28B2
Tandaho Eth 50E2
Tandil Arg 74E5
Tandjung d'Urville, C Indon 27G7
Tandjung Vals, C Indon 27G7
Tando Adam Pak 42B3
Tando Muhammad Khan Pak 42B3
Tandou L Aust 34B2
Tandūr India 44B2
Taneatua NZ 35C1
Tanen Range, Mts Burma/Thai 30B2
Tanezrouft, Desert Region Alg 48B2
Tanga Tanz 50D4
Tanga Is PNG 33E1
Tanganyika,L Tanz/Zaïre 50C4
Tanger = Tangiers
Tanggula Shan, Mts China 39H2
Tangiers Mor 15A2
Tangjin S Korea 28A3
Tangra Yumco, L China 39G2
Tangshan China 31D2
Tanguy USSR 26D1
Tanimbar, Kepulauan, Arch Indon 27G7
Tanjona Ankaboa, C Madag 51E6
Tanjona Anorontany, C Madag 51E5
Tanjona Bobaomby, C Madag 51E5
Tanjona Vilanandro, C Madag 51E5
Tanjona Vohimena, C Madag 51E6
Tanjungbalai Indon 27C6
Tanjungpandan Indon 27D7
Tanjung Priok Indon 27D7
Tanjungredeb Indon 27E6
Tanjung Selatan, Pt Indon 32A1
Tanjungselor Indon 27E6
Tanjung Vals, Pt Indon 32C1
Tank Pak 42C2
Tanna, I Vanuatu 33F2
Tannu Ola, Mts USSR 26C1
Tano, R Ghana 48B4
Tanout Niger 48C3
Tansing Nepal 43E3
Tanta Egypt 49F1
Tan-Tan Mor 48A2
Tanunak USA 54B3
Tanyang S Korea 28A3
Tanzania, Republic Africa 50D4
Tao He, R China 31A3
Taole China 31B2
Taos USA 62A1
Taourirt Mor 48B1
Tapa USSR 20D4
Tapachula Mexico 70C3
Tapajós, R Brazil 73G4
Tapan Indon 27D7
Tapanui NZ 35A3
Tapauá, R Brazil 72E5
Tapi, R India 42D4
Taplejung Nepal 43F3
Tappahannock USA 65D3
Tapuaenuku, Mt NZ 35B2
Tapuaritinga Brazil 75C3
Tapurucuara Brazil 72F4
Taquaral, Serra do, Mts Brazil 75B2
Taquari, R Brazil 75B2
Tara Aust 34D1
Tara USSR 24J4
Tara, R USSR 24J4
Tara, R Yugos 17D2
Taraba, R Nigeria 48D4
Tarabuco Bol 72F7
Tarabulus = Tripoli (Libya)
Taradale NZ 35C1
Tarakan Indon 27E6
Tarancón Spain 15B1
Taransay, I Scot 8B3
Taranto Italy 16D2
Taranto, G di Italy 16D2
Tarapoto Peru 72C5
Tarare France 14C2
Tararua Range, Mts NZ 35C2
Tarasovo USSR 20H2
Tarat Alg 48C2
Tarawera NZ 35C1
Tarazona Spain 15B1
Tarbagatay, Khrebet, Mts USSR 39G1
Tarbat Ness, Pen Scot 8D3
Tarbela Res Pak 42C2
Tarbert, Strathclyde Scot 8C4
Tarbert, Western Isles Scot 8B3
Tarbes France 14B3
Tarboro USA 67C1
Tarcoola Aust 32C4
Tarcoon Aust 34C2
Taree Aust 34D2
Tarfaya Mor 48A2
Targhee P USA 58D2
Tarhunah Libya 49D1
Tarif UAE 41F5
Tarija Bol 72F8
Tarikere India 44B3
Tarim S Yemen 38C4
Tarime Tanz 50D4
Tarim He, R China 39G1
Tarim Pendi, Basin China 39G2
Tarin Kut Afghan 42B2
Tarkastad S Africa 47D3
Tarkio USA 61D2
Tarlac Phil 27F5
Tarma Peru 72C6
Tarn, R France 14C3
Tarnobrzeg Pol 19E2
Tarnów Pol 19E3
Taro, R Italy 16B2
Taroom Aust 32D3
Tarragona Spain 15C1
Tarraleah Aust 34C4
Tarrasa Spain 15C1
Tarrytown USA 68D2
Tarsus Turk 40B2
Tartan, Oilfield N Sea 8E2
Tartarskiy Proliv, Str USSR 26H2
Tartu USSR 20D4
Tartūs Syria 40C3
Tarumirim Brazil 75D2
Tarutung Indon 27C6
Tarvisio Italy 16C1
Taschereau Can 65D1
Tashauz USSR 38D1
Tashigang Bhutan 43G3
Tashkent USSR 39E1
Tashtagol USSR 24K4
Tashtyp USSR 25L4
Tasil Syria 45C2
Tasiussaq Greenland 55N2
Tasker, Well Niger 50B2
Tasman B NZ 35B2
Tasmania, I Aust 32D5
Tasman Mts NZ 35B2
Tasman Pen Aust 34C4
Tasman S NZ/Aust 33E4
Taşova Turk 40C1
Tassili du Hoggar, Desert Region Alg 48C2
Tassili N'jjer, Desert Region Alg 48C2
Tata Mor 48B2
Tatabánya Hung 19D3
Tataouine Tunisia 48D1
Tatar ASSR, Republic USSR 20J4
Tatarsk USSR 24J4
Tateyama Japan 29C3
Tathlina L Can 54G3
Tatnam, Cape Can 55J4
Tatry, Mts Czech/Pol 19D3
Tatsuno Japan 29B4
Tatta Pak 42B4
Tatuí Brazil 75C3
Tatum USA 62B2
Tatvan Turk 40D2
Ta'u, I American Samoa 33H2
Tauá Brazil 73K5
Taubaté Brazil 75C3
Taufstein, Mt W Germ 13E2
Taumarunui NZ 35C1
Taung S Africa 47C2
Taungdwingyi Burma 30B2
Taung-gyi Burma 30B1
Taungup Burma 30A2
Taunsa Pak 42C2
Taunton Eng 7C4
Taunton USA 68E2
Taunus, Mts Turk 40B2
Taunus, Region W Germ 13E2
Taupo NZ 35C1
Taupo,L NZ 35C1
Taurage USSR 19E1
Tauranga NZ 35C1
Tauranga Harbour, B NZ 35C1
Tauroa Pt NZ 35B1
Taurus Mts Turk 40B2
Tavani Can 55J3
Tavda USSR 46H4
Tavda, R USSR 46H4
Taveuni, I Fiji 33H2
Tavira Port 15A2
Tavistock Eng 7B4
Tavoy Burma 30B3
Tavoy Pt Burma 30B3
Tavşanli Turk 40A2
Taw, R Eng 7C4
Tawa NZ 35B2
Tawakoni,L USA 63C2
Tawas City USA 64C2
Tawau Malay 27E6
Taweisha Sudan 50C2
Tawitawi, I Phil 27F6
Taxco Mexico 70C3
Tay, R Scot 8D3
Tayan Indon 27E7
Tay, Loch, L Scot 8C3
Taylor, Michigan USA 64C2
Taylor, Texas USA 63C2
Taylor USA 54B3
Taylor,Mt USA 62A1
Taylorville USA 64B3
Tayma' S Arabia 40C4
Taymura, R USSR 25L3
Taymyr, Ozero, L USSR 25M2
Taymyr, Poluostrov, Pen USSR 25L2
Tay Ninh Viet 30D3
Tayshet USSR 25L4
Tayshir Mongolia 26C2
Tayside, Region Scot 8D3
Taytay Phil 27E5
Taza Mor 48B1
Tazawako Japan 29D3
Tazawa-ko, L Japan 29D3
Tazerbo, Region Libya 49E2
Tazovskiy USSR 24J3
Tbilisi USSR 21G7
Tchibanga Gabon 50B4
Tchigai,Plat du Niger 50B1
Tchin Tabaradene Niger 48C3
Tcholliré Cam 50B3
Tczew Pol 19D2
Te Anau NZ 35A3
Te Anua,L NZ 35A3
Te Aroha NZ 35C1
Te Awamutu NZ 35C1
Tébessa Algeria 16B3
Tébessa, Mts De Tunisia/Alg 16B3
Téboursouk Tunisia 16B3
Tecate Mexico 59C4
Techa, R USSR 20L4
Tecomán Mexico 70B3
Tecpan Mexico 70B3
Tecuci Rom 17F1
Tecumseh USA 61D2
Tedzhen USSR 24H6
Tedzhen, R USSR 24H6
Tees, R Eng 6D2
Tefé Brazil 72F4
Tegucigalpa Honduras 70D3
Tehachapi USA 66C3
Tehachapi Mts USA 66C3
Tehachapi P USA 59C3
Tehek L Can 54J3
Tehrān Iran 41F2
Tehuacán Mexico 70C3
Tehuantepec Mexico 70C3
Tehuantepec, G de Mexico 70C3
Tehuantepec, Istmo de, isthmus Mexico 70C3
Teifi, R Wales 7B3
Teignmouth Eng 7C4
Tejo, R Port 15A2
Tejon P USA 66C3

Tekamah Tongaat

Tekamah *USA* 61D2
Tekapo,L *NZ* 35B2
Tekeli *USSR* 39F1
Tekirdağ *Turk* 40A1
Tekir Dağları, Mts *Turk* 17F2
Teknaf *Bang* 43G4
Te Kuiti *NZ* 35C1
Tela *Honduras* 70D3
Telavi *USSR* 21H7
Tel Aviv Yafo *Israel* 45C2
Telegraph Creek *Can* 54E4
Telén *Arg* 74C5
Telescope Peak, Mt *USA* 59C3
Teles Pires, R *Brazil* 73G5
Telford *Eng* 7C3
Teli *USSR* 25K4
Tell el Meise, Mt *Jordan* 45C3
Teller *USA* 54B3
Tellicherry *India* 44B3
Telok Anson *Malay* 30C5
Telšiai *USSR* 19E1
Telukbetung *Indon* 27D7
Teluk Bone, B *Indon* 27F7
Teluk Cendrawasih, B *Indon* 27G7
Teluk Darvel, B *Malay* 27E6
Teluk Tolo, B *Indon* 27F7
Teluk Tomini, B *Indon* 27F6
Teluk Weda, B *Indon* 27F6
Temagami,L *Can* 64C1
Temblador *Ven* 69E5
Temblor Range, Mts *USA* 66B3
Teme, R *Eng* 7C3
Temerloh *Malay* 30C5
Temir *USSR* 24G5
Temirtau *USSR* 24J4
Temiscaming *Can* 65D1
Témiscouata,L *Can* 65F1
Temora *Aust* 34C2
Tempe *USA* 59D4
Temple *USA* 63C2
Templemore *Irish Rep* 9C3
Templeton *USA* 66B3
Temuco *Chile* 74B5
Temuka *NZ* 35B2
Tena *Ecuador* 72C4
Tenāli *India* 44C2
Tenasserim *Burma* 30B3
Tenby *Wales* 7B4
Tende, Colle de, P *France/Italy* 16B2
Ten Degree Chan *Indian O* 44E4
Tendo *Japan* 29E3
Ténéré, Erg du, Desert Region *Niger* 50B2
Tenerife, I *Canary Is* 48A2
Ténès *Alg* 15C2
Teng, R *Burma* 30B1
Tengger Shamo, Desert *China* 31A2
Tengiz, Ozero, L *USSR* 24H4
Teniente Rodolfo Marsh, Base *Ant* 76G2
Tenkāsi *India* 44B4
Tenke *Zaïre* 51C5
Tenkodogo *Burkina* 48B3
Tennant Creek *Aust* 32C2
Tennessee, R *USA* 63E1
Tennessee, State *USA* 57E3
Tennesse P *USA* 60B3
Tenom *Malay* 27E6
Tenosique *Mexico* 70C3
Tenterfield *Aust* 34D1
Ten Thousand Is *USA* 67B3
Teófilo Otôni *Brazil* 75D2
Tepehuanes *Mexico* 70B2
Tepic *Mexico* 70B2
Teplice *Czech* 18C2
Te Puke *NZ* 35C1
Ter, R *Spain* 15C1
Téra *Niger* 48C3
Teradomari *Japan* 29C3
Teramo *Italy* 16C2
Terceira, I *Azores* 48A1
Terebovlya *USSR* 19F3
Terenos *Brazil* 75B3
Teresina *Brazil* 73K5
Teresópolis *Brazil* 75D3
Teressa, I, Nicobar Is *Indian O* 44E4
Terme *Turk* 40C1
Termez *USSR* 38E2
Términos, L de, Lg *Mexico* 70C3
Termoli *Italy* 16C2
Ternate *Indon* 27F6
Terni *Italy* 16C2
Ternopol *USSR* 19F3
Terpeniya, Zaliv, B *USSR* 26H2
Terra Bella *USA* 66C3
Terrace Bay *Can* 64B1
Terracina *Italy* 16C2
Terrafirma *S Africa* 51C6
Terre Adélie, Region *Ant* 76G8
Terre Bonne B *USA* 63D3
Terre Haute *USA* 64B3
Terrell *USA* 63C2
Terry *USA* 60B1
Terschelling, I *Neth* 18B2
Teruel *Spain* 15B1
Teshekpuk *USA* 54C2
Teshikaga *Japan* 29D2
Teshio, R *Japan* 29E2
Teshio dake, Mt *Japan* 29D2
Tesiyn Gol, R *Mongolia* 25L5
Teslin *Can* 54E3
Tesouro *Brazil* 75B2
Tessalit *Mali* 48C2
Tessaoua *Niger* 48C3
Test, R *Eng* 7D4
Tete *Mozam* 51D5
Teterev, R *USSR* 19F2
Teton, R *USA* 58D1
Teton Range, Mts *USA* 58D2
Tetouan *Mor* 48B1
Tetyushi *USSR* 20H5
Teuco, R *Arg* 72F8
Teuco, R *Par* 74D2
Teulada, C, Sardinia 16B3
Teun, I *Indon* 27F7
Teuri-tō, I *Japan* 29D2
Teutoburger Wald, Hills *W Germ* 13E1
Tevere, R *Italy* 16C2
Teviot, R *Scot* 8D4
Tevriz *USSR* 24J4
Te Waewae B *NZ* 35A3
Tewantin *Aust* 34D1
Tewkesbury *Eng* 7C3
Têwo *China* 31A3
Texarkana *USA* 63D2
Texarkana,L *USA* 63D2
Texas *Aust* 34D1
Texas, State *USA* 56C3
Texas City *USA* 63D3
Texel, I *Neth* 18A2
Texhoma *USA* 62B1
Texoma,L *USA* 63C2
Teyateyaneng *Lesotho* 47D2
Teyvareh *Afghan* 42A2
Tezpur *India* 43G3
Tha, R *Laos* 30C1
Thabana Ntlenyana, Mt *Lesotho* 47D2
Thaba Putsoa, Mt *Lesotho* 47D2
Thabazimbi *S Africa* 47D1
Thagyettaw *Burma* 30B3
Thai Binh *Viet* 30D1
Thailand, Kingdom *S E Asia* 30C2
Thailand,G of *Thai* 30C3
Thai Nguyen *Viet* 30D1
Thakhek *Laos* 30D2
Thal *Pak* 42C2
Thale Luang, L *Thai* 30C4
Thallon *Aust* 34C1
Thames *NZ* 35C1
Thames, R *Eng* 7E4
Thamhar, Wadi ath, R *Iraq* 21G8
Thāne *India* 44A2
Thanh Hoa *Viet* 30D2
Thanjavūr *India* 44B3
Thann *France* 13D4
Thar Desert *India* 42C3
Thargomindah *Aust* 34B1
Thásos, I *Greece* 17E2
Thaton *Burma* 30B2
Thayetmyo *Burma* 30A2
The Broads *Eng* 7E3
The Dalles *USA* 54F5
Thedford *USA* 60C2
The Gambia, Republic *W Africa* 48A3
The Gulf *S W Asia* 41F4
The Hague *Neth* 18A2
Thelon, R *Can* 54H3
The Naze, Pt *Eng* 7E4
Theodore *Aust* 32E3
Theodore Roosevelt L *USA* 59D4
Theodore Roosevelt, R *Brazil* 72F6
The Pas *Can* 54H4
Thermaïkós Kólpos, G *Greece* 17E2
Thermopolis *USA* 58E2
Thesiger B *Can* 54F2
Thessalon *Can* 64C1
Thessaloníki *Greece* 17E2
Thetford *Eng* 7E3
Thetford Mines *Can* 65E1
Theunissen *S Africa* 47D2
Thibodaux *USA* 63D3
Thicket Portage *Can* 54J4
Thief River Falls *USA* 61D1
Thielsen,Mt *USA* 58B2
Thiers *France* 14C2
Thiès *Sen* 48A3
Thika *Kenya* 50D4
Thimphu *Bhutan* 43F3
Thionville *France* 14D2
Thíra, I *Greece* 17F3
Thirsk *Eng* 6D2
Thisted *Den* 12F7
Thitu *S China Sea* 27E5
Thívai *Greece* 17E3
Thiviers *France* 14C2
Thomas A Edison,L *USA* 66C2
Thomaston, Georgia *USA* 67B2
Thomaston, Maine *USA* 65F2
Thomastown *Irish Rep* 9C3
Thomasville, Alabama *USA* 63E2
Thomasville, Georgia *USA* 67B2
Thomasville, N Carolina *USA* 67C1
Thom Bay *Can* 55J2
Thompson *Can* 54J4
Thompson, R *USA* 61E2
Thompson Falls *USA* 58C1
Thompson Landing *Can* 54G3
Thompsonville *USA* 68D2
Thomson *USA* 67B2
Thomson, R *Aust* 32D3
Thon Buri *Thai* 30C3
Thongwa *Burma* 30B2
Thoreau *USA* 62A1
Thornaby *Eng* 6D2
Thorne *Eng* 7D3
Thornhill *Scot* 8D4
Thouars *France* 14B2
Thousand Is *Can/USA* 65D2
Three Forks *USA* 58D1
Three Lakes *USA* 64B1
Three Pagodas P *Thai* 30B2
Three Points, C *Ghana* 48B4
Three Rivers, California *USA* 66C2
Three Rivers, Michigan *USA* 64B2
Three Rivers, Texas *USA* 62C3
Three Sisters, Mt *USA* 58B2
Thule *Greenland* 55M2
Thun *Switz* 16B1
Thunder Bay *Can* 64B1
Thung Song *Thai* 30B4
Thüringer Wald, Upland *E Germ* 18C2
Thurles *Irish Rep* 9C3
Thurso *Scot* 8D2
Thurston I *Ant* 76F4
Thylungra *Aust* 34B1
Tiandong *China* 31B5
Tian'e *China* 31B5
Tianjin *China* 31D2
Tianlin *China* 31B5
Tianqiaoling *China* 28B2
Tian Shan, Mts *China/USSR* 24J5
Tianshui *China* 31B3
Tianzhu *China* 31A2
Tiaret *Alg* 15C2
Tibagi, R *Brazil* 75B3
Tibati *Cam* 48D4
Tiberias *Israel* 45C2
Tiberias,L *Israel* 45C2
Tiber,R = Tevere,R
Tiber Res *USA* 58D1
Tibesti, Mountain Region *Chad* 50B1
Tibet, Autonomous Region *China* 39G2
Tibooburra *Aust* 34B1
Tibrikot *Nepal* 43E3
Tiburón, I *Mexico* 70A2
Tichitt *Maur* 48B3
Tichla *Mor* 48A2
Ticonderoga *USA* 65E2
Ticul *Mexico* 70D2
Tidikelt, Plaine du, Desert Region *Alg* 48C2
Tidjikja *Maur* 48A3
Tidra, Isla *Maur* 48A3
Tiel *Neth* 13C2
Tieling *China* 28A2
Tielt *Belg* 13B2
Tienen *Belg* 13C2
Tiengen *W Germ* 13E4
Tien Shan, Mts *USSR/China* 39G1
Tientsin = Tianjin
Tierp *Sweden* 12H6
Tierra Amarilla *USA* 62A1
Tierra Blanca *Mexico* 70C3
Tierra del Fuego, Territory *Arg* 74C8
Tierra del Fuego, Isla Grande de *Arg/Chile* 74C8
Tietê *Brazil* 75C3
Tiete, R *Brazil* 75B3
Tiffin *USA* 64C2
Tifton *USA* 67B2
Tigil *USSR* 25R4
Tigre, R *Peru* 72C4
Tigre, R *Ven* 72F2
Tigre, Region *Eth* 50D2
Tigris, R *Iraq* 41E3
Tīh, Gebel el, Upland *Egypt* 45B4
Tijuana *Mexico* 59C4
Tikamgarh *India* 42D4
Tikhoretsk *USSR* 21G6
Tikhvin *USSR* 20E4
Tikopia, I *Solomon Is* 33F2
Tikrit *Iraq* 41D3
Tiksi *USSR* 25O2
Tilburg *Neth* 13C2
Tilbury *Eng* 7E4
Tilcara *Arg* 74C2
Tilcha *Aust* 34B1
Tilemis, Vallée du *Mali* 48C3
Tilhar *India* 43K2
Tilin *Burma* 30A1
Tillabéri *Niger* 48C3
Tillamook *USA* 58B1
Tillanchong, I, Nicobar Is *Indian O* 44E4
Tillia *Niger* 48C3
Till, R *Eng* 6D2
Tílos, I *Greece* 17F3
Tilpa *Aust* 34B2
Tilt, R *Scot* 8D3
Timanskiy Kryazh, Mts *USSR* 20H2
Timaru *NZ* 35B2
Timashevsk *USSR* 21F6
Timbákion *Greece* 17E3
Timbalier B *USA* 63D3
Timbédra *Maur* 48B3
Timbuktu = Tombouctou
Timétrine Monts, Mts *Mali* 48B3
Timia *Niger* 48C3
Timimoun *Alg* 48C2
Timişoara *Rom* 17E1
Timmins *Can* 64C1
Timor, I *Indon* 32B1
Timor S *Aust/Indon* 32B2
Timsâh,L *Egypt* 45B3
Tims Ford L *USA* 67A1
Tinaca Pt *Phil* 27F6
Tinaco *Ven* 69D5
Tindivanam *India* 44B3
Tindouf *Alg* 48B2
Tinemaha Res *USA* 66C2
Tinfouchy *Alg* 48B2
Tin Fouye *Alg* 48C2
Tingmiarmiut *Greenland* 55O3
Tingo María *Peru* 72C5
Tingrela *Ivory Coast* 48B3
Tingri *China* 43F3
Tinharé, Ilha de *Brazil* 75E1
Tinian *Pacific O* 27H5
Tinogasta *Arg* 74C3
Tínos, I *Greece* 17F3
Tinsukia *India* 43H3
Tintagel Head, Pt *Eng* 7B4
Tin Tarabine, Watercourse *Alg* 48C2
Tintinara *Aust* 34B3
Tin Zaouaten *Alg* 48C2
Tioga *USA* 60C1
Tioga, R *USA* 68B2
Tioga P *USA* 66C2
Tioman, I *Malay* 30C5
Tioughnioga, R *USA* 68B1
Tipperary *Irish Rep* 10B3
Tipperary, County *Irish Rep* 9C3
Tipton, California *USA* 66C2
Tipton, Missouri *USA* 61E3
Tiptūr *India* 44B3
Tiranë *Alb* 17D2
Tiraspol *USSR* 21D6
Tir'at el Ismâilîya, Canal *Egypt* 45A3
Tire *Turk* 17F3
Tirebolu *Turk* 40C1
Tiree, I *Scot* 8B3
Tîrgovişte *Rom* 17F2
Tîrgu Jiu *Rom* 17E1
Tîrgu Mureş *Rom* 17E1
Tirich Mir, Mt *Pak* 42C1
Tiris, Region *Mor* 48A2
Tirlyanskiy *USSR* 20K5
Tîrnăveni *Rom* 17E1
Tírnavos *Greece* 17E3
Tirodi *India* 42D4
Tirso, R, Sardinia 16B2
Tiruchchendūr *India* 44B4
Tiruchchirāppalli *India* 44B3
Tirunelveli *India* 44B4
Tirupati *India* 44B3
Tiruppattūr *India* 44B3
Tiruppur *India* 44B3
Tiruvannāmalai *India* 44B3
Tishomingo *USA* 63C2
Tisiyah *Syria* 45D2
Tisza, R *Hung* 19E3
Titicaca, Lago *Bol/Peru* 72E7
Titlagarh *India* 43E4
Titograd *Yugos* 17D2
Titova Mitrovica *Yugos* 17E2
Titovo Užice *Yugos* 17D2
Titov Veles *Yugos* 17E2
Titule *Zaïre* 50C3
Titusville *USA* 67B3
Tiumpan Head, Pt *Scot* 8B2
Tiverton *Eng* 7C4
Tivoli *Italy* 16C2
Tiyeglow *Somalia* 50E3
Tizimín *Mexico* 70D2
Tizi Ouzou *Alg* 15C2
Tiznit *Mor* 48B2
Tlañaro *Madag* 51E6
Tlemcen *Alg* 48B1
Toamasina *Madag* 51E5
Toba *Japan* 29C4
Toba and Kakar Ranges, Mts *Pak* 42B2
Tobago, I *Caribbean S* 69E4
Tobelo *Indon* 27F6
Tobermory *Can* 64C1
Tobermory *Scot* 8B3
Tobi, I *Pacific O* 27G6
Tobin,Mt *USA* 59C2
Tobi-shima, I *Japan* 29C3
Toboah *Indon* 27D7
Tobol, R *USSR* 24H4
Toboli *Indon* 27F7
Tobol'sk *USSR* 24H4
Tobruk = Tubruq
Tobseda *USSR* 20J2
Tocantins, R *Brazil* 73J4
Toccoa *USA* 67B2
Tocopilla *Chile* 74B2
Tocorpuri *Bol/Chile* 74C2
Tocuyo, R *Ven* 72E1
Toda *India* 42D3
Todong *S Korea* 28B3
Todos os Santos, Baia de, B *Brazil* 73L6
Todos Santos *Mexico* 56B4
Todos Santos,B de *Mexico* 59C4
Tofua, I *Tonga* 33H2
Togian, Kepulauan, I *Indon* 32B1
Togo, Republic *W Africa* 48C4
Togtoh *China* 31C1
Tohatchi *USA* 62A1
Tokachi, R *Japan* 29E2
Tokamachi *Japan* 29C3
Tokar *Sudan* 50D2
Tokara Retto, Arch *Japan* 26F4
Tokat *Turk* 40C1
Tok-do, I *S Korea* 28B3
Tokelau Is *Pacific O* 33H1
Tokmak *USSR* 39F1
Tokomaru Bay *NZ* 35C1
Tokuno, I, Ryukyu Is *Japan* 26F4
Tokushima *Japan* 29C4
Tokuyama *Japan* 28B4
Tōkyō *Japan* 29D3
Tolaga Bay *NZ* 35C1
Toledo *Brazil* 73H8
Toledo *Spain* 15B2
Toledo *USA* 64C2
Toledo Bend Res *USA* 63D2
Toliara *Madag* 51E6
Tolina, Mt *Colombia* 72C2
Tolochin *USSR* 19F2
Tolosa *Spain* 15B1
Tolsan-do, I *S Korea* 28A4
Toltén *Chile* 74B5
Toluca *Mexico* 70C3
Tol'yatti *USSR* 20H5
Tomah *USA* 64A2
Tomahawk *USA* 64B1
Tomakomai *Japan* 29E2
Tomar *Port* 15A2
Tomaszów Mazowiecka *Pol* 19E2
Tombigbee, R *USA* 63E2
Tomboco *Angola* 51B4
Tombos *Brazil* 75D3
Tombouctou *Mali* 48B3
Tombstone *USA* 59E4
Tomburke *S Africa* 47D1
Tomé *Chile* 74B5
Tomelloso *Spain* 15B2
Tomie *Japan* 28A4
Tomintoul *Scot* 8D3
Tomkinson Range, Mts *Aust* 32B3
Tommot *USSR* 25O4
Tomorrit, Mt *Alb* 17E2
Tomsk *USSR* 24K4
Toms River *USA* 68C3
Tonalá *Mexico* 70C3
Tonasket *USA* 58C1
Tonawanda *USA* 65D2
Tonbridge *Eng* 7E4
Tonga, Is, Kingdom *Pacific O* 33H3
Tongaat *S Africa* 47E2

Tongatapu Tyrone

Tongatapu, I *Tonga* 33H3
Tongatapu Group, Is *Tonga* 33H3
Tonga Trench *Pacific O* 33H3
Tongchang *N Korea* 28A2
Tongcheng *China* 31D3
Tongchuan *China* 31B2
Tongde *China* 31A2
Tongeren *Belg* 13C2
Tonggu Jiao, I *China* 30E2
Tonghai *China* 31A5
Tonghua *China* 28B2
Tongjosŏn-Man, S *N Korea* 28B3
Tongkin,G of *China/Viet* 30D1
Tongliao *China* 31E1
Tongling *China* 31D3
Tongnae *S Korea* 28A3
Tongo *Aust* 34B2
Tongren, Guizhou *China* 31B4
Tongren, Qinghai *China* 31A2
Tongsa *Bhutan* 43G3
Tongta *Burma* 30B1
Tongtian He, R *China* 26C3
Tongue *Scot* 8C2
Tongue, R *USA* 60B1
Tong Xian *China* 31D2
Tongxin *China* 31B2
Tongyuanpu *China* 28A2
Tongzi *China* 31B4
Tonhil *Mongolia* 25L5
Tónichi *Mexico* 56C4
Tonj *Sudan* 50C3
Tonk *India* 42D3
Tonkawa *USA* 63C1
Tonle Sap, L *Camb* 30C3
Tonnerre *France* 13C4
Tono *Japan* 29D3
Tonopah *USA* 59C3
Tooele *USA* 58D2
Toogoolawah *Aust* 34D1
Toompine *Aust* 34B1
Toowoomba *Aust* 34D1
Topaz L *USA* 66C1
Topeka *USA* 61D3
Topock *USA* 59D4
Topolobampo *Mexico* 56C4
Topozero, L *USSR* 20E2
Toppenish *USA* 58B1
Topsfield *USA* 68E1
Torbalı *Turk* 17F3
Torbat-e-Heydariyeh *Iran* 41G2
Torbay *Eng* 7C4
Tordesillas *Spain* 15A1
Torgau *E Germ* 18C2
Torhout *Belg* 13B2
Tori *Eth* 50D3
Tori, I *Japan* 26H3
Torino = Turin
Torit *Sudan* 50D3
Torixoreu *Brazil* 75B2
Tormes, R *Spain* 15A1
Torne, R *Sweden* 12J5
Torneträsk, L *Sweden* 12H5
Torngat, Mts *Can* 55M4
Tornio *Fin* 12J5
Toro, Cerro del, Mt *Arg/Chile* 74C3
Toronto *Can* 65D2
Toropets *USSR* 20E4
Tororo *Uganda* 50D3
Toros, Dağları = Taurus Mts
Torquay *Eng* 7C4
Torrance *USA* 66C4
Torrão *Port* 15A2
Torreblanca *Spain* 15C1
Torre del Greco *Italy* 16C2
Torrelavega *Spain* 15B1
Torremolinos *Spain* 15B2
Torrens, L *Aust* 32C4
Torreón *Mexico* 70B2
Torres Is *Vanuatu* 33F2
Torres Str *Aust* 32D2
Torres Vedras *Port* 15A2
Torridge, R *Eng* 7B4
Torridon, Loch, Inlet *Scot* 8C3
Torrington, Connecticut *USA* 68D2
Torrington, Wyoming *USA* 60C2
Tórshavn *Faeroes* 12D3
Tortosa *Spain* 15C1
Tortosa, Cabo de, C *Spain* 15C1
Tortugas, Golfo de *Colombia* 72C3
Torūd *Iran* 41G2
Toruń *Pol* 19D2
Tory I *Irish Rep* 10B2
Tory Sol *Irish Rep* 9B2
Torzhok *USSR* 20E4
Tosa *Japan* 29B4
Tosashimizu *Japan* 28C4
Tosa-Wan, B *Japan* 29C4
To-shima, I *Japan* 29C4
Tosno *USSR* 12L7
Tosno *USSR* 20E4
Tosu *Japan* 28B4
Tosya *Turk* 40B1
Totana *Spain* 15B2
Tot'ma *USSR* 20G3
Totnes *Eng* 7C4
Totness *Surinam* 73G2
Tottenham *Aust* 34C2
Tottori *Japan* 29C3
Touba *Ivory Coast* 48B4
Touba *Sen* 48A3
Toubkal, Mt *Mor* 48B1
Toucy *France* 13B4
Tougan *Burkina* 48B3
Touggourt *Alg* 48C1
Tougué *Guinea* 48A3
Toul *France* 13C3
Toulon *France* 14D3
Toulouse *France* 14C3
Toumodi *Ivory Coast* 48B4
Toungoo *Burma* 30B2
Tourcoing *France* 13B2
Tourine *Maur* 48A2
Tournai *Belg* 13B2
Tours *France* 14C2
Touws River *S Africa* 47C3
Towada *Japan* 29E2
Towada-ko, L *Japan* 29E2
Towanda *USA* 68B2
Towne P *USA* 66D2
Towner *USA* 60C1
Townsend *USA* 58D1
Townsville *Aust* 32D2
Towson *USA* 68B3
Towy, R *Wales* 7C4
Toyah *USA* 62B2
Toya-ko, L *Japan* 29D2
Toyama *Japan* 29D3
Toyama-wan, B *Japan* 29C3
Toyohashi *Japan* 29C4
Toyonaka *Japan* 29C4
Toyooka *Japan* 29B3
Toyota *Japan* 29D3
Tozeur *Tunisia* 48C1
Traben-Trarbach *W Germ* 13D3
Trâblous = Tripoli, L
Trabzon *Turk* 40C1
Tracy, Minnesota *USA* 61D2
Tracy *USA* 66B2
Trafalgar, Cabo, C *Spain* 15A2
Trail *Can* 54G5
Tralee *Irish Rep* 10B3
Tramore *Irish Rep* 9C3
Tranås *Sweden* 12G7
Trang *Thai* 30B4
Trangan, I *Indon* 27G7
Trangie *Aust* 34C2
Transantarctic Mts *Ant* 76E3
Transkei, Self-governing homeland *S Africa* 47D3
Transvaal, Province *S Africa* 47D1
Transylvanian Alps, Mts = Munţii Carpaţii Meridionali
Trapani *Italy* 16C3
Traralgon *Aust* 34C3
Trarza, Region *Maur* 48A3
Trat *Thai* 30C3
Traveller's L *Aust* 34B2
Travemünde *W Germ* 18C2
Traverse City *USA* 64B2
Travers,Mt *NZ* 35B2
Travis,L *USA* 62C2
Třebíč *Czech* 18D3
Trebinje *Yugos* 17D2
Trebon *Czech* 18C3
Treinta y Tres *Urug* 74F4
Trelew *Arg* 74C6
Trelleborg *Sweden* 12G7
Tremadog B *Wales* 7B3
Tremblant,Mt *Can* 65E1
Tremiti, Is *Italy* 16D2
Tremont *USA* 68B2
Tremonton *USA* 58D2
Trenčín *Czech* 19D3
Trenque Lauquén *Arg* 74D5
Trent, R *Eng* 7D3
Trento *Italy* 16C1
Trenton *Can* 65D2
Trenton, Missouri *USA* 61E2
Trenton, New Jersey *USA* 68C2
Trepassey *Can* 55N5
Tres Arroyos *Arg* 74D5
Três Corações *Brazil* 75C3
Tres Forcas, Cabo, C *Mor* 15B2
Três Lagoas *Brazil* 74F2
Tres Pinos *USA* 66B2
Tres Puntas, Cabo *Arg* 74C7
Três Rios *Brazil* 75D3
Treviso *Italy* 16C1
Trevose Hd, Pt *Eng* 7B4
Treysa *W Germ* 13E2
Tribune *USA* 62B1
Trichūr *India* 44B3
Trida *Aust* 34C2
Trier *W Germ* 13D3
Trieste *Italy* 16C1
Trikomo *Cyprus* 45B1
Trim *Irish Rep* 9C3
Trincomalee *Sri Lanka* 44C4
Trindade, I *Atlantic O* 52G6
Trinidad *Bol* 72F6
Trinidad *Urug* 74E4
Trinidad *USA* 62B1
Trinidad, I *Caribbean S* 69E4
Trinidad & Tobago, Is Republic *Caribbean S* 69E4
Trinity *USA* 63C2
Trinity, R *USA* 56D3
Trinity B *Can* 55N5
Trion *USA* 67A2
Tripoli *Leb* 45C1
Tripoli *Libya* 49D1
Trípolis *Greece* 17E3
Tripura, State *India* 43G4
Tristan da Cunha, Is *Atlantic O* 52H6
Trivandrum *India* 44B4
Trnava *Czech* 19D3
Trobriand Is *PNG* 32E1
Trois Pistoles *Can* 65F1
Trois-Riviéres *Can* 65E1
Troitsk *USSR* 24H4
Troitsko Pechorsk *USSR* 20K3
Trollhättan *Sweden* 12G7
Trollheimen, Mt *Nor* 12F6
Tromelin, I *Indian O* 46K9
Trompsburg *S Africa* 47D3
Tromsø *Nor* 12H5
Trona *USA* 66D3
Trondheim *Nor* 12G6
Trondheimfjord, Inlet *Nor* 12G6
Troödos Range, Mts *Cyprus* 45B1
Troon *Scot* 8C4
Tropic of Cancer 52J3
Tropic of Capricorn 52K6
Troudenni *Mali* 48B2
Trout L, Ontario *Can* 55J4
Trout Peak, Mt *USA* 58E2
Trout Run *USA* 68B2
Trowbridge *Eng* 7C4
Troy, Alabama *USA* 67A2
Troy, Montana *USA* 58C1
Troy, New York *USA* 68D1
Troy, Ohio *USA* 64C2
Troy, Pennsylvania *USA* 68B2
Troyan *Bulg* 17E2
Troyes *France* 13C3
Troy Peak, Mt *USA* 59C3
Trucial Coast, Region *UAE* 41F5
Truckee, R *USA* 59B3
Trujillo *Honduras* 70D3
Trujillo *Peru* 72C5
Trujillo *Spain* 15A2
Trujillo *Ven* 72D2
Trumbull,Mt *USA* 59D3
Trundle *Aust* 34C2
Truro *Can* 55M5
Truro *Eng* 7B4
Truth or Consequences *USA* 62A2
Tsagaan Nuur, L *Mongolia* 26C2
Tsagan-Tologoy *USSR* 26C1
Tsaratanana *Madag* 51E5
Tsau *Botswana* 51C6
Tsavo *Kenya* 50D4
Tsavo Nat Pk *Kenya* 50D4
Tschida,L *USA* 60C1
Tselinograd *USSR* 24J4
Tses *Namibia* 47B2
Tsetserleg *Mongolia* 26C2
Tsetserleg *Mongolia* 26D2
Tsévié *Togo* 48C4
Tshabong *Botswana* 47C2
Tshane *Botswana* 47C1
Tshela *Zaïre* 50B4
Tshibala *Zaïre* 51C4
Tshikapa *Zaïre* 50C4
Tshuapa, R *Zaïre* 50C4
Tsimlyanskoye Vodokhranilishche, Res *USSR* 21G6
Tsinan = Jinan
Tsingtao = Qingdao
Tsiombe *Madag* 51E6
Tsiroanomandidy *Madag* 51E5
Tsna, R *USSR* 19F2
Tsogt Ovoo *Mongolia* 31B1
Tsomo *S Africa* 47D3
Tsu *Japan* 29C4
Tsubata *Japan* 29C3
Tsuchiura *Japan* 29E3
Tsugarū-kaikyo, Str *Japan* 29E2
Tsumeb *Namibia* 51B5
Tsumis *Namibia* 51B6
Tsuruga *Japan* 29D3
Tsurugi *Japan* 29C3
Tsuruoka *Japan* 29D3
Tsushima *Japan* 29C3
Tsushima, Is *Japan* 28B4
Tsushima-Kaikyo = Korea Str
Tsuyama *Japan* 29C3
Tua, R *Port* 15A1
Tuamotu, Îles *Pacific O* 37M5
Tuapse *USSR* 21F7
Tuatapere *NZ* 35A3
Tuba City *USA* 59D3
Tubai, Îles *Pacific O* 37M6
Tubarão *Brazil* 74G3
Tubas *Israel* 45C2
Tübingen *W Germ* 18B3
Tubruq *Libya* 49E1
Tuckerton *USA* 68C3
Tucson *USA* 59D4
Tucumán, State *Arg* 74C3
Tucumcari *USA* 62B1
Tucupita *Ven* 72F2
Tudela *Spain* 15B1
Tudmur *Syria* 40C3
Tugela, R *S Africa* 47E2
Tuggerah L *Aust* 34D2
Tuguegarao *Phil* 27F5
Tugur *USSR* 25P4
Tuhai He, R *China* 31D2
Tukangbesi, Kepulauan, Is *Indon* 32B1
Tukangbesi, Kepulauan, Is *Indon* 27F7
Tuktoyaktuk *Can* 54E3
Tukums *USSR* 19E1
Tukuringra, Khrebet, Mts *USSR* 25O4
Tukuyu *Tanz* 51D4
Tukzar *Afghan* 42B1
Tula *USSR* 20F5
Tulare *USA* 66C2
Tulare Lake Bed *USA* 66C2
Tularosa *USA* 62A2
Tulcán *Ecuador* 72C3
Tulcea *Rom* 21D6
Tul'chin *USSR* 19F3
Tule, R *USA* 66C2
Tuli *Zim* 51C6
Tuli, R *Zim* 47D1
Tulia *USA* 62B2
Tulkarm *Israel* 45C2
Tullahoma *USA* 67A1
Tullarnore *Irish Rep* 9C3
Tulle *France* 14C2
Tullos *USA* 63D2
Tullow *Irish Rep* 9C3
Tully *USA* 68B1
Tulsa *USA* 63C1
Tuluá *Colombia* 72C3
Tulul ash Shamiyah, Desert Region *Iran/Syria* 40C3
Tulun *USSR* 25M4
Tumaco *Colombia* 72C3
Tumany *USSR* 25R3
Tumbarumba *Aust* 34C3
Tumbes *Ecuador* 72B4
Tumen *China* 28B2
Tumen R *China/N Korea* 28B2
Tumkūr *India* 44B3
Tumpat *Malay* 30C4
Tumsar *India* 42D4
Tumu *Ghana* 48B3
Tumucumaque, Serra, Mts *Brazil* 73H3
Tumut *Aust* 34C3
Tumut, R *Aust* 34C3
Tunapuna *Trinidad* 69L1
Tunbridge Wells, Royal *Eng* 7E4
Tunceli *Turk* 40C2
Tunduma *Zambia* 51D4
Tunduru *Tanz* 51D5
Tundzha, R *Bulg* 17F2
Tungabhadra, R *India* 44B2
Tungkang *Taiwan* 26E4
Tungnafellsjökull, Mts *Iceland* 12B2
Tunguska, R *USSR* 25M3
Tuni *India* 44C2
Tunis *Tunisia* 16C3
Tunis, G de *Tunisia* 16C3
Tunisia, Republic *N Africa* 48C1
Tunja *Colombia* 72D2
Tunkhannock *USA* 68C2
Tunxi *China* 31D4
Tuolumne Meadows *USA* 66C2
Tupā *Brazil* 75B3
Tupaciguara *Brazil* 75C2
Tupelo *USA* 63E2
Tupik *USSR* 19G1
Tupiza *Bol* 72E8
Tupman *USA* 66C3
Tupper Lake *USA* 65E2
Tupungato, Mt *Arg* 74C4
Tura *India* 43G3
Tura *USSR* 25L3
Tura, R *USSR* 20L4
Turan *Iran* 41G2
Turan *USSR* 25L4
Turayf *S Arabia* 40C3
Turbat *Pak* 38E3
Turbo *Colombia* 72C2
Turda *Rom* 17E1
Turfan Depression *China* 24K5
Turgay *USSR* 24H5
Turgen Uul, Mt *Mongolia* 25L5
Turgutlu *Turk* 40A2
Turhal *Turk* 40C1
Türi *USSR* 12K7
Turia, R *Spain* 15B2
Turin *Italy* 16B1
Turinsk *USSR* 20L4
Turiy *USSR* 26G2
Turkana, L *Eth/Kenya* 50D3
Turkestan, Region *C Asia* 38E1
Turkey, Republic *W Asia* 40C2
Turkmenskiy Zaliv, B *USSR* 41F2
Turkmen SSR, Republic *USSR* 38D1
Turks Is *Caribbean S* 69C2
Turku *Fin* 12J6
Turkwel, R *Kenya* 50D3
Turlock *USA* 66B2
Turlock L *USA* 66B2
Turnagain,C *NZ* 35C2
Turneffe I *Belize* 70D3
Turners Falls *USA* 68D1
Turnhout *Belg* 13C2
Turnu Măgurele *Rom* 17E2
Turnu-Severin *Rom* 17E2
Turpan *China* 25K5
Turquino, Mt *Cuba* 69B2
Turriff *Scot* 8D3
Turtkul' *USSR* 38E1
Turtle Creek Res *USA* 61D3
Turukhansk *USSR* 25K3
Turuntayevo *USSR* 26D1
Turvo, R, Goias *Brazil* 75B2
Turvo, R, São Paulo *Brazil* 75C3
Tur'ya, R *USSR* 19E2
Tuscaloosa *USA* 63E2
Tuscarora Mt *USA* 68B2
Tuscola, Illinois *USA* 64B3
Tuscola, Texas *USA* 62C2
Tuscumbia *USA* 63E2
Tusharik *Iran* 41G3
Tussey Mt *USA* 68A2
Tuticorin *India* 44B4
Tutrakan *Bulg* 17F2
Tuttlingen *W Germ* 18B3
Tutuila, I *American Samoa* 33H2
Tuul Gol, R *Mongolia* 26D2
Tuva ASSR, Republic *USSR* 25L4
Tuvalu, Is *Pacific O* 33G1
Tuwayīlel Haj, Mt *Jordan* 45C4
Tuxpan *Mexico* 70B2
Tuxpan *Mexico* 70C2
Tuxtla Gutiérrez *Mexico* 70C3
Túy *Spain* 15A1
Tuy Hoa *Viet* 30D3
Tuz Gölü, Salt L *Turk* 40B2
Tuz Khurmatu *Iraq* 41D3
Tuzla *Yugos* 17D2
Tweed, R *Eng/Scot* 8D4
Tweed Heads *Aust* 34D1
Tweedsmuir Hills *Scot* 8D4
Twentynine Palms *USA* 59C4
Twillingate *Can* 55N5
Twin Bridges *USA* 58D1
Twin Buttes Res *USA* 62B2
Twin Falls *USA* 58D2
Twins,The, Mt *NZ* 35B2
Twitchell Res *USA* 66B3
Two Harbors *USA* 64A1
Two Medicine, R *USA* 58D1
Two Rivers *USA* 64B2
Tygda *USSR* 25O4
Tyler *USA* 63C2
Tymovskoye *USSR* 26H1
Tynda *USSR* 26F1
Tyne, R *Eng* 6D2
Tyne and Wear, Metropolitan County *Eng* 6D2
Tynemouth *Eng* 6D2
Tynset *Nor* 12G6
Tyr = Tyre
Tyre *Leb* 45C2
Tyrone, New Mexico *USA* 62A2
Tyrone, Pennsylvania *USA* 68A2

Tyrone Vembanad L

Tyrone, County *N Ire* **9C2**
Tyrrell,L *Aust* **34B3**
Tyrrhenian S *Italy* **16C2**
Tyuleni, Ova, Is *USSR* **21J7**
Tyumen' *USSR* **24H4**
Tyung, R *USSR* **25O3**
Tywyn *Wales* **7B3**
Tzaneen *S Africa* **47E1**
Tzoumérka, Mt *Greece* **17E3**

U

Uarsciek *Somalia* **50E3**
Ubá *Brazil* **75D3**
Ubaí *Brazil* **75D2**
Ubaitaba *Brazil* **75E1**
Ubangi, R *CAR/Congo/Zaïre* **50B3**
Ubayyid, Wadi al, Watercourse *Iraq* **40D3**
Ube *Japan* **28B4**
Ubeda *Spain* **15B2**
Ubekendt Ejland, I *Greenland* **55N2**
Uberaba *Brazil* **75C2**
Uberaba, Lagoa *Brazil* **75A2**
Uberlândia *Brazil* **75C2**
Ubon Ratchathani *Thai* **30D2**
Ubort, R *USSR* **19F2**
Ubundu *Zaïre* **50C4**
Ucayali, R *Peru* **72D5**
Uch *Pak* **42C3**
Uchar, R *USSR* **25P4**
Uchiura-wan, B *Japan* **29E2**
Uchte *W Germ* **13E1**
Ucluelet *Can* **58A1**
Uda, R *USSR* **26C1**
Udaipur *India* **42C4**
Udaipur Garhi *Nepal* **43F3**
Uddevalla *Sweden* **12G7**
Uddjaur, L *Sweden* **12H5**
Udgir *India* **44B2**
Udhampur *India* **42D2**
Udine *Italy* **16C1**
Udmurt ASSR, Republic *USSR* **20J4**
Udon Thani *Thai* **30C2**
Udskaya Guba, B *USSR* **25P4**
Udupi *India* **44A3**
Udzha *USSR* **25N2**
Ueda *Japan* **29C3**
Uele, R *Zaïre* **50C3**
Uelen *USSR* **25U3**
Uelzen *W Germ* **18C2**
Uere, R *Zaïre* **50C3**
Ufa *USSR* **20K5**
Ufa, R *USSR* **20K4**
Ugab, R *Namibia* **51B6**
Ugaila, R *Tanz* **50D4**
Uganda, Republic *Africa* **50D3**
'Ugeiqa, Wadi *Jordan* **45C3**
Uglegorsk *USSR* **26H2**
Uglich *USSR* **20F4**
Uglovoye *USSR* **28C2**
Ugra, R *USSR* **20F5**
Uig *Scot* **8B3**
Uige *Angola* **51B4**
Üijŏngbu *S Korea* **28A3**
Uil *USSR* **21J6**
Uinta Mts *USA* **58D2**
Üiryŏng *S Korea* **28A3**
Uisŏng *S Korea* **28A3**
Uitenhage *S Africa* **47D3**
Újfehértó *Hung* **19E3**
Uji *Japan* **29C4**
Ujiji *Tanz* **50C4**
Ujina *Chile* **74C2**
Ujjain *India* **42D4**
Ujung Pandang *Indon* **32A1**
Ukerewe I *Tanz* **50D4**
Ukhrul *India* **43G3**
Ukhta *USSR* **20J3**
Ukiah, California *USA* **59B3**
Ukiah, Oregon *USA* **58C1**
Ukiah *USA* **56A3**
Ukmerge *USSR* **19E1**
Ukrainian SSR, Republic *USSR* **21D6**
Uku-jima, I *Japan* **28A4**
Ulaanbaatar *Mongolia* **26D2**
Ulaangom *Mongolia* **26C2**
Ulaan Uul *Mongolia* **31C1**
Ulan Bator = Ulaanbaatar
Ulangar Hu, L *China* **39G1**
Ulanhot *China* **26F2**
Ulan Ude *USSR* **26D1**
Ulan Ul Hu, L *China* **26C3**
Ul'beya, R *USSR* **25Q3**
Ulchin *S Korea* **28B3**
Ulcinj *Yugos* **17D2**
Uldz *Mongolia* **26E2**
Uliastay *Mongolia* **26C2**
Ulithi, I *Pacific O* **27G5**
Ulla *USSR* **19F1**
Ulladulla *Aust* **34D3**
Ullapool *Scot* **8C3**
Ullsfjorden, Inlet *Nor* **12H5**
Ullswater, L *Eng* **6C2**
Ullung-do, I *Japan* **28C3**
Ulm *W Germ* **18C3**
Uloowaranie,L *Aust* **34A1**
Ulsan *S Korea* **28B3**
Ulster, Region *N Ire* **9C2**
Ulungur He, R *China* **24K5**
Ulungur Hu, L *China* **24K5**
Ulva, I *Scot* **8B3**
Ulverston *Eng* **6C2**
Ulverstone *Aust* **34C4**
Ulya, R *USSR* **25Q4**
Ulyanovka *USSR* **19G3**
Ul'yanovsk *USSR* **20H5**
Ulysses *USA* **62B1**
Uman' *USSR* **21E6**
Umanak *Greenland* **55N2**
Umaria *India* **43E4**
Umarkot *Pak* **42B3**
Umatilla *USA* **58C1**
Umba *USSR* **20E2**
Umba, R *Tanz/Kenya* **50D4**
Umboi I *PNG* **32D1**
Ume, R *Sweden* **12H6**
Umea *Sweden* **12J6**
Um ed Daraj, Jebel, Mt *Jordan* **45C2**
Um el Hashim, Jebel, Mt *Jordan* **45C4**
Umfolozi, R *S Africa* **47E2**
Umiat *USA* **54C3**
Um Ishrin, Jebel, Mt *Jordan* **45C4**
Umkomaas, R *S Africa* **47E3**
Umm al Qaiwain *UAE* **41G4**
Umm Bell *Sudan* **50C2**
Umm Keddada *Sudan* **50C2**
Umm Lajj *S Arabia* **40C4**
Umm Ruwaba *Sudan* **50D2**
Umm Sa'id *Qatar* **41F5**
Umniaiti, R *Zim* **51C5**
Umpqua, R *USA* **58B2**
Umred *India* **42D4**
Umtali = Mutare
Umtata *S Africa* **47D3**
Umuarama *Brazil* **75B3**
Umzimkulu *S Africa* **47D3**
Umzimkulu, R *S Africa* **47E3**
Umzimvubu, R *S Africa* **47D3**
Umzingwane, R *Zim* **47D1**
Una *Brazil* **75E2**
Una, R *Yugos* **16D1**
Unadilla *USA* **68C1**
Unadilla, R *USA* **68C1**
Unaí *Brazil* **75C2**
Unalakleet *USA* **54B3**
Unayzah *S Arabia* **41D4**
Uncasville *USA* **68D2**
Uncompahgre Plat *USA* **60B3**
Underberg *S Africa* **47D2**
Underwood *USA* **60C1**
Unecha *USSR* **20E5**
Uneisa *Jordan* **45C3**
Ungava B *Can* **55M4**
Unggi *N Korea* **28C2**
União de Vitória *Brazil* **74F3**
Union, Missouri *USA* **63D1**
Union, S Carolina *USA* **67B2**
Union City, Pennsylvania *USA* **65D2**
Union City, Tennessee *USA* **63E1**
Uniondale *S Africa* **47C3**
Union of Soviet Socialist Reps *Asia* **22D3**
Union Springs *USA* **67A2**
Uniontown *USA* **65D3**
United Arab Emirates *Arabian Pen* **41F5**
United Kingdom of Gt Britain & N Ireland *N W Europe* **4E3**
United States of America **53H4**
United States Range, Mts *Can* **55K1**
Unity *USA* **58C2**
University Park *USA* **62A2**
Unna *W Germ* **13D2**
Unnão *India* **43E3**
Unsan *N Korea* **28A2**
Unst, I *Scot* **8E1**
Ünye *Turk* **40C1**
Unzha, R *USSR* **20G4**
Upata *Ven* **72F2**
Upemba Nat Pk *Zaïre* **51C4**
Upernavik *Greenland* **55N2**
Upington *S Africa* **47C2**
Upland *USA* **66D3**
Upolu, I *Western Samoa* **33H2**
Upper Hutt *NZ* **35C2**
Upper Klamath L *USA* **58B2**
Upper L *USA* **58B2**
Upper Lough Erne, L *N Ire* **9C2**
Upper Manzanilla *Trinidad* **69L1**
Upper Red L *USA* **61E1**
Upper Seal,L *Can* **55L4**
Upperville *USA* **68B3**
Uppsala *Sweden* **12H7**
Upsala *Can* **61E1**
Upton *USA* **60C2**
'Uqlat as Suqur *S Arabia* **40D4**
Uraba, Golfo de *Colombia* **72C2**
Urad Qianqi *China* **31B1**
Urairah *S Arabia* **41E4**
Urakawa *Japan* **29D2**
Ural, R *USSR* **21J5**
Uralla *Aust* **34D2**
Ural Mts *USSR* **20M4**
Ural'sk *USSR* **21J5**
Ural'skiy Khrebet, Mts *USSR* **24G4**
Urandi *Brazil* **75D1**
Uranium City *Can* **54H4**
Urapunga *Aust* **27G8**
Uravan *USA* **60B3**
Urawa *Japan* **29C3**
Uray *USSR* **20L3**
Urbana, Illinois *USA* **64B2**
Urbana, Ohio *USA* **64C2**
Urbino *Italy* **16C2**
Urbion, Sierra de, Mt *Spain* **15B1**
Ure, R *Eng* **6C2**
Uren' *USSR* **20H4**
Urfa *Turk* **40C2**
Urgench *USSR* **38E1**
Urgun *Afghan* **42B2**
Urla *Turk* **17F3**
Uroševac *Yugos* **17E2**
Uruaçu *Brazil* **75C1**
Uruapan *Mexico* **70B3**
Urucuia, R *Brazil* **75C2**
Uruguaiana *Brazil* **74E3**
Uruguay, R *Urug/Arg* **74E4**
Uruguay, Republic *S America* **74E4**
Urumiyeh *Iran* **41E2**
Ürümqi *China* **39G1**
Urup, I, Kuril Is *USSR* **26J2**
Uruzgan *Afghan* **42B2**
Uryu-ko, L *Japan* **29D2**
Uryupinsk *USSR* **21G5**
Urzhum *USSR* **20J4**
Urziceni *Rom* **17F2**
Usa *China* **39G1**
Usa *Japan* **28B4**
Usa, R *USSR* **20L2**
Uşak *Turk* **40A2**
Usakos *Namibia* **47B1**
Ushakova, Ostrov, I *USSR* **24J1**
Ushashi *Tanz* **50D4**
Ush Tobe *USSR* **24J5**
Ushuaia *Arg* **74C8**
Ushumun *USSR* **25O4**
Usk, R *Wales* **7C4**
Üsküdar *Turk* **40A1**
Usogorsk *USSR* **20H3**
Usol'ye Sibirskoye *USSR* **25M4**
Ussuri, R *China/USSR* **26G2**
Ussuriysk *USSR* **28C2**
Ust'-Belaya *USSR* **25T3**
Ust'Bol'sheretsk *USSR* **25R4**
Ustica, I, *Sicily* **16C3**
Ústi-nad-Laben *Czech* **18C2**
Ust'Ishim *USSR* **24J4**
Ustka *Pol* **18D2**
Ust'Kamchatsk *USSR* **25S4**
Ust'-Kamenogorsk *USSR* **24K5**
Ust' Kara *USSR* **20L2**
Ust Karabula *USSR* **25L4**
Ust' Katav *USSR* **20K5**
Ust'-Kut *USSR* **25M4**
Ust Labinsk *USSR* **21F6**
Ust'Maya *USSR* **25P3**
Ust' Nem *USSR* **20K3**
Ust'Nera *USSR* **25Q3**
Ust'Nyukzha *USSR* **25N4**
Ust'Ordynskiy *USSR* **25M4**
Ust' Tsil'ma *USSR* **20J2**
Ust-'Umal'tu *USSR* **25P4**
Ust'ya, R *USSR* **20G3**
Ust' Yuribey *USSR* **20M2**
Ustyurt, Plato, Plat *USSR* **24G5**
Usuki *Japan* **28B4**
Usumacinta, R *Guatemala/Mexico* **70C3**
Usutu, R *Swaziland* **47E2**
Usuyŏng *S Korea* **28A4**
Usvyaty *USSR* **19G1**
Utah, State *USA* **56B3**
Utah L *USA* **59D2**
Utena *USSR* **19F1**
Uthal *Pak* **42B3**
Utica *USA* **68C1**
Utiel *Spain* **15B2**
Utrecht *Neth* **18B2**
Utrecht *S Africa* **47E2**
Utrera *Spain* **15A2**
Utsjoki *Fin* **12K5**
Utsonomiya *Japan* **29D3**
Uttaradit *Thai* **30C2**
Uttar Pradesh, State *India* **43E3**
Uttoxeter *Eng* **7D3**
Uusikaupunki *Fin* **12J6**
Uvalde *USA* **62C3**
Uvat *USSR* **24H4**
Uvéa, I *New Caledonia* **33F3**
Uvinza *Tanz* **50D4**
Uvira *Zaïre* **50C4**
Uvkusigssat *Greenland* **55N2**
Uvs Nuur, L *Mongolia* **26C1**
Uwajima *Japan* **28C4**
Uweinat, Jebel, Mt *Sudan* **50C1**
Uxin Qi *China* **31B2**
Uyandina, R *USSR* **25Q3**
Uyar *USSR* **25L4**
Uyuni *Bol* **72E8**
Uyûn Mûsa, Well *Egypt* **45B4**
Uzbek SSR, Republic *USSR* **38E1**
Uzerche *France* **14C2**
Uzh, R *USSR* **19F2**
Uzhgorod *USSR* **19E3**
Uzlovaya *USSR* **20F5**
Uzunköprü *Turk* **40A1**

V

Vaal, R *S Africa* **47C2**
Vaal Dam, Res *S Africa* **47D2**
Vaalwater *S Africa* **47D1**
Vaasa *Fin* **12J6**
Vác *Hung* **19D3**
Vacaria *Brazil* **74F3**
Vacaria, R, Mato Grosso do *Brazil* **75B3**
Vacaria, R, Minas Gerais *Brazil* **75D2**
Vacaville *USA* **59B3**
Vadodara *India* **42C4**
Vadsø *Nor* **12K4**
Vaduz *Liech* **16B1**
Vaga, R *USSR* **20G3**
Váh, R *Czech* **19D3**
Vahel *Israel* **45C3**
Vaigai, R *India* **44B3**
Vaila, I *Scot* **8E1**
Vaitupu, I *Tuvalu* **33G1**
Valcheta *Arg* **74C6**
Valday *USSR* **20E4**
Valdayskaya Vozvyshennost', Upland *USSR* **20E4**
Val de la Pascua *Ven* **72E2**
Valdepeñas *Spain* **15B2**
Valdez *USA* **54D3**
Valdivia *Chile* **74B5**
Val d'Oise, Department *France* **13B3**
Val-d'Or *Can* **65D1**
Valdosta *USA* **67B2**
Vale *USA* **58C2**
Valença, Bahia *Brazil* **75E1**
Valença, Rio de Janeiro *Brazil* **75D3**
Valence *France* **14C3**
Valencia *Spain* **15B2**
Valencia *Ven* **72E1**
Valencia, Region = Comunidad Valenciana
Valencia de Alcantara *Spain* **15A2**
Valencia, Golfo de, G *Spain* **15C2**
Valenciennes *France* **13B2**
Valentine, Nebraska *USA* **60C2**
Valentine, Texas *USA* **62B2**
Vale of Pickering *Eng* **6D2**
Vale of York *Eng* **6D2**
Valera *Ven* **72D2**
Valga *USSR* **12K7**
Valjevo *Yugos* **17D2**
Valkeakoski *Fin* **12J6**
Valladolid *Mexico* **70D2**
Valladolid *Spain* **15B1**
Valle de la Pascua *Ven* **69D5**
Valledupar *Colombia* **72D1**
Valle Grande *Bol* **72F7**
Vallejo *USA* **66A1**
Vallenar *Chile* **74B3**
Valle Pequeno *Brazil* **75D1**
Valley City *USA* **61D1**
Valley Falls *USA* **58B2**
Valleyfield *Can* **65E1**
Valls *Spain* **15C1**
Valmiera *USSR* **19F1**
Valognes *France* **14B2**
Valparaíso *Brazil* **75B3**
Valparaiso *Chile* **74B4**
Valparaiso *USA* **67A2**
Vals, R *S Africa* **47D2**
Valsad *India* **42C4**
Valuyki *USSR* **21F5**
Valverde del Camino *Spain* **15A2**
Vammala *Fin* **12J6**
Van *Turk* **41D2**
Vanavara *USSR* **25M3**
Van Buren, Arkansas *USA* **63D1**
Van Buren, Maine *USA* **65F1**
Vancouleurs *France* **13C3**
Vancouver *Can* **54F5**
Vancouver *USA* **58B1**
Vancouver I *Can* **54F5**
Vandalia, Illinois *USA* **64B3**
Vandalia, Ohio *USA* **64C3**
Vanderhoof *Can* **54F4**
Van Diemen,C *Aust* **27G8**
Van Diemen G *Aust* **32C2**
Vänern, L *Sweden* **12G7**
Vänersborg *Sweden* **12G7**
Van Etten *USA* **68B1**
Vangaindrano *Madag* **51E6**
Van Gölü, Salt L *Turk* **40D2**
Vangou *USSR* **29C2**
Vang Vieng *Laos* **30C2**
Van Horn *USA* **62B2**
Vanier *Can* **65D1**
Vanikoro, I *Solomon Is* **33F2**
Vanino *USSR* **26G2**
Vankarem *USSR* **25U3**
Vännäs *Sweden* **12H6**
Vannes *France* **14B2**
Vanrhynsdorp *S Africa* **47B3**
Vansittart I *Can* **55K3**
Vanua Lava, I *Vanuatu* **33F2**
Vanua Levu, I *Fiji* **33G2**
Vanuatu, Is, Republic *Pacific O* **37K5**
Van Wert *USA* **64C2**
Vanwyksvlei *S Africa* **47C3**
Var, R *France* **14D3**
Varamin *Iran* **41F2**
Varanasi *India* **43E3**
Varandey *USSR* **20K2**
Varangerfjord, Inlet *Nor* **12K4**
Varangerhalvøya, Pen *Nor* **12L4**
Varazdin *Yugos* **16D1**
Varberg *Sweden* **12G7**
Varde *Den* **12F7**
Vardø *Nor* **12L4**
Varel *W Germ* **13E1**
Varėna *USSR* **19E2**
Varese *Italy* **16B1**
Varginha *Brazil* **75C3**
Varkaus *Fin* **12K6**
Varna *Bulg* **17F2**
Värnamo *Sweden* **12G7**
Varnek *USSR* **20K2**
Varnville *USA* **67B2**
Várzea da Palma *Brazil* **75D2**
Vashka, R *USSR* **20H3**
Vasil'kov *USSR* **21E5**
Vassar *USA* **64C2**
Västerås *Sweden* **12H7**
Västervik *Sweden* **12H7**
Vasto *Italy* **16C2**
Vaticano, Citta del *Italy* **16C2**
Vatnajökull, Mts *Iceland* **12B2**
Vatra Dornei *Rom* **17F1**
Vättern, L *Sweden* **12G7**
Vaughn *USA* **62A2**
Vaupés, R *Colombia* **72D3**
Vava'u Group, Is *Tonga* **33H2**
Vavuniya *Sri Lanka* **44C4**
Växjö *Sweden* **12G7**
Vaygach, Ostrov, I *USSR* **24G2**
Vecht, R *Neth/W Germ* **13D1**
Vechta *W Germ* **13E1**
Veendam *Neth* **13D1**
Vega *USA* **62B1**
Vega, I *Nor* **12G5**
Vejer de la Frontera *Spain* **15A2**
Vejle *Den* **12F7**
Velddrif *S Africa* **47B3**
Velebit, Mts *Yugos* **16D2**
Velenje *Yugos* **16D1**
Velhas, R *Brazil* **75D2**
Velikaya, R, Rossiyskaya *USSR* **25T3**
Velikaya, R, RSFSR *USSR* **19F1**
Velikaya, R *USSR* **12K7**
Velikiye Luki *USSR* **20E4**
Velikiy Ustyug *USSR* **20H3**
Veliko Tŭrnovo *Bulg* **17F2**
Vélingara *Sen* **48A3**
Velizh *USSR* **19G1**
Vella Lavella, I *Solomon Is* **33E1**
Vellore *India* **44B3**
Velmerstat, Mt *W Germ* **13E2**
Vel'sk *USSR* **20G3**
Veluwe, Region *Neth* **13C1**
Velva *USA* **60C1**
Vembanad L *India* **44B4**

Venado Tuerto Ware

Venado Tuerto *Arg* 74D4
Vençeslau Braz *Brazil* 75C3
Vendeuvre-sur-Barse *France* 13C3
Vendôme *France* 14C2
Venezia = Venice
Venezia, G di *Italy* 16C1
Venezuela, Republic *S America* 72E2
Venezuela,G de *Ven* 69C4
Vengurla *India* 44A2
Venice *Italy* 16C1
Venkatagiri *India* 44B3
Venlo *Neth* 18B2
Venta, R *USSR* 19E1
Ventersburg *S Africa* 47D2
Ventnor *Eng* 7D4
Ventspils *USSR* 19E1
Ventuari, R *Ven* 72E3
Ventura *USA* 66C3
Vepsovskaya Vozvyshennost', Upland *USSR* 20E3
Vera *Arg* 74D3
Vera *Spain* 15B2
Veracruz *Mexico* 70C3
Verá, L *Par* 75A4
Verāval *India* 42C4
Vercelli *Italy* 16B1
Vérde, R *Brazil* 75A1
Verde, R, Goias *Brazil* 75B2
Verde, R, Mato Grosso do Sul *Brazil* 75B2
Verde, R *USA* 59D4
Verde,C = Vert, Cap
Verde Grande, R *Brazil* 75D2
Verden *W Germ* 13E1
Verdon, R *France* 14D3
Verdun *France* 13C3
Vereeniging *S Africa* 47D2
Vereshchagino *USSR* 24K3
Verga,C *Guinea* 48A3
Verin *Spain* 15A1
Verissimo Sarmento *Angola* 51C4
Verkh Angara, R *USSR* 25N4
Verkhneural'sk *USSR* 20K5
Verkhnevilyuysk *USSR* 25O3
Verkhnyaya Toyma *USSR* 20H3
Verkhoyansk *USSR* 25P3
Verkhoyanskiy Khrebet, Mts *USSR* 25O3
Verkneimbatskoye *USSR* 25K3
Verkola *USSR* 20H3
Vermelho, R *Brazil* 75B2
Vermenton *France* 13B4
Vermilion *Can* 54G4
Vermilion L *USA* 61E1
Vermillion *USA* 61D2
Vermont, State *USA* 57F2
Vernal *USA* 58E2
Vernalis *USA* 66B2
Verneuk Pan, Salt L *S Africa* 47C3
Vernon *Can* 54G4
Vernon *USA* 62C2
Vero Beach *USA* 67B3
Véroia *Greece* 17E2
Verona *Italy* 16C1
Versailles *France* 13B3
Vert, Cap, C *Sen* 48A3
Verulam *S Africa* 47E2
Verviers *Belg* 13C2
Vervins *France* 13B3
Veselinovo *USSR* 19G3
Vesle, R *France* 13C3
Vesoul *France* 14D2
Vesterålen, Is *Nor* 12G5
Vestfjorden, Inlet *Nor* 12G5
Vestmannaeyjar *Iceland* 12A2
Vesuvio, Vol *Italy* 16C2
Veszprém *Hung* 19D3
Vetlanda *Sweden* 12H7
Vetluga, R *USSR* 20G4
Veurne *Belg* 13B2
Vevey *Switz* 16B1
Vézelise *France* 13C3
Viana do Castelo *Port* 15A1
Viareggio *Italy* 16C2
Viborg *Den* 12F7
Vibo Valentia *Italy* 16D3
Vice-commodoro Marambio, Base *Ant* 76G2
Vicenza *Italy* 16C1
Vich *Spain* 15C1
Vichada, R *Colombia/Ven* 72E3
Vichuga *USSR* 20G4
Vichy *France* 14C2
Vicksburg *USA* 63D2
Vicosa *Brazil* 75D3
Victor Harbor *Aust* 32C4
Victoria *Hong Kong* 31C5
Victoria *USA* 63C3
Victoria, R *Aust* 32C2
Victoria, State *Aust* 34B3
Victoria de las Tunas *Cuba* 69B2
Victoria Falls *Zambia/Zim* 51C5
Victoria I *Can* 54G2
Victoria,L *Aust* 34B2
Victoria,L *C Africa* 50D4
Victoria Land, Region *Ant* 76F7
Victoria,Mt *Burma* 43G4
Victoria,Mt *PNG* 27H7
Victoria Nile, R *Uganda* 50D3
Victoria Range, Mts *NZ* 35B2
Victoria River Downs *Aust* 32C2
Victoria Str *Can* 54H3
Victoriaville *Can* 65E1
Victoria West *S Africa* 47C3
Victorville *USA* 59C4
Vidalia *USA* 67B2
Videle *Rom* 17F2
Vidin *Bulg* 17E2
Vidisha *India* 42D4
Vidzy *USSR* 19F1
Viedma *Arg* 74D6
Viedma, Lago *Arg* 74B7
Viejo *Costa Rica* 69A4
Viella *Spain* 15C1
Vienna *Austria* 18D3
Vienna, Illinois *USA* 64B3
Vienna, W Virginia *USA* 64C3
Vienne *France* 14C2
Vienne, R *France* 14C2
Vientiane *Laos* 30C2
Vierzon *France* 14C2
Vieste *Italy* 16D2
Vietnam, Republic *S E Asia* 27D5
Vietri *Viet* 30D1
Vieux Fort *St Lucia* 69P2
Vigan *Phil* 27F5
Vignemale, Mt *France/Spain* 14B3
Vigo *Spain* 15A1
Vijayawāda *India* 44C2
Vijosë, R *Alb* 17D2
Vikhren, Mt *Bulg* 17E2
Vikna, I *Nor* 12G6
Vila da Maganja *Mozam* 51D5
Vila Machado *Mozam* 51D5
Vilanculos *Mozam* 51D6
Vila Real *Port* 15A1
Vila Vasco da Gama *Mozam* 51D5
Vila Velha *Brazil* 75D3
Vileyka *USSR* 19F2
Vilhelmina *Sweden* 12H6
Vilhena *Brazil* 73G6
Viljandi *USSR* 20D4
Viljoenskroon *S Africa* 47D2
Vilkitskogo, Proliv, Str *USSR* 25L2
Vilkovo *USSR* 19F3
Villa Ahumada *Mexico* 62A2
Villaba *Spain* 15A1
Villach *Austria* 16C1
Villa Dolores *Arg* 74C4
Villa Gesell *Arg* 74E5
Villa Hayes *Par* 75A4
Villahermosa *Mexico* 70C3
Villa Huidobro *Arg* 74D4
Villa María *Arg* 74D4
Villa Montes *Bol* 72F8
Villa Nova de Gaia *Port* 15A1
Villanueva de la Serena *Spain* 15A2
Villanueva-y-Geltrú *Spain* 15C1
Villarreal *Spain* 15B2
Villarrica *Par* 74E3
Villarrobledo *Spain* 15B2
Villa Unión, Coahuila *Mexico* 62B3
Villavicencio *Colombia* 72D3
Villefranche *France* 14C2
Ville-Marie *Can* 55L5
Villena *Spain* 15B2
Villeneuve-St-Georges *France* 13B3
Villeneuve-sur-Lot *France* 14C3
Villeneuve-sur-Yonne *France* 13B3
Ville Platte *USA* 63D2
Villers-Cotterêts *France* 13B3
Villeurbanne *France* 14C2
Villiers *S Africa* 47D2
Villingen-Schwenningen *W Germ* 13E3
Villupuram *India* 44B3
Vilnius *USSR* 19F2
Vilyuy, R *USSR* 25N3
Vilyuysk *USSR* 25O3
Vinaroz *Spain* 15C1
Vincennes *USA* 64B3
Vindel, R *Sweden* 12H5
Vindhya Range, Mts *India* 42D4
Vineland *USA* 68C3
Vineyard Haven *USA* 68E2
Vinh *Viet* 30D2
Vinh Cam Ranh, B *Viet* 30D3
Vinh Loi *Viet* 30D4
Vinh Long *Viet* 30D3
Vinita *USA* 63C1
Vinkovci *Yugos* 17D1
Vinnitsa *USSR* 19F3
Vinson Massif, Upland *Ant* 76F3
Vinton *USA* 61E2
Viõna del Mar *Chile* 74B4
Virei *Angola* 51B5
Virgem da Lapa *Brazil* 75D2
Virgin, R *USA* 59D3
Virginia *S Africa* 47D2
Virginia *USA* 61E1
Virginia, State *USA* 57F3
Virginia Beach *USA* 65D3
Virginia City *USA* 59C3
Virgin Is *Caribbean S* 69E3
Viroqua *USA* 64A2
Virovitica *Yugos* 16D1
Virton *Belg* 13C3
Virudunagar *India* 44B4
Vis, I *Yugos* 16D2
Visalia *USA* 66C2
Visby *Sweden* 12H7
Viscount Melville Sd *Can* 54H2
Višegrad *Yugos* 17D2
Viseu *Port* 15A1
Vishakhapatnam *India* 44C2
Vishera, R *USSR* 20K3
Viso, Monte, Mt *Italy* 16B2
Vista *USA* 59C4
Vistula, R = Wisła
Vite *India* 44A2
Vitebsk *USSR* 19G1
Viterbo *Italy* 16C2
Vitigudino *Spain* 15A1
Vitim, R *USSR* 25N4
Vitória *Brazil* 73K8
Vitoria *Spain* 15B1
Vitória da Conquista *Brazil* 73K6
Vitré *France* 14B2
Vitry-le-François *France* 13C3
Vittangi *Sweden* 12J5
Vittel *France* 13C3
Vittoria, Sicily 16C3
Vityaz Depth *Pacific O* 26J2
Vivero *Spain* 15A1
Vivi, R *USSR* 25L3
Vizcaya, Golfo de *Spain* 15B1
Vizhne-Angarsk *USSR* 25N4
Vizianagaram *India* 44C2
Vizinga *USSR* 20J3
Vladeasa, Mt *Rom* 17E1
Vladimir *USSR* 24F4
Vladimir Volynskiy *USSR* 19E2
Vladivostok *USSR* 28C2
Vlieland, I *Neth* 18A2
Vlissingen *Neth* 13B2
Vloosdrift *S Africa* 47B2
Vlorë *Alb* 17D2
Vltara, R *Czech* 18C3
Vöcklabruck *Austria* 18C3
Voeune Sai *Camb* 30D3
Vogelsberg, Region *W Germ* 13E2
Vohemar = Inaraña
Vohibinany = Ampasimanolotra
Voi *Kenya* 50D4
Voinjama *Lib* 48B4
Voiron *France* 14D2
Volborg *USA* 60B1
Volcán Barú, Mt *Panama* 69A5
Volcano Is = Kazan Retto
Volchansk *USSR* 20K4
Volga, R *USSR* 21H6
Volgodonsk *USSR* 21G6
Volgograd *USSR* 21G6
Volgogradskoye Vodokhranilishche, Res *USSR* 21H5
Volkhov *USSR* 20E4
Volkhov, R *USSR* 20E4
Volkovysk *USSR* 19E2
Volksrust *S Africa* 47D2
Volochanka *USSR* 25L2
Vologda *USSR* 20G4
Vólos *Greece* 17E3
Vol'sk *USSR* 21H5
Volta *USA* 66B2
Volta Blanche, R *Burkina/Ghana* 48B3
Volta, L *Ghana* 48B4
Volta Noire, R *W Africa* 48B3
Volta Redonda *Brazil* 75D3
Volta Rouge, R *Burkina/Ghana* 48B3
Volzhskiy *USSR* 21G6
Vonguda *USSR* 20F3
Vopnafjörður *Iceland* 55R3
Vordingborg *Den* 18C1
Voriái, I *Greece* 21C8
Vorkuta *USSR* 24H3
Vorma, R *Nor* 12G6
Voronezh *USSR* 21F5
Voron'ya, R *USSR* 12M5
Voroshilovgrad *USSR* 21F6
Voru *USSR* 12K7
Vosges, Department *France* 13D3
Vosges, Mts *France* 14D2
Voss *Nor* 12F6
Vostochnyy Sayan, Mts *USSR* 25L4
Vostok, Base *Ant* 76F9
Votkinsk *USSR* 20J4
Vouziers *France* 13C3
Voyageurs Nat Pk *USA* 61E1
Voy Vozh *USSR* 20K3
Voznesensk *USSR* 21E6
Vranje *Yugos* 17E2
Vratsa *Bulg* 17E2
Vrbas *Yugos* 17D1
Vrbas, R *Yugos* 16D2
Vrbovsko *Yugos* 16C1
Vrede *S Africa* 47D2
Vredendal *S Africa* 47B3
Vreed en Hoop *Guyana* 73G2
Vriddhachalam *India* 44B3
Vršac *Yugos* 17E1
Vrtoče *Yugos* 16D2
Vryburg *S Africa* 47C2
Vryheid *S Africa* 47E2
Vukovar *Yugos* 17D1
Vuktyl' *USSR* 20K3
Vulcano, I *Italy* 16C3
Vung Tau *Viet* 30D3
Vuollerim *Sweden* 12J5
Vyartsilya *USSR* 20E3
Vyatka, R *USSR* 20J4
Vyazemskiy *USSR* 26G2
Vyaz'ma *USSR* 20E4
Vyazniki *USSR* 20G4
Vyborg *USSR* 20D3
Vygozero, L *USSR* 20F3
Vym, R *USSR* 20J3
Vyrnwy, R *Wales* 7C3
Vyshniy-Volochek *USSR* 20E4
Vyškov *Czech* 18D3
Vytegra *USSR* 20F3

W

Wa *Ghana* 48B3
Waal, R *Neth* 13C2
Wabasca, R *Can* 54G4
Wabash *USA* 64B2
Wabash, R *USA* 64B3
Wabatongushi L *Can* 64C1
Wabowden *Can* 54J4
Wabush *Can* 55M4
Waccasassa B *USA* 67B3
Wachusett Res *USA* 68E1
Waco *USA* 63C2
Wad *Pak* 42B3
Waddan *Libya* 49D2
Waddenzee, S *Neth* 13C1
Waddington,Mt *Can* 54F4
Wadebridge *Eng* 7B4
Wadena *USA* 61D1
Wadi es Sir *Jordan* 45C3
Wadi Halfa *Sudan* 50D1
Wadi Musa *Jordan* 45C3
Wad Medani *Sudan* 50D2
Waegwan *S Korea* 28A3
Wafang *China* 28A2
Wafra *Kuwait* 41E4
Wageningen *Neth* 13C2
Wager B *Can* 55K3
Wager Bay *Can* 55J3
Wagga Wagga *Aust* 34C3
Wagin *Aust* 32A4
Wagner *USA* 61D2
Waha *Libya* 49D2
Wahiawa *Hawaiian Is* 66E5
Wahoo *USA* 61D2
Wahpeton *USA* 61D1
Wai *India* 44A2
Waialua *Hawaiian Is* 66E5
Waiau *NZ* 35B2
Waiau, R *NZ* 35B2
Waigeo, I *Indon* 27G6
Waihi *NZ* 35C1
Waikaremoana,L *NZ* 35C1
Waikato, R *NZ* 35C1
Waikerie *Aust* 34A2
Waikouaiti *NZ* 35B3
Wailuku *Hawaiian Is* 66E5
Waimakariri, R *NZ* 35B2
Waimate *NZ* 35B2
Waimea *Hawaiian Is* 66E5
Waingapu *Indon* 32B1
Wainwright *Can* 54G4
Wainwright *USA* 54B2
Waioura *NZ* 35C1
Waipara *NZ* 35B2
Waipukurau *NZ* 35C2
Wairarapa,L *NZ* 35C2
Wairau, R *NZ* 35B2
Wairoa *NZ* 35C1
Wairoa, R *NZ* 35C1
Waitaki, R *NZ* 35B2
Waitara *NZ* 35B1
Waitomo *NZ* 35C1
Waiuku *NZ* 35B1
Wajima *Japan* 29C3
Wajir *Kenya* 50E3
Wakasa-wan, B *Japan* 29C3
Wakatipu,L *NZ* 35A3
Wakayama *Japan* 29D4
Wa Keeney *USA* 60D3
Wakefield *Eng* 7D3
Wakefield *Jamaica* 69H1
Wakefield, Michigan *USA* 64B1
Wakefield, Rhode Island *USA* 68E2
Wakema *Burma* 30B2
Wakkanai *Japan* 29E1
Wakool, R *Aust* 34B3
Wałbrzych *Pol* 18D2
Walcha *Aust* 34D2
Wałcz *Pol* 18D2
Waldbröl *W Germ* 13D2
Walden *USA* 68C2
Waldia *Eth* 50E2
Waldshut *W Germ* 13E4
Wales *USA* 54B3
Wales, Principality *U K* 7C3
Wales I *Can* 55K3
Walgett *Aust* 34C2
Walgreen Coast, Region *Ant* 76F4
Walikale *Zaïre* 50C4
Walker *USA* 61E1
Walker L *USA* 66C1
Walker Pass *USA* 66C3
Walkerton *Can* 64C2
Wall *USA* 60C2
Wallace *USA* 58C1
Wallaroo *Aust* 32C4
Walla Walla *Aust* 34C3
Walla Walla *USA* 58C1
Wallingford *USA* 68D2
Wallis and Futuna, Is *Pacific O* 37K5
Wallis, Îles *Pacific O* 33H2
Wallowa *USA* 58C1
Wallowa Mts *USA* 58C1
Wallumbilla *Aust* 34C1
Walney, I *Eng* 6C2
Walnut Ridge *USA* 63D1
Walpole *USA* 68D1
Walsall *Eng* 7D3
Walsenburg *USA* 62B1
Walterboro *USA* 67B2
Walter F George Res *USA* 67A2
Walters *USA* 62C2
Waltham *USA* 68E1
Walton *USA* 68C1
Walton-on-the Naze *Eng* 7E4
Walvis Bay *S Africa* 47A1
Walvis Ridge *Atlantic O* 52J6
Wamba *Nigeria* 48C4
Wamba, R *Zaïre* 50B4
Wamego *USA* 61D3
Wamsutter *USA* 58E2
Wana *Pak* 42B2
Wanaaring *Aust* 34B1
Wanaka *NZ* 35A2
Wanaka,L *NZ* 35A2
Wanapitei L *Can* 64C1
Wando *S Korea* 28A4
Wandoan *Aust* 34C1
Wanganella *Aust* 34B3
Wanganui *NZ* 35B1
Wanganui, R *NZ* 35C1
Wangaratta *Aust* 34C3
Wangerooge, I *W Germ* 13D1
Wangqing *China* 28B2
Wanjialing *China* 28A3
Wankie = Hwange
Wanle Weyne *Somalia* 50E3
Wanning *China* 30E2
Wanpaca *USA* 64B2
Wanparti *India* 44B2
Wansbeck, R *Eng* 6D2
Wantage *Eng* 7D4
Wanxian *China* 31B3
Wanyuan *China* 31B3
Wappapello,L *USA* 63D1
Wappingers Falls *USA* 68D2
Wapsipinicon, R *USA* 61E2
Warangal *India* 44B2
Waratah *Aust* 34C4
Waratah B *Aust* 34C3
Warburg *W Germ* 13E2
Warburton *Aust* 34C3
Ward, R *Aust* 34C1
Warden *S Africa* 47D2
Wardha *India* 42D4
Ward,Mt *NZ* 35A3
Ware *Can* 54F4
Ware *USA* 68D1

Wareham Winchester

Wareham *Eng* 7C4
Wareham *USA* 68E2
Warendorf *W Germ* 13D2
Warialda *Aust* 34D1
Warin Chamrap *Thai* 30D2
Warmbad *Namibia* 47B2
Warmbad *S Africa* 51C6
Warminster *Eng* 7C4
Warminster *USA* 68C2
Warm Springs *USA* 59C3
Warnemünde *E Germ* 18C2
Warner Mts *USA* 58B2
Warner Robins *USA* 67B2
Warracknabeal *Aust* 34B3
Warrego, R *Aust* 32D3
Warren, Arkansas *USA* 63D2
Warren *Aust* 34C2
Warren, Massachusetts *USA* 68E2
Warren, Minnesota *USA* 61D1
Warren, Ohio *USA* 64C2
Warren, Pennsylvania *USA* 65D2
Warrenpoint *N Ire* 9C2
Warrensburg *USA* 61E3
Warrenton *S Africa* 47C2
Warrenton *USA* 65D3
Warri *Nigeria* 48C4
Warrington *Eng* 7C3
Warrington *USA* 63E2
Warrnambool *Aust* 34B3
Warroad *USA* 61D1
Warsaw *Pol* 19E2
Warsaw *USA* 68A1
Warszawa = Warsaw
Warta, R *Pol* 19D2
Warwick *Aust* 34D1
Warwick *Eng* 7D3
Warwick, New York *USA* 68C2
Warwick, Rhode Island *USA* 68E2
Warwick, County *Eng* 7D3
Wasatch Range, Mts *USA* 59D3
Wasbank *S Africa* 47E2
Wasco *USA* 66C3
Waseca *USA* 61E2
Washburn *USA* 64A1
Washburn L *Can* 54H2
Washburn,Mt *USA* 58D2
Wāshim *India* 42D4
Washington, District of Columbia *USA* 57F3
Washington, Georgia *USA* 67B2
Washington, Indiana *USA* 64B3
Washington, Iowa *USA* 61E2
Washington, Missouri *USA* 61E3
Washington, N Carolina *USA* 67C1
Washington, New Jersey *USA* 68C2
Washington, Pennsylvania *USA* 64C2
Washington, Utah *USA* 59D3
Washington, State *USA* 56A2
Washington Court House *USA* 64C3
Washington Land *Can* 55M1
Washington,Mt *USA* 65E2
Washita, R *USA* 62C1
Wash,The, B *Eng* 7E3
Washuk *Pak* 42A3
Waspán *Nic* 69A4
Wassuk Range, Mts *USA* 66C1
Wassy *France* 13C3
Watampone *Indon* 27F7
Waterberge, Mts *S Africa* 47D3
Waterbury *USA* 68D2
Waterford *Irish Rep* 10B3
Waterford, County *Irish Rep* 9C3
Waterford Harbour *Irish Rep* 9C3
Waterloo *Belg* 13C2
Waterloo *USA* 61E2
Watersmeet *USA* 64B1
Waterton-Glacier International Peace Park *USA* 58D1
Watertown, New York *USA* 65D2
Watertown, S Dakota *USA* 61D2
Watertown, Wisconsin *USA* 64B2
Waterval-Boven *S Africa* 47E2
Waterville, Maine *USA* 65F2
Waterville, New York *USA* 68C1
Watervliet *USA* 68D1
Waterways *Can* 54G4
Watford *Eng* 7D4
Watford City *USA* 60C1
Watkins Glen *USA* 68B1
Watonga *USA* 62C1
Watrous *Can* 56C1
Watrous *USA* 62B1
Watsa *Zaïre* 50C3
Watson Lake *Can* 54F3
Watsonville *USA* 66B2
Wau *PNG* 27H7
Wau *Sudan* 50C3
Wauchope *Aust* 34D2
Wauchula *USA* 67B3
Waukegan *USA* 64B2
Waukesha *USA* 64B2
Waupun *USA* 64B2
Waurika *USA* 63C2
Wausau *USA* 64B2
Wauwatosa *USA* 64B2
Wave Hill *Aust* 32C2
Waveney, R *Eng* 7E3
Waverly, Iowa *USA* 60E2
Waverly, New York *USA* 68B1
Waverly, Ohio *USA* 64C3
Wavre *Belg* 13C2
Wawa *Can* 64C1
Wāw Al Kabir *Libya* 49D2
Wāw an Nāmūs, Well *Libya* 49D2
Wawona *USA* 66C2
Waxahachie *USA* 63C2
Waycross *USA* 67B2
Wayne *USA* 61D2
Waynesboro, Georgia *USA* 67B2
Waynesboro, Mississippi *USA* 63E2
Waynesboro, Pennsylvania *USA* 68B3
Waynesboro, Virginia *USA* 65D3
Waynesville, Missouri *USA* 63D1
Waynesville, N Carolina *USA* 67B1
Wazi Khwa *Afghan* 42B2
W Burra, I *Scot* 8E1
Weald,The, Upland *Eng* 7E4
Wear, R *Eng* 6C2
Weatherford, Oklahoma *USA* 62C1
Weatherford, Texas *USA* 63C2
Weaverville *USA* 58B2
Webbwood *Can* 64C1
Webster, New York *USA* 68B1
Webster, S Dakota *USA* 61D1
Webster *USA* 68E1
Webster City, Massachusetts *USA* 61E2
Webster Groves *USA* 64A3
Weddell, I *Falkland Is* 74D8
Weddell Sea *Ant* 76G2
Weed *USA* 58B2
Weedville *USA* 68A2
Weenen *S Africa* 47E2
Wee Waa *Aust* 34C2
Weichang *China* 31D1
Weiden *W Germ* 18C3
Weifang *China* 31D2
Weihai *China* 31E2
Wei He, R, Henan *China* 31C3
Wei He, R, Shaanxi *China* 31C2
Weilmoringle *Aust* 34C1
Weinheim *W Germ* 13E3
Weining *China* 31A4
Weipa *Aust* 32D2
Weirton *USA* 64C2
Weiser *USA* 58C2
Weishan Hu, L *China* 31D3
Weissenfels *E Germ* 18C2
Weiss L *USA* 67A2
Welch *USA* 64C3
Weldon *USA* 66C3
Welkom *S Africa* 47D2
Welland *Can* 65D2
Welland, R *Eng* 7D3
Wellesley Is *Aust* 32C2
Wellfleet *USA* 68E2
Wellingborough *Eng* 7D3
Wellington *Aust* 34C2
Wellington, Colorado *USA* 60C2
Wellington *Eng* 7C4
Wellington, Kansas *USA* 63C1
Wellington, Nevada *USA* 66C1
Wellington *NZ* 35B2
Wellington *S Africa* 47B3
Wellington, Texas *USA* 62B2
Wellington Chan *Can* 55J2
Wellington, Isla *Chile* 74B7
Wells *Eng* 7C4
Wells, Nevada *USA* 58D2
Wells, New York *USA* 68C1
Wellsboro *USA* 68B2
Wellsford *NZ* 35B1
Wells,L *Aust* 32B3
Wells-next-the-Sea *Eng* 7E3
Wellsville *USA* 68B1
Wels *Austria* 18C3
Welshpool *Wales* 7C3
Welwyn Garden City *Eng* 7D4
Wemindji *Can* 55L4
Wenatchee *USA* 58B1
Wenatchee, R *USA* 58C1
Wenchi *Ghana* 48B4
Wendeng *China* 31E2
Wendover *USA* 58D2
Wenling *China* 31E4
Wenshan *China* 31A5
Wensleydale *Eng* 6D2
Wensum, R *Eng* 7E3
Wentworth *Aust* 34B2
Wen Xian *China* 31A3
Wenzhou *China* 31E4
Wenzhu *China* 31C4
Wepener *S Africa* 47D2
Werda *Botswana* 47C2
Werder *Eth* 50E3
Werra, R *E Germ* 18C2
Werris Creek *Aust* 34D2
Wesel *W Germ* 13D2
Weser, R *W Germ* 18B2
Weskan *USA* 60C3
Weslaco *USA* 63C3
Wesleyville *Can* 55N5
Wessel Is *Aust* 32C2
Wessington Springs *USA* 60D2
West Allis *USA* 64B2
West Australian Basin *Indian O* 36F5
West Australian Ridge *Indian O* 36F6
West B *USA* 63E3
West Bengal, State *India* 43F4
West Branch Delaware, R *USA* 68C1
West Branch Susquehanna, R *USA* 68A2
West Bromwich *Eng* 7D3
Westbrook *USA* 65E2
Westby *USA* 64A2
West Chester *USA* 68C3
West End *Bahamas* 67C3
Westend *USA* 66D3
Westerburg *W Germ* 13D2
Westerland *W Germ* 18B2
Westerly *USA* 68E2
Western Australia, State *Aust* 32B3
Western Ghats, Mts *India* 44A2
Western Isles, Region *Scot* 8B3
Western Sahara, Region *Mor* 48A2
Western Samoa, Is *Pacific O* 33H2
Westerschelde, Estuary *Neth* 13B2
Westerstede *W Germ* 13D1
Westerwald, Region *W Germ* 13D2
Westfalen, Region *W Germ* 14D1
West Falkland, Is *Falkland Is* 74D8
Westfield, Massachusetts *USA* 68D1
Westfield, New York *USA* 65D2
Westfield, Pennsylvania *USA* 68B2
West Frankfort *USA* 64B3
Westgate *Aust* 34C1
West Germany, Republic *Europe* 18B2
West Glamorgan, County *Wales* 7C4
West Grand L *USA* 65F1
West Indies, Is *Caribbean S* 52E3
West Liberty *USA* 64C3
West Lorne *Can* 64C2
Westmeath, County *Irish Rep* 9C3
West Memphis *USA* 63D1
West Midlands, County *Eng* 7D3
Westminster *Eng* 7D4
Westminster, Maryland *USA* 68B3
Westminster, S Carolina *USA* 67B2
West Nicholson *Zim* 47D1
Weston *Malay* 27E6
Weston *USA* 64C3
Weston-super-Mare *Eng* 7C4
West Palm Beach *USA* 67B3
West Plains *USA* 63D1
West Point, California *USA* 66B1
West Point, Mississippi *USA* 63E2
West Point, Nebraska *USA* 61D2
West Point, New York *USA* 68D2
Westport *NZ* 35B2
Westray, I *Scot* 10C2
West Sole, Oilfield *N Sea* 6E3
West Virginia, State *USA* 57E3
West Walker, R *USA* 66C1
West Wyalong *Aust* 34C2
West Yellowstone *USA* 58D2
West Yorkshire, County *Eng* 7D3
Wetar, I *Indon* 27F7
Wetaskiwin *Can* 54G4
Wete *Tanz* 50D4
Wetter, R *W Germ* 13E2
Wetzlar *W Germ* 13E2
Wevok = Lisburne, Cape
Wewak *PNG* 32D1
Wewoka *USA* 63C1
Wexford *Irish Rep* 9C3
Wexford, County *Irish Rep* 9C3
Weybridge *Eng* 7D4
Weyburn *Can* 54H5
Weymouth *Eng* 7C4
Weymouth *USA* 68E1
Whakatane *NZ* 35C1
Whakatane, R *NZ* 35C1
Whalsay, I *Scot* 8E1
Whangarei *NZ* 35B1
Wharfe, R *Eng* 6D3
Wharton *USA* 63C3
Wheatland *USA* 60B2
Wheaton, Maryland *USA* 68B3
Wheaton, Minnesota *USA* 61D1
Wheeler Peak, Mt, Nevada *USA* 59D3
Wheeler Peak, Mt, New Mexico *USA* 62A1
Wheeler Ridge *USA* 66C3
Wheeling *USA* 64C2
Whitby *Can* 65D2
Whitby *Eng* 6D2
Whitchurch *Eng* 7C3
White, R, Arkansas *USA* 63D1
White, R, Colorado *USA* 60B2
White, R, Indiana *USA* 64B3
White, R, S Dakota *USA* 60C2
White B *Can* 55N4
White Butte, Mt *USA* 60C1
White Cliffs *Aust* 34B2
White Coomb, Mt *Scot* 10C2
Whitefish *USA* 58D1
Whitefish Pt *USA* 64B1
Whitegull L *Can* 55M4
Whitehall, New York *USA* 65E2
Whitehall, Pennsylvania *USA* 68C2
Whitehall, Wisconsin *USA* 64A2
Whitehaven *Eng* 6C2
Whitehorse *Can* 54E3
White I *NZ* 35C1
White L *USA* 63D3
Whitemark *Aust* 34C4
White Mountain Peak, Mt *USA* 59C3
White Mountain Peak, Mt *USA* 66C2
White Mts, California *USA* 66C2
White Mts, New Hampshire *USA* 65E2
White Nile = Bahr el Abiad
White Nile, R *Sudan* 50D2
White Plains *USA* 68D2
White River *Can* 55K5
White River *USA* 60C2
White River Junction *USA* 65E2
White Russia = Belorussian SSR
White Salmon *USA* 58B1
White Sea *USSR* 24E3
White Sulphur Springs *USA* 58D1
Whiteville *USA* 67C2
White Volta *W Africa* 48B4
Whitewater *USA* 64B2
Whithorn *Scot* 8C4
Whitmire *USA* 67B2
Whitney,Mt *USA* 66C2
Whittier, California *USA* 66C4
Whittlesey *Eng* 7D3
Wholdaia *Can* 54H3
Whyalla *Aust* 32C4
Wiarton *Can* 64C2
Wiay, I *Scot* 8B3
Wibaux *USA* 60C1
Wichita *USA* 63C1
Wichita, R *USA* 62C2
Wichita Falls *USA* 62C2
Wichita Mts *USA* 62C2
Wick *Scot* 8D2
Wickenburg *USA* 59D4
Wicklow *Irish Rep* 9C3
Wicklow, County *Irish Rep* 9C3
Wicklow Hd, Pt *Irish Rep* 9C3
Wicklow Mts *Irish Rep* 9C3
Widgeegoara, R *Aust* 34C1
Widnes *Eng* 7C3
Wied, R *W Germ* 13D2
Wielun *Pol* 19D2
Wien = Vienna
Wiener Neustadt *Austria* 18D3
Wieprz, R *Pol* 19E2
Wiesbaden *W Germ* 13E2
Wiese, R *W Germ* 13D4
Wigan *Eng* 7C3
Wiggins *USA* 63E2
Wight, I of, County *Eng* 7D4
Wigton *Eng* 6C2
Wigtown *Scot* 8C4
Wigtown B *Scot* 8C4
Wilbur *USA* 58C1
Wilcannia *Aust* 34B2
Wildcat Peak, Mt *USA* 59C3
Wildeshausen *W Germ* 13E1
Wildspitze, Mt *Austria* 16C1
Wildwood, Florida *USA* 67B3
Wildwood, New Jersey *USA* 68C3
Wiley *USA* 62B1
Wilge, R *S Africa* 47D2
Wilhelm,Mt *PNG* 32D1
Wilhelmshaven *W Germ* 18B2
Wilkes-Barre *USA* 68C2
Wilkes Land, Region *Ant* 76F8
Willamette, R *USA* 58B2
Willandra, R *Aust* 34B2
Willapa B *USA* 58B1
Willcox *USA* 59E4
Willemstad *Curaçao* 69D4
William,Mt *Aust* 34B3
Williams, Arizona *USA* 59D3
Williams, California *USA* 59B3
Williamsburg *USA* 65D3
Williams Lake *Can* 54F4
Williamson *USA* 64C3
Williamsport *USA* 68B2
Williamston *USA* 67C1
Williamstown, Massachusetts *USA* 68D1
Williamstown, W Virginia *USA* 64C3
Willimantic *USA* 68D2
Willingboro *USA* 68C2
Willis Group, Is *Aust* 32E2
Williston, Florida *USA* 67B3
Williston, N Dakota *USA* 60C1
Williston *S Africa* 47C3
Willmar *USA* 61D1
Willoughby,C *Aust* 34A3
Willow Bunch *Can* 60B1
Willowmore *S Africa* 47C3
Willow Ranch *USA* 58B2
Willows *USA* 59B3
Willow Springs *USA* 63D1
Wilmington *Aust* 34A2
Wilmington, Delaware *USA* 68C3
Wilmington, N Carolina *USA* 67C2
Wilmington, Vermont *USA* 68D1
Wilson, Kansas *USA* 60D3
Wilson, N Carolina *USA* 67C1
Wilson, New York *USA* 68A1
Wilson, R *Aust* 34B1
Wilson,C *Can* 55K3
Wilson L *USA* 60D3
Wilson,Mt, California *USA* 66C3
Wilson,Mt, Colorado *USA* 62A1
Wilson,Mt, Oregon *USA* 58B1
Wilson's Promontory, Pen *Aust* 34C3
Wilstedt *W Germ* 13E1
Wiltshire, County *Eng* 7D4
Wiltz *Lux* 13C3
Wiluna *Aust* 32B3
Winamac *USA* 64B2
Winburg *S Africa* 47D2
Wincanton *Eng* 7C4
Winchendon *USA* 68D1
Winchester *Can* 65D1
Winchester *Eng* 7D4
Winchester, Kentucky *USA* 64C3
Winchester, New Hampshire *USA* 68D1
Winchester, Virginia *USA* 65D3

ACKNOWLEDGEMENTS

PICTURE CREDITS
The sources for the photographs and illustrations appearing in the atlas are listed below.

page
48–61 Physical maps by Duncan Mackay, copyright © Times Books Ltd., London

62 *Venus* US Geological Survey, Flagstaff, Arizona
Mercury NSSDC/NASA
Mars NSSDC/NASA
Jupiter NSSDC/NASA
Saturn NASA
Uranus Jet Propulsion Laboratory/NASA

63 *Rock and Hydrological Cycles* Encyclopaedia Universalis Editeur, Paris

90 *Manhattan* Adapted from map by Nicholson Publications Ltd.

94–99 Robert Harding Picture Library Ltd.

BIBLIOGRAPHY
G.L. Fitzpatrick and M.J. Modlin: *Direct Line Distances. International Edition* Metuchen N.J. and London, 1986

The Europa Year Book 1987 London, 1987

Ed. J. Paxton: *The Statesman's Year-book 1987–88.* London, 1987

CITY DISTANCE TABLES

ABU DHABI	AMSTERDAM	ATHENS	AUCKLAND	BANGKOK	BARCELONA	BEIJING	BERLIN	BOMBAY	BOSTON	BRUSSELS	BUENOS AIRES	CAIRO	CALCUTTA	CAPE TOWN	CHICAGO	COPENHAGEN	DELHI	GENEVA	HAMBURG	HONG KONG	HONOLULU	ISTANBUL	JERUSALEM	LONDON	LOS ANGELES
ABU DHABI	5167	3260	14244	4975	5142	5972	4637	2003	10735	5158	13534	2367	3471	7498	11688	4845	2317	4903	4892	6071	13865	2987	2043	5478	13481
3211	**AMSTERDAM**	2164	18728	9185	1237	7841	577	6864	5575	174	11424	3282	7620	9647	6628	623	6368	690	367	9300	11676	2213	3350	359	8963
2026	1345	**ATHENS**	16775	7933	1822	7633	1803	5179	7639	2092	11677	1120	6325	7979	8765	2136	5019	1710	2026	8560	13439	562	1256	2394	11118
8851	11637	10424	**AUCKLAND**	9566	19204	10388	17743	12294	14478	18279	10372	16573	11176	11796	13181	17525	12482	18609	17813	9121	7052	17042	16287	18330	10479
3091	5707	4930	5944	**BANGKOK**	9692	3291	8613	3010	13733	9263	16885	7279	1610	10144	13789	8628	2917	9249	8824	1723	10634	7477	6895	9544	13319
3195	769	1132	11933	6023	**BARCELONA**	8822	1500	7044	5881	1063	10447	2897	8084	8502	7101	1760	6782	624	1473	10087	12766	2238	3122	1138	9677
3711	4872	4743	6455	2045	5482	**BEIJING**	7375	4760	10860	7983	19265	7557	3271	12947	10626	7218	3788	8223	7492	1972	8171	7072	7135	8160	10082
2881	358	1120	11025	5352	932	4583	**BERLIN**	6298	6098	654	11890	2891	7045	9588	7103	355	5791	876	255	8770	11782	1739	2903	934	9332
1245	4265	3218	7639	1870	4377	2958	3914	**BOMBAY**	12275	6891	14937	4363	1664	8216	12976	6430	1156	6725	6544	4311	12928	4818	4017	7205	14021
6671	3464	4747	8996	8534	3654	6748	3789	7628	**BOSTON**	5598	8619	8737	12517	12411	1369	5904	11504	5929	5843	12831	8191	7783	8884	5280	4179
3205	108	1300	11358	5756	661	4961	406	4282	3479	**BRUSSELS**	11282	3212	7689	9490	6679	769	6427	533	491	9416	11825	2185	3302	320	9055
8410	7099	7256	6445	10492	6492	11971	7388	9282	5356	7011	**BUENOS AIRES**	11811	16535	6891	8978	12046	15800	11045	11773	18463	12160	12235	12236	11105	9828
1471	2039	696	10298	4523	1800	4696	1796	2711	5429	1996	7339	**CAIRO**	5708	7208	9881	3206	4436	2816	3125	8158	14239	1234	426	3513	12223
2157	4735	3930	6945	1000	5023	2033	4378	1034	7778	4778	10275	3547	**CALCUTTA**	9684	12861	7083	1307	7651	7264	2654	11357	5867	5314	7978	13141
4659	5995	4958	7330	6303	5283	8045	5958	5105	7712	5897	4282	4479	6018	**CAPE TOWN**	13658	9942	9284	8958	9725	11867	18562	8367	7481	9635	16054
7263	4119	5447	8191	8568	4413	6603	4414	8063	851	4150	5579	6140	7992	8487	**CHICAGO**	6860	12047	7069	6850	12560	6849	8834	9978	6371	2810
3011	387	1327	10890	5361	1094	4485	221	3996	3669	478	7485	1992	4401	6178	4263	**COPENHAGEN**	5857	1145	289	8688	11428	2021	3191	958	9026
1440	3957	3119	7756	1813	4214	2354	3599	718	7148	3994	9818	2757	812	5769	7486	3640	**DELHI**	6363	6020	3770	11930	4560	4032	6724	12882
3047	429	1063	11563	5747	388	5110	544	4179	3684	331	6863	1750	4754	5566	4393	712	3954	**GENEVA**	862	9544	12358	1921	2959	748	9519
3040	228	1259	11069	5483	915	4655	159	4066	3631	305	7291	1942	4514	6043	4257	180	3741	536	**HAMBURG**	8934	11629	1988	3150	723	9098
3772	5779	5319	5668	1071	6268	1225	5450	2679	7973	5851	11473	5069	1649	7374	7805	5399	2343	5931	5552	**HONG KONG**	8945	8034	7740	9646	11674
8616	7255	8351	4382	6608	7933	5077	7321	8033	5090	7348	7556	8848	7057	11534	4256	7101	7413	7679	7226	5558	**HONOLULU**	13068	13969	11653	4125
1856	1375	349	10590	4646	1391	4394	1081	2994	4836	1358	7603	767	3646	5199	5489	1256	2834	1194	1235	4992	8120	**ISTANBUL**	1170	2504	11043
1270	2082	781	10121	4285	1940	4434	1804	2496	5520	2052	7603	265	3302	4649	6200	1983	2505	1839	1957	4810	8680	727	**JERUSALEM**	3615	12210
3404	223	1488	11390	5931	707	5071	580	4477	3281	199	6901	2183	4957	5987	3959	595	4178	465	449	5994	7241	1556	2246	**LONDON**	8778
8377	5570	6909	6512	8276	6013	6265	5799	8713	2597	5627	6107	7595	8166	9976	1746	5609	8005	5915	5653	7254	2563	6862	7587	5455	**LOS ANGELES**

Additional city rows (city labels continue beyond LOS ANGELES):

3500	921	1475	12174	6336	314	5744	1163	4688	3410	818	6229	2085	5337	5304	4191	1289	4529	637	1111	6562	7874	1705	2238	785	5833
7263	10280	9289	1634	4573	10458	5650	9924	6096	10521	10325	7226	8678	5547	6424	9673	9930	6333	10271	10057	4593	5507	9090	8521	10503	7930
8932	5739	7024	6802	9739	5909	7754	6056	9739	2279	5757	4577	7700	9504	8515	1691	5921	9121	5962	5898	8796	3789	7114	7800	5560	1549
2893	514	910	11482	5614	452	5031	523	4029	3838	434	6943	1599	4619	5493	4542	720	3816	155	560	5823	7764	1041	1685	597	6051
6616	3428	4737	8935	8337	3677	6518	3740	7522	251	3451	5593	5427	7615	7919	744	3606	7013	3677	3581	7744	4918	4803	5502	3256	2469
2321	1337	1386	10063	4393	1873	3610	1002	3129	4498	1404	8365	1801	3443	6277	4984	971	2702	1504	1109	4672	7048	1091	1660	1557	6085
2126	4133	2828	8678	4485	3652	5727	3948	2816	7190	4066	6472	2186	3839	2542	8010	4155	3373	3764	4080	5449	10741	2952	2276	4229	9664
6860	3654	4937	8816	8668	3842	6843	3979	7808	191	3669	5276	5618	7936	7799	713	3857	7319	3874	3820	8068	4969	5026	5711	3471	2451
4808	5742	5797	5532	2615	6421	1110	5494	3956	6871	5840	9786	5796	2955	8906	6500	5363	3415	6036	5541	1549	4104	5448	5535	5919	5724
6692	3512	4825	8835	8353	3772	6509	3820	7582	313	3536	5612	5516	7649	8010	645	3682	7061	3766	3661	7734	4819	4887	5588	3342	2366
3260	266	1306	11521	5877	517	5118	547	4365	3446	163	6853	1998	4892	5783	4143	639	4102	257	464	5996	7449	1405	2075	212	5658
5614	8779	7628	3312	3301	8788	4944	8427	4514	11621	8793	7839	6992	4163	5416	10979	8499	4877	8660	8579	3728	6777	7467	6850	8989	9337
7310	5937	6033	7636	9993	5294	10766	6207	8338	4829	5844	1223	6141	9372	3775	5284	6321	8749	5673	6147	11005	8291	6380	6405	5750	6294
2674	804	655	11433	5494	534	5061	735	3845	4102	729	6919	1327	4495	5230	4821	951	3684	433	813	5779	8038	857	1435	891	6346
8145	5468	6792	6517	7930	5963	5918	567	8405	2699	5532	6453	7466	7828	10245	1859	5474	7693	5833	5533	6910	4261	672	7436	5369	347
9097	7452	7797	6021	10968	6923	11842	7772	9984	5217	7375	705	7954	10961	4946	5294	7835	10518	7274	7677	11607	6861	8136	2005	7240	5578
7527	6077	6221	7483	10196	5452	10933	6356	8558	4795	5985	1044	6345	9592	3949	5209	6462	8967	5826	6290	11221	8090	6567	6610	5885	6149
4299	5332	5305	5963	2312	5982	595	5064	3488	6815	5425	12073	5284	2514	8519	6546	4948	2920	5601	5123	1303	4549	4956	5023	5519	5968
4068	5530	5318	5815	1784	6119	669	5233	3131	7314	5616	12190	5199	2113	8053	7081	5143	2640	5753	5310	755	4955	4973	4934	5731	6507
3669	6526	5629	5227	887	6767	2775	6169	2428	9410	6566	9873	5139	1794	6009	9375	6195	2574	6525	6306	1600	6726	5376	4924	6748	8784
2978	701	1497	10565	5143	1417	4179	505	3878	3753	799	7793	2115	4204	6421	4286	325	3467	1032	505	5122	6872	1352	2064	892	5531
6085	2875	9523	1343	4675	10677	5545	9998	6305	10092	10404	7345	8957	5668	6856	9242	9963	6472	10422	10111	4566	5065	9286	8778	10557	7497
5018	5788	5922	5475	2865	6487	1307	5556	4195	6718	5888	11412	5957	3200	9157	6311	5415	3640	6101	5594	1798	3858	5574	5699	5956	5486
6905	3728	5044	8624	8480	3989	6594	4035	7777	431	3754	5545	5734	7810	8134	437	3896	7243	3985	3877	7815	4659	5103	5806	3560	2176
2635	582	797	11094	5251	1026	4647	326	3721	4045	570	7328	1480	4262	5653	4698	541	3465	500	462	5437	7634	794	1504	769	6116
7063	3858	5141	8621	8806	4044	6941	4181	8002	395	3873	5194	5822	8102	7892	595	4058	7501	4075	4023	8163	4838	5231	5915	3676	2300

MILES